Antwerp

Demer R.

Louvain

Brussels

BELGIUM

Maas R.

Namur

Meuse R.

Liege

ADVANCE

▪ ▪ ▪ 18 JULY 1918

━━━ 11 NOVEMBER 1918

- - - INTERNATIONAL
BORDER

ARDENNES FOREST

GERMANY

LUXEMBOURG

Our R.

Moselle R.

Sedan

✱ Luxembourg

Meuse R.

Saar R.

(AREA ENLARGED
ON BACK
INSIDE COVER)

ARGONNE FOREST

Suippes

Verdun

Metz

Châlons-sur-Marne

St.
Mihiel

Bar-le-Duc

Marne R.

Moselle R.

WORLD WAR I AND AMERICA

WORLD WAR I
AND AMERICA

TOLD BY THE
AMERICANS WHO LIVED IT

A. Scott Berg, *editor*

THE LIBRARY OF AMERICA

World War I and America:
Told by the Americans Who Lived It
is published in memory of

PVT. SAMUEL B. ROSE
(1889–1964)

Company G
322nd Infantry Regiment
81st (Wildcat) Division
American Expeditionary Forces
France 1918

with a gift from his son
Elihu Rose

.

World War I and America:
Told by the Americans Who Lived It
is kept in print by a gift from

MARY CARR PATTON

to the Guardians of American Letters Fund
established by Library of America
to ensure that every volume in the series
will be permanently available.

Contents

Introduction

*"I came to see the First World War . . . as the great seminal
catastrophe of this century—the event which . . . lay at the heart
of the failure and decline of this Western civilization."*
—GEORGE F. KENNAN (1904–2005)

LIKE the headwaters of a great river, several influences con-
verged in 1914 until they created an unstoppable flow of
events that produced one of the most cataclysmic torrents
mankind had ever experienced. Streams of imperialism, nationalism, and militarism joined; and soon they surged through
an intricate system of alliances until they created the First World
War. It engulfed much of two continents and engaged the rest
of the globe for four years; and its effects continue to permeate
twenty-first-century politics, economics, geography, and psychology.

Through the writings of Americans who lived it, this volume
attempts to show how the United States confronted World War I.
It reveals the country's strained metamorphosis—from concerned
observer to tide-turning participant and finally to a global force
hoping to prevent the recurrence of another such catastrophe. All
the authors presented here were eyewitnesses to the events depicted or participants therein; and though this collection com-
prises a diverse assortment of firsthand commentary—news
articles, speeches, memoirs, poems, songs, editorials, letters, diaries, and histories—most of these pieces share a common thread,
an often overlooked theme that accounts for much of what caused
the war and much of what resulted: the affirmation of identity.

This impetus is as ancient as the Bible, suggested in the
Book of Numbers when the Lord commanded Moses to count
and name the members of each tribe; and thousands of years
later, the United States Constitution issued a similar mandate
—to take a census. Such tabulations did more than determine
military power or how to apportion representatives; the numbers
—today, as in earliest times—validate the people themselves, assuring them, as they are counted, that they count. Individual
lives mattered; and virtually every selection in this anthology

addresses that theme of identity, directly or indirectly—that desire for self-definition that helps us determine who we are as individuals, and as nations.

By the start of the twentieth century, Europe was prospering in the general calm that had lingered since Napoleon's downfall. A handful of empires had steadily grown, often conglomerating populations even where they did not fit. Four dinosaurian autocracies ruled most of the Continent and into Asia.

The Austro-Hungarian Empire was a dual monarchy ruled by the House of Habsburg; and Emperor Franz Josef's subjects included a large assortment of not just Germans and Magyars but also Czechs, Slovaks, Slovenes, Serbs, and Croats. The Romanov dynasty dated back three hundred years, and its territory stretched from the Arctic Ocean in the north to the Black Sea in the south, from the mouth of the Danube River to the Pacific Ocean—more than 8.5 million square miles that were home to Ukrainians, Belarusians, Moldavians, Finns, Azerbaijanis, Georgians, Kazakhs, Kirghizes, Turkmen, Uzbeks, Lithuanians, Estonians, Latvians, and Poles, among many other nationalities. Adjacent to both realms, the seven-hundred-year-old Ottoman Empire united Asia and Europe at Constantinople and spread east to Persia and south as far as the Gulf of Aden, encompassing Palestine, Syria, Mesopotamia, and Arabia. While much of the empire was not arable, the entire world was beginning to appreciate not only its strategic location but also the oil beneath its sand. And finally the Hohenzollern dynasty, for centuries the kings of Prussia, ruled the new German Empire that had dominated the center of the continent since its creation in 1871. Fearing encirclement by Russia, France, and Britain, Germany's autocratic rulers believed their survival depended on their military power and expanding navy. And though its population was far more ethnically homogeneous than those of the other empires, the rising tide of socialism was seeping into the national consciousness; and the leaders feared that in a crisis, class identity might prevail over national identity.

Thus hundreds of millions of people lived under the rule of four families. Ironically, greater consanguinity existed among the competitive crowned heads themselves—many of whom were first cousins—than between the sovereigns and their subjects. Outside castle walls, the discontent of those living under heedless autocrats intensified, and disaffected populations sowed the seeds of revolt. The Poles, for example, whose territory had been partitioned among Russia, Prussia, and Austria, felt no special affinity for any of those imperial powers; and political borders drawn after the Franco-Prussian War in 1871 meant less to the people of Alsace-Lorraine than did the language they spoke or the boundaries imposed by the Rhine River. Ignored masses in polyglot empires invariably clung to their ethnic identities.

So it proved on June 28, 1914, when a teenage member of a small group of terrorists in the southern corner of the vast Austro-Hungarian Empire shot the archduke and his wife. The assassin was a Bosnian Serb associated with a movement composed of other Serbs, as well as Croats and Bosnian Muslims. With no allegiance to leaders in Vienna or Budapest, he asserted both his motive and his identity at his trial, declaring: "I am a Yugoslav nationalist, aiming for the unification of all Yugoslavs, and I do not care what form of state, but it must be freed from Austria."

Commitments established in preexisting treaties and ententes sprang into motion. Germany and Austria-Hungary quickly found themselves at war with France, Great Britain, Russia, and Japan. The Ottoman Empire, Italy, Bulgaria, and Romania would later choose sides, while a host of countries—including the Netherlands and much of Scandinavia—remained neutral.

With a long-standing tradition of avoiding foreign entanglements, the United States naturally resisted involvement in this international conflict. But President Woodrow Wilson, who would become the dominant voice in the world during the war years, had deeper reasons for not wanting his country to participate in the war, as America's evolving foreign policy tapped into his personal history, his very identity.

Besides being the most scholarly President in American history (to this day the nation's only chief executive to have earned a doctorate) and the most religious, Wilson was the first Southerner elected to the presidency since the Civil War.

Born in 1856 in Virginia and raised during Reconstruction in Georgia and South Carolina, he remains the only President to have grown up in a country that had lost a war—the Confederate States of America. Wilson had experienced not just the devastation and deprivation of war but also the degradation—all of which provided bitter memories that dictated his policy of avoiding war at all redeemable costs. "I came from the South and I know what war is, for I have seen its terrible wreckage and ruin," he would later say. "It is easy for me as President to declare war. I do not have to fight, and neither do the gentlemen on the Hill . . . It is some poor farmer's boy, or the son of some poor widow . . . who will have to do the fighting and dying." Furthermore, millions of Wilson's constituents were "hyphenated" Americans, immigrants with family members on either side of the war in Europe.

From its start, the President exhorted Americans to remain "impartial," not only in their action but even in their thought. This proved hardest on Wilson himself, a lifelong Anglophile. At the same time, he faced increasing opposition from stateside jingoists—most especially former President Theodore Roosevelt, whom he had defeated in the 1912 election. With each passing month of neutrality, more Americans grew restless. The harrowing reportage from overseas—especially the accounts of Germany's wanton destruction of Belgium—stirred moral outrage; and daily arguments ripened into the greatest debate in the United States since the Civil War, a profound national conversation. The adolescent nation—only fourteen decades old—was searching for its identity; protected by an ocean on either side, the United States questioned whether it should impose itself in a world fast shrinking because of advancements in communication and transportation, a world seemingly hell-bent just then on destroying itself.

The fighting in World War I ranged from Kilimanjaro to Kosovo, from Transylvania to Tsingtao, from Basra to Riga; and for most of the American population, such places existed only in atlases. They related more readily to the fighting in Western Europe, from where the great majority of America's immigrants had set sail. Great Britain and France, with their democratic governments, felt most like the United States; and for humanitarian or political reasons, or just because they sought adventure, many Americans joined the French Foreign Legion or the Lafayette Escadrille or one of several volunteer ambulance services so that they could be part of the action on the Western Front.

The opening offensives of the war resulted in massive casualties on both sides and ended in stalemate. By 1915, the evenly matched Allied Powers and Central Powers looked to the sea for an advantage: the British Royal Navy blockaded Germany, in hopes of starving that nation into submission; and the German Kaiserliche Marine launched a counter-blockade with persistently aggressive submarine warfare.

For the United States, the fighting remained a world away—until May 7, when a German U-boat torpedoed the British ocean liner RMS *Lusitania*, taking the lives of almost 1,200 passengers and crew, 128 Americans among them. This disaster politicized the war for the United States. While Wilson himself continued to practice neutrality, he increasingly preached Americanism and Preparedness, as the small peacetime army of his isolationist nation gradually expanded. By the start of 1916, the President had rid himself of a pacifistic secretary of state and raised his rhetoric to new levels of patriotism; that June, he officially proclaimed Flag Day. The national debate raged.

"He kept us out of war" was a campaign slogan that helped re-elect Wilson in November; but within weeks of his second inauguration—at which he proclaimed, "We are provincials no longer"—American entry into the war felt imminent. Germany had reneged on earlier pledges and resumed unrestricted submarine warfare; and then interception of a telegram from the German foreign minister revealed his country's attempt to enlist Mexico in fighting against the United States. On April 2, 1917, Wilson asked Congress for a declaration of war against Germany. In his request he introduced a moral component to American foreign policy, one that has provided the foundation for the country's international diplomacy ever since. In suggesting a mission of spreading democracy around the world, Wilson directed the United States to play a leading role in global politics.

Rising above the usual reasons that drew countries into war—territory, treasure, or simply long-standing tribal rivalry—President Wilson summoned Americans to fight for universal principles. He enumerated them in a speech in January 1918. Several of his points were general matters of diplomacy—such as arms reduction and self-determination; others were specific territorial matters. In no instance did the United States seek any specific gains for itself; he thought the country should fight for supra-national interests, most especially his fourteenth point—an Arthurian notion of a League of Nations, a table at which all countries would settle disagreements before they could mushroom into wars.

It took a year before the United States had armed and trained enough soldiers to engage in battle; and in the six months that followed, the fresh American Expeditionary Forces fought across rivers and through villages, towns, woods, and forests north and east of Paris, their charming names becoming synonyms for blood-soaked battlefields. By then, almost four years in the trenches, artillery bombardments, machine guns, chemical warfare, and disease—notably an influenza pandemic—had exhausted both sides; but the Allied forces won.

With the Armistice in November 1918, Wilson realized his toughest fights lay ahead—in crafting a peace treaty. The world was a jump ball, what with the demise of the four autocratic empires and their former territories up for grabs, economies in crisis, and measurable percentages of populations decimated. Wilson hoped the war had unknotted enough foreign entanglements to allow a new world order to be knitted together.

The President of the United States spent the next six months outside the country—in Paris, wangling to get his Fourteen Points incorporated into the Treaty of Versailles, all the while arguing with the Allied leaders to lessen their punitive demands of Germany. By the end of his stay, Wilson had made certain compromises to ensure the inclusion of his League, for he believed the "future peace and policy of the world" depended upon an entirely new political model—that there must no longer be a "balance of power, but a community of power; not organized rivalries, but an organized common peace."

Wars are game changers, and the First World War catalyzed transformations in America that altered the country's nature—from the halls of government to the wheat fields then feeding the world. Upon America's entering battle, President Wilson had told Congress, "Politics is adjourned"; but every one of the wartime issues that would actually change America's identity invoked intense partisan debate and sometimes provoked violence. Redefinitions of government operations (if not new vocabulary altogether) left traces that exist to this day.

Almost overnight, the federal government enlarged—creating an alphabet soup of thousands of boards, agencies, committees, and commissions. The President recruited America's business titans to work in conjunction with the armed forces, establishing an infrastructure for a military-industrial complex.

This sudden growth demanded a reconstruction of the economy, as the federal deficit had bounced from $1 billion to $9 billion. The government sharply raised the tax rates on extreme wealth and added to its coffers by selling war bonds. Washington courted Hollywood—a new American industry built on the premise that people enjoyed watching flickering images of larger-than-life people; and recruitment of these movie stars contributed to the bonds' hugely successful subscription. So that the Department of the Treasury did not have to go to Congress every time it wanted to float a bond, the legislature established what it called a "debt ceiling," a roof they kept raising.

For the first time, the United States had militarized on a scale grand enough to fight an overseas war—expanding an army of 130,000 "doughboys," as they were called, to some four million and a navy that increased almost tenfold to 500,000 sailors. In order to muster an army of this magnitude, the government created the Selective Service System, a nationwide network of local boards that would determine the fitness of its community members to serve. It became a great social equalizer that might place a scion of a great family in the same trench with a dirt-poor farm boy. Many rural high school students were excused from class to work their land, producing the additional food necessary for the troops and the starving civilians overseas. The government authorized Daylight Saving Time, creating an extra hour of productivity each day.

This great military mobilization affected all races in America —separately and not always equally. Four hundred thousand African Americans were inducted, and many considered their service a path to full citizenship. Surely, they thought, making the world safe for democracy meant an end to disenfranchisement, Jim

Crow laws, and lynching at home in the United States. But military units, trenches, and burials remained segregated; and in 1917, African American soldiers experienced a death rate twice that of whites, performing the lowliest duties while receiving inferior medical care. Stateside, a need for labor in the North spurred a Great Migration of African Americans, who imagined greater fortune ahead. But when black soldiers returned from the war, they found their opportunities were the same as when they had left, or worse; and whites across the country who feared the creeping acceptance of racial equality incited the most brutal race riots the nation had ever seen.

Female identity underwent several significant changes as a result of the war. With so much of the male population in military service, women took to working outside the home. Black women were able to find employment as something other than domestics—serving as waitresses and elevator operators. Most important, while President Wilson had long considered woman suffrage a states' rights issue, he went to Congress to argue that passage of the Nineteenth Amendment to the Constitution was essential to winning the war and fulfilling the nation's democratic goals. After decades of speeches, petitions, and demonstrations, women finally received the vote for which they had long fought.

And the war revived an aspect of the American character that had lain dormant for years—xenophobia. Fear of German subversion had sparked the adoption of draconian espionage and sedition laws that not only established a framework for protecting national security but also dangerously curtailed free speech. After the Armistice, a spate of anarchist bombings prompted a nationwide surge of arrests, imprisonments, and deportations that came to be considered perilously excessive in their disregard for civil liberties and due process.

In the wake of the Allied victory, America was perceived as the world's first modern superpower, and its president was received in Paris, where the peace talks were held, as its savior. With several empires dismantled, everybody waited to see how Wilson thought the maps of the world should be redrawn. His concept of "self-determination" raised old questions of identity, especially when it came to defining nations. Such factors as geography, ethnicity, language, religion, economy, and history all had to be considered. Censuses were taken, and numbers in almost every imaginable category were totaled. Much of America's future identity would also be determined at those peace conference tables, as several members of its next generation of leaders played roles in Paris—including two future Presidents (Herbert Hoover and Franklin D. Roosevelt), two future secretaries of state (John Foster Dulles and Christian Herter), and numerous future ambassadors and heads of agencies.

The Treaty of Versailles ended the war with Germany on June 28, 1919, but then the next battle began. While the United States Constitution allowed the President to make treaties, it required Senate approval; and a rancorous Republican upper chamber intended to shred Woodrow Wilson's idealistic accord, which included the League of Nations. Before a vote could be taken, he took his argument to the people by embarking on a month-long whistle-stop tour of the country. He made the cause one of identity—melding his with that of his nation. "Sometimes people call me an idealist," he told a crowd in South Dakota. "Well, that is the way I know I am an American." And if the Senate did not accept this treaty, he warned, "I can predict with absolute certainty that within another generation there will be another world war."

Before the tour had ended, the President collapsed. Rushed back to Washington, he suffered a stroke days later. His vision of bringing America into the League died, and his prophecy lived: the victors and the vanquished went to war twenty years later, fighting over many of the same battlefields as before. Many argue that the severe terms of the Treaty ruined Germany, guaranteeing its desire for revenge; others contend that Germany never even made a dent in its reparation bills and that its refusal to accept its defeat in 1918 caused the second global conflagration. Several of the reconfigured countries after the First World War held for the better part of a century—including Yugoslavia, Czechoslovakia, and various states in the Middle East. But people's undeniable need for identity keeps returning, begging acknowledgment; and new nations continue to emerge a century later.

While this collection focuses on factual writing, its coda acknowledges a related cultural phenomenon: World War I stimulated a landmark era in American fiction. The war became the defining moment for "the lost generation"—those young people who served in the war and spent the next several years searching for their identities. While the United States reveled in a decade of prosperity and madcap behavior, its most serious novelists explored the themes of postwar disillusionment, creating some of the most enduring fiction in the American canon: Fitzgerald's Jay Gatsby meets Daisy Fay at Camp Taylor in Louisville; Hemingway's Jake Barnes struggles with his war wound from Italy; Faulkner's self-destructive Bayard Sartoris, his twin brother killed in action, returns from the war to Yoknapatawpha County.

Several of America's most significant novelists appear in this collection, but not in their customary roles. Here they join the ranks of the nonfiction writers as correspondents—for major periodicals or just in sending letters home—recording their firsthand experiences of the war. Many thoughtful histories of World War I have appeared over the last century, as each generation has extracted new information and examined it under the lens of its era; they tend to magnify those moments of the past that especially address the present.

All the selections that follow capture moments of the past when they *were* the present. One hundred years after the events depicted in these pages, readers know the outcomes of World War I; but the authors of these pieces did not. The immediacy of their observations and the rawness of their emotions are all fraught with electrifying uncertainty.

It remains difficult to mark the conclusion of the First World War as the world continues to live in its aftermath, still fighting over many of the same places and issues of one hundred years ago. In the end, the ancients proved wise in urging censuses, as time tends to reduce history to its basic numbers; and the horrifying statistics of this war should never be forgotten. The reckoning comes to 10 million soldiers killed, 23 million more wounded, and another 6 million civilians dead directly because of the war or disease. (And those numbers do not include the tens of millions who succumbed to the war-related influenza pandemic.) The Congressional Research Service tallied 116,708 American military deaths. One of those souls has been specially memorialized at Arlington National Cemetery—a body that got counted but could never be identified, an American who eternally remains "the Unknown Soldier."

World War I forever altered America's character. After supplying humanitarian relief to faraway countries during the early part of the war, the United States proceeded to act further on a moral imperative, offering the commitment of an entire nation in the name of peace and freedom. In years thereafter, America's confident stride on the world stage would often become a swagger, and peacemaking efforts would evolve into peacekeeping. But fundamentally, the enduring legacy of this war for Americans lies in its commitment to the belief that all people forging their identities, no matter how small their numbers, are entitled to the privilege of self-determination and to the principle that all people are created equal and are endowed with certain unalienable rights. The war gave Americans that new sense of their own national identity, one that emboldened them to help others realize theirs.

—A. Scott Berg
July 2016

The New York Times:
Heir to Austria's Throne Is Slain

Europe greeted the twentieth century at peace with itself and full of hope. Even so, some of its empires showed signs of buckling under the pressure of national minorities who sought to shake off the old autocratic order. In 1908, Austria-Hungary annexed Bosnia and Herzegovina, angering Serbian nationalists, who comprised much of the population and sought to create a Greater Serbia. Victories in the Balkan Wars of 1912–1913 heightened both pan-Serbian passions and Austrian fears for the empire's future. When Archduke Franz Ferdinand and his wife, Sophie, arrived in the provincial capital of Sarajevo on June 28, 1914, members of a pan-Slavic nationalist movement called Young Bosnia ambushed them. *The New York Times* reported the fatal visit on its front page but moved on to other news after the Archduke's funeral on July 3.

HEIR TO AUSTRIA'S THRONE IS SLAIN WITH HIS WIFE BY A BOSNIAN YOUTH TO AVENGE SEIZURE OF HIS COUNTRY

Francis Ferdinand Shot During State Visit to Sarajevo.

TWO ATTACKS IN A DAY

Archduke Saves His Life First Time by Knocking Aside a Bomb Hurled at Auto.

SLAIN IN SECOND ATTEMPT

Lad Dashes at Car as the Royal Couple Return from Town Hall and Kills Both of Them.

LAID TO A SERVIAN PLOT

Heir Warned Not to Go to Bosnia,
Where Populace Met Him with Servian Flags.

AGED EMPEROR IS STRICKEN

Shock of Tragedy Prostrates Francis
Joseph—Young Assassin
Proud of His Crime.

SARAJEVO, Bosnia, June 28, (By courtesy of the Vienna Neue Freie Presse.)—Archduke Francis Ferdinand, heir to the throne of Austria-Hungary, and his wife, the Duchess of Hohenberg, were shot and killed by a Bosnian student here today. The fatal shooting was the second attempt upon the lives of the couple during the day, and is believed to have been the result of a political conspiracy.

This morning, as Archduke Francis Ferdinand and the Duchess were driving to a reception at the Town Hall a bomb was thrown at their motor car. The Archduke pushed it off with his arm.

The bomb did not explode until after the Archduke's car had passed on, and the occupants of the next car, Count von Boos-Waldeck and Col. Morizzi, the Archduke's aide de camp, were slightly injured. Among the spectators, six persons were more or less seriously hurt.

The author of the attempt at assassination was a compositor named Gabrinovics, who comes from Trebinje.

After the attempt upon his life the Archduke ordered his car to halt, and after he found out what had happened he drove to the Town Hall, where the Town Councillors, with the Mayor at their head, awaited him. The Mayor was about to begin his address of welcome, when the Archduke interrupted him angrily, saying:

"Herr Burgermeister, it is perfectly outrageous! We have come to Sarajevo on a visit and have had a bomb thrown at us."

The Archduke paused a moment, and then said: "Now you may go on."

Thereupon the Mayor delivered his address and the Archduke made a suitable reply.

The public by this time had heard of the bomb attempt, and burst into the hall with loud cries of "Zivio!" the Slav word for "hurrah."

After going around the Town Hall, which took half an hour, the Archduke started for the Garrison Hospital to visit Col. Morizzi, who had been taken there after the outrage.

As the Archduke reached the corner of Rudolf Street two pistol shots were fired in quick succession by an individual who called himself Gavrio Princip. The first shot struck the Duchess in the abdomen, while the second hit the Archduke in the neck and pierced the jugular vein. The Duchess became unconscious immediately and fell across the knees of her husband. The Archduke also lost consciousness in a few seconds.

The motor car in which they were seated drove straight to the Konak, where an army Surgeon rendered first aid, but in vain. Neither the Archduke nor the Duchess gave any sign of life, and the head of the hospital could only certify they were both dead.

The authors of both attacks upon the Archduke are born Bosnians. Gabrinovics is a compositor, and worked for a few weeks in the Government printing works at Belgrade. He returned to Sarajevo a Servian chauvinist, and made no concealment of his sympathies with the King of Servia. Both he and the actual murderer of the Archduke and the Duchess expressed themselves to the police in the most cynical fashion about their crimes.

ARCHDUKE IGNORED WARNING.

Servian Minister Feared Trouble if
Heir Went to Bosnia.
Special Cable to THE NEW YORK TIMES.
[Dispatch to The London Daily Mail.]

VIENNA, June 28.—When the news of the assassination of the Archduke Francis Ferdinand and the Duchess was broken to the aged Emperor Francis Joseph he said: "Horrible, horrible! No sorrow is spared me."

The Emperor, who yesterday left here for Ischl, his favorite Summer resort, amid acclamations of the people, will return to Vienna at once, in spite of the hardships of the journey in the terrible heat.

The Archduke, who was created head of the army, went to

Bosnia to represent the Emperor at the grand manoeuvres there. This was the first time the Archduke had paid an official visit to Bosnia. The Emperor visited the provinces immediately after their annexation, in 1908, and the manner in which he mixed freely with the people was much criticised at the time, as those in his party were always afraid lest some Slav or Mohammedan fanatic might attempt the monarch's life. The Emperor's popularity, however, saved him from all danger of this kind.

Before the Archduke went to Bosnia last Wednesday the Servian Minister here expressed doubt as to the wisdom of the journey, saying the country was in a very turbulent condition and the Servian part of the population might organize a demonstration against the Archduke. The Minister said if the Archduke went himself he certainly ought to leave his wife at home, because Bosnia was no place for a woman in its present disturbed state.

The Minister's word proved correct. The people of Sarajevo welcomed the Archduke with a display of Servian flags, and the authorities had some difficulty in removing them before the Archduke made his state entry into the city yesterday, after the conclusion of the manoeuvres. In these manoeuvres were the famous Fifteenth and Sixteenth Army Corps, which were stationed on the frontier throughout the recent Balkan war, and they carried out the evolutions before the Archduke.

GREETED WITH CHEERS.

The details of the tragedy, as received in Vienna, were as follows: The Archduke was driving in a motor car toward the Town Hall in Sarajevo, with the Duchess of Hohenberg by his side. A large crowd assembled to watch them go by. The Archduke, raising his hand to his military cap, acknowledged the cheers, while the Duchess was smiling and bowing, her pretty face framed by her blonde hair.

Suddenly the Archduke's sharp eye caught sight of a bomb hurling through the air. His first thought was for his wife, and he threw up his arm in time to catch the bomb, which thus was turned aside from its course and fell on the pavement and exploded. The Archduke's motor car hastened on its way, its occupants unharmed, but the two Adjutants who were seated in the next motor car were injured by splinters from the bomb. Several persons on the pavement were very seriously hurt by the explosion of the bomb, which was thrown by a young man named Tabrinovitch, (Gabrinovics,) who is a typist from Trebenje, in Herzegovina, and is of Servian nationality. He was arrested some twenty minutes later.

The Archduke and his wife left the Town Hall, intending to visit those who had been injured by the bomb, when a schoolboy 19 years old, named Prinzip, who came from Grahovo, fired a shot at the Archduke's head. The boy fired from the shelter of a projecting house.

WORE BULLET-PROOF COAT.

The boy must have been carefully instructed in his part, for it was a well-guarded secret that the Archduke always wore a coat of silk strands which were woven obliquely, so that no weapon or bullet could pierce it. I once saw a strip of this fabric used for a motor-car tire, and it was puncture-proof. This new invention enabled the Archduke to brave attempts on his life, but his head naturally was uncovered.

The Duchess was shot in the body. The boy fired several times, but only two shots took effect. The Archduke and his wife were carried to the Konak, or palace, in a dying condition.

Later details show that the assassin darted forth from his hiding place behind a house and actually got on the motor car in which the Archduke and his wife were sitting. He took close aim first at the Archduke, and then at the Duchess. The fact that no one stopped him, and that he was allowed to perpetrate the dastardly act indicate that the conspiracy was carefully planned and that the Archduke fell a victim to a political plot. The aspiration of the Servian population in Bosnia to join with Servia and form a great Servian kingdom is well known. No doubt today's assassination was regarded as a means of forwarding this plan.

BREAK NEWS TO CHILDREN.

The Archduke's children are at Glumex, in Bohemia, and relatives already have left Vienna to break the news to them. The Duke of Cumberland motored to Ischl immediately upon receipt of the news and was received by the Emperor, who will arrive in Vienna at 6 o'clock tomorrow. The bodies of the Archduke and his wife will not be brought to Vienna until tomorrow a week.

The Archduke Charles Francis Joseph, the new heir to the

throne, is at Reichenau, near Vienna, with his wife, Princess Zita of Parma, and their little son and daughter. He is expected in Vienna tonight.

When the first news of the assassination became known in Vienna, early this afternoon, crowds collected in solemn silence and discussed the report, which was not credited at first. Every one connected with the press was stormed by crowds asking whether confirmation had been received, and on hearing the truth they said, "How awful!" and then dispersed, to go about their ordinary business or pleasure. The newspapers are getting out extra editions, and the whole city talks of nothing else.

New Heir Popular.

The Archduke Charles Francis Joseph, who is now heir to the throne, always has enjoyed great popularity. He was trained for the throne from the first, although he was kept somewhat in the background, being sent to country garrisons. He was not allowed to undertake to act as the representative of the Duchy of Vienna to as great an extent as the Viennese would have wished. This, however, did not detract from his popularity, while the Princess Zita, his wife, won all hearts before she married the heir to the throne, and the birth of a son two years ago completed her popularity, if, indeed, anything was lacking.

General opinion here connects the assassins with the Servian faction, and it is feared that it will lead to serious complications with that unruly kingdom, and may have far-reaching results. The future of the empire is a subject of general discussion. It is felt that the Servians have been treated too leniently, and some hard words are being said about the present foreign policy.

All the public buildings are draped in long black streamers and the flags are all at half-mast.

BRAVERY OF ARCHDUKE.

Gave First Aid to Those Wounded by the Bomb.

Sarajevo, Bosnia, June 28.—Archduke Francis Ferdinand, heir to the Austro-Hungarian throne, and the Duchess of Hohenberg, his morganatic wife, were shot dead in the main street of the Bosnian capital by a student today while they were making an apparently triumphant progress through the city on their annual visit to the annexed provinces of Bosnia and Herzegovina.

The Archduke was hit full in the face and the Duchess was shot through the abdomen and throat. Their wounds proved fatal within a few minutes after they reached the palace, whence they were hurried with all speed.

Those responsible for the assassination took care that it would prove effective, as there were two assailants, the first armed with a bomb and the other with a revolver. The bomb was thrown at the royal automobile as it was proceeding to the Town Hall, where a reception was to be held, but the Archduke saw the deadly missile coming and warded it off with his arm. It fell outside the car and exploded, slightly wounding two aids de camp in a second car, and half a dozen spectators. It was on the return of the procession that the tragedy was added to the long list of those that have darkened the pages of the recent history of the Hapsburgs.

As the royal automobile reached a prominent point in the route to the palace, an eighth grade student, Gavrio Prinzip, sprang out of the crowd and poured a fusillade of bullets from an automatic pistol at the Archduke and the Duchess. Both fell mortally wounded.

Prinzip and a fellow-conspirator, a compositor from Trebinje, Nedeljo Gabrinovics, barely escaped lynching by the infuriated spectators and were finally seized by the police, who afforded them protection. Both men are natives of the annexed province of Herzegovina.

WARDS OFF THE BOMB.

The first attempt against the Archduke occurred just outside the Girls' High School. The Archduke's car had restarted after a brief pause for an inspection of the building, when Gabrinovics hurled the bomb. This was so successfully warded off by the Archduke that it fell directly beneath the following car, the occupants of which, Count von Boos-Waldeck and Col. Merizzo, were struck by splinters of iron.

Archduke Francis Ferdinand stopped his car, and after making inquiries as to the injuries of his aids and lending what aid he could, continued his journey to the Town Hall. There the

Mayor began the customary address, but the Archduke sharply interrupted and snapped out, "Herr Burgomeister, we have come here to pay you a visit and bombs have been thrown at us. This is altogether an amazing indignity."

After a pause, the Archduke said: "Now you may speak."

On leaving the hall the Archduke and his wife announced their intention of visiting the wounded members of their suite at the hospital on their way back to the palace. They were actually bound on their mission of mercy when, at the corner of Rudolf Street and Franz Josef Street, Prinzip opened his deadly fusillade.

A bullet struck the Archduke in the face. The Duchess was wounded in the abdomen and another bullet struck her in the throat, severing an artery. She fell unconscious across her husband's knees. At the same moment the Archduke sank to the floor of the car.

PLUNGES INTO RIVER.

After his unsuccessful attempt to blow up the imperial visitors Gabrinovics sprang into the River Miljachka in an effort to escape, but witnesses plunged after him and seized him.

A few yards from the scene of the shooting an unexploded bomb was found, which, it is suspected, was thrown away by an accomplice after he had noted the success of Prinzip's attack.

The assassins were questioned by the police during the course of the afternoon, and both seemed to glory in their exploit. Prinzip said he had studied for a time at Belgrade. He declared he had long intended to kill some eminent person from nationalist motives. He was awaiting the Archduke at a point where he knew the automobile would slacken speed, turning into Franz Josef Street. The presence of the Duchess in the car caused him to hesitate, but only for a moment. Then his nerve returned and he emptied his pistol at the couple. He denied that he had any accomplices.

Prinzip is 18 years old and Nedeljo Gabrinovics is 21. Gabrinovics told the police that he had obtained the bomb from Anarchists at Belgrade, whose names he did not know. He similarly denied that he had accomplices and treated the whole tragedy with cynical indifference.

Anti-Servian demonstrations began tonight. The crowds

knelt in the streets and sang the national anthem. The Mayor of Sarajevo issued a proclamation to the inhabitants of the city denouncing the crime, and declaring that by the confessions of the assassins it was shown beyond all doubt that the bomb thrown at the Archduke's car came from Belgrade.

It is said that after the attempt with the bomb the Duchess tried to dissuade the Archduke from venturing in the motor car again. To allay her fears M. Potiorek, Governor of Bosnia, said: "It's all over now. We have not more than one murderer in Sarajevo," whereupon the Archduke decided to go on.

At a meeting of the provincial Diet tonight the President of the Chamber expressed Bosnia's profound sorrow and indignation over the outrage and paid a glowing tribute to the Archduke and the Duchess. He also declared his devotion to the Emperor and the ruling house.

The New York Times, June 29, 1914

Hugh Gibson: from
A Journal from Our Legation in Belgium

To America's 100 million citizens, the datelines on the stories from Europe suggested a distant foreign entanglement that did not impact them directly. But within a month, the major European powers found themselves trammeled in an intricate net of political and military alliances from prior treaties. When Austrian authorities arrested several of the Sarajevo perpetrators, they learned that an officer in Serbian military intelligence had supplied their weapons. The Austro-Hungarian foreign minister then enlisted the backing of the Habsburgs' ally Germany, which pledged to support Austria-Hungary against Serbia, even at the risk of war with Russia. On July 28, 1914, Austria-Hungary declared war on Serbia and began shelling Belgrade. Hugh Gibson, an American diplomat who had served in Honduras, London, Cuba, and Santo Domingo before being posted to Brussels in 1914 as secretary of the U.S. legation, observed the first days of the European conflict.

———————

July 28, 1914.—Well, the roof has fallen in. War was declared this afternoon by Austria. The town is seething with excitement and everybody seems to realise how near they are to the big stage. Three classes of reserves have already been called to the colours to defend Belgian neutrality. A general mobilisation is prepared and may be declared at any time. The Bourse has been closed to prevent too much play on the situation, and let things steady themselves. In every other way the hatches have been battened down and preparations made for heavy weather.

To-night the streets are crowded and demonstrations for and against war are being held. The Socialists have Jaurès, their French leader, up from Paris, and have him haranguing an anti-war demonstration in the Grande Place, where a tremendous crowd has collected. Nobody on earth can see where it will all lead. England is trying hard to localise the conflict, and has valuable help. If she does not succeed * * *

An advance guard of tourists is arriving from France, Germany, and Switzerland, and a lot of them drop in for advice as to whether it is safe for them to go to various places in Europe. And most of them seem to feel that we really have authoritative information as to what the next few days are to bring forth, and resent the fact that we are too disobliging to tell them the inside news. A deluge of this sort would be easier for a full-sized Embassy to grapple with, but as Belgium is one of those places where nothing ever happens we have the smallest possible organisation, consisting on a peace basis of the Minister and myself, with one clerk. We shall have somehow to build up an emergency force to meet the situation.

July 30th.—No line on the future yet. Brussels is beginning to look warlike. Troops are beginning to appear. The railway stations have been occupied, and the Boy Scouts are swarming over the town as busy as bird dogs. A week ago there was hardly a tourist in Brussels. Now the Legation hall is filled with them, and they all demand precise information as to what is going to happen next and where they can go with a guarantee from the Legation that they will not get into trouble.

July 31st.—No, my recent remarks about nothing ever happening in Brussels were not intended as sarcasm. I thought Belgium was the one place where I could be sure of a quiet time, and here we are right in the centre of it. Even if nothing more happens we have had enough excitement to last me for some time. The doings of the past few days have brought out some idea of what a general European war would mean—and it is altogether too dreadful to think of.

Saturday, Aug. 1st.—Last night when I went home, at about midnight, I found the police going about with the orders for mobilisation, ringing the door bells and summoning the men to the colours. There was no time to tarry, but each man tumbled out of bed into his clothes and hurried away to his regiment. Two of my neighbours were routed out a little after midnight, and got away within the hour. There was a good deal of weeping and handshaking and farewelling, and it was not the sort of thing to promote restful sleep.

This morning I got down to the chancery at a quarter past eight, and found that Omer, our good messenger, had been summoned to the colours. He had gone, of course, and had left a note for me to announce the fact. He had been ill, and could perfectly well have been exempted. The other day, when we had discussed the matter, I had told him that there would be no difficulty in getting him off. He showed no enthusiasm, however, and merely remarked, without heroics, that it was up to him.

Colonel Falls, 7th Regiment, of the National Guard of New York, came in, having been sent back from the frontier. He had the pleasure of standing all the way as the trains were packed.

Millard Shaler, the American mining engineer, who had just come back from the Congo, came in with his amusing Belgian friend who had been telling us for weeks about the wonderful new car in which he was investing. This time he came around to let me have a look at it, he having been advised that the car was requisitioned and due to be taken over to-day.

We have done a land-office business in passports, and shall probably continue to turn them out by the dozen.

Sunday, August 2d.—Another hectic day with promise of more to come.

This morning I came down a little earlier than usual and found the Minister already hard at it. He had been routed out of bed and had not had time to bathe or shave. There was nothing to show that it was a Sunday—nearly twice as many callers as yesterday, and they were more exacting.

Mrs. A— B— C— came in airily and announced that she had started from Paris yesterday on a motor tour through France and Belgium. Having got this far, some rude person had told her that her motor might be seized by the Government for military purposes and that an order had been promulgated forbidding any one to take cars out of the country. She came around confidently to have us assure her that this was a wicked lie—and needless to say was deeply disappointed in us when we failed to back her up. We had refrained from asking the Government to release our own servants from their military obligations and have refused to interfere for anybody else, but that was not enough for her. She left, a highly indignant lady.

The story is around town this afternoon that the Germans have already crossed the frontier without the formality of a declaration of war—but that remains to be seen. Brussels was put under martial law last night, and is now patrolled by grenadiers and lancers.

The money situation is bad. All small change has disappeared in the general panic, and none of it has dared show its head during the past few days. The next thing done by panicky people was to pass round word that the Government bank notes were no good and would not be honoured. Lots of shops are refusing to accept bank notes, and few places can make any change. The police are lined up outside the banks keeping people in line. People in general are frantic with fear, and are trampling each other in the rush to get money out of the banks before the crash that probably will not come. Travelers who came here with pockets bulging with express checks and bank notes are unable to get a cent of real money, and nobody shows any enthusiasm over American paper. I have a few bank notes left, and this evening when I went into a restaurant I have patronised ever since my arrival the head waiter refused to change a note for me, and I finally had to leave it and take credit against future meals to be eaten there. We may have our troubles when our small store is gone, but probably the situation will improve and I refuse to worry. And some of our compatriots don't understand why the Legation does not have a cellar full of hard money to finance them through their stay in Europe.

Communications, with such parts of the world as we still speak to, are getting very difficult on account of mobilisation, the military having right of way. This morning's Paris papers have not come in this evening, and there are no promises as to when we shall see them. The news in the local papers is scarce and doubtful, and I hope for a word from Paris.

Word has just come in that the Government has seized the supplies of bread, rice, and beans, and will fix prices for the present. That is a sensible and steadying thing, and should have a good effect.

Nobody seems to remember that a few days ago Serbia was playing a star rôle in this affair. She seems to have faded away behind the scenes. A few days ago, Mexico loomed large in the papers and now we have forgotten that she ever existed. Albania supplied a lot of table talk, and now we think about as much about her and her troubles as we do about Thibet.

This afternoon I went around to the Rue Ducale to take a look at the French Legation. The tricolor was flying in the fresh breeze, and there was a big crowd outside cheering itself hoarse. It was made up of men who were called to the colors and were waiting to enroll themselves and get instructions as to where they should report for duty. The air was electric, and every now and then the military band struck up the Marseillaise and the crowd instantly became happily delirious. Some of them had been standing in the sun for hours waiting to get in and get their orders, but they were just as keenly responsive to the music and the mood of the crowd as anybody. All the crowd in the Legation had been working day and night for days, and was dead with fatigue; but, some way, they kept going, and managed to be civil and friendly when I had business with them. How they do it I don't know. A Frenchman's politeness must be more deeply ingrained than even I had supposed.

On the way back from the Legation this evening, I saw von Below, the German Minister, driving home from the Foreign Office to his Legation. He passed close to me, and I saw that the perspiration was standing out on his forehead. He held his hat in his hand and puffed at a cigarette like a mechanical toy, blowing out jerky clouds of smoke. He looked neither to left nor right, and failed to give me his usual ceremonious bow. He is evidently not at ease about the situation, although he continues to figure in the newspapers as stating that all is well, that Germany has no intention of setting foot on Belgian soil, and that all Belgium has to do is to keep calm. In an interview given to *Le Soir* he sums up his reassuring remarks by saying: "Your neighbour's house may burn but yours will be safe."

Walter Hines Page: Memorandum

On July 30 Tsar Nicholas II ordered the mobilization of the Russian army. The next day the German government demanded that the Tsar cancel the mobilization, and it called upon France to forsake its alliance with Russia and remain neutral in a Russo-German war. Both ultimatums were rejected; and on August 1, Germany declared war on Russia as France mobilized its army. In 1913, Woodrow Wilson had appointed his longtime friend Walter Hines Page—a journalist and newspaper editor from North Carolina who had become a successful book publisher—America's ambassador to Great Britain.

Bachelor's Farm, Ockham, Surrey.
Sunday, August 2, 1914.

THE Grand Smash is come. Last night the German Ambassador at St. Petersburg handed the Russian Government a declaration of war. To-day the German Government asked the United States to take its diplomatic and consular business in Russia in hand. Herrick, our Ambassador in Paris, has already taken the German interests there.

It is reported in London to-day that the Germans have invaded Luxemburg and France.

Troops were marching through London at one o'clock this morning. Colonel Squier came out to luncheon. He sees no way for England to keep out of it. There is no way. If she keep out, Germany will take Belgium and Holland, France would be betrayed, and England would be accused of forsaking her friends.

People came to the Embassy all day to-day (Sunday), to learn how they can get to the United States—a rather hard question to answer. I thought several times of going in, but Greene and Squier said there was no need of it. People merely hoped we might tell them what we can't tell them.

Returned travellers from Paris report indescribable confusion—people unable to obtain beds and fighting for seats in railway carriages.

It's been a hard day here. I have a lot (not a big lot either) of routine work on my desk which I meant to do. But it has been impossible to get my mind off this Great Smash. It holds one in spite of one's self. I revolve it and revolve it—of course getting nowhere.

It will revive our shipping. In a jiffy, under stress of a general European war, the United States Senate passed a bill permitting American registry to ships built abroad. Thus a real emergency knocked the old Protectionists out, who had held on for fifty years! Correspondingly the political parties here have agreed to suspend their Home Rule quarrel till this war is ended. Artificial structures fall when a real wind blows.

The United States is the only great Power wholly out of it. The United States, most likely, therefore, will be able to play a helpful and historic part at its end. It will give President Wilson, no doubt, a great opportunity. It will probably help us politically and it will surely help us economically.

The possible consequences stagger the imagination. Germany has staked everything on her ability to win primacy. England and France (to say nothing of Russia) really ought to give her a drubbing. If they do not, this side of the world will henceforth be German. If they do flog Germany, Germany will for a long time be in discredit.

I walked out in the night a while ago. The stars are bright, the night is silent, the country quiet—as quiet as peace itself. Millions of men are in camp and on warships. Will they all have to fight and many of them die—to untangle this network of treaties and alliances and to blow off huge debts with gunpowder so that the world may start again?

Hugo Münsterberg to the Boston Herald

Germans comprised the largest ethnic group in the American melting pot, accounting for about 10 percent of its population. Born in Danzig, Prussia, and educated at Leipzig and Heidelberg, the psychologist Hugo Münsterberg had joined the Harvard faculty in 1892 at the encouragement of his friend William James. A prolific writer and popular lecturer, Münsterberg became a well-known public intellectual, one who never lost affection for his homeland. German plans called for a quick decisive victory over France by invading neutral Belgium and enveloping the French armies massed along the Franco-German frontier. When Germany prepared to enter Belgium and declared war on France on August 3, Münsterberg responded to the anti-German sentiment in the American press. The *Boston Herald* published "Fair Play!" on August 5, 1914; and it was reprinted in more than fifty American newspapers and in Münsterberg's book *The War and America*, published in September 1914.

FAIR PLAY!

THE European war broke into the calm of our summer quick and unexpected, but still quicker and still more unexpected by any lover of fair play was the vehement turn of the American press for the Slavs and against the Germans. Whatever Germany or Austria did was seen through the spectacles of the enemy. Their motives appeared tainted, their actions against the rules of the game, they had no just cause and no morals, they were not worthy of American sympathy. Of course, some pretext can be found for every partiality, and it is not difficult to foresee how this game can be played on. If Germany's enemies are defeated the American nation must be with them because it is always with the weakest, always with the under dog; but if they are victorious the American nation will be with them, too, because it loves a spirited fighter and a triumphant power. Yet it is just Germany which dares a spirited fight and which is the weaker, forced to fight, two nations against five.

The naked news which the cable brings helps on this cruel game. The average American reader has no idea how much anti-German feeling is infused into the so-called facts which are sent over the ocean. He sees that the news is dated from Vienna or Berlin and he does not know that most of the American correspondents on the continent for many years have been enthusiastic Englishmen, who serve first of all their home papers. And even the few American journalists on the spot devote most of their energies to London papers and receive from there the daily advice and the daily prejudice of English rivalry.

But does the news at least find fair play when it arrives? What the French or the English government proclaims stands gloriously on the first page; what the German government replies is hidden somewhere in a corner of the fifth. When England interprets German action in Luxemburg as the violation of agreements it is told in inch-large letters; when Germany proves that it had the right it comes out in the smallest print. When Germany goes through Belgium, America shares the indignation of England, to which it serves as a welcome pretext. But that France went through Belgium and Holland first is kept a secret in most American papers. This means playing the reporter's game with loaded dice.

Yet even the kind of news which is dumped on us does not justify the editorial temper with which especially the New York papers appeal to our sense of superiority over mediaeval Germany. Typical is the way in which the decisions and deeds of the emperors are always treated as if they were purely personal autocratic caprices without inner contact with the national life. This better than anything whips up the democratic spirit of the new world. Who stops to consider that in the hour of war, and even of danger before the war, the American President has more personal power than any emperor except the Czar, and even he would be swept away if he obstructed the will of the people? Children like to fancy that kings run about with golden crowns on their heads and with purple cloaks. It is hardly less childlike to imagine that a proclamation like that of the Emperor Franz Josef was written by him personally, and to construe it as if he made war on Servia because he wanted to take personal vengeance for the murder of his heir. Even the distant spectator ought to have seen that the whole tremendous pressure of the Austrian nation was necessary to force the old Emperor into a war which he resisted with all the instincts of a man who has suffered much and who wants at last his peace and rest.

Is it really possible to doubt that Emperor William desired nothing but honorable peace with all the world? For twenty-five years he has been the most efficient power for European peace. He has done more for it than all the European peace societies together, and, however often the world seemed at the verge of war, his versatile mind averted the danger. He knew too well, and the whole German people knew too well, that the incomparable cultural and industrial growth of the nation since the foundation of the young empire would be horribly threatened by the risks of war. Can any sane man really believe the slander that all was a long-prepared game which Austria was to start, and in which Germany would wilfully force the furies of war into the Russian realm?

No; this time every effort was in vain, and all good will for peace was doomed because the issue between the onrushing Slavic world and the German world had grown to an overpowering force. The struggle between the two civilizations was imminent, and where such a historic world conflict arises the will of individuals is crushed until they serve the will of the nations. The Slavs of the southeast, the Servians, had defeated their oppressors, the Turks. It was inevitable that their new strength should push them to ambitious plans. It was necessary that they should aim toward a new great Slavic empire which would border the sea and embrace Austria's Slavic possessions. That had to mean the end of Austria, the crumbling of its historic power. Such an inner, passionate conflict, such an issue of existence must lead to explosions. Servians killed the Archduke. That was Austria's opportunity for an effort to crush the power which aimed toward its downfall. But it was no less historically necessary that the largest Slavic nation, the Russians, should feel that Servia's cause was their own. Russia knew well that while it had recovered from the wounds of the Japanese war the Slavic strength was still unequal to that of the German nations, but it knew also that it could rely on France's latent longing to revenge itself for Alsace and on England's grumbling jealousy of the great German rival in the world's markets. At last the chances seemed splendid to strike the long delayed blow of the Slavic world against the German. The Czar was unable to resist the gigantic pressure of the hour, his government mobilized against both Austria and Germany.

Is there really any sense in blaming the German Emperor for actually declaring war, when the Russian hostile preparation was evident, before its slow mobilization was completed and before Germany by such loss of time would have been brought to certain destruction? Four times he urged the Czar to abstain from the moving of the Russian troops to the frontier; most willingly he undertook to urge Austria to new negotiations. But the world contrast of the two civilizations was too deep; Russia could not forego its unique chances, and so it continued passionately to its armaments, trusting that the French guns would start of themselves. The German Emperor would have shamefully neglected his duties if he had quietly waited until the Russian armies were brought together from the far East. He had to strike as soon as the war was certain. He therefore had to go through the formality of declaring war, but it was Russia which made the war, and it was part of Russia's war-making that it forced Germany to declare the war first. America undertook without such a deep inner conflict a punitive expedition against Mexico, not unlike that of Austria against Servia. If at that time Japan had declared that it could not tolerate such hostility to Mexico and had sent all its warships toward California, would the President have genially waited until the Japanese cruisers entered the Golden Gate instead of putting an ultimatum to the Mikado saying that unless the ships stopped it would mean war?

In this historic situation neither Russia nor Germany could really act otherwise. The great conflict of civilizations was necessarily stronger than the mere wishes of peaceful individuals. But if it is such a gigantic conflict of Slavic and Germanic culture, the sympathies of the progressive American nation ought not to be so wilfully misled and ought not to be whipped into the camp of the Cossacks. Americans ought not to rejoice when the uncultured hordes of the East march over the frontier and aim toward the most eastern German city, toward Konigsberg, the town of Immanuel Kant.

If this war means such an inevitable conflict of the Slavic and the Germanic world, at least it ought to be clear to every one who can think historically that it belongs to the type of war for which the world as yet knows no substitute, the one type of war which in spite of the terrible losses is ultimately moral. Surely no comment on this fight of the nations is more absurd than the frivolous cry that this is an immoral war. Every war for commercial ends or for personal glory or for mere aggrandizement or for revenge may be called immoral, and thus the feelings with which Frenchmen and Englishmen join the Slavic forces might justly be accused. But both Slavs and Germans stand here on moral ground, as both are willing to sacrifice labor and life for the conservation of their national culture and very existence. Since the days of Napoleon Germany has never gone into a war which was more justified by the conscience of history.

To be sure, there is no lack of elements in this war which do hurt the moral feeling. In victory or defeat Germans will hardly forget the flight of Italy which, under the flimsiest subterfuges, has deserted its allies in the hour of need. And immoral above all is the effort of the world to strangle the spirit of Germany by the mere number of enemies. That truly is no fair, no moral fight, if Germany and Austria are not to stand against Russia and Servia alone, which together have a population equal to that of the two opponents, but are also attacked from behind by France and England, perhaps by Roumania and Japan, and last, but not least, by the misled public opinion of America.

And this answers at once the pointed question which many American papers have discussed since the war began, the question whether the whole system is not fundamentally wrong, whether the armaments which were planned to protect the countries and to keep the balance and harmony have not thrown them into a destructive war, and whether it would not have been better to rely on international arbitration throughout the world. The grouping of this war shows why Germany would have trampled on her own sacred rights if she had laid

the armor away and relied on the judgment of the other nations. Would she have had the slightest chance for a fair judgment if political jealousy, economic rivalry, in England, the
vanity of revenge and the aversion of a lower culture had been
combined against her in an unholy alliance? The jury would
have been packed, prejudices would have swept the courtroom.
No: unless the Cossacks with their pogroms were to crush the
culture of Germany she had simply no resort left but to trust
in her sword and in her prayer.

Clifton, Mass., Aug. 4, 1914.

Walter Hines Page to Woodrow Wilson

The Treaty of London, signed in 1839 by Great Britain, France, Russia, Austria, Prussia, and the Netherlands, had guaranteed the independence and neutrality of Belgium. Thus, the German invasion of Belgium presented the British government with a challenge to international morality and national honor, while the possibility of Germany gaining naval bases on the Channel coast offered a further threat to its national security. Britain warned Germany on August 4 that it would go to war if the invasion of Belgium continued. When the British ambassador met with German Chancellor Theobald von Bethmann Hollweg that evening, the latter announced his disbelief that Britain and Germany would enter battle over "a scrap of paper." Upon the expiration of the ultimatum at 11 P.M. that night, the entire British Empire, including India and the Dominions of Canada, Newfoundland, South Africa, Australia, and New Zealand, went to war. Five days later, Ambassador Page wrote to President Wilson of the impact the expanded conflict was having on the U.S. Embassy in London.

Belated, I fear, beyond any value or interest.

Dear Mr. President: London, Sunday, August 9, 1914.

God save us! What a week it has been! Last Sunday (Aug. 2) I was down here at the cottage I have taken for the summer—an hour out of London—uneasy because of the apparent danger and of what Sir Edward Grey had told me. During the day people began to go to the Embassy but not in great numbers —merely to ask what they should do in case of war. The Secretary whom I had left in charge on Sunday telephoned me every few hours and laughingly told funny experiences with nervous women who came in and asked absurd questions. Of course, we all knew the grave danger that war might come, but nobody could, by the wildest imagination, guess at what awaited us. On Monday I was at the Embassy earlier than I think I had ever been there before, and every member of the staff was already on duty. Before breakfast-time the place was filled— packed like sardines. This was two days before war was declared. There was no chance to talk to individuals, such was

23

the jam. I got on a chair and explained that I had already telegraphed to Washington—on Saturday—suggesting the sending of money and ships, and asking them to be patient. I made
a speech to them several times during the day, and kept the
Secretaries doing so at intervals. More than 2,000 Americans
crowded into those offices (which are not large) that day. We
were kept there till two o'clock in the morning. The Embassy
has not been closed since.

Mr. Kent of the Bankers' Trust Co. in New York volunteered
to form an American Citizens' Relief Committee. He and
other men of experience and influence organized themselves at
the Savoy Hotel. The hotel gave the use of nearly a whole
floor. They organized themselves quickly and admirably and
got information about steamships and currency, etc. We began
to send callers at the Embassy to this Committee for such information. The banks were all closed for four days. These men
got money enough—put it up themselves and used their English banking friends for help—to relieve all cases of actual
want of cash that came to them. Tuesday the crowd at the
Embassy was still great but less. The big space at the Savoy
Hotel gave them room to talk to one another and to get relief
for immediate needs. By that time I had accepted the volunteer
service of five or six men* to help us explain to the people—
and they have all worked manfully day and night. We now have
an orderly organization at four places—the Embassy, the
Consul-General's Office, the Savoy, and The American Society
in London, and everything is going well. We now have offices
for inquiries & for disbursing agents also. Those two first days,
there was, of course, great confusion. Crazy men and weeping
women were imploring and cursing and demanding—God
knows it was bedlam turned loose. I have been called a man of
the greatest genius for an emergency by some, by others a
d—d fool, by others every epithet between these extremes.
Men shook English banknotes in my face and demanded U. S.
money and swore our Government and its agents ought all to
be shot. Women expected me to hand them steamship tickets
home. When some found out they could not get tickets on the

---

* There are now, I think, 14 extra men at work, besides the relief-group of as
many more.

transports (which they assumed would sail the next day) they accused me of favoritism. European folk regard an Ambassador as a man who represents their government; Americans, as a personal servant to secure them state-rooms! These absurd experiences will give you a hint of the panic. But now it has worked out all right, thanks to the Savoy Committee and other helpers.

Meantime, of course, our telegrams and mail increased almost as much as our callers. I have filled the place with stenographers, I have got the Savoy people to answer certain classes of letters, and we have caught up. My own time and the time of two of the Secretaries has been almost wholly taken with governmental problems: hundreds of questions have come in from every quarter that were never asked before. But even with them we have now practically caught up—it has been a wonderful week!

Then the Austrian Ambassador came to give us his Embassy —to take over his business. Every detail was arranged. The next morning I called on him to assume charge and to say good bye, when he told me that he was not yet going! That was a stroke of genius by Sir Edward Grey who informed him that Austria had not given England cause for war. That *may* work out, or it may not. Pray Heaven it may! Poor Mensdorff, the Austrian Ambassador, does not know where he is. He is practically shut up in his guarded Embassy, weeping and waiting the decree of fate.

Then came the declaration of war, most dramatically. Tuesday night five minutes after the ultimatum expired the Admiralty telegraphed to the fleet "Go." In a few minutes the answer came back "Off." Soldiers began to march through the city going to the railway stations. An indescribable crowd so blocked the streets about the Admiralty, the War Office, and the Foreign Office, that at one o'clock in the morning I had to drive in my car by other streets to get home.

The next day the German Embassy was turned over to me. I went to see the German Ambassador at three o'clock in the afternoon. He came down in his pajamas—a crazy man. I feared he might literally go mad. He is of the anti-war party and he had done his best and utterly failed. This interview was one of the most pathetic experiences of my life. The poor man had not slept for several nights. Then came the crowds of frightened Germans, afraid that they would be arrested. They besieged the German Embassy and our Embassy. A servant in the German Embassy who went over the house with one of our men came to the desk of Princess Lichnowsky, the Ambassador's wife. A photo of the German Emperor lay on the desk, face down. The man said: "She threw it down and said: 'That is the swine that did this,'" and she drew a pig on the blotting pad, wh. is still there. I put one of our naval officers in the German Embassy, put the U. S. on the door to protect it, and we began business there, too. Our naval officer has moved in—sleeps there. He has an assistant, a stenographer, a messenger; and I gave him the German automobile and chauffeur and two English servants that were left there. He has the job well in hand now, under my and Laughlin's supervision. But this has brought still another new lot of diplomatic and governmental problems—a lot of them. Three enormous German banks in London have, of course, been closed. Their managers pray for my aid. Howling women come and say their innocent German husbands have been arrested as spies. English, Germans, Americans—everybody has daughters and wives and invalid grandmothers alone in Germany. In God's name, they ask, what can I do for them? Here come stacks of letters sent under the impression that I can send them to Germany. But the German business is already well in hand and I think that that will take little of my own time and will give little trouble. I shall send a report about it in detail to the Department the very first day I can find time to write it. In spite of the effort of the English Government to remain at peace with Austria, I fear I shall yet have the Austrian Embassy too. But I can attend to it.

Now, however, comes the financial job of wisely using the $300,000 which I shall have tomorrow. I am using Mr. Chandler Anderson as counsel, of course. I have appointed a Committee —Skinner, the Consul-General, Lieut. Commander McCrary of our Navy, Kent of the Bankers' Trust Co., N. Y., and one other man yet to be chosen—to advise, after investigation, about every proposed expenditure. Anderson has been at work all day today drawing up proper forms etc. to fit the Department's very excellent instructions. I have the feeling that more of that money may be wisely spent in helping to get people off the continent (except in France, where they seem admirably to be managing it, under Herrick) than is immediately needed in England. All this merely to show you the diversity and multiplicity of the job.

I am having a card catalogue, each containing a sort of who's who, of all Americans in Europe of whom we hear. This will be ready by the time the Tennessee comes. Fifty or more stranded Americans—men and women—are doing this work free. I have a member of Congress in the general reception room of the Embassy answering people's questions—three other volunteers as well.

We had a world of confusion for two or three days. But all this work is now well organized and it can be continued without confusion or cross-purposes. I meet committees and lay plans and read and write telegrams from the time I wake till I go to bed. But, since it is now all in order, it is easy. Of course I am running up the expenses of the Embassy—there is no help for that; but the bill will be really exceedingly small because of the volunteer work—for awhile. I have not and shall not consider the expense of whatever it seems absolutely necessary to do—of other things, I shall always consider the expense most critically. Everybody is working with everybody else in the finest possible spirit. I have made out a sort of military order to the Embassy staff, detailing one man with clerks for each night and forbidding the others to stay there till midnight. None of us slept more than a few hours last week. It was not the work that kept them after the first night or two, but the sheer excitement of this awful cataclysm. All London has been awake for a week. Soldiers are marching day and night; immense throngs block the streets about the government offices; thousands and thousands throng before the Palace every night till the King comes out on the balcony. But they are all very orderly. Every day Germans are arrested on suspicion; and several of them have committed suicide. Yesterday one poor American woman yielded to the excitement and cut her throat. I find it hard to get about much. People stop me on the street, follow me to luncheon, grab me as I come out of any committee meeting—to know my opinion of this or that—how can they get home? Will such-and-such a boat fly the American flag? Why did I take the German Embassy? I receive yet a great deal of criticism for having the German Embassy—from

Americans chiefly. I have to fight my way about and rush to an automobile. I have had to buy me a second one to keep up the racket. Buy? no—only bargain for it, for I have not any money. But everybody is considerate, and that makes no matter for the moment. This little cottage in an out-of-the-way place 25 miles from London where I am trying to write and sleep has been found by people today, who come in automobiles to know how they may reach their sick kinspeople in Germany. I had not had a bath for three days: as soon as I got in the tub, the telephone rang an "urgent" call!

Upon my word, if one could forget the awful tragedy, all this experience would be worth a life-time of common-place. One surprise follows another so rapidly that one loses all sense of time: it seems an age since last Sunday.

I shall never forget Sir Edward Grey's telling me of the ultimatum—while he wept; nor the poor German Ambassador who has lost in his high game—almost a demented man; nor the King as he declaimed at me for half-an-hour and threw up his hands and said, "My God, Mr. Page, what else could we do?" Nor the Austrian Ambassador's wringing his hands and weeping and crying out "My dear Colleague, my dear colleague."

Along with all this tragedy come two reverend American peace-delegates who got out of Germany by the skin of their teeth and complain that they lost all the clothes they had except what they had on. "Don't complain," said I, "but thank God you saved your skins." Everybody has forgotten what war means—forgotten that folks get hurt. But they are coming around to it now. A U. S. Senator telegraphs me "Send my wife and daughter home on the first ship." Ladies and gentlemen filled the steerage of that ship, not a bunk left; and his wife and daughter are found three days later sitting in a swell hotel waiting for me to bring them state-room tickets on a silver tray! One of my young fellows in the Embassy rushes into my office saying that a man from Boston with letters of introduction from Senators and Governors and Secretaries et al. was demanding tickets of admission to a picture-gallery, and a Secretary to escort him there. "What shall I do with him?" "Put his proposal to a vote of the 200 Americans in the room and see them draw and quarter him." I have not yet heard what happened. A woman writes me four pages to prove how dearly she loves my sister and invites me to her hotel—5 miles away—"please to tell her about the sailing of the steamships." Six American preachers pass a resolution unanimously "urging our Ambassador to telegraph our beloved, peace-loving President to stop this awful war"; and they come with simple solemnity to present their resolution. Lord save us, what a world!

And this awful tragedy moves on to—what? We do not know what is really happening, so strict is the censorship. But it seems inevitable to me that Germany will be beaten, after a long while, that the horrid period of alliances and armaments will not come again, that England will gain even more of the earth's surface, that Russia may next play the menace; that all Europe (so much as survives) will be bankrupt; that relatively *we* shall be immensely stronger financially and politically—there must surely come many great changes—very many, yet undreamed of. Be ready; for you will be called on to compose this huge quarrel. I thank Heaven for many things—first, the Atlantic Ocean; second, that you refrained from war in Mexico; third, that we kept our treaty—the canal tolls victory, I mean. Now, when all this half of the world will suffer the unspeakable brutalization of war, we shall preserve our moral strength, our political power, and our ideals.

God save us!   Yours faithfully   Walter H. Page

Woodrow Wilson: Statement on Neutrality

"It would be the irony of fate if my administration had to deal chiefly with foreign affairs," President-elect Woodrow Wilson had told a former Princeton colleague while preparing for his move to Washington. The election of 1912—in which he faced the Republican incumbent William Howard Taft, former President Theodore Roosevelt, who had formed the Progressive "Bull Moose" Party, and the Socialist candidate, Eugene V. Debs—was almost entirely about domestic issues. Upon his election, Wilson pressed forward with his progressive agenda, known as "the New Freedom"; but within a few months in office, he found himself drawn into an expanding quagmire of international incidents, starting with several incursions into Mexico. The tragic death on August 6, 1914, of Ellen Axson Wilson, his beloved wife of twenty-nine years, added to his distress. Just two days prior, the President had issued a formal proclamation of American neutrality; two weeks later, a depressed and distraught Wilson delivered a stronger appeal in a written statement.

My fellow countrymen:

I suppose that every thoughtful man in America has asked himself during these last troubled weeks what influence the European war may exert upon the United States, and I take the liberty of addressing a few words to you in order to point out that it is entirely within our own choice what its effects upon us will be and to urge very earnestly upon you the sort of speech and conduct which will best safeguard the nation against distress and disaster.

The effect of the war upon the United States will depend upon what American citizens say and do. Every man who really loves America will act and speak in the true spirit of neutrality, which is the spirit of impartiality and fairness and friendliness to all concerned. The spirit of the nation in this critical matter will be determined largely by what individuals and societies and those gathered in public meetings do and say, upon what newspapers and magazines contain, upon what ministers utter in their pulpits, and men proclaim as their opinions on the street.

The people of the United States are drawn from many nations, and chiefly from the nations now at war. It is natural and inevitable that there should be the utmost variety of sympathy and desire among them with regard to the issues and circumstances of the conflict. Some will wish one nation, others another, to succeed in the momentous struggle. It will be easy to excite passion and difficult to allay it. Those responsible for exciting it will assume a heavy responsibility, responsibility for no less a thing than that the people of the United States, whose love of their country and whose loyalty to its government should unite them as Americans all, bound in honor and affection, to think first of her and her interests—may become divided in camps of hostile opinion, hot against each other, involved in the war itself in impulse and opinion, if not in action. Such divisions among us would be fatal to our peace of mind and might seriously stand in the way of the proper performance of our duty as the one great nation at peace, the one people holding itself ready to play a part of impartial mediation and speak the counsels of peace and accommodation, not as a partisan, but as a friend.

I venture, therefore, my fellow countrymen, to speak a solemn word of warning to you against that deepest, most subtle, most essential breach of neutrality which may spring out of partisanship, out of passionately taking sides. The United States must be neutral in fact as well as in name during these days that are to try men's souls. We must be impartial in thought as well as in action, must put a curb upon our sentiments as well as upon every transaction that might be construed as a preference of one party to the struggle before another.

My thought is of America. I am speaking, I feel sure, the earnest wish and purpose of every thoughtful American that this great country of ours, which is, of course, the first in our thoughts and in our hearts, should show herself in this time of peculiar trial a nation fit beyond others to exhibit the fine poise of undisturbed judgment, the dignity of self-control, the efficiency of dispassionate action; a nation that neither sits in judgment upon others nor is disturbed in her own counsels and which keeps herself fit and free to do what is necessary and disinterested and truly serviceable for the peace of the world.

Shall we not resolve to put upon ourselves the restraints which will bring to our people the happiness and the great and lasting influence for peace we covet for them?

August 18, 1914

Richard Harding Davis to the
New York Tribune

The Germans captured Brussels on August 20 as they fought the French along the Alsace-Lorraine border. Behind the front lines, the invaders brutally retaliated for alleged attacks by civilian snipers, executing some 5,500 Belgian and 900 French civilians in the early months of the war; in fact, the supposed guerrilla attacks were the products of fear, rumor, and panic. The worst massacre occurred on August 23 in Dinant, where 674 Belgian men, women, and children were shot. The fate of the university town of Louvain inflicted even more damage upon Germany's international reputation. On the night of August 25, reports of a Belgian army counterattack caused German troops to open fire; the garrison then destroyed the town, killing 248 of its inhabitants and burning more than 1,000 buildings, including the university's landmark medieval library. Star reporter Richard Harding Davis was known as much for his good looks and derring-do as for his writing. The most famous American war correspondent of his day, he had covered the Greco-Turkish, Spanish-American, Boer, and Russo-Japanese conflicts.

SAW GERMAN ARMY ROLL ON LIKE FOG

Richard Harding Davis Cables Vivid Picture of the
Kaiser's Great Gray Force, Which Was 26
Hours in Passing Through Brussels

BRUSSELS, Friday, Aug. 21, 2 P.M.—The entrance of the German army into Brussels has lost the human quality. It was lost as soon as the three soldiers who led the army bicycled into the Boulevard du Regent and asked the way to the Gare du Nord. When they passed the human note passed with them.

What came after them, and twenty-four hours later is still coming, is not men marching, but a force of nature like a tidal wave, an avalanche or a river flooding its banks. At this minute it is rolling through Brussels as the swollen waters of the Conemaugh Valley swept through Johnstown.

At the sight of the first few regiments of the enemy we were thrilled with interest. After for three hours they had passed in one unbroken steel gray column we were bored. But when hour after hour passed and there was no halt, no breathing time, no open spaces in the ranks, the thing became uncanny, inhuman. You returned to watch it, fascinated. It held the mystery and menace of fog rolling toward you across the sea.

The gray of the uniforms worn by both officers and men helped this air of mystery. Only the sharpest eye could detect among the thousands that passed the slightest difference. All moved under a cloak of invisibility. Only after the most numerous and severe tests at all distances, with all materials and combinations of colors that give forth no color could this gray have been discovered. That it was selected to clothe and disguise the German when he fights is typical of the German staff in striving for efficiency to leave nothing to chance, to neglect no detail.

Uniforms Suggest Fog

After you have seen this service uniform under conditions entirely opposite you are convinced that for the German soldier it is his strongest weapon. Even the most expert marksman cannot hit a target he cannot see. It is a gray green, not the blue gray of our Confederates. It is the gray of the hour just before daybreak, the gray of unpolished steel, of mist among green trees.

I saw it first in the Grand Place in front of the Hotel de Ville. It was impossible to tell if in that noble square there was a regiment or a brigade. You saw only a fog that melted into the stones, blended with the ancient house fronts, that shifted and drifted, but left you nothing at which you could point.

Later, as the army passed below my window, under the trees of the Botanical Park, it merged and was lost against the green leaves. It is no exaggeration to say that at a hundred yards you can see the horses on which the Uhlans ride, but cannot see the men who ride them.

If I appear to overemphasize this disguising uniform it is because of all the details of the German outfit it appealed to me as one of the most remarkable. The other day, when I was with the rear guard of the French Dragoons and Cuirassiers and they threw out pickets, we could distinguish them against the yellow wheat or green gorse at half a mile, while these men passing in the street, when they have reached the next crossing, become merged into the gray of the paving stones and the earth swallows them. In comparison the yellow khaki of our own American army is about as invisible as the flag of Spain.

Yesterday Major General von Jarotzky, the German Military Governor of Brussels, assured Burgomaster Max that the German army would not occupy the city, but would pass through it. It is still passing. I have followed in campaigns six armies, but, excepting not even our own, the Japanese or the British, I have not seen one so thoroughly equipped. I am not speaking of the fighting qualities of any army, only of the equipment and organization. The German army moved into this city as smoothly and as compactly as an Empire State Express. There were no halts, no open places, no stragglers.

GERMANS SING ON THE MARCH.

This army has been on active service three weeks, and so far there is not apparently a chinstrap or horseshoe missing. It came in with the smoke pouring from cookstoves on wheels, and in an hour had set up postoffice wagons, from which mounted messengers galloped along the line of column distributing letters and at which soldiers posted picture postcards.

The infantry came in in files of five, two hundred men to each company; the Lancers in columns of four, with not a pennant missing. The quick firing guns and field pieces were one hour at a time in passing, each gun with its caisson and ammunition wagon taking twenty seconds in which to pass.

The men of the infantry sang "Fatherland, My Fatherland." Between each line of song they took three steps. At times two thousand men were singing together in absolute rhythm and beat. When the melody gave way the silence was broken only by the stamp of iron-shod boots and then again the song rose. When the singing ceased the bands played marches. They were followed by the rumble of siege guns, the creaking of wheels and of chains clanking against the cobble stones and the sharp bell-like voices of the bugles.

For seven hours the army passed in such solid column that not once might a taxicab or trolley car pass through the city. Like a river of steel it flowed, gray and ghostlike. Then, as dusk came and as thousands of horses' hoofs and thousands of iron boots continued to tramp forward, they struck tiny sparks from the stones, but the horses and the men who beat out the sparks were invisible.

At midnight pack wagons and siege guns were still passing. At 7 this morning I was awakened by the tramp of men and bands playing jauntily. Whether they marched all night or not I do not know; but now for twenty-six hours the gray army has rumbled by with the mystery of fog and the pertinacity of a steam roller.

New York Tribune, August 24, 1914

HORRORS OF LOUVAIN TOLD BY EYEWITNESS; CIRCLED BURNING CITY

Vandalism and Atrocities on Women and
Children Committed in Name of War,
Says Richard Harding Davis.

OFFICER SHOT, IS GERMAN EXCUSE

Asserted That Burgomaster's Son Fired on Chief of
Staff and Surgeons—Six-Hundred-Year-Old Town
Turned Into a Wilderness.

[*Richard Harding Davis, the Tribune correspondent, was arrested as a spy, and, after being held for four days, was allowed to go. The dispatch below indicates that he was held in the train at Louvain during the burning of the town.*]

LONDON, Aug. 30.—I left Brussels on Thursday afternoon and have just arrived in London. For two hours on Thursday night I was in what for six hundred years had been the City of Louvain. The Germans were burning it, and to hide their work

kept us locked in the railroad carriages. But the story was
written against the sky, was told to us by German soldiers inco-
herent with excesses; and we could read it in the faces of
women and children being led to concentration camps and of
citizens on their way to be shot.

The Germans sentenced Louvain on Wednesday to become
a wilderness, and with the German system and love of thoroughness they left Louvain an empty, blackened shell. The
reason for this appeal to the torch and the execution of
non-combatants, as given to me on Thursday morning by
General Von Lutwitz, military governor of Brussels, was this:
On Wednesday while the German military commander of the
troops in Louvain was at the Hotel de Ville talking to the
burgomaster a son of the burgomaster with an automatic pistol
shot the chief of staff and German staff surgeons.

Lutwitz claims this was the signal for the civil guard, in civilian clothes on roofs, to fire upon the German soldiers in the
open square below. He said also the Belgians had quick-firing
guns, brought from Antwerp. As for a week the Germans had
occupied Louvain and closely guarded all approaches, the
story that there was any gunrunning is absurd.

Fifty Germans were killed and wounded. For that, said Lutwitz, Louvain must be wiped out. So in pantomime with his
fist he swept the papers across his table.

"The Hotel de Ville," he added, "was a beautiful building; it
is a pity it must be destroyed."

Educated Many American Priests.

Ten days ago I was in Louvain when it was occupied by
Belgian troops and King Albert and his staff. The city dates
from the eleventh century and the population was 42,000.
The citizens were brewers, lacemakers and manufacturers of
ornaments for churches. The university once was the most
celebrated in European cities, and still is, or was, headquarters
of the Jesuits.

In the Louvain college many priests now in America have
been educated, and ten days ago over the great yellow walls of
the college I saw hanging two American flags. I found the city
clean, sleepy and pretty, with narrow, twisting streets and smart

shops and cafés set in flower gardens of the houses, with red roofs, green shutters and white walls.

Over those that faced south had been trained pear trees, their branches heavy with fruit spread out against the walls like branches of candelabra. The Town Hall was very old and very beautiful, an example of Gothic architecture, in detail and design more celebrated even than the Town Hall of Bruges or Brussels. It was five hundred years old, and lately had been repaired with great taste and at great cost.

Opposite was the Church of St. Pierre, dating from the fifteenth century, a very noble building, with many chapels filled with carvings of the time of the Renaissance in wood, stone and iron. In the university were 150,000 volumes.

Near it was the bronze statue of Father Damien, priest of the leper colony in the South Pacific, of which Robert Louis Stevenson wrote. All these buildings now are empty, exploded cartridges. Statues, pictures, carvings, parchments, archives— all are gone.

COMPARED WITH UNITED STATES IN MEXICO.

No one defends the sniper. But because ignorant Mexicans when their city was invaded fired upon our sailors, we did not destroy Vera Cruz. Even had we bombarded Vera Cruz, money could have restored it. Money can never restore Louvain. Great architects and artists, dead these six hundred years, made it beautiful, and their handiwork belonged to the world. With torch and dynamite the Germans have turned these masterpieces into ashes, and all the Kaiser's horses and all his men cannot bring them back again.

When by troop train we reached Louvain, the entire heart of the city was destroyed and fire had reached the Boulevard Tirlemont, which faces the railroad station. The night was windless, and the sparks rose in steady, leisurely pillars, falling back into the furnace from which they sprang. In their work the soldiers were moving from the heart of the city to the outskirts, street by street, from house to house.

In each building, so German soldiers told me, they began at the first floor, and when that was burning steadily passed to the one next. There were no exceptions—whether it was a store, chapel or private residence it was destroyed. The occupants had been warned to go, and in each deserted shop or house the furniture was piled the torch was stuck under it, and into the air went the savings of years, souvenirs of children, of parents, heirlooms that had passed from generation to generation.

The people had time only to fill a pillowcase and fly. Some were not so fortunate, and by the thousands, like flocks of sheep, they were rounded up and marched through the night to concentration camps. We were not allowed to speak to any citizen of Louvain, but the Germans crowded the windows, boastful, gloating, eager to interpret.

WAR ON THE DEFENCELESS.

We were free to move from one end of the train to the other, and in the two hours during which it circled the burning city war was before me in its most hateful aspect.

In other wars I have watched men on one hilltop, without haste, without heat, fire at men on another hill, and in consequence on both sides good men were wasted. But in those fights there were no women or children, and the shells struck only vacant stretches of veldt or uninhabited mountainsides.

At Louvain it was war upon the defenceless, war upon churches, colleges, shops of milliners and lacemakers; war brought to the bedside and the fireside; against women harvesting in the fields, against children in wooden shoes at play in the streets.

At Louvain that night the Germans were like men after an orgy.

There were fifty English prisoners, erect and soldierly. In the ocean of gray the little patch of khaki looked pitifully lonely, but they regarded the men who had outnumbered but not defeated them with calm but uncurious eyes. In one way I was glad to see them there. Later they will bear witness as to how the enemy makes a wilderness and calls it war. It was a most weird picture.

On the high ground rose the broken spires of the Church of St. Pierre and the Hotel de Ville, and descending like steps were row beneath row of houses, roofless, with windows like blind eyes. The fire had reached the last row of houses, those

on the Boulevard de Jodigne. Some of these were already
cold, but others sent up steady, straight columns of flame. In
others at the third and fourth stories the window curtains
still hung, flowers still filled the window boxes, while on the
first floor the torch had just passed and the flames were leaping. Fire had destroyed the electric plant, but at times the
flames made the station so light that you could see the second
hand of your watch, and again all was darkness, lit only by
candles.

Men to be Shot Marched Past.

You could tell when an officer passed by the electric torch he
carried strapped to his chest. In the darkness the gray uniforms
filled the station with an army of ghosts. You distinguished
men only when pipes hanging from their teeth glowed red or
their bayonets flashed.

Outside the station in the public square the people of Louvain passed in an unending procession, women bareheaded,
weeping, men carrying the children asleep on their shoulders,
all hemmed in by the shadowy army of gray wolves. Once they
were halted, and among them were marched a line of men.
They well knew their fellow townsmen. These were on their
way to be shot. And better to point the moral an officer halted
both processions and, climbing to a cart, explained why the
men were to die. He warned others not to bring down upon
themselves a like vengeance.

As those being led to spend the night in the fields looked
across to those marked for death they saw old friends, neighbors of long standing, men of their own household. The officer
bellowing at them from the cart was illuminated by the headlights of an automobile. He looked like an actor held in a
spotlight on a darkened stage.

It was all like a scene upon the stage, so unreal, so inhuman,
you felt it could not be true that the curtain of life, purring
and crackling and sending up hot sparks to meet the kind,
calm stars, was only a painted backdrop, that the reports of
rifles from the dark rooms came from blank cartridges, and
that these trembling shopkeepers and peasants ringed in bayonets would not in a few minutes really die, but that they

themselves and their homes would be restored to their wives and children.

You felt it was only a nightmare, cruel and uncivilized. And then you remembered that the German Emperor has told us what it is. It is his Holy War.

New York Tribune, August 30, 1914

Theodore Roosevelt to Hugo Münsterberg

Although his third-party effort in 1912 failed to return him to the White House, Theodore Roosevelt remained an international figure, the most famous living American. Beloved by many at home, he never stepped out of the political spotlight nor stopped considering a third term as president. During the four years of the war, Roosevelt would invariably define his political positions in opposition to the man who had prevented his reclaiming the presidency, as his antipathy toward Woodrow Wilson soured into bitter enmity. Roosevelt had been corresponding since 1901 with Münsterberg, who had just sent him a copy of his book *The War and America*. Despite mounting criticism from American supporters of the Allies, Münsterberg maintained his public defense of Germany until his sudden death in December 1916.

Personal   Oyster Bay, October 3, 1914
My dear Professor Münsterberg: I have received your very interesting book and it impresses me very much. But, my dear Münsterberg, there are two or three points that you leave out of calculation. The first and most essential is that when a nation faces immediate death or humiliation because of the deed of another nation, it cannot look to the future with lofty philosophy, see the possible resulting good of its own ruin, and disregard the moral question of the moment. I firmly believe that in 1812 it was an essential thing to overthrow Napoleonic France. I feel that the German movement against France and the English resistance to France represented the struggle for light. (Let me remind you that Russia, that Asia, as you call it, was then on the side of Germany and that Germany could have done nothing without Russia and would have acted inexcusably if she had remained under France's yoke because it could be truthfully said that France represented far more enlightenment than Russia.) At that time the United States made war on England and by just so much gave comfort and strength to the Napoleonic side in the European struggle. Yet the ac-

tion of the United States was absolutely necessary. My criticism
of the United States in 1812 is heavy but it is not because she
went to war with England; it is because she did not prepare
effectively in advance for the war and wage it effectively; and
indeed, as far as I am concerned, I think she ought to have
declared war on both France and England.

Now, this is the exact case with Belgium today. The more I
have studied the case, the more keenly I have felt that there
can be no satisfactory peace until Belgium's wrongs are redressed and until there is some kind of effective guaranty
against the repetition of them as against her and others. I do
not for a moment believe that the predominant German motive in this war was aggression. I regard the talk about the
Kaiser "wishing a blood-bath" as preposterous. I am sure that
nine tenths of the German people have acted primarily from
fear—from an honorable fear, just as you phrase it, that German civilization would be wiped out if they did not strike their
foes. But, my dear Münsterberg, there was a ten per cent remainder, including the bulk of the men high up, who have for
fifty years cultivated a theory in international matters quite as
aggressive, quite as regardless of the rights of others and of all
questions of international morality, as that which the French
and to an only less extent the English had cultivated in the
preceding seventy years. This country was strongly anti-En-
glish for a generation after the Civil War, because of the attitude of England and (also France) during the Civil War. But
you probably do not realize the deep impression made upon
this country by the attitude of Germany toward us in the
Spanish War, especially in connection with Admiral Diederichs
at Manila, and also by the attitude of Germany in South
America.

Now, not for publication, but frankly between ourselves, do
you not believe that if Germany won in this war, smashed the
English Fleet and destroyed the British Empire, within a year
or two she would insist upon taking the dominant position in
South and Central America and upon treating the United
States precisely as she treated Japan when she joined with Russia
and France against Japan twenty years ago and took Kiaochow
as her share? I believe so. Indeed I know so. For the great Germans with whom I have talked, when once we could talk

intimately, accepted this view with a frankness that bordered on the cynical; just exactly as the big Russians with whom I have talked took the view that international morality had no place where Russian interests were concerned.

I am under no illusions as to any friendship for the United States that England or France may entertain. It would be worthless to us in any crisis unless it was greatly to the interest of France and England to support us. But it does seem to me that England had to act as she did when Belgium was invaded; and that as regards Belgium there are no two sides to the question.

I am not much interested in trying to get at the truth about the alleged outrages on individuals. The unquestioned fact is that Belgium has been ruined, that wonderful and beautiful old cities have been destroyed, that millions of entirely unoffending plain people have been reduced to the last pitch of misery, because Germany deemed it to its interest to inflict upon Belgium the greatest wrong one nation can inflict upon another. I grant you that Germany sincerely believed that this was necessary to her own existence; but surely we are not to be excused if we do not try to prevent the possibility of the recurrence of such incidents.

What the outcome of this war may be no human being can tell. At the moment it looks as if both sides might hammer themselves into a state of absolute exhaustion. If the allies should win and should then wish to dismember Germany and reduce her to impotence, whatever I could do would be done to prevent such a deed. I would regard it as a frightful calamity to civilization; and if Austria falls to pieces, I very earnestly hope that the German portion and all the other portions that are willing will join the Germanic body—the German Empire. But most emphatically I hope that ample reparation will be made to Belgium and that an effectual guarantee against the repetition of such wrongs as those that she has suffered will be arranged.

Now, as to the Russian. You speak very bitterly of him, and indeed of the Slav as a whole. I freely admit that the Russian is backward. They have a long way to go, those Russians, before they leave far enough behind them the days of Tartar dominion and the days when Tartar dominion was only overthrown through the upgrowth of a government such as that of Ivan the Terrible. The attitude of the Russian toward the Finn, the Caucasian, the Pole, the Jew and the Slavonian German in the past has too often been an evil attitude. But I think that liberal ideas are gaining in Russia. The gain is slow but on the whole it seems to me that it is evident. I do not believe the Russian will become an Asiatic. I think he will in the long run be the most effective means of preventing a recrudescence of Asiatic rule over Europe. Down at bottom, my dear Münsterberg, the Russian is just about like you or like me. The Englishman thinks of the German as an alien by race and innate disposition. I know better, for I have some English and some German blood in me, not to speak of other strains. In exactly the same way I find that here in America the descendants of the Slavonic immigrants become men precisely like ourselves. Surely in the end we can aim for a better understanding between German, Englishman and Slav; and such an understanding must be based on justice and no one of them must feel for the others either fear or contempt.

You will not misunderstand me. I am not an ultrapacificist. I regard the Wilson-Bryan attitude of trusting to fantastic peace treaties, to impossible promises, to all kinds of scraps of paper without any backing in efficient force, as abhorrent. It is infinitely better for a nation and for the world to have the Frederick the Great and Bismarck tradition as regards foreign policy than to have the Bryan or Bryan-Wilson attitude as a permanent national attitude, for the Bryan-Wilson attitude is one that would Chinafy the country and would reduce us to the impotence of Spain when it was under the leadership of Godoy—"The Prince of Peace," as he was officially entitled. A milk-and-water righteousness unbacked by force is to the full as wicked as and even more mischievous than force divorced from righteousness. But surely there is a goal different from either toward which we can strive. Surely we can strive for an international peace of justice, based on ability to guard ourselves from injustice, and determination not to do injustice to others, a peace in which some step shall have been taken toward putting international force behind an international desire to secure at least a reasonable approximation toward justice and fair play. *Sincerely yours*

W.E.B. Du Bois:
World War and the Color Line

The first African American to receive a PhD from Harvard University, William Edward Burghardt Du Bois was the most prominent black intellectual in America. Teacher, sociologist, historian, writer, and political activist, he was a founder of the National Association for the Advancement of Colored People and the editor of its monthly magazine, *The Crisis*. At a pan-African conference held in London in 1900, Du Bois stated that "the problem of the twentieth century is the problem of the color line," a prophecy that reverberated in his initial response to the war. While most African Americans struggled to find a place in American society, Du Bois asked black people to consider their place in the world.

———————

MANY colored persons, and persons interested in them, may easily make the mistake of supposing that the present war is far removed from the color problem of America and that in the face of this great catastrophe we may forget for a moment such local problems and give all attention and contributions to the seemingly more pressing cause.

This attitude is a mistake. The present war in Europe is one of the great disasters due to race and color prejudice and it but foreshadows greater disasters in the future.

It is not merely national jealousy, or the so-called "race" rivalry of Slav, Teuton and Latin, that is the larger cause of this war. It is rather the wild quest for Imperial expansion among colored races between Germany, England and France primarily, and Belgium, Italy, Russia and Austria-Hungary in lesser degree. Germany long since found herself shut out from acquiring colonies. She looked toward South America, but the "Monroe Doctrine" stood in her way. She started for Africa and by bulldozing methods secured one good colony, one desert and two swamps. Her last efforts looked toward North Africa and Asia-Minor. Finally, she evidently decided at the first opportunity to seize English or French colonies and to this end feverishly expanded her navy, kept her army at the highest point of efficiency and has been for twenty years the bully of Europe with a chip on her shoulder and defiance in her mouth.

The colonies which England and France own and Germany covets are largely in tropical and semi-tropical lands and inhabited by black, brown and yellow peoples. In such colonies there is a chance to confiscate land, work the natives at low wages, make large profits and open wide markets for cheap European manufactures. Asia, Africa, the South Sea Islands, the West Indies, Mexico and Central America and much of South America have long been designated by the white world as fit field for this kind of commercial exploitation, for the benefit of Europe and with little regard for the welfare of the natives. One has only to remember the forced labor in South Africa, the outrages in Congo, the cocoa-slavery in Portuguese Africa, the land monopoly and peonage of Mexico, the exploitation of Chinese coolies and the rubber horror of the Amazon to realize what white imperialism is doing to-day in well-known cases, not to mention thousands of less-known instances.

In this way a theory of the inferiority of the darker peoples and a contempt for their rights and aspirations has become all but universal in the greatest centers of modern culture. Here it was that American color prejudice and race hatred received in recent years unexpected aid and sympathy. To-day civilized nations are fighting like mad dogs over the right to own and exploit these darker peoples.

In such case where should our sympathy lie? Undoubtedly, with the Allies—with England and France in particular. Not that these nations are innocent. England was in the past blood-guilty above all lands in her wicked and conscienceless rape of darker races. England was primarily responsible for American slavery, for the starvation of India, and the Chinese opium traffic. But the salvation of England is that she has the ability to learn from her mistakes. To-day no white nation is fairer in its treatment of darker peoples than England. Not that England is yet fair. She is not yet just, and she still nourishes much disdain for colored races, erects contemptible and humiliating political and social barriers and steals their land and labor; but as compared with Germany England is an angel of light. The record of Germany as a colonizer toward weaker and darker people is the most barbarous of any civilized people and grows worse instead of better. France is less efficient than England as an administrator of colonies and has consequently been guilty of much neglect and injustice; but she is nevertheless the most kindly of all European nations in her personal relations with colored folk. She draws no dead line of color and colored Frenchmen always love France.

Belgium has been as pitiless and grasping as Germany and in strict justice deserves every pang she is suffering after her unspeakable atrocities in Congo. Russia has never drawn a color line but has rather courted the yellow races, although with ulterior motives. Japan, however, instilled wholesome respect in this line.

Undoubtedly, then the triumph of the allies would at least leave the plight of the colored races no worse than now. Indeed, considering the fact that black Africans and brown Indians and yellow Japanese are fighting for France and England it may be that they will come out of this frightful welter of blood with new ideas of the essential equality of all men.

On the other hand, the triumph of Germany means the triumph of every force calculated to subordinate darker peoples. It would mean triumphant militarism, autocratic and centralized government and a studied theory of contempt for everything except Germany—"Germany above everything in the world." The despair and humiliation of Germany in the eighteenth century has brought this extraordinary rebound of self-exaltation and disdain for mankind. The triumph of this idea would mean a crucifixion of darker peoples unparalleled in history.

The writer speaks without anti-German bias; personally he has deep cause to love the German people. They made him believe in the essential humanity of white folk twenty years ago when he was near to denying it. But even then the spell of militarism was in the air, and the Prussian strut had caught the nation's imagination. They were starting on the same road with the southern American whites toward a contempt toward human beings and a faith in their own utter superiority to all other breeds. This feeling had not then applied itself particularly to colored folk and has only begun to to-day; but it is going by leaps and bounds. Germany needs but the rôle of world conquest to make her one of the most contemptible of "Nigger" hating nations. Just as we go to press, the *Berliner Tageblatt* publishes a proclamation by "German representatives of Science and Art to the World of Culture" in which men like Harnack, Bode, Hauptmann, Suderman, Roentgen, Humperdink, Wundt and others, insult hundreds of millions of human beings by openly sneering at "Mongrels and Niggers."

As colored Americans then, and as Americans who fear race prejudice as the greatest of War-makers, our sympathies in the awful conflict should be with France and England; not that they have conquered race prejudice, but they have at least begun to realize its cost and evil, while Germany exalts it.

If so great a catastrophe has followed jealousies and greed built on a desire to steal from and oppress people whom the dominant culture dispises, how much wilder and wider will be the conflict when black and brown and yellow people stand up together shoulder to shoulder and demand recognition as men!

Let us give then our sympathies to those nations whose triumph will most tend to postpone if not to make unnecessary a world war of races.

The Crisis, November 1914

Nellie Bly to the New York Evening Journal

Austria-Hungary began the war with simultaneous invasions of Serbia and of Russian Galicia and faced disastrous results. By year's end, its armies had been driven back on both fronts with more than 1.2 million men killed, wounded, sick, or captured. Into this havoc ventured one of America's most intrepid journalists: Nellie Bly, the pen name of Elizabeth Cochrane Seaman. A pioneering member of Joseph Pulitzer's reporting team at the *New York World*, Bly had feigned insanity in order to be committed to the Blackwell Island's Asylum for ten days in 1887 and had traveled around the world in seventy-two days in 1889–90. In August 1914 she traveled to Austria to raise funds for the manufacturing business she had inherited from her husband. During the fall, Bly wrote twenty-one dispatches for the *New York Evening Journal*, including reports from the fortress city of Przemyśl in Austrian Galicia (now in Poland) and from military hospitals in Budapest.

NELLIE BLY ON THE BATTLEFIELD

Hides in Trenches as Russ Shells Rain About Her

SOLDIERS FIVE DAYS WITHOUT FOOD

Following is a continuation of the article by Miss Nellie Bly, special correspondent for the Evening Journal at Przemyśl, in Austria:

PRZEMYŚL, Oct. 30.—We left the battery and proceeded along the muddy road. There was Colonel John, Baron Mednyanszky, a painter of renown; Cesare Santoro, a writer, editor and owner of a newspaper in Rome, Italy; Alexander Exax, photographer, and myself. In Herr Hollitzer's cape! That meant labor.

Along the road were deep, muddy trenches, and into these

we were ordered to go and follow our leader in single file, thirty feet apart.

We were on ground plainly visible to the Russians, who fire as soon as they see anything move or that looks like a human being.

The trench was muddy and filthy. I slipped and slid and held my breath—all I had. The weight of Herr Hollitzer's cape, which I had to carry in folds over my arms to keep from soiling it, had left me little breath to hold.

I almost despaired of getting out of the trench. At that particular spot it was fully eight feet high and as slippery as a greased pole. I had no nails in my shoes, and as I made a step I slid back.

Baron Mednyanszky had missed me and turned back. His head and walking stick were visible above the edge of the trench. He held out the curved end to me. I grasped it and was quickly pulled up the slippery bank.

We darted across the road, expecting a Russian bullet to greet the two of us in the worst exposed spot.

NOWHERE TO HIDE AND AS SLIPPERY AS ICE!

But none came. And now we were on a bare, muddy hill. Not a blade of grass, not a tree or shrub, nothing but shiny, smooth-worn mud, more slippery than ice.

It seemed to be laid out in terraces, and each terrace was but a series of half-dug graves. Just the size of a grave, and the shape, and possibly three feet deep.

I looked at them in horror. Were they filled graves which had sunk? Were they graves half-prepared, waiting for the next battle?

Down where the slope ended in the valley were long lines of rude crosses made from tree branches. They marked plainly visible graves.

In some of these open graves was straw. In some were empty cartridges. In others bullets not yet taken from their pasteboard boxes. Here were bloody bandages, a lost shoe, a piece of a coat, an abandoned cooking pan, another with a bullet hole through it, a buckle from a belt. Then I realized where I was. I was on a battlefield. These were not half-dug or sunken graves. They were the trenches in which the soldiers had lain for three weeks fighting constantly.

Each of these hundreds of grave-like holes had been the tent, the home, the retreat of a soldier. Here they ate when food could reach them. Here they starved when food could not be had. Here they killed and were killed.

I have spoken to soldiers who were in trenches for five days without food. That does not mean supplies were exhausted. Food may have been in sight, yet could not be brought to them for the constant rain of the enemy's bullets.

Under Fire for Weeks in the Rain and Cold

In rain, in cold, in wind—hungry, wet, weary, under constant fire for weeks! Is it surprising that cholera, dysentery and all other ills, including insanity, seize them?

And what is here in the Austrian army is as bad, perhaps worse, in the Russian front. The wild, primitive country in which these two nations fight make conditions most terrible and suffering unspeakable to man and beast.

I could only view the bloody bandages with the most helpless horror. It is as if the last day had come and one could not change or better the inevitable torture. Imagine a man with a bullet in his lungs or head or arm, or a bit of shrapnel in his chest or abdomen, or his arms or feet torn off, lying in the trench for days without one soul to help tie up his gaping wounds or hand him a bite to eat.

Dr. Kling told me of a soldier whose shoulder blade was torn out by shrapnel, leaving a gaping wound bigger than two fists, and that man lay in a trench for six days in that condition without aid.

Picked Out Bullets with Pocketknife

He told me of others who had been for days with bullets buried in them and when they reached him they let him dig the bullets out with a pocketknife. No ether or cocaine to ease the pain, yet never cry or moan.

I saw one man whose jaws were broken in thirty-two pieces by a shrapnel. It hung shapeless on his chest.

That man lay in a trench six days after he was injured. No food, no aid and rain all the while. His jaw has been mended by silver wire, is growing together and he is walking around the hospital.

It was growing dark. We retraced our steps. I was saddened and heartsick by what I had seen. I felt indifferent to the constant bellowing of cannon and whizzing of shells through the air. Campfires were glowing and the smell of smoke made the land more wholesome. The shapeless, huddled mass of men by the cholera hovels lay still, silently motionless in the straw. I turned my eyes away.

The air was chilled. The last glimmer of sun tinted the black clouds with a golden edge. Two officers on horseback met on the brow of the hill and were outlined against the sky like statues. Hundreds of cattle and horses were standing in vast groups in the valley, eating. Wagons were unhitched and in line. Men were eating in groups or standing around small fires. To the southwest a long balloon, cigar-shaped, hung motionless in the sky.

And Suddenly War Let Loose Its Furies

It was a scene of peaceful nightfall. Then suddenly the most terrific explosion of the day bellowed out just back of us. We turned. We saw a cloud of black smoke rise in the air, apparently from the place we had just left—the trenches where, three weeks ago, the Russians left and retreated before the fire of the Austrians.

We heard a Russian shell come singing through the air. Then—it fell on our left, less than 200 feet away! We could not see it; like the men who shoot, it is not visible to the eye. But the shower of black mud showed where it struck. It missed a stable and the edge of a camp by 50 feet only.

The spraying mud had hardly returned to earth until the whole scene had changed from stillness to the utmost animation. The cattle were driven westward on a run—campfires were deserted, horses were hitched to wagons and whipped into the fastest speed. From the stables horses were led running in groups. Everything seemed moving with the greatest rapidity and at an instant's notice.

Colonel John yelled for us to fly to the trenches. But like the famous lady who turned to salt, I turned to look!

Another frightful explosion in the east, another cloud of black smoke and one after the other six shells fell and buried themselves in the same soft earth.

Then I got into the trench. Two hundred feet was near enough for me. I was not afraid, I would not run. Yet my mind was busy. I thought another shot would follow. It will doubtless be better aimed. If it does, we shall die.

And, if so, what then?

December 8, 1914

NELLIE BLY AT FRONT

Visits Wounded in Budapest

SEES HORRORS OF WAR

While in Budapest Miss Nellie Bly, Special Correspondent for the Evening Journal in the Austrian fighting zone, paid a visit to some of the hospitals. The following relates some of what she experienced and saw:

BUDAPEST, Nov. 10.—Ten languages are spoken in the hospital, and nurses, German, Austrian, Gulitzin, Hungarian and Servian are employed, so that patients will always have nurses who speak their language.

They have also a series of chapels, Catholic, Protestant and Hebrew. Off each ward are small soundproof rooms called "Death Chambers."

Patients at the point of death are removed to these rooms to spare the feelings of their fellow comrades. Smoking rooms, glass partitioned, are also an adjunct to each ward.

This hospital accommodates 2,000 wounded. The kitchen is superb and needs a column to properly describe it. They showed with pride a large American refrigerator. The doctors and nurses each have their sleeping, eating and rest departments. One large hall, gaily decorated with the national colors, is used for the amusement of the convalescent. Even kino shows are given and concerts.

Men were being received from a train, so we went down to see them. We talked to them, as detachments of twenty were taken at a time to the bath.

I cannot praise too highly the wonderful executive ability of those who conceived and established the astounding perfection of those two hospitals. Nothing is wanting to aid and assist nature to save and heal what man is so inhumanely torturing and destroying.

We had scarcely reached the Astoria when I had a telephone call from Dr. MacDonald.

CALLED TO HOSPITAL

"I want you to get in a taxi and come here, Miss Bly," he said. "I have received just now the worst cases I have ever seen in my entire life. They may interest you."

I rushed to the American Red Cross Hospital. It is located in Mexico street in a large building, formerly used as a home for the blind. I flew in the door and up the stairs over which floats a fifty-foot American flag.

Dr. MacDonald, grave and sad, met us at the head of the stairs.

"Come into the operating room," he said, taking my hand. "I have the most frightful case I ever saw."

Mr. Schriner, who had enough misery for one day, had tried to induce me not to come. Failing he had come along. Silently he kept at my side.

The operating room was in confusion. On the floor was blood. Filling pails and in piles were bloody bandages. I tried not to see. I began to wish I had not come.

Four American Red Cross nurses stood gravely around an operating table. Dr. MacDonald pointed to two bandaged stumps. I could see one foot was gone at the ankle, the other apparently half way to the knee.

"This is a Russian," said the doctor. "He was wounded by a shot through his body. For eight days he lay in the trench unattended. His feet froze. He was put on a freight train and when we received him an hour ago his feet had dropped off, doubtless in the car, for we never saw them, and the last blood the poor fellow had was pouring from his open veins. We carried him here and bandaged him up, but he cannot live many minutes longer. He has no pulse now. Come, look at him."

A Dreadful Sight

Come, look, reader, with me! My whole soul shrank from the sight. The doctor took me by the hand. I kept my eyes away from the face I was afraid to look upon.

"Look at this body," said the doctor. I looked—I shuddered. The clay pallor of death. The ribs cutting the skin. Bones, bones, no flesh anywhere.

The head turned. Great, hollow black eyes looked into mine. Transfixed I stood, heartsick, soul-sad. Those great hollow eyes searched mine. They tried to question me. They spoke soul language to soul. The lips parted, a moan, a groan of more than physical agony. He spoke. I could not understand. His words were a sound my ears shall never forget. The appeal, the longing, the knowledge!

"What does he say?" I cried, unable to stand it. "Can no one understand? Can't you find someone to speak to him?"

A nurse smoothed his forehead. An attendant held fast the pale, pale hands.

"The attendant understands," the doctor said; and to him, "What does he say?"

Asked for Children

"He is asking for his children," was the low reply.

The hollow, black eyes turned again to search mine. I could not endure their question. I had no answer to give.

"Let me go!" I said to the doctor.

The low moans seemed to call me back, but I walked steadfastly toward the door and down the corridor.

"Could Emperors and Czars and Kings look on this torturing slaughter and ever sleep again?" I asked the doctor.

"They do not look," he said gently. "Only by witnessing such horrors can one realize them."

"Miss Bly," cried von Leidenfrost, running down the hall, "that poor fellow just died!"

This is only one case. Travel the roads from the scene of battle; search the trains; wounded, frozen, starved thousands are dying by agonizing torture—not hundreds, but thousands. And as they die thousands are being rushed into their pest-filled trenches to be slaughtered in the same way.

Oh, we Christians!

January 19, 1915

George Santayana: The Logic of Fanaticism

The war in Europe entered everybody's mind, as people debated among themselves and sometimes with themselves. Spanish-born philosopher George Santayana came to the United States as a child and was educated at Harvard, where he taught for the next quarter of a century. He retired to Europe, traveling around France, Spain, Italy, and England. In a private letter on August 5, 1914, as war was breaking out, he wrote that his "sympathies are naturally with France and England, and with the blameless unfortunate Belgians; yet I feel no anger against the Germans. They are carrying out a brave and heroic determination to be the masters of Europe and to rule by force of arms, industry and character." "The Logic of Fanaticism" records some of his own internal argument about Germany's belligerent conduct. Remaining in England throughout the war, he wrote to *The New Republic* in January 1916, calling for a peace that would "teach Germany that aggression does not pay."

———————

AMONG the sweeping judgments, boasts, insults, recriminations, and falsehoods that dishonor the present war, two are often heard which, though flatly contradictory in form and in animus, yet curiously enough designate the same substantive fact. One of these assertions is that the Germans are barbarians, the other that they possess and defend the highest *Kultur*. Why should anyone call the Germans barbarians when they evidently share to the full in the arts and traditions of Christendom? Because, incidentally, their policy and methods are ruthless, appealing deliberately and even from a sense of duty to any and every means which is expected to further their national purposes; and again on the deeper ground that they are singly determined to carry out an *a priori* impulse or Absolute Will, which their philosophers have found to be agitating the whole universe and more particularly their own bosoms; a will to which they attribute infinite authority and value, so that it must be heroically executed, in disdain of liberty, security, and delight, both within and without their own borders.

And why do the Germans claim the highest *Kultur*, and claim it with the deepest conviction, backed by the most elaborate historical and philosophical arguments? Almost for the same reason for which they are called barbarians by their enemies. Have they not renounced individualism in the interests of organization, recast their institutions and subdued their souls for the better service of the State? Have they not scoured the sciences and tormented the arts, so as to strengthen and express their national energies? Evidently their alleged barbarism is but the inevitable operation of their boasted *Kultur*; and the bias of the two opposite designations cannot alter the formidable fact to which both equally apply.

The sword of Islam and the zeal of the Inquisition were similarly denounced and similarly justified. Those who think they have hold on an absolute good must necessarily be ruthless. That the end justifies the means passes for an immoral maxim; but taken in one sense it is the very principle of order and rational sacrifice. A supreme social good is hardly to be secured without foregoing many sweets and inflicting many stripes on one's own back and even more on one's neighbor's. It is true that a rigid control of life in the service of ends freely chosen would not curtail freedom, but rather set freedom in motion where only chance and alternating impulses prevailed before.

Yet the maturer and disillusioned portion of mankind are hardly wrong in smelling a danger whenever an absolute and supreme end is proposed and pursued to the serious inconvenience of everybody. They know how likely it is that such a dazzling celestial light should be but heat-lightning. The pursuit of any single end, ravishing and incomparable as it may seem to the enthusiast, strains and impoverishes human nature, and sometimes, by detaching it too much from common and humble feelings, actually debauches it. Indeed, the inhumanity of fanaticism does not lie chiefly in the conscientious crimes which it dictates here and there; it lies rather in the miserable imaginary end itself, for the sake of which those crimes are committed. A "truth," a "salvation," a *Kultur*, which wars and persecutions hope to diffuse is presumably spurious. Men presently will cry out to be saved from that salvation and enlightened out of that truth; they will gasp to escape from the heavy regimen of that *Kultur*, so as to see this green world for themselves, and live and learn after their own fashion. If the end does not justify the means, it is because this end is too often worthless, or at least no more valuable than what it bids us renounce for its sake. Nothing will repay a man for becoming inhuman. The aim of life is some way of living, as flexible and gentle as human nature; so that ambition may stoop to kindness, and philosophy to candor and to humor. Neither prosperity nor empire nor heaven can be worth winning at the price of a virulent temper, bloody hands, an anguished spirit, and a vain hatred of the rest of the world.

The New Republic, November 28, 1914

Alfred Bryan:
I Didn't Raise My Boy to Be a Soldier

The war of words over America's role in the European war broke out everywhere in the United States—even Tin Pan Alley. Canadian-born Alfred Bryan worked as a newspaper reporter in Chicago before moving to New York to become a lyricist. He made his name with such hits as "Come, Josephine in My Flying Machine" and "Peg O' My Heart." In 1915, as the United States was starting to discuss the need for military "preparedness," he wrote his biggest hit: "I Didn't Raise My Boy to Be a Soldier," which sold 650,000 copies in three months. While his song expressed the majority opinion at the time, dozens of parodies argued otherwise over the next year, including "I Didn't Raise My Boy to Be a Molly-Coddle" and "I Did Not Rear My Boy to Be a Coward."

Ten million soldiers to the war have gone,
Who may never return again.
Ten million mothers' hearts must break
For the ones who died in vain.
Head bowed down in sorrow in her lonely years,
I heard a mother murmur thro' her tears:

"I didn't raise my boy to be a soldier,
I brought him up to be my pride and joy,
Who dares to place a musket on his shoulder,
To shoot some other mother's darling boy?
Let nations arbitrate their future troubles,
It's time to lay the sword and gun away,
There'd be no war today,
If mothers all would say,
"I didn't raise my boy to be a soldier."

What victory can cheer a mother's heart,
When she looks at her blighted home?

What victory can bring her back
All she cared to call her own?
Let each mother answer in the years to be,
Remember that my boy belongs to me!

"I didn't raise my boy to be a soldier,
I brought him up to be my pride and joy,
Who dares to place a musket on his shoulder,
To shoot some other mother's darling boy?
Let nations arbitrate their future troubles,
It's time to lay the sword and gun away,
There'd be no war today,
If mothers all would say,
"I didn't raise my boy to be a soldier."

Edith Wharton: In Argonne

By the start of 1915, the Western Front extended 475 miles, a continuous line of trenches and outposts from the North Sea to the Swiss border. Germany occupied most of Belgium and a small patch of France that accounted for almost half the country's coal production and a majority of its steel and iron output. Perhaps the unlikeliest correspondent to cover the war at this time was Edith Wharton—the daughter of a socially prominent New York family, a noted garden and interior designer, and one of America's most celebrated writers of fiction. She had been living in Paris for several years when the war began; and, instead of fleeing for safety, she remained, founding the American Hostels for Refugees, raising funds for refugee relief, and visiting the front in the Verdun-Argonne region in February and March 1915, in Lorraine and the Vosges in May, and near the Channel coast in June. Wharton wrote about these trips and the impact of the war on Paris in four articles for *Scribner's Monthly* that were published as *Fighting France, from Dunkerque to Belfort* in November 1915.

I

THE PERMISSION to visit a few ambulances and evacuation hospitals behind the lines gave me, at the end of February, my first sight of War.

Paris is no longer included in the military zone, either in fact or in appearance. Though it is still manifestly under the war-cloud, its air of reviving activity produces the illusion that the menace which casts that cloud is far off not only in distance but in time. Paris, a few months ago so alive to the nearness of the enemy, seems to have grown completely oblivious of that nearness; and it is startling, not more than twenty miles from the gates, to pass from such an atmosphere of workaday security to the imminent sense of war.

Going eastward, one begins to feel the change just beyond Meaux. Between that quiet episcopal city and the hill-town of Montmirail, some forty miles farther east, there are no sensational evidences of the great conflict of September—only, here and there, in an unploughed field, or among the fresh brown furrows, a little mound with a wooden cross and a wreath on it. Nevertheless, one begins to perceive, by certain negative signs, that one is already in another world. On the cold February day when we turned out of Meaux and took the road to the Argonne, the change was chiefly shown by the curious absence of life in the villages through which we passed. Now and then a lonely ploughman and his team stood out against the sky, or a child and an old woman looked from a doorway; but many of the fields were fallow and most of the doorways empty. We passed a few carts driven by peasants, a stray wood-cutter in a copse, a road-mender hammering at his stones; but already the "civilian motor" had disappeared, and all the dust-coloured cars dashing past us were marked with the Red Cross or the number of an army division. At every bridge and railway-crossing a sentinel, standing in the middle of the road with lifted rifle, stopped the motor and examined our papers. In this negative sphere there was hardly any other tangible proof of military rule; but with the descent of the first hill beyond Montmirail there came the positive feeling: *This is war!*

Along the white road rippling away eastward over the dimpled country the army motors were pouring by in endless lines, broken now and then by the dark mass of a tramping regiment or the clatter of a train of artillery. In the intervals between these waves of military traffic we had the road to ourselves, except for the flashing past of despatch-bearers on motor-cycles and of hideously hooting little motors carrying goggled officers in goat-skins and woollen helmets.

The villages along the road all seemed empty—not figuratively but literally empty. None of them has suffered from the German invasion, save by the destruction, here and there, of a single house on which some random malice has wreaked itself; but since the general flight in September all have remained abandoned, or are provisionally occupied by troops, and the rich country between Montmirail and Châlons is a desert.

The first sight of Châlons is extraordinarily exhilarating. The old town lying so pleasantly between canal and river is the headquarters of an army—not of a corps or of a division, but of a whole army—and the network of grey provincial streets about the Romanesque towers of Notre Dame rustles with the movement of war. The square before the principal hotel—the incomparably named "Haute Mère-Dieu"—is as vivid a sight as any scene of modern war can be. Rows of grey motor-lorries and omnibuses do not lend themselves to as happy groupings as a detachment of cavalry, and spitting and spurting motor-cycles and "torpedo" racers are no substitute for the glitter of helmets and the curvetting of chargers; but once the eye has adapted itself to the ugly lines and the neutral tints of the new warfare, the scene in that crowded clattering square becomes positively brilliant. It is a vision of one of the central functions of a great war, in all its concentrated energy, without the saddening suggestions of what, on the distant periphery, that energy is daily and hourly resulting in. Yet even here such suggestions are never long out of sight; for one cannot pass through Châlons without meeting, on their way from the station, a long line of "éclopés"—the unwounded but battered, shattered, frost-bitten, deafened and half-paralyzed wreckage of the awful struggle. These poor wretches, in their thousands, are daily shipped back from the front to rest and be restored; and it is a grim sight to watch them limping by, and to meet the dazed stare of eyes that have seen what one dare not picture.

If one could think away the "éclopés" in the streets and the wounded in the hospitals, Châlons would be an invigorating spectacle. When we drove up to the hotel even the grey motors and the sober uniforms seemed to sparkle under the cold sky. The continual coming and going of alert and busy messengers, the riding up of officers (for some still ride!), the arrival of much-decorated military personages in luxurious motors, the hurrying to and fro of orderlies, the perpetual depleting and refilling of the long rows of grey vans across the square, the movements of Red Cross ambulances and the passing of detachments for the front, all these are sights that the pacific stranger could forever gape at. And in the hotel, what a clatter of swords, what a piling up of fur coats and haversacks, what a grouping of bronzed energetic heads about the packed tables in the restaurant! It is not easy for civilians to get to Châlons, and almost every table is occupied by officers and soldiers—for, once off duty, there seems to be no rank distinction in this happy democratic army, and the simple private, if he chooses to treat himself to the excellent fare of the Haute Mère-Dieu, has as good a right to it as his colonel.

The scene in the restaurant is inexhaustibly interesting. The mere attempt to puzzle out the different uniforms is absorbing. A week's experience near the front convinces me that no two uniforms in the French army are alike either in colour or in cut. Within the last two years the question of colour has greatly preoccupied the French military authorities, who have been seeking an invisible blue; and the range of their experiments is proved by the extraordinary variety of shades of blue, ranging from a sort of greyish robin's-egg to the darkest navy, in which the army is clothed. The result attained is the conviction that no blue is really inconspicuous, and that some of the harsh new slaty tints are no less striking than the deeper shades they have superseded. But to this scale of experimental blues, other colours must be added: the poppy-red of the Spahis' tunics, and various other less familiar colours—grey, and a certain greenish khaki—the use of which is due to the fact that the cloth supply has given out and that all available materials are employed. As for the differences in cut, the uniforms vary from the old tight tunic to the loose belted jacket copied from the English, and the emblems of the various arms and ranks embroidered on these diversified habits add a new element of perplexity. The aviator's wings, the motorist's wheel, and many of the newer symbols, are easily recognizable—but there are all the other arms, and the doctors and the stretcher-bearers, the sappers and miners, and heaven knows how many more ramifications of this great host which is really all the nation.

The main interest of the scene, however, is that it shows almost as many types as uniforms, and that almost all the types are so good. One begins to understand (if one has failed to before) why the French say of themselves: "*La France est une nation guerrière.*" War is the greatest of paradoxes: the most senseless and disheartening of human retrogressions, and yet the stimulant of qualities of soul which, in every race, can seemingly find no other means of renewal. Everything depends, therefore, on the category of impulses that war excites in a people. Looking at the faces at Châlons, one sees at once in which sense the French are "une nation guerrière." It is not too much to say that war has given beauty to faces that were interesting, humorous, acute, malicious, a hundred vivid and expressive things, but last and least of all beautiful. Almost all the faces about these crowded tables—young or old, plain or handsome, distinguished or average—have the same look of quiet authority: it is as though all "nervosity," fussiness, little personal oddities, meannesses and vulgarities, had been burnt away in a great flame of self-dedication. It is a wonderful example of the rapidity with which purpose models the human countenance. More than half of these men were probably doing dull or useless or unimportant things till the first of last August; now each one of them, however small his job, is sharing in a great task, and knows it, and has been made over by knowing it.

Our road on leaving Châlons continued to run north-eastward toward the hills of the Argonne.

We passed through more deserted villages, with soldiers lounging in the doors where old women should have sat with their distaffs, soldiers watering their horses in the village pond, soldiers cooking over gypsy fires in the farm-yards. In the patches of woodland along the road we came upon more soldiers, cutting down pine saplings, chopping them into even lengths and loading them on hand-carts, with the green boughs piled on top. We soon saw to what use they were put, for at every cross-road or railway bridge a warm sentry-box of mud and straw and plaited pine-branches was plastered against a bank or tucked like a swallow's nest into a sheltered corner. A little farther on we began to come more and more frequently on big colonies of "Seventy-fives." Drawn up nose to nose, usually against a curtain of woodland, in a field at some distance from the road, and always attended by a cumbrous drove of motor-vans, they looked like giant gazelles feeding among elephants; and the stables of woven pine-boughs which stood near by might have been the huge huts of their herdsmen.

The country between Marne and Meuse is one of the regions on which German fury spent itself most bestially during the abominable September days. Half way between Châlons and Sainte Menehould we came on the first evidence of the invasion: the lamentable ruins of the village of Auve. These pleasant villages of the Aisne, with their one long street, their half-timbered houses and high-roofed granaries with espaliered gable-ends, are all much of one pattern, and one can easily picture what Auve must have been as it looked out, in the blue September weather, above the ripening pears of its gardens to the crops in the valley and the large landscape beyond. Now it is a mere waste of rubble and cinders, not one threshold distinguishable from another. We saw many other ruined villages after Auve, but this was the first, and perhaps for that reason one had there, most hauntingly, the vision of all the separate terrors, anguishes, uprootings and rendings apart involved in the destruction of the obscurest of human communities. The photographs on the walls, the twigs of withered box above the crucifixes, the old wedding-dresses in brass-clamped trunks, the bundles of letters laboriously written and as painfully deciphered, all the thousand and one bits of the past that give meaning and continuity to the present—of all that accumulated warmth nothing was left but a brick-heap and some twisted stove-pipes!

As we ran on toward Sainte Menehould the names on our map showed us that, just beyond the parallel range of hills six or seven miles to the north, the two armies lay interlocked. But we heard no cannon yet, and the first visible evidence of the nearness of the struggle was the encounter, at a bend of the road, of a long line of grey-coated figures tramping toward us between the bayonets of their captors. They were a sturdy lot, this fresh "bag" from the hills, of a fine fighting age, and much less famished and war-worn than one could have wished. Their broad blond faces were meaningless, guarded, but neither defiant nor unhappy: they seemed none too sorry for their fate.

Our pass from the General Head-quarters carried us to Sainte Menehould on the edge of the Argonne, where we had to apply to the Head-quarters of the division for a farther extension. The Staff are lodged in a house considerably the worse for German occupancy, where offices have been improvised by means of wooden hoardings, and where, sitting in a bare passage on a frayed damask sofa surmounted by theatrical posters and faced by a bed with a plum-coloured counterpane, we listened for a while to the jingle of telephones, the rat-tat of typewriters, the steady hum of dictation and the coming and going of hurried despatch-bearers and orderlies. The extension

to the permit was presently delivered with the courteous request that we should push on to Verdun as fast as possible, as
civilian motors were not wanted on the road that afternoon;
and this request, coupled with the evident stir of activity at
Head-quarters, gave us the impression that there must be a
good deal happening beyond the low line of hills to the north.
How much there was we were soon to know.

We left Sainte Menehould at about eleven, and before twelve
o'clock, we were nearing a large village on a ridge from which
the land swept away to right and left in ample reaches. The
first glimpse of the outlying houses showed nothing unusual;
but presently the main street turned and dipped downward,
and below and beyond us lay a long stretch of ruins: the cal-
cined remains of Clermont-en-Argonne, destroyed by the
Germans on the 4th of September. The free and lofty situation
of the little town—for it was really a good deal more than a
village—makes its present state the more lamentable. One can
see it from so far off, and through the torn traceries of its
ruined church the eye travels over so lovely a stretch of country! No doubt its beauty enriched the joy of wrecking it.

At the farther end of what was once the main street another
small knot of houses has survived. Chief among them is the
Hospice for old men, where Sister Gabrielle Rosnet, when the
authorities of Clermont took to their heels, stayed behind to
defend her charges, and where, ever since, she has nursed an
undiminishing stream of wounded from the eastern front. We
found Sœur Rosnet, with her Sisters, preparing the midday
meal of her patients in the little kitchen of the Hospice: the
kitchen which is also her dining-room and private office. She
insisted on our finding time to share the *filet* and fried potatoes
that were just being taken off the stove, and while we lunched
she told us the story of the invasion—of the Hospice doors
broken down "à coups de crosse" and the grey officers bursting in with revolvers, and finding her there before them, in the
big vaulted vestibule, "alone with my old men and my Sisters."
Sœur Gabrielle Rosnet is a small round active woman, with a
shrewd and ruddy face of the type that looks out calmly from
the dark background of certain Flemish pictures. Her blue
eyes are full of warmth and humour, and she puts as much
gaiety as wrath into her tale. She does not spare epithets in

talking of "ces satanés Allemands"—these Sisters and nurses of the front have seen sights to dry up the last drop of sentimental pity—but through all the horror of those fierce September days, with Clermont blazing about her and the helpless remnant of its inhabitants under the perpetual threat of massacre, she retained her sense of the little inevitable absurdities of life, such as her not knowing how to address the officer in command "because he was so tall that I couldn't see up to his shoulder-straps."—"*Et ils étaient tous comme ça*," she added, a sort of reluctant admiration in her eyes.

A subordinate "good Sister" had just cleared the table and poured out our coffee when a woman came in to say, in a matter-of-fact tone, that there was hard fighting going on across the valley. She added calmly, as she dipped our plates into a tub, that an obus had just fallen a mile or two off, and that if we liked we could see the fighting from a garden over the way. It did not take us long to reach that garden! Sœur Gabrielle showed the way, bouncing up the stairs of a house across the street, and flying at her heels we came out on a grassy terrace full of soldiers.

The cannon were booming without a pause, and seemingly so near that it was bewildering to look out across empty fields at a hillside that seemed like any other. But luckily somebody had a field-glass, and with its help a little corner of the battle of Vauquois was suddenly brought close to us—the rush of French infantry up the slopes, the feathery drift of French gun-smoke lower down, and, high up, on the wooded crest along the sky, the red lightnings and white puffs of the German artillery. Rap, rap, rap, went the answering guns, as the troops swept up and disappeared into the fire-tongued wood; and we stood there dumbfounded at the accident of having stumbled on this visible episode of the great subterranean struggle.

Though Sœur Rosnet had seen too many such sights to be much moved, she was full of a lively curiosity, and stood beside us, squarely planted in the mud, holding the field-glass to her eyes, or passing it laughingly about among the soldiers. But as we turned to go she said: "They've sent us word to be ready for another four hundred to-night"; and the twinkle died out of her good eyes.

Her expectations were to be dreadfully surpassed; for, as we learned a fortnight later from a three column *communiqué*, the scene we had assisted at was no less than the first act of the successful assault on the high-perched village of Vauquois, a point of the first importance to the Germans, since it masked their operations to the north of Varennes and commanded the railway by which, since September, they have been revictualling and reinforcing their army in the Argonne. Vauquois had been taken by them at the end of September and, thanks to its strong position on a rocky spur, had been almost impregnably fortified; but the attack we looked on at from the garden of Clermont, on Sunday, February 28th, carried the victorious French troops to the top of the ridge, and made them masters of a part of the village. Driven from it again that night, they were to retake it after a five days' struggle of exceptional violence and prodigal heroism, and are now securely established there in a position described as "of vital importance to the operations." "But what it cost!" Sœur Gabrielle said, when we saw her again a few days later.

II

The time had come to remember our promise and hurry away from Clermont; but a few miles farther our attention was arrested by the sight of the Red Cross over a village house. The house was little more than a hovel, the village—Blercourt it was called—a mere hamlet of scattered cottages and cow-stables: a place so easily overlooked that it seemed likely our supplies might be needed there.

An orderly went to find the *médecin-chef*, and we waded after him through the mud to one after another of the cottages in which, with admirable ingenuity, he had managed to create out of next to nothing the indispensable requirements of a second-line ambulance: sterilizing and disinfecting appliances, a bandage-room, a pharmacy, a well-filled wood-shed, and a clean kitchen in which "tisanes" were brewing over a cheerful fire. A detachment of cavalry was quartered in the village, which the trampling of hoofs had turned into a great morass, and as we picked our way from cottage to cottage in the doctor's wake he told us of the expedients to which he had been put to secure even the few hovels into which his patients were

crowded. It was a complaint we were often to hear repeated along
this line of the front, where troops and wounded are packed in
thousands into villages meant to house four or five hundred; and
we admired the skill and devotion with which he had dealt with
the difficulty, and managed to lodge his patients decently.

We came back to the high-road, and he asked us if we should
like to see the church. It was about three o'clock, and in the low
porch the curé was ringing the bell for vespers. We pushed open
the inner doors and went in. The church was without aisles, and
down the nave stood four rows of wooden cots with brown
blankets. In almost every one lay a soldier—the doctor's "worst
cases"—few of them wounded, the greater number stricken
with fever, bronchitis, frost-bite, pleurisy, or some other form of
trench-sickness too severe to permit of their being carried farther from the front. One or two heads turned on the pillows as
we entered, but for the most part the men did not move.

The curé, meanwhile, passing around to the sacristy, had
come out before the altar in his vestments, followed by a little
white acolyte. A handful of women, probably the only "civil"
inhabitants left, and some of the soldiers we had seen about
the village, had entered the church and stood together between the rows of cots; and the service began. It was a sunless
afternoon, and the picture was all in monastic shades of black
and white and ashen grey: the sick under their earth-coloured
blankets, their livid faces against the pillows, the black dresses
of the women (they seemed all to be in mourning) and the
silver haze floating out from the little acolyte's censer. The
only light in the scene—the candle-gleams on the altar, and
their reflection in the embroideries of the curé's chasuble—
were like a faint streak of sunset on the winter dusk.

For a while the long Latin cadences sounded on through
the church; but presently the curé took up in French the Can-
ticle of the Sacred Heart, composed during the war of 1870,
and the little congregation joined their trembling voices in the
refrain:

> "*Sauvez, sauvez la France,*
> *Ne l'abandonnez pas!*"

The reiterated appeal rose in a sob above the rows of bodies in
the nave: "*Sauvez, sauvez la France,*" the women wailed it near

the altar, the soldiers took it up from the door in stronger tones; but the bodies in the cots never stirred, and more and more, as the day faded, the church looked like a quiet grave-yard in a battle-field.

After we had left Sainte Menehould the sense of the nearness and all-pervadingness of the war became even more vivid. Every road branching away to our left was a finger touching a red wound: Varennes, Le Four de Paris, le Bois de la Grurie, were not more than eight or ten miles to the north. Along our own road the stream of motor-vans and the trains of ammunition grew longer and more frequent. Once we passed a long line of "Seventy-fives" going single file up a hillside, farther on we watched a big detachment of artillery galloping across a stretch of open country. The movement of supplies was continuous, and every village through which we passed swarmed with soldiers busy loading or unloading the big vans, or clustered about the commissariat motors while hams and quarters of beef were handed out. As we approached Verdun the cannonade had grown louder again; and when we reached the walls of the town and passed under the iron teeth of the portcullis we felt ourselves in one of the last outposts of a mighty line of defense. The desolation of Verdun is as impressive as the feverish activity of Châlons. The civil population was evacuated in September, and only a small percentage have returned. Nine-tenths of the shops are closed, and as the troops are nearly all in the trenches there is hardly any movement in the streets.

The first duty of the traveller who has successfully passed the challenge of the sentinel at the gates is to climb the steep hill to the citadel at the top of the town. Here the military authorities inspect one's papers, and deliver a "permis de séjour" which must be verified by the police before lodgings can be obtained. We found the principal hotel much less crowded than the Haute Mère-Dieu at Châlons, though many of the officers of the garrison mess there. The whole atmosphere of the place was different: silent, concentrated, passive. To the chance observer, Verdun appears to live only in its hospitals; and of these there are fourteen within the walls alone. As darkness fell, the streets became completely deserted, and the cannonade seemed to grow nearer and more incessant. That first night the hush was so intense that every reverberation from the dark hills beyond the walls brought out in the mind its separate vision of destruction; and then, just as the strained imagination could bear no more, the thunder ceased. A moment later, in a court below my windows, a pigeon began to coo; and all night long the two sounds strangely alternated . . .

On entering the gates, the first sight to attract us had been a colony of roughly-built bungalows scattered over the miry slopes of a little park adjoining the railway station, and surmounted by the sign: "Evacuation Hospital No. 6." The next morning we went to visit it. A part of the station buildings has been adapted to hospital use, and among them a great roofless hall, which the surgeon in charge has covered in with canvas and divided down its length into a double row of tents. Each tent contains two wooden cots, scrupulously clean and raised high above the floor; and the immense ward is warmed by a row of stoves down the central passage. In the bungalows across the road are beds for the patients who are to be kept for a time before being transferred to the hospitals in the town. In one bungalow an operating-room has been installed, in another are the bathing arrangements for the newcomers from the trenches. Every possible device for the relief of the wounded has been carefully thought out and intelligently applied by the surgeon in charge and the *infirmière major* who indefatigably seconds him. Evacuation Hospital No. 6 sprang up in an hour, almost, on the dreadful August day when four thousand wounded lay on stretchers between the railway station and the gate of the little park across the way; and it has gradually grown into the model of what such a hospital may become in skilful and devoted hands.

Verdun has other excellent hospitals for the care of the severely wounded who cannot be sent farther from the front. Among them St. Nicolas, in a big airy building on the Meuse, is an example of a great French Military Hospital at its best; but I visited few others, for the main object of my journey was to get to some of the second-line ambulances beyond the town. The first we went to was in a small village to the north of Verdun, not far from the enemy's lines at Cosenvoye, and was fairly representative of all the others. The dreary muddy village was crammed with troops, and the ambulance had been installed at haphazard in such houses as the military authorities could spare. The arrangements were primitive but clean, and even the dentist had set up his apparatus in one of the rooms. The men lay on mattresses or in wooden cots, and the rooms were heated by stoves. The great need, here as everywhere, was for blankets and clean underclothing; for the wounded are brought in from the front encrusted with frozen mud, and usually without having washed or changed for weeks. There are no women nurses in these second-line ambulances, but all the army doctors we saw seemed intelligent, and anxious to do the best they could for their men in conditions of unusual hardship. The principal obstacle in their way is the over-crowded state of the villages. Thousands of soldiers are camped in all of them, in hygienic conditions that would be bad enough for men in health; and there is also a great need for light diet, since the hospital commissariat of the front apparently supplies no invalid foods, and men burning with fever have to be fed on meat and vegetables.

In the afternoon we started out again in a snow-storm, over a desolate rolling country to the south of Verdun. The wind blew fiercely across the whitened slopes, and no one was in sight but the sentries marching up and down the railway lines, and an occasional cavalryman patrolling the lonely road. Nothing can exceed the mournfulness of this depopulated land: we might have been wandering over the wilds of Poland. We ran some twenty miles down the steel-grey Meuse to a village about four miles west of Les Eparges, the spot where, for weeks past, a desperate struggle had been going on. There must have been a lull in the fighting that day, for the cannon had ceased; but the scene at the point where we left the motor gave us the sense of being on the very edge of the conflict. The long straggling village lay on the river, and the trampling of cavalry and the hauling of guns had turned the land about it into a mud-flat. Before the primitive cottage where the doctor's office had been installed were the motors of the surgeon and the medical inspector who had accompanied us. Near by stood the usual flock of grey motor-vans, and all about was the coming and going of cavalry remounts, the riding up of officers, the unloading of supplies, the incessant activity of mud-splashed sergeants and men.

The main ambulance was in a grange, of which the two stories had been partitioned off into wards. Under the cobwebby
rafters the men lay in rows on clean pallets, and big stoves
made the rooms dry and warm. But the great superiority of
this ambulance was its nearness to a canal-boat which had been
fitted up with hot douches. The boat was spotlessly clean, and
each cabin was shut off by a gay curtain of red-flowered chintz.
Those curtains must do almost as much as the hot water to
make over the *moral* of the men: they were the most comforting sight of the day.

Farther north, and on the other bank of the Meuse, lies another large village which has been turned into a colony of
éclopés. Fifteen hundred sick or exhausted men are housed
there—and there are no hot douches or chintz curtains to
cheer them! We were taken first to the church, a large feature-
less building at the head of the street. In the doorway our
passage was obstructed by a mountain of damp straw which a
gang of hostler-soldiers were pitchforking out of the aisles.
The interior of the church was dim and suffocating. Between
the pillars hung screens of plaited straw, forming little enclo-
sures in each of which about a dozen sick men lay on more
straw, without mattresses or blankets. No beds, no tables, no
chairs, no washing appliances—in their muddy clothes, as they
come from the front, they are bedded down on the stone floor
like cattle till they are well enough to go back to their job. It
was a pitiful contrast to the little church at Blercourt, with the
altar lights twinkling above the clean beds; and one wondered
if, even so near the front, it had to be. "The African village, we
call it," one of our companions said with a laugh: but the African village has blue sky over it, and a clear stream runs between
its mud huts.

We had been told at Sainte Menehould that, for military
reasons, we must follow a more southerly direction on our return to Châlons; and when we left Verdun we took the road to
Bar-le-Duc. It runs southwest over beautiful broken country,
untouched by war except for the fact that its villages, like all
the others in this region, are either deserted or occupied by
troops. As we left Verdun behind us the sound of the cannon
grew fainter and died out, and we had the feeling that we were
gradually passing beyond the flaming boundaries into a more

normal world; but suddenly, at a cross-road, a sign-post snatched us back to war: *St. Mihiel*, 18 *Kilomètres*. St. Mihiel, the danger-spot of the region, the weak joint in the armour! There it lay, up that harmless-looking bye-road, not much more than ten miles away—a ten minutes' dash would have brought us into the thick of the grey coats and spiked helmets! The shadow of that sign-post followed us for miles, darkening the landscape like the shadow from a racing storm-cloud.

Bar-le-Duc seemed unaware of the cloud. The charming old town was in its normal state of provincial apathy: few soldiers were about, and here at last civilian life again predominated. After a few days on the edge of the war, in that intermediate region under its solemn spell, there is something strangely lowering to the mood in the first sight of a busy unconscious community. One looks instinctively, in the eyes of the passers-by, for a reflection of that other vision, and feels diminished by contact with people going so indifferently about their business.

A little way beyond Bar-le-Duc we came on another phase of the war-vision, for our route lay exactly in the track of the August invasion, and between Bar-le-Duc and Vitry-le-François the high-road is lined with ruined towns. The first we came to was Laimont, a large village wiped out as if a cyclone had beheaded it; then comes Revigny, a town of over two thousand inhabitants, less completely levelled because its houses were more solidly built, but a spectacle of more tragic desolation, with its wide streets winding between scorched and contorted fragments of masonry, bits of shop-fronts, handsome doorways, the colonnaded court of a public building. A few miles farther lies the most piteous of the group: the village of Heiltz-le-Maurupt, once pleasantly set in gardens and orchards, now an ugly waste like the others, and with a little church so stripped and wounded and dishonoured that it lies there by the roadside like a human victim.

In this part of the country, which is one of many cross-roads, we began to have unexpected difficulty in finding our way, for the names and distances on the mile-stones have all been effaced, the sign-posts thrown down and the enamelled *plaques* on the houses at the entrance to the villages removed. One report has it that this precaution was taken by the inhabitants at the approach of the invading army, another that the Germans themselves demolished the sign-posts and plastered over the mile-stones in order to paint on them misleading and encouraging distances. The result is extremely bewildering, for, all the villages being either in ruins or uninhabited, there is no one to question but the soldiers one meets, and their answer is almost invariably: "We don't know—we don't belong here." One is in luck if one comes across a sentinel who knows the name of the village he is guarding.

It was the strangest of sensations to find ourselves in a chartless wilderness within sixty or seventy miles of Paris, and to wander, as we did, for hours across a high heathery waste, with wide blue distances to north and south, and in all the scene not a landmark by means of which we could make a guess at our whereabouts. One of our haphazard turns at last brought us into a muddy bye-road with long lines of "Seventy-fives" ranged along its banks like grey ant-eaters in some monstrous menagerie. A little farther on we came to a bemired village swarming with artillery and cavalry, and found ourselves in the thick of an encampment just on the move. It seems improbable that we were meant to be there, for our arrival caused such surprise that no sentry remembered to challenge us, and obsequiously saluting *sous-officiers* instantly cleared a way for the motor. So, by a happy accident, we caught one more war-picture, all of vehement movement, as we passed out of the zone of war.

We were still very distinctly in it on returning to Châlons, which, if it had seemed packed on our previous visit, was now quivering and cracking with fresh crowds. The stir about the fountain, in the square before the Haute Mère-Dieu, was more melodramatic than ever. Every one was in a hurry, every one booted and mud-splashed, and spurred or sworded or despatch-bagged, or somehow labelled as a member of the huge military beehive. The privilege of telephoning and telegraphing being denied to civilians in the war-zone, it was ominous to arrive at night-fall on such a crowded scene, and we were not surprised to be told that there was not a room left at the Haute Mère-Dieu, and that even the sofas in the reading-room had been let for the night. At every other inn in the town we met with the same answer; and finally we decided to ask permission to go on as far as Epernay, about twelve miles off. At Head-quarters we were told that our request could not be granted. No motors are allowed to circulate after night-fall in the zone of war, and the officer charged with the distribution of motor-permits pointed out that, even if an exception were made in our favour, we should probably be turned back by the first sentinel we met, only to find ourselves unable to reenter Châlons without another permit! This alternative was so alarming that we began to think ourselves relatively lucky to be on the right side of the gates; and we went back to the Haute Mère-Dieu to squeeze into a crowded corner of the restaurant for dinner. The hope that some one might have suddenly left the hotel in the interval was not realized; but after dinner we learned from the landlady that she had certain rooms permanently reserved for the use of the Staff, and that, as these rooms had not yet been called for that evening, we might possibly be allowed to occupy them for the night.

At Châlons the Head-quarters are in the Préfecture, a coldly handsome building of the eighteenth century, and there, in a majestic stone vestibule, beneath the gilded ramp of a great festal staircase, we waited in anxious suspense, among the orderlies and *estafettes,* while our unusual request was considered. The result of the deliberation was an expression of regret: nothing could be done for us, as officers might at any moment arrive from the General Head-quarters and require the rooms. It was then past nine o'clock, and bitterly cold—and we began to wonder. Finally the polite officer who had been charged to dismiss us, moved to compassion at our plight, offered to give us a *laissez-passer* back to Paris. But Paris was about a hundred and twenty-five miles off, the night was dark, the cold was piercing—and at every cross-road and railway crossing a sentinel would have to be convinced of our right to go farther. We remembered the warning given us earlier in the evening, and, declining the offer, went out again into the cold. And just then chance took pity on us. In the restaurant we had run across a friend attached to the Staff, and now, meeting him again in the depth of our difficulty, we were told of lodgings to be found near by. He could not take us there, for it was past the hour when he had a right to be out, or we either, for that matter, since curfew sounds at nine at Châlons. But he told us how to find our way through the maze of little unlit streets about the Cathedral; standing there beside the motor, in the icy darkness of the deserted square, and whispering hastily, as he turned to leave us: "You ought not to be out so late; but the word to-night is *Jéna*. When you give it to the chauffeur, be sure no sentinel overhears you." With that he was up the wide steps, the glass doors had closed on him, and I stood there in the pitch-black night, suddenly unable to believe that I was I, or Châlons Châlons, or that a young man who in Paris drops in to dine with me and talk over new books and plays, had been whispering a password in my ear to carry me unchallenged to a house a few streets away! The sense of unreality produced by that one word was so overwhelming that for a blissful moment the whole fabric of what I had been experiencing, the whole huge and oppressive and unescapable fact of the war, slipped away like a torn cobweb, and I seemed to see behind it the reassuring face of things as they used to be.

The next morning dispelled that vision. We woke to a noise of guns closer and more incessant than even the first night's cannonade at Verdun; and when we went out into the streets it seemed as if, overnight, a new army had sprung out of the ground. Waylaid at one corner after another by the long tide of troops streaming out through the town to the northern suburbs, we saw in turn all the various divisions of the unfold-ing frieze: first the infantry and artillery, the sappers and min-ers, the endless trains of guns and ammunition, then the long line of grey supply-waggons, and finally the stretcher-bearers following the Red Cross ambulances. All the story of a day's warfare was written in the spectacle of that endless silent flow to the front: and we were to read it again, a few days later, in the terse announcement of "renewed activity" about Suippes, and of the bloody strip of ground gained between Perthes and Beauséjour.

Scribner's Monthly, June 1915

John Reed:
Goutchevo and the Valley of Corpses

With a personality as big as the stories he covered, John "Jack" Reed made his way to New York City after his graduation from Harvard in 1910 and embarked upon a career in journalism. A group of reform-minded writers, whom Theodore Roosevelt had called "muck-rakers," had been chronicling injustices in America just as progressivism was taking root in the country. Reed had met one of the prime practitioners of this new journalism—Lincoln Steffens, who helped him find work as he settled into a decidedly Bohemian life in Greenwich Village. Often becoming the subject of his own stories, Reed reported on a strike of silk workers in Paterson, New Jersey, for *The Masses* in 1913, went to Mexico to report on its revolution for *Metropolitan*, and spent four months with the army of Pancho Villa. His articles from that experience, published as *Insurgent Mexico* in 1914, made him famous. Reed spent several months investigating battle-torn Europe, including a visit in early 1915 to a section of the German trenches in occupied France. Returning to the United States in late January, he published four articles on the war in *Metropolitan*, before visiting Serbia in April during a lull in the fighting. Between August and December 1914, the Serbs had repelled three Austro-Hungarian offensives, driving the invaders from their country. The Serbian victories had come at the cost of 165,000 men killed, wounded, or missing, and another 160,000 soldiers and civilians died as typhus, cholera, and diphtheria swept through the country. Reed's description of his visit to the battlefield on Gučevo Mountain in northwestern Serbia appeared as a chapter in his book *The War in Eastern Europe* (1916).

———————

BEFORE DAWN next morning we were on horseback, galloping out of Losnitza on the way to Goutchevo Mountain, which towered in a lofty series of wooded crests three thousand feet up to the south. It was the summit of Goutchevo that the Austrians seized and intrenched at the time of the second invasion. In the face of their withering fire the Serbians climbed its eastern side, foot by foot, until their trenches were also upon the narrow crest, and along a front of ten miles on top of a savage mountain was fought that strange Battle Above the Clouds which lasted fifty-four days, and ended with the retirement of the Serbs, only because the third invasion had broken their lines down by Krupaign. After the rout at Valievo the Austrians abandoned Goutchevo without a stand.

The genial young captain who escorted us had once been a *comitadji* officer, sent by the government to organize revolt—first in Macedonia, and then in Austrian Bosnia and Herzegovina.

"Before we volunteered for *comitadji* service," he said, "we were sent to the universities in Berlin and Vienna to study the organization of revolutions, particularly of the Italian *Risorgimento.* . . ."

Our road turned to rough country way, deep in mud, then to a mere track where only mules and pedestrians could pass—winding upward through immense oaks and ashes, lost in swift mountain brooks and choked with brush. An hour's hard climb brought us to the summit of the first mountain, from which we could see the precipitous peak of Eminove Vode —"Waters of Emin," as the old Turks named it—rising tremendous from the little valley that lay between, and splendid with the vivid green of young leaves, and great shining knobs of black rock.

In the high valley of the hills the white houses of a village lay half hidden in a sea of riotous plum blossoms. Their windows gaped wide—their doors swung idly to and fro. Behind some wall which we could not see a feminine voice was wailing shrilly, flatly, with hysterical catches, the monotonous song of mourning for the dead. The captain pulled up his horse and hallooed loudly—finally a thin, gaunt woman came slowly through the orchard.

"Have you *rackia*, sister?"

"*Ima*. I have." She went back and returned with a stone jug and a long-necked vase for us to drink from.

"What is this place?"

"It is the Rich Village of the Rackia-Makers."

"Where are all the people?"

"They are dead, of the spotted heat (typhus)."

We spurred forward through the golden silence, heavy with the scent of the plum-trees and with humming bees. The wailing died behind. Here the travelled road ended, and beyond was a mountain path untravelled save by hunters and the goatherds of high Goutchevo, but now scarred and rutted by the feet of thousands, and the passage of heavy bodies dragged through the rocks and brush.

"By here the army climbed Goutchevo," said the captain, "and those marks are the marks of cannon that we took up there." He pointed to the towering height of Eminove Vode. "Horses were no good here—and the oxen fell dead of fatigue. So we pulled them up by men—a hundred and twenty to each gun."

The path wound upward along the flank of the mountain and through a leaping stream which we waded. Here it ceased; but on the other side the deeply scored hillside rose almost straight for five hundred feet. We dismounted and led the stumbling, winded mountain horses, zigzagging from shelf to shelf of earth and crumbling rock.

"It took them three days to haul the cannon up here," panted the captain.

Resting and walking, and for level spaces riding a short distance, we climbed up through the forest of the mounting crest perhaps a thousand feet higher, over ground strewn with brass cartridge-shells, trace-leathers, bits of Serbian uniforms, and the wheels of shattered cannon limbers. Everywhere in the woods were deserted huts thatched with leaves and the branches of trees, and caves in the ground, where the Serbian army had lived for two months in the snow. Higher up we noticed that the lower parts of the trees were covered with leaves, but that their tops were as if dead; slowly as we climbed the dead part descended, until half the forest lifted gaunt, broken spikes where the vicious hail of bullets had torn off their tops—and then came trees naked of branches. We crossed two lines of deep trenches, and emerged on the bare summit of Goutchevo, which had also once been wooded, but where now nothing but jagged stumps studded with glistening lead remained.

On one side of this open space were the Serbian trenches, on the other side the Austrian. Barely twenty yards separated the two. Here and there both trenches merged into immense pits, forty feet around and fifty feet deep, where the enemy had undermined and dynamited them. The ground between was

humped into irregular piles of earth. Looking closer, we saw a
ghastly thing: from these little mounds protruded pieces of
uniform, skulls with draggled hair, upon which shreds of flesh
still hung; white bones with rotting hands at the end, bloody
bones sticking from boots such as the soldiers wear. An awful
smell hung over the place. Bands of half-wild dogs slunk at the
edge of the forest, and far away we could see two tearing at
something that lay half-covered on the ground. Without a
word the captain pulled out his revolver and shot. One dog
staggered and fell thrashing, then lay still—the other fled
howling into the trees; and instantly from the depths of the
wood all around came a wolfish, eerie howling in answer,
dying away along the edge of the battle-field for miles.

We walked on the dead, so thick were they—sometimes our
feet sank through into pits of rotting flesh, crunching bones.
Little holes opened suddenly, leading deep down and swarming with gray maggots. Most of the bodies were covered only
with a film of earth, partly washed away by the rain—many
were not buried at all. Piles of Austrians lay as they had fallen
in desperate charge, heaped along the ground in attitudes of
terrible action. Serbians were among them. In one place the
half-eaten skeletons of an Austrian and a Serbian were entangled, their arms and legs wrapped about each other in a death-
grip that could not even now be loosened. *Behind* the front
line of Austrian trenches was a barbed-wire barricade, significant of the spirit of the men pinned in that death-trap—for
they were mostly Serbians from the Austrian Slav provinces,
driven at the point of a revolver to fight their brothers.

For six miles along the top of Goutchevo the dead were
heaped like that—ten thousand of them, said the captain.
From here we could see for forty miles around—the green
mountains of Bosnia across the silver Drina, little white villages
and flat roads, planes of fields green and yellow with new crops
and brown with ploughing, and the towers and bright houses
of Austrian Svornik, gleaming among lovely trees at the bend
of the river; southward in long lines that seemed to move, so
living were they, lifted and broke the farther peaks of
Goutchevo, along which wriggled to the end of vision the
double line of trenches and the sinister field between . . .

We rode through fruit orchards heavy with blossoms,

between great forests of oaks and beeches and blooming chestnuts; under high wooded hills, whose slopes broke into a hundred rippling mountain meadows that caught the sun like silk. Everywhere springs poured from the hollows, and clear streams leaped down canyons choked with verdure, from Goutchevo, which the Turks called "Mountain of Waters"— from Goutchevo, saturated with the rotting dead. All this part of Serbia was watered by the springs of Goutchevo; and on the other side they flowed into the Drina, thence into the Save and the Danube, through lands where millions of people drank and washed and fished in them. To the Black Sea flowed the poison of Goutchevo. . . .

Late in the afternoon we descended into the main highroad to Valievo, by which the Austrian army had entered the heart of the country, and at evening, clattered down the main street of the white little village of Krupaign, where the subprefect, the chief of police, the president of the town, and the officers of the divisional staff came to meet us, dressed in their best uniforms. Our dinner consisted of roast young pig torn in fragments, beer, wine, *rackia*, cognac, and *pitta smesson*, chopped meat fried in greasy pastry.

Through the warm dark of the spring evening came the squealing of bagpipes, the stamping and shuffling of feet, and short, wild shouts. We leaned from the window. Up the cobbled street marched a big gypsy with the Serbian pipes swelling under his arm, and behind him came hundreds of soldiers, hand in hand, sidling along in a sort of rough polka step—the *kolo*, which is danced all over this part of the world. They swayed along, whooping, until they reached the village square; there they formed a huge, irregular circle, with the gypsy in the middle. The tune changed to a swifter, wilder measure. The dancers flung their legs high and leaped faster in all sorts of variations—each one the specialty of a different village—and as they danced they sang a short chorus with much laughter.

"Every Sunday the peasants all over Serbia gather in their village squares and dance the *kolo*," explained the captain. "There are *kolos* for marriages, *kolos* for christenings, *kolos* for every occasion. And each political party has a separate *kolo* for elections. This one they are dancing now is the Radical *kolo* (the government in power)—and the song they are singing is the Radical song:

> "'If you will pay my taxes for me
> Then I will vote for you! . . .'"

At a quarter to five in the morning our breakfast appeared—a glass of cognac, a glass of tea, and a tiny cup of Turkish coffee. This was to last us perhaps all day, for between here and Valievo was all devastated country. At five we climbed into an ox-cart covered over with a bowed top of matting like the roof of a prairie-schooner, so low that we could not sit up straight. The wagon was not only springless, but built so that every unevenness was magnified one hundred times and communicated to every part. And our route lay over the worst road in Serbia, now rendered impassable by the double passage of two great armies in the winter. The greater part of the trip consisted of a jolting crawl over huge bowlders lying in bottomless mud—and eighty kilometres lie between Krupaign and Valievo.

"*Haide!*" roared the driver, lashing the horses. He was a miserably dressed soldier, dirty and covered with fleas—who soon were holding a banquet on Robinson and me. We tore down the cobbled street at a terrible pace, bouncing up to the roof with shaking bones, in the frightful clatter of the cart over the rocks.

"See those horses go!" cried the soldier, beaming with pride. "The finest horses in all Serbia! This stallion I have named Voyvoda Michitch, and the mare, I call her King Peter."

He pulled up with a flourish at the last café in the village, got down and sat down at a table, rapping loudly for a glass of wine. And there he stayed for half an hour, embracing the hostess, patting the children on the head, and sipping his wine amid an admiring circle of girls who greeted his sallies with giggles. Finally we fell furiously upon Johnson, demanding that he call the driver.

"Excuse me, sair!" returned our guide. "You must have patience. Thees is war!"

Off again at top speed, bouncing over the stones and sinking in the mud.

"I am behind time!" explained the driver. "We must hurry!"

"Well, why did you stay at that café so long?"

He stared at us with bland surprise. "Because I wanted to talk and drink!"

Finally the horses were too tired to run, and the road became so horrible that we walked, the drivers pulling at the bridles with shouts, and lashing their beasts through mire and over heaps of great stones.

All along the débris of the Austrian retreat still littered both sides of the way—hundreds of transport wagons, cannon limbers, broken guns, heaps of rusty rifles and of unshot cartridges, uniforms, caps, hairy knapsacks, and leather ammunition-belts. The road ran along the edge of a canyon through which a river fell down the valley. A sickening stench rose from it. Into this river had been thrown the bodies of men and horses found dead along the line of the retreat. Here the river widened out and poured thunderously over an immense dam; and looking down, we could see the clear water running above a mass of sodden cloth and bodies bloated gray—from the falls themselves a bone stuck straight out, with strings of flesh and pieces of clothing waving in the current.

This nightmare journey continued for five hours, until we reached the hideous, ruined, looted village of Zavlaka. Faint with hunger, we besought Johnson to get something to eat. He roused himself from a light slumber and began: "Excuse me, sair! Thees is——"

"I don't care whether it's war or not!" screamed Robinson. "You get out and rustle some eggs! *Haide!*"

We got our eggs and again started. All that day we crawled down the valley, which is nothing but a fifty-mile grave of dead Austrians.

Late at night we rounded a wooded hill where the camp-fires of the first army stretched under immense oak-trees for miles, and the soldiers lay about them singing epics of the war, and found ourselves in the streets of Valievo.

Valievo had been one of the worst typhus pest-holes in all Serbia. Even now, when the disease had diminished so greatly, the streets of Valievo were nothing but avenues of hospitals. We were taken to one of these.

"Now," said the Serbian doctor who was in charge, "you

shall see a good Serbian hospital. You have seen the bad ones, where we were hampered by the lack of all necessities. But *my* hospital is equal to the American hospital at Belgrade."

We entered a whitewashed hall, clean as it could be made, and smelling of disinfectant. In the wards, where the patients had each his own bed and lay in clean blankets in new clean nightclothes, all the windows were open to the sun and air. The doctor put on a white blouse over his uniform, washed his hands with sublimate, and made us do the same. We were enchanted. But in the centre of the hospital was an open-air court, whitewashed with lime, where the convalescents walked slowly about. At one side was a small open shed, and within lay five dead men, clothed in the filthy rags in which they had entered the hospital. They had lain there for two days, for Serbians will not bury a man until a coffin is made—and in Valievo the coffin-makers were behind with their orders. On the other side of the court were the open toilets. And the court sloped down to the middle, *where was the well for drinking water!*

Here was a horrible room full of men with post-typhus gangrene, that awful disease that follows typhus in almost fifty per cent of soldier cases, in which the flesh rots away and the bones crumble. The only hope of stopping it is by amputating the afflicted part—and this room was full of men without arms and legs, of men with rotting faces and breasts. They moaned and screamed, crying, "*Kuku Mayka!* Holy Mother, help me!" For most of them there was nothing to be done. Their flesh would slough away until it reached their hearts or brains, and death would come in dreadful agony.

We wandered around Valievo for two days, noting the sanitary measures that had been taken to stop the epidemic. They consisted largely in throwing disinfectant over everything. In the street and in every courtyard were piles of filth and garbage. Little attempt had been made to remove these; there were even new piles on top of the old—but freshly sprinkled with lime. This is the key to the Serbian attitude toward sanitation. They do not understand it—they haven't the slightest conception what it means. It is something modern, something European, something that the civilized world uses to prevent disease; so they splash disinfectant about, with a half-contemptuous sneer at people who are so cowardly as to take such precautions, and go on accumulating filth as they always have done.

We went down to the railway-station late at night, to take the train for Nish and Russia. In the light of blue electric arcs, long chains of Austrian prisoners were unloading flour to feed the desolate country until the harvests could be sown and gathered. And as we waited on the platform, I thought with wonder of these Serbians, their origin, and their destiny. They alone of all the Balkan peoples have been one unmixed race since first they came into this country eight centuries ago—and they alone have built their own civilization, unmodified by any other. The Romans had a string of mountain fortresses through the region—they settled no colonies here. The Crusaders passed them by. They held their narrow passes against the Tartars of Bulgaria, the Dacians of Rumania, the Huns and Tcheks of the North—and long before their neighbors, with the armed help of European nations, threw off the yoke of the Turk, Serbia made herself free. When Europe imposed foreign dynasties on Bulgaria, Rumania, and Greece, Serbia was ruled by her own house. With such a stock, with such a history, with the imperialistic impulse growing daily, hourly, in the hearts of her peasant soldiers, into what tremendous conflicts will Serbia's ambition lead her!

There was a soldier standing on guard at the platform—a tall, wiry, bearded man, dressed in the fragments of a uniform and shoes with sandals of cowhide and high socks embroidered with flowers. He was leaning on an Austrian rifle, staring out over the heads of the sweating workmen to those dim mountains lost in the dark beyond. And as he looked he sang, swaying lightly to the rhythm, that most ancient Serbian ballad of all, which begins:

"How is it with thee, O Serbia, my dear mother?"

Charles E. Lauriat, Jr.:
from The Lusitania's Last Voyage

From the outset of the war, Britain's navy had blockaded the North Sea, restricting Germany's overseas trade and its ability to import food. The outnumbered Kaiserliche Marine could not break the blockade, but with its fleet of "U-boats"—short for *Unterseeboots*—it could retaliate. On February 4, 1915, Germany declared that hostile merchant shipping entering the war zone around the British Isles would be subject to underwater attack without warning and that neutral ships would enter the war zone at their own peril. Sinking ships without warning violated the international rules of naval warfare, which dictated that enemy merchant ships could be sunk only after their passengers and crews had been safely loaded into lifeboats. With British ships sometimes feigning neutrality by raising American flags, the Germans issued public warnings in newspapers to Americans considering Atlantic crossings. On May 1, 1915, the *U-30* torpedoed the American tanker *Gulflight* in the Irish Sea, causing the drowning deaths of two crewmen who jumped overboard. That same day, the British Cunard liner *Lusitania*, one of the largest and fastest luxury ships afloat, left New York for Liverpool. On May 7 the *U-20* fired a torpedo into the *Lusitania* as it neared the Irish Sea. The ship sank in eighteen minutes, with the loss of 1,198 lives, 128 of them American. First-class passenger Charles Lauriat, Jr., a successful Boston bookseller, had seen the German newspaper notice warning passengers but gave it "no serious thought" because he "did not think any human being with a drop of red blood in his veins, called a man, could issue an order to sink a passenger steamer without at least giving the women and children a chance to get away." On May 7 he learned otherwise.

AFTER LUNCH I went to my stateroom and put on my sweater under the coat of the knickerbocker suit that I was wearing and went up on deck for a *real walk*. I came up the main companion-way and stepped out on the port side of the steamer and saw Mr. and Mrs. Elbert Hubbard standing by the rail, a little for'ard of the entrance. I joined them and was conversing with them when the torpedo struck the ship. In fact, Mr. Hubbard had just jokingly remarked that he didn't believe he would be a welcome traveller to Germany, owing to the little essay he had written entitled "Who Lifted the Lid Off Hell." Mr. Hubbard had not more than finished this remark when the shock came. This "essay" appeared in the "Philistine" for October, 1914, and Mr. Hubbard had given me a copy earlier on the voyage. If you want to read a piece of vitriolic English, I suggest that you send for a copy.

Where I stood on deck the shock of the impact was not severe; it was a heavy, rather muffled sound, but the good ship trembled for a moment under the force of the blow; a second explosion quickly followed, but I do not think it was a second torpedo, for the sound was quite different; it was more likely a boiler in the engine room.

As I turned to look in the direction of the explosion I saw a shower of coal and steam and some débris hurled into the air between the second and third funnels, and then heard the fall of gratings and other wreckage that had been blown up by the explosion.

Remember that I was standing well for'ard on the port side, and consequently looked back at the scene of the explosion, at an angle across to the starboard side; therefore, although the débris showed between the second and third funnels, I think the blow was delivered practically in line with the fourth funnel.

I looked immediately at my watch and it was exactly 8 minutes past 9 (A.M.) Boston time, which means 8 minutes past 2 Greenwich time.

I turned to the Hubbards and suggested that they go to their stateroom to get their life jackets. Their cabin was on deck B, on the port side, at the foot of the main companion-way, and they had ample time to go there and get back to the deck; but Mr. Hubbard stayed by the rail affectionately holding his arm around his wife's waist and both seemed unable to act.

I went straight down to my stateroom, which, as you will remember, was the most for'ard one on deck B on the starboard side. The boat had taken a list to starboard, but it was not acute, and so I had no difficulty in making my way to and from my cabin. I tied on a life belt, took the others in the room and my small leather case containing my business papers, and went up on deck to the port side. I went back to the spot where I had left the Hubbards, but they had gone, and I never saw them again.

I found those who needed the life belts, put them on, tied them properly, and then went aft along the port side of the ship, for I was confident that all hands would naturally rush to the starboard side and so there would be more opportunity to help along the port side. I turned and walked for'ard toward the bridge, and Captain Turner and Captain Anderson were both calling in stentorian tones not to lower away the boats, ordering all passengers and sailors to get out of them, saying that there was no danger and that the ship would float. A woman passenger beside me called out to Captain Turner in a perfectly clear and calm voice, "Captain, what do you wish us to do?" "Stay right where you are, Madam, she's all right." Then the woman asked him, "Where do you get your information?" —and he replied in rather a severe and commanding voice, "From the engine room, Madam." She and I turned and walked quietly aft and tried to reassure the passengers we met.

As I looked around to see to whom I could be of the greatest help it seemed to me that about everyone who passed me wearing a life belt had it on incorrectly. In their hurry they put them on every way except the right way: one man had his arm through one armhole and his head through the other; others had them on around the waist and upside down; but very few had them on correctly. I stopped these people and spoke to them in a calm voice and persuaded them to let me help them on with the belts, for they certainly stood no show in the water rigged as they were. At first they thought I was trying to take their jackets from them, but on reassuring them they let me straighten them out.

I had been watching carefully the list of the steamer, and by now I was confident that she wouldn't float and that the end was coming fast. I remembered one or two personal things in my stateroom which I very much wanted, and I figured that I had time to go down and get them. If I didn't come through the final plunge, I wanted to feel I had them with me, and if I did get through, I was just as sure I wanted them, so there didn't seem anything to do but to get them, which I did.

There was a companion-way for'ard of the main staircase, about half-way between it and my stateroom, so I went along the port passage inside of deck A, down that companion-way, and along the starboard passage to my stateroom. It was not until I walked along this passage that I realized how acute was the list of the ship. My stateroom was an inside one without a porthole, and consequently could be lighted only by electricity. I pressed the switch, but the light had gone, so I put my hand on a box of matches; for each night when I retired I placed a box in a particular place, just in case I needed it. With the aid of these matches I found the little article for which I was looking, opened my travelling bag, and took out some papers which included my passport and other envelopes that could easily be slipped into my inside pocket.

I had kept my drafts on my person, for I figured that there was no use in giving them to the purser, except as a precaution against theft, and that was negligible. If what had happened was to happen, I knew there would be no time to reclaim them from the purser.

I made my way back along the passage, walking in the angle formed by the floor and the side walls of the staterooms rather than the floor, and went back up the for'ard companion-way, the same that I came down. Going along the passage (on deck B) I looked down some of the cross passages that lead to the staterooms, and at the bottom of the ones I passed I saw that the portholes were open and that the water could not have been more than a few feet from them. Here let me state that I consider it most extraordinary that the portholes on the lower decks should not have been *closed* and *sealed* as we steamed through the war zone. At luncheon the portholes in the dining-saloon on deck D were open, and so I doubt not that all the others on that deck were open. I mean those in the staterooms. I cannot speak with certainty in regard to the portholes on deck E. I believe that the first list the ship took brought her down to these open ports on the starboard side and that she sank much more quickly from filling through them.

On my return to the deck I felt that the steamer must make her final plunge any moment now, and as there was nothing more that could be done on the port side—for there was no discipline or order with which to do it—I passed through to the starboard side. Men were striving to lower the boats and were putting women and children into them, but it seemed to me that it only added horror to the whole situation to put people into a boat that you knew never would be cleared and which would go down with the steamer; better leave them on the deck to let them take their chance at a piece of wreckage.

True, there was no panic, in the sense that anyone crowded or pushed his way to the lifeboats, but there was infinite confusion, and there seemed no one to take command of any one boat.

As I came out on the starboard side, I saw, a little aft of the main entrance, a lifeboat well filled with people, principally women and children, that no one had attempted to clear from the davits. The steamer was rapidly sinking, and I realized that the boat must be cleared at once if the people were to be saved.

I climbed into the stern of the boat, which was floating flush with the rail of deck B, so far had the steamer settled, and helped clear the fall. We freed our end and swung the ropes clear, but we couldn't make anyone for'ard understand what to do or how to do it.

I remember looking for'ard and seeing someone, I think it was a steward, bravely cutting away at the thick ropes with a pocket knife. How I wish he had had an axe! What would I have given for one real sailor man for'ard; we could have saved that boatload of people. I started to go for'ard, but it was impossible to climb through that boatload of people, mixed up as they were with oars, boat hooks, kegs of water, rope ladders, sails, and God knows what—everything that seemed to hinder progress to getting for'ard. The steamer was all the time rapidly settling, and to look at the tremendous smokestack hanging out over us only added to the terror of the people in the boat. I certainly did not blame them, for it was a harrowing sight, even to one as familiar with the ocean as I am. However, I should have gone for'ard and made the try, except that the stern end of the boat was raised by a small swell of the ocean and I was impressed by the nearness of the davit by getting a blow on the back which nearly knocked me overboard.

Then I admit that I saw the hopelessness of ever clearing the for'ard davit in time to get the boat away, so I stepped out and made a try for it by swimming. I spoke to several and urged them to come; but truly they were petrified, and only my training from boyhood up, in the water and under it, gave me the courage to jump. I swam about 100 feet away from the ship and then turned around to see if anyone was following to whom I could lend a hand, and found several who needed encouragement. Also I wanted to see when the final plunge of the steamer came, that I might be the more ready to fight against the vortex and tell the others. The Lusitania did not go down anything like head first: she had, rather, settled along her whole water line. This convinces me that practically all the ports must have been open, even those as far down as Deck E. The stern did not rise to anything like a perpendicular, nor did it rise so high that I could see a single one of the propellers or even the end of her rudder. Not one of her funnels fell.

The last I saw of the lifeboat out of which I jumped was that she was being pulled down, bow first, as the tackle had not been freed and the stern of the boat was rising high in the air. While the people were thrown out, they were not so violently thrown as those from some of the lifeboats that were dropped when half lowered into the water.

There was very little vortex; there was rather a shooting out from the ship instead of a sucking in, after she sank; this I am told was *partly* caused by the water rushing into her funnels and being blown out again by explosions made by the mixing of the cold water of the sea with the steam of the boilers. I saw an interesting statement in one of the papers, purporting to have come from Captain Turner, in which he stated that the small amount of suction was probably due to the fact that the bow of the boat was already resting on the bottom when the stern went down. This seems quite feasible, as she sank in about 60 fathoms (360 feet) of water and she was 755 feet long.

The sea was wonderfully smooth, and it seemed to me that if one could keep clear of the wreck and pick up a lifeboat, that it could be manned and that we could go back and get many survivors. I was able to work this out quite as I planned.

As I waited for the final plunge something caught me on the top of my head and slipped down to my shoulders, pressing me under the water; I couldn't imagine what it was, but on turning to see I found that it was one of the aërials of the wireless that stretched from topmast to topmast.

The present style of life belt, or rather jacket, is not the old-fashioned kind filled with hard cork, but a larger and more bulky affair filled with fibre, and when you have it on you look and feel like a padded football player, especially around the shoulders. When I shook this wire off my head, it caught me around the shoulders on the soft pad, and I couldn't shake it off. It took me down under the water and turned me upside down. I tell you I "kicked." I came up none the worse for my ducking, for it simply reminded me of one of my various trips down to see "Susy the Mermaid" when I was a youngster at Camp Asquam and the older boys used to duck us youngsters anywhere from five to fifteen times a day, according to the unpardonable sins we were supposed to have committed; and these weren't mere "duckings" either. They used to push us under, put their feet on our shoulders, and then give a good shove, so that we went down anywhere from six to sixteen feet under water. I hated the duckings at that time, but they proved mighty good training!

When I came up, after shaking the Marconi wire, the waves bearing the wreckage and people were upon me. After swimming around and helping those I could by pushing them pieces of wreckage to which to cling, I saw a short distance away a collapsible lifeboat floating right side up, swam to it, and climbed aboard. A seaman quickly followed, and a fine husky chap he proved to be. I heard my name called, and for the moment I didn't realize whether it was a call from Heaven or Hell, but when I turned in the direction of the voice I found the man to be G——, one of the three men with whom I had played cards each evening. I pulled him up on the boat, and we three got out our jackknives and went at a kind of can-opening operation, which was really the removing of the canvas cover of the boat.

They call that invention a "boat," but to start with, it is nothing but a "raft." Let me try to draw you a word picture and see if you will understand it.

Suppose you floated a real lifeboat in the water, and at the water line cut down the sides so that the bottom of the boat that was left floated flush with the water. Then deck over and make watertight this part of the boat that is left. This gives you a round bottomed, watertight raft, floating almost flush with the water.

Take a long piece of about 24-inch high (or wide) canvas that will reach all around the sides from one end back to the same end. Nail the lower edge of this canvas to the outside edge of the "raft." To enable you to raise these "collapsible" canvas sides and to keep them in place, make a stout rail that will be curved to the shape of the floor of the "raft" and nail the top edge of the canvas on to it.

This now "collapsible boat," with its folding canvas sides, is of course shallow, and about three or four of them can be nested on the deck of a steamer in the space occupied by a "real lifeboat." There is a canvas cover laced down over the top of these boats, the same as on regular boats.

Before you can do anything with a collapsible lifeboat you must make it a "real boat" by lifting up its canvas sides and lashing them in place so they can't collapse. Until this is done you have nothing but a "raft." It is almost impossible to lift the rail into place if there are people hanging on to it, as that would mean lifting the people as well. Also, you can't lift the sides, which automatically raise the cross seats, if there is any-one lying across the boat, and you can't get on the "raft" without getting on the seats. We tried to persuade the people who were hanging on to the rail to take off their hands and hang on to the life ropes—but that was impossible. Never have I heard a more distressing cry of despair than when I tried to tell one of them that that was what we were doing. In their condition I don't wonder they thought we were trying to push them off. So we had to take some aboard, those who were in the most panicky condition, and try to get up the sides with the "raft" half covered with people.

The seats of these boats are attached to an iron brace which is supposed to slide on a metal run in the middle of the boat. A wooden brace at either end is held in place by a pin when the sides are raised to their proper height, but, as the saying is, "There warn't no pin" and the wooden brace in my end of the boat was broken and the metal run for the iron braces of the

seats was so rusted and corroded that it wasn't a "run;" so
there we were, back to a raft again.

Not an oar in the boat, nor even a stick with which to reach
wreckage so that we could block up the seats. We must get
those seats braced up to give us the protection of the canvas
sides, and they mustn't fall down either, because then the
"boat" became a "raft," the people became a little more panicky, and the falling seats hurt and slightly injured the people
sitting between them, for of course we had to seat those too
exhausted to pull and haul on the floor between the seats. We
had to have some oars too to make the boat navigable, so we
fished round in the wreckage and were fortunate to get five
oars (one broken, but that served me as a steering oar) and
some blocks. Then with a long heave and a heave all together
we raised the blasted seats as far as possible, but not to their
proper height, and jammed the blocks under them. We were
lucky to get blocks that act as supports to a *real* lifeboat, which,
as you know, have notches cut on the long side. These blocks
are like little steps, so that we were able to shove them under
the seats to the limit.

About the fifth man aboard the boat was a chap named
B——; he was a husky, no mistake. He weighed about 200
pounds and was all good material. This man G—— was another good one too; he deserved his name. By this time we
must have had fifteen people in our now "*non*-collapsible
boat." Let us thank God for the "non."

I went aft and took the steering oar and my two huskies,
B—— and the sailor man, rowed the heavy sweeps, and G——
stayed for'ard to help the people in. We headed back into the
wreckage and picked up those who seemed most urgently in
need.

I won't enter into the detail of the condition of the poor
souls we got, but two instances of nerve stand out so clearly in
my mind that I must tell them. Both pertain to women, and never
have I seen greater courage and patience shown by anyone.

I heard a call near my end of the boat and told the boys to
back water, and I reached over and pulled in a woman who I
thought at first glance was a negress; I never believed a white
woman could be so black. I learned afterwards that she and
her husband had got into a lifeboat, and while he was busy

helping to clear it she got panic-stricken by the tremendous overhanging funnels and jumped back on to the steamer without her husband knowing it. She was aboard when the final plunge came, and the suction took her part way down one of the funnels, but the thankful explosion blew her forth, out into clear water, in among the wreckage, where she could hang on. The clothes were almost blown off the poor woman, and there wasn't a white spot on her except her teeth and the whites of her eyes. Marvellous to say she wasn't hurt and proved a great help in cheering us all by her bright talk.

For coolness I think this second case is even more remarkable. We had about as many in our boat as we ought to take when I heard a woman's voice say, in just as natural a tone of voice as you would ask for another slice of bread and butter, "Won't you take me next? you know I can't swim." When I looked over into the mass of wreckage from which this voice emanated all I could see was a woman's head, with a piece of wreckage under her chin and with her hair streaming out over other pieces of wreckage. She was so jammed in she couldn't even get her arms out, and with it all she had a half smile on her face and was placidly chewing gum. The last I saw of her when I helped her off the boat at Queenstown was that she was still chewing that piece of gum, and I shouldn't be surprised if she had it yet. Of course, we couldn't leave her, and as there was no possible way that I dared try to get her without going into the water for her, I told her that if she'd keep cool I'd come after her. To my surprise she said it was not at all necessary, just hand her an oar and she'd hang on. That is the last thing in the world I should ever have dared to do, for naturally I thought, in view of the fact that she could not swim, that as soon as I cleared away the wreckage with an oar she'd get rattled and sink. After what she had said I got my huskies to back through the wreckage till my oar would reach to her. Then I placed it as close to her face as I could and she wriggled around and got her two hands on the oar, held fast, and we pulled her through.

Then we rowed for the shore. G—— took the for'ard port oar, and somewhere in the shuffle we had picked up a couple of the stokers, and while they weren't very big men they were red-headed   cockneys   and   they   were   trumps.   Their conversation was something to remember; I shall never forget it. They two rowed the for'ard starboard oar, B—— rowed the after port oar, and the sailor man rowed the after starboard oar. Others helped push on the oars and so we had a good crew. I steered for a lighthouse on the coast, for I didn't know whether the Marconi operator had had time to send out an S. O. S., or if he had, whether or not it had been picked up. It was a good long row ashore and I knew we could not get there until after dark, and it was much better to land on a shore, however barren, near a lighthouse than to land on that part where there might not be an inhabitant for miles; also I saw the sail of a fisherman between us and the lighthouse, so I had two goals for which to steer.

The lighthouse for which we were steering was that on the Head of Old Kinsale. There were already two real lifeboats between us and the shore. We had stayed around and picked up everyone who seemed to be in the most helpless condition. Those we were forced to leave were as safe as if we had over-crowded them into our flimsy craft. The calmness of the sea was the only thing that enabled us to take on so many, with any degree of safety.

We must have rowed about a quarter of a mile toward shore, when off in the distance I saw one lone man floating around by himself. He seemed to prefer his own society to anyone's else by going off "on his own," but apparently he had changed his mind and got lonesome, for he sure did yell. He looked safe enough, as he had one of the big round white lifebuoys around his body, under his arms, and he was perfectly safe from sinking. I was pretty sure that according to the rules of the blessed "Board of Trade" we had all the people in our boat that our license would allow us to carry. Still I headed for the chap, for you couldn't go off and leave that one more soul floating around. It was lucky we went for him for he was in pretty bad shape, but recovered all right after we got him ashore. This chap turned out to be McM——, a fine Canadian fellow and a man of some experience in shipwreck, for he was on the Republic when she sank.

After rowing about two miles we came up to the fishing smack, and although they had already taken on two boatloads, they made room for us. Before anyone left our boat I counted heads and found we had 32 aboard! It wasn't just the time to hunt souvenirs, but I took my steersman's oarlock with me; it will do for a paper weight.

Aboard the fisherman I witnessed one of the most affecting scenes of all. It seems that the husband of the temporary negress we picked up was aboard, and as we approached she recognized him and called to him; but he stood at the rail with a perfectly blank expression on his face and refused to recognize his own wife. Not until we were directly alongside and he could lean over and look the woman squarely in the face did he realize that his wife had been given back to him.

1915

Woodrow Wilson: Address to Naturalized Citizens at Convention Hall

Americans could ignore the war no longer, as the sinking of the *Lusitania* galvanized the national debate. Jingoes now had ammunition in arguing for U.S. entry into the war. Colonel Edward M. House, President Wilson's chief adviser, sought immediate assurances that such attacks against American civilians would never occur again and asserted that the United States "must determine whether she stands for civilized or uncivilized warfare." One citizen wired the White House, "In the name of God and humanity, declare war on Germany." An offended Wilson told his secretary, "War isn't declared in the name of God; it is a human affair entirely." In that moment, a human affair of another kind had taken hold of Wilson. The bereft fifty-eight-year-old widower had suddenly fallen in love with Edith Bolling Galt, a forty-two-year-old Washington widow, and was in the middle of an obsessive courtship, writing her two or three love letters a day. When he arrived in Philadelphia three days after the sinking of the *Lusitania* to address an audience of 15,000 (4,000 newly naturalized citizens among them), he was hardly thinking straight. He spoke, as he generally did, from a basic outline, offering a message of peace with his reasons for maintaining American neutrality. He later confessed to Edith that his mind was elsewhere that day.

———————

Mr. Mayor, fellow citizens: It warms my heart that you should give me such a reception; but it is not of myself that I wish to think tonight, but of those who have just become citizens of the United States.

This is the only country in the world which experiences this constant and repeated rebirth. Other countries depend upon the multiplication of their own native people. This country is constantly drawing strength out of new sources by the voluntary association with it of great bodies of strong men and forward-looking women out of other lands. And so, by the gift of the free will of independent people, it is being constantly renewed from generation to generation by the same process by which it was originally created. It is as if humanity had determined to see to it that this great nation, founded for the benefit of humanity, should not lack for the allegiance of the people of the world.

You have just taken an oath of allegiance to the United States. Of allegiance to whom? Of allegiance to no one, unless it be God—certainly not of allegiance to those who temporarily represent this great government. You have taken an oath of allegiance to a great ideal, to a great body of principles, to a great hope of the human race. You have said, "We are going to America, not only to earn a living, not only to seek the things which it was more difficult to obtain where we were born, but to help forward the great enterprises of the human spirit—to let men know that everywhere in the world there are men who will cross strange oceans and go where a speech is spoken which is alien to them, if they can but satisfy their quest for what their spirits crave; knowing that, whatever the speech, there is but one longing and utterance of the human heart, and that is for liberty and justice." And, while you bring all countries with you, you come with a purpose of leaving all other countries behind you—bringing what is best of their spirit, but not looking over your shoulders and seeking to perpetuate what you intended to leave behind in them. I certainly would not be one even to suggest that a man cease to love the home of his birth and the nation of his origin—these things are very sacred and ought not to be put out of our hearts. But it is one thing to love the place where you were born, and it is another thing to dedicate yourself to the place to which you go. You cannot dedicate yourself to America unless you become in every respect and with every purpose of your will thorough Americans. You cannot become thorough Americans if you think of yourselves in groups. America does not consist of groups. A man who thinks of himself as belonging to a particular national group in America has not yet become an American, and the man who goes among you to trade upon your nationality is no worthy son to live under the Stars and Stripes.

My urgent advice to you would be, not only always to think first of America, but always, also, to think first of humanity.

You do not love humanity if you seek to divide humanity into jealous camps. Humanity can be welded together only by love, by sympathy, by justice—not by jealousy and hatred. I am sorry for the man who seeks to make personal capital out of the passions of his fellow men. He has lost the touch and ideal of America, for America was created to unite mankind by those passions which lift, and not by the passions which separate and debase. We came to America, either ourselves or in the persons of our ancestors, to better the ideals of men, to make them see finer things than they had seen before, to get rid of the things that divide, and to make sure of the things that unite. It was but an historical accident, no doubt, that this great country was called the "United States"; and yet I am very thankful that it has that word "united" in its title, and the man who seeks to divide man from man, group from group, interest from interest in the United States is striking at its very heart.

It is a very interesting circumstance to me, in thinking of those of you who have just sworn allegiance to this great government, that you were drawn across the ocean by some beckoning finger of hope, by some belief, by some vision of a new kind of justice, by some expectation of a better kind of life. No doubt you have been disappointed in some of us. Some of us are very disappointing. No doubt you have found that justice in the United States goes only with a pure heart and a right purpose, as it does everywhere else in the world. No doubt what you have found here did not seem touched for you, after all, with the complete beauty of the ideal which you had conceived beforehand. But remember this: If we had grown at all poor in the ideal, you brought some of it with you. A man does not go out to seek the thing that is not in him. A man does not hope for the thing that he does not believe in. And if some of us have forgotten what America believed in, you, at any rate, imported in your own hearts a renewal of the belief. That is the reason that I, for one, make you welcome. If I have in any degree forgotten what America was intended for, I will thank God if you will remind me. I was born in America. You dreamed dreams of what America was to be, and I hope you brought the dreams with you. No man that does not see visions will ever realize any high hope or undertake any high enterprise. Just because you brought dreams with you, America is more likely to realize dreams such as you brought. You are enriching us if you came expecting us to be better than we are.

See, my friends, what that means. It means that Americans must have a consciousness different from the consciousness of every other nation in the world. I am not saying this with even the slightest thought of criticism of other nations. You know how it is with a family. A family gets centered on itself if it is not careful and is less interested in the neighbors than it is in its own members. So a nation that is not constantly renewed out of new sources is apt to have the narrowness and prejudice of a family, whereas America must have this consciousness— that on all sides it touches elbows and touches hearts with all the nations of mankind. The example of America must be a special example. The example of America must be the example, not merely of peace because it will not fight, but of peace because peace is the healing and elevating influence of the world, and strife is not. There is such a thing as a man being too proud to fight. There is such a thing as a nation being so right that it does not need to convince others by force that it is right.

So, if you come into this great nation, as you have come, voluntarily seeking something that we have to give, all that we have to give is this: We cannot exempt you from work. No man is exempt from work anywhere in the world. I sometimes think he is fortunate if he has to work only with his hands and not with his head. It is very easy to do what other people give you to do, but it is very difficult to give other people things to do. We cannot exempt you from work; we cannot exempt you from the strife and the heartbreaking burden of the struggle of the day—that is common to mankind everywhere. We cannot exempt you from the loads that you must carry. We can only make them light by the spirit in which they are carried, because that is the spirit of hope, it is the spirit of liberty, it is the spirit of justice.

When I was asked, therefore, by the Mayor and the committee that accompanied him to come up from Washington to meet this great company of newly admitted citizens, I could not decline the invitation. I ought not to be away from Washington, and yet I feel that it has renewed my spirit as an

American. In Washington, men tell you so many things every day that are not so, and I like to come and stand in the presence of a great body of my fellow citizens, whether they have been my fellow citizens a long time or a short time, and drink, as it were, out of the common fountains with them and go back feeling what you have so generously given me—the sense of your support and of the living vitality in your hearts of the great ideals which have made America the hope of the world.

May 10, 1915

The New York Times:
Roosevelt for Prompt Action

Only four words reverberated from President Wilson's speech at Convention Hall—"too proud to fight." Henry Cabot Lodge, the senior Republican on the Senate Foreign Relations Committee and Wilson's chief rival, insisted this was not a moment for "false idealism" and called Wilson's phrase justifying neutrality the most "unfortunate" the President "ever coined." Lodge's friend and political ally Theodore Roosevelt had even more to say. Always looking for an opportunity to raise his political stock—especially if it allowed him to sell Wilson short—Roosevelt wasted no time in mocking the President's pusillanimity. Privately, he would write his son Archibald: "As a nation, we have thought very little about foreign affairs; we don't realize that the murder of the thousand men, women and children on the *Lusitania* is due, solely, to Wilson's abject cowardice and weakness in failing to take energetic action when the *Gulflight* was sunk but a few days previously." He vented his public feelings to *The New York Times.*

ROOSEVELT FOR PROMPT ACTION

Ex-President Says We Must
Remember There Are Worse
Things Than War.

WHEN PEACE IS WORTHY

Only When It Is the Handmaiden of
Righteousness and National Self-Respect.

READS WILSON'S SPEECH

And Says China Is Entitled to Draw
All the Comfort She Can from It.

SYRACUSE, N. Y., May 11.—Colonel Theodore Roosevelt announced today what action, in his opinion, this country should take toward Germany because of the sinking of the Lusitania. Colonel Roosevelt earnestly said that the time for deliberation was past, and that within twenty-four hours this country could and should take effective action by declaring that all commerce with Germany forthwith be forbidden and that all commerce of every kind permitted and encouraged with France, England, and "the rest of the civilized world."

Colonel Roosevelt said that for America to take this step would not mean war, as the firm assertion of our rights could not be so construed, but he added that we would do well to remember that there were things worse than war.

The Colonel has been reading President Wilson's speech carefully, and what seemed to impress him more than anything else was this passage from it:

"There is such a thing as a man being too proud to fight. There is such a thing as a nation being so right that it does not need to convince others by force that it is right."

Asked if he cared to make any comment upon the speech of the President, Mr. Roosevelt said:

"I think that China is entitled to draw all the comfort she can from this statement, and it would be well for the United States to ponder seriously what the effect upon China has been of managing her foreign affairs during the last fifteen years on the theory thus enunciated.

IN CHINA'S POSITION.

"If the United States is satisfied with occupying some time in the future the precise international position that China now occupies, then the United States can afford to act on this theory. But it cannot act on this theory if it desires to retain or regain the position won for it by the men who fought under Washington and by the men who, in the days of Abraham Lincoln, wore the blue under Grant and the gray under Lee.

"I very earnestly hope that we will act promptly. The proper time for deliberation was prior to sending the message that our Government would hold Germany to a strict accountability if it did the things it has now actually done. The 150 babies drowned on the Lusitania; the hundreds of women drowned with them, scores of these women and children being Americans, and the American ship, the Gulflight, which was torpedoed, offer an eloquent commentary on the actual working of the theory that force is not necessary to assert and, that a policy of blood and iron can with efficacy be met by a policy of milk and water.

RIGHT TO SHIP ARMS.

"I see it stated in the press dispatches from Washington that Germany now offers to stop the practice on the high seas, committed in violation of the neutral rights that she is pledged to observe, if we will abandon further neutral rights, which by her treaty she has solemnly pledged herself to see that we exercise without molestation. Such a proposal is not even entitled to an answer. The manufacturing and shipment of arms and ammunition to any belligerent is moral or immoral according to the use to which the arms and munitions are to be put. If they are to be used to prevent the redress of the hideous wrongs inflicted on Belgium, then it is immoral to ship them. If they are to be used for the redress of those wrongs and the restoration of Belgium to her deeply wronged and unoffending people, then it is eminently moral to send them.

"Without twenty-four hours' delay this country could and should take effective action by declaring that in view of Germany's murderous offenses against the rights of neutrals, all commerce with Germany shall be forthwith forbidden, and all commerce of every kind permitted and encouraged with France, England, and the rest of the civilized world. This would not be a declaration of war. It would merely prevent munitions of war being sent to a power which, by its conduct, has shown willingness to use munitions to slaughter American men and women and children. I do not believe the assertion of our rights means war, but we will do well to remember there are things worse than war.

"Let us, as a nation, understand that peace is worthy only when it is the handmaiden of international righteousness and of national self-respect."

ROOSEVELT URGES VIGOR.

Failure to Act with Decision
Failure of Duty, He Says.

Advance copies of an article entitled, "Murder on the High Seas," written by
Theodore Roosevelt on May 9—two days after the sinking of the Lusitania—
were given out yesterday at the office of the Metropolitan Magazine, 432
Fourth Avenue. The article, which was not to have appeared until the June
number of the magazine, was made public yesterday with Colonel Roosevelt's
consent. Here it is:

THE German submarines have established no effective blockade of the British and French coast lines. They have endeavored to prevent the access of French, British, and neutral ships
to Britain and France by attacks upon them which defy every
principle of international law as laid down in innumerable existing treaties, including the Hague Conventions. Many of
these attacks have represented pure piracy; and not a few of
them have been accompanied by murder on an extended scale.
In the case of the Lusitania the scale was so vast that the murder became wholesale.

A number of American ships had already been torpedoed in
similar fashion. In one case the lives lost included those not only
of the American Captain but of his wife and little daughter.
When the Lusitania sank some twelve hundred non-combatants,
men, women, and children, were drowned, and more than a
hundred of these were Americans. Centuries have passed since
any war vessel of a civilized power has shown such ruthless
brutality toward non-combatants, and especially toward women
and children. The pirates of the Barbary Coast behaved at
times in similar fashion, until the civilized nations joined in
suppressing them; and the pirates who were outcasts from
among these civilized nations also at one time perpetrated
similar deeds, until they were sunk or hung. But none of these
old-time pirates committed murder on so vast a scale as in the
case of the Lusitania.

The day after the tragedy the newspapers reported in one
column that in Queenstown there lay by the score the bodies
of women and children, some of the dead women still clasping
the bodies of the little children they held in their arms when
death overwhelmed them. In another column they reported

the glee expressed by the Berlin journals at this "great victory of German naval policy." It was a victory over the defenseless and the unoffending, and its signs and trophies were the bodies of the murdered women and children.

Our treaties with Prussia in 1785, 1799, and 1828, still in force in this regard, provide that "if one of the contracting parties should be at war with any other power the free intercourse and commerce of the subjects or citizens of the party remaining neutral with the belligerent powers shall not be interrupted." Germany has treated this treaty as she has treated other "scraps of paper."

But the offense goes far deeper than this. The action of the German submarines in the cases cited can be justified only by a plea which would likewise justify the wholesale poisoning of wells in the path of a hostile army or the shipping of infected rags into the cities of a hostile country; a plea which would justify the torture of prisoners and the reduction of captured women to the slavery of concubinage. Those who advance such a plea will accept but one counter plea—strength, the strength and courage of the just man armed.

When those who guide the military policy of a State hold up to the soldiers of their army, the "Huns," and the terror once caused by the Huns, for their imitation, they thereby render themselves responsible for any Hunnish deed which may follow. The destruction of cities like Louvain and Dinant, the scientific vivisection of Belgium as a warning to other nations, the hideous wrongdoing to civilians, men, women, and children in Belgium and Northern France, in order thereby to terrorize the civilian population—all these deeds, and those like them, done on the land, have now been paralleled by what has happened on the sea.

In the teeth of those things, we earn as a nation measureless scorn and contempt if we follow the lead of those who exalt peace above righteousness, if we heed the voices of those feeble folk who bleat to high Heaven that there is peace when there is no peace. For many months our Government has preserved between right and wrong a "neutrality" which would have excited the emulous admiration of Pontius Pilate—the arch-typical neutral of all time. We have urged as a justification for failing to do our duty in Mexico that to do so would benefit "American dollars." Are we now to change faces and advance the supreme interest of "American dollars" as a justification for continuance in the refusal to do the duty imposed on us in connection with the world war?

Unless we act with immediate decision and vigor we shall have failed in the duty demanded by humanity at large and demanded even more clearly by the self-respect of the American Republic.

The New York Times, May 12, 1915

William Jennings Bryan
to Gottlieb von Jagow

A dynamic amalgam of progressive politics and Protestant fundamentalism, Secretary of State William Jennings Bryan was a three-time Democratic candidate for president who had received his cabinet position largely because he had helped Wilson secure their party's nomination in 1912. A pacifist who had seen much of the world before it had gone to war, he did all he could to maintain the neutrality Wilson advocated. Bryan learned that the *Lusitania* had been transporting 4,200 cases of rifle cartridges and 1,250 cases of inert shrapnel shells, as well as potentially explosive aluminum powder. He believed the United States should rebuke not only Germany but also Great Britain for interfering in international shipping, especially for "using our citizens to protect her ammunition." In consultation with the President and Robert Lansing, his deputy at the State Department, Bryan cabled Ambassador James Watson Gerard in Berlin with a message for the German foreign minister.

The Secretary of State to the Ambassador in Germany (Gerard)
Washington, May 13, 1915.

1664. Please call on the Minister of Foreign Affairs and, after reading to him this communication, leave him with a copy:

In view of recent acts of the German authorities in violation of American rights on the high seas which culminated in the torpedoing and sinking of the British steamship *Lusitania* on May 7, 1915, by which over 100 American citizens lost their lives, it is clearly wise and desirable that the Government of the United States and the Imperial German Government should come to a clear and full understanding as to the grave situation which has resulted.

The sinking of the British passenger steamer *Falaba* by a German submarine on March 28, through which Leon C. Thrasher, an American citizen was drowned; the attack on April 28 on the American vessel *Cushing* by a German aeroplane; the torpedoing on May 1 of the American vessel *Gulflight* by a German submarine, as a result of which two or more American citizens met their death; and, finally, the torpedoing and sinking of the steamship *Lusitania*, constitute a series of events which the Government of the United States has observed with growing concern, distress, and amazement.

Recalling the humane and enlightened attitude hitherto assumed by the Imperial German Government in matters of international right, and particularly with regard to the freedom of the seas; having learned to recognize the German views and the German influence in the field of international obligation as always engaged upon the side of justice and humanity; and having understood the instructions of the Imperial German Government to its naval commanders to be upon the same plane of humane action prescribed by the naval codes of other nations, the Government of the United States was loath to believe—it can not now bring itself to believe—that these acts, so absolutely contrary to the rules, the practices, and the spirit of modern warfare, could have the countenance or sanction of that great Government. It feels it to be its duty, therefore, to address the Imperial German Government concerning them with the utmost frankness and in the earnest hope that it is not mistaken in expecting action on the part of the Imperial German Government which will correct the unfortunate impressions which have been created, and vindicate once more the position of that Government with regard to the sacred freedom of the seas.

The Government of the United States has been apprised that the Imperial German Government considered themselves to be obliged by the extraordinary circumstances of the present war and the measures adopted by their adversaries in seeking to cut Germany off from all commerce, to adopt methods of retaliation which go much beyond the ordinary methods of warfare at sea, in the proclamation of a war zone from which they have warned neutral ships to keep away. This Government has already taken occasion to inform the Imperial German Government that it can not admit the adoption of such measures or such a warning of danger to operate as in any degree an abbreviation of the rights of American shipmasters or of American citizens bound on lawful errands as passengers on merchant ships of belligerent nationality; and that it must hold the Imperial German Government to a strict accountability for any infringement of those rights, intentional or incidental. It does not understand the Imperial German Government to question those rights. It assumes, on the contrary, that the Imperial Government accept, as of course, the rule that the lives of non-combatants, whether they be of neutral citizenship or citizens of one of the nations at war, can not lawfully or rightfully be put in jeopardy by the capture or destruction of an unarmed merchantman, and recognize also, as all other nations do, the obligation to take the usual precaution of visit and search to ascertain whether a suspected merchantman is in fact of belligerent nationality or is in fact carrying contraband of war under a neutral flag.

The Government of the United States, therefore, desires to call the attention of the Imperial German Government with the utmost earnestness to the fact that the objection to their present method of attack against the trade of their enemies lies in the practical impossibility of employing submarines in the destruction of commerce without disregarding those rules of fairness, reason, justice, and humanity, which all modern opinion regards as imperative. It is practically impossible for the officers of a submarine to visit a merchantman at sea and examine her papers and cargo. It is practically impossible for them to make a prize of her; and, if they can not put a prize crew on board of her, they can not sink her without leaving her crew and all on board of her to the mercy of the sea in her small boats. These facts it is understood the Imperial German Government frankly admit. We are informed that, in the instances of which we have spoken, time enough for even that poor measure of safety was not given, and in at least two of the cases cited, not so much as a warning was received. Manifestly submarines can not be used against merchantmen, as the last few weeks have shown, without an inevitable violation of many sacred principles of justice and humanity.

American citizens act within their indisputable rights in taking their ships and in traveling wherever their legitimate business calls them upon the high seas, and exercise those rights in what should be the well-justified confidence that their lives will not be endangered by acts done in clear violation of universally acknowledged international obligations, and certainly in the confidence that their own Government will sustain them in the exercise of their rights.

There was recently published in the newspapers of the United States, I regret to inform the Imperial German Government, a formal warning, purporting to come from the Imperial German Embassy at Washington, addressed to the people of the United States, and stating, in effect, that any citizen of the United States who exercised his right of free travel upon the seas would do so at his peril if his journey should take him within the zone of waters within which the Imperial German Navy was using submarines against the commerce of Great Britain and France, notwithstanding the respectful but very earnest protest of his Government, the Government of the United States. I do not refer to this for the purpose of calling the attention of the Imperial German Government at this time to the surprising irregularity of a communication from the Imperial German Embassy at Washington addressed to the people of the United States through the newspapers, but only for the purpose of pointing out that no warning that an unlawful and inhumane act will be committed can possibly be accepted as an excuse or palliation for that act or as an abatement of the responsibility for its commission.

Long acquainted as this Government has been with the character of the Imperial German Government and with the high principles of equity by which they have in the past been actuated and guided, the Government of the United States can not believe that the commanders of the vessels which committed these acts of lawlessness did so except under a misapprehension of the orders issued by the Imperial German naval authorities. It takes it for granted that, at least within the practical possibilities of every such case, the commanders even of submarines were expected to do nothing that would involve the lives of non-combatants or the safety of neutral ships, even at the cost of failing of their object of capture or destruction. It confidently expects, therefore, that the Imperial German Government will disavow the acts of which the Government of the United States complains, that they will make reparation so far as reparation is possible for injuries which are without measure, and that they will take immediate steps to prevent the recurrence of anything so obviously subversive of the principles of warfare for which the Imperial German Government have in the past so wisely and so firmly contended.

The Government and the people of the United States look to the Imperial German Government for just, prompt, and enlightened action in this vital matter with the greater confidence because the United States and Germany are bound together not only by special ties of friendship but also by the explicit stipulations of the treaty of 1828 between the United States and the Kingdom of Prussia.

Expressions of regret and offers of reparation in case of the destruction of neutral ships sunk by mistake, while they may satisfy international obligations, if no loss of life results, can not justify or excuse a practice, the natural and necessary effect of which is to subject neutral nations and neutral persons to new and immeasurable risks.

The Imperial German Government will not expect the Government of the United States to omit any word or any act necessary to the performance of its sacred duty of maintaining the rights of the United States and its citizens and of safeguarding their free exercise and enjoyment.

Henry Morgenthau
to William Jennings Bryan

Known as the "Young Turks," members of the Committee of Union and Progress had ruled the Ottoman Empire since 1913. The CUP led the empire into the war as allies of Germany and Austria-Hungary on October 29, 1914, when the Ottoman navy attacked the Russian fleet in the Black Sea. A winter offensive into the Russian Caucasus from December 1914 to January 1915 resulted in the deaths of 60,000 Ottoman soldiers, many of them frozen to death in the mountains. On April 25, 1915, British, Australian, New Zealand, and French troops landed on the Gallipoli peninsula in an attempt to open the Dardanelles—the sea route to the Ottoman capital at Constantinople —to Allied warships. Born in Mannheim, Germany, Henry Morgenthau enjoyed a successful legal career in New York City, where he became active in the Jewish community and in Democratic politics. Believing that a Jewish envoy could remain vigilant toward his coreligionists and neutral between Muslims and Christians, President Wilson appointed him ambassador to the Ottoman Empire, which then included Palestine. In late May 1915 Morgenthau wrote to the secretary of state about the increasingly perilous situation of the Armenian population of the Ottoman Empire.

AMERICAN EMBASSY
CONSTANTINOPLE

STRICTLY CONFIDENTIAL
No. 310

May 25, 1915

The Honorable
The Secretary of State,
Washington.

Sir:

I have the honor to bring to your notice, certain aspects of policy adopted by the present Government towards the

Armenian community. The sharp oscillations in the treatment to which it has been subjected since the Turkish Revolution have taken a markedly unfavorable turn by reason of the War. The fact is that the present Ottoman Government no longer count on the Armenians as loyal to them. The hardships and oppression the Armenians have suffered in recent years, compared with the most favorable treatment received in Russia has caused them not unnaturally to contrast their lot with that of their co-religionists there. The first glamour of the constitutional era here, soon disappeared, while the recollection of the Adana Massacre in 1909 is still fresh in their minds. It is therefore not unlikely to suppose that the great majority of the Armenians in common with all non-Moslem communities, as well as many Turks ardently hope for a change in Government. Between the wish and the ability to realize this there lies, however, a wide gulf. Apart from the mountainous region in Eastern Armenia, and the Zeitoun district, North of Alexandretta, the Armenians no more than other dissatisfied communities, possess the means or the determination to give expression to their wishes. In the Zeitoun, where a few tried to escape from military service, a movement of savage repression has lately been carried out. Its details are in great part ignored here, but enough is known (See Despatch from Mr. Consul Jackson of April 21st) to make it certain that entire villages have been destroyed, with the invariable accompaniments of murder, rape and pillage. A more systematic policy than has been customary in the past, appears to have been pursued, in the wholesale deportation of the population. Only the other day, I received word (see Enclosure No. 1 letter from Dr. Dodd) of the arrival of 4,000 homeless refugees from this district at Konia, where they find themselves in the most pitiable state. Our Red Cross relief which was preferred, was refused by the Turkish authorities who announced that the refugees will be distributed in the neighboring country. The policy pursued in this case appears to be one of breaking up a compact Armenian community which had hitherto been able to preserve a certain liberty owing to living in mountainous fastness, and by wholesale deportations which must deprive them of their ordinary means of livelihood locating them among purely Turkish villages where those who survived their ill-treatment need no longer be feared by the Government.

In the Eastern regions of the Empire, although news is extremely scarce and unreliable, it would seem as if an Armenian insurrection to help the Russians had broken out in Van. Thus a former deputy here, one Pastermadjian who had assisted our proposed railway concessions some years ago, is now supposed to be fighting the Turks with a legion of Armenian volunteers. These insurgents are said to be in possession of a part of Van and to be conducting a guerrilla warfare in a country where regular military operations are extremely difficult. To what extent they are organized or what success they have gained it is impossible for me to say; their numbers have been variously estimated but none puts them at less than ten thousand and twenty-five thousand is probably closer to the truth.

At all events, these doings have not unnaturally cast suspicion on the peaceful Armenian communities elsewhere and notably in the capital. Partly because of the suspicion that these are in connivance with the insurgents, partly because of the policy to destroy all vestiges of organization other than its own, the Government as I telegraphed you lately, has proceeded to the arrest and exile of several hundred Armenians in this city. In the towns of the interior similar repressive measures have been undertaken, while the same carried out in Armenian villages by brutal subordinates have doubtless given rise to excesses. I do not believe that as yet there have been any massacre on a large scale, but the repression and coercive measures employed have undoubtedly been responsible for some loss of life. They have been brutal enough to alarm a nervous and excitable population who are prone moreover to give credence to startling reports. It is very difficult by reason of circumstances which the Department will appreciate to investigate the truth of the rumors of real or proposed massacres which constantly reach our ears. Correspondence with the interior is practically stopped or else written with a view to the censor's eye. Travel is permitted only exceptionally and taken place with great difficulty. The Armenians in common with everyone not in sympathy with the ruling party, are afraid of expressing themselves. Even if they do so, they have not the means of making heard their complaints. The Government invariably denies these or invests them with a totally different complexion. We hear at times through our Missionaries in the interior, but the difficulties and dangers of correspondence are so great as to render their news only fragmentary and occasional.

The situation is one of mutual fear. Fear on the part of the Armenians who recall the past massacres and fear on the part of the Government at alleged or dreaded conspiracies. Their distrust of all non-Moslems which may often be more apparent than real in order to create rifts in the population has recently been manifested in various ways. In the army they have for the most part been disarmed in common with the Greek soldiers and employed in manual employment. Here a most stringent regulation compelling all inhabitants to deliver their weapons to the authorities under penalty of death, has I understand, been applied differently in the case of Moslems who have been authorized to retain their arms. The recent expulsion measures against the non-Moslem inhabitants of the Bosphorus have caused grave hardships to an eminently peaceful community. Hardly a day passes without hearing of some new measures of vexation. Short of the actual taking of life, of which there appear as yet to have been but a few cases, the period we are traversing is one of very severe repression. Those out of sympathy with the Committee of Union and Progress, describe it as a reign of terror. It is a situation which at a time like this when restraining elements are few may easily lead to the most serious and the saddest consequences.

I have the honor to be, Sir,
Your obedient servant,

H. Morgenthau

Enclosure: as stated.

W.E.B. Du Bois: Lusitania

Debate over the sinking of the *Lusitania* raged for weeks, as the press stoked war fervor. The *New York Herald* called the incident "the blackest and greatest crime in the annals of history"; *The Nation* said, "the law of nations and the law of God have been alike trampled upon"; "the worst crime against civilization and humanity that the modern world has ever known," said the *Boston Post*. And *The Continent*, a Presbyterian periodical, called the incident "the worst crime of a responsible government since the crucifixion of Christ." In the pages of *The Crisis*, Du Bois weighed in on the controversy.

THE LAST horror of a horrible war is come! It puts a period to what we have already said: European civilization has failed. Its failure did not come with this war but with this war it has been made manifest. Whatever of brutality and inhumanity, of murder, lust and theft has happened since last summer is but counterpart of the same sort of happenings hidden in the wilderness and done against dark and helpless people by white harbingers of human culture. But when Negroes were enslaved, or the natives of Congo raped and mutilated, or the Indians of the Amazon robbed, or the natives of the South Seas murdered, or 2,732 American citizens lynched—when all this happened in the past and men knew it was happening and women fatted and plumed themselves on the ill-gotten gains, and London and Berlin and Paris and New York flamed with orgies of extravagance which the theft of worlds made possible, when all this happened, we civilized folk turned deaf ears. We explained that these "lesser breeds without the law" were given to exaggeration and had to be treated this way. They could not understand "civilization;" but as for the White World, there humanity and Christianity and loving kindness reigned. This was a lie and we know it was a lie. The Great War is the lie unveiled. This world is a miserable pretender toward things which it might accomplish if it would be humble and

gentle and poor and honest. It is a great privilege in the midst
of this frightful catastrophe to belong to a race that can stand
before Heaven with clean hands and say: we have not oppressed, we have been oppressed; we are not thieves, we are
victims; we are not murderers, we are lynched!

Robert Lansing to Gottlieb von Jagow

The President believed he could get immediate congressional approval to go to war; but having grown up in war-ravaged southern states himself, he was determined to try settling the German situation by every method that was possible and peaceable. "I am the trustee of this nation," he said, "and the cost of it all must be considered in the reckoning before we go forward." Wilson drafted his nation's response to the German naval aggression, reducing his secretary of state to little more than a messenger. In truth, Bryan disagreed with the tone of Wilson's note, believing it should also condemn Allied violations, particularly the British blockade. The German foreign minister, Gottlieb von Jagow, responded on May 28, 1915, expressing regret but insisting they were acting in self-defense against British attempts to starve the German population. When Wilson's reply came down even harder, Bryan tendered his resignation. Robert Lansing, the Counselor (second in command) for the State Department, was appointed Bryan's successor, and he affixed his name to Wilson's note of June 9, 1915. A month later, the Germans would send a reply deemed inadequate; and Wilson and Lansing drafted a third note, on July 21, warning that any further violation of American rights would be regarded as "deliberately unfriendly." A German U-boat would sink the British liner *Arabic* off the coast of Ireland on August 19, killing forty-four passengers, two of them Americans. Fearing American entry into the war, the German government issued a pledge on September 1, 1915, not to sink passenger ships without warning.

---

*The Secretary of State ad interim to
the Ambassador in Germany (Gerard)*

Washington, June 9, 1915.

1803.   You are instructed to deliver textually the following note to the Minister of Foreign Affairs:

In compliance with your excellency's request I did not fail to transmit to my Government immediately upon their receipt your note of May 28 in reply to my note of May 15 [13], and your supplementary note of June 1, setting forth the conclusions so far as reached by the Imperial German Government concerning the attacks on the American steamers *Cushing* and *Gulflight*. I am now instructed by my Government to communicate the following in reply:

The Government of the United States notes with gratification the full recognition by the Imperial German Government, in discussing the cases of the *Cushing* and the *Gulflight*, of the principle of the freedom of all parts of the open sea to neutral ships and the frank willingness of the Imperial German Government to acknowledge and meet its liability where the fact of attack upon neutral ships "which have not been guilty of any hostile act" by German aircraft or vessels of war is satisfactorily established; and the Government of the United States will in due course lay before the Imperial German Government, as it requests, full information concerning the attack on the steamer *Cushing*.

With regard to the sinking of the steamer *Falaba*, by which an American citizen lost his life, the Government of the United States is surprised to find the Imperial German Government contending that an effort on the part of a merchantman to escape capture and secure assistance alters the obligation of the officer seeking to make the capture in respect of the safety of the lives of those on board the merchantman, although the vessel had ceased her attempt to escape when torpedoed. These are not new circumstances. They have been in the minds of statesmen and of international jurists throughout the development of naval warfare, and the Government of the United States does not understand that they have ever been held to alter the principles of humanity upon which it has insisted. Nothing but actual forcible resistance or continued efforts to escape by flight when ordered to stop for the purpose of visit on the part of the merchantman has ever been held to forfeit the lives of her passengers or crew. The Government of the United States, however, does not understand that the Imperial German Government is seeking in this case to relieve itself of liability, but only intends to set forth the circumstances which led the commander of the submarine to allow himself to be hurried into the course which he took.

Your excellency's note, in discussing the loss of American lives resulting from the sinking of the steamship *Lusitania*, adverts at some length to certain information which the Imperial German Government has received with regard to the character and outfit of that vessel, and your excellency expresses the fear that this information may not have been brought to the attention of the Government of the United States. It is stated in the note that the *Lusitania* was undoubtedly equipped with masked guns, supplied with trained gunners and special ammunition, transporting troops from Canada, carrying a cargo not permitted under the laws of the United States to a vessel also carrying passengers, and serving, in virtual effect, as an auxiliary to the naval forces of Great Britain. Fortunately, these are matters concerning which the Government of the United States is in a position to give the Imperial German Government official information. Of the facts alleged in your excellency's note, if true, the Government of the United States would have been bound to take official cognizance in performing its recognized duty as a neutral power and in enforcing its national laws. It was its duty to see to it that the *Lusitania* was not armed for offensive action, that she was not serving as a transport, that she did not carry a cargo prohibited by the statutes of the United States, and that, if in fact she was a naval vessel of Great Britain, she should not receive clearance as a merchantman; and it performed that duty and enforced its statutes with scrupulous vigilance through its regularly constituted officials. It is able, therefore, to assure the Imperial German Government that it has been misinformed. If the Imperial German Government should deem itself to be in possession of convincing evidence that the officials of the Government of the United States did not perform these duties with thoroughness, the Government of the United States sincerely hopes that it will submit that evidence for consideration.

Whatever may be the contentions of the Imperial German Government regarding the carriage of contraband of war on board the *Lusitania* or regarding the explosion of that material by the torpedo, it need only be said that in the view of this Government these contentions are irrelevant to the question of the legality of the methods used by the German naval authorities in sinking the vessel.

But the sinking of passenger ships involves principles of humanity which throw into the background any special circumstances of detail that may be thought to affect the cases, principles which lift it, as the Imperial German Government will no doubt be quick to recognize and acknowledge, out of the class of ordinary subjects of diplomatic discussion or of international controversy. Whatever be the other facts regarding the *Lusitania*, the principal fact is that a great steamer, primarily and chiefly a conveyance for passengers, and carrying more than a thousand souls who had no part or lot in the conduct of the war, was torpedoed and sunk without so much as a challenge or a warning, and that men, women, and children were sent to their death in circumstances unparalleled in modern warfare. The fact that more than one hundred American citizens were among those who perished made it the duty of the Government of the United States to speak of these things and once more, with solemn emphasis, to call the attention of the Imperial German Government to the grave responsibility which the Government of the United States conceives that it has incurred in this tragic occurrence, and to the indisputable principle upon which that responsibility rests. The Government of the United States is contending for something much greater than mere rights of property or privileges of commerce. It is contending for nothing less high and sacred than the rights of humanity, which every Government honors itself in respecting and which no Government is justified in resigning on behalf of those under its care and authority. Only her actual resistance to capture or refusal to stop when ordered to do so for the purpose of visit could have afforded the commander of the submarine any justification for so much as putting the lives of those on board the ship in jeopardy. This principle the Government of the United States understands the explicit instructions issued on August 3, 1914, by the Imperial German Admiralty to its commanders at sea to have recognized and embodied, as do the naval codes of all other nations, and upon it every traveler and seaman had a right to depend. It is upon this principle of humanity as well as upon the law founded upon this principle that the United States must stand.

The Government of the United States is happy to observe that your excellency's note closes with the intimation that the Imperial German Government is willing, now as before, to accept the good offices of the United States in an attempt to come to an understanding with the Government of Great Britain by which the character and conditions of the war upon the sea may be changed. The Government of the United States would consider it a privilege thus to serve its friends and the world. It stands ready at any time to convey to either Government any intimation or suggestion the other may be willing to have it convey and cordially invites the Imperial German Government to make use of its services in this way at its convenience. The whole world is concerned in anything that may bring about even a partial accommodation of interests or in any way mitigate the terrors of the present distressing conflict.

In the meantime, whatever arrangement may happily be made between the parties to the war, and whatever may in the opinion of the Imperial German Government have been the provocation or the circumstantial justification for the past acts of its commanders at sea, the Government of the United States confidently looks to see the justice and humanity of the Government of Germany vindicated in all cases where Americans have been wronged or their rights as neutrals invaded.

The Government of the United States therefore very earnestly and very solemnly renews the representations of its note transmitted to the Imperial German Government on the 15th of May, and relies in these representations upon the principles of humanity, the universally recognized understandings of international law, and the ancient friendship of the German nation.

The Government of the United States can not admit that the proclamation of a war zone from which neutral ships have been warned to keep away may be made to operate as in any degree an abbreviation of the rights either of American shipmasters or of American citizens bound on lawful errands as passengers on merchant ships of belligerent nationality. It does not understand the Imperial German Government to question those rights. It understands it, also, to accept as established beyond question the principle that the lives of non-combatants can not lawfully or rightfully be put in jeopardy by the capture or destruction of an unresisting merchantman, and to recognize the obligation to take sufficient precaution to ascertain whether a suspected merchantman is in fact of belligerent nationality or is in fact carrying contraband of war under a neutral flag. The Government of the United States therefore deems it reasonable to expect that the Imperial German Government will adopt the measures necessary to put these principles into practice in respect of the safeguarding of American lives and American ships, and asks for assurances that this will be done.

LANSING

John Reed: Zalezchik the Terrible

With his drive for adventure, John Reed traveled with the artist
Boardman Robinson from Serbia through neutral Romania and then
across the Prut River into the Austrian province of Bukovina, which
the Russians had occupied in August 1914. In late January 1915, Austro-Hungarian troops launched a counteroffensive that further devastated the region. Traversing Bukovina in early June, Reed observed
that many villages "were deserted, smashed, and black with fire—
especially those where Jews had lived"—the result of the brutal
anti-Semitism of the Tsarist army. Crossing the Dniester River into
Austrian Galicia, Reed arrived in Zalezchik (now Zalishchyky in
Ukraine). Occupied by the Russians since the preceding August, the
city had endured three battles that spring.

———————————

IT WAS ON the other side of Zastevna, where we stopped beside
some ruined houses for a drink, that we saw the Austrian prisoners. They came limping along the road in the hot sun, about
thirty of them, escorted by two Don Cossacks on horseback;
gray uniforms white with dust, bristly faces drawn with fatigue.
One man had the upper left-hand part of his face bound up, and
the blood had soaked through; another's hand was bandaged,
and some jerked along on improvised crutches. At a sign from
the Cossacks, who dismounted, they reeled and stumbled to
the side of the road, and sullenly threw themselves down in the
shade. Two dark-faced men snarled at each other like beasts.
The man with the wounded head groaned. He with the
bandaged hand began tremblingly to unwrap the gauze. The Cossacks good-naturedly waved us permission to talk with them,
and we went over with handfuls of cigarettes. They snatched at
them with the avidity of smokers long deprived of tobacco—all
except one haughty-faced youth, who produced a handsome
case crammed with gold-tipped cigarettes, declined ours frig-
idly, and took one of his own, without offering any to the
others.

"He is a Count," explained a simple, peasant-faced boy with awe.

The man with the wounded hand had got his bandage off at last, and was staring at his bloody palm with a sort of fascination.

"I think this had better be dressed again," said he at last, glancing diffidently at a stout, sulky-looking person who wore a Red Cross arm-band. The latter looked across with lazy contempt and shrugged his shoulders.

"We've got some bandages," I began, producing one. But one of the Cossacks came over, scowling and shaking his head at me. He kicked the Red Cross man with a look of disgust, and pointed to the other. Muttering something, the stout man fumbled angrily in his case, jerked out a bandage, and slouched across.

There were thirty of them, and among that thirty five races were represented: Tcheks, Croats, Magyars, Poles, and Austrians. One Croat, two Magyars, three Tcheks could speak absolutely not a word of any language but their own, and, of course, none of the Austrians knew a single word of Bohemian, Croatian, Hungarian, or Polish. Among the Austrians were Tyroleans, Viennese, and a half-Italian from Pola. The Croats hated the Magyars, and the Magyars hated the Austrians—and as for the Tcheks, no one would speak to them. Besides, they were all divided up into sharply defined social grades, each of which snubbed its inferiors. . . . As a sample of Franz Joseph's army the group was most illuminating.

They had been taken in a night attack along the Pruth, and marched more than twenty miles in two days. But they were all enthusiastic in praise of their Cossack guards.

"They are very considerate and kind," said one man. "When we stop for the night the Cossacks personally go around to each man, and see that he is comfortable. And they let us rest often. . . ."

"The Cossacks are fine soldiers," another broke in; "I have fought with them, and they are very brave. I wish we had cavalry like them!"

A young volunteer of the Polish legion asked eagerly if Rumania was coming in. We replied that it seemed like it, and suddenly he burst out, quivering:

"My God! My God! What can we do? How long can this awful war last? All we want is peace and quiet and rest! We are beaten—we are honorably beaten. England, France, Russia, Italy, the whole world is against us. We can lay down our arms with honor now! Why should this useless butchery go on?"

And the rest sat there, gloomily listening to him, without a word. . . .

Toward evening we were rattling down a steep gully between high cliffs. A stream plunged down beside the road, turning a hundred water-wheels whose mills lay shattered by artillery fire; shacks in partial ruin shouldered each other along the gully, and on top of the eastern cliff we could see disembowelled trenches and an inferno of twisted, snarled barbed wire, where the Russians had bombarded and stormed the Austrian defenses a month before. Hundreds of men were at work up there clearing away the wreckage and building new works. We rounded a corner suddenly and came out upon the bank of the Dniester, just below where the tall railroad bridge plunged into the water its tangle of dynamited girders and cables. Here the river made a huge bend, beneath earthen cliffs a hundred feet high, and across a pontoon bridge choked with artillery the once lovely town of Zalezchik lay bowered in trees. As we crossed, naked Cossacks were swimming their horses in the current, shouting and splashing, their powerful white bodies drenched with golden light. . . .

Zalezchik had been captured, burned, and looted three times by two armies, shelled for fifteen days, and the major portion of its population wiped out by both sides because it had given aid and comfort to the enemy. Night was falling when we drove into the market-place, surrounded with the shocking débris of tall houses. A sort of feeble market was going on there under miserable tilted shacks, where sad-eyed peasant women spread their scanty vegetables and loaves of bread, the centre of a mob of soldiers. A few Jews slunk about the corners. Ivan demanded a hotel, but the man smiled and pointed to a tall crumbling brick wall with "Grand Hotel" painted boldly across it—all that remained. Where could we get something to eat?

"Something to eat? There is not enough food in this town to feed my wife and children."

An atmosphere of terror hung over the place—we could feel it in the air. It was in the crouching figures of the Jews, stealing furtively along the tottering walls; in the peasants as they got out of the way of our carriage, doffing their hats; in the faces of cringing children, as soldiers went by. It got dark, and we sat in the carriage, debating what to do.

An "Apteka"—apothecary shop—stood on the corner, comparatively undamaged, with a light inside. I found the druggist alone, a Jew who spoke German.

"What are you?" he asked suspiciously, peering at me.

"An American."

"There is no hotel here," he burst out suddenly. "There is no place to stay and nothing to eat. A month ago the Russians came in here—they slaughtered the Jews, and drove the women and children out there." He pointed west. "There is no place here——"

"Then," I said, "the military commandant must take care of us. Where can I find him?"

"I will send my assistant with you," he answered. His face stiffened with fear. "You will not say to them what I have told, noble *Herr*? You will not——"

The entry of two Russian soldiers interrupted him, and he rose, addressing me insolently for their benefit:

"I can't drive you out of the shop. It's a public shop. But remember, I assume no responsibility for you. I didn't ask you to come here. I don't know you." For, after all, we might be undesirable people.

We bestowed upon Ivan a two-rouble piece, which, after biting, he put away in his pocket with hoarse sounds betokening gratitude. And we left him sitting on his vehicle in the middle of the square, gazing at nothing. When we came out of the Apteka he was still there, hunched over in the same position, and an hour later, when we issued from the colonel's headquarters, he had not moved, though it was quite dark. What was passing in that swampy mind? Perhaps he was trying to remember the name of Novo Sielitza, his home—perhaps he was merely wondering how to get there. . . .

We sat long over dinner with the genial colonel and his staff, chattering politics and gossip in intensely fragmentary German.

Among other officers were a young Finnish lieutenant and an old Cossack major with a wrinkled Mongolian face like the pictures of Li Hung Chang, who were very much excited over the sinking of the *Lusitania*, and sure that America would go to war.

"What can we do for you?" asked the colonel.

We said that we would like to visit this part of the front, if there were any fighting going on.

"That, I am afraid, is impossible from here," he regretted. "But if you will go to Tarnopol, the general commanding this army will surely give you permission. Then you must return here, and I shall be glad to accompany you myself. A train for Tarnopol leaves to-night at eleven."

Could he give us any idea what was happening along the front?

"With pleasure," said he eagerly, telling an orderly to bring the maps. He spread them out on the table. "Now here, near Zadagora, we have ten big guns placed in these positions, to stop the Austrian flanking column that is rolling up from the Pruth. Over here, near Kaluz, the Austrians imagine that we have nothing but cavalry, but in about three days we'll throw three regiments across this little stream at this point——"

I remarked that all those maps seemed to be German or Austrian maps.

"Oh, yes," he replied. "At the beginning of the war we had no maps at all of Bucovina or Galicia. We didn't even know the lay of the land until we had captured some. . . ."

From The War in Eastern Europe (1916)

Edith Wharton: In the North

With the same unerring eye she had once cast upon privileged members of society in New York ballrooms, Wharton shifted her gaze to the battlefields of the Western Front. In June 1915 she visited the ruins of Ypres, the Flemish city that had already braved two major battles. In the fall of 1914, French, British, and Indian troops had paid a heavy price in defending the town against a series of German offensives that threatened the French Channel ports at Dunkirk and Calais. In the spring of 1915, French, British, and Canadian troops stopped a German attack that began with the release of chlorine gas. Wharton's report from Flanders appeared in *Scribner's Magazine* in November 1915 and in *Fighting France, from Dunkerque to Belfort*, published the same month.

June 19th, 1915.

ON THE WAY from Doullens to Montreuil-sur-Mer, on a shining summer afternoon. A road between dusty hedges, choked, literally strangled, by a torrent of westward-streaming troops of all arms. Every few minutes there would come a break in the flow, and our motor would wriggle through, gain a few yards and be stopped again by a widening of the torrent that jammed us into the ditch and splashed a dazzle of dust into our eyes. The dust was stifling—but through it, what a sight!

Standing up in the car and looking back, we watched the river of war wind toward us. Cavalry, artillery, lancers, infantry, sappers and miners, trench-diggers, road-makers, stretcher-bearers, they swept on as smoothly as if in holiday order. Through the dust, the sun picked out the flash of lances and the gloss of chargers' flanks, flushed rows and rows of determined faces, found the least touch of gold on faded uniforms, silvered the melancholy grey of mitrailleuses and munition waggons. Close as the men were, they seemed allegorically splendid: as if, under the arch of the sunset, we had been watching the whole French army ride straight into glory . . .

Finally we left the last detachment behind, and had the

country to ourselves. The ravage of war has not touched the fields of Artois. The thatched farmhouses dozed in gardens crowded with roses and hollyhocks, and the hedges above the duck-ponds were weighed down with layers of elder-blossom. Wheat-fields skirted with woodland went billowing away under the breezy light that seemed to carry a breath of the Atlantic on its beams. The road ran up and down as if our motor were a ship on a deep-sea swell; and such a sense of space and light was in the distances, such a veil of beauty over the whole world, that the vision of that army on the move grew more and more fabulous and epic.

The sun had set and the sea-twilight was rolling in when we dipped down from the height of Montreuil to the valley below, where the towers of an ancient abbey-church rise above terraced orchards. The gates at the end of the drive were thrown open, and suddenly the motor was in a monastery court full of box and roses. Everything was sweet and secluded in this mediæval place; and from the shadow of cloisters and arched passages bevies of nuns fluttered out, nuns all black or all white, gliding, peering and standing at gaze. It was as if we had plunged back into a century to which motors were unknown and our car had been some monster cast up from a Barbary shipwreck; and the startled attitudes of these holy women did the more credit to their sense of the picturesque since the Abbey of Neuville is now a great Belgian hospital, and such monsters frequently intrude on its seclusion . . .

Sunset, and summer dusk, and the moon. Under the monastery windows a sharply drawn walled garden with stone pavilions at the angles, and below it tiers of orchard-terraces fading into a great moon-confused plain that might be either fields or sea . . .

June 20th.

Today our way ran north-east, through a landscape so English that there was no incongruity in the sprinkling of khaki along the road. Even the villages are English: the same plum-red brick of tidy self-respecting houses behind gardens bursting with flowers, everything neat, demure and freshly painted, the landscape hedgerowed and willowed and fed with innumerable water-courses, the people's faces square and pink and honest, and the signs over the shops in a language astride between English and German. Only the architecture of the towns is French, of a Frenchness northern and reserved and robust, but unmistakeably in the great continental tradition.

War still seemed so far off that one had time for these digressions as the motor flew over the undulating miles. But presently we came on an aviation camp spreading its sheds over a big green plateau. Here the khaki throng was thicker and the familiar military stir enlivened the landscape. A few miles farther, and we were seemingly in a big English town oddly grouped about a nucleus of French churches. This was St. Omer, grey, spacious, coldly clean in its Sunday emptiness. At the street crossings English sentries stood mechanically directing the absent traffic with gestures familiar to Piccadilly; and the signs of the British Red Cross and St. John's Ambulance hung on club-like façades that might almost have claimed a home in Pall Mall.

The Englishness of things was increased, as we passed out through the suburbs, by the look of the crowd on the canal bridges and along the dusty roads. Every nation has its own way of loitering, and there is nothing so unlike the French way as the English. Even if all these tall youths had not been in khaki, and the girls with them so wholesomely pink and countrified, one would instantly have recognized the passive northern way of letting a holiday soak in instead of squeezing out its juices with feverish fingers.

When we turned westward from St. Omer, across the same pastures and water-courses, we were faced by two isolated hills standing up out of the plain; and on the top of one rose the walls and towers of a compact mediæval town. As we took the windings that led up to it a sense of Italy began to penetrate the persistent impression of being somewhere near the English Channel. It might have been a queer dream-blend of Winchelsea and San Gimignano that we were climbing to; but when we entered the gates of Cassel we were in a town so intensely itself that all analogies dropped out of mind.

It was not surprising to learn from the guide-book that Cassel has the most extensive view of any town in Europe: one felt at once that it differed in all sorts of marked and self-assertive ways from every other town, and would be almost sure to have the best things going in every line. And the line of an illimitable horizon is exactly the best to set off its own obvious limits.

We found our hotel in the most charming of little market squares, with a Renaissance town-hall on one side, and on the other a miniature Spanish palace with a front of rosy brick and twisted grey carvings. The square was crowded with English army motors and beautiful prancing chargers; and the restaurant of the inn (which has the luck to face the pink and grey palace) swarmed with khaki tea-drinkers turning indifferent shoulders to the widest view in Europe. It is one of the most detestable things about war that everything connected with it, except the death and ruin that result, is such a heightening of life, so visually stimulating and absorbing. "It was gay and terrible," is the phrase forever recurring in "War and Peace"; and the gaiety of war was everywhere in Cassel, transforming the lifeless little town into a romantic stage-setting full of the flash of arms and the virile animation of young faces.

From the park on top of the hill we looked down on another picture. All about us was the great plain, its rim merged in northern sea-mist; and through the mist, in the glitter of the afternoon sun, far-off towns and shadowy towers lay steeped, as it seemed, in summer peace. For a moment, while we looked, the vision of war shrivelled up like a painted veil; then we caught the names pronounced by a group of young English soldiers leaning over the parapet at our side. "That's Dunkerque" —one of them pointed it out with his pipe—"and there's Poperinghe, just under us; that's Furnes beyond, and Ypres and Dixmude, and Nieuport . . ." And at the mention of those names the scene grew dark again, and we felt the passing of the Angel to whom was given the Key of the Bottomless Pit.

That night we went up once more to the rock of Cassel. The moon was full, and as civilians are not allowed out alone after dark a staff-officer had offered to show us the view from the roof of the disused Casino on top of the rock. It was the queerest of sensations to push open a glazed door and find ourselves in a spectral painted room with soldiers dozing in the moonlight on polished floors, their kits stacked on the gaming tables. We passed through a white vestibule among more soldiers lounging in the half-light, and up a long staircase to the roof where a watcher challenged us and then let us approach the parapet. Below lay the unlit mass of the town. To the northwest a single sharp hill, the "Mont des Cats," stood against the sky; the rest of the horizon was unbroken, and floating in misty moonlight. The outline of the ruined towns had vanished and peace seemed to have won back the world. But far off to the northwest a red flash started suddenly out of the mist; then another and another flickered up at different points of the long curve. "Luminous bombs thrown up along the lines," our guide explained; and just then, far off, a white light opened like a tropical flower, spread to full bloom and drew itself back into the night. "A flare," we were told; and another white flower bloomed out farther down. Below us, the grey roofs of Cassel slept their provincial sleep, the moonlight picking out every leaf in the hushed gardens; while, far off, those infernal flowers opened and shut along the curve of death. It was one of the moments when the beauty of war seems more intolerable than all its horror.

June 21st.

On the road from Cassel to Poperinghe. Heat, dust, crowds, confusion, all the sordid shabby rear-view of war. The road running across the plain between white-powdered hedges was ploughed up by numberless motor vans, supply-waggons and Red Cross ambulances. Labouring through between them came detachments of British artillery, clattering gun-carriages, stalwart young figures on glossy horses, long Phidian lines of youths so ingenuously fair that one wondered how they could have looked on the Medusa face of war and lived. Men and beasts, in spite of the stifling dust, were as fresh and sleek as if they had come from a bath; and everywhere along the wayside were improvised camps, with tents made of waggon-covers, where the ceaseless indomitable work of cleaning was being carried out in all its searching details. Shirts were drying on elder-bushes, kettles boiling over gipsy fires, men shaving, blacking their boots, cleaning their guns, rubbing down their horses, greasing their saddles, polishing their stirrups and bits: on all sides a general cheery struggle against the prevailing dust, discomfort and disorder. Here and there a young soldier leaned against a garden paling to talk to a girl among the hollyhocks, or an older soldier initiated a group of children into some mystery of military housekeeping; and everywhere were the same signs of inarticulate understanding with the owners of the fields and gardens.

From the thronged high-road we passed into the emptiness of Poperinghe, and out again on the way to Ypres. Beyond the flats and wind-mills to our left were the invisible German lines, and the staff-officer who was with us leaned forward to caution our chauffeur: "*No* tooting between here and Ypres." There was still a good deal of movement on the road, though it was less crowded with troops than near Poperinghe; but as we passed through the last village and approached the long low line of houses ahead, the silence and emptiness widened about us. That long low line was Ypres; every monument that marked it, that gave it an individual outline, is gone. It is a town without a profile.

The motor slipped through a suburb of low brick houses and was stopped under cover of some tallish buildings. Another military motor waited there, the chauffeur relic-hunting in the gutted houses.

We got out and walked toward the centre of the Cloth Market. We had seen evacuated towns—Verdun, Badonviller, Raon-l'Étape—but we had seen no emptiness like this. Not a human being was in the streets. Endless lines of empty houses looked down on us from vacant windows. Our footsteps echoed like the tramp of a crowd, our lowered voices seemed to shout. In one street we came on three English soldiers who were carrying a piano out of a house and lifting it onto a hand-cart. They stopped in amazement to stare at us, and we stared back. It seemed an age since we had seen a living being! One of the soldiers scrambled into the cart and tapped out a tune on the cracked key-board, and we all laughed with relief at the foolish noise . . . Then we passed on and were alone again.

We had seen other ruined towns, but none like this. The towns of Lorraine were blown up, burnt down, deliberately erased from the earth. At worst they are like stone-yards, at best like Pompeii. But Ypres has been bombarded to death, and the outer walls of its houses are still standing, so that it presents the distant semblance of a living city, while near by it is seen to be a corpse disembowelled and embalmed. Every window-pane is smashed, nearly every building unroofed, and some house-fronts are cut clean off, with the different stories exposed, as if for the stage-setting of a farce. And in these exposed interiors the poor little household gods shiver and blink like owls surprised in a hollow tree. A hundred signs of intimate and humble tastes, of humdrum pursuits, of family association, cling desperately to the unmasked walls. Whiskered photographs fade on morning glory wall-papers, little plaster saints pine under glass bells, antimacassars droop from plush sofas, yellowing diplomas display their seals on office walls. It was all so still and familiar that it seemed as if the people for whom these things had a meaning might at any moment come back and take up their daily business. And then—crash! the guns began, slamming out volley after volley all along the English lines, and the poor frail web of things that had made up the lives of a vanished city-full hung dangling before us in that blast of death.

We had just reached the square before the Cathedral when the cannonade began, and its roar seemed to build a roof of iron over the glorious ruins of Ypres. The singular distinction of Ypres is that it is destroyed but not abased. The walls of the Cathedral, the long bulk of the Cloth Market, still lift themselves above the market-place with a majesty that seems to reject compassion. The sight of those scarred façades, so proud in death, recalled a phrase used soon after the fall of Liège by Belgium's Foreign Minister—"*La Belgique ne regrette rien*," —which ought some day to serve as the motto of the renovated city.

We were turning to go when we heard a whirr overhead, followed by a stinging volley of mitrailleuse. High up in the blue, over the centre of the dead city, flew a German aeroplane; and all about it hundreds of white shrapnel tufts burst out in the summer sky like the miraculous snow-fall of Italian legend. Up and up they flew, on the trail of the Taube, and on flew the Taube, faster still, till quarry and pack were lost in mist, and the barking of the mitrailleuse died out. So we left Ypres to the death-silence in which we had found her.

The afternoon carried us back to Poperinghe, where I was bound on a quest for lace-cushions of the special kind required by our Flemish refugees. The model is unobtainable in France, and I had been told—with few and vague indications—that I might find the cushions in a certain convent of the city. But in which?

Poperinghe, though little injured, is almost empty. In its tidy desolation it looks like a town on which a wicked enchanter has laid a spell. We roamed from quarter to quarter, hunting for some one to show us the way to the convent I was looking for, till at last a passer-by led us to a door which seemed the right one. At our knock the bars were drawn and a cloistered face looked out. No, there were no cushions there; and the nun had never heard of the order we named. But there were the Penitents, the Benedictines—we might try. Our guide agreed to show us the way and we went on. From one or two windows, wondering heads looked out and vanished; but the streets were lifeless. At last we came to a convent where there were no nuns left, but where, the caretaker told us, there were cushions—a great many. He led us through pale blue passages, up cold stairs, through rooms that smelt of linen and lavender. We passed a chapel with plaster saints in white niches above paper flowers. Everything was cold and bare and blank: like a mind from which memory has gone. We came to a big classroom with lines of empty benches facing a blue-mantled Virgin; and here, on the floor, lay rows and rows of lace-cushions. On each a bit of lace had been begun—and there they had been dropped when nuns and pupils fled. They had not been left in disorder: the rows had been laid out evenly, a handkerchief thrown over each cushion. And that orderly arrest of life seemed sadder than a scene of desperate disarray. It symbolized the senseless paralysis of a whole nation's activities. Here were a houseful of women and children, yesterday engaged in a useful task and now aimlessly astray over the earth. And in hundreds of such houses, in dozens, in hundreds of open towns, the hand of time had been stopped, the heart of life had ceased to beat, all the currents of hope and happiness and industry been choked—not that some great military end might be gained, or the length of the war curtailed, but that, wherever the shadow of Germany falls, all things should wither at the root.

The same sight met us everywhere that sad afternoon. Over Furnes and Bergues, and all the little intermediate villages, the evil shadow lay. Germany had willed that these places should die, and wherever her bombs could not reach her malediction had carried. Only Biblical lamentation can convey a vision of this life-drained land. "Your country is desolate; your cities are burned with fire; your land, strangers devour it in your presence, and it is desolate, as overthrown by strangers."

Presently we came to Dunkerque, lying peacefully between its harbour and canals. The bombardment of the previous month had emptied it, and though no signs of damage were visible, the same spellbound air lay over everything. As we sat alone at tea in the big hall of the hotel on the Place Jean Bart, and looked out on the silent square and its lifeless shops and cafés, some one suggested that the hotel would be a convenient centre for the excursions we had planned, and we decided to return there the next evening. Then we motored back to Cassel.

June 22nd.

My first waking thought was: "How time flies! It must be the Fourteenth of July!" I knew it could not be the Fourth of that specially commemorative month, because I was just awake enough to be aware that I was not in America; and the only other event to justify such a terrific clatter was the French national anniversary. I sat up and listened at the patriotic popping of guns till a completer sense of reality stole over me, and I realized that I was in the inn of the Wild Man at Cassel, and that it was not the fourteenth of July but the twenty-second of June.

Then, what—? Why, a Taube, of course! And all the guns in the place were cracking at it! By the time this mental process was complete, I had scrambled up and got downstairs and across the court, had unbolted the heavy doors and rushed out into the square. It was about four in the morning, the heavenliest moment of a summer dawn, and in spite of the tumult Cassel still apparently slept. Only a few soldiers stood in the square, looking up at a drift of white cloud behind which—they averred—a Taube had just slipped out of sight. Cassel was evidently used to Taubes, and I had the sense of having overdone my excitement and not being exactly in tune; so after staring a moment at the white cloud I slunk back into the court, barred the door and mounted to my room. At a window on the stairs I paused to look out over the sloping roofs of the town, the gardens, the plain; and suddenly there was another crash and a drift of white smoke blew up from the fruit-trees just under the window. It was a last shot at the fugitive, from a gun hidden in one of those quiet provincial gardens between the houses; and its secret presence there was more startling than all the clatter of mitrailleuses from the rock.

Silence and sleep came down again on Cassel; but an hour or two later the hush was broken by a roar like the last trump. This time it was no question of mitrailleuses. The Wild Man rocked on its base, and every pane in my windows beat a tattoo. What was that incredible, unimagined sound? Why it could be nothing, of course, but the voice of the big siege-gun of Dixmude! Five times, while I was dressing, the thunder shook my windows, and the air was filled with a noise that may be compared—if the human imagination can stand the strain— to the simultaneous closing of all the shop-shutters in the world. The odd part was that—apart from the first start of surprise—as far as the Wild Man and its inhabitants were concerned no visible effects resulted, and dressing, packing and coffee-drinking went on comfortably in the strange parentheses between the roars.

We set off early for a neighbouring Head-Quarters, and it was not till we turned out of the gates of Cassel that we came on signs of the bombardment: the smashing of a gas-house and the converting of a cabbage-field into a crater which, for some time to come, will spare seismological photographers the trouble of climbing Vesuvius. There was consolation in the discrepancy between the noise and the damage.

At Head-Quarters we learned more of the morning's incidents. Dunkerque, it appeared, had first been visited by the Taube which afterward came to take the range of Cassel; and the big gun had then turned all its fury on the French sea-port. The bombardment was still going on; and we were asked, and in fact bidden, to give up our plan of going to Dunkerque for the night.

After luncheon we turned north, toward the dunes. The villages we traversed were all evacuated, some quite lifeless, others occupied by troops. Presently we came to a group of military motors drawn up by the roadside, and a field black with wheeling troops. "Admiral Ro'narch!" our companion from Head-Quarters exclaimed; and we understood that we had had the good luck to come on the hero of Dixmude in the act of reviewing the marine fusiliers and territorials whose magnificent defense gave that much-besieged town another lease of glory.

We stopped the motor and climbed to a ridge above the field. A high wind was blowing, bringing with it the booming of the guns along the front. A sun half-veiled in sand-dust shone on pale meadows, sandy flats, grey wind-mills. The scene was deserted, except for the handful of troops deploying before the officers on the edge of the field. Admiral Ro'narch, white-gloved and in full-dress uniform, stood a little in advance, a young naval officer at his side. He had just been distributing decorations to his fusiliers and territorials, and they were marching past him, flags flying and bugles playing. Every one of those men had a record of heroism, and every face in those ranks had looked on horrors unnameable. They had lost Dixmude—for a while—but they had gained great glory, and the inspiration of their epic resistance had come from the quiet officer who stood there, straight and grave, in his white gloves and gala uniform.

One must have been in the North to know something of the tie that exists, in this region of bitter and continuous fighting, between officers and soldiers. The feeling of the chiefs is almost one of veneration for their men; that of the soldiers, a kind of half-humorous tenderness for the officers who have faced such odds with them. This mutual regard reveals itself in a hundred undefinable ways; but its fullest expression is in the tone with which the commanding officers speak the two words oftenest on their lips: "My men."

The little review over, we went on to Admiral Ro'narch's quarters in the dunes, and thence, after a brief visit, to another brigade Head-Quarters. We were in a region of sandy hillocks feathered by tamarisk, and interspersed with poplar groves slanting like wheat in the wind. Between these meagre thickets the roofs of gimcrack bungalows shewed above the dunes; and before one of these we stopped, and were led into a pitch-pine sitting-room full of maps and aeroplane photographs. One of the officers of the brigade telephoned to ask if the way was clear to Nieuport; and the answer was that we might go on.

Our road ran through the "Bois Triangulaire," a bit of woodland exposed to constant shelling. Half the poor spindling trees were down, and patches of blackened undergrowth and ragged hollows marked the path of the shells. If the trees of a cannonaded wood are of strong inland growth their fallen trunks have the majesty of a ruined temple; but there was something humanly pitiful in the frail trunks of the Bois Triangulaire, lying there like slaughtered immature troops.

A few miles more brought us to Nieuport, most lamentable of the victim towns. It is not empty as Ypres is empty: troops are quartered in the cellars, and at the approach of our motor knots of cheerful zouaves came swarming out of the ground like ants. But Ypres is majestic in death, poor Nieuport gruesomely comic. About its noble nucleus of mediæval architecture a modern town had grown up; and nothing stranger can be pictured than the contrast between the streets of flimsy houses, twisted like curl-papers, and the spectral ruins of the Gothic Cathedral and the Cloth Market. It is like passing from a smashed toy to the august survival of a cataclysm.

Modern Nieuport seems to have died in a colic. No less homely image expresses the contractions and contortions of the disembowelled houses reaching out the appeal of their desperate chimney-pots and agonized girders. There is one view along the exterior of the town like nothing else on the war-front. On the left, a line of convulsed and palsied houses leads like a string of cowering crutch-propped beggars to the mighty ruin of the Templars' Tower; on the right the flats reach away to the almost imperceptible humps of masonry that were St. George, Ramscappelle, Pervyse. And over it all the incessant crash of the guns stretches a sounding-board of steel.

In front of the cathedral a German shell has dug a crater thirty feet across, overhung by splintered tree-trunks, burnt shrubs, vague mounds of rubbish; and a few steps beyond lies the peacefullest spot in Nieuport, the grave-yard where the zouaves have buried their comrades. The dead are laid in rows under the flank of the cathedral, and on their carefully set grave-stones have been placed groups of pious images collected from the ruined houses. Some of the most privileged are guarded by colonies of plaster saints and Virgins so numerous that they cover the whole slab; and over the handsomest Virgins and the most gaily coloured saints the soldiers have placed the glass bells that probably once protected the clocks and wedding-wreaths in the same houses.

From sad Nieuport we motored on to a little seaside colony where gaiety prevails. Here the big hotels and the gimcrack villas along the beach are filled with troops just back from the trenches: it is one of the "rest cures" of the front. When we drove up, the regiment "au repos" was assembled in the wide sandy space between the principal hotels, and in the centre of the jolly crowd the band was playing. The Colonel and his officers stood listening to the music, and presently the soldiers broke into the wild "chanson des zouaves" of the ——th zouaves. It was the strangest of sights to watch that throng of dusky merry faces, under their red fezes, against the background of sunless northern sea. When the music was over some one with a kodak suggested "a group": we struck a collective attitude on one of the hotel terraces, and just as the camera was being aimed at us the Colonel turned and drew into the foreground a little grinning pock-marked soldier. "He's just been decorated—he's got to be in the group." A general exclamation of assent from the other officers, and a protest from the hero: "Me? Why, my ugly mug will smash the plate!" But it didn't——

Reluctantly we turned from this interval in the day's melancholy round, and took the road to La Panne. Dust, dunes, deserted villages: my memory keeps no more definite vision of the run. But at sunset we came on a big seaside colony, stretching out above the longest beach I ever saw: along the sea-front, an esplanade bordered by the usual foolish villas, and behind it a single street filled with hotels and shops. All the life of the desert region we had traversed seemed to have taken refuge at La Panne. The long street was swarming with throngs of dark-uniformed Belgian soldiers, every shop seemed to be doing a thriving trade, and the hotels looked as full as bee-hives.

June 23rd. LA PANNE.

The particular hive that has taken us in is at the extreme end of the esplanade, where asphalt and iron railings lapse unaffectedly into sand and sea-grass. When I looked out of my window early this morning I saw only the endless stretch of brown sand against the grey roll of the Northern Ocean, and, on a crest of the dunes, the figure of a solitary sentinel. But presently there was a sound of martial music, and long lines of troops came marching along the esplanade and down to the beach. The sands stretched away to east and west, a great "field of Mars" on which an army could have manœuvred; and presently the morning exercises of cavalry and infantry began. Against the brown beach the regiments in their dark uniforms were as black as silhouettes; and when the cavalry galloped by in single file they looked like the black frieze of warriors encircling the dun-coloured flanks of an Etruscan vase. For hours these long-drawn-out movements of troops went on, to the wail of bugles, and under the eye of the lonely sentinel on the sand-crest; then the soldiers poured back into the town, and La Panne was once more a busy common-place "bain-de-mer." The common-placeness, however, was only on the surface; for as one walked along the esplanade one discovered that the town had become a citadel, and that all the little doll's-house villas with their silly gables and sillier names—"Seaweed," "the Sea-gull," "Mon Repos," and the rest—were really a continuous line of barracks swarming with cheerful Belgian soldiers. In the main street there were hundreds of soldiers, pottering along in couples, chatting in groups, romping and wrestling like a crowd of school-boys, or bargaining in the shops for shell-work souvenirs and sets of post-cards; and between the dark-green and crimson uniforms was a frequent sprinkling of khaki, with the occasional pale blue of a French officer's tunic.

Before luncheon we motored over to Dunkerque. The road runs along the canal, between grass-flats and prosperous villages. No signs of war were noticeable except on the road, which was crowded with motor vans, ambulances, and troops. Presently the walls and gates of Dunkerque rose before us, as calm and undisturbed as when we entered the town the day before yesterday. But within the gates we were in a desert. The bombardment had ceased the previous evening, but a death-hush lay on the town. Every house was shattered and the streets were empty. We drove to the Place Jean Bart, where

two days ago we sat at tea in the hall of the hotel. Now there
was not a whole pane of glass in the windows of the square, the
doors of the hotel were closed, and every now and then some
one came out carrying a basketful of plaster from fallen ceilings. The whole surface of the square was covered with a mo-
saic of glass from the hundreds of broken windows, and at the
foot of David's statue of Jean Bart, just where our motor had
stood while we had tea, the siege-gun of Dixmude had scooped
out a hollow as big as the crater at Nieuport.

Though not a house on the square was touched, the scene
was one of unmitigated desolation. It was the first time we had
seen the raw wounds of a bombardment, and the freshness of
the havoc seemed to accentuate its cruelty. We wandered down
the street behind the hotel to the graceful Gothic church of St.
Eloi, of which one aisle had been shattered; then, turning another corner, we came on a poor house that had had its whole
front torn away. The squalid sight of caved-in floors, smashed
wardrobes, dangling bedsteads, heaped-up blankets, topsy-turvy
chairs and stoves and wash-stands was somehow far more painful than the sight of the wounded church. St. Eloi was draped in
the indestructible dignity of martyrdom, but the poor little
house reminded one of some shy humdrum person suddenly
exposed in the glare of a great misfortune.

A few people stood in silent clusters looking up at the ruins, or
strayed aimlessly about the streets. Not a loud word was heard.
The air seemed heavy with the suspended breath of a great city's
activities: the mournful hush of Dunkerque was more oppressive
than the death-silence of Ypres. But when we came back to the
Place Jean Bart the unbreakable human spirit had begun to reassert itself. A handful of children were playing in the bottom of the
crater, collecting "specimens" of glass and splintered brick; and
about its rim the market-people, quietly and as a matter of course,
were setting up their stalls. In a few minutes the signs of German
havoc would be hidden behind stacks of crockery and household
utensils, and some of the pale women we had left in mournful
contemplation of the ruins would be bargaining as astutely as ever
for a saucepan or a butter-tub. Not once but a thousand times has
the attitude of the average French civilian on the front reminded
me of the gallant cry of Calanthea in *The Broken Heart*: "Let me

die smiling!" I should have liked to stop and spend all I had in the market of Dunkerque . . .

All the afternoon we wandered about La Panne. The exercises of the troops had begun again, and the deploying of those endless black lines along the beach was a sight of the strangest beauty. The sun was veiled, and heavy surges rolled in under a northerly gale. Toward evening the sea turned to cold tints of jade and pearl and tarnished silver. Far down the beach a mysterious fleet of fishing boats was drawn up on the sand, with black sails bellying in the wind; and the black riders galloping by might have landed from them, and been riding into the sunset, out of some wild northern legend. Presently a knot of buglers took up their stand on the edge of the sea, facing inward, their feet in the surf, and began to play; and their call was like the call of Roland's horn, when he blew it down the pass against the paynim. And on the sand-crest below my window the lonely sentinel still watched . . .

June 24th.

It is like coming down from the mountains to leave the front. I never had the feeling more strongly than when we passed out of Belgium this afternoon. I had it most strongly as we drove by a cluster of villas standing apart in a lonely region of grass and sand. In one of them, for nearly a year, two hearts at the highest pitch of human constancy have held up a light to the world. It is impossible to pass that house without a sense of awe. Because of the light that comes from it dead faiths have come to life, weak convictions have grown strong, fiery impulses have turned to long endurance, and long endurance has kept the fire of impulse. In the harbour of New York there is a pompous statue of a goddess with a torch, designated as "Liberty enlightening the World." It seems as though the title on her pedestal might well, for the time, be transferred to the lintel of that quiet villa in the dunes.

On leaving St. Omer we took a short cut southward across rolling country. It was a happy accident that caused us to leave the main road, for presently, over the crest of a hill, we saw surging toward us a mighty movement of British and Indian troops. It was a radiant afternoon and a great bath of silver sunlight lay on the wheat-fields, the clumps of woodland and the hilly blue horizon. In that slanting radiance the cavalry rode toward us, regiment after regiment of slim turbaned Indians, with delicate proud faces like the faces of Princes in Persian miniatures. Then came a long train of artillery; splendid horses, clattering gun-carriages, clear-faced English youths galloping by all aglow in the sunset. The stream of them seemed never ending. Now and then it was checked by a train of ambulances and supply-waggons, or caught and congested in the crooked streets of a village where the children and girls had come out with bunches of flowers, and bakers were selling hot loaves to the sutlers; then we extricated ourselves from the crowd, and climbing another hill came on another cavalcade surging toward us through the silver wheat-fields. For over an hour the procession poured by, so like and yet so unlike the French division we had met on the move as we went north a few days ago; so that we seemed to have passed to the front, and away from it, through a great gateway in the long wall of armies that are guarding the civilized world from the North Sea to the Vosges.

Henry James to Herbert Henry Asquith

The war forced millions to question their identities, particularly their nationalities. As he was born in 1843 at 21 Washington Place in New York City, raised there and in Newport, Rhode Island, Henry James's roots were indubitably American; but as a child he also lived abroad in Geneva, Paris, and London, where he was schooled by tutors and governesses before studying at Harvard. Although his prodigious writing career budded in America, he lighted in Paris in his thirties and then settled in London, where his literary life blossomed. James had been living in England for almost four decades when the war broke out. On August 10, 1914, six days after Britain joined the conflict, he wrote a friend: "Black and hideous to me is the tragedy that gathers, and I'm sick beyond cure to have lived on to see it." Not two weeks later he found himself swelling with pride over Britain's defense of Belgium, writing, "never has England in all her time, gone at anything with cleaner hands or a cleaner mind and slate." He visited wounded soldiers in London hospitals and raised money for Belgian refugees as well as for an American volunteer ambulance corps in France. James had known the Liberal statesman Herbert Henry Asquith since the 1890s, and after Asquith became prime minister in 1908, James would occasionally dine with him at 10 Downing Street. At age seventy-two, less than a year before his death, James asked and answered a major question for himself.

––––––––––

> 21 Carlyle Mansions, S.W.
> June 28*th* 1915

My dear Prime Minister and Illustrious Friend.

I am venturing to trouble you with the mention of a fact of my personal situation, but I shall do so as briefly and considerately as possible. I desire to offer myself for naturalization in this country, that is, to change my status from that of American citizen to that of British subject. I have assiduously and happily spent here all but forty years, the best years of my life, and I find my wish to testify at this crisis to the force of my attachment and devotion to England, and to the cause for which she is fighting, finally and completely irresistible. It brooks at least no inward denial whatever. I can only testify by laying at her feet my explicit, my material and spiritual allegiance, and throwing into the scale of her fortune my all but imponderable moral weight—"a poor thing but mine own." Hence this respectful appeal. It is necessary (as you may know) that for the purpose I speak of four honorable householders should bear witness to their kind acquaintance with me, to my apparent respectability, and to my speaking and writing English with an approach of propriety. What I presume to ask of you is whether you will do me the honour to be the pre-eminent one of that gently guaranteeing group? Edmund Gosse has benevolently consented to join it. The matter will entail on your part, as I understand, no expenditure of attention at all beyond your letting my solicitor wait upon you with a paper for your signature —the affair of a single moment; and the "going through" of my application will doubtless be proportionately expedited. You will thereby consecrate my choice and deeply touch and gratify yours all faithfully,

Henry James

Leslie Davis to Henry Morgenthau

Wartime is a difficult period for any diplomat, especially one with little experience who is suddenly exposed to unimaginable horrors. Leslie Davis, a lawyer from New York, joined the State Department in 1912 and found himself two years later as the U.S. consul to the twin cities of Harput and Mamuret-ul-Aziz (now Elâziğ) in eastern Anatolia. Mamuret-ul-Aziz was the capital of the *vilayet* (province) of the same name, one of six Ottoman provinces with a large Armenian population. From the spring of 1915 on, Davis regularly reported to Morgenthau on the atrocities being committed against the Armenians, describing his province as "the 'Slaughterhouse Vilayet' of Turkey." He provided safe haven in the consulate for as many as eighty Armenian survivors at a time and helped them escape into hiding. In May 1917 he left the Ottoman Empire after it broke diplomatic relations with the United States and returned to his home on Long Island. The following February he submitted a 132-page report to the State Department chronicling his service in Harput with greater specificity than his prior correspondence had allowed because of fears that the Turks were reading his mail. In his report he detailed a visit to nearby Lake Hazar in October 1915, when he had seen the bodies of 10,000 murdered Armenians around its shores.

No. 62

American Consulate
Mamouret-ul-Aziz (Harput)
June 30, 1915

Honorable Henry Morgenthau,
American Ambassador
Constantinople

Sir:

I have the honor to report to the Embassy about one of the severest measures ever taken by any government and one of the greatest tragedies in all history. If the Embassy had not already learned about it from other sources, my telegrams of

June 27th and 28th and my brief dispatch of June 29th will have brought the matter to the attention of the Embassy.

The attention of the Embassy has been called, in previous dispatches from this Consulate, to the very critical situation here. My dispatches of April 19th, May 5th and June 2nd referred to the general conditions and the fears of the people that a massacre was being planned. I have reported in frequent dispatches the hostile attitude of the local authorities during the last few months toward the American missionaries and the complete interruption of all work in the American schools. In my dispatch of June 12th I spoke of the actual danger in which the American missionaries in this part of Turkey are now placed and in my cipher dispatch of June 24th I gave some further details of what has been happening here.

As stated in some of the above mentioned dispatches, a revolutionary movement on the part of some of the Armenians was discovered and severe measures were taken to check it. These were undertaken in a wholesale matter, little distinction being made between people who were entirely innocent and those who were suspected of being participants in the movement. Practically every male Armenian of any consequence at all here has been arrested and put in prison. A great many of them were subjected to the most cruel tortures under which some of them died. Several hundred of the leading Armenians were sent away at night and it seems to be clearly established that most, if not all, of them were killed. Last week there were well founded rumors of a threatened massacre. I think there is very little doubt that one was planned.

Another method was found, however, to destroy the Armenian race. This is no less than the deportation of the entire Armenian population, not only from this Vilayet, but, I understand, from all six Vilayets comprising Armenia. There are said to be about sixty thousand Armenians in this Vilayet and about a million in the six Vilayets. All of these are to be sent into exile; an undertaking greater, probably, than anything of the kind in all history. For several days last week there were rumors of this but it seemed incredible.

On Saturday, June 28th, it was publicly announced that all Armenians and Syrians were to leave after five days. The town of

Mamouret-ul-Aziz and the city of Harput were divided into districts and notice was given at each house of the day when the occupants must leave. Two days are given for Mamouret-ul-Aziz, July 1st and third. Three days are given for Harput, July 4th, 5th and 6th. In these two towns, supposed to contain a population of about 40,000, there are probably not less than 15,000 or 18,000 Armenians, or at least three thousand families. There are as many more in the neighbouring villages and these are to leave a few days later.

The full meaning of such an order can scarcely be imagined by those who are not familiar with the peculiar conditions of this isolated region. A massacre, however horrible the word may sound, would be humane in comparison with it. In a massacre many escape but a wholesale deportation of this kind in this country means a lingering and perhaps even more dreadful death for nearly every one. I do not believe it possible for one in hundred to survive, perhaps not one in thousand.

The alleged destination of those sent from here is Urfa, but I know very well this does not mean the city of Urfa. It may mean the Mesopotamia plain to the southeast of that city, a region almost uninhabitable for man or beast. Whatever the destination may be, the journey from here in that direction at this season of the year is very difficult for one who has made careful preparations and travels by wagon. It is for the most part over an extremely hot plain in which there is very little water or vegetation. There are places where there is no water at all during an entire day's journey by wagon. A crowd of women and children on foot will, of course, require several days to traverse the same distance. They cannot go from here to Urfa in less than fifteen or twenty days. There are only two towns and two or three small villages on this route. It would be impossible to find in these villages food for more than twenty or thirty people and there will be days and days when neither food nor water can be obtained. People on foot cannot carry enough food and water on their backs to last them between towns. Under the most favorable conditions the journey is a very fatiguing one (I am speaking from experience, as I traversed that route twice last summer on my attempted trip to America and my return to Harpout). For people traveling as these Armenians who are going into exile will be obliged to travel it is certain death for by far the greater part of them.

It must be borne in mind that wagons and horses are practically unavailable. There are probably not more than twenty-five wagons that can be found for the five or six thousand families who are leaving from this immediate locality. There are several hundred ox-carts and quite a good many small donkeys, while some people are planning to take a cow on which to carry a little food and a blanket or two. This represents every available means of transportation in this region at the present time. There are not nearly enough animals of any kind to enable each family to have one and it is obvious that nearly every one will have to travel on foot. A few of the more fortunate families will have an animal or two on which the women and children can take turns riding, but there will be many cases where a mother with a babe in arms and several small children, and no husband, will have no animal at all.

The fate of these people can readily be imagined. The method is perhaps a little more cultured than a massacre but it will be far more effective and thorough. It is quite probable that many of them will be robbed and murdered en route as the roads are now filled with bands of pillaging Kurds. I asked the Vali the other day what measures were being taken for the protection of these people. He replied that there would be plenty of gendarmes with them so as to avoid a repetition of the fate which had befallen the prisoners who had been sent away from here before, and added that they had met some Kurds who had treated them rather unpleasantly. There is little doubt that these Kurds had been engaged to dispose of them. Many think, and it is by no means improbable, that the same fate is being prepared for those who are now leaving. It is quite possible that the men may be killed, the more attractive women carried off as slaves, and the other women and children left to perish in the desert. In any case, it is quite certain that almost all will die in one way or another before they ever reach their destination.

One thing that increases the doubt about their safe arrival anywhere is that quite a good many people who have been deported from Erzurum and Erzincan have been expected here, but with the exception of one small party from the latter place, none have arrived as yet, while there have been many rumors that these parties have been attacked and killed by Kurds. Money has been sent here from different ones but no one of them has ever appeared to claim it.

Another bad omen is that the Vali has refused permission for any of the Americans to accompany the parties leaving here. Some of the missionaries decided that they would like to go with them in order to be of assistance to those who might need help. On Sunday, the 27th, I called on the Vali about this and other matters. This request he refused absolutely saying it could not be granted but that after the people reached their destination the Americans might then join them if they wished. As probably very few, if any, of them will ever reach their destination this was a safe offer. If it were intended to give these people a safe-conduct to any place there would probably be no objection to the Americans accompanying them. On the other hand, as the roads are decidedly unsafe now, it may be that the Vali did not want to take the responsibility of allowing the Americans to risk their lives in this way. Or, perhaps, the Vali's suggestion that the Americans might join these people later was an intimation that the missionaries also may be invited to leave in the near future.

In my telegrams of June 27th and 28th and in a telegram from Mr. Riggs to Mr. Peet on the 28th we spoke of the need for relief at the destination and I suggested asking aid from America. To what extent it may be possible to aid these people and how it can be done is a problem. There is great danger that they may nearly all be killed or allowed to perish en route. If they arrive anywhere it is still doubtful if they will be within communication. My opinion is that the few who survive the journey will be taken to some remote part of the Mesopotamian plain many days' journey from Urfa or any other town. Should they be within reach of Urfa relief might be arranged through the American Mission in that town or through our Consulate at Aleppo. In any case, there is going to be terrible suffering and great need to help among those who survive the journey. Those who were formerly rich and the poor will alike be destitute. If any possible measures can be taken for their relief I feel that now is the time to begin.

It is impossible for me to give any adequate idea of the panic in this locality that has resulted from the announcement of this order of expulsion. The people have been given four or six days to dispose of everything they have and leave. For the merchants to wind up their affairs in that short time is difficult. It is also difficult for householders to dispose of their household and personal effects. The result has been a panic such as has never been known here or in few other places. Every one who is obliged to leave is trying to get together a little money to take on the journey. The Turks are, of course, taking advantage of the situation to get things at practically nothing. Robbery and looting were never undertaken in a more wholesale manner. Turkish men and Turkish women are entering the houses of all the Armenians and taking things at almost any price. As nearly half the population are leaving they have to take what they can get. This is rarely more than five or ten per cent, of the value. All the furniture in a house, costing originally one or two hundred pounds will be sold for ten or fifteen pounds. Rugs that cost five or ten pounds are sold for fifty or seventy-five piasters. The people are glad to get anything at all for their merchandise or effects. The streets are full of camels carrying off the loot and of rich Turks and Turkish women dressed in their finest gowns, who are making a holiday of the occasion. The scene reminds one of a lot of hungry vultures hovering over the remains of those who have fallen by the way. A more disgusting sight than that which is taking place here now can scarcely be imagined.

The difficulty for people to get ready to leave at such short notice was so great that on Tuesday six of us, comprising practically the entire foreign male population of the town, called on the Vali unofficially to enquire if it would be possible to have a greater length of time given the people before leaving. He received us very courteously but said that was impossible. We did succeed, however, in having a clear understanding that we could help the people in certain ways. The Vali said that there was no objection to our buying things from them or having them leave their money in our care. The Kaimakam has interfered in carrying out this purpose, but on the whole we have been able to do quite a good deal. The Missionaries have also tried to furnish the people with medicine and other useful articles for their journey and some of the poorer and needier ones have been given cash.

During the last three days crowds of people have visited the Consulate and the American Mission for help of some kind. Many have wanted financial assistance, while others have wanted to leave things in our care. They have brought money, documents, jewelry, furniture, and many other things. I have taken documents and some money, while the missionaries have taken much more than I have. Some have left money to be paid in any case to relatives in America, but most have left it on condition that if nothing is heard from them in four or six months it is then to be sent to their relatives. I have never seen a more pathetic or tragic scene. All feel that they are going to certain death and they certainly have good reason to feel that way. Their confidence in the American missionaries and in the Consulate is touching. Some of them don't even want to count the money they are leaving. They hand over the savings of a lifetime with the simple request that if they are not heard from after a few months to send their money if possible to their relatives.

All real estate belonging to Armenians will be confiscated by the Government. Many people will be unable to dispose of their personal property and will probably walk out leaving their houses and stores with all their contents. Those who have made fortunes will lose everything. Some will, of course, take a moderate amount of money with them, but all fear being robbed and very few will dare take much money with them. For those who are feeble and have no money at all, it is a question what will become of them. The Government has offered to furnish donkeys for them, but charges an enormous price per day for every donkey. A man who starts out with only one or two liras will find after a few days that all his money is gone and will be absolutely stranded.

The effect industrially and commercially of the expulsion of the Armenians from this region is going to be to throw it back in the middle ages. It is officially stated that ninety per cent of the trade and of the business carried on through the banks is that of Armenians. Business of all kind will now be destroyed beyond the possibility of its being restored. In some trades there will be no mechanics or workmen at all. It is difficult to understand how those Turks who have had any taste of civilisation at all will be able to live unless exceptions are made and there does not seem to be any indication of that. There will be no banks, no Christian schools, no Christian churches. With one stroke the country is set back two three hundred years. The same will be true of Diyarbakir and of all other parts of this consular district.

There is no doubt in my mind that all the American Missionaries will be obliged to leave. It will not surprise me at all if they are ordered to go but whether they are expelled or not there will be nothing for them to do here. The labors of the missionaries at Harput, which have continued during more than sixty years, have come to an end and I see no way in which they will be able to continue their work here.

With the destruction of all business and the departure of the Missionaries, there will be no object in maintaining a consulate either here or at Diyarbakir or in any other part of this region. There is great danger that I may lose at this time two indispensable employees, both of whom have been with the Consulate for more than ten years, but they are both Armenians, I have asked the Vali to allow them to remain, but the only promise he would give me was that they would not be obliged to go with the first lot. He said they could remain here for a few days and in the meantime he would ask for instructions from Constantinople about them. In my telegram of June 28th, I asked the Embassy to request exemption for them, but I do not believe my telegram ever reached the Embassy.

In my telegram of June 27th, I asked the Embassy to wire me also if it would be possible to secure exemption for the naturalized American citizens who are here. I spoke to the Vali about this at once but he has been very evasive. I hope to receive some reply from the Embassy in time, if it is going to be possible to do anything to save any of these people and their children. There is one class of citizens who are certainly entitled to protection. There are women whose husbands are naturalized American citizens and are now in America, while they have returned here for a short time to visit relatives. There are several of these and nearly all of them have children with them who were born in America. I shall certainly do everything possible to save these.

Tomorrow the exodus of one-half of the population of this region commences. Were the people not so entirely subdued I should expect to see some stirring scenes. As it is, I can hardly think it possible that the authorities will succeed in sending everyone into exile, but as yet there does not seem to be any sign of their relenting or of their granting many exemptions.

I have the honor to be, Sir,
Your obedient servant,
Leslie A. Davis,
Consul.

American Consulate
Mamouret-ul-Aziz (Harput), Turkey
July 11, 1915

Honorable Henry H. Morgenthau,
American Ambassador,
Constantinople

Sir:

I have the honor to supplement my report of June 30th in regard to the expulsion of the Armenians from this region, as follows:

On July 1st a great many people left and on July 3rd several thousand more started from here. Others left on subsequent days. There is no way of obtaining figures but many thousand have already left. The departure of those living at Harput was postponed, however, and many women and children were allowed to remain temporarily. People began to hope that the worst was over and that those who remained might be left alone. Now it has just been announced by the public crier that on Tuesday, July 13th, every Armenian without exception, must go.

If it were simply a matter of being obliged to leave here to go somewhere else it would not be so bad, but everyone knows it is a case of going to one's death. If there was any doubt about it, it has been removed by the arrival of a number of parties, aggregating several thousand people, from Erzurum and Erzinggan. The first ones arrived a day or two after my last report was written. I have visited their encampment a number of times and talked with some of the people. A more pitiable sight cannot be imagined. They were almost without exception ragged, filthy, hungry and sick. That is not surprising in view of the fact that they have been on the road for nearly two months with no change of clothing, no chance to wash, no shelter and little to eat. The Government has been giving them some scanty rations here. I watched them one time when their food was brought. Wild animals could not be worse. They rushed upon the guards who carried the food and the guards beat them back with clubs hitting hard enough to kill them sometimes. To watch them one could hardly believe that these people were human beings.

As one walks through the camp mothers offer their children and beg one to take them. In fact, the Turks have been taking their choice of these children and girls for slaves, or worse. In fact, they have even had their doctors there to examine the more likely girls and thus secure the best ones.

There are very few men among them, as most of them have been killed on the road. All tell the same story of having been attacked and robbed by the Kurds. Most of them were attacked over and over again and a great many of them, especially the men, were killed. Women and children were also killed. Many died, of course, from sickness and exhaustion on the way and there have been deaths each day that they have been here. Several different parties have arrived and after remaining a day or two have been pushed on with no apparent destination. Those who have reached here are only a small portion, however, of those who started. By continuing to drive these people on in this way it will be possible to dispose of all of them in a comparatively short time. Among those with whom I have talked were three sisters. They had been educated at Constantinople and spoke excellent English. They said their family was the richest in Erzurum and numbered twenty-five when they left but there were now only fourteen survivors. The other eleven, including the husband of one of them and their old grandmother had been butchered before their eyes by the Kurds. The oldest male survivor of the family was eight years of age. When they left Erzurum they had money, horses and personal effects but they had been robbed of everything, including even their clothing. They said some of them had been left absolutely naked and others with only a single garment. When they reached a village their gendarmes obtained clothes for them from some of the native women. Another girl with whom I talked is the daughter of the Protestant pastor of Erzurum. She said every member of her family with her had been killed and she was left entirely alone. These and some others are a few survivors of the better class of people who have been exiled. They are being detained in an abandoned schoolhouse just outside of the town and no one is allowed to enter it. They said they practically are in prison, although they were allowed to visit a spring just outside the building. It was there that I happened to see them. All the others are camped in a large open field with no protection at all from the sun.

The condition of these people indicates clearly the fate of those who have left and are about to leave from here. I believe nothing has been heard from any of them as yet and probably very little will be heard. The system that is being followed seems to be to have bands of Kurds awaiting them on the road to kill the men especially and incidentally some of the others. The entire movement seems to be the most thoroughly organized and effective massacre this country has ever seen.

Not many men have been spared, however, to accompany those who are being sent into exile, for a more prompt and sure method has been used to dispose of them. Several thousand Armenian men have been arrested during the past few weeks. These have been put in prison and each time that several hundred had been gathered up in that way they were sent away during the night. The first lot was sent away during the night of June 23rd. Among them were some of the professors in the American college and other prominent Armenians, including the Prelate of the Armenian Gregorian Church of Harput. There have been frequent rumors that all of these were killed and there is little doubt that they were. All Armenian soldiers have likewise been sent away in the same manner. They have been arrested and confined in a building at one end of the town.

No distinction has been made between those who had paid their military exemption tax and those who had not. Their money was accepted and then they were arrested and sent off with the others. It was said that they were to go somewhere to work on the roads but no one has heard from them and that is undoubtedly false.

The fate of all the others has been pretty well established by reliable reports of a similar occurrence on Wednesday, July 7th. On Monday many men were arrested both at Harput and Mezreh and put in prison. At daybreak Tuesday morning they were taken out and made to march towards an almost uninhabited mountain. There were about eight hundred in all and they were tied together in groups of fourteen each. That afternoon they arrived in a small Kurdish village where they were kept over night in the mosque and other buildings. During all this time they were without food or water. All their money and much of their clothing had been taken from them. On Wednesday morning they were taken to a valley a few hours' distant where they were all made to sit down. Then the gendarmes began shooting them until they had killed nearly all of them. Some who had not been killed by bullets were then disposed of with knives and bayonets. A few succeeded in breaking the rope with which they were tied to their companions and running away, but most of these were pursued and killed. A few succeeded in getting away, probably not more than two or three. Among those who were killed was the Treasurer of the American College. Many other estimable men were among the number. No charge of any kind had ever been made against any of these men. They were simply arrested and killed as part of the general plan to dispose of the Armenian race.

Last night several hundred more men, including both men arrested by the civil authorities and those enrolled as soldiers, were taken in a different direction and murdered in a similar manner. It is said this happened at a place not two hours' distance from here. I shall ride out that way some day when things become a little quieter and try to verify it for myself.

The same thing has been done systematically in the villages.

A few weeks ago about three hundred men were gathered together at Itchme and Haboosi, two villages four and five hours' distant from here, and then taken up into the mountains and massacred. This seems to be fully established. Many women from those villages have been here since and told about it. There have been rumors of similar occurrences in other places.

There seems to be a definite plan to dispose of all the Armenian men, but after the departure of the families during the first few days of the enforcement of the order it was announced that women and children with no men in the family might remain here for the present and many hoped that the worst was over. The American missionaries began considering plans to aid the women and children who would be left here with no means of support. It was thought that perhaps an orphanage could be opened to care for some of the children especially those who had been born in America and then brought here by their parents and also those who belonged to parents who had been connected in some way with the American Mission and schools. There would be plenty of opportunity, although there might not be sufficient means, to care for children who reached here with the exiles from other Vilayets and whose parents had died on the way. I went to see the Vali about this matter yesterday and was met with a flat refusal. He said we could aid these people if we wished to do so, but the Government was establishing orphanages for the children and we could not undertake any work of that nature. An hour after I left the Vali the announcement was made that all the Armenians remaining here, including women and children must leave on July 13th.

The evident plan of the Government is to give no opportunity for any educational or religious work to be done here by foreign missionaries. Some Armenian women will be taken as Moslem wives and some children will be brought up as Moslems, but none of them will be allowed to come under foreign influences. The country is to be purely Moslem and nothing else. Some of the missionaries think they would like to remain here and try to work among Moslems. I not only think it would be very dangerous for them to undertake it but do not believe they will be allowed to do anything along that line. I shall not be surprised, as I have said before, if all the American missionaries are ordered to leave here in the near future. If they are not, they will be so effectually prevented from doing any kind of work that it will be entirely useless for them to remain here. Furthermore, they will be annoyed in many ways by the local officials. I do not think for a moment that they will be allowed to open any of the schools again and it's quite probable that the hospital may be ordered closed. It is very probable also that both the school and the hospital buildings may be seized by the Government. It seems certain that there will not be any work for them to do here and that they will not be permitted to do any work.

Under the circumstances, I think the only wise and safe thing for them to do is to consider the matter of leaving here, temporarily at least, as soon as it may be possible. I realize that it is a serious matter for them to abandon their work, but the present situation is serious too and I fully believe there is nothing else for them to do. It would probably not be best for all of them to leave together, but I am going to advise that some of them leave as soon as it may be safe to go. In the meantime I earnestly recommend that the Embassy bring to the attention of Mr. Peet and the board the possible necessity of all of them leaving here.

I do not think that any of them should go now. In fact, some of them have been quite firmly of the opinion that some one should go at once for the purpose of trying to raise a relief fund for these unfortunate people. To go now would be almost certain death, with bands of Kurds awaiting travelers on every road. I asked the Vali, however, if it would be all right for one or two of the Americans to leave here now to go to Constantinople and then to America and he said very plainly that it would not be safe. He said that no matter how much a guard he gave them it would be dangerous for them to travel at the present moment and advised waiting a few weeks. This confirms the general fear as to the fate of those who are sent away from here. It also indicated that perhaps the authorities do not wish any real harm to befall the Americans. On the other hand, the Vali intimated that possibly the Americans might not be permitted to leave here. Some of them think that we know too much about what is happening in the interior of Turkey and the authorities do not intend to let any Americans leave here alive to tell about it. I do not think that, but I do think the life of every American here is in danger and that the danger is increasing. If all of the missionaries can get away safely I shall feel greatly relieved. It is not only that the present situation is very critical, but they are constantly doing things that are more or less imprudent. The entire colony may suffer for the imprudence of one person. It is quite natural that they should sympathize with the people among whom they have been working and want to aid and protect them, but there is great danger of carrying their zeal too far and getting into trouble themselves.

With reference to the need of funds for the relief of these exiles, which I mentioned in my telegrams of June 27th and 28th and my dispatch of June 30th I am inclined to believe that there will be no occasion for raising funds. It looks as though there were not going to be any people who can be helped. All who are sent away will probably be killed or die on the road within the next few months and the women and children who are left will probably have to become Moslems.

My attention has just been called to the fact that the post office at Mamouret-ul-Aziz has refused to pay out money to the Americans that has been sent them from Erzurum and Erzincan for the exiles who have come here. It is probable that the Government will confiscate this money. I do not know whether the Embassy would care to take any measures about this or not. The money is addressed to the Americans, but it is intended for the Armenian exiles.

Embassy's telegrams Nos. 19 and 20 have been received. I have seen the Vali about the naturalized American citizens and their children and about the consular staff. He said he had received no instructions about them, as I telegraphed this morning. I have now just received word that the consular staff and two or three women whose husbands are in America may stay here for the present. There seems to be nothing very definite about any of it. I shall be very glad to have these women leave as soon as it is reasonably safe for them to go. I hope it can be arranged for the employees of the Consulate, however, to remain here permanently, or at least as long as there may be a Consulate. It would be impossible to find any one to take their place.

I have the honor to be, Sir,
your obedient servant,
Leslie A. Davis
Consul

Henry Morgenthau to Robert Lansing

Based on reports he received from American consuls and from the missionaries who ran schools and hospitals across the Ottoman Empire, Ambassador Morgenthau kept the new secretary of state informed on the progress of the "campaign of racial extermination" being waged against the Armenians. (Not until 1944 did the refugee Polish legal scholar Raphael Lemkin, who had studied the systematic extermination of the Armenians, coin the word "genocide.")

WSB

GREEN CIPHER
From Constantinople
Dated July 16, 1915.
Rec'd. 30, 8:10 A.M.

Secretary of State,
Washington.

858, July 16, 1 P.M.
CONFIDENTIAL
Have you received my 841? Deportation of and excesses against peaceful Armenians is increasing and from harrowing reports of eye witnesses it appears that a campaign of race extermination is in progress under a pretext of reprisal against rebellion.

Protests as well as threats are unavailing and probably incite the Ottoman government to more drastic measures as they are determined to disclaim responsibility for their absolute disregard of Capitulations and I believe nothing short of actual force which obviously United States are not in a position to exert would adequately meet the situation. Suggest you inform belligerent nations and mission boards of this.

AMERICAN AMBASSADOR
CONSTANTINOPLE

Jane Addams: The Revolt Against War

A powerful movement infused American life around the time of the war—"the Social Gospel," a Protestant impulse to ameliorate society's ills through Christian ethics. Jane Addams, born in Illinois in 1860, was one of its adherents. She spent her life fighting poverty, crime, alcoholism, and racial inequality, working initially from Hull-House, the settlement house in Chicago she co-founded in 1889. Her agenda went well beyond the walls of that tumble-down mansion, as she recognized that in order to grapple with social conditions, women needed the vote. On January 10, 1915, with leading suffragist Carrie Chapman Catt, she held a meeting in Washington, D.C., which 3,000 women attended. It resulted in the Woman's Peace Party—a sister-hood of social reformers and suffragists—which Addams chaired. At the end of April 1915, Addams attended the International Congress of Women in The Hague, where delegates from twelve countries—some neutral (such as the United States), some belligerent (such as Great Britain, Germany, and Austria-Hungary)—gathered to call for a ne-gotiated end to the war. That spring, Addams met heads of govern-ment in Britain, Germany, Austria-Hungary, France, and Italy, which declared war on Austria-Hungary on May 23, 1915. She returned to the United States on July 5, delivering a report of her trip four days later at Carnegie Hall. It appeared in *The Survey*, a social reform journal, the following week.

IT IS DIFFICULT to formulate your experience when brought face to face with so much genuine emotion and high patriotism as Europe exhibits at the present moment. You become very much afraid of generalizing. The situation is so confused, so many wild and weird things are said about it, that you are afraid to add one word that is not founded upon absolutely first-hand impressions and careful experience; because, for the world, you would not add a bit to this already overwhelming confusion. And you do not come back,—at least I do not,—from these various warring countries with any desire to let loose any more emotion upon the world. You feel that what is needed above all else is some careful understanding,—some human touch, if you please, in this over-involved and over-talked-of situation in which so much of the world finds itself in dire confusion and bloodshed. You get afraid of tall talk; you do not know where words may lead the people to whom you are speaking. They seem to have acquired such a fearful significance and seem to have power over the very issues of life and death itself.

And so I should like, if I might, for a few moments, to tell as simply as I can, the experiences which we had at The Hague. Some have been much too kind to call me the leader of that movement, for I was not, in any sense of the word. It was convened and called together by a group of European women, and only after all the arrangements were made did we know about it in America, and consent to go. They were anxious to have a woman from a neutral country to serve as president, and it was safer to have the neutral country as far away as possible, and America was the furthest away. Therefore, I think America was chosen.

The women who called the congress were sure that, although during this last year none of the great international congresses, in science and arts or the most abstract subjects, had dared to meet; they were quite sure that the women who had been meeting during many years, in such conventions as Dr. Shaw has described, that at least a few of them could come together and in all sobriety and in all friendliness discuss their common aims and the terrible stake which they all had together in this war. That faith as you know, was well grounded, and for three days and a half with much less friction than is usual in the ordinary meetings of men or women, so far as I know them, the women met there at The Hague and formulated their series of resolutions. I will confess that the first day we were a little cautious. We skated, as it were, more or less on thin ice, because we did not know how far we dared venture in freedom of expression. One of the Dutch committee came to me and whispered almost in a stage whisper: "I think you ought to know that the hall is full of police, not only those supplied by The Hague, but some of them supplied by the government itself because they fear trouble." We told them we should be happy to have the police there to listen to our deliberations, and to call upon them if needed! It seemed as if every

one was nervous, and I will admit that there was an element of
risk, if you please, in asking women to come; but they did
come from twelve different countries, in the midst of the strain
under which Europe is now laboring.

On the last day of that conference it was suggested that the
resolutions be carried by committees to the various governments of Europe, and to the President of the United States.
Some of us felt that the congress had ended very happily, that
we had proceeded day by day in good will and understanding,
and that it was perhaps unfortunate to venture further. But the
resolution was passed, and two committees set forth. One
committee to the north, consisting of a woman from the side
of the allies, and a woman from the side of the Germans, and
also two women from the neutral nations, have visited the
Scandinavian countries and Russia. We have had cables from
them from time to time. They were received by the prime
ministers and members of Parliament in all of the countries as
well as by the ministers of foreign affairs. They have been reported in Italy and Holland, and will arrive in America we
hope within a week or two. You cannot tell how long it may
take to cross the ocean now because you may quite easily be
held up in the English channel or some other crucial trade
route for some ten or twelve days.

The other committee consisting of the vice-president and
the president of the congress, women from the two neutral
nations, from Holland and from America, set forth to visit the
other countries.

We were received in each of the capitals, in London, in Berlin, in Budapest, in Rome, in Paris and in Havre, where the
Belgian government is now established. We took in also Switzerland and Holland, although they are neutral, and Rome
should be counted twice for we visited the Vatican; or nine
visits in all. We were received in each case by the minister of
foreign affairs, and by the chancellor or prime minister, and in
all of the countries we saw members of Parliament and other
men who are responsible for governmental policies.

It is too much to hope to reach the mind of everyone in a
huge audience like this, but I should like to reproduce in the
minds of some of you some of the impressions made by this
pilgrimage of ours, if you choose to call it so, going to and fro

from one government to another, as we did to nine governments in the space of five weeks.

The first thing which was striking is this, that the same causes
and reasons for the war were heard everywhere. Each warring
nation solemnly assured you it is fighting under the impulse of
self-defense. Each of the warring nations I assure you feels it is
fighting to preserve its own traditions and its own ideals from
those who would come in and disturb and destroy those high
traditions and those ideals. And in one tongue or another, or
translated into English, we heard the identical phrases. Going
as rapidly as we did, from one country to another, I almost
knew what to expect and what phrases were coming next, after
a foreign minister had begun.

Another thing which we found very striking was that in practically all of the foreign offices including those two foreign offices, one of which I suppose to be leading one side and one
the other side of this conflict, the men said—again in very
similar phrases,—that a nation at war cannot make negotiations and that a nation at war cannot even express willingness
to receive negotiations, for if it does either, the enemy will at
once construe it as a symptom of weakness; and when the
terms are made the side which first suggested negotiations will
suffer as being construed the side that was weaker and was
suing for peace.

But they said, in all of these foreign offices, that if some
other power presented propositions,—if neutral people, however
they might be gotten together, people who would command the
respect of the foreign offices to whom their propositions would
be presented—if a small conference were willing to get together to study the situation seriously and to make propositions, one, two, three—even if they were turned down over
and over again until something were found upon which negotiations might commence, *there is none of the warring nations
that would not be glad to receive such service.* Now that came to
us unequivocally.

We presented to each of the chancelleries our resolutions,
but we talked for the most part about the possibility of substi-
tuting negotiations for military processes. Now, it is very easy

for a minister to say: "This country will never receive negotiations; we are going to drive the enemy out inch by inch," but it is pretty hard for him to say it to one or two or three or four women who are sitting there, and asking: "If a proposition were presented to you, which seemed to you feasible,—if something were presented to you which might mean the beginning of further negotiations between yourselves and your enemies, would you decline such a proposition? Would you feel justified to go on sacrificing the young men of your country in order to obtain through bloodshed what might be obtained through negotiations,—the very thing for which your foreign office was established?" No minister, of course, is willing to say that he would. No minister would be willing, of course, to commit himself for a moment to such a policy. That we found everywhere.

There was another thing which was impressed upon us all of the time, and in all of the countries which we visited. Although each is tremendously united at the present moment, although there is no break that can be seen or heard anywhere on the part of the people fighting together—that they wish the war to cease or that they are going to divide into parties; one party to oppose the other—while they are thus united in this tremendous national consciousness, there was manifested in every country two general lines of approach. One finds expression in the military party which believes that the matter can be settled only upon a military basis; the other, a civil party, which very much deprecates this exaltation of militarism, which says that the longer the war runs on, the more the military parties are being established as censors of the press and in all sorts of other places which they ordinarily do not occupy; that the longer the war goes on the more the military power is breaking down all of the safeguards of civil life and of civil government, and that consequently the harder will it be for civil life and for the rights of civil life to re-establish themselves over the rights and power of the military. The more desperately they cling to their army, the more absolute is the power and the glory of that army. The people who represent the civil view of life, in the midst of this patriotic fervor, in the midst of this devotion to the army, see that and long for some other form of settlement,

—for some other form of approach to this terrible, confused situation,—long for it one month more than they did the month before.

As you go from one country to another, you can only say for yourself and say it to the citizens as you have opportunity, that if this war is ever to be settled through negotiations,—and sometime it must be, heaven knows when,—but sometime men must stop fighting and return to their normal existence— you say to these men: "Why not begin now before the military becomes even further entrenched? Why not begin now when you still have enough power to hold them to their own state- ments, to hold them to their own purposes, and not allow them to rule and control the absolute destinies of the nation?"

Now, I am quite aware that in every country we met, broadly speaking, the civil people and not the military people. I am quite aware that it was natural for us to see the pacifists, if you please,—although they are hardly known under that name;— that it was more natural for us to meet and know the people who were on that side of life, instead of the military side of life. But because we did meet dozens of them, I am willing to be- lieve that there must be many more of the same type of mind in every country; quite as loyal as the military people, quite as eager for the growth and development of their own ideals and their own standard of living; but believing with all their hearts that the military message is a wrong message, which cannot in the end establish those things which are so dear to their hearts.

Now, that is something to work upon. When peace comes, it must come through the people within those countries having some sort of claim to the same type of mind and the same type of people who are dwelling in other countries.

At present they have no means of communication. They say that under the censorship of the press one man cannot tell how many other men are feeling as he does or believing as he does. Although he is a comrade in mind, and may be living in the next street, or in the next town, he does not know how many there are. He cannot get them together. In our modern cities with their huge agglomeration of human beings, we communicate largely through the daily press. We cannot find out public opinion in any other way. Poor method as it seems, it is, after all, all that we have worked out as yet. And in the warring countries nothing goes into the press except those things which the military censors deem fit and proper.

So as we went about, people would say to us, in regard to the press, if you see So and So, say a word about lessening the censorship. And we said, No, we can talk about but this one thing. We cannot carry messages from the citizens to their governments. But over and over again this request was made. And as we got back to one country from another, they would say: "Are people talking like that there? That is just the way we are talking here." But they do not know each other from one country to another. And the individuals cannot find each other within the country itself.

In each of the warring nations there is this other point of similarity. Generally speaking, we heard everywhere that this war was an old man's war; that the young men who were dying, the young men who were doing the fighting, were not the men who wanted the war, and were not the men who believed in the war; that somewhere in church and state, somewhere in the high places of society, the elderly people, the middle-aged people, had established themselves and had convinced themselves that this was a righteous war, that this war must be fought out, and the young men must do the fighting.

Now, this is a terrible indictment, and I admit that I cannot substantiate it. I can only give it to you as an impression, but I should like to bring one or two details before you to back it up, so to speak.

I thought when I got up I shouldn't mention the word German or the word allies, but perhaps if I give an example from Germany and then an example from the allies, I will not get into trouble.

We met a young man in Switzerland. He had been in the trenches for three months, had been wounded and had been sent to Switzerland to be cured. He had developed tuberculosis and the physician among us thought he would scarcely live three months. But he thought he was being cured, and he was speaking his mind before he went back to the trenches. He was, I suppose, what one would call a fine young man, but not an exceptional young man. He had had a gymnasium education. He had been in business with his father, had traveled in South Africa; had traveled in France, England, and Holland, in the line of business. He had come to know men as *mensch*, that *gute menschen* were to be found in every land. And now here he was, at twenty-eight, facing death because he was quite sure when he went back to the trenches that death awaited him. This is what he said: Never during that three months and a half had he once shot his gun in a way that could possibly hit another man. He said that nothing in the world could make him kill another man. He could be ordered into the trenches; he could be ordered to go through the motions, but the final act was in his own hands and with his own conscience. And he said: "My brother is an officer." (He gave the name of his brother, gave his title; he wasn't concealing anything; he was quite too near death's door to have any shifting and concealing). "He never shoots anything; he never shoots in a way that will kill. And I know dozens and dozens of young men who do not."

We had a list given to us by the woman at the head of a hospital in one German city of five young Germans who had been cured and were ready to be sent back to the trenches, when they committed suicide, not because they were afraid of being killed, but because they were afraid they might be put into a position where they would have to kill someone else.

We heard stories of that sort from France. We talked with nurses in hospitals; we talked with convalescent soldiers; we talked to the mothers of soldiers who had come back on furlough and had gone into the trenches; and in all of these countries we learned that there are surprising numbers of young men and old men who will not do any fatal shooting because they think that no one has the right to command them to do that thing.

In order to be quite fair and square, I shall next give my testimony from England. I quote a letter published in the *Cambridge Magazine* at Cambridge University and written by a young man who had gone to the front. I didn't visit Cambridge, but I did visit Oxford. The universities are almost depleted of young men. The great majority of them have gone into the war. This is what this young man wrote:

"The greatest trial that this war has brought is that it has released the old men from all restraining influences, and has let them loose upon the world. The city editors, the retired majors, the amazons [women are included, you see] and last, but I fear, not least, the venerable archdeacons, have never been so free from contradiction. Just when the younger generation was beginning to take its share in the affairs of the world, and was hoping to counteract the Victorian influences of the older generation, this war has come to silence us,—permanently or temporarily as the case may be. Meanwhile, the old men are having field days on their own. In our name, and for our sakes as they pathetically imagine, they are doing their very utmost, it would seem, to perpetuate, by their appeals to hate, intolerance and revenge, those very follies which have produced the present conflagration."

I am not going to tell of many things that were said because I think there have been, for the present, too many things said: but the mothers would say to us: "It was hard to see that boy go because he did not believe in war; he did not belong to a generation that believes in war."

One of the leading men of Europe, whose name you would instantly recognize if I felt at liberty to give it, said: "If this war could have been postponed for ten years—perhaps," he said, "I will be safe and say, twenty years,—war would have been impossible in Europe, because of the tremendous revolt against it in the schools and the universities."

I am quite sure when I say that, that it is a partial view. I am quite sure that there are thousands of young men in the trenches feeling that they are performing the highest possible duties. I am quite sure that the spirit of righteousness is in the hearts of most of them, at least of many of them; but that throughout there are to be found these other men who are doing violence to the highest teachings which they know.

It seemed to me at times as if the difference between the older generation and the new, is something we apprehended dimly in each country,—that the older men believed more in abstractions, shall I say; that when they talked of patriotism, when they used certain theological or nationalistic words, these meant more to them than they did to the young men; that the young men had come to take life much more from the point of view of experience; that they were much more—pragmatic (I suppose I could have said in Boston: I don't know how well it will go in New York)—that they had come to take life much more empirically; and when they went to the trenches and tested it out, they concluded that it did not pay, that it was not what they wanted to do with their lives.

I saw an old Quaker in England who said: "My sons are not fighting, they are sweeping mines." The Quakers are very clever in distinguishing between what they will or will not do. This Quaker explained to me that his sons allow themselves to sweep mines but they do not allow themselves to fire mines. They are doing this, that and the other thing. "It is strange to me," he said, "because they never went to Quaker meetings, but they are awfully keen now on being consistent." Now, there you are. I think it was the difference again between the older generation and the new. This again may be a superficial impression, but such as it is, we had it in every single country, one after the other.

Let me say just a word about the women in the various countries. The belief that a woman is against war simply and only because she is a woman and not a man, does not, of course, hold. In every country there are many, many women who believe that the war is inevitable and righteous, and that the highest possible service is being performed by their sons who go into the army; just as there are thousands of men believing that in every country; the majority of women and men doubtless believe that.

But the women do have a sort of pang about it. Let us take the case of an artist, an artist who is in an artillery corps, let us say, and is commanded to fire upon a wonderful thing, say St. Mark's at Venice, or the duomo at Florence, or any other great architectural and beautiful thing. I am sure he would have just a little more compunction than the man who had never given himself to creating beauty and did not know the cost of it. There is certainly that deterrent on the part of the women, who have nurtured these soldiers from the time they were little things, who brought them into the world and brought them up to the age of fighting, and now see them destroyed. That curious revolt comes out again and again, even in the women who are most patriotic and who say: "I have five sons and a son-in-law in the trenches. I wish I had more sons to give." Even those women, when they are taken off their guard, give a certain protest, a certain plaint against the whole situation which very few men I think are able to formulate.

Now, what is it that these women do in the hospitals? They nurse the men back to health and send them to the trenches, and the soldiers say to them: "You are so good to us when we are wounded, you do everything in the world to make life possible and to restore us; why do you not have a little pity for us when we are in the trenches? Why do you not put forth a little of this same effort and this same tenderness to see what might be done to pull us out of those miserable places?"

That testimony came to us, not from the nurses of one country, and not from the nurses who were taking care of the soldiers on one side, but from those who were taking care of them upon every side.

And it seems to make it quite clear that whether we are able to recognize it or not, there has grown up a generation in Europe, as there has doubtless grown up a generation in America, who have revolted against war. It is a god they know not of, that they are not willing to serve; because all of their sensibilities and their training upon which their highest ideals depend, revolt against the whole situation.

Now it seems to me this:—and bear in mind that the papers were much too kind when they said that I was going to advise the President. I never dreamed of advising him or of formulating plans. That last will have to be done when the others have returned—I should never venture alone to do anything of the sort. But this, it seems to me, broadly speaking, might be true, that a set of people could be gotten together who are international, out of their own experience. You know, of course, that the law is the least international thing we have! We have an international body of science; a man takes the knowledge of the science to which he is devoted, and deals with that knowledge, and he doesn't ask whether it was gathered together by Englishmen or Germans. We have an international postal system, a tremendous international commerce, and a tremendous international finance; internationalism in all sorts of fields. But the law lags behind, and perhaps will lag behind for a long time, quite as many of our most settled customs have never been embodied in law at all.

If men could be brought together who have had international experience, who have had it so long and so unconsciously that they have come to think not merely in internationalistic terms, but in the realities of the generation in which they have been doing the thing—whether business or labor or any other thing which has become so tremendously international—if they could be brought together, they could be asked to try to put the very best mind they have not as representing one country or another country, but as representing human life and human experience as it has been lived during the last ten years in Europe.

They could be asked what it is that has brought about this situation. Does Servia need a seaport? Is that what is the matter with Servia? I won't mention any of the other warring countries because I might get into difficulties; but is this thing or that thing needed? What is it from the human standpoint, from the social standpoint? Is it necessary to feed the people of Europe—who are, as you know, so underfed in all of the southern portions of Europe—is it necessary, in order to feed them, to get the wheat out of Russia? Then in heaven's name, let us have warm water harbors in order to get that wheat out of Russia.

Let us not consider it from the point of view of the claims of Russia, or of the counterclaims of someone else; but consider it from the point of view of the needs of Europe. If men with that temper, and that experience, and that sort of understanding of life were to begin to make propositions to the various governments, men who would not placate the claims of one government and set them over against the claims of another government, but would look at the situation from a humane standpoint,—I am sure, at the least (from my knowledge of dozens of men in all of the countries who talked with me about the situation) that that sort of negotiation would be received. Now that does not seem an impossible thing.

Perhaps the most shocking impression left upon one's mind is this, that in the various countries the temper necessary for continuing the war is worked up and fed largely by the things which have occurred in the war itself. Germany has done this; the allies have done that; somebody tried to do this and somebody else tried to do that, and we foiled them by doing that. Now, I submit that no, shall I say, plain mother who found two children fighting,—not for any cause which they stated, but because "he did that" and "I did this, and therefore he did that to me,"—that such a woman would say "this can't go on." It leads to nothing but continuous hatred and quarreling.

Let us say that there are two groups of boys in a boys' club, and I have much experience of that sort in boys' clubs to draw upon. If one says, "We did this because the other fellows did that," you will simply have to say, "I won't go into the rights and wrongs of this, but this thing must stop, because it leads nowhere and gets nowhere." And so with larger groups. We all know the strikes that have gone on for weeks, with the original cause quite lost sight of. I submit that something of the same sort is happening in Europe now.

They are going on because of the things which have been done in the war; but that certainly is a very curious cause for continuing the war. And what it needs, it seems to me, and to many of us, is a certain touch of human nature. The human nature in the trenches would heal them over; the kindly people in the various countries would not support the war longer, and the foreign offices themselves would resume their own business, —that of negotiation versus that of military affairs,—if human nature can be released instead of being kept at the boiling pitch as it is all the time by outrages here and there and somewhere else. I do not know how that is to be brought about, and I admit that this is a very simple analysis of a very serious and complex situation. But when you go about and see the same sort of sorrow everywhere, see the tremendous loss of life in these countries, when you find that you can't talk to a woman on any subject, however remote from the war, without finding at once that she is in the deepest perplexity,—that while she is carrying herself bravely and going on with her accustomed activities because she thinks thereby that she is serving her country, her heart is being torn all the time,—it is borne in upon you that at last human nature must revolt. The fanatical feeling which is so high in every country, and which is so fine in every country, cannot last. The wave will come down. The crest cannot be held indefinitely. Then men must see the horrible things which have happened; they will have to soberly count up the loss of life, and the debt they have settled upon themselves for years to come.

I could go on and tell many things that we saw. The Pope himself gave us an audience of half an hour. The men with religious responsibility feel keenly what has happened in Europe —that while the various countries see in the war a throwback of civilization, the church sees it as a throwback to religion— breeding animosities and tearing and rending the work of years. And yet we are all apparently powerless to do the one thing which might end it. I do not say end it. We did not talk peace as we went about. It would merely confuse the issue. (And, in truth, isn't it hideous that whole nations find the word peace intolerable?) We said: "Why not see what can be done to arrive at some form of coming together—to discover what might be done—in the place of the settlement which is now being fought out through military processes?" And that was as far as we were able to go with clearness and safety, and upon that platform we were met with the greatest—someone said courtesy—it was to my mind more than courtesy. It was received, as one Englishman expressed it, like a breath of fresh air, this coming in at last of someone to talk of something that was not of war. We went into the room of one of the prime ministers of Europe, a large, grizzled, formidable man. We told him our little story and he said nothing. I never have a great deal of self-confidence—I am never so dead sure I am doing the right thing, and I said to him:

"This perhaps seems to you very foolish, to have women going about in this way; but after all, the world itself is so strange in this new war situation that our mission may be no more strange or foolish than the rest."

He banged his fist on the table. "Foolish?" he said, "Not at all. These are the first sensible words that have been uttered in this room for ten months."

He said: "That door opens from time to time, and people come in to say, 'Mr. Minister, we must have more men, we must have more ammunition, we must have more money. We

cannot go on with this war without more of something else.'
At last the door opens and two people walk in and say, 'Mr.
Minister, why not settle by means of negotiations instead of by
fighting?' They are the sensible ones."

Other people, of course, said he was an old man, this prime
minister, that he was without power. Yet he was an officer of
the government in a high place, and that is what he said. I give
it to you for what it is worth. And there are other testimonials
of the same sort from all kinds of people in office and out of
office; they are part of the peoples who are at war, and unable
to speak for themselves.

There is one more thing I should like to say and I will close;
and that is that one feels that the talk against militarism, and
the belief that it can be crushed by a counter-militarism is, as
has been uttered so many times, one of the greatest illusions
which can possibly seize the human mind. England likes to talk
and does talk sharply against what it calls militarism, but if they
have conscription in England, then the militarism which they
think they are fighting will, at least for the moment, have
conquered Britain itself, which has always been so proud that
it had a free army and not a conscripted army. And if all of the
young men of France between certain ages come to their
deaths in their effort to move people out of trenches from
which they cannot be moved (because they are absolutely built
in of concrete on both sides, and even military men say you
cannot budge them without tremendous loss of life)—if these
young men are convinced that France must arm as never before, that she must turn herself into a military camp, as they
are fond of saying, then, of course, the militaristic idea has
conquered France.

The old notion that you can drive a belief into a man at the
point of a bayonet is in force once more. It is quite as foolish
to think that if militarism is an idea and an ideal, it can be
changed and crushed by counter-militarism or by a bayonet
charge. And the young men in these various countries say of
the bayonet charges: "That is what we cannot think of." We
heard in all countries similar statements in regard to the necessity for the use of stimulants before men would engage in
bayonet charges—that they have a regular formula in Germany,

that they give them rum in England and absinthe in France; that they all have to give them the "dope" before the bayonet charge is possible. Well, now, think of that.

No one knows who is responsible for the war; all the warring nations are responsible, and they indict themselves. But in the end human nature must reassert itself. The old elements of human understanding and human kindliness among them must come to the fore, and then it may well be that they will reproach the neutral nations and will say: "What was the matter with the rest of the world that you kept quiet while this horrible thing was happening, and our men for a moment had lost their senses in this fanaticism of national feeling all over Europe?" They may well say: "You were far enough away from it not to share in it, and yet you wavered until we lost the flower of the youth of all Europe."

That is what the women said in various tongues and according to their various temperaments at The Hague, and that is what enabled them to leave their countries when they were at war, believing as they did in the causes for which they were fighting. The women who came to the congress were women who were impelled by a genuine feeling for life itself.

Please do not think we are overestimating a very slight achievement or taking too seriously the kindness with which we were received abroad. We do wish to record ourselves as being quite sure that the peoples in these various countries were grateful for the effort, trifling as it was. The people say they do not want this war, they say that the governments are making this war. And the governments say they do not want this war. They say, "We will be grateful to anybody who would help us to stop the war." We did not reach the military, but we did talk to a few military men, some of whom said they were sick to death of the war, and I have no doubt there were many others who, if they spoke freely, would say the same thing.

"Without abandoning your causes, and without lowering, if you please, the real quality of your patriotism,"—the women's resolutions, which we carried, said to these various nations, and we said it to their representatives as long as they permitted us to talk—"whatever it is you want, and whatever it is you feel you ought to have in honor, why in the world can't you submit your case to a tribunal of fair-minded men? If your case is as good as you are sure it is, certainly those men will find the righteousness which adheres within it."

And they all say that if the right medium can be found, the case will be submitted.

Richard Harding Davis to
The New York Times

The legendary Davis had returned to the United States to publish *With the Allies* in December 1914. The following year he went overseas again, visiting France, Greece, and Serbia. Davis would return home to Mount Kisco, New York, in early 1916 and publish *With the French in France and Salonika* that April, shortly before dying of a heart attack one week shy of his fifty-second birthday.

Mount Kisco, N. Y., July 11, 1915.
To the Editor of The New York Times:
　On Friday night at Carnegie Hall Miss Jane Addams stated that in the present war, in order to get soldiers to charge with the bayonet, all nations are forced first to make them drunk. I quote from *The Times* report:

> In Germany they have a regular formula for it [she said.] In England they use rum and the French resort to absinthe. In other words, therefore, in the terrible bayonet charges they speak of with dread, the men must be doped before they start.

　In this war the French or English soldier who has been killed in a bayonet charge gave his life to protect his home and country. For his supreme exit he had prepared himself by months of discipline. Through the Winter in the trenches he has endured shells, disease, snow, and ice. For months he had been separated from his wife, children, friends—all those he most loved. When the order to charge came it was for them he gave his life, that against those who destroyed Belgium they might preserve their home, might live to enjoy peace.

　Miss Addams denies him the credit of his sacrifice. She strips him of honor and courage. She tells his children, "Your father did not die for France, or for England, or for you; he died because he was drunk."

　In my opinion, since the war began, no statement has been

so unworthy or so untrue and ridiculous. The contempt it shows for the memory of the dead is appalling; the credulity and ignorance it displays are inconceivable.

Miss Addams does not know that even from France they have banished absinthe. If she doubts that in this France has succeeded let her ask for it. I asked for it, and each maître d'hôtel treated me as though I had proposed we should assassinate General Joffre.

If Miss Addams does know that the French Government has banished absinthe, then she is accusing it of openly receiving the congratulations of the world for destroying the drug while secretly using it to make fiends of the army. If what Miss Addams states is true, then the French Government is rotten, French officers deserve only court-martial, and French soldiers are cowards.

If we are to believe her, the Canadians at Ypres, the Australians in the Dardanelles, the English and the French on the Aisne made no supreme sacrifice, but were killed in a drunken brawl.

Miss Addams desires peace. So does every one else. But she will not attain peace by misrepresentation. I have seen more of this war and other wars than Miss Addams, and I know all war to be wicked, wasteful, and unintelligent, and where Miss Addams can furnish one argument in favor of peace I will furnish a hundred. But against this insult, flung by a complacent and self-satisfied woman at men who gave their lives for men, I protest. And I believe that with me are all those women and men who respect courage and honor.

RICHARD HARDING DAVIS.

The New York Times, July 13, 1915

Alan Seeger:
Diary, September 16–24, 1915, and to Elsie Simmons Seeger

Alan Seeger graduated from Harvard College in the remarkable class of 1910 that also produced T. S. Eliot, John Reed, and Walter Lippmann; and his life beyond Harvard Yard quickly became as artistic and bohemian and politically engaged as any of theirs. Trying his hand at poetry, he lived in Greenwich Village for the next two years and in Paris for two years after that. He enlisted in the French Foreign Legion in August 1914, along with fifty other Americans. By the fall he was serving in the trenches, and on December 8, he wrote to the *New York Sun*: "for the poor common soldier it is anything but romantic. His rôle is simply to dig himself a hole in the ground and to keep hidden in it as tightly as possible. Continually under the fire of the opposing batteries, he is yet never allowed to get a glimpse of the enemy. Exposed to all the dangers of war, but with none of its enthusiasms or splendid *élan*, he is condemned to sit like an animal in its burrow and hear the shells whistle over his head and take their little daily toll from his comrades." His first major battle experience came with the French offensive in Champagne, which began on September 25, 1915, as he had anticipated in his diary entries during the preceding days.

———————

Suippes, September 16.—Left Plancher-Bas for good, day before yesterday evening. The fine weather which had lasted without a break for several weeks came to an end, and the gray skies corresponded with the melancholy that many of us felt at breaking forever with associations that had grown so dear to us. Marched away after dark in the rain, our rifles decorated with bouquets and our *musettes* filled with presents from the good townspeople. The *Tirailleurs* and Zouaves, coming from the direction of Giromagny, preceded us. We entrained at Champagney, about 45 men in a car. Terrible discomfort. Impossible to stretch legs or lie out flat. Several fights; had a fight myself with the corporal. Found ourselves next morning at Vesoul and from there followed the same route as on coming, that is, up through Langres, Chaumont, Vitry-le-François, to Châlons. We had been hearing for some time of the big concentration of troops at the Camp de Châlons and were not surprised when we turned north and stopped at the way station of St.-Hilaire. Everything bore testimony of the big offensive in preparation, troops cantonned in the villages, the railroad lines congested with trains of cannon and material, but most sinister and significant, the newly constructed evacuation sheds for the wounded, each one labelled "*blessés assis*" or "*blessés couchés.*" Violent cannonade as we disembarked.

Marched seven or eight kilometers up a national road and then made a *grande halte* at sundown for soup. Pleasant country that we marched through, the *Champagne pouilleuse* with its broad plains and vast distances. The good weather had come back and the waxing moon hung in the south. After the *grande halte* we resumed the march at ten o'clock. Everyone in good spirits and full of excitement at the prospect of the big action in preparation that everything bore evidence of. Heavy cannonading continued during the entire march and the northern skies were lit up continually with the German *fusées*. During our last *pose*, just before entering Suippes, several heavy German shells fell into the town with terrific explosions. The flashes of the cannon lit up all the sky like summer lightning. Marched into the dark, silent town about two o'clock in the morning. The civils apparently have all been evacuated. Marched on and bivouacked in an open field beyond the town. Slept well on the ground.

This morning we moved up here into a big grove and pitched tents, the first time we have done this on the front. Do not know whether we are to go up to the trenches or wait here until we go into action. The *2me Etranger* ought certainly to be first. It is going to be a grandiose affair and the cannonade will doubtless be a thing beyond imagination. The attack this time will probably be along a broad front. Our immediate object ought to be Vouziers and the line of the Aisne, but it is probably the object of the *Etat-Major* to expel the Germans from Northern France entirely. They are fortunate who have lasted to see this, and I thrill at the certain prospect of being in the thick of it.

September 18.—Took pick and shovel yesterday evening and marched up to the front—the whole regiment—where we worked all night. Our road lay again through dark and silent Suippes, where the moonlight, less covered tonight, revealed the heaps of ruins—rent walls, shells of burnt-out buildings, and a whole quarter completely razed by the fire the Germans must have started before evacuating the town a year ago. Took the Vouziers road northward toward the trenches, where the sky was lit continually with the *fusées éclairantes* and the flash of the cannon. At one time during our first *pose* there must have been an attack of some sort, for the German rockets began popping up like "flower pots" of our Fourth of Julys, and the cannon flashes redoubled, but we could hear no fusillade for the continual rumble of traffic on the highroad beside us.

Turned off a side road after a while in the direction of Perthes-les-Hurlus. Climbed a long, gradual ascent. Our batteries fired occasionally close at hand. During last *pose* a half dozen heavy German shells—probably 210s—fell near a battery emplacement near us with the most terrific explosion, the singing shell-fragments falling among us. Walked through the pine groves at the summit of the crest and then came out through a deep-cut *boyau* to a magnificent spectacle. The position here is a valuable one that must once have been fiercely disputed, for it dominates all the low rolling country to the north. Here, illuminated by the German *fusées* that shot up continually from their trenches a mile or so off, lay the vast battlefield that in a few days is to see one of the most tremendous actions ever fought. The clouds had blown off, the stars were all out, the night was a glorious one. We formed a long file, one man with a pick and one with a shovel at five yard intervals down the open northern slope and started digging an immense *boyau* to rush troops up through for the attack. Worked all night, then marched back and arrived at bivouac at dawn. A fatiguing night but can sleep late and rest all day.

September 19.—Went up and worked again last night. Beautiful starry night; bright moonlight. A pleasure walking up, but the work was tiring and the road long. A violent artillery duel. Our advanced batteries of heavy guns fired continually. The Germans replied less frequently, but when their heavy shells fell by twos and fours the explosions were terrific beyond anything I have heard before on the front. They covered the lines with smoke, through which the *fusées* glimmered, blurred and reddened. The smell of powder was heavy in the air. It was daybreak when we returned. . . .

Today at *rapport* the captain read the order from Joffre announcing to the troops the great general attack. The company drew close around him, and he spoke to us of our reasons for confidence in success and a victory that would drive the enemy definitely out of France. The German positions are to be overwhelmed with a hurricane of artillery fire and then great assaults will be delivered all along the line. The chances for success are good. It will be a battle without precedent in history.

September 21.—About twenty heavy shells fell yesterday evening around the Suippes station, which is right near the park where we are bivouacking. Went out to watch them burst; no serious damage. Went up to work after supper. The dead and wounded were being carried in litters through the streets of Suippes, which had been bombarded, too. The fine weather is continuing, and it was a beautiful moonlit night, but frosty. Hard work until two o'clock digging communication ditches. Officers went down to the trenches to reconnoitre the *terrain.* The captain spoke to us again at *rapport* today, and gave us his impressions of this visit. The Colonials apparently are to lead the attack; we ought to come in the third or fourth wave. Our objective is the Ferme de Navarin, about 3½ kilometers behind the German lines. Here we will halt to reform, while the entire 8th Corps, including numerous cavalry, will pass through the breach we have made. These will be sublime moments; there are good chances of success and even of success without serious losses.

September 22.—The day ought to be near at hand. The artillery is becoming more and more violent and tonight as I write here by candlelight in our tent the cannonade is extremely violent down the line toward Reims. The Germans continue to bombard Suippes and the Suippes station. Luckily they have not discovered our bivouac, for the French keep continual patrols in the air and no German aeroplane dares to come over here. Should they bombard us here the execution of these terrific 210 shells would be appalling. Today several fell in the park, not more than fifty yards from the tent. I thought they were going to bother us, but these were really bad shots at the station that had gone astray. Spend a hard night at work yesterday, leaving here at 6 P.M. and not getting back till 6 this morning. This afternoon walked to Somme-Suippe to try and buy something, but there is nothing to be had. The fine weather continues. We have received steel casques in place of the *képis.*

September 23.—Bombardment of the station resumed this morning. Went out to the gate to watch the shells burst. The men of the *génie* "beat it" as usual into the fields near by, but a few nervy ones remained to take the little Décauville engines and a trainload of shells out of danger. When the bombardment seemed over I noticed them all running back and commencing digging. Went over and joined them and helped disinter three men who had been buried alive. They had taken refuge in a deep trench that had been dug for the purpose. But a big shell had fallen right beside this trench and covered the unfortunate men with dirt. We dug and dug and finally came upon a piece of cloth. With difficulty we uncovered one after another and pulled them out, but it was too late. They had been smothered to death. . . . Wild rumors are reaching us of victories on other parts of the line. It is said the French have taken the plateau of Craonne and that the English are at Lille.

September 24.—We are to attack tomorrow morning. Gave in our blankets this morning; they are to be carried on the wagons. Also made bundles, in order to lighten the sack of all unnecessary articles, including the second pair of shoes. We are admirably equipped, and if we do not succeed it will not be the fault of those responsible for supplying us. A terrific cannonade has been going on all night and is continuing. It will grow in violence until the attack is launched, when we ought to find at least the first enemy line completely demolished. What have

they got up their sleeves for us? Where shall we find the strongest resistance? I am very confident and sanguine about the
result and expect to march right up to the Aisne, borne on in
an irresistible *élan*. I have been waiting for this moment for
more than a year. It will be the greatest moment in my life. I
shall take good care to live up to it.

To Elsie Simmons Seeger

October 25, 1915.

The regiment is back in *repos* after the battle in Champagne,
in which we took part from the beginning, the morning of the
memorable 25th September. We are billeted in a pleasant little
village not far from Compiègne, quite out of hearing of the cannon. It seems that absurd rumors were current about the fate
of Americans in the Legion, so I hasten to let you know that I
am all right. Quite a few Americans were wounded, but none
killed, to my knowledge.

The part we played in the battle is briefly as follows. We
broke camp about 11 o'clock the night of the 24th, and
marched up through ruined Souain to our place in one of the
numerous *boyaux* where the *troupes d'attaque* were massed.
The cannonade was pretty violent all that night, as it had been
for several days previous, but toward dawn it reached an intensity unimaginable to anyone who has not seen a modern battle.
A little before 9.15 the fire lessened suddenly and the crackle of
the fusillade between the reports of the cannon told us that
the first wave of assault had left and the attack begun. At the
same time we received the order to advance. The German artillery had now begun to open upon us in earnest. Amid the
most infernal roar of every kind of fire-arms and through an
atmosphere heavy with dust and smoke, we marched up
through the *boyaux* to the *tranchées de départ*. At shallow
places and over breaches that shells had made in the bank we
caught momentary glimpses of the blue lines sweeping up
the hillside or silhouetted on the crest where they poured into
the German trenches. When the last wave of the Colonial brigade had left, we followed. *Baïonnette au canon*, in lines of
tirailleurs, we crossed the open space between the lines, over

the barbed wire, where not so many of our men were lying as I had feared (thanks to the efficacy of the bombardment) and over the German trench, knocked to pieces and filled with their dead. In some places they still resisted in isolated groups. Opposite us, all was over, and the herds of prisoners were being already led down as we went up. We cheered, more in triumph than in hate, but the poor devils, terror-stricken, held up their hands, begged for their lives, cried "Kamerad," "Bon Français," even "Vive la France." We advanced and lay down in columns by two behind the second crest. Meanwhile, bridges had been thrown across trenches and *boyaux*, and the artillery, leaving the emplacements where they had been anchored a whole year, came across and took position in the open, a magnificent spectacle. Squadrons of cavalry came up. Suddenly the long, unpicturesque *guerre de tranchées* was at an end and the field really presented the aspect of the familiar battle pictures— the battalions in manœuvre, the officers, superbly indifferent to danger, galloping about on their chargers. But now the German guns, moved back, began to get our range and the shells to burst over and around batteries and troops, many with admirable precision. Here my best comrade was struck down by shrapnel at my side—painfully but not mortally wounded.

I often envied him after that. For now our advanced troops were in contact with the German second-line defenses, and these proved to be of a character so formidable that all further advance without a preliminary artillery preparation was out of the question. And our rôle, that of troops in reserve, was to lie passive in an open field under a shell fire that every hour became more terrific, while aeroplanes and captive balloons, to which we were entirely exposed, regulated the fire.

That night we spent in the rain. With portable picks and shovels each man dug himself in as well as possible. The next day our concentrated artillery again began the bombardment, and again the fusillade announced the entrance of the infantry into action. But this time only the wounded appeared coming back, no prisoners. I went out and gave water to one of these, eager to get news. It was a young soldier, wounded in the hand. His face and voice bespoke the emotion of the experience he had been through in a way that I will never forget.

"*Ah, les salauds!*" he cried, "They let us come right up to the barbed wire without firing. Then a hail of grenades and balls. My comrade fell, shot through the leg, got up, and the next moment had his head taken off by a grenade before my eyes." "And the barbed wire, wasn't it cut down by the bombardment?" "Not at all in front of us." I congratulated him on having a *blessure heureuse* and being well out of the affair. But he thought only of his comrade and went on down the road toward Souain, nursing his mangled hand, with the stream of wounded seeking their *postes de secours*.

The afternoon of the 28th should have been our turn. We had spent four days under an almost continual bombardment. The regiment had been decimated, though many of us had not fired a shot. After four such days as I hope never to repeat, under the strain of sitting inactive, listening to the slow whistle of 210-millimetre shells as they arrived and burst more or less in one's proximity, it was a real relief to put *sac au dos* and go forward. We marched along in columns by two, behind a crest, then over and across an exposed space under the fire of their 77's, that cost us some men, and took formation to attack on the border of a wood, somewhere behind which they were entrenched. And here we had a piece of luck. For our colonel, a soldier of the old school, stronger for honor than expediency, had been wounded in the first days of the action. Had he been in command, we all think that we should have been sent into the wood (and we would have gone with *élan*) notwithstanding that the 1*er Etranger* had just attacked gallantly but unsuccessfully and had been badly cut up. The commandant of our battalion, who had succeeded him in command, when he heard, after a reconnaissance, that the wire had not been sufficiently cut, refused to risk his regiment. So you have him to thank.

The last days of the week we went up into first line to relieve the tired *troupes d'attaque*. It was an abandoned German artillery position, full of souvenirs of the recent occupants and of testimony to their hasty departure. They did not counterattack on this sector and we finished this first period in comparative tranquillity.

Then two days *repos* in the rear and we came back to the battle field. The attack of the 6th October netted us some substantial gains but not enough to call into action the *troupes de poursuite* among which we were numbered. It became more and more evident that the German second line of defense presented obstacles too serious to attempt overcoming for the moment, and we began going up at night to work at consolidating our advanced trenches and turning them into a new permanent line. We spent two weeks on the front this time. But as luck would have it, the bombardment that thundered continually during this period did not fall very heavily on the wood where we were sheltered and we did not suffer seriously in comparison with the first days.

And now we are back in the far rear again, the battle is over, and in the peace of our little village we can sum up the results of the big offensive in which we took part. No one denies that they are disappointing. For we know, who heard and cheered the order of Joffre to the army before the battle, that it was not merely a fight for a position, but a supreme effort to pierce the German line and liberate the invaded country; we know the immense preparation for the attack, what confidence our officers had in its success, and what enthusiasm ourselves. True, we broke their first line along a wide front, advanced on an average of three or four kilometers, took numerous prisoners and cannon. It was a satisfaction at last to get out of the trenches, to meet the enemy face to face, and to see German arrogance turned into suppliance. We knew many splendid moments, worth having endured many trials for. But in our larger aim, of piercing their line, of breaking the long deadlock, of entering Vouziers in triumph, of course we failed.

This check, in conjunction with the serious turn that affairs have taken in the Balkans, makes the present hour a rather grave one for us. Yet it cannot be said to be worse than certain moments that arrived even much later in the course of our Civil War, when things looked just as critical for the North, though in the end of a similar *guerre d'usure* they pulled out victorious.

But perhaps you will understand me when I say that the matter of being on the winning side has never weighed with me in comparison with that of being on the side where my sympathies lie. This affair only deepened my admiration for, my loyalty to, the French. If we did not entirely succeed, it was not the fault of the French soldier. He is a better man, man for man, than the German. Any one who had seen the charge of the Marsouins at Souain would acknowledge it. Never was anything more magnificent. I remember a captain, badly wounded in the leg, as he passed us, borne back on a litter by four German prisoners. He asked us what regiment we were, and when we told him, he cried "Vive la Légion," and kept repeating "Nous les avons eus. Nous les avons eus." He was suffering, but oblivious of his wound, was still fired with the enthusiasm of the assault and all radiant with victory. What a contrast with the German wounded, on whose faces was nothing but terror and despair. What is the stimulus in their slogans of "Gott mit uns" and "für König und Vaterland" beside that of men really fighting in defense of their country? Whatever be the force in international conflicts of having justice and all the principles of personal morality on one's side, it at least gives the French soldier a strength that's like the strength of ten against an adversary whose weapon is only brute violence. It is inconceivable that a Frenchman, forced to yield, could behave as I saw German prisoners behave, trembling, on their knees, for all the world like criminals at length overpowered and brought to justice. Such men have to be driven to the assault, or intoxicated. But the Frenchman who goes up is possessed with a passion beside which any of the other forms of experience that are reckoned to make life worth while seem pale in comparison. The modern prototype of those whom history has handed down to the admiration of all who love liberty and heroism in its defense, it is a privilege to march at his side—so much so that nothing the world could give could make me wish myself anywhere else than where I am.

Most of the other Americans have taken advantage of the permission to pass into a regular French regiment. There is much to be said for their decision, but I have remained true to the Legion, where I am content and have good comrades. I have a pride particularly in the Moroccan division, whereof we are the first brigade. Those who march with the Zouaves and the Algerian *tirailleurs* are sure to be where there is most honor. We are *troupes d'attaque* now, and so will assist at all the big *coups*, but be spared the monotony of long periods of inactive guard in the trenches, such as we passed last winter.

I am glad to hear that Thwing has joined the English. I used to know him at Harvard. He refused to be content, no doubt, with lesser emotions while there are hours to be lived such as are being lived now by young men in Flanders and Champagne. It is all to his credit. There should really be no neutrals in a conflict like this, where there is not a people whose interests are not involved. To neutrals who have stomached what America has consented to stomach from Germany—whose ideals are so opposite to hers—who in the event of a German victory would be so inevitably embroiled, the question he put to himself and so resolutely answered will become more and more pertinent.

James Norman Hall: Damaged Trenches

Fighting in Champagne lasted until November 6. Although the French advanced 2.5 miles in places, they failed to break through the German defenses and lost 143,000 men killed, wounded, or missing in the effort; German losses totaled 85,000. At the same time, the British launched their largest offensive to date, at Loos in the Artois; but they could not break through the German defenses either. In just three weeks of fighting there, 50,000 British soldiers were killed or wounded or went missing. Among those who survived was a pretender of sorts: James Norman Hall, a 1910 graduate of Grinnell College from Colfax, Iowa. He had worked in Boston as an agent for the Society for the Prevention of Cruelty to Children before vacationing in Britain in the summer of 1914. Swept away by the "spirit of adventure," Hall claimed to be Canadian so that he could enlist in the British army that August. Trained as a machine gunner, he served with the 9th Royal Fusiliers at Loos before being discharged in December 1915, when his true nationality was revealed. He returned to the United States, published his memoir, *Kitchener's Mob: The Adventures of an American in the British Army*, and then went back to France, where he would fly in the Lafayette Escadrille.

THE BRIEF RESPITE which we enjoyed during our first night soon came to an end. We were given time, however, to make our trenches tenable. Early the following morning we set to work removing the wreckage of human bodies. Never before had death revealed itself so terribly to us. Many of the men had been literally blown to pieces, and it was necessary to gather the fragments in blankets. For weeks afterward we had to eat and sleep and work and think among such awful sights. We became hardened to them finally. It was absolutely essential that we should.

The trenches and dugouts had been battered to pieces by the British artillery fire before the infantry assault, and since their capture the work of destruction had been carried on by the German gunners. Even in their wrecked condition we could see how skillfully they had been constructed. No labor had been spared in making them as nearly shell-proof and as comfortable for living quarters as it is possible for such earth-works to be. The ground here was unusually favorable. Under a clayish surface soil, there was a stratum of solid chalk. Advantage of this had been taken by the German engineers who must have planned and supervised the work. Many of the shell-proof dugouts were fifteen and even twenty feet below the surface of the ground. Entrance to these was made in the front wall of the trench on a level with the floor. Stairways just large enough to permit the passage of a man's body led down to them. The roofs were reinforced with heavy timbers. They were so strongly built throughout that most of them were intact, although the passageways leading up to the trench were choked with loose earth.

There were larger surface dugouts with floors but slightly lower than that of the trench. These were evidently built for living quarters in times of comparative quiet. Many of them were six feet wide and from twenty to thirty feet long, and quite palaces compared to the wretched little "funk-holes" to which we had been accustomed. They were roofed with logs a foot or more in diameter placed close together and one on top of the other in tiers of three, with a covering of earth three or four feet thick. But although they were solidly built they had not been proof against the rain of high explosives. Many of them were in ruins, the logs splintered like kindling wood and strewn far and wide over the ground.

We found several dugouts, evidently officers' quarters, which were almost luxuriously furnished. There were rugs for the wooden floors and pictures and mirrors for the walls; and in each of them there was the jolliest little stove with a removable lid. We discovered one of these underground palaces at the end of a blind alley leading off from the main trench. It was at least fifteen feet underground, with two stairways leading down to it, so that if escape was cut off in one direction, it was still possible to get out on the other side. We immediately took possession, built a roaring fire, and were soon passing canteens of hot tea around the circle. Life was worth while again. We all agreed that there were less comfortable places in which to have breakfast on rainy autumn mornings than German officers' dugouts.

The haste with which the Germans abandoned their trenches was evidenced by the amount of war material which they left behind. We found two machine guns and a great deal of small-arms ammunition in our own limited sector of frontage. Rifles, intrenching tools, haversacks, canteens, greatcoats, bayonets were scattered everywhere. All of this material was of the very best. Canteens, water-bottles, and small frying-pans were made of aluminum and most ingeniously fashioned to make them less bulky for carrying. Some of the bayonets were saw-edged. We found three of these needlessly cruel weapons in a dugout which bore the following inscription over the door:—

"Gott tret' herein. Bring' glück herein."

It was an interesting commentary on German character. Tommy Atkins never writes inscriptions of a religious nature over the doorway of his splinter-roof shelter. Neither does he file a saw edge on his bayonet.

We found many letters, picture post-cards, and newspapers; among the latter, one called the "Krieg-Zeitung," published at Lille for the soldiers in the field, and filled with glowing accounts of battles fought by the ever victorious German armies.

Death comes swiftly in war. One's life hangs by a thread. The most trivial circumstance saves or destroys. Mac came into the half-ruined dugout where the off-duty machine gunners were making tea over a fire of splintered logs.

"Jamie," he said, "take my place at sentry for a few minutes, will you? I've lost my water-bottle. It's 'ere in the dugout somew'ere. I'll be only a minute."

I went out to the gun position a few yards away, and immediately afterward the Germans began a bombardment of our line. One's ear becomes exact in distinguishing the size of shells by the sound which they make in traveling through the air; and it is possible to judge the direction and the probable place of their fall. Two of us stood by the machine gun. We heard at the same time the sound which we knew meant danger, possibly death. It was the awful whistling roar of a high explosive. We dropped to the floor of the trench at once. The explosion blackened our faces with lyddite and half-blinded us. The dugout which I had left less than a moment ago was a mass of wreckage. Seven of our comrades were inside.

One of them crawled out, pulling himself along with one arm. The other arm was terribly crushed and one leg was hanging by a tendon and a few shreds of flesh.

"My God, boys! Look wot they did to me!"

He kept saying it over and over while we cut the cords from our bandoliers, tied them about his leg and arm and twisted them up to stop the flow of blood. He was a fine, healthy lad. A moment before he had been telling us what he was going to do when we went home on furlough. Now his face was the color of ashes, his voice grew weaker and weaker, and he died while we were working over him.

High explosive shells were bursting all along the line. Great masses of earth and chalk were blown in on top of men seeking protection where there was none. The ground rocked like so much pasteboard. I heard frantic cries for "Picks and shovels!" "Stretcher-bearers! Stretcher-bearers this way, for God's sake!" The voices sounded as weak and futile as the squeaking of rats in a thunderstorm.

When the bombardment began, all off-duty men were ordered into the deepest of the shell-proof dugouts, where they were really quite safe. But those English lads were not cowards. Orders or no orders, they came out to the rescue of their comrades. They worked without a thought of their own danger. I felt actually happy, for I was witnessing splendid heroic things. It was an experience which gave one a new and unshakable faith in his fellows.

The sergeant and I rushed into the ruins of our machine-gun dugout. The roof still held in one place. There we found Mac, his head split in two as though it had been done with an axe. Gardner's head was blown completely off, and his body was so terribly mangled that we did not know until later who he was. Preston was lying on his back with a great jagged, blood-stained hole through his tunic. Bert Powel was so badly hurt that we exhausted our supply of field dressings in bandaging him. We found little Charlie Harrison lying close to the side of the wall, gazing at his crushed foot with a look of incredulity and horror pitiful to see. One of the men gave him first aid with all the deftness and tenderness of a woman.

The rest of us dug hurriedly into a great heap of earth at the other end of the shelter. We quickly uncovered Walter, a lad who had kept us laughing at his drollery on many a rainy night. The earth had been heaped loosely on him and he was still conscious.

"Good old boys," he said weakly; "I was about done for."

In our haste we dislodged another heap of earth which completely buried him again, and it seemed a lifetime before we were able to remove it. I have never seen a finer display of pure grit than Walter's.

"Easy now!" he said. "Can't feel anything below me waist. I think I'm 'urt down there."

We worked as swiftly and as carefully as we could. We knew that he was badly wounded, for the earth was soaked with blood; but when we saw, we turned away sick with horror. Fortunately, he lost consciousness while we were trying to disentangle him from the fallen timbers, and he died on the way to the field dressing-station. Of the seven lads in the dug-out, three were killed outright, three died within half an hour, and one escaped with a crushed foot which had to be amputated at the field hospital.

What had happened to our little group was happening to others along the entire line. Americans may have read of the bombardment which took place that autumn morning. The dispatches, I believe, described it with the usual official brevity, giving all the information really necessary from the point of view of the general public.

"Along the Loos–La Bassée sector there was a lively artillery action. We demolished some earthworks in the vicinity of Hulluch. Some of our trenches near Hill 70 were damaged."

"Damaged!" It was a guarded admission. Our line was a shambles of loose earth and splintered logs. At some places it was difficult to see just where the trench had been. Had the Germans launched a counter-attack immediately after the bombardment, we should have had difficulty in holding the position. But it was only what Tommy called "a big 'ap'orth o' 'ate." No attempt was made to follow up the advantage, and we at once set to work rebuilding. The loose earth had to be put into sandbags, the parapets mended, the holes, blasted out by shells, filled in.

The worst of it was that we could not get away from the sight of the mangled bodies of our comrades. Arms and legs stuck out of the wreckage, and on every side we saw distorted human faces, the faces of men we had known, with whom we had lived and shared hardships and dangers for months past. Those who have never lived through experiences of this sort cannot possibly know the horror of them. It is not in the heat of battle that men lose their reason. Battle frenzy is, perhaps, a temporary madness. The real danger comes when the strain is relaxed. Men look about them and see the bodies of their comrades torn to pieces as though they had been hacked and butchered by fiends. One thinks of the human body as inviolate, a beautiful and sacred thing. The sight of it dismembered or disemboweled, trampled in the bottom of a trench, smeared with blood and filth, is so revolting as to be hardly endurable.

And yet, we had to endure it. We could not escape it. Whichever way we looked, there were the dead. Worse even than the sight of dead men were the groans and entreaties of those lying wounded in the trenches waiting to be taken back to the dressing-stations.

"I'm shot through the stomach, matey! Can't you get me back to the ambulance? Ain't they *some* way you can get me back out o' this?"

"Stick it, old lad! You won't 'ave long to wite. They'll be some of the Red Cross along 'ere in a jiffy now."

"Give me a lift, boys, can't you? Look at my leg! Do you think it'll 'ave to come off? Maybe they could save it if I could get to 'ospital in time! Won't some of you give me a lift? I can 'obble along with a little 'elp."

"Don't you fret, sonny! You're a-go'n' to ride back in a stretcher presently. Keep yer courage up a little w'ile longer."

Some of the men, in their suffering, forgot every one but themselves, and it was not strange that they should. Others, with more iron in their natures, endured fearful agony in silence. During memorable half-hours, filled with danger and death, many of my gross misjudgments of character were made clear to me. Men whom no one had credited with heroic qualities revealed them. Others failed rather pitiably to live up to one's expectations. It seemed to me that there was strength or weakness in men, quite apart from their real selves, for which they were in no way responsible; but doubtless it had always been there, waiting to be called forth at just such crucial times.

During the afternoon I heard for the first time the hysterical cry of a man whose nerve had given way. He picked up an arm and threw it far out in front of the trenches, shouting as he did so in a way that made one's blood run cold. Then he sat down and started crying and moaning. He was taken back to the rear, one of the saddest of casualties in a war of inconceivable horrors. I heard of many instances of nervous breakdown, but I witnessed surprisingly few of them. Men were often badly shaken and trembled from head to foot. Usually they pulled themselves together under the taunts of their less susceptible comrades.

From *Kitchener's Mob* (1916)

Henry Morgenthau to Robert Lansing

The genocide of the Armenians continued throughout 1915, as the Ottoman interior ministry organized mass deportations and the Committee of Union and Progress arranged for Kurdish tribesmen and criminal gangs to commit mass slaughter. In February 1916 Morgenthau returned to the United States on leave, only to resign his post to help raise funds for Armenian relief and to work on President Wilson's reelection campaign. As many as one million Armenians were estimated to have been killed or otherwise left to die from hunger and disease during the deportations of 1915–16. The Ottoman Empire would break relations with the United States in May 1917 after America declared war on Germany, but the United States never joined the Allies in their war against the Ottomans.

———————

AMERICAN EMBASSY
CONSTANTINOPLE

November 4, 1915
PRIVATE AND STRICTLY CONFIDENTIAL

My dear Mr. Lansing:

In compliance with your cable, I shall send you frequent confidential and personal letters concerning the general conditions here, and shall keep the copies, as requested, on my personal file, hoping that you will do the same in Washington, as their publication might affect my usefulness here. I take it for granted that you want me to write very frankly and unreservedly.

At the present time, conditions here are extremely precarious. The Sultan is absolutely powerless. He has to simply affix his signature to whatever Iradés are submitted to him. The Grand Vezier never exercised much power, and now that he has turned over his portfolio of Minister for Foreign Affairs to Halil, he has become merely ornamental. The real governing force in this country is in the hands of the Committee of the

Union and Progress Party, consisting of about forty members, of whom the following nine are the leading spirits: Dr. Nazim, Chairman of the Committee; Midhat Chukri, General Secretary; Talaat, Minister of Interior; Enver, Minister of War; Djemal, Minister of Marine and Commander-in-Chief of the 4th Army; Ayoub Sabri (now prisoner of war at Malta); Halil, Minister for Foreign Affairs; Hadji Adil Bey, President of the Chamber of Deputies; Beha-ed-din Chakir.

The real power is exercised by the entire forty or a majority thereof, which is changeable and therefore never definitely fixed. Whenever anyone of the men assumes too much authority, as has occurred several times recently, the majority combine against him and no matter how important his position may be, he is compelled to obey the orders of the Committee and abandon all efforts to become the supreme ruler. This is where their government distinctly differs from the Boss Rule in the United States, and it is intensely interesting to observe its development.

All the important and even some unimportant questions are submitted to this Committee for its consideration. The Committee has at present absolute control of the army, navy and civil government of the country. They have removed many governors of interior vilayets who would not obey their orders. They also completely control the Chamber of Deputies, whose members are absolutely selected by them and the people have no choice but to go through the formality of electing the candidates of the Committee. In the Senate the majority are independent of them, as Senatorship is a position for life and most senators were elected by Kiamil Pasha and appointed by Abdul Hamid in 1908. Recently, when Senator Ahmed Riza Bey, an ex-Union and Progress man, wanted to champion the cause of the Armenians and questioned their treatment and also wanted to interpellate the Cabinet on the question of the control of the sale and distribution of food supply and the title of "Conqueror" conferred upon the Sultan, I was informed that Talaat sent word to him that if he really wanted to benefit the Armenians, he had better stop his agitation; for, if he continued it, he, Talaat, would publish statements about the Armenians that would incite the Turkish population against them and they would thereupon fare worse than before. From other sources it is stated that the Cabinet promised to modify their attitude towards the Armenians if Ahmed Riza and his friends would agree not to interpellate the Government. This Ahmed Riza and his friends did.

The Committee of Union and Progress have very few actual followers among the people of the Empire. They have some adherents in Constantinople and Smyrna and a few other centers. They rule through the fact that they are in possession of most of the offices and the army, and are so exercising their power that they have frightened almost everyone into submission. They have reinstated the spy system so prevalent under Abdul Hamid. By their treatment of the Armenians, they have so cowed the people that they have succeeded for the time being in suppressing all opposition to them, and they are so determined to retain possession of the government, that they will not hesitate to use any means that will enable them to do so. The only members of the Cabinet, and I believe of the inner Committee, that had any decent standing or possessed of any property prior to the Revolution, were the Grand Vezier and perhaps Halil Bey. When I arrived here two years ago, only one of these nine was a member of Cabinet: that was Talaat. The Cabinet then had amongst its members Djavid Bey, a Deunmé, as Minister of Finance; Oscan Effendi, an Armenian, as Minister of Posts and Telegraphs; Mahmoud Pasha, a Circassian, as Minister of Marine; Bustany Effendi, a Christian Arab, as Minister of Commerce and Agriculture. But at the time Turkey entered the war a year ago, all these men resigned because they could not assent to the war, and the Union and Progress men themselves did not want in the Cabinet anyone except most faithful adherents of the Committee. There is no opposition party in existence. The press is carefully censored and must obey the wishes of the Union and Progress Party. The people have absolutely no part in the government and therefore their opinions and wishes are totally disregarded and only the good of the party is considered. They have gradually filled the various posts with the trusted and leading members of the Union and Progress Committee and are continually strengthening themselves. Last year Enver was made Minister of War, and a little later Djemal was made Minister of Marine; Talaat, besides being Minister of Interior, acted and is still

acting as Minister of Finance; Chukri, the Minister of Public
Instruction, took also charge of the Ministry of Posts and
Telegraphs after the resignation of Oscan; only last week Halil
was given the Ministry for Foreign Affairs and Hadji Adil, former General Secretary of the Committee and ex-Governor
General of Adrianople, was made President of the Chamber of
Deputies. It is expected here that shortly either Enver or Talaat
will be made Grand Vezier. It is a personal government and
not one of policy, but unfortunately no one of them has full
power, and as there are so many of them attempting to exercise
power, absolute confusion and anarchy is resulting therefrom.
The most glaring instance of this fact is Djemal Pasha, who at
the beginning of the war was Minister of Marine and now is
Commander of the 4th Army and has established himself as
absolute dictator in Palestine and Syria. Repeatedly, when I
have asked Enver to do something for me in that district, he
told me that he would recommend it to Djemal and if he had
no objection thereto, my request would be granted. I have
begged Enver several times to order it done, and he said that
he could not do so as military reasons might exist which would
justify Djemal to object thereto.

At present the clique in power feel that they have succeeded
in abrogating, without bloodshed or fighting, the Capitulations and thereby freed themselves from the control of the six
Powers; that they have been able with their own resources
(except five million pounds borrowed from Germany) to put
an army of over one million men into the field and to successfully defend themselves against the four big nations arrayed
against them. They claim with pride that they are the nation
that have shown that the English fleet was not unconquerable,
and that the Russians, who have for generations held the big
stick over them, are unable to carry out their threat to punish
them. They have devised a method by which they could put
this tremendous army into the field with practically no cash
expenditure. They pay some of their soldiers the ridiculous
sum of 20 cents a month, and even from that they deduct a
share for taxes etc., while others get neither pay nor food.
They have requisitioned, without paying for it, a great part of
the materials and articles that they required (and even things
they did not require) to dress and feed part of their army, and

thus demonstrated how to conduct a war almost without cost to the Government.

These men seven years ago were looked upon as a set of irresponsible revolutionists and adventurers, and have now usurped and maintain this tremendous power: you can therefore readily understand that they have become dizzy from success. From a desperate band playing a desperate game, they have become allies and friends of two of the important nations of the world and are convinced that they have been of greater service to their allies than their allies have been to them. They claim, and justly so, that they have compelled England and France to employ 500,000 troops to try and force the Dardanelles and to use a tremendous fleet, sacrifice numerous ships and spend millions of pounds worth of ammunition, all of which greatly diminished their power to defeat the Germans. They feel at present that they have successfully kept the great Powers at bay and are very proud of the achievement.

The oriental temperament and mode of thinking is so different from ours, that no one who has not lived here can understand them. Their absolute frankness (sometimes taking the form of impudence) about all their actions, no matter how brutal or criminal they may be, is at times surprising. They speak of their determination to destroy the Armenian race as though it were a perfectly justifiable action. A number of the leaders have told me that after the war if they have won, their faults and excesses will be forgotten; if they have lost, they will be destroyed no matter how kind or considerate they might have been towards their enemies. They admit that they have no friends and they do not expect any consideration except such as their position and strength will entitle them to. As a nation, both their hatreds and their friendships are merely superficial and change continually. They have been very much influenced by the Germans who have used them to create this tremendous diversion against the English and French, and who are still thinking and scheming to create uprisings of the Moslem populations in Egypt, India and Persia.

At the present moment, the authorities would be very glad to have this war end. They begin to realize that economically they have injured their country tremendously through these high handed, indiscriminate and mismanaged requisitions. They have destroyed the producing and earning power of their country. Thousands of farmers were deprived of all their animals. The authorities foolishly did not even leave them single pairs of cattle so that the farmers could have a beginning for new herds. They have drawn from the fields the male population and thereby destroyed their agricultural communities. They have annihilated or displaced at least two thirds of the Armenian population and thereby deprived themselves of a very intelligent and useful race. They have used the railroads almost exclusively for military purposes and the ordinary roads have become so unsafe that the little that has been produced cannot be brought to markets. All the products that used to be exported are at their places of production and selling at considerably less than their usual-prices; this particularly applies to tobacco, opium, silk and figs.

I have given you the conclusions first, as I would have done in a first interview with you, and am going to write you special letters on some of the different topics, such as the effects of the abrogation of the Capitulations; the present conduct of their courts of justice and the management of prisons; public debt and internal financial conditions; the educational institutions and the new regulations under which they will probably be compelled to administer them; the Armenian atrocities; the management of the sale of food, bread, meat and other foodstuffs; the diplomatic representatives here, their influence or lack of influence with the authorities; the evils resulting from an invisible and irresponsible government as now conducted here, etc. etc.

With my kindest personal regards, I remain,

Yours very sincerely,

Morgenthau

Theodore Roosevelt to William Castle, Jr.

Beneath his feelings toward the Germans for sinking the *Lusitania* seethed Roosevelt's contempt for Wilson, whose measured policy of diplomacy struck him as nothing more than dithering. The United States was unprepared for war, he maintained in speeches and articles, as he bugled for universal military training and the expansion of the army and navy. "Wilson is at heart an abject coward," Roosevelt wrote his son Kermit, "or else he has a heart so cold and selfish that he is entirely willing to sacrifice the honor and the interest of the country to his own political advancement." He railed to anybody he could, in this case to William Castle, Jr., the wealthy scion of Hawaiian landowners, who edited the *Harvard Graduates' Magazine* from 1915 until 1917.

Private

Oyster Bay, Long Island, N.Y.
November 13th, 1915

My dear Castle:

I am sending you a copy of the Metropolitan Magazine, in which I take up the question of the Hague Treaties and their obligations upon us. For your private information I will say that this article was submitted to Dr. James Brown Scott, probably the best authority on international law in this country, and approved by him. If the Hague Conventions don't represent international law, then there is no such thing as international law, and it is absurd to have Professors lecture on the subject.

Down at bottom, the case is perfectly simple. A number of nations, including our own, went into a joint and several agreement. Now either we meant something by that agreement or we did not. If the conduct of Germany toward Belgium is not a violation of that agreement, of course it is an absolute physical impossibility to violate it or to violate any other agreement. The question, therefore, is merely whether we meant something or did not mean something when we signed that Hague Convention. It has turned out that the Convention means absolutely nothing. Everything done at the two Hague Conferences, everything done at the Geneva Conventions and the like, all the things supposed to be provided for in the way of preventing barbarity in war, all have proved absolutely futile. They have proved futile because the one big neutral, the United States, and of course very naturally the smaller neutrals, have not ventured to take action of any kind to protest against the violation. If your friends of the Somerset Club and the Professor you quote are correct and this inaction is proper, then it was a peculiarly silly bit of meaningless hypocrisy to hold the conventions at all. If they are right in saying that no action was called for by us, then it was a sheer waste of money and a good deal worse than a waste of money, because we encouraged people to believe that there was some alternative to international wrongdoing, some way of taking effective steps against international wrong-doers. Of course, to my mind the people who take this stand are sinning against international righteousness and against the honor of this country and are aiding the powers of evil in peculiarly contemptible fashion; but, if they are right, then it can only be on the assumption that never again must this nation go into international agreements of any kind for the betterment of international conditions and the securing of the peace of justice.

To my mind the argument is not only nonsense but such a vicious absurdity that it is very hard for me to believe that it can now be accepted by people, excepting as an excuse to cover either timid or selfish avoidance of duty. A year and a half ago I did not believe anyone would have accepted the argument. Certainly the pacifists who now use it would not have accepted it. A year and a half ago the argument of these pacifists was that the Hague Conventions removed all necessity for preparedness on the part of nations, because they gave a chance for international public opinion to express itself, by whatever means were necessary, with such force that brutal wars of aggression and brutal international wrong-doing were things of the past.

According to my view, the attitude of these worthy people, such as those you mention, affords the clearest kind of proof that this nation has not and will not have anything but its own strength to protect it from international wrong-doing and that it must therefore fully prepare. If not only timid and selfish people but honest and high-minded people, unconsciously influenced by their own instinctive effort to avoid personal or national risk, can interpret the Hague Conventions as being entirely meaningless and not calling for any kind of action by the United States when most flagrantly broken, then it is perfectly clear that no conceivable international promise can be made, couched in any possible terms, which would not also be explained away as not binding by good people of similar type. Words must be taken in their ordinary sense, in the way in which they would appeal to ordinary people of common sense. It is exactly like that unspeakably base song so popular in peace-at-any-price circles, "I Didn't Raise My Boy To Be A Soldier." The creature who wrote this song has been explaining that by it he was endeavoring to attack German militarism and that it was meant to convert the hearts of all German women and other women living in military despotisms to make them somehow or other, by song or otherwise, in manner unspecified, forthwith procure the abandonment of militarism by the Kaiser and others. Of course, the song had not, and never could have, and never under any possible circumstances would have, and could not be imagined to have, any, even the smallest, effect on Germany or on any other militarist country. Its only possible effect and the only effect that any rational man writing it or singing it could have in view was in non-military nations, to help in the creation of a sentiment for shirking duty and for the avoidance of risk, which would tend to leave these peaceful, non-militaristic countries at the mercy of any aggressor.

In just the same way President Wilson's statement about "being too proud to fight" could have had and did have but one possible result, the furnishing of an excuse to the people in this country who were ignobly afraid of just war and the arousing of the heartiest contempt for us in foreign countries. Dave Goodrich has just come back from England; and he says that whenever he went to a music hall or any entertainment of the kind there, he had to brace himself for the fact that some comedian in the course of the entertainment would make some grinning allusion to "not being too proud to fight"; and it always brought down the house with laughter at the American people. No ballad-singer can do the cause of decency and humanity and the cause of his own country worse damage than securing popularity for such a song as "I Didn't Raise My Boy To Be A Soldier." No President could utter a more ignoble sentiment or one calculated to do more permanent harm to the country than the phrase about being "too proud to fight." Finally, no nominal friends of peace and righteousness, no nominal believers, or real but misguided and foolish believers, in justice and courage and decency and fair dealing, could possibly do more damage to the cause of international good faith and humanity than by championing the view, equally foolish and wicked, that when the United States signed the Hague Conventions it meant nothing and was justified in preserving neutrality "not only in deed but in thought" when with ruthless and brutal cynicism Germany violated these conventions and inflicted upon Belgium a far greater wrong than any civilized power has inflicted on any other since the close of the Napoleonic Wars.

Faithfully yours,
Theodore Roosevelt

William R. Castle, Jr. Esq.,
3 Gray's Hall,
Cambridge, Mass.

P.S. Wilson's note to England is both wicked and contemptible when his cowardice about the Lusitania has just resulted in the sinking of the Ancona and when he has supinely permitted the German activities which have resulted in the blowing up of our munition plants.

Emma Goldman:
Preparedness, the Road
to Universal Slaughter

By the fall of 1915, not only jingoists advocated preparedness. In a speech in New York City on November 4, President Wilson called for expanding the navy and enlisting 400,000 volunteers in a reserve army. "All Europe is embattled," he said. "Force everywhere speaks out with a loud and imperious voice," requiring the United States "to be prepared, not for war, but only for defense." Strong opposition persisted, particularly from Emma Goldman, an immigrant from Lithuania who had lived in New York since 1885. Goldman lectured and wrote in favor of anarchism, socialism, free speech, free love, and birth control; and she took her stand against preparedness in the December 1915 number of *Mother Earth*, the magazine she had founded in 1906.

EVER SINCE the beginning of the European conflagration, the whole human race almost has fallen into the deathly grip of the war anesthesis, overcome by the mad teaming fumes of a blood soaked chloroform, which has obscured its vision and paralyzed its heart. Indeed, with the exception of some savage tribes, who know nothing of Christian religion or of brotherly love, and who also know nothing of dreadnaughts, submarines, munition manufacture and war loans, the rest of the race is under this terrible narcosis. The human mind seems to be conscious of but one thing, murderous speculation. Our whole civilization, our entire culture is concentrated in the mad demand for the most perfected weapons of slaughter.

Ammunition! Ammunition! O, Lord, thou who rulest heaven and earth, thou God of love, of mercy and of justice, provide us with enough ammunition to destroy our enemy. Such is the prayer which is ascending daily to the Christian heaven. Just like cattle, panic-stricken in the face of fire, throw themselves into the very flames, so all of the European people

217

have fallen over each other into the devouring flames of the furies of war, and America, pushed to the very brink by unscrupulous politicians, by ranting demagogues, and by military sharks, is preparing for the same terrible feat.

In the face of this approaching disaster, it behooves men and women not yet overcome by the war madness to raise their voice of protest, to call the attention of the people to the crime and outrage which are about to be perpetrated upon them.

America is essentially the melting pot. No national unit composing it, is in a position to boast of superior race purity, particular historic mission, or higher culture. Yet the jingoes and war speculators are filling the air with the sentimental slogan of hypocritical nationalism, "America for Americans," "America first, last, and all the time." This cry has caught the popular fancy from one end of the country to another. In order to maintain America, military preparedness must be engaged in at once. A billion dollars of the people's sweat and blood is to be expended for dreadnaughts and submarines for the army and the navy, all to protect this precious America.

The pathos of it all is that the America which is to be protected by a huge military force is not the America of the people, but that of the privileged class; the class which robs and exploits the masses, and controls their lives from the cradle to the grave. No less pathetic is it that so few people realize that preparedness never leads to peace, but that it is indeed the road to universal slaughter.

With the cunning methods used by the scheming diplomats and military cliques of Germany to saddle the masses with Prussian militarism, the American military ring with its Roosevelts, its Garrisons, its Daniels, and lastly its Wilsons, are moving the very heavens to place the militaristic heel upon the necks of the American people, and, if successful, will hurl America into the storm of blood and tears now devastating the countries of Europe.

Forty years ago Germany proclaimed the slogan: "Germany above everything. Germany for the Germans, first, last and always. We want peace; therefore we must prepare for war. Only a well armed and thoroughly prepared nation can maintain peace, can command respect, can be sure of its national integrity." And Germany continued to prepare, thereby forcing the other nations to do the same. The terrible European war is only the culminating fruition of the hydra-headed gospel, military preparedness.

Since the war began, miles of paper and oceans of ink have been used to prove the barbarity, the cruelty, the oppression of Prussian militarism. Conservatives and radicals alike are giving their support to the Allies for no other reason than to help crush that militarism, in the presence of which, they say, there can be no peace or progress in Europe. But though America grows fat on the manufacture of munitions and war loans to the Allies to help crush Prussians the same cry is now being raised in America which, if carried into national action, would build up an American militarism far more terrible than German or Prussian militarism could ever be, and that because nowhere in the world has capitalism become so brazen in its greed and nowhere is the state so ready to kneel at the feet of capital.

Like a plague, the mad spirit is sweeping the country, infesting the clearest heads and staunchest hearts with the deathly germ of militarism. National security leagues, with cannon as their emblem of protection, naval leagues with women in their lead have sprung up all over the country, women who boast of representing the gentler sex, women who in pain and danger bring forth life and yet are ready to dedicate it to the Moloch War. Americanization societies with well known liberals as members, they who but yesterday decried the patriotic clap-trap of to-day, are now lending themselves to befog the minds of the people and to help build up the same destructive institutions in America which they are directly and indirectly helping to pull down in Germany—militarism, the destroyer of youth, the raper of women, the annihilator of the best in the race, the very mower of life.

Even Woodrow Wilson, who not so long ago indulged in the phrase "A nation too proud to fight," who in the beginning of the war ordered prayers for peace, who in his proclamations spoke of the necessity of watchful waiting, even he has been whipped into line. He has now joined his worthy colleagues in the jingo movement, echoing their clamor for preparedness and their howl of "America for Americans." The difference between Wilson and Roosevelt is this: Roosevelt, a born bully, uses the club; Wilson, the historian, the college professor, wears the smooth polished university mask, but underneath it he, like Roosevelt, has but one aim, to serve the big interests, to add to those who are growing phenomenally rich by the manufacture of military supplies.

Woodrow Wilson, in his address before the Daughters of the American Revolution, gave his case away when he said, "I would rather be beaten than ostracized." To stand out against the Bethlehem, du Pont, Baldwin, Remington, Winchester metallic cartridges and the rest of the armament ring means political ostracism and death. Wilson knows that; therefore he betrays his original position, goes back on the bombast of "too proud to fight" and howls as loudly as any other cheap politician for preparedness and national glory, the silly pledge the navy league women intend to impose upon every school child: "I pledge myself to do all in my power to further the interests of my country, to uphold its institutions and to maintain the honor of its name and its flag. As I owe everything in life to my country, I consecrate my heart, mind and body to its service and promise to work for its advancement and security in times of peace and to shrink from no sacrifices or privation in its cause should I be called upon to act in its defence for the freedom, peace and happiness of our people."

To uphold the institutions of our country—that's it—the institutions which protect and sustain a handful of people in the robbery and plunder of the masses, the institutions which drain the blood of the native as well as of the foreigner, and turn it into wealth and power; the institutions which rob the alien of whatever originality he brings with him and in return gives him cheap Americanism, whose glory consists in mediocrity and arrogance.

The very proclaimers of "America first" have long before this betrayed the fundamental principles of real Americanism, of the kind of Americanism that Jefferson had in mind when he said that the best government is that which governs least; the kind of America that David Thoreau worked for when he proclaimed that the best government is the one that doesn't govern at all; or the other truly great Americans who aimed to make of this country a haven of refuge, who hoped that all the disinherited and oppressed people in coming to these shores would give character, quality and meaning to the country. That is not the America of the politician and munition speculators. Their America is powerfully portrayed in the idea of a young New York Sculptor; a hard cruel hand with long, lean, merciless fingers, crushing in over the heart of the immigrant, squeezing out its blood in order to coin dollars out of it and give the foreigner instead blighted hopes and stulted aspirations.

No doubt Woodrow Wilson has reason to defend these institutions. But what an ideal to hold out to the young generation! How is a military drilled and trained people to defend freedom, peace and happiness? This is what Major General O'Ryan has to say of an efficiently trained generation: "The soldier must be so trained that he becomes a mere automation; he must be so trained that it will destroy his initiative; he must be so trained that he is turned into a machine. The soldier must be forced into the military noose; he must be jacked up; he must be ruled by his superiors with pistol in hand."

This was not said by a Prussian Junker; not by a German barbarian; not by Treitschke or Bernhardi, but by an American Major General. And he is right. You cannot conduct war with equals; you cannot have militarism with free born men; you must have slaves, automatons, machines, obedient disciplined creatures, who will move, act, shoot and kill at the command of their superiors. That is preparedness, and nothing else.

It has been reported that among the speakers before the Navy League was Samuel Gompers. If that is true, it signalizes the greatest outrage upon labor at the hands of its own leaders. Preparedness is not directed only against the external enemy; it aims much more at the internal enemy. It concerns that element of labor which has learned not to hope for anything from our institutions, that awakened part of the working people which has realized that the war of classes underlies all wars among nations, and that if war is justified at all it is the war against economic dependence and political slavery, the two dominant issues involved in the struggle of the classes.

Already militarism has been acting its bloody part in every economic conflict, with the approval and support of the state.

Where was the protest of Washington when "our men, women and children" were killed in Ludlow? Where was that high sounding outraged protest contained in the note to Germany? Or is there any difference in killing "our men, women and children" in Ludlow or on the high seas? Yes, indeed. The men, women and children at Ludlow were working people, belonging to the disinherited of the earth, foreigners who had to be given a taste of the glories of Americanism, while the passengers of the Lusitania represented wealth and station—therein lies the difference.

Preparedness, therefore, will only add to the power of the privileged few and help them to subdue, to enslave and crush labor. Surely Gompers must know that, and if he joins the howl of the military clique, he must stand condemned as a traitor to the cause of labor.

Just as it is with all the other institutions in our confused life, which were supposedly created for the good of the people and have accomplished the very reverse, so it will be with preparedness. Supposedly, America is to prepare for peace; but in reality it will be the cause of war. It always has been thus—all through blood-stained history, and it will continue until nation will refuse to fight against nation, and until the people of the world will stop preparing for slaughter. Preparedness is like the seed of a poisonous plant; placed in the soil, it will bear poisonous fruit. The European mass destruction is the fruit of that poisonous seed. It is imperative that the American workers realize this before they are driven by the jingoes into the madness that is forever haunted by the spectre of danger and invasion; they must know that to prepare for peace means to invite war, means to unloose the furies of death over land and seas.

That which has driven the masses of Europe into the trenches and to the battlefields is not their inner longing for war; it must be traced to the cut-throat competition for military equipment, for more efficient armies, for larger warships, for more powerful cannon. You cannot build up a standing army and then throw it back into a box like tin soldiers. Armies equipped to the teeth with weapons, with highly developed instruments of murder and backed by their military interests, have their own dynamic functions. We have but to examine into the nature of militarism to realize the truism of this contention.

Militarism consumes the strongest and most productive elements of each nation. Militarism swallows the largest part of the national revenue. Almost nothing is spent on education, art, literature and science compared with the amount devoted to militarism in times of peace, while in times of war everything else is set at naught; all life stagnates, all effort is curtailed; the very sweat and blood of the masses are used to feed this insatiable monster—militarism. Under such circumstances, it must become more arrogant, more aggressive, more bloated with its own importance. If for no other reason, it is out of surplus energy that militarism must act to remain alive; therefore it will seek an enemy or create one artificially. In this civilized purpose and method, militarism is sustained by the state, protected by the laws of the land, is fostered by the home and the school, and glorified by public opinion. In other words, the function of militarism is to kill. It cannot live except through murder.

But the most dominant factor of military preparedness and the one which inevitably leads to war, is the creation of group interests, which consciously and deliberately work for the increase of armament whose purposes are furthered by creating the war hysteria. This group interest embraces all those engaged in the manufacture and sale of munition and in military equipment for personal gain and profit. For instance, the family Krupp, which owns the largest cannon munition plant in the world; its sinister influence in Germany, and in fact in many other countries, extends to the press, the school, the church and to statesmen of highest rank. Shortly before the war, Carl Liebknecht, the one brave public man in Germany now, brought to the attention of the Reichstag that the family Krupp had in its employ officials of the highest military position, not only in Germany, but in France and in other countries. Everywhere its emissaries have been at work, systematically inciting national hatreds and antagonisms. The same investigation brought to light an international war supply trust who cares not a hang for patriotism, or for love of the people, but who uses both to incite war and to pocket millions of profits out of the terrible bargain.

It is not at all unlikely that the history of the present war will trace its origin to this international murder trust. But is it always necessary for one generation to wade through oceans of blood and heap up mountains of human sacrifice that the next generation may learn a grain of truth from it all? Can we of to-day not profit by the cause which led to the European war, can we not learn that it was preparedness, thorough and efficient preparedness on the part of Germany and the other countries for military aggrandizement and material gain; above all can we not realize that preparedness in America must and will lead to the same result, the same barbarity, the same senseless sacrifice of life? Is America to follow suit, is it to be turned over to the American Krupps, the American military cliques? It almost seems so when one hears the jingo howls of the press, the blood and thunder tirades of bully Roosevelt, the sentimental twaddle of our college-bred President.

The more reason for those who still have a spark of libertarianism and humanity left to cry out against this great crime, against the outrage now being prepared and imposed upon the American people. It is not enough to claim being neutral; a neutrality which sheds crocodile tears with one eye and keeps the other riveted upon the profits from war supplies and war loans, is not neutrality. It is a hypocritical cloak to cover, the countries' crimes. Nor is it enough to join the bourgeois pacifists, who proclaim peace among the nations, while helping to perpetuate the war among the classes, a war which in reality, is at the bottom of all other wars.

It is this war of the classes that we must concentrate upon, and in that connection the war against false values, against evil institutions, against all social atrocities. Those who appreciate the urgent need of co-operating in great struggles must oppose military preparedness imposed by the state and capitalism for the destruction of the masses. They must organize the preparedness of the masses for the overthrow of both capitalism and the state. Industrial and economic preparedness is what the workers need. That alone leads to revolution at the bottom as against mass destruction from on top. That alone leads to true internationalism of labor against Kaiserdom, Kingdom, diplomacies, military cliques and bureaucracy. That alone will give the people the means to take their children out of the slums, out of the sweat shops and the cotton mills. That alone will enable them to inculcate in the coming generation a new ideal of brotherhood, to rear them in play and song and beauty; to bring up men and women, not automatons. That alone will enable woman to become the real mother of the race, who will give to the world creative men, and not soldiers who destroy. That alone leads to economic and social freedom, and does away with all wars, all crimes, and all injustice.

George E. Riis *to* The Brooklyn Daily Eagle

Politics proverbially makes strange bedfellows, seldom unlikelier than those that gathered around the idealistic mission known as the Peace Ship. Thomas Edison and William Jennings Bryan supported the vision, but Henry Ford underwrote the voyage. Although he would later become a notorious purveyor of anti-Semitism, in 1915 Ford allied himself with Rosika Schwimmer, a Hungarian Jewish journalist and suffragist active in the Woman's Peace Party. She had traveled with Jane Addams to The Hague in the spring of 1915 and now sought to return to Europe and establish a Conference for Continuous Mediation between the belligerent governments. Ford chartered an ocean liner that sailed for Scandinavia from Hoboken, New Jersey, on December 4, 1915, carrying himself, Schwimmer, a large delegation of peace activists, and a host of journalists. George Riis of *The Brooklyn Daily Eagle* sent this dispatch from Kirkwall, the port in the Orkneys where the British cleared neutral ships seeking to enter the North Sea. Ford fell ill in Norway and left the delegation on December 23. Upon returning to the United States, he said that while he "didn't get much peace" on the voyage, he was encouraged to hear "that Russia might well become a huge market for tractors." The remaining delegates made no progress in ending the war.

CROWD OF DREAMERS
ON THE PEACE ARK;
FORD IS SINCERE

Hungarian Zealot, With Hatred of War,
Found Another Visionary in Him.

QUEER PEOPLE IN PARTY.

One Woman Started for Arctice Regions With
Handkerchiefs and Spare Shirtwaist.

ON BOARD STEAMSHIP OSCAR II, December 15—A band played, "I Didn't Raise My Boy to Be a Soldier." It was a Danish band, too. With the first strains the Henry Ford peace pilgrims tumbled from a cold couch—pilgriming for peace up near the outer edge of the Arctic Circle is no joke—and prepared to take stock of one another. There they were and it was too late to get off the boat—peace-at-any-price men, single-taxers, Socialists, suffragists and vegetarians. All differences were breached in the unity of one great common cause, for whether they believed in eating grass for breakfast or in the affinity of molecules, they were all determined to stop the war.

This is, indeed, a strange assortment of men and women. They haven't anything except a vague idea of why they are going—that is, so far as details are concerned—but they are on their way. All they know is that Henry Ford and Mme. Schwimmer are going to do something, somehow, to bring about peace and they are going to help. One hundred and sixty-five men and women will present a solid phalanx against Europe in arms. Three days in Norway, three in Sweden, a similar length of time in Copenhagen, a few conferences at The Hague ending with the appointment of a handful of permanent delegates, and all will be settled.

A zealot from Hungary, in whose breast there burned a consuming hatred of war, found a dreamer, a supreme idealist, in America whose dream was that some day universal brotherhood would reign among the peoples of the earth, engines of war become scrap iron, and swords be beaten into plowshares. The dreamer had great wealth and a dream. The zealot had something more than a dream—a definite plan. For months she had been looking for a man with money to back the plan and she had found him.

The two chartered a steamship—or, to be more correct— bought the first and second cabins, gathered about them a little circle of men and women who had been prominent in work for peace, and with 165 laymen and women, most of them idealists like themselves, set out on what in many respects is the most remarkable cruise in history. They went away to bring a world at arms to its senses as confidently as if they were merely on a Sunday school excursion to Rockaway and expected to return before dark.

That is how the unique voyage of Henry Ford, manufacturer, and one of the world's richest men, and Mme. Rosika

Schwimmer, Hungarian suffragist and peace lecturer, shapes itself. Jason Ford is after the Golden Fleece. Will he get it?

PARTY DOESN'T REPRESENT
ANYTHING IN PARTICULAR.

The 165 are representative of nobody in particular, unless you except the college students. Although they are on their way to a continent where preparedness has been a cardinal virtue many of them have joined the ship in such a hurry that they have lost trunks and grips in their haste. One woman came from Philadelphia via taxicab to Newark with a set of handkerchiefs and a spare shirtwaist, but no heavy coat. She was on her way to Norway, which is not a long way from the Arctic Circle, and where the snow will be lying on the mountains when we get there. Others, like Senator Helen Ring Robinson of Colorado, have had to abandon missing trunks in the wild chase for a ship. This chase to bring Europe to her senses reminds one, in lost impedimenta at any rate, of an army's flight.

One cannot laugh at their earnestness, however. It is pathetic in some instances. There are those among them who appear to believe that if a hand is held up to fighting Europe the cannons roar will end and the chimes of peace ring out over a glad world.

A strange, impractical lot for the most part. Visionary among visionaries—the cream of the idealists of America. Stop and ask many of them just how they mean to go about settling the war and you discover that they have their heads in the clouds. They haven't any real plan; they are trusting to Henry Ford, Mme. Schwimmer, Louis Lochner, Dr. Aked and old Dr. Jenkin Lloyd Jones of Chicago, to lead them out of the wilderness of conflict into a land where no one carries a big stick but all speak softly. There are to be no more warships, no more guns —the nations will settle all their quarrels in a World Court of Arbitration or something. Really, we haven't thought out the details, you know.

FORD'S IDEAS HAVE BEEN MISINTERPRETED AT HOME.

Ford is sincere. There is not the slightest doubt of that. He has done many remarkable things when people ridiculed him and he is convinced that he can succeed in this, the greatest thing he ever attempted. Ford has been misinterpreted at home.

This may be due to the fact that he shows up poorly in an interview. He doesn't talk. He failed to answer questions well. To listen to him, you would set him down as the most impractical of men when it comes to a mission such as this, whatever he may be in his business.

The cruise of "Henry the Dreamer" is based upon faith. That is the only large asset he gives this expedition besides his money. He is ready to spend every last cent of his huge fortune to back up his faith. He has the nerve of a gambler stacking his all on the last card. They say he has more ready money available than any other man in America—about $95,000,000 in assets which he could convert into cash quickly—and he owes nothing.

There does not seem reasonable room for the belief that Ford is trying to advertise himself. His income is said to be $50,000 a day. Wherefore advertise himself, say his friends.

Such a cosmopolitan company it is—a Governor, a Lieutenant Governor, a judge, educators, a dean of St. Paul's Cathedral, now head of the sociological department of the Ford works—a fine, level-headed man—a group of college students from West, South and East, a sprinkling of single-taxers and Socialists and more than fifty newspapermen and women and magazine writers.

Mixed in with the visionaries there is an element of men and women who do not go so far as advocating sweeping disarmament, a subject dear to the heart of Lochner and Mme. Schwimmer, but joined because they are more than half convinced that some good may be accomplished by a trip which all the world is ridiculing. Judge Lindsey is one of these and so is Governor Hanna of North Dakota. Dean Marquis of St. Paul's Cathedral, a long-time friend of Ford's, and Lieutenant Governor Bethea of South Carolina.

FORD SINCERE IN HIS BELIEF
HE CAN STOP THE WAR.

They know that Ford is sincere, they are his friends and want to stand by him when a world ridicules, and they are hypnotized by that abiding faith of his in human nature which nothing has succeeded in shaking yet. He is an optimist of first water.

"I believe there are very few bad men in this world," said Ford to an Eagle correspondent. "I believe that if you follow a man with your human sympathy you can bring out the good that is in him and it is surely there in every man. I have many men working for me who have been in prison and out of 600 such cases that I have handled I have only known of three men who failed to live up to my expectations."

But he talks vaguely of adopting his idea of "community spirit" in Europe. He says at one minute that it may be necessary for the country to have a modified form of protection—citizen police—perhaps—and the next moment he talks uncompromisingly of universal disarmament. He tells you that the greatest thing said in this war was the statement of Lord Rosebery that he was sorry to see the United States arming against that which Great Britain is trying to crush out. He declares that the world war had its roots laid away back in Napoleon's time and that the Kaiser has it in him to be the greatest man of all time. One cannot get away from the idea that Henry Ford, as a peace apostle, is a fine manufacturer.

He talks about world politics like a little child. One feels sorry for the man while one admires his sublime audacity in setting sail across the wintry seas to set a world askew back in the straight path again by the power of his personality and the potent force of his money.

An honest man with a dream. That is a correct interpretation of Ford. Did ever crusader launch a bolder enterprise under more untoward circumstances?

The Daily Brooklyn Eagle, January 6, 1916

Alan Seeger:
I Have a Rendezvous with Death

Seeger probably wrote this poem in early 1916, in anticipation of renewed fighting later that year. That Fourth of July, during the first
week of the Anglo-French offensive along the Somme River, Seeger's
regiment of the Foreign Legion attacked the village of Belloy-en-
Santerre. Struck several times by machine-gun fire, Seeger reportedly
cheered on his comrades in their successful advance before he died.
His *Poems* were published posthumously in December 1916, and his
Letters and Diaries appeared in May 1917; some reviewers compared
him to the Romantic English poet Rupert Brooke, who had died
from blood poisoning in 1915 while serving with the Royal Navy in
the Aegean. American supporters of the Allies lauded Seeger as a
hero; his brother, Charles, a prominent musicologist (and future
father of the folksinger Pete Seeger), became an outspoken opponent
of intervention.

I have a rendezvous with Death
At some disputed barricade,
When Spring comes back with rustling shade
And apple-blossoms fill the air—
I have a rendezvous with Death
When Spring brings back blue days and fair.

It may be he shall take my hand
And lead me into his dark land
And close my eyes and quench my breath—
It may be I shall pass him still.
I have a rendezvous with Death
On some scarred slope of battered hill,
When Spring comes round again this year
And the first meadow-flowers appear.

God knows 'twere better to be deep
Pillowed in silk and scented down,
Where Love throbs out in blissful sleep,

Pulse nigh to pulse, and breath to breath,
Where hushed awakenings are dear . . .
But I've a rendezvous with Death
At midnight in some flaming town,
When Spring trips north again this year,
And I to my pledged word am true,
I shall not fail that rendezvous.

Ellen N. La Motte: Alone

Born in Louisville, Kentucky, Ellen Newbold La Motte trained as a nurse at Johns Hopkins University at a time when nursing was one of the few professions open to women who wished to pursue careers and independent lives. She became an expert in caring for tuberculosis patients and published *The Tuberculosis Nurse* (1914). After spending the first winter of the war in Paris, in July 1915 she departed for a French military field hospital run by American heiress Mary Borden in Rousbrugge, Belgium, about six miles behind the front lines. La Motte left the hospital a year later, returning to America, where she published *The Backwash of War: The Human Wreckage of the Battle-field as Witnessed by an American Hospital Nurse* in December. In the summer of 1918 her book was withdrawn by the publisher under government pressure. "Truth, it appears," La Motte later wrote, "has no place in war."

ROCHARD died to-day. He had gas gangrene. His thigh, from knee to buttock, was torn out by a piece of German shell. It was an interesting case, because the infection had developed so quickly. He had been placed under treatment immediately too, reaching the hospital from the trenches about six hours after he had been wounded. To have a thigh torn off, and to reach first-class surgical care within six hours, is practically immedi-ately. Still, gas gangrene had developed, which showed that the Germans were using very poisonous shells. At that field hospi-tal there had been established a surgical school, to which young men, just graduated from medical schools, or old men, graduated long ago from medical schools, were sent to learn how to take care of the wounded. After they had received a two months' experience in this sort of war surgery, they were to be placed in other hospitals, where they could do the work themselves. So all those young men who did not know much, and all those old men who had never known much, and had forgotten most of that, were up here at this field hospital, learning. This had to be done, because there were not enough good doctors to go round, so in order to care for the wounded at all, it was necessary to furbish up the immature and the senile. However, the *Médecin Chef* in charge of the hospital and in charge of the surgical school, was a brilliant surgeon and a good administrator, so he taught the students a good deal. Therefore, when Rochard came into the operating room, all the young students and the old students crowded round to see the case. It was all torn away, the flesh from that right thigh, from knee to buttock, down to the bone, and the stench was awful. The various students came forward and timidly pressed the upper part of the thigh, the remaining part, all that remained of it, with their fingers, and little crackling noises came forth, like bubbles. Gas gangrene. Very easy to diagnose. Also the bacteriologist from another hospital in the region happened to be present, and he made a culture of the material discharged from that wound, and afterwards told the *Médecin Chef* that it was positively and absolutely gas gangrene. But the *Médecin Chef* had already taught the students that gas gangrene may be recognized by the crackling and the smell, and the fact that the patient, as a rule, dies pretty soon.

They could not operate on Rochard and amputate his leg, as they wanted to do. The infection was so high, into the hip, it could not be done. Moreover, Rochard had a fractured skull as well. Another piece of shell had pierced his ear, and broken into his brain, and lodged there. Either wound would have been fatal, but it was the gas gangrene in his torn-out thigh that would kill him first. The wound stank. It was foul. The *Médecin Chef* took a curette, a little scoop, and scooped away the dead flesh, the dead muscles, the dead nerves, the dead blood-vessels. And so many blood-vessels being dead, being scooped away by that sharp curette, how could the blood circulate in the top half of that flaccid thigh? It couldn't. Afterwards, into the deep, yawning wound, they put many compresses of gauze, soaked in carbolic acid, which acid burned deep into the germs of the gas gangrene, and killed them, and killed much good tissue besides. Then they covered the burning, smoking gauze with absorbent cotton, then with clean, neat bandages, after which they called the stretcher bearers, and Rochard was carried from the operating table back to the ward.

The night nurse reported next morning that he had passed a night of agony.

"*Cela pique! Cela brule!*" he cried all night, and turned from side to side to find relief. Sometimes he lay on his good side; sometimes he lay on his bad side, and the night nurse turned him from side to side, according to his fancy, because she knew that on neither one side nor the other would he find relief, except such mental relief as he got by turning. She sent one of the orderlies, Fouquet, for the *Médecin Chef*, and the *Médecin Chef* came to the ward, and looked at Rochard, and ordered the night nurse to give him morphia, and again morphia, as often as she thought best. For only death could bring relief from such pain as that, and only morphia, a little in advance of death, could bring partial relief.

So the night nurse took care of Rochard all that night, and turned him and turned him, from one side to the other, and gave him morphia, as the *Médecin Chef* had ordered. She listened to his cries all night, for the morphia brought him no relief. Morphia gives a little relief, at times, from the pain of life, but it is only death that brings absolute relief.

When the day nurse came on duty next morning, there was Rochard in agony. "*Cela pique! Cela brule!*" he cried. And again and again, all the time, "*Cela pique! Cela brule!*", meaning the pain in his leg. And because of the piece of shell, which had penetrated his ear and lodged in his brain somewhere, his wits were wandering. No one can be fully conscious with an inch of German shell in his skull. And there was a full inch of German shell in Rochard's skull, in his brain somewhere, for the radiographist said so. He was a wonderful radiographist and anatomist, and he worked accurately with a beautiful, expensive machine, given him, or given the field hospital, by Madame Curie.

So all night Rochard screamed in agony, and turned and twisted, first on the hip that was there, and then on the hip that was gone, and on neither side, even with many ampoules of morphia, could he find relief. Which shows that morphia, good as it is, is not as good as death. So when the day nurse came on in the morning, there was Rochard strong after a night of agony, strong after many *picqures* of strychnia, which kept his heart beating and his lungs breathing, strong after many *picqures* of morphia which did not relieve his pain. Thus the science of healing stood baffled before the science of destroying.

Rochard died slowly. He stopped struggling. He gave up trying to find relief by lying upon the hip that was there, or the hip that was gone. He ceased to cry. His brain, in which was lodged a piece of German shell, seemed to reason, to become reasonable, with break of day. The evening before, after his return from the operating room, he had been decorated with the *Médaille Militaire*, conferred upon him, *in extremis*, by the General of the region. Upon one side of the medal, which was pinned to the wall at the head of the bed, were the words: *Valeur et Discipline*. Discipline had triumphed. He was very good and quiet now, very obedient and disciplined, and no longer disturbed the ward with his moanings.

Little Rochard! Little man, gardener by trade, aged thirty-nine, widower, with one child! The piece of shell in his skull had made one eye blind. There had been a hæmorrhage into the eyeball, which was all red and sunken, and the eyelid would not close over it, so the red eye stared and stared into space. And the other eye drooped and drooped, and the white showed, and the eyelid drooped till nothing but the white showed, and that showed that he was dying. But the blind, red eye stared beyond. It stared fixedly, unwinkingly, into space. So always the nurse watched the dull, white eye, which showed the approach of death.

No one in the ward was fond of Rochard. He had been there only a few hours. He meant nothing to any one there. He was a dying man, in a field hospital, that was all. Little stranger Rochard, with one blind, red eye that stared into Hell, the Hell he had come from. And one white, dying eye, that showed his hold on life, his brief, short hold. The nurse cared for him very gently, very conscientiously, very skilfully. The surgeon came many times to look at him, but he had done for him all that could be done, so each time he turned away with a shrug. Fouquet, the young orderly, stood at the foot of the bed, his feet far apart, his hands on his hips, and regarded Rochard, and said: "*Ah! La la! La la!*" And Simon, the other orderly, also stood at the foot of the bed, from time to time, and regarded Rochard, and said: "*Ah! C'est triste! C'est bien triste!*"

So Rochard died, a stranger among strangers. And there were many people there to wait upon him, but there was no one there to love him. There was no one there to see beyond the horror of the red, blind eye, of the dull, white eye, of the vile, gangrene smell. And it seemed as if the red, staring eye was looking for something the hospital could not give. And it seemed as if the white, glazed eye was indifferent to everything the hospital could give. And all about him was the vile gangrene smell, which made an aura about him, and shut him into himself, very completely. And there was nobody to love him, to forget about that smell.

He sank into a stupor about ten o'clock in the morning, and was unconscious from then till the time the nurse went to lunch. She went to lunch reluctantly, but it is necessary to eat. She instructed Fouquet, the orderly, to watch Rochard carefully, and to call her if there was any change.

After a short time she came back from lunch, and hurried to see Rochard, hurried behind the flamboyant, red, cheerful screens that shut him off from the rest of the ward. Rochard was dead.

At the other end of the ward sat the two orderlies, drinking wine.

Paris,
April 15, 1916.

Woodrow Wilson: Address to Congress

The first president to address Congress in person since John Adams, Wilson spoke before a joint session of both houses twenty-six times, more than any president before or since. On March 24, 1916, a U-boat torpedoed the French cross-Channel passenger steamer *Sussex* without forewarning, taking fifty lives, none of them American. This aggressive action was an apparent violation of the *Arabic* pledge in which the Germans had promised not to attack passenger ships without notice. Secretary of State Lansing advised breaking relations with Germany, but the president decided to issue an ultimatum first and delivered his admonition before a joint session of Congress on April 19. Determined to avoid war with the United States, the German government pledged on May 4 that it would adhere to the established rules of naval warfare—that U-boats would sink merchant ships only after their passengers and crew were safely in lifeboats, unless the ship offered resistance or tried to escape.

———————————

19 April, 1916.

Gentlemen of the Congress: A situation has arisen in the foreign relations of the country of which it is my plain duty to inform you very frankly.

It will be recalled that in February, 1915, the Imperial German Government announced its intention to treat the waters surrounding Great Britain and Ireland as embraced within the seat of war and to destroy all merchant ships owned by its enemies that might be found within any part of that portion of the high seas, and that it warned all vessels, of neutral as well as of belligerent ownership, to keep out of the waters it had thus proscribed or else enter them at their peril. The Government of the United States earnestly protested. It took the position that such a policy could not be pursued without the practical certainty of gross and palpable violations of the law of nations, particularly if submarine craft were to be employed as its instruments, inasmuch as the rules prescribed by that law, rules founded upon principles of humanity and established for the protection of the lives of non-combatants at sea, could not in the nature of the case be observed by such vessels. It based its protest on the ground that persons of neutral nationality and vessels of neutral ownership would be exposed to extreme and intolerable risks, and that no right to close any part of the high seas against their use or to expose them to such risks could lawfully be asserted by any belligerent government. The law of nations in these matters, upon which the Government of the United States based its protest, is not of recent origin or founded upon merely arbitrary principles set up by convention. It is based, on the contrary, upon manifest and imperative principles of humanity and has long been established with the approval and by the express assent of all civilized nations.

Notwithstanding the earnest protest of our Government, the Imperial German Government at once proceeded to carry out the policy it had announced. It expressed the hope that the dangers involved, at any rate the dangers to neutral vessels, would be reduced to a minimum by the instructions which it had issued to its submarine commanders, and assured the Government of the United States that it would take every possible precaution both to respect the rights of neutrals and to safeguard the lives of non-combatants.

What has actually happened in the year which has since elapsed has shown that those hopes were not justified, those assurances insusceptible of being fulfilled. In pursuance of the policy of submarine warfare against the commerce of its adversaries, thus announced and entered upon by the Imperial German Government in despite of the solemn protest of this Government, the commanders of German undersea vessels have attacked merchant ships with greater and greater activity, not only upon the high seas surrounding Great Britain and Ireland but wherever they could encounter them, in a way that has grown more and more ruthless, more and more indiscriminate as the months have gone by, less and less observant of restraints of any kind; and have delivered their attacks without compunction against vessels of every nationality and bound upon every sort of errand. Vessels of neutral ownership, even vessels of neutral ownership bound from neutral port to neutral port, have been destroyed along with vessels of belligerent ownership in constantly increasing numbers. Sometimes the merchantman attacked has been warned and summoned to surrender before being fired on or torpedoed; sometimes passengers or crews have been vouchsafed the poor security of being allowed to take to the ship's boats before she was sent to the bottom. But again and again no warning has been given, no escape even to the ship's boats allowed to those on board. What this Government foresaw must happen has happened. Tragedy has followed tragedy on the seas in such fashion, with such attendant circumstances, as to make it grossly evident that warfare of such a sort, if warfare it be, cannot be carried on without the most palpable violation of the dictates alike of right and of humanity. Whatever the disposition and intention of the Imperial German Government, it has manifestly proved impossible for it to keep such methods of attack upon the commerce of its enemies within the bounds set by either the reason or the heart of mankind.

In February of the present year the Imperial German Government informed this Government and the other neutral governments of the world that it had reason to believe that the Government of Great Britain had armed all merchant vessels of British ownership and had given them secret orders to attack any submarine of the enemy they might encounter upon the seas, and that the Imperial German Government felt justified in the circumstances in treating all armed merchantmen of belligerent ownership as auxiliary vessels of war, which it would have the right to destroy without warning. The law of nations has long recognized the right of merchantmen to carry arms for protection and to use them to repel attack, though to use them, in such circumstances, at their own risk; but the Imperial German Government claimed the right to set these understandings aside in circumstances which it deemed extraordinary. Even the terms in which it announced its purpose thus still further to relax the restraints it had previously professed its willingness and desire to put upon the operations of its submarines carried the plain implication that at least vessels which were not armed would still be exempt from destruction without warning and that personal safety would be accorded their passengers and crews; but even that limitation, if it was ever practicable to observe it, has in fact constituted no check at all upon the destruction of ships of every sort.

Again and again the Imperial German Government has

given this Government its solemn assurances that at least passenger ships would not be thus dealt with, and yet it has again and again permitted its undersea commanders to disregard those assurances with entire impunity. Great liners like the LUSITANIA and the ARABIC and mere ferryboats like the SUSSEX have been attacked without a moment's warning, sometimes before they had even become aware that they were in the presence of an armed vessel of the enemy, and the lives of non-combatants, passengers and crew have been sacrificed wholesale, in a manner which the Government of the United States cannot but regard as wanton and without the slightest colour of justification. No limit of any kind has in fact been set to the indiscriminate pursuit and destruction of merchantmen of all kinds and nationalities within the waters, constantly extending in area, where these operations have been carried on; and the roll of Americans who have lost their lives on ships thus attacked and destroyed has grown month by month until the ominous toll has mounted into the hundreds.

One of the latest and most shocking instances of this method of warfare was that of the destruction of the French cross-Channel steamer SUSSEX. It must stand forth, as the sinking of the steamer LUSITANIA did, as so singularly tragical and unjustifiable as to constitute a truly terrible example of the inhumanity of submarine warfare as the commanders of German vessels have for the past twelvemonth been conducting it. If this instance stood alone, some explanation, some disavowal by the German Government, some evidence of criminal mistake or wilful disobedience on the part of the commander of the vessel that fired the torpedo might be sought or entertained; but unhappily it does not stand alone. Recent events make the conclusion inevitable that it is only one instance, even though it be one of the most extreme and distressing instances, of the spirit and method of warfare which the Imperial German Government has mistakenly adopted, and which from the first exposed that Government to the reproach of thrusting all neutral rights aside in pursuit of its immmediate objects.

The Government of the United States has been very patient. At every stage of this distressing experience of tragedy after tragedy in which its own citizens were involved it has sought to be restrained from any extreme course of action or of protest by a thoughtful consideration of the extraordinary circumstances of this unprecedented war, and actuated in all that it said or did by the sentiments of genuine friendship which the people of the United States have always entertained and continue to entertain towards the German nation. It has of course accepted the successive explanations and assurances of the Imperial German Government as given in entire sincerity and good faith, and has hoped, even against hope, that it would prove to be possible for the German Government so to order and control the acts of its naval commanders as to square its policy with the principles of humanity as embodied in the law of nations. It has been willing to wait until the significance of the facts became absolutely unmistakable and susceptible of but one interpretation.

That point has now unhappily been reached. The facts are susceptible of but one interpretation. The Imperial German Government has been unable to put any limits or restraints upon its warfare against either freight or passenger ships. It has therefore become painfully evident that the position which this Government took at the very outset is inevitable, namely, that the use of submarines for the destruction of an enemy's commerce is of necessity, because of the very character of the vessels employed and the very methods of attack which their employment of course involves, incompatible with the principles of humanity, the long established and incontrovertible rights of neutrals, and the sacred immunities of non-combatants.

I have deemed it my duty, therefore, to say to the Imperial German Government that if it is still its purpose to prosecute relentless and indiscriminate warfare against vessels of commerce by the use of submarines, notwithstanding the now demonstrated impossibility of conducting that warfare in accordance with what the Government of the United States must consider the sacred and indisputable rules of international law and the universally recognized dictates of humanity, the Government of the United States is at last forced to the conclusion that there is but one course it can pursue; and that unless the Imperial German Government should now immediately declare and effect an abandonment of its present methods of warfare against passenger and freight carrying vessels this

Government can have no choice but to sever diplomatic relations with the Government of the German Empire altogether.

This decision I have arrived at with the keenest regret; the possibility of the action contemplated I am sure all thoughtful Americans will look forward to with unaffected reluctance. But we cannot forget that we are in some sort and by the force of circumstances the responsible spokesmen of the rights of humanity, and that we cannot remain silent while those rights seem in process of being swept utterly away in the maelstrom of this terrible war. We owe it to a due regard for our own rights as a nation, to our sense of duty as a representative of the rights of neutrals the world over, and to a just conception of the rights of mankind to take this stand now with the utmost solemnity and firmness.

I have taken it, and taken it in the confidence that it will meet with your approval and support. All sober-minded men must unite in hoping that the Imperial German Government, which has in other circumstances stood as the champion of all that we are now contending for in the interest of humanity, may recognize the justice of our demands and meet them in the spirit in which they are made.

William B. Seabrook:
from Diary of Section VIII

While the United States remained out of the war, a number of young Americans wanted to support the Allied cause and venture close to the front. Many volunteered as ambulance drivers, some for the American Ambulance Field Service, which was founded in April 1915 to aid the French army. More than 2,000 Americans would volunteer for the service, including William Seabrook, a graduate of Newberry College in South Carolina who had worked in journalism and advertising. Seabrook described his section's actions in Champagne.

ON SATURDAY, May 27, Section 8 received its baptism of fire.

Three cars were called to St. Hilaire, our evacuation post eight kilometres from Mourmelon and about two and a half kilometres behind the first-line trenches. Dodge, Seabrook, and Shattuck drove, and with them went Iasigi, Davison, and Section-Chief Mason.

St. Hilaire, a village which has changed hands several times and now finds itself in front of the French batteries in easy sight and range of the German guns on the slopes opposite, is what the poilus call a "*mauvais coin*."

It is a mass of ruins, but evidently was once a charming spot, and the approach by the road from Mourmelon is still beautiful, though the fields on both sides of the route are scarred with bomb-craters and honeycombed with abandoned trenches. For practically the entire distance the road is protected from German observation by a screen formed of pine limbs and small pine saplings strung on wires and rising well over the top of the tallest auto truck.

This road is in easy distance for the German artillery, but there is only one point which they have been shelling during the past month, to wit, the abandoned farm of St. Hilaire, three kilometres back from the village and now nothing more than an abandoned mass of crumbled masonry. However, no shells fell as we passed the farm, and in another five minutes we turned a curve and caught our first sight of a French village totally destroyed by heavy-artillery fire. The approach is through a grove, over a lovely little stream with a picturesque mill at the left, and one emerges rather sharply from the trees into full view of the town. To one who had never before seen the effect of heavy high-explosive shells the scene was appalling. Some among us had seen big floods, fires, tornados and railroad wrecks, but there is no form of devastation on earth that can compare to a town deliberately and completely wrecked by continuous artillery fire. On one side of the street the houses were blown into shapeless masses; the stone was not only scattered, but often crumbled into dust; the iron was tortured into fantastic shapes; the woodwork was ashes; on the opposite side were wrecks of houses with one wall or one triangular corner standing; others had holes blown through them big enough for a two-horse team to drive in, yet still upright; here and there a single house had escaped destruction, but served only to emphasize the devastation around it; the roof of the church is gone, one half of the nave and entire transept is crushed in, and the tower is tottering; it was as if the huge hand of some demon from the clouds had lifted the entire village to unthinkable heights and in wanton rage dashed it back to earth.

These impressions crowded on us in the instant that we were traversing the village to reach the entrance to the trenches and bombproof shelters in which the evacuation *poste* is located. The entrance is immediately beside the road, emerging from the village behind a half-destroyed house that furnishes shelter from Bosche binoculars if not from their big guns. The sergeant on duty was standing in the road at the entrance to his dugout, smoking a pipe, and half a dozen of his stretcher-bearers were sitting around under the trees. There had been little if any firing that morning.

They told us they had several "*blessés*" (even the Americans and English call them that in France) to be transported back to the hospital near Mourmelon, and we made ready to load them into Dodge's car.

While we were still talking a German shell, and then another, and still another, screamed high over our heads and exploded somewhere in the woods behind St. Hilaire. In another instant the French batteries located a few hundred yards behind us opened up a terrific bombardment, while more German guns joined in the duel.

The fire was not directed at St. Hilaire. The enemy was firing just over our heads to the woods 300 and 400 yards behind us, "feeling" for the batteries they knew were masked among the trees.

"They are not firing at us," explained the sergeant, "but a shell timed a fraction of a second early, or fired a fraction of a centimetre lower, might land here by accident, so we had better get our *blessés* loaded and away."

The few more minutes we remained, however, were ample to furnish experiences we shall never forget. Scarcely had the sergeant ceased speaking when a German shell fell far short of its mark and short of us, too, in the field beyond St. Hilaire; another broke to the right a hundred yards or so above our heads, and a third and fourth broke so close that the fragments sprayed the road where we were standing. One of our party picked up a jagged piece still sizzling hot from the explosion. Then the Bosche gunners readjusted their range, and the shells began to break again, as they intended, in the woods behind.

Descriptions of how one feels under shell fire are always inadequate and malapropos, because every man feels differently. Close observation of the men of our section on this and subsequent occasions seems to show that they are alike in only one respect—they all hold their ground. For instance, there is one of us, a man of unquestioned courage, who "ducks" his head and shoulders every time a shell screams over his head; it seems to be an involuntary muscular reaction. Another becomes garrulous, laughing loud and keeping up a rapid fire of jokes, possibly like the negro who whistles as he traverses a graveyard. Another man in the section turns quite pale, yet keeps his hand and voice as steady and his eye as clear as one of Napoleon's grenadiers.

It may possibly all be summed up in the comment often made in other wars that a man who is not afraid of a big shell is simply a fool, and that courage consists not in foolhardy nonchalance, but in standing your ground and doing your duty.

The noise of an artillery duel has been described by thousands of writers, yet it comes as a surprise to each man who hears it for the first time. The crashing reports of the French soixante-quinze, the roar of the bigger guns, the sharp crack of the small shells, and the muffled boom of the exploding bombs—all these can easily be reproduced in the imagination, by simply multiplying the din of any practice cannonading you may have happened to hear at close range in time of peace. But what nobody can describe is the shrieking and screaming of the shells as they fly through the air over your head before bursting. It cannot be described, because there is no sound with which it can be compared. It is a sound which has no place in things human—a shrieking, crescendo scream from the shells that are arriving—the last diminishing wail of a lost soul from the shells as they depart—all mingled at times in an ear-splitting, high-keyed symphony of hell in which the bursting bombs and rumbling guns furnish the deep bass tones.

Well, after all, they weren't firing directly at us, and we all got back to Mourmelon.

From *Diary of Section VIII* (1917)

Victor Chapman to John Jay Chapman

For the first time in the war, some Americans found their military adventures in the air, by joining a French fighter squadron known as the Lafayette Escadrille. In 1914 airplanes were used only for reconnaissance and token bombing raids; but the next year, belligerents on both sides introduced aircraft with forward-firing machine guns specially designed for aerial combat. Victor Chapman had graduated from Harvard in 1913 and was studying architecture in Paris when the war broke out. He joined the French Foreign Legion and served in trenches for a year before taking to the sky. Chapman began training with the French air service in September 1915 and became one of the first seven American volunteer pilots in the Lafayette Escadrille. Flying a French Nieuport 11, Chapman took part in the first patrol of the new squadron on May 13, 1916. He wrote his father about flying over the Verdun battlefield, where the French and Germans had been engaged in a massive battle for more than three months.

———————

June 1st, 1916.
Dear Papa: This flying is much too romantic to be real modern war with all its horrors. There is something so unreal and fairy like about it, which ought to be told and described by Poets, as Jason's Voyage was, or that Greek chap who wandered about the Gulf of Corinth and had giants try to put him in beds that were too small for him, etc.

Yesterday afternoon it was bright but full of those very thick fuzzy clouds like imaginary froth of gods or genii. We all went out. All but I and the Captain got lost and turned back, so we two flitted about over mountains of fleecy snow full of shadow and mist. He reminded me of the story of the last fly on a polar expedition as I followed his black silhouette. I went down to a field near the front and flew again at five o'clock. Then it was marvelous. At 3000 metres one floated secure on a purple sea of mist. Up through it, here and there, voluminous clouds resembling those thick water plants that grow in ponds; and far over this ocean, other white rounded ones just protruding, like strands on some distant mainland. Deep below me I could just distinguish enough of the land now and again to know my whereabouts,—the winding Meuse in its green flood banks or that smouldering Etna, Douaumont. But off to the north, hovering and curveting over one of the bleached coral strands like seagulls—not Nieuports surely! They were the modern harpies: the German machines for the chase. In the still gray mist below now and again I caught sight of a Farman or Caudron sweeping over the corner of the lines to see some battery fire. But as I peered down, a livid white object moved under me going south, with the tail of a skate. "There is my fish and prey," I thought as I pointed down after the German *réglage* machine, "but prudence first." So I searched in the water-plant clouds. Yes, sure enough the venomous creatures are there, as dark specks resembling the larvae one sees in brackish water,— three of them moving the same way. Those are the Fokkers. I did not want to have them fall on my neck when I dived on the fat greasy Boche!

This morning we all started off at three, and, not having made concise enough arrangements, got separated in the morning mist. I found Prince, however, and we went to Douaumont where we found two German *réglage* machines unprotected and fell upon them. A skirmish, a spitting of guns, and we drew away. It had been badly executed that manœuvre! But ho! another Boche heading for Verdun! Taking the direction stick between my knees I tussled and fought with the *mitrailleuse* and finally charged the *rouleau*, all the while eyeing my Boche and moving across Vaux towards Etain. I had no altitude with which to overtake him, but a little more speed. So I got behind his tail and spit till he dived into his own territory. Having lost Norman, I made a tour to the Argonne and on the way back saw another fat Boche. "No protection machine in sight." I swooped, swerved to the right, to the left, almost lost, but then came up under his lee keel by the stern. (It's the one position they cannot shoot from.) I seemed a dory alongside a schooner. I pulled up my nose to let him have it. Crr—Crr— Crr—a cartridge jammed in the barrel. He jumped like a frog and fled down to his grounds. Later in the morning I made another stroll along the lines. Met a flock of Nieuports, and saw across the way a squad of white-winged L. V. G. How like a game of prisoner's base it all is! I scurry out in company, and they run away. They come into my territory and I being alone, take to my heels. They did come after me once too! Faster they are than I, but I had height so they could but leer up at me with their dead-white wings and black crosses like sharks, and they returned to their own domain.

This afternoon we left together, it being our turn for the lines at 12:30. The rolly-poly cotton wool clouds were thick again. Popping in and out of them, I ran upon some blue puffs such as one sees when the artillery has been shooting at aeroplanes. "Strange phenomena, perhaps there exist blue puffs like that." Yesterday I had fruitlessly chased about such puffs to find the Avions. More smoke balls! There above me, like a black beetle, was the Boche! But well above me, and heading for his lines. For twenty minutes I followed that plane ever in front of me, and inch by inch, almost imperceptibly I gained in height and distance. He veered off to give me a broadside; I ducked away behind his tail; he turned off again; I repeated, but I did not have enough extra speed to manœuvre close to him, though I temporarily cut off his retreat. After three passages-at-arms he got away. Then like a jack-ass I went on to Verdun and found no one. On my return what tales were told! The Boches had come over Bar-le-Duc and plentifully shelled it; two of our pilots had their reservoirs pierced and one had not returned. The town, the station, the aviation field all shelled—40 killed, including ten school children. (And we had word this morning that Poincaré has formally forbidden bombardment of every description, even on arm factories—it might kill civilians.) Yes, this is what comes of getting notoriety. There were disgusting notices about us in the papers two days ago,—even yesterday. I am ashamed to be seen in town today if our presence here has again caused death and destruction to innocent people. It would seem so. That Boche at Luxeuil, by the way, came again after we left, on the day and at the hour when the funeral services were being held. But through telephone they got out a Nieuport *escadrille* and cut off his retreat, bringing him down on the French trenches. By the papers on him he was identified as a one-time waiter in the Lion Vert now, of course, a German officer.

Mary Borden: Conspiracy

A Chicago-born heiress and Vassar graduate, Mary Borden had married George Douglas Turner, a Scottish missionary, in 1908. Already the mother of three children, the author of two pseudonymous novels, and a committed suffragist, Borden funded and managed the French military hospital at Rousbrugge, Belgium, which began operations in July 1915 with a staff of seventeen, including the American nurse Ellen N. La Motte. Borden became the director of another military hospital at Bray-sur-Somme in August 1916, treating the wounded from the ongoing Somme campaign. In 1929 she published *The Forbidden Zone*, a collection of sketches and poems drawn from her wartime experiences. The undated "Conspiracy" appears in the second part of the book, titled "The Somme—Hospital Sketches."

———————————

IT IS ALL carefully arranged. Everything is arranged. It is arranged that men should be broken and that they should be mended. Just as you send your clothes to the laundry and mend them when they come back, so we send our men to the trenches and mend them when they come back again. You send your socks and your shirts again and again to the laundry, and you sew up the tears and clip the ravelled edges again and again, just as many times as they will stand it. And then you throw them away. And we send our men to the war again and again, just as long as they will stand it; just until they are dead, and then we throw them into the ground.

It is all arranged. Ten kilometres from here along the road is the place where men are wounded. This is the place where they are mended. We have all the things here for mending, the tables and the needles, and the thread and the knives and the scissors, and many curious things that you never use for your clothes.

We bring our men up along the dusty road where the bushes grow on either side and the green trees. They come by in the mornings in companies, marching with strong legs, with firm steps. They carry their knapsacks easily. Their knapsacks and their guns and their greatcoats are not heavy for them. They wear their caps jauntily, tilted to one side. Their faces are ruddy and their eyes bright. They smile and call out with strong voices. They throw kisses to the girls in the fields.

We send our men up the broken road between bushes of barbed wire and they come back to us, one by one, two by two in ambulances, lying on stretchers. They lie on their backs on the stretchers and are pulled out of the ambulances as loaves of bread are pulled out of the oven. The stretchers slide out of the mouths of the ambulances with the men on them. The men cannot move. They are carried into a shed, unclean bundles, very heavy, covered with brown blankets.

We receive these bundles. We pull off a blanket. We observe that this is a man. He makes feeble whining sounds like an animal. He lies still; he smells bad; he smells like a corpse; he can only move his tongue; he tries to moisten his lips with his tongue.

This is the place where he is to be mended. We lift him on to a table. We peel off his clothes, his coat and his shirt and his trousers and his boots. We handle his clothes that are stiff with blood. We cut off his shirt with large scissors. We stare at the obscene sight of his innocent wounds. He allows us to do this. He is helpless to stop us. We wash off the dry blood round the edges of his wounds. He suffers us to do as we like with him. He says no word except that he is thirsty and we do not give him to drink.

We confer together over his body and he hears us. We discuss his different parts in terms that he does not understand, but he listens while we make calculations with his heart beats and the pumping breath of his lungs.

We conspire against his right to die. We experiment with his bones, his muscles, his sinews, his blood. We dig into the yawning mouths of his wounds. Helpless openings, they let us into the secret places of his body. We plunge deep into his body. We make discoveries within his body. To the shame of the havoc of his limbs we add the insult of our curiosity and the curse of our purpose, the purpose to remake him. We lay odds on his chances of escape, and we combat with Death, his saviour.

It is our business to do this. He knows and he allows us to

do it. He finds himself in the operating room. He lays himself
out. He bares himself to our knives. His mind is annihilated.
He pours out his blood, unconscious. His red blood is spilled
and pours over the table onto the floor while he sleeps.

After this, while he is still asleep, we carry him into another
place and put him to bed. He awakes bewildered as children
do, expecting, perhaps, to find himself at home with his
mother leaning over him, and he moans a little and then lies
still again. He is helpless, so we do for him what he cannot do
for himself, and he is grateful. He accepts his helplessness. He
is obedient. We feed him, and he eats. We fatten him up, and
he allows himself to be fattened. Day after day he lies there and
we watch him. All day and all night he is watched. Every day
his wounds are uncovered and cleaned, scraped and washed
and bound up again. His body does not belong to him. It belongs to us for the moment, not for long. He knows why we
tend it so carefully. He knows what we are fattening and cleaning it up for; and while we handle it he smiles.

He is only one among thousands. They are all the same.
They all let us do with them what we like. They all smile as if
they were grateful. When we hurt them they try not to cry
out, not wishing to hurt our feelings. And often they apologise
for dying. They would not die and disappoint us if they could
help it. Indeed, in their helplessness they do the best they can
to help us get them ready to go back again.

It is only ten kilometres up the road, the place where they
go to be torn again and mangled. Listen; you can hear how
well it works. There is the sound of cannon and the sound of
the ambulances bringing the wounded, and the sound of the
tramp of strong men going along the road to fill the empty
places.

Do you hear? Do you understand? It is all arranged just as it
should be.

Herbert Bayard Swope:
Boelcke, Knight of the Air

In the first presentation of the Pulitzer Prizes in 1917, the award for reporting went to Herbert Bayard Swope of the *New York World* for a series of articles he had written in Germany and occupied France in the fall of 1916. These pieces included vivid accounts of the German pilot Oswald Boelcke, the commander of Jasta (fighter squadron) 2 and a renowned innovator of fighter tactics. Boelcke died on October 28, 1916, when his Albatros D II collided with another German plane. Much of his fame rests on his having mentored Manfred von Richtofen —the "Red Baron"—who scored eighty aerial victories, the most of any World War I pilot, before his death in combat on April 21, 1918. Swope's reports from Germany were published in January 1917 as *Inside the German Empire, in the Third Year of the War.*

———————————

IT IS GIVEN to few men in this war of bitterness and hatred to achieve popularity both among their own people and the enemy, and it is rarer among the Germans, who generally scorn the arts leading to it. Hindenburg, Mackensen, Muller of the *Emden*, Weddigen of the U-9 are four Germans who have attained this goal in their own country and in England and France, and to this list must be added the name of Captain Boelcke of the German Flying Corps, who shot down thirty-eight enemy aëroplanes before he was killed by a collision with a German machine behind his own lines in late October.

The day that Boelcke scored his twentieth victory I talked with him for an hour. It was early in October, near Bapaume, and the drum-fire of the Somme Battle, which had been raging since June 23, rolled and crashed about us, a thing alive and monstrous. The air was fairly dotted with skymen, while he, the chief of them all, sat quietly under a hangar and let me learn why he was held in such high esteem by friend and foe. For his charm and modesty commanded respect and affection apart from his ability as a fighting flier, and in that capacity he was the greatest the war has produced. He made his record in the face of the English dominance of the air, for that, apart from Zeppelins, the English surely possess. And in building his fame he built a technique of war aviation that is a standard for all tacticians of the clouds. So the story of Boelcke is the story of a man and a master. When he "went," the English and French fliers threw flowers behind the German lines in his memory, and his casket, when he was buried, bore a great wreath from British prisoners in the empire. Only among the aviators of the fighting armies is one certain to find that chivalry which once was never dissociated from war. Theirs is the special heritage of preserving the knightly tradition. The extraordinary bitterness of the other arms of the service makes the contrast all the sharper.

I came into contact with something like thirty or forty German fliers and several English and French airmen along the Somme front, and Boelcke was a fair representative of the lot. His twentieth "bag," made just before I saw him, illustrates the regard the English have for him. Captain Wilson of the Royal Flying Corps, attached to a station near Pozières, was flying over the German lines when Boelcke rose to meet him. Boelcke outguessed, out manœuvered, and outshot the Englishman, who dropped safely to the ground after having a wing broken. Boelcke landed near him, and in surrendering, the Englishman asked the name of his captor.

"Boelcke," replied the German.

The chagrin and humiliation of defeat and capture were forgotten for a moment as the Englishman put out his hand and, as Boelcke shook it, said:

"If I had to be shot down, I am glad it was by so good a man."

Wilson was sent back to Cambrai. The next day Boelcke invited him to lunch with the officers at the flying park, where the captured flier expressed appreciation of the exceptional treatment he had received and told of the high regard in which the English held the German fliers. That night he was sent to a German prison camp.

When I talked with Boelcke, through the courtesy of the German general staff, which usually makes a rule against personal exploitation, I found him to be a good-looking young chap, twenty-five years old, of the thin, wiry, quick, and graceful type usually associated with airmen. His manner of thought was simple and direct, and his conversation modest and responsive.

We met at his station at an old château only a few kilometers from the heaviest fighting, in which he was daily engaged; but his appearance was neat, as is that of all the German officers, his face newly shaved, his uniform clean, and ornamented only with the Iron Cross of the first class. In talking of his work he made it plain that he held it to be a duty, not a sport, as do most of the Englishmen, to the bewilderment of the Germans.

"How many of the twenty that you shot down lived after the fight?" I asked him after congratulating him on his skill and courage and telling him of America's interest in his heroism.

"Only two, unfortunately," he replied with feeling. "All fought so well that I was sorry luck was against them. I think most of the eighteen were killed by bullets from my machine or died in the fall, a few meeting death when they smashed to the ground. One Englishman, Wilson, and a French officer remained alive. The others died for their country."

When I asked for a comparison between the English and the French fliers Boelcke hesitated, and then said he had noticed no great difference. Both, he said, were courageous and skilful, with perhaps a distinction to be observed in the spirit animating them, the English never lacking the spirit of sport, so inexplicable to the German mind, while the French took it fatalistically and with grim earnestness.

Boelcke stood about five feet seven, clean-shaven and red-cheeked, with gray-blue eyes that never left the questioner. He had a thin Roman nose, a soft voice, and rather quick enunciation. He carried a cane of necessity because of a recent wound. He had been wounded several times, but never seriously.

He wore the field-gray uniform of an infantry captain, with propellers on the shoulder straps as insignia of the service. Before the war he was attached to the infantry, and in common with other flying officers, he clung to the old regimental uniform because of the traditions behind it. Only those younger men who have joined the fliers since the war began wear a distinctive flying-corps uniform. All the others wear their old outfit.

Before we talked of his work he said half jestingly:

"Since you will write for America, you might straighten out one point. The London papers credit me with having lived in America and been a lift-boy there, getting my flying experience in that way. I was never in America, and never happened to be a lift-boy. Just before the war began I lived in Dessau, and did some flying there. I liked the work, and when I was called out to join the Prussian forces I went into the flying branch. I hope to visit America for the first time after the war."

When Boelcke went into flying he was first an observer and later a pilot; then he was shifted because of his steady eye, sure nerves, and splendid courage, into the fighting detachment, where he did nothing but fight off hostile aëroplanes scouting over the German lines or go to the relief of his own people attacked while on observation duty.

He always flew alone. There was an observer's seat in his machine, but he never used it. In fact, most of the German fighting fliers travel alone. This is to minimize the risk, and, by engaging the enemy, give the observation machines a chance to get back with information.

"The English say that no German fighters and few observers cross their lines; but that they fly over their own troops," I said to Boelcke.

"That isn't true as regards the observers," he answered earnestly. "They have done much good work over the enemy's forces. It used to be true in part about the fighters. That was at first, because there were several parts of our new Fokkers that we wanted to keep secret; and second, because it was important that we remain on guard in our own territory to prevent the enemy's observers gaining information. Lately circumstances have changed, and we fly everywhere. Obviously, it is the best tactics to bring your man down behind your own lines, so he can be made a prisoner if alive and his machine kept from the chance of the enemy repairing it. Each of us follows the fight through now, no matter where it takes us."

Boelcke's modesty kept him from saying that five of his quarries were shot down inside their own lines. His brother officers, by whom he was much liked, said that the English always tried to seek out the neighborhood in which he was supposed to be, in the hope of having a go with him. But he held to the strictest duty, and never went into action unless directed to do so. In other words, he held to the spirit that is a striking characteristic of the whole German army—teamwork. That is what made Boelcke so well liked.

Boelcke paid a high tribute to Lieutenant Immelmann, who had been killed shortly before, after making his twelfth score, and added that what he and Immelmann had done was possible with equal luck for all the other flying officers. But that there is more to Boelcke's record than mere luck was shown the day after he shot down his twentieth prize, when two of his companions, Rosencrantz and Falbusch, were shot down in trying to stop an English raiding party of eight aëroplanes bombing railroad stations. The courage with which they took on a fight with so superior a force was typical of the German fliers.

When I asked Boelcke about the methods he used in his big-game hunting, he replied:

"I use no special formula except to try to get my man before he gets me. Almost all fighting aëroplanes are similarly rigged, with a machine-gun fixed in front of the pilot. As the gun is stationary, to get it into position I must manœuver my machine, and this is done best by outflying the enemy and coming into him from the rear. I am violating no military secrets in saying this because air fighting, regardless of nationality, is almost always conducted on similar lines. I do not try to out-climb my adversary and come down on him, shooting as I come, but rather to outspeed and outsteer him, gaining the rearward position, where my shots go home while he has nothing to shoot at. I turn as he does, for if he made a quicker or shorter bank than I, he would be able to rake me. To gain speed, we Germans fly light, and as speed is essential in the fighting end, the fighting fliers usually fly alone."

Boelcke had had five machines smashed under him, but always volplaned to earth successfully until the fatal trip late in October, 1916. His favorite machine had the lines of a bird. Even close at hand it looked tiny, being much smaller than the French and British planes.

He used a specially cooled machine-gun, firing ordinary rifle ammunition. The gun had a pistol grip and trigger, and he fired it with one hand, steering with his feet and balancing with the free hand on the wheel. Boelcke and the other

German fliers declined to use anything but regular rifle ammunition fed by the usual web belt, and shooting at a speed that is greater than that of the ordinary automatic pistol, sometimes exceeding five hundred shots a minute.

It was a matter of ammunition that, after two years of chivalry among the knights of the air, threatened to lead to great bitterness. The Germans accused the English fliers of using incendiary bullets in their machine-guns. These cartridges, slightly larger than the usual rifle-shell, carry an explosive chamber that ignites in flight and inflames the substance against which it is shot. As aëroplane wings are oil-coated, they are highly combustible, and several disasters overtook German fliers in this way. The German military authorities resented the new tactics, and talked of making an example of captured Englishmen who had employed what Germany held to be an unfair and illegal method. Rosencrantz and Falbusch were shot down in this way.

It was in this connection that it became my good fortune to be of service in possibly saving the lives of two young English flying officers. They had just been captured and when the prison-yard commandant at Cambrai gave me permission to speak to them, he added that I might tell them that they were to be court-martialed, and probably shot, on the ground that they had been using the so-called illegal ammunition. I was unwilling to be the bearer of such unhappy news, and I did not tell them. Instead, as I had not been placed under any confidence by the German officers, I informed Ambassador Gerard of their danger, when I returned to Berlin, as he is charged with the British interests in Germany. Through the Foreign Office the ambassador immediately requested permission to have the Englishmen represented by counsel at their trial. This permission was granted, although it had been declined in the case of Captain Fryatt. Before I left Germany, I was given to understand that even if the two men were court-martialed, it was highly improbable that they would be executed. They were Ronald Walker, first lieutenant of the Royal Flying Corps, of March Rectory, Cambridgeshire, and Lieutenant C. Smith of Cemetery Road, York. When I spoke with them their first request was to notify their families, and their second for chocolate and cigarettes.

Another Englishman whom I met in the Cambrai prison gave me an English view of the German fliers. He was Captain H. G. Salmond of Bedford, England, whose heavy flying-goggles had been cracked, but not splintered, by a bullet just before he was captured.

"All of us think the German fliers are very good," he said, "and that this chap Boelcke is top hole, but I'm bound to say it's jolly hard to get fight out of them. We have to hang over their parks for hours at a time before we can tempt them to come up and have a go. I've never seen a German machine over our lines; they always wait for us to bring the fight to them.

"The officers here at the prison are decent fellows as far as they can be, but it is rotten to be here without a single change of togs, without a chance for a shave except a hack that a Tommy does for me by renting a razor from a German soldier, and without a sou of money. Naturally, I flew without money, and now I find that my prisoner's pay doesn't start until I'm shifted to Germany.

"I hope they'll hurry up. Here I can't even keep my windows open at night. I had some ripping bad luck in being bagged, though I must say my man was a game one. One of his shots glanced and broke my wind frame. I almost keeled over, but righted, and managed to get down without hurting myself much except for the wound and the bruises I got in landing."

The captain, too, next to having word sent to his family of his safety, wanted most of all chocolate and cigarettes.

The Germans call their anti-aircraft guns "*flak*," deriving the nickname from *Flieger-abschuss-kanonen*. Every park has its own equipment of protective armament, and every series of observation balloons has at a central strategical point a "*flak*" battery. The abbreviation style they lifted from the British "Anzac"—Australian–New Zealand Army Corps.

"I hope to see you again in happier times," said Boelcke in parting. "We Germans don't want to fight, but so long as we are forced to, you may be sure we will, and fight so that we shall never be beaten." And with a wave of his hand Boelcke turned to his quarters to climb into flying-clothes. Three weeks later they dressed him in his shroud.

Theodore Roosevelt: Speech at Cooper Union

When the Progressive Party renominated Roosevelt for president in June 1916, he declined to run, endorsing instead the Republican candidate, Charles Evan Hughes. A former governor of New York and an associate justice of the U.S. Supreme Court, Hughes stepped down from the bench to run on a platform that called for a "strict and honest neutrality" but denounced the administration for having "humiliated us in our own eyes" by failing to defend American rights abroad. Wilson's supporters countered with the slogan "he kept us out of war." Roosevelt could hardly think of a worse reason for re-electing anybody, and said as much at Cooper Union in New York City just days before the election. The results of one of the closest contests in American history hung in the balance for three days. At last the 3,806-vote margin in California made the difference, giving Wilson 277 electoral votes to Hughes's 254.

I AM GLAD to speak in this historic building, at the request of men of such high standing as those who have asked me to speak; and I thank them for having asked me to speak on the most vital of all present-day questions, the "Nation's Crisis," a crisis preeminently moral and spiritual.

There can be no greater misfortune for a free nation than to find itself under incapable leadership when confronted by a great crisis. This is peculiarly the case when the crisis is not merely one in its own history, but is due to some terrible world cataclysm—such a cataclysm as at this moment has overwhelmed civilization. The times have needed a Washington or a Lincoln. Unfortunately we have been granted only another Buchanan.

The appeal is made on behalf of Mr. Wilson that we should not change horses in crossing a stream. The worth of such an appeal is not obvious when the horse, whenever he comes to a stream, first pretends he is going to jump it, then refuses to enter it, and when he has reached the middle alternately moves feebly forward and feebly backward, and occasionally lies down.

We had just entered the greatest crisis in our history when we "swapped horses" by exchanging Buchanan for Lincoln; and if we had not made the exchange we would never have crossed the stream at all. The failure now to change Mr. Wilson for Mr. Hughes would be almost as damaging.

Washington and Lincoln confronted crises of different types, and therefore in any given crisis it is now the example of one, now the example of the other, which it is most essential for us to follow. Each stood absolutely for the National ideal, for a full Union of all our people, perpetual and indestructible, and for the full employment of our entire collective strength to any extent that was necessary in order to meet the nation's needs. Lincoln had to deal with vital questions of internal reform, and with the overturning of internal forces tending toward the destruction of the Union. Washington had to deal primarily, not only with the creation of our Union, but with the maintenance of our liberty against all adverse forces from without. This country must learn the lessons taught by both careers, and must apply the principles established by those careers to the ever-changing conditions of the present, or sooner or later it will go down in utter ruin.

The lesson of nationalism and therefore of efficient action through the national government is taught by both careers. At the present moment we need to apply this principle in our social and industrial life to a degree far greater than was the case in either Washington's day or Lincoln's.

The expansion of our people across the continent has gone hand in hand with their immense concentration in great cities, and with gigantic changes in the machinery of communication, transportation, and production; changes which have worked a business revolution almost as vast as that worked by all similar revolutions put together since the days of the Roman Empire. Therefore we are now forced to face problems not only new in degree, but new in kind. We must face these problems in the spirit of Washington and Lincoln; but our methods in industrial life must differ as completely from those that obtained in the times of those two great men of the past as the weapons of warfare now differ from the flintlocks of Washington's soldiers, or the muzzle-loading smooth-bores of Lincoln's day. We must quit the effort to meet modern conditions by flintlock legislation. We must recognize, as modern Germany has recognized, that it is folly either to try to cripple business by making it ineffective, or to fail to insist that the wage-worker and consumer must be given their full share of the prosperity that comes from the successful application and use of modern industrial instrumentalities. Both capitalists and wageworkers must understand that the performance of duties and the enjoyment of rights go hand in hand. Any shirking of obligation toward the nation, and towards the people that make up the nation, deprives the offenders of all moral right to the enjoyment of privileges of any kind. This applies alike to corporations and to labor unions, to rich men and poor men, to big men and little men.

There can be no genuine feeling of patriotism of the kind that makes all men willing and eager to die for the land, unless there has been some measure of success in making the land worth living in for all alike, whatever their station, so long as they do their duty; and on the other hand, no man has a right to enjoy any benefits whatever from living in the land in time of peace, unless he is trained physically and spiritually so that if duty calls he can and will do his part to keep the land against all alien aggression. Every citizen of this land, every American of whatever creed or national origin, should keep in mind the injunction of George Washington to his nephews, when in his will dated July 9th, 1799, he bequeathed to each of them a sword, making the bequest in the following words:

> "The swords are accompanied with an injunction not to unsheathe them for the purpose of shedding blood, except it be for self-defense, or in defense of their country and its rights; and in the latter case to keep them unsheathed and prefer falling with them in their hands to the relinquishment thereof."

These are noble words. Remember that they gained their nobility only because the deeds of Washington had been such that he had a right to utter them. His sword had been sheathed until he drew it on behalf of national liberty and of humanity, and then it was kept unsheathed until victory came. His sword was a terror to the powers of evil. It was a flame of white fire in the eyes of those who fought for what was right.

Washington loved peace. Perhaps Lincoln loved peace even

more. But when the choice was between peace and righteousness, both alike trod undaunted the dark path that led through terror and suffering and the imminent menace of death to the shining goal beyond. We treasure the lofty words these men spoke. We treasure them because they were not merely words, but the high expression of deeds still higher; the expression of a serene valor that was never betrayed by a cold heart or a subtle and selfish brain. We treasure what Washington enjoined on his blood-kin as their duty when they should inherit his swords; but we do so only because Washington's own sword never slipped from a hand made irresolute by fear. We treasure the words that Lincoln spoke at Gettysburg, and in his second inaugural; words spoken with the inspiration of a prophet of old, standing between the horns of the altar, while the pillars of the temple reeled round about. The words spoken by Lincoln were spoken when he was weighed down by iron grief, and yet was upheld by an iron will, so that he stood erect while the foundations of the country rocked beneath his feet, and with breaking heart and undaunted soul poured out, as if it were a libation, the life blood of the best and bravest of the land. We cherish these words of his only because they were made good by his deeds. We remember that he said that a government dedicated to freedom should not perish from the earth. We remember it only because he did not let the government perish. We remember that he said that the bondman should be free at whatever cost. We remember it only because he paid the cost and set the bondman free.

When Lincoln accepted the nomination of the Republican Party in 1860, he spoke of the platform of that party as follows:

> "The declaration of principles and sentiments which accompanies your letter meets my approval, and it shall be my care not to violate or disregard them in any part."

This was a short statement. It derived its value from the fact that it was a promise that was kept. I ask you to compare this record of Lincoln's with the cynicism shown by Mr. Wilson at different times in repudiating almost every promise he has ever made on any matter of vital importance. He has repudiated the promises of the platform on which he was elected. He has repudiated the promises he made on the stump to further his own election. He has now repudiated about all the promises which he has made since he became President.

I have been assailed because I have criticised Mr. Wilson. I have not said one thing of him that was not absolutely accurate and truthful. I have not said one thing of him which I did not deem it necessary to say because of the vital interests of this Republic. I have criticised him because I believe he has dragged in the dust what was most sacred in our past, and has jeopardized the most vital hopes of our future. I have never spoken of him as strongly as Abraham Lincoln in his day spoke of Buchanan and Pierce when they were Presidents of the United States. I spoke of him at all, only because I have felt that in this great world crisis he has played a more evil part than Buchanan and Pierce ever played in the years that led up to and saw the opening of the Civil War. I criticise him now because he has adroitly and cleverly and with sinister ability appealed to all that is weakest and most unworthy in the American character; and also because he has adroitly and cleverly and with sinister ability sought to mislead many men and women who are neither weak nor unworthy, but who have been misled by a shadow dance of words. He has made our statesmanship a thing of empty elocution. He has covered his fear of standing for the right behind a veil of rhetorical phrases. He has wrapped the true heart of the nation in a spangled shroud of rhetoric. He has kept the eyes of the people dazzled so that they know not what is real and what is false, so that they turn, bewildered, unable to discern the difference between the glitter that veneers evil and the stark realities of courage and honesty, of truth and strength. In the face of the world he has covered this nation's face with shame as with a garment.

I hardly know whether to feel the most burning indignation at those speeches of his wherein he expresses lofty sentiments which his deeds belie, or at those other speeches wherein he displays a frank cynicism of belief in, and of appeal to, what is basest in the human heart. In a recent speech at Long Branch he said to our people, as reported in the daily press, that "You cannot worship God on an empty stomach, and you cannot be a patriot when you are starving." No more sordid untruth was ever uttered. Is it possible that Mr. Wilson, who professes to be a historian, who has been a college president, and passes for a man of learning, knows nothing either of religion or of patriotism? Does he not know that never yet was there a creed worth having, the professors of which did not fervently worship God whether their stomachs were full or empty? Does he not know that never yet was there a country worth living in which did not develop among her sons something at least of that nobility of soul which makes men not only serve their country when they are starving, but when death has set its doom on their faces?

Such a sentence as this could be uttered only by a President who cares nothing for the nation's soul, and who believes that the nation itself puts its belly above its soul. No wonder that when such a doctrine is preached by the President, his Secretary of War should compare Washington and Washington's soldiers with the bandit chiefs of Mexico and their followers who torture men and murder children, and commit nameless outrages on women. This sentence is as bad as anything Secretary Baker himself said. I call the attention of these apostles of the full belly, of these men who jeer at the nation's soul, I call the attention of President Wilson and his Secretary of War and his Secretary of the Navy, to what Washington said of his own soldiers when he spoke of them in a letter to Congress on April 21st, 1778:

"Without arrogance or the slightest deviation from truth, it may be said that no history now extant can furnish an instance of an army's suffering such uncommon hardships as ours has done and bearing them with the same patience and fortitude. To see men without clothes to cover their nakedness, without blankets to lie on, without shoes for the want of which their marches might be traced by the blood from their feet, and almost as often without provisions as with them, marching through the frost and snow and at Christmas taking up their winter quarters within a day's march of the enemy without a house or a hut to cover them till they could be built, and submitting without a murmur, is a proof of patience and obedience which, in my opinion, can scarce be paralleled."

That is what Washington said. Does Mr. Wilson think that these men of Valley Forge were not patriots, because they were starving? Is his own soul so small that he cannot see the

greatness of soul of Washington and of the Continental soldiers whose feet left bloody tracks upon the snow as they
marched towards the enemy? They were clad in rags; their eyes
were hollow with famine; their bodies were numbed with cold
and racked with fever; but they loved their country; they stood
for the soul of the nation and not for its belly. Mr. Baker and
Mr. Daniels have done evil to this country only because they
stood where their master, Mr. Wilson, had placed them. Mr.
Baker has preached the doctrine of contempt for the men of
the Revolution only because he has followed the lead of the
President, who says that religion is merely a matter of a full
stomach, and that patriotism vanishes when heroes feel the
pinch of famine. I call your attention to these statements not
only because they are foul slanders on everything that is good
in human nature, not only because they are a foul slander on
every American worth calling an American, but because they
show the character of Mr. Wilson himself.

So much for Mr. Wilson when he says what he really feels.
Now a word about what he says when he speaks what it is
quite impossible that he really believes. On last Saturday afternoon, with an effrontery that is literally dumbfounding, he
said that when he "started in one direction" he "would never
turn around and go back," and that he "had acted upon this
principle all his life," and that he "intended to act upon it in
the future," and that he "did not see any obstacle that would
make him turn back." Why, his whole record has consisted in
turning back at every point when he was bidden to do so by
either fear or self-interest. He has reversed himself on almost
every important position he has ever taken. There is not a
bandit leader in Mexico who does not know that if he can
show enough strength he can at any moment make Mr. Wilson
not merely turn back, but humbly kiss his hand; kiss the hand
that is red with the blood of our men, women and children.
Mr. Wilson says that he "never turns back!" Why, he has been
conducting his whole campaign on the appeal that he has
"kept us out of war"; and yet last Thursday, without a moment's notice, and only ten days before election, after having
been going full speed in one direction, he turned around and
went full speed in the reverse direction on this very point;
saying, forsooth, that if there was another war we must not

keep out of it! He has been claiming credit because in the case of Belgium he has preserved a neutrality that would make Pontius Pilate quiver with envy; and yet in this speech last Thursday he said that never again must we be neutral! He has kept us absolutely unprepared; so that now we are as absolutely unprepared, after he has been in office three and a half years, as we were when he took office; and yet he now says that we must enter the next war whenever one comes! He has looked on without a single throb of his cold heart, without the least quickening of his tepid pulse, while gallant Belgium was trampled into bloody mire, while the Turk inflicted on the Armenian and Syrian Christians wrongs that would have blasted the memory of Attila, and he has claimed credit for his neutral indifference to their suffering; and yet now, ten days before election, he says the United States must hereafter refuse to allow small nations to be mishandled by big, powerful nations. Do it now, Mr. Wilson! If you mean what you say, Mr. Wilson, show that you mean it by your action in the present.

There is no more evil lesson that can be taught this people than to cover up failure in the performance of duty in the present by the utterance of glittering generalities as to the performance of duty in the nebulous future. With all my heart I believe in seeing this country prepare its own soul and body so that it can stand up for the weak when they are oppressed by the strong. But before it can do so it must fit itself to defend its own rights, and it must stand for the rights of its citizens. During the last three years and a half, hundreds of American men, women and children have been murdered on the high seas, and in Mexico. Mr. Wilson has not dared to stand up for them. He has let them suffer without relief, and without inflicting punishment upon the wrongdoers. When he announces that in some dim future he intends to stand up for the rights of others, let him make good in the present by now standing up for the rights of our own people. He wrote Germany that he would hold her to "strict accountability" if an American lost his life on an American or neutral ship by her submarine warfare. Forthwith the Arabic and the Gulflight were sunk. But Mr. Wilson dared not take any action to make his threat effective. He held Germany to no accountability, loose or strict.

Germany despised him; and the Lusitania was sunk in consequence. Thirteen hundred and ninety-four people were
drowned, one hundred and three of them babies under two
years of age. Two days later, while the dead mothers with their
dead babies in their arms lay by scores in the Queenstown
morgue, Mr. Wilson selected the moment as opportune to
utter his famous sentence about being "Too proud to fight."
Mr. Wilson now dwells at Shadow Lawn. There should be shadows enough at Shadow Lawn; the shadows of men, women
and children who have risen from the ooze of the ocean bottom and from graves in foreign lands; the shadows of the
helpless whom Mr. Wilson did not dare protect lest he might
have to face danger; the shadows of babies gasping pitifully as
they sank under the waves; the shadows of women outraged
and slain by bandits; the shadows of Boyd and Adair and their
troopers who lay in the Mexican desert, the black blood
crusted round their mouths, and their dim eyes looking upward, because President Wilson had sent them to do a task,
and had then shamefully abandoned them to the mercy of foes
who knew no mercy. Those are the shadows proper for Shadow
Lawn; the shadows of deeds that were never done; the shadows
of lofty words that were followed by no action; the shadows of
the tortured dead.

The titanic war still staggers to and fro across the continent
of Europe. The nations engaged in the death wrestle still show
no sign of letting up. Some time in the next four years the end
will come, and then no human being can tell what this nation
will have to face. If we were ready and able to defend ourselves
and to do our duty to others, and if our abilities were backed
by an iron willingness to show courage and good faith on behalf both of ourselves and of others, not only would our own
place in the world be secure, but we might render incalculable
service to other nations. If we elect Mr. Wilson it will be serving
notice on the world that the traditions, the high moral standards, the courageous purposes of Washington and Lincoln
have been obscured, and that in their stead we have deliberately elected to show ourselves for the time being a sordid, soft
and spineless nation; content to accept any and every insult;
content to pay no heed to the most flagrant wrongs done to

the small and weak; allowing our men, women and children to be murdered and outraged; anxious only to gather every dollar that we can, to spend it in luxury, and to replace it by any form of moneymaking which we can follow with safety to our own bodies.

We cannot for our own sakes, we cannot for the sake of the world at large, afford to take such a position. In place of the man who is now in the White House, who has wrought such shame on our people, let us put in the Presidential chair the clean and upright Justice of the Supreme Court, the fearless Governor of New York, whose whole public record has been that of a man straightforward in his thoughts and courageous in his actions, who cannot be controlled to do what is wrong, and who will do what is right no matter what influences may be brought against him.

November 3, 1916

John Jay Chapman
to the Harvard Alumni Bulletin

Victor Chapman was shot down June 23, 1916, near Verdun—the first American aviator killed in combat during the war. When Harvard, both his and his father's alma mater, announced that it would build a memorial to the university men who had died in the war, John Jay Chapman—a lawyer, impassioned social reformer, and idiosyncratic essayist—made his views known.

———————

Editor, HARVARD ALUMNI BULLETIN:

I take advantage of your permission to give my views on the proposed memorial to Harvard men who have given their lives in the war. The Harvard Corporation on November 27 voted to include in one memorial both those who fell fighting for the cause of Germany and those who fell in the cause of the Allies.

It may be that I am over-influenced by personal feelings due to my son's death in France, or to an ineradicable sentiment that I am bound up with Harvard and that her fair fame is my business. In either case you will be able to discount any extravagance of statement which I may fall into.

Monuments are the earliest recorded language of mankind, and the nature of the appeal which they make is deeper than consciousness and deeper than all explanation. Every monument that men put up commemorates an idea, or a cause. This fact made the difficulty which Charles Francis Adams experienced some years ago in advocating a monument to that very noble gentleman, Robert E. Lee. A monument to Robert E. Lee would proclaim to the world the right of secession.

For a monument always proclaims an abstract idea. A monument to a scientist commemorates science; to a musician, music; to a lawyer, law, etc. If you should erect a monument to any two ideas that are mutually exclusive, e.g., to Theseus *and* the Minotaur, to St. George *and* the dragon, to the Greeks who fell at Thermopylae *and* the Persians who slew them, to George Washington *and* George III, your monument would become a symbol of zero. No matter what you intended to express by your monument it would express zero on the issue.

It happens that the struggle now going on in Europe is the great struggle between good and evil, of which all the myths of Theseus, and St. George, and all the contests for freedom, at Thermopylae, at Valley Forge, etc., have been faint prefigurations. Germany exhibits tyranny, brutality, cruelty, craft, cynicism, and an open determination to rule the world. No one ever dreamed that so much evil existed as Germany has revealed to mankind.

It happens also that quite a number of Harvard men have seen this evil, and have given their lives in an endeavor to oppose and destroy it for the world's sake. To erect a single monument to commemorate these men as well as any Harvard men who fought for Germany would be to announce to the world that Harvard sees no difference between the cause of Germany and the cause of the Allies.

The Harvard men who died for France certainly deserve no credit except the credit they gain from the cause of France. Harvard in this resolution proclaims that she has no interest in the cause of France. Then why erect a monument?

But the matter is deeper still and subtler still. The proposed memorial, by the declaration of its indifference to the cause of the Allies for which these men fell, casts a slur upon their cause,—if not an insult upon their memory. It is, to be sure, an unconscious insult, an unintended slur; and perhaps this phase of the matter is transitory, and historically unimportant. Yet there is a permanent side to the situation.

The Corporation's resolution of November 27 is at this moment a little enduring monument to zero erected in the sanctum of the Corporation,—zero on the moral aspects of the war. The question arises in any thoughtful mind, and is certain to be raised in public before long: What has a university to teach its students, or to stand for in the public consciousness, which can compete for a moment in importance with the moral questions of the war,—these very questions which in this resolution are rated at zero?

JOHN JAY CHAPMAN, '84.

Barrytown, N. Y.

January 4, 1917

Robert Frost: Not to Keep

Robert Frost had moved in 1912 to Beaconsfield, Buckinghamshire, England, where he befriended the essayist, biographer, and critic Edward Thomas. With Frost's encouragement, Thomas began to write poetry, and the two men drew so close that they spoke of raising their families next to each other in America. Frost returned to New England in 1915, and Thomas became an artillery officer in the British army. His letters to Frost inspired this poem, which was published a few months before Thomas was killed in action on April 9, 1917, in the battle of Arras.

They sent him back to her. The letter came
Saying . . . and she could have him. And before
She could be sure there was no hidden ill
Under the formal writing, he was in her sight—
Living.—They gave him back to her alive—
How else? They are not known to send the dead—
And not disfigured visibly. His face?—
His hands? She had to look—to ask
"What was it, dear?" And she had given all
And still she had all—*they* had—they the lucky!
Wasn't she glad now? Everything seemed won,
And all the rest for them permissible ease.
She had to ask "What was it, dear?"
                                    "Enough,
Yet not enough. A bullet through and through,
High in the breast. Nothing but what good care
And medicine and rest—and you a week,
Can cure me of to go again." The same
Grim giving to do over for them both.
She dared no more than ask him with her eyes
How was it with him for a second trial.
And with his eyes he asked her not to ask.
They had given him back to her, but not to keep.

The Yale Review, January 1917

Woodrow Wilson: Address to the Senate

After more than two years, the war appeared to have reached a bloody impasse. On December 12, 1916, the German government expressed a willingness to negotiate peace, and a week later Wilson asked both sides to state their terms. The Germans declined, waiting to hear first from the Allies. On January 10, 1917, Britain and France offered specific conditions, which included returning Alsace-Lorraine, restoring all occupied territory with indemnities, and requiring freedom for nationalities within Austria-Hungary—all of which was unacceptable to the Central Powers. Wilson could see a path forward only if the United States took the diplomatic initiative. He articulated his vision for a peace settlement in an address to the Senate.

Gentlemen of the Senate: 22 January, 1917.

   On the eighteenth of December last I addressed an identic note to the governments of the nations now at war requesting them to state, more definitely than they had yet been stated by either group of belligerents, the terms upon which they would deem it possible to make peace. I spoke on behalf of humanity and of the rights of all neutral nations like our own, many of whose most vital interests the war puts in constant jeopardy. The Central Powers united in a reply which stated merely that they were ready to meet their antagonists in conference to discuss terms of peace. The Entente Powers have replied much more definitely and have stated, in general terms, indeed, but with sufficient definiteness to imply details, the arrangements, guarantees, and acts of reparation which they deem to be the indispensable conditions of a satisfactory settlement. We are that much nearer a definite discussion of the peace which shall end the present war. We are that much nearer the discussion of the international concert which must thereafter hold the world at peace. In every discussion of the peace that must end this war it is taken for granted that that peace must be followed by some definite concert of power which will make it virtually impossible that any such catastrophe should ever overwhelm us again. Every lover of mankind, every sane and thoughtful man must take that for granted.

I have sought this opportunity to address you because I thought that I owed it to you, as the council associated with me in the final determination of our international obligations, to disclose to you without reserve the thought and purpose that have been taking form in my mind in regard to the duty of our Government in the days to come when it will be necessary to lay afresh and upon a new plan the foundations of peace among the nations.

It is inconceivable that the people of the United States should play no part in that great enterprise. To take part in such a service will be the opportunity for which they have sought to prepare themselves by the very principles and purposes of their polity and the approved practices of their Government ever since the days when they set up a new nation in the high and honourable hope that it might in all that it was and did show mankind the way to liberty. They cannot in honour withhold the service to which they are now about to be challenged. They do not wish to withhold it. But they owe it to themselves and to the other nations of the world to state the conditions under which they will feel free to render it.

That service is nothing less than this, to add their authority and their power to the authority and force of other nations to guarantee peace and justice throughout the world. Such a settlement cannot now be long postponed. It is right that before it comes this Government should frankly formulate the conditions upon which it would feel justified in asking our people to approve its formal and solemn adherence to a League for Peace. I am here to attempt to state those conditions.

The present war must first be ended; but we owe it to candour and to a just regard for the opinion of mankind to say that, so far as our participation in guarantees of future peace is concerned, it makes a great deal of difference in what way and upon what terms it is ended. The treaties and agreements which bring it to an end must embody terms which will create a peace that is worth guaranteeing and preserving, a peace that will win the approval of mankind, not merely a peace that will serve the several interests and immediate aims of the nations engaged. We shall have no voice in determining what those terms shall be, but we shall, I feel sure, have a voice in determining whether they shall be made lasting or not by the guarantees of a universal covenant; and our judgment upon what is fundamental and essential as a condition precedent to permanency should be spoken now, not afterwards when it may be too late.

No covenant of cooperative peace that does not include the peoples of the New World can suffice to keep the future safe against war; and yet there is only one sort of peace that the peoples of America could join in guaranteeing. The elements of that peace must be elements that engage the confidence and satisfy the principles of the American governments, elements consistent with their political faith and the practical convictions which the peoples of America have once for all embraced and undertaken to defend.

I do not mean to say that any American government would throw any obstacle in the way of any terms of peace the governments now at war might agree upon, or seek to upset them when made, whatever they might be. I only take it for granted that mere terms of peace between the belligerents will not satisfy even the belligerents themselves. Mere agreements may not make peace secure. It will be absolutely necessary that a force be created as a guarantor of the permanency of the settlement so much greater than the force of any nation now engaged or any alliance hitherto formed or projected that no nation, no probable combination of nations could face or withstand it. If the peace presently to be made is to endure, it must be a peace made secure by the organized major force of mankind.

The terms of the immediate peace agreed upon will determine whether it is a peace for which such a guarantee can be secured. The question upon which the whole future peace and policy of the world depends is this: Is the present war a struggle for a just and secure peace, or only for a new balance of power? If it be only a struggle for a new balance of power, who will guarantee, who can guarantee, the stable equilibrium of the new arrangement? Only a tranquil Europe can be a stable Europe. There must be, not a balance of power, but a community of power; not organized rivalries, but an organized common peace.

Fortunately we have received very explicit assurances on this point. The statesmen of both of the groups of nations now arrayed against one another have said, in terms that could not be misinterpreted, that it was no part of the purpose they had in mind to crush their antagonists. But the implications of these assurances may not be equally clear to all,—may not be the same on both sides of the water. I think it will be serviceable if I attempt to set forth what we understand them to be.

They imply, first of all, that it must be a peace without victory. It is not pleasant to say this. I beg that I may be permitted to put my own interpretation upon it and that it may be understood that no other interpretation was in my thought. I am seeking only to face realities and to face them without soft concealments. Victory would mean peace forced upon the loser, a victor's terms imposed upon the vanquished. It would be accepted in humiliation, under duress, at an intolerable sacrifice, and would leave a sting, a resentment, a bitter memory upon which terms of peace would rest, not permanently, but only as upon quicksand. Only a peace between equals can last. Only a peace the very principle of which is equality and a common participation in a common benefit. The right state of mind, the right feeling between nations, is as necessary for a lasting peace as is the just settlement of vexed questions of territory or of racial and national allegiance.

The equality of nations upon which peace must be founded if it is to last must be an equality of rights; the guarantees exchanged must neither recognize nor imply a difference between big nations and small, between those that are powerful and those that are weak. Right must be based upon the common strength, not upon the individual strength, of the nations upon whose concert peace will depend. Equality of territory or of resources there of course cannot be; nor any other sort of equality not gained in the ordinary peaceful and legitimate development of the peoples themselves. But no one asks or expects anything more than an equality of rights. Mankind is looking now for freedom of life, not for equipoises of power.

And there is a deeper thing involved than even equality of right among organized nations. No peace can last, or ought to last, which does not recognize and accept the principle that governments derive all their just powers from the consent of the governed, and that no right anywhere exists to hand peoples about from sovereignty to sovereignty as if they were property. I take it for granted, for instance, if I may venture upon a single example, that statesmen everywhere are agreed that there should be a united, independent, and autonomous Poland, and that henceforth inviolable security of life, of worship, and of industrial and social development should be guaranteed to all peoples who have lived hitherto under the power of governments devoted to a faith and purpose hostile to their own.

I speak of this, not because of any desire to exalt an abstract political principle which has always been held very dear by those who have sought to build up liberty in America, but for the same reason that I have spoken of the other conditions of peace which seem to me clearly indispensable,—because I wish frankly to uncover realities. Any peace which does not recognize and accept this principle will inevitably be upset. It will not rest upon the affections or the convictions of mankind. The ferment of spirit of whole populations will fight subtly and constantly against it, and all the world will sympathize. The world can be at peace only if its life is stable, and there can be no stability where the will is in rebellion, where there is not tranquillity of spirit and a sense of justice, of freedom, and of right.

So far as practicable, moreover, every great people now struggling towards a full development of its resources and of its powers should be assured a direct outlet to the great highways of the sea. Where this cannot be done by the cession of territory, it can no doubt be done by the neutralization of direct rights of way under the general guarantee which will assure the peace itself. With a right comity of arrangement no nation need be shut away from free access to the open paths of the world's commerce.

And the paths of the sea must alike in law and in fact be free. The freedom of the seas is the *sine qua non* of peace, equality, and cooperation. No doubt a somewhat radical reconsideration of many of the rules of international practice hitherto thought to be established may be necessary in order to make the seas indeed free and common in practically all circumstances for the use of mankind, but the motive for such changes

is convincing and compelling. There can be no trust or intimacy between the peoples of the world without them. The
free, constant, unthreatened intercourse of nations is an essential part of the process of peace and of development. It need
not be difficult either to define or to secure the freedom of the
seas if the governments of the world sincerely desire to come
to an agreement concerning it.

It is a problem closely connected with the limitation of naval
armaments and the cooperation of the navies of the world in
keeping the seas at once free and safe. And the question of
limiting naval armaments opens the wider and perhaps more
difficult question of the limitation of armies and of all pro-
grammes of military preparation. Difficult and delicate as these
questions are, they must be faced with the utmost candour and
decided in a spirit of real accommodation if peace is to come
with healing in its wings, and come to stay. Peace cannot be
had without concession and sacrifice. There can be no sense of
safety and equality among the nations if great preponderating
armaments are henceforth to continue here and there to be
built up and maintained. The statesmen of the world must
plan for peace and nations must adjust and accommodate their
policy to it as they have planned for war and made ready for pitiless contest and rivalry. The question of armaments, whether on
land or sea, is the most immediately and intensely practical
question connected with the future fortunes of nations and of
mankind.

I have spoken upon these great matters without reserve and
with the utmost explicitness because it has seemed to me to be
necessary if the world's yearning desire for peace was anywhere
to find free voice and utterance. Perhaps I am the only person
in high authority amongst all the peoples of the world who is
at liberty to speak and hold nothing back. I am speaking as an
individual, and yet I am speaking also, of course, as the responsible head of a great government, and I feel confident that I
have said what the people of the United States would wish me
to say. May I not add that I hope and believe that I am in effect
speaking for liberals and friends of humanity in every nation
and of every programme of liberty? I would fain believe that I
am speaking for the silent mass of mankind everywhere who
have as yet had no place or opportunity to speak their real

hearts out concerning the death and ruin they see to have come already upon the persons and the homes they hold most dear.

And in holding out the expectation that the people and Government of the United States will join the other civilized nations of the world in guaranteeing the permanence of peace upon such terms as I have named I speak with the greater boldness and confidence because it is clear to every man who can think that there is in this promise no breach in either our traditions or our policy as a nation, but a fulfillment, rather, of all that we have professed or striven for.

I am proposing, as it were, that the nations should with one accord adopt the doctrine of President Monroe as the doctrine of the world: that no nation should seek to extend its polity over any other nation or people, but that every people should be left free to determine its own polity, its own way of development, unhindered, unthreatened, unafraid, the little along with the great and powerful.

I am proposing that all nations henceforth avoid entangling alliances which would draw them into competitions of power, catch them in a net of intrigue and selfish rivalry, and disturb their own affairs with influences intruded from without. There is no entangling alliance in a concert of power. When all unite to act in the same sense and with the same purpose all act in the common interest and are free to live their own lives under a common protection.

I am proposing government by the consent of the governed; that freedom of the seas which in international conference after conference representatives of the United States have urged with the eloquence of those who are the convinced disciples of liberty; and that moderation of armaments which makes of armies and navies a power for order merely, not an instrument of aggression or of selfish violence.

These are American principles, American policies. We could stand for no others. And they are also the principles and policies of forward looking men and women everywhere, of every modern nation, of every enlightened community. They are the principles of mankind and must prevail.

H. L. Mencken: "The Diary of a Retreat"

In 1916 the German offensive at Verdun failed to break the French army, while the Anglo-French offensive on the Somme forced the Germans to fight a debilitating defensive battle against an enemy with growing material superiority. Severe food shortages increased unrest on the home front in Germany and Austria-Hungary. Faced with the prospect of losing a prolonged war of attrition, the German military leadership launched a new U-boat campaign aimed at British imports of food and raw materials. Although the resumption of unrestricted submarine warfare risked drawing the United States into the war, Germany believed it could defeat Great Britain before America could effectively intervene. Despite the opposition of Chancellor Bethmann Hollweg, who believed America's entry into the conflict would seal Germany's fate, the Kaiser endorsed the new policy on January 9, 1917. Henry Louis Mencken, former editor of the *Baltimore Evening Sun*, co-editor of *The Smart Set*, and America's premier social critic, arrived in Berlin in late January to report on the war for the *Sun*. The grandson of German immigrants, Mencken had already sparked controversy in the United States with his pro-German sympathies. He now found himself in Berlin at a turning point in American-German relations.

BERLIN, Feb. 1.

ACROSS the front page of the *Tageblatt* this morning ran the long-awaited, hat-in-the-ring-throwing, much-pother-through-out-the-world-up-stirring headline: *Verkündung des unein-geschränkten U-Boot-Krieges!*—Proclamation of the Unrestrained U-Boat War! At last, by dam! The adjective used to be *rücksichtslos*, which is to say, reckless. Lately it has been *verschärften*: sharpened. Now it is *uneingeschränkten*: unrestrained, unlimited, fast and loose, knock him down and drag him out, without benefit of clergy. But whatever the term used to designate it, the thing in itself remains, and out of that thing in itself, unless I lose my guess, a lot of trouble is going to arise. If the United States accepts this new slaughter of ships without giving Dr. Bernstorff his walking papers, it will be a miracle. If it goes another month without horning into the war, it will be two miracles . . .

282

I got back to Berlin from Vilna late last night, tired, rheumatic and half-frozen, and rolled into bed at once. This morning I turned out just in time for the fireworks. The first man I encountered was Raymond Swing, of the Chicago *Daily News*. I had borrowed a heavy overcoat and a pair of leather *Gamaschen* from him, and went to his office in Unter den Linden to thank him for them, and to give him a *Leberwurst*—a souvenir of the army slaughter house at Novo Aleksandrowsk. "Pack your bags!" said Swing. "The jig is up. We'll be kicked out in five days." "But no, my dear Mon Chair! Surely"——"But yes, my dear Herr Kollege! This is the finish. *Exeunt omnes!*" . . . Swing's chief, Oswald Schütte, came in. A far more optimistic fellow. Schütte believes that the United States will keep hands off—that the new rough-house will promote peace. The other American correspondents, he says, are about evenly divided. As for me!——

I have spoken of fireworks. Let me be exact: I have seen none on the German side. The calm of the Germans is amazing, almost staggering. They know very well that they are challenging the United States to join their enemies, and not only the United States, but also Denmark, Holland, Norway and even Switzerland, and yet they show no anxiety whatever, and scarcely any interest. Outside the *Lokal-Anzeiger* office, in Unter den Linden, the crowd about the bulletin board has never got beyond 15 or 20 persons all day. Not a single newspaper has printed an extra. No unusual display of the news is visible. The *Lokal-Anzeiger* publishes a brief statement by Admiral von Scheer in a box on its front page—and that is all. The other papers content themselves with the pronunciamento of Von Hindenburg, in small type and on inside pages.

> Our front is secure on all sides. We have the necessary reserves everywhere. The morale of our troops is sound and unshaken. The general military situation is such that we can accept safely all consequences of an unrestrained U-boat war. And inasmuch as this U-boat war offers us the means of doing the maximum of damage to our foes we must begin it forthwith.

It would be impossible to overestimate the effect of this statement. It is almost alone responsible, I dare say, for the calm which hangs over Berlin—and for the unmistakable jauntiness under the calm. Hindenburg is not only the hero and idol of the Germans; he has become their prophet and oracle, and his rare and austere utterances are accepted as inspired and impeccable. If he proposed an invasion of England in motorboats, I doubt that a single *Feldgrau* would hang back; or even harbor a qualm. He is credited with astounding prodigies—and many of them he has actually performed. . . . More, he is a very careful fellow. Three or four times today I picked up the rumor that Falkenhayn, with three army corps from Roumania, is already on the Danish frontier. Two weeks ago, coming down from Copenhagen, I saw the Danes digging trenches feverishly—and all the way from the German border back to the very gates of their capital.

* * *

At noon I went to the Military Bureau of the Foreign Office and called on Rittmeister *(i.e.,* Cavalry Captain) Freiherr von Plettenberg. Plettenberg is the Father Superior of the American correspondents. He speaks American (not English, but American) perfectly, and knows the United States very well, for in his early days he worked for the North German Lloyd on the Hoboken docks and later he rose to be a director of the company. Now he looks after newspaper men who want to go to the front, and is in charge of the map room in which the doings of the army are explained to them, and keeps a jug of Scotch whisky for their refreshment. I found him in conference with another old North German Lloyd official, Hauptmann (that is, Captain) von Vignau. The two hailed me hospitably and got out the jug.

"Well," said the Rittmeister, "what is it going to be?"

I ventured the guess that the finish was in sight.

The Rittmeister looked thoughtful.

"I hope not," he said, "but maybe you are right. In any case, it's too late to turn back. England has escaped too long. We must give her a taste of steel."

"But if the United States enters the war?"

The Rittmeister lighted a cigarette.

"We have considered that, of course," he replied. "We have had to consider it for two years past. It's a pity. But it's now too late to go back. . . . Meanwhile, let us be hopeful. Maybe the United States will see our point of view, after all. We have no desire to hurt Americans. All we ask is that they keep out of the way while we tackle England. They have done as much for the English. Perhaps they'll do as much for us."

"And if not?"

The Rittmeister achieved a shrug.

"Who can say?" he replied. "All I know is that we are ready to fight as long as it is necessary."

The Hauptmann then spoke up.

"You have seen the German Army in the field," he said. "Did you find any sign that it was *Kriegsmüde* (war-weary)?"

Half an hour's conversation followed, always circling back to the same arguments. Plettenberg and Vignau profess to be optimistic, but it is obvious that both of them expect Bernstorff to be given his passports, and that a declaration of war by the United States would not surprise them. I have met other officers today, and find them all talking the same way. It is difficult to define their mood precisely. I expected a certain amount of anxiety, for they all realize that they are at the parting of the ways, but failed to discover it. They cultivate stoicism, serenity, a dispassionate manner. The air is full of electricity, but there are no sparks.

* * *

At the Foreign Office in the Wilhelmstrasse I found Dr. Roediger at his interminable labors. Dr. Roediger is to the American correspondents in civil matters what the gentlemen of the Military Bureau are to them in military matters. He is the man one sees if one desires to investigate the potato situation, or to look into diplomatic papers, or to arrange for credit with the wireless authorities, or to get advice and consolation. An Oxford man and smooth-shaven, he looks the Englishman far more than the German, and speaks English perfectly. He inhabits a bare room near the entrance of the Wilhelmstrasse barn, and Americans hammer on his door all day.

"We haven't a word," he said. "Our note has been delivered, but that's all we know."

"And what do you expect?"

"Expect? We don't expect. We merely wait."

* * *

Up stairs I found Consul-General Thiel, one of the few men in the Wilhelmstrasse who actually know anything about the United States, and the American point of view, and American ways of thinking. Significantly enough, I found him packing his traps; he is ordered to some new field of labor. Is his job here done? Have they given up trying to win their case in America? . . . The Consul-General himself was somewhat vague about it, but he was willing enough to discuss the general situation, and he gave me the clearest statement of the German position that I have yet got hold of.

"This new submarine war," he said, "is the only way to an early peace. Germany's peace proposal was perfectly sincere. If the Allies had asked for our terms they would have been surprised by their moderation. Instead, they offered us not only a flat refusal, but also an insult so gross that no self-respecting people could be expected to bear it. We now accept the situation. It is, as they say, a fight to a finish—and we fully expect to be on our legs at that finish.

"Personally, I am very sorry that the United States seems likely to join our enemies, but I see no way to avoid it. The United States, in point of fact, has been on the side of our enemies for a long while, and it has already done us more damage than most of them. To me, at least, this seems quite natural. The sympathies of nations go with their interests, and England's control of the seas makes American interests identical with her own. The only thing we can do is to make that control of the seas as precarious and hollow as possible, and this we propose to do. So long as England is uninjured by the war, she will keep it going, for it is to her interest to have every other nation damaged as much as possible, including her allies. The one way out is to bring the war home to her—to make her suffer as she is trying to make us suffer. This is what we intend to do."

"But suppose the United States goes to her aid?"

"I am still in hope," replied the Consul-General, "that the United States won't. We have no quarrel with the American people, and do not want to injure them. We offer them a safe conduct for neutral and necessary business. All we ask of them is that they cease to give active aid to our chief enemy. There is a chance that they may yet see our point of view, and so keep out of what is not their fight, but England's fight. However, if they do not, we shall have to face the fact. It will take the United States six months to make ready for an effective blow. During those six months we will accomplish our plans against England."

"And what then? You will simply have the United States to fight, and the United States can raise and equip five million men."

"True," replied the Consul-General. "But how will the United States get them to Europe?"

* * *

So much for Consul-General Thiel. I sat with him an hour, bombarding him with objections, problems and dilemmas. To every one he offered a pat answer. Obviously, the whole thing has been thought out to nine or ten places of decimals. I have talked to half a dozen. Thiel is by far the cleverest of them. They all say the same things; it is like a lesson learned. The one novelty I encountered I dredged out of an officer—more, a marine officer.

"The trouble with this new U-boat campaign," he said, "is that it promises too much. The German people probably expect a clean-up of the English merchant fleet in six months. They will be disappointed. Say 40 ships come out of a given harbor in a day. We'll be lucky if we sink one. Starving England will be a hard job—maybe, like starving Germany, a quite impossible job."

* * *

No such doubts, however, are on tap in the newspapers. There the tune is one of extreme optimism, even of complacency. Prussian discipline is showing itself; even those who were against the "sharpened" U-boat war a week ago are now in favor of it and preaching it. Among them, for example, is Herr Gutmann, head of the great Dresdner Bank. He used to be a leader of the anti-U-boatistas; today he told one of the American correspondents that he is hot for the slaughter.

In yesterday's papers was a statement by the official Wolff Telegraph Bureau, obviously designed to prepare the way for this morning's announcement. It showed the doings of the U-boats in 1916. During December, it appears, they disposed of 217 ships, of a total tonnage of 415,500. Of these ships, 152 flew enemy flags and 65 were neutrals carrying contraband. The English loss was 240,000 tons. All this in December alone. In November the bag was 408,500 tons. But I had better copy the figures for the whole year from yesterday's *Lokal-Anzeiger*:

	Tons.
January–February	238,000
March–April	432,000
May–June	219,000
July–August	273,779
September	254,600
October	393,500
November	408,500
December	415,500
Total	2,634,879

The "sharpened" U-boat war, so it is gossiped, is estimated to dispose of 1,000,000 tons a month. A large bite, indeed. What of the chewing thereof?

* * *

The cold here is intense. It is positively painful to walk down Unter den Linden. Soldiers, schoolboys, old men, women and even girls are digging away at the frozen snow. In some of the Berlin boroughs the authorities are calling for volunteers. . . . As for me, I am pretty well banged up. The cold came very near fetching me in Lithuania, and now I have a game foot and my nose shows signs of frostbite. What if my beauty is ruined forever?

* * *

Gerard seems very pessimistic. The other correspondents say that he is always pessimistic—that he has been preaching disaster for a year past. But this time, I fancy, he has good excuse for his mood.

The Baltimore Sun, March 10, 1917

Robert Lansing:
Memorandum on the Severance of
Diplomatic Relations with Germany

Shortly after the resurgence of unrestricted German submarine warfare, Secretary of State Lansing wrote a long memorandum recording the administration's response.

February 4, 1917.

During the forenoon of Wednesday, January 31, 1917, the German Ambassador telephoned my office and arranged an interview for four o'clock that afternoon. He did not indicate his purpose and my own idea was that he probably desired to talk over confidentially the terms on which Germany would make peace.

That afternoon I was working on a letter to the President in regard to the arming of merchant vessels on the ground that Germany was undoubtedly preparing to renew vigorous submarine warfare. Before I had completed the letter the German Ambassador was announced.

When he entered my room at ten minutes after four I noticed that, though he moved with his usual springy step, he did not smile with his customary assurance. After shaking hands and sitting down in the large easy chair by the side of my desk he drew forth from an envelope, which he carried, several papers. Selecting one he held it out saying that he had been instructed to deliver it to me. As I took the paper he said that he had had for convenience an English translation made. He then handed me three documents in English consisting of a note and two accompanying memoranda.

He asked me if he should read them to me or if I would read them to myself before he said anything about them. I replied that I would read the papers, which I did slowly and carefully for as the nature of the communication was disclosed I realized that it was of very serious import and would probably bring on the gravest crisis which this Government had had to face during the war. The note announced the renewal on the next day of indiscriminate submarine warfare, and the annulment of the assurances given this Government by Germany in the note of May 4, 1916, following the SUSSEX affair.

While I had been anticipating for nearly three months this very moment in our relations with Germany and had given expression to my conviction in the public statement which I made concerning our note of December 18th, for which I had been so generally criticized, I was nevertheless surprised that Germany's return to ruthless methods came at this time. I knew that all her shipyards had been working to their full capacity in constructing submarines for the past seven months and that thousands of men were being trained to handle their complex mechanism, but I assumed that on account of the difficulties of using submarines in northern waters during midwinter the campaign would not begin before March and probably not until April. It was therefore with real amazement that I read the note and memoranda handed me. I can only account for the premature announcement of indiscriminate warfare on the ground that the food situation in Germany had reached such a pass that the Imperial Government had to do something to satisfy public opinion.

As I finished my deliberate perusal of the papers, I laid them on the desk and turned toward Count Bernstorff. "I am sorry" he said, "to have to bring about this situation but my Government could do nothing else."

I replied, "That is of course the excuse given for this sudden action, but you must know that it cannot be accepted."

"Of course; of course," he said, "I understand that. I know it is very serious, very, and I deeply regret that it is necessary."

"I believe you do regret it," I answered, "for you know what the result will be. But I am not blaming you personally."

"You should not," he said with evident feeling, "you know how constantly I have worked for peace."

"I do know it," I said, "I have never doubted your desire or failed to appreciate your efforts."

"I still hope," he said speaking with much earnestness, "that with a full realization of Germany's situation your Government will in justice decide that the notification of blockade is entirely warranted."

I answered him that I could not discuss the merits until I had thoroughly digested the documents, but I would say that the first reading had made a very bad impression, and that to give only eight hours notice without any previous warning of intention was in my opinion an unfriendly and indefensible act.

He exclaimed, "I do not think it was so intended; I am sure it was not."

"I regret that I must differ with you," I replied, "but this has come so suddenly that I am sure you will understand I do not wish to discuss the matter further."

"Of course, of course; I quite understand," he said rising and extending his hand which I took with a feeling almost of compassion for the man, whose eyes were suffused and who was not at all the jaunty care-free man-of-the-world he usually was. With a ghost of a smile he bowed as I said "Good afternoon" and turning left the room.

Immediately on his departure I called in Polk and Woolsey, and read the communication which I had received. We all agreed that the only course which seemed open was to break off diplomatic relations. I think we all expressed indignation at the shortness of the notice and the repudiation of the SUSSEX assurance.

I telephoned to the White House and found the President was out. I then wrote him a short letter transmitting the papers, and sent it by Sweet to the White House, who between five and five-thirty left it with the usher to be put in the President's hands as soon as he returned. Through some confusion with other papers the President did not get the papers until after eight o'clock. He then telephoned me to come to the White House.

From a quarter to nine until half past ten we conferred in his study beneath the picture of Secretary Day and the French Ambassador signing the preliminaries of peace with Spain. Throughout the conference I maintained that we must pursue the course which we had declared we would pursue in our SUSSEX note of April 18, 1916, namely to break off relations with Germany if she practiced ruthless submarine warfare; that any lesser action would be impossible; and that the only question in my mind was whether we ought not to go further and declare that the actual renewal of indiscriminate submarine attack affecting our citizens or ships would be considered by us to be an act of war.

The President, though deeply incensed at Germany's insolent notice, said, that he was not yet sure what course we must pursue and must think it over; that he had been more and more impressed with the idea that "white civilization" and its domination in the world rested largely on our ability to keep this country intact, as we would have to build up the nations ravaged by the war. He said that as this idea had grown upon him he had come to the feeling that he was willing to go to any lengths rather than to have the nation actually involved in the conflict.

I argued with him that, if the break did not come now, it was bound to do so in very short time, and that we would be in a much stronger position before the world if we lived up to our declared purpose than if we waited until we were further humiliated. I said that if we failed to act I did not think we could hold up our heads as a great nation and that our voice in the future would be treated with contempt by both the Allies and Germany.

The President said that he was not sure of that; that, if he believed that it was for the good of the world for the United States to keep out of the war in the present circumstances, he would be willing to bear all the criticism and abuse which would surely follow our failure to break with Germany; that contempt was nothing unless it impaired future usefulness; and that nothing could induce him to break off relations unless he was convinced that viewed from every angle it was the wisest thing to do.

I replied to this that I felt that the greatness of the part which a nation plays in the world depends largely upon its character and the high regard of other nations; that I felt that to permit Germany to do this abominable thing without firmly following out to the letter what we had proclaimed to the world we would do, would be to lose our character as a great power and the esteem of all nations; and that to be considered a "bluffer" was an impossible position for a nation which cherished self-respect.

There was of course much more said during our conference. The President showed much irritation over the British disregard for neutral rights and over the British plan (asserted by Germany) to furnish British merchant ships with heavy guns. I told him that so far as proof of this we had none, but it seemed to me that Germany's declaration in any event justified such a practice. He replied that he was not certain that the argument was sound but he did not think it worth while to discuss it now in view of the present crisis.

After some further talk it was agreed that I should prepare a note to Bernstorff setting out the breach of faith by Germany and breaking off diplomatic relations. This was to be a tentative draft and a basis for further consideration of the subject.

On returning home I immediately prepared a draft in rough form, and the next morning (Thursday) redrew it in my own handwriting using for the quoted parts clippings from the printed correspondence. (This note with practically no changes was the one finally sent.)

Although many diplomats called at the Department I denied myself to them all as I did not care to discuss the situation. However I had to see Senator Hitchcock, who in the absence of Senator Stone was the ranking Democrat on the Committee of Foreign Relations. He suggested that we ask the belligerents of both sides for a ten-days armistice. I asked him what good that would do. He said "To gain time." "Well, and then what?" I asked. He had nothing to offer and I told him that I did not think that it would get us anywhere, but that, even if there was some benefit to be gained, I was sure that Germany would decline and the Allies would probably do the same. He went away in a dispirited frame of mind, saying that he saw no other way of avoiding the trouble.

At noon on Thursday (the 1st of February) I went over to the White House and with Col. House, who had arrived early that morning, conferred with the President for about an hour in his study. We went over substantially the same ground, which the President and I had covered the night before. The Colonel, as is customary with him, said very little, but what he did say was in support of my views.

I went further in this conference than I did in the previous one by asserting that in my opinion peace and civilization depended on the establishment of democratic institutions throughout the world, and that this would be impossible if Prussian militarism after the war controlled Germany. The President said that he was not sure of this as it might mean the disintegration of German power and the destruction of the German nation. His argument did not impress me as very genuine, and I concluded that he was in his usual careful way endeavoring to look at all sides of the question.

When I left the conference I felt convinced that the President had almost reached a decision to send Bernstorff home. It was not any particular thing which he said but rather a general impression gained from the entire conversation. At any rate I felt very much better than I had the night before when the President's tone of indecision had depressed me. Probably I misjudged him because he did not at once fall in with my views, which were certainly radical.

Thursday evening I wrote out at considerable length an arraignment of Germany on her submarine methods and the faithlessness of the German Government in giving its assurance of May 4, 1916, in the SUSSEX case. I wrote it as I felt without softening the harshness of my thoughts, and, as I intended to send it to the President, I wished him to know exactly how I felt.

The next morning (Friday, the 2nd) I read to Mr. Polk my arraignment of Germany, which he heartily approved, and then sent it to the President. Three times that morning the President and I conferred over our private wire. We discussed the issuance of passports, the sailing of American ships for the "danger zone" and the possibility of securing identic action by other neutrals in case of a break with Germany.

At 2:30 Friday afternoon the Cabinet met and sat until 4:45. The entire time was given to a discussion of the crisis with Germany. The discussion was very general although it was chiefly confined to the subjects which the President and I had been over in our conferences.

I felt all the time that, while the President was holding back in the traces, he was not unwilling to be urged forward by argument favoring a strong policy. He appeared to be resisting the idea of a break with Germany. In this he was supported by Secretary Wilson, and Burleson seemed more or less sympathetic. All the rest were united in support of severing relations, McAdoo and Houston being particularly outspoken. I am not at all sure that the President urged his arguments in good faith. I do not mean anything invidious by this, only that I have often seen him in Cabinet meetings oppose action, which I was sure he favored, in order to draw out arguments on both sides. Indeed I am morally certain his mind was made up when he came to the meeting.

Just at the close of the session he read the note which I had drafted saying that if it seemed best to sever relations it was proposed to send this note which avoided a general attack on lawless submarine warfare and dealt only with Germany's broken promise.

I think that the part of the discussion which most deeply shocked some of the members was the President's comment on a remark which I made concerning the future peace of the world. I said that I was convinced that an essential of permanent peace was that all nations should be politically liberalized; that the only surety of independence for small nations was that the great and powerful should have democratic institutions because democracies were never aggressive or unjust. I went on to say that it seemed to me there could be no question but that to bring to an end absolutism the Allies ought to succeed, and that it was for our interest and for the interest of the world that we should join the Allies and aid them if we went into the war at all.

To this the President replied, "I am not so sure of that." He then went on to argue that probably greater justice would be done if the conflict ended in a draw. This did not make so painful an impression on me as it did on others who heard it, for I was sure it was done to draw out arguments. Furthermore I knew that the President agreed with me about democracy being the only firm foundation for universal peace.

When we left the Cabinet room some of my colleagues remarked that I seemed very cheerful. I told them I was cheerful for I was sure that it would all come out right. They shook their heads dubiously and said that they could not see it that way.

Friday was a day of extreme tension. From morning till night officials and newspaper men were fairly on tiptoe with suppressed excitement. Fully eighty of the correspondents were present at my interview in the morning, and they were swarming in the corridors when I returned to the Department at five o'clock. I slept soundly that night feeling sure that the President would act vigorously.

Saturday morning (the 3rd) soon after I reached the Department Polk and I discussed the situation. He was doubtful and distressed, and I assured him that I was certain the President would act that day.

A little after ten Senator Stone, who had arrived from the West on Friday noon and had taken part in the conferences which the President held in his room at the Capitol soon after the Cabinet meeting, came in, but as I had just been summoned by telephone to the White House we had only a word together.

At 10:30 I reached the President's study and we conferred for half an hour. He told me that he had decided to hand Bernstorff his passports and to recall Gerard, and that at two o'clock that afternoon he would address Congress laying before them in a little more elaborate form the substance of the note which I had drafted together with a statement that he would come before them again and ask for powers in case Germany should carry out her threats. I congratulated him on his decision saying I was sure that he was right and that the American people almost to a man would stand behind him.

It was arranged that at the hour when the President began his address to Congress Count Bernstorff would receive his passports. I told the President that in view of the routine preparation of the note and passport and of the necessity of getting of telegrams to Berlin and neutral countries inviting their identic action, it would be impossible for me to go to the Capitol at two o'clock. He replied that he understood perfectly and that in any event the essential part of his address was in the note which I had drafted.

On leaving the White House I met Tumulty in front of the Executive Offices. He had just returned from the Capitol, where he had been to arrange for the President's appearance there at two o'clock. I then hurried over to the Department, called in Polk and Woolsey and later Phillips and Sweet. The necessary papers were prepared as rapidly as possible and I read and signed them. Everything was carried through according to schedule. At two the President spoke at the Capitol in the House of Representatives. Three minutes before two Woolsey delivered the note and passports to Count Bernstorff at the Embassy; and the necessary telegrams were put on the wires.

Even so serious an act as the severing of diplomatic relations with Germany was a great relief from the intense anxiety of the two preceding days. From the reception of the German notification Wednesday afternoon I had felt that such action was the only possible one to take and to preserve the Honor, dignity and prestige of the United States. I did not really doubt but that the President would ultimately reach the same conclusion, but I feared that the delay would create the impression that he was wavering and undecided. When, therefore, he announced his decision on Saturday morning I was thankful that the period of uncertainty was over, that the die was cast, and that Germany's insolent challenge had been met with firmness. That it would be received with the universal approval by the American people was not a matter of doubt. Whatever may be the consequences no other course was open to a self-respecting nation.

New York Tribune: *Germany Asks Mexico to Seek Alliance with Japan for War on U.S.*

The violent and unstable politics in Mexico since its revolution in 1910 had challenged both the Taft and Wilson administrations. Tensions between the United States and the dictatorship of General Victoriano Huerta led to fighting in Veracruz in April 1914, in which nineteen U.S. Marines and sailors and more than 150 Mexican soldiers were killed. On March 9, 1916, the Mexican rebel Pancho Villa, angered by American support for Huerta's successor, Venustiano Carranza, raided Columbus, New Mexico, killing eighteen American soldiers and civilians. Wilson responded by sending General John J. Pershing across the border with 5,000 men in what would prove to be an unsuccessful attempt to capture Villa. The expedition, which lasted until early February 1917, angered Carranza and led to two skirmishes between Pershing's troops and Carranza's soldiers. German foreign minister Arthur Zimmermann sought to exploit the situation by sending a coded telegram containing a highly provocative proposal to the German ambassador in Mexico. British naval intelligence intercepted and decrypted the telegram and then presented it to Ambassador Page in London on February 24, 1917. Wilson released it to the press four days later.

GERMANY ASKS MEXICO TO SEEK ALLIANCE WITH JAPAN FOR WAR ON U.S.

Message from Foreign Secretary Zimmermann to Carranza
Reveals Astounding Plot to Attack from Border if This
Nation Should Go to War with Teutons; Texas, New Mexico
and Arizona Promised as Reward

Tokio Called Upon to Desert Allies and Form Alliance with Central
Powers—Bernstorff Got Instructions from Berlin on January 19
and Sent Them to Minister von Eckhardt—Money and Share
in "Victorious Peace" Pledged to Carranza,
Together with "Lost Territory"

WASHINGTON, Feb. 28.—The Associated Press is enabled to reveal that Germany, in planning unrestricted submarine warfare and counting its consequences, proposed an alliance with Mexico and Japan to make war on the United States, if this country should not remain neutral. Japan, through Mexican mediation, was to be urged to abandon her allies and join in the attack on the United States.

Mexico, for her reward, was to receive general financial support from Germany, reconquer Texas, New Mexico and Arizona —lost provinces—and share in the victorious peace terms Germany contemplated.

Details were left to German Minister von Eckhardt in Mexico City, who by instructions signed by German Foreign Minister Zimmermann at Berlin on January 19, 1917, was directed to propose the alliance with Mexico to General Carranza and suggest that Mexico seek to bring Japan into the plot.

These instructions were transmitted to von Eckhardt through Count von Bernstorff, former German Ambassador here, now on his way home to Germany under a safe conduct obtained from his enemies by the country against which he was plotting war. Germany pictured to Mexico by broad intimation England and the Entente Allies defeated, Germany and her allies triumphant and in world domination by the instrument of unrestricted submarine warfare.

ZIMMERMANN'S INSTRUCTIONS

A copy of Zimmermann's instructions to von Eckhardt, sent through von Bernstorff, is in possession of the United States Government. It is as follows:

Berlin, January 19, 1917.

On the 1st of February we intend to begin submarine warfare unrestricted. In spite of this, it is our intention to endeavor to keep neutral the United States of America.

If this attempt is not successful, we propose an alliance on the following basis with Mexico: That we shall make war together and together make peace. We shall give general financial support, and it is understood that Mexico is to reconquer the lost territory in New Mexico, Texas and Arizona. The details are left to you for settlement.

You are instructed to inform the President of Mexico of the

above in the greatest confidence as soon as it is certain that there will be an outbreak of war with the United States, and suggest that the President of Mexico, on his own initiative, should communicate with Japan suggesting adherence at once to this plan; at the same time, offer to mediate between Germany and Japan.

Please call to the attention of the President of Mexico that the employment of ruthless submarine warfare now promises to compel England to make peace in a few months.

(Signed)   ZIMMERMANN.

United States Kept Document Secret

This document has been in the hands of the government since President Wilson broke off diplomatic relations with Germany. It has been kept secret, while the President has been asking Congress for full authority to deal with Germany, and while Congress has been hesitating.

It was in the President's hands while Chancellor von Bethmann-Hollweg was declaring that the United States had placed an interpretation on the submarine declaration "never intended by Germany" and that Germany had promoted and honored friendly relations with the United States "as an heirloom from Frederick the Great."

Of itself, if there were no other, it is considered a sufficient answer to the German Chancellor's plaint that the United States "brusquely" broke off relations without giving "authentic" reasons for its action.

There was an intimation that Germany's astounding proposal that Japan turn traitor to her Allies had been answered by Tokio.

The document supplies the missing link to many separate chains of circumstances, which until now have seemed to lead to no definite point. It sheds new light upon the frequently reported but indefinable movements of the Mexican government to couple its situation with the friction between the United States and Japan.

It adds another chapter to the celebrated report of Jules Cambon, French Ambassador in Berlin before the war, of Germany's world-wide plans for stirring strife on every continent where it might aid her in the struggle for world domination, which she dreamed was close at hand.

It adds a climax to the operations of Count von Bernstorff and the German Embassy in this country, which have been colored with passport frauds, charges of dynamite plots and intrigue, the full extent of which never has been published.

It gives new credence to persistent reports of submarine bases on Mexican territory in the Gulf of Mexico; it takes cognizance of a fact long recognized by American army chiefs —that if Japan ever undertook to invade the United States it probably would be through Mexico, over the border and into the Mississippi Valley to split the country in two.

It recalls that Count von Bernstorff, when handed his passports, was very reluctant to return to Germany, but expressed a preference for asylum in Cuba. It gives a new explanation to the repeated arrests on the border of men charged by American military authorities with being German intelligence agents.

Last of all, it seems to show a connection with General Carranza's recent proposal to neutrals that exports of food and munitions to the Entente Allies be cut off, and an intimation that he might stop the supply of oil, so vital to the British navy, which is exported from the Tampico fields.

What Congress will do, and how members of Congress who openly have sympathized with Germany in their opposition to clothing the President with full authority to protect American rights will regard the revelation of Germany's machinations to attack the United States, is the subject to-night of the keenest interest.

Such a proposal as Germany instructed her minister to make to Mexico borders on an act of war if, actually, it is not one.

MEXICANS KNEW OF PLOT

No doubt exists here now that the persistent reports during the last two years of the operations of German agents not alone in Mexico, but all through Central America and the West Indies, are based on fact. There is now no doubt whatever that the proposed alliance with Mexico was known to high Mexican officials who are distinguished for their anti-Americanism. Among them are Rafael Zubaran, Carranza's Minister to Germany, and Luis Cabrera, Carranza's Minister of Finance.

It is apparent that the proposal had taken definite form when Zubaran returned to Mexico City from Berlin recently.

His return from his foreign post was covered by the fact that Carranza had called in many of his diplomats for "conferences." Some time before that Cabrera while still at Atlantic City in the conference of the American-Mexican Joint Commission, had suggested in a guarded way to a member of the American section that he regretted that the commission had not succeeded fully in settling the difficulties between Mexico and the United States, for, he said, he had hoped it might continue its work and make peace for the world.

When pressed for some details of how the commission could restore world peace, Cabrera suggested that the American republics controlled the destiny of the war by controlling a large part of its supplies. Mexico, he intimated, might do her part by cutting off exports of oil. The American commissioners dismissed his ideas as visionary.

Almost coincident with Zubaran's return from Germany Cabrera returned to Mexico City, open in his expressions of anti-Americanism. Zubaran, before being sent abroad, had represented General Carranza here while the Niagara mediation conferences were proceeding, and was no less avowedly anti-American than Cabrera.

Von Schoen Sent to Mexico

Meanwhile, Baron von Schoen, secretary of the German Embassy here, was transferred to the legation in Mexico City. No explanation could be obtained of the reason for his transfer, and such investigation as was possible failed to develop why a secretary from the United States should be sent to the German Legation in Mexico.

Baron von Schoen's association with the moves, if any at all, does not appear. The only outward indication that he might have been connected with them is found in the fact that he recently had been detached from the German Embassy in Tokio and was well acquainted with the Japanese Minister in Mexico City.

Carranza's peace proposal was openly pronounced an evidence of German influence in Mexico by officials here, who declared it was intended only to embarrass the United States. Then, apparently, some influences showed their effect on the course of the Mexican government, and on February 25

Cabrera, the Minister of Finance, issued a statement describing the "amazement" of the Mexican government that the American newspapers should have interpreted General Carranza's proposal to cut off exports of munitions as a suggestion that he might cut off shipments of British oil. They were, Cabrera declared, "entirely groundless," and that feature of the situation ended.

AMBASSADOR DIRECTED SCHEME

Count von Bernstorff's connection with the plot, further than serving as the channel of communication, is intensified by the fact that the German Embassy here was not merely the medium of delivering a message in this instance, but was really a sort of headquarters for all the German missions to Central and South America.

The German naval attaché, Captain Boy-Ed, and the military attaché, Captain von Papen, whose recall was forced by the State Department because of their military activities in this country, also were accredited to Mexico, and between the outbreak of the war and their departure from this country made at least one visit there.

For months many naval officers here have believed that the mysterious German sea raiders of the South Atlantic must have found a base somewhere on the Mexican coast, and that such a base could not be maintained without the knowledge and consent of Mexican officials. Last November the British charge at Mexico City presented to the Carranza Foreign Office a notification that if it was discovered that the Mexican neutrality thus had been violated the Allies would take "drastic measures" to prevent a continuance of that situation.

MEXICO SENT INSOLENT REPLY

In a note almost insolent in tone, Foreign Minister Aguilar replied to the charge that, in effect, it was the business of the Allies to keep German submarines out of Western waters, and that if they were not kept out Mexico would adopt whatever course the circumstances might commend.

To German influences also have been attributed in some quarters the vigorous steps taken by the de facto Finance Minister to force loans from the Banco Nacional and the Bank of London and Mexico, owned by French and British capital.

The institutions were closed by the Mexican officials and some of their officers imprisoned and held for weeks, despite repeated protests by France, Great Britain and the United States.

Envoy on "Secret Mission"

Reports of German machine guns and German gunners in the Carranza army also have been persistent. It is recalled tonight, too, that last November, when the Mexican-American Joint Commission was making its futile effort to adjust the difficulties between the two countries the Austro-Hungarian Ambassador at Mexico City, Count Kalman Votkanya, made a trip to the United States on what he described as a "secret mission."

A suggestion interpreted by some officials as an indication that Germany might have made approaches to Mexico at that time was made by Cabrera in an address at Philadelphia on November 10.

"The foes of the United States will certainly assume to be friends of Mexico," said Mr. Cabrera, "and will try to take advantage of any sort of resentment Mexico may have against the United States. Mexico, nevertheless, understands that in case of a conflict between the United States and any other nation outside America her attitude must be one of continental solidarity."

Germans Incite Raids

It has been an open secret that Department of Justice agents in their investigations of plots to violate American neutrality by setting on foot armed expeditions in Mexico more than once have uncovered what appeared to be trails of the German Secret Service.

A few days ago Fred Kaiser, suspected of being a German agent, was arrested at Nogales on charges brought under the neutrality statutes, Department of Justice agents declaring he had attempted to obtain military information on the American side of the border and had cultivated the society of American army officers with an apparent intention of promoting those efforts.

Last July, when W. H. Schweibz, who claimed to be a former Germany army officer, escaped into Mexico at Nogales after

arrest on similar charges, the deputy marshal who tried to follow him was stopped by Mexican authorities.

EVIDENCE WILL AMAZE PUBLIC

The full extent of the evidence of Germany's plotting against
the United States, gathered by the American Secret Service,
may become known only according to the course of the future
relations between the two countries. It is known that much
evidence of the operations of the German Embassy and persons who were responsible to it never has been permitted to
come out, because officials preferred to guard against inflam-
ing the public mind in the tense situation with Germany. The
public amazement which a full exposition of the evidence in
the hands of the government would cause cannot be overesti-
mated.

Only to-day the Council of National Defence, created by act
of Congress, issued an appeal to all Americans to show every
consideration for aliens in this country.

"We call upon all citizens," said the appeal, "if untoward
events should come upon us, to present to these aliens, many
of whom to-morrow will be Americans, an attitude of neither
suspicion nor aggressiveness. We urge upon all Americans to
meet these millions of foreign born with unchanged manner
and with unprejudiced mind."

New York Tribune, March 1, 1917

Edmond C. C. Genet:
Diary, March 19–24, 1917

The great-great-grandson of Edmond "Citizen" Genet, the first minister sent by Revolutionary France to the United States, Edmond C. C. Genet had deserted the U.S. Navy in 1915 in order to join the French Foreign Legion. He fought in the Champagne offensive that September. Accepted for flight training by the French aviation service in May 1916, Genet joined the Lafayette Escadrille in January 1917. While flying a Nieuport 17 near St. Quentin, he would be shot down and killed by anti-aircraft fire on April 16, 1917.

Mon. 19   959. Cloudy windy day. Escadrille on duty this A.M. MacConnell, I and Parsons went out for 3rd Patrol at 9 o'clock to protect French reconnaissance machine around Ham. Parsons had to return before we reached the lines on account of motor trouble. "Mac" and I kept on—he leading. We stayed under 2000 metres and patroled around Ham over the French reglage avions until about 10 o'clock. Then "Mac" headed north towards St. Quentin and I followed to the rear and above him. North of Ham I discovered two German machines much higher than we coming towards us to attack. One was much nearer than the other and began to come towards "Mac." I immediately started up towards it and met it at 2200 metres—leaving Mac to take care of the end. The German Avion was a biplace and his gunner opened fire on me at 200 yds. as the pilot began to circle around me. I opened fire with my incendiary bullets and headed directly for them. The German's first few shots cut one main wing support in half and an explosive bullet hit the guiding rod of the left aileron and cut open a nice hole in my left cheek. I scarcely noticed it and kept on firing until we were scarcely 25 yds apart. We passed close and I peaked down. The German didn't follow but an anti-aircraft battery shelled me for quite awhile. At 1000 metres I stopped and circled around for 15 minutes in search of Mac and the second Boche but the clouds were thick and I saw nothing. I was afraid my supports would break entirely and my wound was hurting some so I headed for St. Just at a low altitude reaching there at 10:45 hoping all the way back that Mac had preceeded me but when I arrived I found he had not and tho Lufberry and Lt. de Laage have been out over the region north of Ham with their Spads this afternoon to look for him (de Laage also landed to ask the troops if they saw him brought down) they found nothing and the chances are Mac was either brought down by the German machine or else wounded in combat and forced to land in their territory and so is a prisoner. Its the best we can hope for—that he is at least alive. I feel dreadfully—my wound, tho a bit painful, is nothing compared with my grief for poor "Mac's" loss. The Commandant told me, when I described the combat to him this morning, that I fought bravely. I wish I had been able to do more for MacConnell. The French and English forces are advancing beyond Nesle, Ham, and Noyon and with few losses. Perhaps to-morrow will bring forth better news of "Mac." if the advance continues. British troops have taken Peronne and the French have gained the Heights north of Soissons. The enemy are retreating back to St. Quentin and the Hindenburg line. Thaw landed beside Nesle this morning to give information to the British cavalry patrols and had lunch with a French woman and her daughters who have been 31 months behind German lines. The civilians left by the Germans in the recaptured towns are wild with joy and relief at being once again with their own people. The German troops before retiring have torn up all roads, railroads, cut down all trees, flooded a lot of land, fired all important buildings in every town, insulted the women— carrying off many of the younger women and old men with them, and destroying all stores they couldn't carry with them. They are fiends if ever there were any! All the territory at present in their hands towards St. Quentin is in flames. Its horrible to see. German submarines have torpedoed 3 more vessels carrying the American Flag. Now will any action be taken! The French are trying to form a new cabinet and the revolution in Russia has quieted down with the installation of the new popular government. My machine has been nearly repaired this afternoon, and as my wound is scarcely grave enough to bother over I hope I shall be out on service again either to-morrow afternoon or at least the following day. Thank God I escaped so luckily to-day but I do wish I had brought down that damned Boche machine and that poor MacConnell was back safely with us to-night. If he was killed I know he met his end bravely fighting. God grant he isn't dead!

Tues. 20 960th day of the war. This is dear old Dad's birthday. Very high wind all day and plenty of low clouds kept us from going out all today. We've been hoping and waiting all day for news of poor MacConnell but not a word has come and it seems certain that he has met his fate at the hands of those damned Huns within their lines. I feel horribly depressed over it. If I had only been able to get to him and save him from his fate! Would that I had a dozen such wounds as I have and he were back here with us all safe and sound. Sent the news to Major Parker to-day and Lovell. Wrote to Paul Rockwell. Poor Paul will feel dreadfully over it. Walked down to St. Just late in P.M. but came back in time for tea. Rocle and another chap were around for dinner. Wrote a long letter to dear little Mother before dinner. She'll be worried, I'm afraid, when she reads in it of my wound but I think it is best I told her. The doctor redressed it this A.M., and it seems better—only pains rather dully. French and British advance continued today. We may move further east soon as now we are much too far from the new lines. Three American ships sunk the day before yesterday seem to have brought the crisis almost to a climax and war seems surer than ever. Feeling mighty blue and lonely for darling beloved Gertrude tonight. Ever hearing from her again has certainly become to seem utterly hopeless. The old dear letters of love and devotion from her coming at these trying times would mean so much to me. Can she realize that and yet not write? I can't believe that. Am on first Patrol at 10 o'clock tomorrow morning. Asked Lieut. de Laage to go out on the first patrol and he put me on it. I'm out after blood now in grim earnest to avenge poor MacConnell.

Wed. 21 961. Too windy and cloudy to permit flying all the day. Was put out about that as I wished very much to go out over the lines this morning. I wish I could do something really

worth while for the English and thus get them willing to give
me the English Military Cross. Captain Thenault to-day proposed me for a citation a'l'ordre d'armee which will bring me
the Croix de Guerre with a palm. Poor MacConnell is proposed for a citation also but I'm afraid he is where he will never
know of it or receive his decoration. No news of any sort of
him to-day. Wrote a long letter this morning to Paul Rockwell
telling him about Mac's fate as best I could and my fight. Got
a letter from Cousin Hugh Eastburn but not as cordial a one
as I would like. He expects to get a leave the latter part of April
but may go to Rome if possible. Wrote to Mrs. Wheeler late
this afternoon. She and Dave will be glad to learn I've been
cited at last. Mr. and Mrs. Hoskier, Ronald's parents came out
to visit him and the Escadrille to-day. Dugan came out from
Plessis Belleville to get a machine from the 67th Escadrille to
take back to the G.D.E. and is staying over night with us. We
had 17 persons at the table for dinner to-night. Mr. and Mrs.
Hoskier and Dugan were the guests. Am on service at 6:45
to-morrow morning and from 5:20 P.M. until dark. From all
reports there seem to be big chances of finding Boche machines along the lines now where the present offensive is. Poor
MacConnell and I surely had little trouble finding two on
Monday. I wish I could find one mighty soon and bring it
down within our lines so as to avenge "Mac". I guess there will
be no such luck for me tho.

Thurs. 22   962. Big French success reported to-night towards
St. Quentin. Internal riots also reported in Berlin. Fair in
morning but clouded up heavily and snow fell quite a number
of times during the afternoon. Went out with Lieut de Laage,
Lovell, and Willis from 7 to 8:30 for trip along the lines around
Ham and St. Simon. Very cold and my machine gun got
jammed so I came back. The others followed soon after. Saw
no German machines. Willis got his face badly frozen. Volunteered to go out with a patrol at 11:30. Patrol consisted of 2
Spads (the Captain and Hoskier) and 5 of us with Nieuports.
On account of the heavy thick clouds we got pretty well separated along the lines. Was with Haviland and Hinkle until my
oil clutch began to freeze while we were at 3000 metres where
the cold was very severe and then went down over Ham alone,

made some observations, and came back thru snow and sleet arriving at 1:05. Haviland and Hinkle forced to land near Compeigne for lack of gasoline. Bigelow back before me. Hoskier landed at Mondider because of motor trouble. Parsons had to land at an English aviation field north of the Somme and got back late in the afternoon, and the Captain had to land east of Amiens on account of motor trouble. We had a patrol to make at 5:15 this afternoon consisting of Thaw, Johnson, Lovell and myself. We got all ready to leave but were ordered back at the last minute on account of a big wind storm approaching. It would have made my third flight to-day—a record for me. Was quite satisfied to remain on the ground tho on account of the bad weather. Wrote to Major Parker this morning about "Mac" not having been heard from up to to-day. Soubiran went to Paris this afternoon so I gave him the letter to mail there. Used an hour or so before dinner to write to Ralph Cooper and Miss Mooney. Miss Mooney, as my motherly marraine will be glad to learn that I've won a citation. No more news to-day about MacConnell. Rumor got to Paris yesterday that he was killed and I wounded by a bullet in my shoulder, was lying between life and death in the Amer. Ambulance at Nuilly. Don't mind that report except that it will probably get to New York papers and cause a lot of anxiety to Mother and Rivers and the rest.

Fri. 23   963. Windy and cloudy. Escadrille on service both A.M. and P.M. but none went out until noon. Had to go then on account of expected German attack towards St. Quentin. Report came in from Regiment of French cavalry that they saw the fight MacConnell and I had on Monday morning and that Mac, instead of being attacked by one Boche machine, was attacked by two and was brought down towards St. Quentin and the chances are 9 to 10 that he is dead and not a prisoner. Had I seen all 3 enemy machines I certainly would have stayed close beside Mac and not gone up to attack the nearest but I only saw two and both were coming down towards Mac. The third must have been further back and hidden in the heavy mist. Wrote to Helen Harper late this morning and to Major Parker about MacConnell. Went out with Hoskier and Hinkle at 5 o'clock this afternoon for a short trip along our lines around

Ham and St. Simon, Hinkle turned back soon after we started. Strong northeast wind was blowing a very thick mist and we had to fly very low to find our way at all and I had difficulty in following Hoskier at all. Back at 6 o'clock after being unable to make any adequate observations. Wrote to Paul Rockwell telling him the news about poor Mac. Mrs. Weeks certainly will grieve when she learns of it. Paul will write her about it she is still in the States. All America seems bent on declaring war on Germany very soon. Pres. Wilson has called Congress to session at an early date and will undoubtedly take strong measures. U.S. troops may be sent over to fight on French or Belgian soil and U. S. warships will probably have a naval base in one or more of the Allied Ports over here.

Sat. 24   Dreamed last night that I received a loving letter from beloved Gertrude with her photograph, Oh if that dream will only come true. Cold, windy and misty. News came in this morning that a body of French Cavalry found yesterday at Bois L'Abbe S.E. of Flavy Le Martel a badly smashed Nieuport with the body of MacConnell, dead about 3 days inside with no papers on him and a number of bullet wounds. The Germans evidently only searched his body for papers and then left him unburied. Bois L'Abbe was just back of the German lines up there the 20th. Went out on a reconnaisance patrol with the Captain, Hoskier, Parsons, Hinkle and Bigelow at 10:30. Went along the lines south and southeast of St. Quentin. Saw no Boche machines and little activity on the lines. Very windy and cold in the air. Left patrol when the rest headed back and went over to Bois L'Abbe to find Mac's machine. Went very low and finally found the machine completely wrecked in a tiny orchard just on the southern edge of a town just west of Bois L'Abbé Detroit-Blue, by name. Circled over it and saw lots of French soldiers gathered around it. Mac certainly must have been killed in the air for he never would have attempted to make a landing in that small field. Walked down to St. Just late in afternoon for some exercise. Another American vessel sunk without warning by a German U-boat and 19 American lives lost. Teddy Roosevelt is trying to raise 100,000 volunteers to fight on European soil in case the States declare war and wants all Americans now serving France to be with him to help train the troops. Wish *Teddy would* come over here. Letter from Mr. Grundy demanding definite news about Mac so I have written him a full account of the affair. It was reported in N.Y. papers three days ago that Mac had either been killed or was missing after a flight over the lines. Captain went over to see about Mac's body to-day and found he had been terribly mangled with the wreckage, his papers, boots, cap and flying suit taken by the Boches and his body left unburied beside his machine. He will be buried to-morrow in a coffin and placed in a grave beside the road where he fell. Village there is Petit Detroit instead of Detroit Blue. I made a mistake in the name on the map this morning. All honor to gallant Mac.

Woodrow Wilson:
Address to Congress on War with Germany

Wilson addressed Congress on February 26, asking for the authority to arm American merchant ships. The House of Representatives approved the measure by a vote of 403–13 on March 1, but a Senate filibuster led by Robert "Fighting Bob" La Follette, the progressive Republican from Wisconsin, blocked its passage before the 64th Congress adjourned on March 4. Enraged, Wilson denounced the "little group of willful men" who had "rendered the great Government of the United States helpless and contemptible" and imposed an executive order to arm the ships; but this new policy of armed neutrality failed to stop the Germans from sinking American vessels. On March 20 the cabinet unanimously recommended asking Congress for a declaration of war; and the next day Wilson requested that a joint session convene on April 2. The last president to write his own speeches, he toiled over multiple drafts right up until the morning of his address. On the evening of April 2, Wilson arrived at the Capitol to deliver one of the most important speeches in American history, contending that a war of choice had become one of necessity. Eight words embedded in his argument—"The world must be made safe for democracy"—have remained the cornerstone of American foreign policy for a century. The speech received thunderous approval, which depressed the President. "My message to-day was a message of death for our young men," he said to one of his advisers. "How strange it seems to applaud that." A moment later, Wilson laid his head on the Cabinet table and sobbed.

---

2 April, 1917 8.30 P.M.

Gentlemen of the Congress: I have called the Congress into extraordinary session because there are serious, very serious, choices of policy to be made, and made immediately, which it was neither right nor constitutionally permissible that I should assume the responsibility of making.

On the third of February last I officially laid before you the extraordinary announcement of the Imperial German Government that on and after the first day of February it was its purpose to put aside all restraints of law or of humanity and use its submarines to sink every vessel that sought to approach either the ports of Great Britain and Ireland or the western coasts of Europe or any of the ports controlled by the enemies of Germany within the Mediterranean. That had seemed to be the object of the German submarine warfare earlier in the war, but since April of last year the Imperial Government had somewhat restrained the commanders of its undersea craft in conformity with its promise then given to us that passenger boats should not be sunk and that due warning would be given to all other vessels which its submarines might seek to destroy, when no resistance was offered or escape attempted, and care taken that their crews were given at least a fair chance to save their lives in their open boats. The precautions taken were meagre and haphazard enough, as was proved in distressing instance after instance in the progress of the cruel and unmanly business, but a certain degree of restraint was observed. The new policy has swept every restriction aside. Vessels of every kind, whatever their flag, their character, their cargo, their destination, their errand, have been ruthlessly sent to the bottom without warning and without thought of help or mercy for those on board, the vessels of friendly neutrals along with those of belligerents. Even hospital ships and ships carrying relief to the sorely bereaved and stricken people of Belgium, though the latter were provided with safe conduct through the proscribed areas by the German Government itself and were distinguished by unmistakable marks of identity, have been sunk with the same reckless lack of compassion or of principle.

I was for a little while unable to believe that such things would in fact be done by any government that had hitherto subscribed to the humane practices of civilized nations. International law had its origin in the attempt to set up some law which would be respected and observed upon the seas, where no nation had right of dominion and where lay the free highways of the world. By painful stage after stage has that law been built up, with meagre enough results, indeed, after all was accomplished that could be accomplished, but always with a clear view, at least, of what the heart and conscience of mankind demanded. This minimum of right the German Government has swept aside under the plea of retaliation and necessity and because it had no weapons which it could use at sea except these which it is impossible to employ as it is employing them without throwing to the winds all scruples of humanity or of respect for the understandings that were supposed to underlie the intercourse of the world. I am not now thinking of the loss of property involved, immense and serious as that is, but only of the wanton and wholesale destruction of the lives of non-combatants, men, women, and children, engaged in pursuits which have always, even in the darkest periods of modern history, been deemed innocent and legitimate. Property can be paid for; the lives of peaceful and innocent people cannot be. The present German submarine warfare against commerce is a warfare against mankind.

It is a war against all nations. American ships have been sunk, American lives taken, in ways which it has stirred us very deeply to learn of, but the ships and people of other neutral and friendly nations have been sunk and overwhelmed in the waters in the same way. There has been no discrimination. The challenge is to all mankind. Each nation must decide for itself how it will meet it. The choice we make for ourselves must be made with a moderation of counsel and a temperateness of judgment befitting our character and our motives as a nation. We must put excited feeling away. Our motive will not be revenge or the victorious assertion of the physical might of the nation, but only the vindication of right, of human right, of which we are only a single champion.

When I addressed the Congress on the twenty-sixth of February last I thought that it would suffice to assert our neutral rights with arms, our right to use the seas against unlawful interference, our right to keep our people safe against unlawful violence. But armed neutrality, it now appears, is impracticable. Because submarines are in effect outlaws when used as the German submarines have been used against merchant shipping, it is impossible to defend ships against their attacks as the law of nations has assumed that merchantmen would defend themselves against privateers or cruisers, visible craft giving chase upon the open sea. It is common prudence in such circumstances, grim necessity, indeed, to endeavour to destroy them before they have shown their own intention. They must be dealt with upon sight, if dealt with at all. The German

Government denies the right of neutrals to use arms at all within the areas of the sea which it has proscribed, even in the defense of rights which no modern publicist has ever before questioned their right to defend. The intimation is conveyed that the armed guards which we have placed on our merchant ships will be treated as beyond the pale of law and subject to be dealt with as pirates would be. Armed neutrality is ineffectual enough at best; in such circumstances and in the face of such pretensions it is worse than ineffectual: it is likely only to produce what it was meant to prevent; it is practically certain to draw us into the war without either the rights or the effectiveness of belligerents. There is one choice we cannot make, we are incapable of making: we will not choose the path of submission and suffer the most sacred rights of our nation and our people to be ignored or violated. The wrongs against which we now array ourselves are no common wrongs; they cut to the very roots of human life.

With a profound sense of the solemn and even tragical character of the step I am taking and of the grave responsibilities which it involves, but in unhesitating obedience to what I deem my constitutional duty, I advise that the Congress declare the recent course of the Imperial German Government to be in fact nothing less than war against the government and people of the United States; that it formally accept the status of belligerent which has thus been thrust upon it; and that it take immediate steps not only to put the country in a more thorough state of defense but also to exert all its power and employ all its resources to bring the Government of the German Empire to terms and end the war.

What this will involve is clear. It will involve the utmost practicable cooperation in counsel and action with the governments now at war with Germany, and, as incident to that, the extension to those governments of the most liberal financial credits, in order that our resources may so far as possible be added to theirs. It will involve the organization and mobilization of all the material resources of the country to supply the materials of war and serve the incidental needs of the nation in the most abundant and yet the most economical and efficient way possible. It will involve the immediate full equipment of the navy in all respects but particularly in supplying it with the best means of dealing with the enemy's submarines. It will involve the immediate addition to the armed forces of the United States already provided for by law in case of war at least five hundred thousand men, who should, in my opinion, be chosen upon the principle of universal liability to service, and also the authorization of subsequent additional increments of equal force so soon as they may be needed and can be handled in training. It will involve also, of course, the granting of adequate credits to the Government, sustained, I hope, so far as they can equitably be sustained by the present generation, by well conceived taxation.

I say sustained so far as may be equitable by taxation because it seems to me that it would be most unwise to base the credits which will now be necessary entirely on money borrowed. It is our duty, I most respectfully urge, to protect our people so far as we may against the very serious hardships and evils which would be likely to arise out of the inflation which would be produced by vast loans.

In carrying out the measures by which these things are to be accomplished we should keep constantly in mind the wisdom of interfering as little as possible in our own preparation and in the equipment of our own military forces with the duty,—for it will be a very practical duty,—of supplying the nations already at war with Germany with the materials which they can obtain only from us or by our assistance. They are in the field and we should help them in every way to be effective there.

I shall take the liberty of suggesting, through the several executive departments of the Government, for the consideration of your committees, measures for the accomplishment of the several objects I have mentioned. I hope that it will be your pleasure to deal with them as having been framed after very careful thought by the branch of the Government upon which the responsibility of conducting the war and safeguarding the nation will most directly fall.

While we do these things, these deeply momentous things, let us be very clear, and make very clear to all the world what our motives and our objects are. My own thought has not been driven from its habitual and normal course by the unhappy events of the last two months, and I do not believe that the thought of the nation has been altered or clouded by them.

I have exactly the same things in mind now that I had in mind when I addressed the Senate on the twenty-second of January last; the same that I had in mind when I addressed the Congress on the third of February and on the twenty-sixth of February. Our object now, as then, is to vindicate the principles of peace and justice in the life of the world as against selfish and autocratic power and to set up amongst the really free and self-governed peoples of the world such a concert of purpose and of action as will henceforth ensure the observance of those principles. Neutrality is no longer feasible or desirable where the peace of the world is involved and the freedom of its peoples, and the menace to that peace and freedom lies in the existence of autocratic governments backed by organized force which is controlled wholly by their will, not by the will of their people. We have seen the last of neutrality in such circumstances. We are at the beginning of an age in which it will be insisted that the same standards of conduct and of responsibility for wrong done shall be observed among nations and their governments that are observed among the individual citizens of civilized states.

We have no quarrel with the German people. We have no feeling towards them but one of sympathy and friendship. It was not upon their impulse that their government acted in entering this war. It was not with their previous knowledge or approval. It was a war determined upon as wars used to be determined upon in the old, unhappy days when peoples were nowhere consulted by their rulers and wars were provoked and waged in the interest of dynasties or of little groups of ambitious men who were accustomed to use their fellow men as pawns and tools. Self-governed nations do not fill their neighbour states with spies or set the course of intrigue to bring about some critical posture of affairs which will give them an opportunity to strike and make conquest. Such designs can be successfully worked out only under cover and where no one has the right to ask questions. Cunningly contrived plans of deception or aggression, carried, it may be, from generation to generation, can be worked out and kept from the light only within the privacy of courts or behind the carefully guarded confidences of a narrow and privileged class. They are happily impossible where public opinion commands and insists upon full information concerning all the nation's affairs.

A steadfast concert for peace can never be maintained except by a partnership of democratic nations. No autocratic government could be trusted to keep faith within it or observe its covenants. It must be a league of honour, a partnership of opinion. Intrigue would eat its vitals away; the plottings of inner circles who could plan what they would and render account to no one would be a corruption seated at its very heart. Only free peoples can hold their purpose and their honour steady to a common end and prefer the interests of mankind to any narrow interest of their own.

Does not every American feel that assurance has been added to our hope for the future peace of the world by the wonderful and heartening things that have been happening within the last few weeks in Russia? Russia was known by those who knew it best to have been always in fact democratic at heart, in all the vital habits of her thought, in all the intimate relationships of her people that spoke their natural instinct, their habitual attitude towards life. The autocracy that crowned the summit of her political structure, long as it had stood and terrible as was the reality of its power, was not in fact Russian in origin, character, or purpose; and now it has been shaken off and the great, generous Russian people have been added in all their naive majesty and might to the forces that are fighting for freedom in the world, for justice, and for peace. Here is a fit partner for a League of Honour.

One of the things that has served to convince us that the Prussian autocracy was not and could never be our friend is that from the very outset of the present war it has filled our unsuspecting communities and even our offices of government with spies and set criminal intrigues everywhere afoot against our national unity of counsel, our peace within and without, our industries and our commerce. Indeed it is now evident that its spies were here even before the war began; and it is unhappily not a matter of conjecture but a fact proved in our courts of justice that the intrigues which have more than once come perilously near to disturbing the peace and dislocating the industries of the country have been carried on at the instigation, with the support, and even under the personal direction of official agents of the Imperial Government accredited to the Government of the United States. Even in checking these things and trying to extirpate them we have sought to put the most generous interpretation possible upon them because we knew that their source lay, not in any hostile feeling or purpose of the German people towards us (who were, no doubt as ignorant of them as we ourselves were), but only in the selfish designs of a Government that did what it pleased and told its people nothing. But they have played their part in serving to convince us at last that that Government entertains no real friendship for us and means to act against our peace and security at its convenience. That it means to stir up enemies against us at our very doors the intercepted note to the German Minister at Mexico City is eloquent evidence.

We are accepting this challenge of hostile purpose because we know that in such a government, following such methods, we can never have a friend; and that in the presence of its organized power, always lying in wait to accomplish we know not what purpose, there can be no assured security for the democratic governments of the world. We are now about to accept gauge of battle with this natural foe to liberty and shall, if necessary, spend the whole force of the nation to check and nullify its pretensions and its power. We are glad, now that we see the facts with no veil of false pretense about them, to fight thus for the ultimate peace of the world and for the liberation of its peoples, the German peoples included: for the rights of nations great and small and the privilege of men everywhere to choose their way of life and of obedience. The world must be made safe for democracy. Its peace must be planted upon the tested foundations of political liberty. We have no selfish ends to serve. We desire no conquest, no dominion. We seek no indemnities for ourselves, no material compensation for the sacrifices we shall freely make. We are but one of the champions of the rights of mankind. We shall be satisfied when those rights have been made as secure as the faith and the freedom of nations can make them.

Just because we fight without rancour and without selfish object, seeking nothing for ourselves but what we shall wish to share with all free peoples, we shall, I feel confident, conduct our operations as belligerents without passion and ourselves observe with proud punctilio the principles of right and of fair play we profess to be fighting for.

I have said nothing of the governments allied with the Imperial Government of Germany because they have not made war upon us or challenged us to defend our right and our honour. The Austro-Hungarian Government has, indeed, avowed its unqualified endorsement and acceptance of the reckless and lawless submarine warfare adopted now without disguise by the Imperial German Government, and it has therefore not been possible for this Government to receive Count Tarnowski, the Ambassador recently accredited to this Government by the Imperial and Royal Government of Austria-Hungary; but that Government has not actually engaged in warfare against citizens of the United States on the seas, and I take the liberty, for the present at least, of postponing a discussion of our relations with the authorities at Vienna. We enter this war only where we are clearly forced into it because there are no other means of defending our rights.

It will be all the easier for us to conduct ourselves as belligerents in a high spirit of right and fairness because we act without animus, not in enmity towards a people or with the desire to bring any injury or disadvantage upon them, but only in armed opposition to an irresponsible government which has thrown aside all considerations of humanity and of right and is running amuck. We are, let me say again, the sincere friends of the German people, and shall desire nothing so much as the early re-establishment of intimate relations of mutual advantage between us,—however hard it may be for them, for the time being, to believe that this is spoken from our hearts. We have borne with their present government through all these bitter months because of that friendship,—exercising a patience and forbearance which would otherwise have been impossible. We shall, happily, still have an opportunity to prove that friendship in our daily attitude and actions towards the millions of men and women of German birth and native sympathy who live amongst us and share our life, and we shall be proud to prove it towards all who are in fact loyal to their neighbours and to the Government in the hour of test. They are, most of them, as true and loyal Americans as if they had never known any other fealty or allegiance. They will be prompt to stand with us in rebuking and restraining the few who may be of a different mind and purpose. If there should be disloyalty, it will be dealt with with a firm hand of stern repression; but, if it lifts its head at all, it will lift it only here and there and without countenance except from a lawless and malignant few.

It is a distressing and oppressive duty, Gentlemen of the Congress, which I have performed in thus addressing you. There are, it may be, many months of fiery trial and sacrifice ahead of us. It is a fearful thing to lead this great peaceful people into war, into the most terrible and disastrous of all wars, civilization itself seeming to be in the balance. But the right is more precious than peace, and we shall fight for the things which we have always carried nearest our hearts,—for democracy, for the right of those who submit to authority to have a voice in their own governments, for the rights and liberties of small nations, for a universal dominion of right by such a concert of free peoples as shall bring peace and safety to all nations and make the world itself at last free. To such a task we can dedicate our lives and our fortunes, everything that we are and everything that we have, with the pride of those who know that the day has come when America is privileged to spend her blood and her might for the principles that gave her birth and happiness and the peace which she has treasured. God helping her, she can do no other.

George Norris: Speech in the U.S. Senate

The congressional response to Wilson's speech was not unanimous. With La Follette and George W. Norris, a progressive Republican from Nebraska, leading the opposition, the Senate voted on April 4 to declare war against Germany by a vote of 82–6—with three Democrats and three Republicans opposed. Two days later, the House of Representatives voted 373–50, with thirty-one Republicans, eighteen Democrats, and one Socialist opposed; most of the "nay" votes came from the Midwest.

———————

Mr. NORRIS. Mr. President, while I am most emphatically and sincerely opposed to taking any step that will force our country into the useless and senseless war now being waged in Europe, yet if this resolution passes I shall not permit my feeling of opposition to its passage to interfere in any way with my duty either as a Senator or as a citizen in bringing success and victory to American arms. I am bitterly opposed to my country entering the war, but if, notwithstanding my opposition, we do enter it, all of my energy and all of my power will be behind our flag in carrying it on to victory.

The resolution now before the Senate is a declaration of war. Before taking this momentous step, and while standing on the brink of this terrible vortex, we ought to pause and calmly and judiciously consider the terrible consequences of the step we are about to take. We ought to consider likewise the route we have recently traveled and ascertain whether we have reached our present position in a way that is compatible with the neutral position which we claimed to occupy at the beginning and through the various stages of this unholy and unrighteous war.

No close student of recent history will deny that both Great Britain and Germany have, on numerous occasions since the beginning of the war, flagrantly violated in the most serious manner the rights of neutral vessels and neutral nations under existing international law as recognized up to the beginning of this war by the civilized world.

The reason given by the President in asking Congress to declare war against Germany is that the German Government has declared certain war zones, within which, by the use of submarines, she sinks, without notice, American ships and destroys American lives.

Let us trace briefly the origin and history of these so-called war zones. The first war zone was declared by Great Britain. She gave us and the world notice of it on the 4th day of November, 1914. The zone became effective November 5, 1914, the next day after the notice was given. This zone so declared by Great Britain covered the whole of the North Sea. The order establishing it sought to close the north of Scotland route around the British Isles to Denmark, Holland, Norway, Sweden, and the Baltic Sea. The decree of establishment drew an arbitrary line from the Hebrides Islands along the Scottish coast to Iceland, and warned neutral shipping that it would cross those lines at its peril, and ordered that ships might go to Holland and other neutral nations by taking the English Channel route through the Strait of Dover.

The first German war zone was declared on the 4th day of February, 1915, just three months after the British war zone was declared. Germany gave 15 days' notice of the establishment of her zone, which became effective on the 18th day of February, 1915. The German war zone covered the English Channel and the high sea waters around the British Isles. It sought to close the English Channel route around the British Isles to Holland, Norway, Sweden, Denmark, and the Baltic Sea. The German war zone decreed that neutral vessels would be exposed to danger in the English Channel route, but that the route around the north of Scotland and in the eastern part of the North Sea, in a strip 30 miles wide along the Dutch coast, would be free from danger.

It will thus be seen that the British Government declared the north of Scotland route into the Baltic Sea as dangerous and the English Channel route into the Baltic Sea as safe.

The German Government in its order did exactly the reverse. It declared the north of Scotland route into the Baltic

Sea as safe and the English Channel route into the Baltic Sea as dangerous.

The order of the British Government declaring the North Sea as a war zone used the following language:

> The British Admiralty gives notice that the waters of the North Sea must be considered a military area. Within this area merchant shipping of all kinds, traders of all countries, fishing craft, and other vessels will be exposed to the gravest danger from mines it has been necessary to lay.

The German Government, by its order declaring its war zone around the south of England, declared that the order would be made effective by the use of submarines.

Thus we have the two declarations of the two Governments, each declaring a military zone and warning neutral shipping from going into the prohibited area. England sought to make her order effective by the use of submerged mines. Germany sought to make her order effective by the use of submarines. Both of these orders were illegal and contrary to all international law as well as the principles of humanity. Under international law no belligerent Government has the right to place submerged mines in the high seas. Neither has it any right to take human life without notice by the use of submarines. If there is any difference on the ground of humanity between these two in-strumentalities, it is certainly in favor of the submarines. The submarine can exercise some degree of discretion and judg-ment. The submerged mine always destroys without notice, friend and foe alike, guilty and innocent the same. In carrying out these two policies, both Great Britain and Germany have sunk American ships and destroyed American lives without provocation and without notice. There have been more ships sunk and more American lives lost from the action of subma-rines than from English mines in the North Sea; for the simple reason that we finally acquiesced in the British war zone and kept our ships out of it, while in the German war zone we have refused to recognize its legality and have not kept either our ships or our citizens out of its area. If American ships had gone into the British war zone in defiance of Great Britain's order, as they have gone into the German war zone in defiance of the

German Government's order, there would have been many more American lives lost and many more American ships sunk by the instrumentality of the mines than the instrumentality of the submarines.

We have in the main complied with the demands made by Great Britain. Our ships have followed the instructions of the British Government in going not only to England but to the neutral nations of the world, and in thus complying with the British order American ships going to Holland, Denmark, Norway, and Sweden have been taken by British officials into British ports, and their cargoes inspected and examined. All the mails we have carried even to neutral countries have been opened and censored, and oftentimes the entire cargo confiscated by the Government. Nothing has been permitted to pass to even the most neutral nations except after examination and with the permission of the officials of the British Government.

I have outlined the beginning of the controversy. I have given in substance the orders of both of these great Governments that constituted the beginning of our controversy with each. There have been other orders made by both Governments subsequent to the ones I have given that interfered with our rights as a neutral Nation, but these two that I have outlined constitute the origin of practically the entire difficulty, and subsequent orders have only been modifications and reproductions of those I have already mentioned. It is unnecessary to cite authority to show that both of these orders declaring military zones were illegal and contrary to international law. It is sufficient to say that our Government has officially declared both of them to be illegal and has officially protested against both of them.

The only difference is that in the case of Germany we have persisted in our protest, while in the case of England we have submitted. What was our duty as a Government and what were our rights when we were confronted with these extraordinary orders declaring these military zones? First, we could have defied both of them and could have gone to war against both of these nations for this violation of international law and interference with our neutral rights. Second, we had the technical right to defy one and to acquiesce in the other. Third, we could, while denouncing them both as illegal, have acquiesced in them both and thus remained neutral with both sides, although not agreeing with either as to the righteousness of their respective orders. We could have said to American ship-owners that, while these orders are both contrary to international law and are both unjust, we do not believe that the provocation is sufficient to cause us to go to war for the defense of our rights as a neutral nation, and, therefore, American ships and American citizens will go into these zones at their own peril and risk. Fourth, we might have declared an embargo against the shipping from American ports of any merchandise to either one of these Governments that persisted in maintaining its military zone. We might have refused to permit the sailing of any ship from any American port to either of these military zones. In my judgment, if we had pursued this course, the zones would have been of short duration. England would have been compelled to take her mines out of the North Sea in order to get any supplies from our country. When her mines were taken out of the North Sea then the German ports upon the North Sea would have been accessible to American shipping and Germany would have been compelled to cease her submarine warfare in order to get any supplies from our Nation into German North Sea ports.

There are a great many American citizens who feel that we owe it as a duty to humanity to take part in this war. Many instances of cruelty and inhumanity can be found on both sides. Men are often biased in their judgment on account of their sympathy and their interests. To my mind, what we ought to have maintained from the beginning was the strictest neutrality. If we had done this I do not believe we would have been on the verge of war at the present time. We had a right as a nation, if we desired, to cease at any time to be neutral. We had a technical right to respect the English war zone and to disregard the German war zone, but we could not do that and be neutral. I have no quarrel to find with the man who does not desire our country to remain neutral. While many such people are moved by selfish motives and hopes of gain, I have no doubt but that in a great many instances, through what I believe to be a misunderstanding of the real condition, there are many honest, patriotic citizens who think we ought to engage in this war and who are behind the President in his demand that we should declare war against Germany. I think such people err in judgment and to a great extent have been misled as to the real history and the true facts by the almost unanimous demand of the great combination of wealth that has a direct financial interest in our participation in the war. We have loaned many hundreds of millions of dollars to the allies in this controversy. While such action was legal and countenanced by international law, there is no doubt in my mind but the enormous amount of money loaned to the allies in this country has been instrumental in bringing about a public sentiment in favor of our country taking a course that would make every bond worth a hundred cents on the dollar and making the payment of every debt certain and sure. Through this instrumentality and also through the instrumentality of others who have not only made millions out of the war in the manufacture of munitions, etc., and who would expect to make millions more if our country can be drawn into the catastrophe, a large number of the great newspapers and news agencies of the country have been controlled and enlisted in the greatest propaganda that the world has ever known, to manufacture sentiment in favor of war. It is now demanded that the American citizens shall be used as insurance policies to guarantee the safe delivery of munitions of war to belligerent nations. The enormous profits of munition manufacturers, stockbrokers, and bond dealers must be still further increased by our entrance into the war. This has brought us to the present moment, when Congress, urged by the President and backed by the artificial sentiment, is about to declare war and engulf our country in the greatest holocaust that the world has ever known.

In showing the position of the bondholder and the stockbroker I desire to read an extract from a letter written by a member of the New York Stock Exchange to his customers. This writer says:

> Regarding the war as inevitable, Wall Street believes that it would be preferable to this uncertainty about the actual date of its commencement. Canada and Japan are at war, and are more prosperous than ever before. The popular view is that stocks would have a quick, clear, sharp reaction, immediately upon outbreak of hostilities, and that then they would enjoy

an old-fashioned bull market such as followed the outbreak of war with Spain in 1898. The advent of peace would force a readjustment of commodity prices and would probably mean a postponement of new enterprises. As peace negotiations would be long drawn out, the period of waiting and uncertainty for business would be long. If the United States does not go to war it is nevertheless good opinion that the preparedness program will compensate in good measure for the loss of the stimulus of actual war.

Here we have the Wall Street view. Here we have the man representing the class of people who will be made prosperous should we become entangled in the present war, who have already made millions of dollars, and who will make many hundreds of millions more if we get into the war. Here we have the cold-blooded proposition that war brings prosperity to that class of people who are within the viewpoint of this writer. He expresses the view, undoubtedly, of Wall Street, and of thousands of men elsewhere, who see only dollars coming to them through the handling of stocks and bonds that will be necessary in case of war. "Canada and Japan," he says, "are at war, and are more prosperous than ever before."

To whom does war bring prosperity? Not to the soldier who for the munificent compensation of $16 per month shoulders his musket and goes into the trench, there to shed his blood and to die if necessary; not to the broken-hearted widow who waits for the return of the mangled body of her husband; not to the mother who weeps at the death of her brave boy; not to the little children who shiver with cold; not to the babe who suffers from hunger; nor to the millions of mothers and daughters who carry broken hearts to their graves. War brings no prosperity to the great mass of common and patriotic citizens. It increases the cost of living of those who toil and those who already must strain every effort to keep soul and body together. War brings prosperity to the stock gambler on Wall Street—to those who are already in possession of more wealth than can be realized or enjoyed. Again this writer says that if we can not get war, "it is nevertheless good opinion that the preparedness program will compensate in good measure for the loss of the stimulus of actual war." That is, if we can not get war, let us go as far in that direction as possible. If we can not get war, let us cry for additional ships, additional guns, additional munitions, and everything else that will have a tendency to bring us as near as possible to the verge of war. And if war comes do such men as these shoulder the musket and go into the trenches?

Their object in having war and in preparing for war is to make money. Human suffering and the sacrifice of human life are necessary, but Wall Street considers only the dollars and the cents. The men who do the fighting, the people who make the sacrifices, are the ones who will not be counted in the measure of this great prosperity that he depicts. The stock brokers would not, of course, go to war, because the very object they have in bringing on the war is profit, and therefore they must remain in their Wall Street offices in order to share in that great prosperity which they say war will bring. The volunteer officer, even the drafting officer, will not find them. They will be concealed in their palatial offices on Wall Street, sitting behind mahogany desks, covered up with clipped coupons —coupons soiled with the sweat of honest toil, coupons stained with mothers' tears, coupons dyed in the lifeblood of their fellow men.

We are taking a step to-day that is fraught with untold danger. We are going into war upon the command of gold. We are going to run the risk of sacrificing millions of our countrymen's lives in order that other countrymen may coin their lifeblood into money. And even if we do not cross the Atlantic and go into the trenches, we are going to pile up a debt that the toiling masses that shall come many generations after us will have to pay. Unborn millions will bend their backs in toil in order to pay for the terrible step we are now about to take. We are about to do the bidding of wealth's terrible mandate. By our act we will make millions of our countrymen suffer, and the consequences of it may well be that millions of our brethren must shed their lifeblood; millions of broken-hearted women must weep, millions of children must suffer with cold, and millions of babes must die from hunger, and all because we want to preserve the commercial right of American citizens to deliver munitions of war to belligerent nations.

Mr. REED. Mr. President——

The PRESIDENT pro tempore. Does the Senator from Nebraska yield to the Senator from Missouri?

Mr. NORRIS. I will say to the Senator that I prefer not to yield.

The PRESIDENT pro tempore. Does the Senator yield?

Mr. REED. Of course I can not interrupt under those circumstances.

The PRESIDENT pro tempore. The Senator declines to yield.

Mr. NORRIS. I know that I am powerless to stop it. I know that this war madness has taken possession of the financial and political powers of our country. I know that nothing I can say will stay the blow that is soon to fall. I feel that we are committing a sin against humanity and against our countrymen. I would like to say to this war god, You shall not coin into gold the lifeblood of my brethren. I would like to prevent this terrible catastrophe from falling upon my people. I would be willing to surrender my own life if I could cause this awful cup to pass. I charge no man here with a wrong motive, but it seems to me that this war craze has robbed us of our judgment. I wish we might delay our action until reason could again be enthroned in the brain of man. I feel that we are about to put the dollar sign upon the American flag.

I have no sympathy with the military spirit that dominates the Kaiser and his advisers. I do not believe that they represent the heart of the great German people. I have no more sympathy with the submarine policy of Germany than I have with the mine-laying policy of England. I have heard with rejoicing of the overthrow of the Czar of Russia and the movement in that great country toward the establishment of a government where the common people will have their rights, liberty, and freedom respected. I hope and pray that a similar revolution may take place in Germany, that the Kaiser may be overthrown, and that on the ruins of his military despotism may be established a German republic, where the great German people may work out their world destiny. The working out of that problem is not an American burden. We ought to remember the advice of the Father of our Country and keep out of entangling alliances. Let Europe solve her problems as we have solved ours.

Let Europe bear her burdens as we have borne ours. In the greatest war of our history and at the time it occurred, the greatest war in the world's history, we were engaged in solving an American problem. We settled the question of human slavery and washed our flag clean by the sacrifice of human blood. It was a great problem and a great burden, but we solved it ourselves. Never once did we think of asking Europe to take part in its solution. Never once did any European nation undertake to settle the great question. We solved it, and history has rendered a unanimous verdict that we solved it right. The troubles of Europe ought to be settled by Europe, and wherever our sympathies may lie, disagreeing as we do, we ought to remain absolutely neutral and permit them to settle their questions without our interference. We are now the greatest neutral nation. Upon the passage of this resolution we will have joined Europe in the great catastrophe and taken America into entanglements that will not end with this war, but will live and bring their evil influences upon many generations yet unborn.

April 4, 1917

George M. Cohan: Over There

The most prodigious man of the American theater at that time, George M. Cohan—performer, playwright, producer, and composer —wrote the words and music to this song shortly after the declaration of war, while riding the train from his home in New Rochelle to New York. Enrico Caruso and Nora Bayes made hugely popular recordings of it; but only a few people ever heard perhaps its most moving renditions, as it became President Wilson's favorite song. He sang it in the corridors of the White House, his voice never failing to crack whenever he got to the last line.

———————

Johnnie get your gun, get your gun, get your gun,
Take it on the run, on the run, on the run,
Hear them calling you and me,
Ev'ry son of liberty.
Hurry right away, no delay, go today,
Make your daddy glad to have had such a lad,
Tell your sweetheart not to pine,
To be proud her boy's in line.

Over there over there
Send the word, send the word over there
That the Yanks are coming, the Yanks are coming,
The drums rum-tumming ev'ry where
So prepare say a pray'r
Send the word, send the word to beware
We'll be over, we're coming over,
And we won't come back till it's over, over there!

Johnnie get your gun, get your gun, get your gun,
Johnnie show the Hun you're a son of a gun,
Hoist the flag and let her fly,
Yankee Doodle do or die.
Pack your little kit, show your grit, do your bit,
Yankees to the ranks from the towns and the tanks,

Make your mother proud of you
And the old Red White and Blue.

Over there over there
Send the word, send the word over there
That the Yanks are coming, the Yanks are coming,
The drums rum-tumming ev'ry where
So prepare say a pray'r
Send the word, send the word to beware
We'll be over, we're coming over,
And we won't come back till it's over, over there!

Majority Report of the
St. Louis Socialist Convention

The Socialist Party of America formed in 1901; and in the 1912 presidential election, its candidate, Eugene V. Debs, received 901,551 votes—6 percent of the popular vote. Immediately following the declaration of war, the Socialist Party held an emergency convention in St. Louis to consider its position. The party's minority report stated: "Having failed to prevent the war by our agitation, we can only recognize it as a fact and try to force upon the government, by pressure of public opinion, a constructive program." It called for securing peace on "democratic terms," continued freedom of speech and the press, a national referendum on conscription, and using the war to advance "democratic collectivism." Morris Hillquit, Charles Emil Ruthenberg, and Algernon Lee wrote the majority report, which flatly opposed the war; and by a subsequent vote of 22,345 to 2,752, the Socialist Party thus became the largest political organization to protest American participation.

———————————

THE SOCIALIST PARTY of the United States in the present grave crisis, solemnly reaffirms its allegiance to the principle of internationalism and working class solidarity the world over, and proclaims its unalterable opposition to the war just declared by the government of the United States.

Modern wars as a rule have been caused by the commercial and financial rivalry and intrigues of the capitalist interests in the different countries. Whether they have been frankly waged as wars of aggression or have been hypocritically represented as wars of "defense," they have always been made by the classes and fought by the masses. Wars bring wealth and power to the ruling classes, and suffering, death and demoralization to the workers.

They breed a sinister spirit of passion, unreason, race hatred and false patriotism. They obscure the struggles of the workers for life, liberty and social justice. They tend to sever the vital bonds of solidarity between them and their brothers in other countries, to destroy their organizations and to curtail their civic and political rights and liberties.

The Socialist Party of the United States is unalterably opposed to the system of exploitation and class rule which is upheld and strengthened by military power and sham national patriotism. We, therefore, call upon the workers of all countries to refuse support to their governments in their wars. The wars of the contending national groups of capitalists are not the concern of the workers. The only struggle which would justify the workers in taking up arms is the great struggle of the working class of the world to free itself from economic exploitation and political oppression, and we particularly warn the workers against the snare and delusion of so-called defensive warfare. As against the false doctrine of national patriotism we uphold the ideal of international working-class solidarity. In support of capitalism, we will not willingly give a single life or a single dollar; in support of the struggle of the workers for freedom we pledge our all.

The mad orgy of death and destruction which is now convulsing unfortunate Europe was caused by the conflict of capitalist interests in the European countries.

In each of these countries, the workers were oppressed and exploited. They produced enormous wealth but the bulk of it was withheld from them by the owners of the industries. The workers were thus deprived of the means to repurchase the wealth which they themselves had created.

The capitalist class of each country was forced to look for foreign markets to dispose of the accumulated "surplus" wealth. The huge profits made by the capitalists could no longer be profitably reinvested in their own countries, hence, they were driven to look for foreign fields of investment. The geographical boundaries of each modern capitalist country thus became too narrow for the industrial and commercial operations of its capitalist class.

The efforts of the capitalists of all leading nations were therefore centered upon the domination of the world markets. Imperialism became the dominant note in the politics of Europe. The acquisition of colonial possessions and the extension of spheres of commercial and political influence became the object of diplomatic intrigues and the cause of constant clashes between nations.

The acute competition between the capitalist powers of the earth, their jealousies and distrusts of one another and the fear of the rising power of the working class forced each of them to arm to the teeth. This led to the mad rivalry of armament, which, years before the outbreak of the present war, had turned the leading countries of Europe into armed camps with standing armies of many millions, drilled and equipped for war in times of "peace."

Capitalism, imperialism and militarism had thus laid the foundation of an inevitable general conflict in Europe. The ghastly war in Europe was not caused by an accidental event, nor by the policy or institutions of any single nation. It was the logical outcome of the competitive capitalist system.

The six million men of all countries and races who have been ruthlessly slain in the first thirty months of this war, the millions of others who have been crippled and maimed, the vast treasures of wealth that have been destroyed, the untold misery and sufferings of Europe, have not been sacrifices exacted in a struggle for principles or ideals, but wanton offerings upon the altar of private profit.

The forces of capitalism which have led to the war in Europe are even more hideously transparent in the war recently provoked by the ruling class of this country.

When Belgium was invaded, the government enjoined upon the people of this country the duty of remaining neutral, thus clearly demonstrating that the "dictates of humanity," and the fate of small nations and of democratic institutions were matters that did not concern it. But when our enormous war traffic was seriously threatened, our government calls upon us to rally to the "defense of democracy and civilization."

Our entrance into the European war was instigated by the predatory capitalists in the United States who boast of the enormous profit of seven billion dollars from the manufacture and sale of munitions and war supplies and from the exportation of American food stuffs and other necessaries. They are also deeply interested in the continuance of war and the success of the allied arms through their huge loans to the governments of the allied powers and through other commercial ties. It is the same interests which strive for imperialistic domination of the Western Hemisphere.

The war of the United States against Germany cannot be justified even on the plea that it is a war in defense of American rights or American "honor." Ruthless as the unrestricted submarine war policy of the German government was and is, it is not an invasion of the rights of the American people, as such, but only an interference with the opportunity of certain groups of American capitalists to coin cold profits out of the blood and sufferings of our fellow men in the warring countries of Europe.

It is not a war against the militarist regime of the Central Powers. Militarism can never be abolished by militarism.

It is not a war to advance the cause of democracy in Europe. Democracy can never be imposed upon any country by a foreign power by force of arms.

It is cant and hypocrisy to say that the war is not directed against the German people, but against the Imperial Government of Germany. If we send an armed force to the battlefields of Europe, its cannon will mow down the masses of the German people and not the Imperial German Government.

Our entrance into the European conflict at this time will serve only to multiply the horrors of the war, to increase the toll of death and destruction and to prolong the fiendish slaughter. It will bring death, suffering and destitution to the people of the United States and particularly to the working class. It will give the powers of reaction in this country, the pretext for an attempt to throttle our rights and to crush our democratic institutions, and to fasten upon this country a permanent militarism.

The working class of the United States has no quarrel with the working class of Germany or of any other country. The people of the United States have no quarrel with the people of Germany or any other country. The American people did not want and do not want this war. They have not been consulted about the war and have had no part in declaring war. They have been plunged into this war by the trickery and treachery of the ruling class of the country through its representatives in the National Administration and National Congress, its demagogic agitators, its subsidized press, and other servile instruments of public expression.

We brand the declaration of war by our government as a crime against the people of the United States and against the nations of the world.

In all modern history there has been no war more unjustifiable than the war in which we are about to engage.

No greater dishonor has ever been forced upon a people than that which the capitalist class is forcing upon this nation against its will.

In harmony with these principles, the Socialist Party emphatically rejects the proposal that in time of war the workers should suspend their struggle for better conditions. On the contrary, the acute situation created by war calls for an even more vigorous prosecution of the class struggle, and we recommend to the workers and pledge ourselves to the following course of action:

1. Continuous, active, and public opposition to the war, through demonstrations, mass petitions, and all other means within our power.

2. Unyielding opposition to all proposed legislation for military or industrial conscription. Should such conscription be forced upon the people, we pledge ourselves to continuous efforts for the repeal of such laws and to the support of all mass movements in opposition to conscription. We pledge ourselves to oppose with all our strength any attempt to raise money for payment of war expense by taxing the necessaries of life or issuing bonds which will put the burden upon future generations. We demand that the capitalist class, which is responsible for the war, pay its cost. Let those who kindled the fire, furnish the fuel.

3. Vigorous resistance to all reactionary measures, such as censorship of press and mails, restriction of the rights of free speech, assemblage, and organization, or compulsory arbitration and limitation of the right to strike.

4. Consistent propaganda against military training and militaristic teaching in the public schools.

5. Extension of the campaign of education among the workers to organize them into strong, class-conscious, and closely unified political and industrial organizations, to enable them

by concerted and harmonious mass action to shorten this war and to establish lasting peace.

6. Widespread educational propaganda to enlighten the masses as to the true relation between capitalism and war, and to rouse and organize them for action, not only against present war evils, but for the prevention of future wars and for the destruction of the causes of war.

7. To protect the masses of the American people from the pressing danger of starvation which the war in Europe has brought upon them, and which the entry of the United States has already accentuated, we demand—

(a) The restriction of food exports so long as the present shortage continues, the fixing of maximum prices and whatever measures may be necessary to prevent the food speculators from holding back the supplies now in their hands;

(b) The socialization and democratic management of the great industries concerned with the production, transportation, storage, and the marketing of food and other necessaries of life;

(c) The socialization and democratic management of all land and other natural resources now held out of use for monopolistic or speculative profit.

These measures are presented as means of protecting the workers against the evil results of the present war. The danger of recurrence of war will exist as long as the capitalist system of industry remains in existence. The end of wars will come with the establishment of socialized industry and industrial democracy the world over. The Socialist Party calls upon all the workers to join it in its struggle to reach this goal, and thus bring into the world a new society in which peace, fraternity, and human brotherhood will be the dominant ideals.

April 12, 1917

Walter Lippmann: The World Conflict in Its Relation to American Democracy

Although best remembered for his long career as a nationally syndicated columnist and presidential adviser, Walter Lippmann had already made a name for himself in his mid-twenties as a political scientist. Born in New York City in 1889, Lippmann graduated in the class of 1910 from Harvard, having studied under George Santayana and William James. In 1914, he helped Herbert Croly found *The New Republic*, where he worked as assistant editor. Lippmann delivered these remarks at a meeting of the American Academy of Political and Social Science in Philadelphia on April 20, 1917.

I

THE WAY in which President Wilson directed America's entrance into the war has had a mighty effect on the public opinion of the world. Many of those who are disappointed or pleased say they are surprised. They would not be surprised had they made it their business this last year to understand the policy of their government.

In May, 1916, the President made a speech which will be counted among the two or three decisive utterances of American foreign policy. The Sussex pledge had just been extracted from the German government, and on the surface American neutrality seemed assured. The speech was an announcement that American isolation was ended, and that we were prepared to join a League of Peace. This was the foundation of all that followed, and it was intended to make clear to the world that America would not abandon its traditional policy for imperialistic adventure, that if America had to fight it would fight for the peace and order of the world. It was a great portent in human history, but it was overshadowed at the time by the opening of the presidential campaign.

Through the summer the President insisted again and again

that the time had come when America must assume its share of responsibility for a better organization of mankind. In the early autumn very startling news came from Germany. It was most confusing because it promised peace maneuvers, hinted at a separate arrangement with the Russian court party, and at the resumption of unlimited submarine warfare. The months from November to February were to tell the story. Never was the situation more perplexing. The prestige of the Allies was at low ebb, there was treachery in Russia, and, as Mr. Lansing said, America was on the verge of war. We were not only on the verge of war, but on the verge of a bewildering war which would not command the whole-hearted support of the American people.

With the election past, and a continuity of administration assured, it became President Wilson's task to make some bold move which would clarify the muddle. While he was preparing this move, the German chancellor made his high-handed proposal for a blind conference. That it would be rejected was obvious. That the rejection would be followed by the submarine war was certain. The danger was that America would be drawn into the war at the moment when Germany appeared to be offering the peace for which the bulk of American people hoped. We know now that the peace Germany was prepared to make last December was the peace of a conqueror. But at the time Germany could pose as a nation which had been denied a chance to end the war. It was necessary, therefore, to test the sincerity of Germany by asking publicly for a statement of terms. The President's circular note to the powers was issued. This note stated more precisely than ever before that America was ready to help guarantee the peace, and at the same time it gave all the belligerents a chance to show that they were fighting for terms which could be justified to American opinion. The note was very much misunderstood at first because the President had said that, since both sides claimed to be fighting for the same things, neither could well refuse to define the terms. The misunderstanding soon passed away when the replies came. Germany brushed the President aside, and showed that she wanted a peace by intrigue. The Allies produced a document which contained a number of formulae so cleverly worded that they might be stretched to cover the wildest demands of the extremists or contracted to a moderate and just settlement. Above all the Allies assented to the League of Peace which Germany had dismissed as irrelevant.

The war was certain to go on with America drawn in. On January 22, after submarine warfare had been decided upon but before it had been proclaimed, the President made his address to the Senate. It was an international program for democracy. It was also a last appeal to German liberals to avert a catastrophe. They did not avert it, and on February 1 Germany attacked the whole neutral world. That America would not submit was assured. The question that remained to be decided was the extent of our participation in the war. Should it be merely defensive on the high seas, or should it be a separate war? The real source of confusion was the treacherous and despotic Russian government. By no twist of language could a partnership with that government be made consistent with the principles laid down by the President in his address to the Senate.

The Russian Revolution ended that perplexity and we could enter the war with a clear conscience and a whole heart. When Russia became a Republic and the American Republic became an enemy, the German empire was isolated before mankind as the final refuge of autocracy. The principle of its life is destructive of the peace of the world. How destructive that principle is, the ever-widening circle of the war has disclosed.

II

Our task is to define that danger so that our immense sacrifices shall serve to end it. I cannot do that for myself without turning to the origins of the war in order to trace the logical steps by which the pursuit of a German victory has enlisted the enmity of the world.

We read statements by Germans that there was a conspiracy against their national development, that they found themselves encircled by enemies, that Russia, using Serbia as an instrument, was trying to destroy Austria, and that the Entente had already detached Italy. Supposing that all this were true, it would remain an extraordinary thing that the Entente had succeeded in encircling Germany. Had that empire been a good neighbor in Europe, by what miracle could the old hostility between England and France and Russia have been wiped out so quickly? But there is positive evidence that no such conspiracy existed.

Germany's place in the sun is Asia Minor. By the Anglo-German agreement of June, 1914, recently published, a satisfactory arrangement had been reached about the economic exploitation of the Turkish empire. Professor Rohrbach has acknowledged that Germany was given concessions "which exceeded all expectations," and on December 2, 1914, when the war was five months old, von Bethmann-Hollweg declared in the Reichstag that "this understanding was to lessen every possible political friction." The place in the sun had been secured by negotiation.

But the road to that place lay through Austria-Hungary and the Balkans. It was this highway which Germany determined to control absolutely; and the chief obstacle on that highway was Serbia backed by Russia. Into the complexities of that Balkan intrigue I am not competent to enter. We need, however, do no more than follow Lord Grey in the belief that Austria had a genuine grievance against Serbia, a far greater one certainly than the United States has ever had against Mexico. But Britain had no stake in the Austro-Serbian quarrel itself.

It had an interest in the method which the central powers took of settling the quarrel. When Germany declared that Europe could not be consulted, that Austria must be allowed to crush Serbia without reference to the concert of Europe, Germany proclaimed herself an enemy of international order. She preferred a war which involved all of Europe to any admission of the fact that a coöperative Europe existed. It was an assertion of unlimited national sovereignty which Europe could not tolerate.

This brought Russia and France into the field. Instantly Germany acted on the same doctrine of unlimited national sovereignty by striking at France through Belgium. Had Belgium been merely a small neutral nation the crime would still have been one of the worst in the history of the modern world. The fact that Belgium was an internationalized state has made the invasion the master tragedy of the war. For Belgium repre-

sented what progress the world had made towards coöperation. If it could not survive then no internationalism was
possible. That is why through these years of horror upon horror, the Belgian horror is the fiercest of all. The burning, the
shooting, the starving, and the robbing of small and inoffensive
nations is tragic enough. But the German crime in Belgium is
greater than the sum of Belgium's misery. It is a crime against
the bases of faith at which the world must build or perish.

The invasion of Belgium instantly brought the five British
democracies into the war. I think this is the accurate way to
state the fact. Had the war remained a Balkan war with France
engaged merely because of her treaty with Russia, had the
fighting been confined to the Franco-German frontier, the
British empire might have come into the war to save the balance of power and to fulfill the naval agreements with France
but the conflict would probably never have become a people's
war in all the free nations of the empire. Whatever justice there
may have been in Austria's original quarrel with Serbia and
Russia was overwhelmed by the exhibition of national lawlessness in Belgium.

This led to the third great phase of the war, the phase which
concerned America most immediately. The Allies directed by
Great Britain employed sea power to the utmost. They barred
every road to Germany, and undoubtedly violated many commercial rights of neutrals. What America would do about this
became of decisive importance. If it chose to uphold the rights
it claimed, it would aid Germany and cripple the Allies. If it
refused to do more than negotiate with the Allies, it had,
whatever the technicalities of the case might be, thrown its
great weight against Germany. It had earned the enmity of the
German government, an enmity which broke out into intrigue
and conspiracy on American soil. Somewhere in the winter of
1915, America was forced to choose between a policy which
helped Germany and one which helped the Allies. We were
confronted with a situation in which we had to choose between opening a road to Germany and making an enemy of
Germany. With the proclamation of submarine warfare in 1915
we were told that either we must aid Germany by crippling sea
power or be treated as a hostile nation. The German policy was
very simple: British mastery of the seas must be broken. It

could be broken by an American attack from the rear or by the German submarine. If America refused to attack from the rear, America was to be counted as an enemy. It was a case of he who is not for me is against me.

To such an alternative there was but one answer for a free people to make. To become the ally of the conqueror of Belgium against France and the British democracies was utterly out of the question. Our choice was made and the supreme question of American policy became: how far will Germany carry the war against us and how hard shall we strike back? That we were aligned on the side of Germany's enemies no candid man, I think, can deny. The effect of this alignment was to make sea power absolute. For mastery of the seas is no longer the possession of any one nation. The supremacy of the British navy in this war rests on international consent, on the consent of her allies and of the neutrals. Without that consent the blockade of Germany could not exist, and the decision of America not to resist allied sea power was the final blow which cut off Germany from the world. It happened gradually, without spectacular announcement, but history, I think, will call it one of the decisive events of the war.

The effect was to deny Germany access to the resources of the neutral world, and to open these resources to the Allies. Poetic justice never devised a more perfect retribution. The nation which had struck down a neutral to gain a military advantage found the neutral world a partner of its enemies.

That partnership between the neutral world and Germany's enemies rested on merchant shipping. This suggested a new theory of warfare to the German government. It decided that since every ship afloat fed the resources of its enemies, it might be a good idea to sink every ship afloat. It decided that since all the highways of the world were the communications of the Allies, those communications should be cut. It decided that if enough ships were destroyed, it didn't matter what ships or whose ships, England and France would have to surrender and make a peace on the basis of Germany's victories in Europe.

Therefore, on the 31st of January, 1917, Germany abolished neutrality in the world. The policy which began by denying that a quarrel in the Balkans could be referred to Europe, went on to destroy the internationalized state of Belgium, culminated in indiscriminate attack upon the merchant shipping of all nations. The doctrine of exclusive nationalism had moved through these three dramatic phases until those who held it were at war with mankind.

III

The terrible logic of Germany's policy had a stupendous result. By striking at the bases of all international order, Germany convinced even the most isolated of neutrals that order must be preserved by common effort. By denying that a society of nations exists, a society of nations has been forced into existence. The very thing Germany challenged Germany has established. Before 1914 only a handful of visionaries dared to hope for some kind of federation. The orthodox view was that each nation had a destiny of its own, spheres of influence of its own, and that it was somehow beneath the dignity of a great state to discuss its so-called vital interests with other governments. It was a world almost without common aspiration, with few effective common ideals. Europe was split into shifting alliances, democracies and autocracies jumbled together. America lay apart with a budding imperialism of its own. China was marked as the helpless victim of exploitation. That old political system was one in which the German view was by no means altogether disreputable. Internationalism was half-hearted and generally regarded somewhat cynically.

What Germany did was to demonstrate *ad nauseam* the doctrine of competitive nationalism. Other nations had applied it here and there cautiously and timidly. No other nation in our time had ever applied it with absolute logic, with absolute preparation, and with absolute disregard of the consequences. Other nations had dallied with it, compromised about it, muddled along with it. But Germany followed through, and Germany taught the world just where the doctrine leads.

Out of the necessities of defense men against it have gradually formulated the ideals of a coöperative nationalism. From all parts of the world there has been a movement of ideals working slowly towards one end, towards a higher degree of spiritual unanimity than has ever been known before. China and India have been stirred out of their dependence. The

American Republic has abandoned its isolation. Russia has become something like a Republic. The British empire is moving towards closer federation. The Grand Alliance called into existence by the German aggression is now something more than a military coalition. Common ideals are working through it—ideals of local autonomy and joint action. Men are crying that they must be free and that they must be united. They have learned that they cannot be free unless they coöperate, that they cannot coöperate unless they are free.

I do not wish to underestimate the forces of reaction in our country or in the other nations of the Alliance. There are politicians and commercial groups who see in this whole thing nothing but opportunity to secure concessions, manipulate tariffs and extend the bureaucracies. We shall know how to deal with them. Forces have been let loose which they can no longer control, and out of this immense horror ideas have arisen to possess men's souls. There are times when a prudent statesman must build on a contracted view of human nature. But there are times when new sources of energy are tapped, when the impossible becomes possible, when events outrun our calculations. This may be such a time. The Alliance to which we belong has suddenly grown hot with the new democracy of Russia and the new internationalism of America. It has had an access of spiritual force which opens a new prospect in the policies of the world. We can dare to hope for things which we never dared to hope for in the past. In fact if those forces are not to grow cold and frittered they must be turned to a great end and offered a great hope.

IV

That great end and that great hope is nothing less than the Federation of the World. I know it sounds a little old-fashioned to use that phrase because we have abused it so long in empty rhetoric. But no other idea is big enough to describe the Alliance. It is no longer an offensive-defensive military agreement among diplomats. That is how it started to be sure. But it has grown, and is growing, into a union of peoples determined to end forever that intriguing, adventurous nationalism which has torn the world for three centuries. Good democrats have always believed that the common interests of men were greater than their special interests, that ruling classes can be enemies, but that the nations must be partners. Well, this war is being fought by nations. It is the nations who were called to arms, and it is the force of nations that is now stirring the world to its foundations.

The war is dissolving into a stupendous revolution. A few months ago we still argued about the Bagdad corridor, strategic frontiers, colonies. Those were the stakes of the diplomat's war. The whole perspective is changed today by the revolution in Russia and the intervention of America. The scale of values is transformed, for the democracies are unloosed. Those democracies have nothing to gain and everything to lose by the old competitive nationalism, the old apparatus of diplomacy, with its criminal rivalries in the backward places of the earth. The democracies, if they are to be safe, must coöperate. For the old rivalries mean friction and armament and a distortion of all the hopes of free government. They mean that nations are organized to exploit each other and to exploit themselves. That is the life of what we call autocracy. It establishes its power at home by pointing to enemies abroad. It fights its enemies abroad by dragooning the population at home.

That is why practically the whole world is at war with the greatest of the autocracies. That is why the whole world is turning so passionately towards democracy as the only principle on which peace can be secured. Many have feared, I know, that the war against Prussian militarism would result the other way, that instead of liberalizing Prussia the outcome would be a prussianization of the democracies. That would be the outcome if Prusso-Germany won. That would be the result of a German victory. And that is why we who are the most peaceful of democracies are at war. The success of the submarine would give Germany victory. It was and is her one great chance. To have stood aside when Germany made this terrible bid for victory would have been to betray the hope of free government and international union.

V

There are two ways now in which peace can be made. The first is by political revolution in Germany and Austria-Hungary. It is not for us to define the nature of that revolution. We cannot dictate liberty to the German people. It is for them to decide what political institutions they will adopt, but if peace is to come through revolution we shall know that it has come when new voices are heard in Germany, new policies are proclaimed, when there is good evidence that there has, indeed, been a new orientation. If that is done the war can be ended by negotiation.

The other path to peace is by the definite defeat of every item in the program of aggression. This will mean, at a minimum, a demonstration on the field that the German army is not invincible; a renunciation by Germany of all the territory she has conquered; a special compensation to Belgium; and an acknowledgment of the fallacy of exclusive nationalism by an application for membership in the League of Nations.

Frontier questions, colonial questions, are now entirely secondary, and beyond this minimum program the United States has no direct interest in the territorial settlement. The objects for which we are at war will be attained if we can defeat absolutely the foreign policy of the present German government. For a ruling caste which has been humiliated abroad has lost its glamor at home. So we are at war to defeat the German government in the outer world, to destroy its prestige, to deny its conquests, and to throw it back at last into the arms of the German people marked and discredited as the author of their miseries. It is for them to make the final settlement with it.

If it is our privilege to exert the power which turns the scale, it is our duty to see that the end justifies the means. We can win nothing from this war unless it culminates in a union of liberal peoples pledged to coöperate in the settlement of all outstanding questions, sworn to turn against the aggressor, determined to erect a larger and more modern system of international law upon a federation of the world. That is what we are fighting for, at this moment, on the ocean, in the shipyard and in the factory, later perhaps in France and Belgium, ultimately at the council of peace.

If we are strong enough and wise enough to win this victory, to reject all the poison of hatred abroad and intolerance at home, we shall have made a nation to which free men will turn with love and gratitude. For ourselves we shall stand committed as never before to the realization of democracy in America.

We who have gone to war to insure democracy in the world will have raised an aspiration here that will not end with the overthrow of the Prussian autocracy. We shall turn with fresh interests to our own tyrannies—to our Colorado mines, our autocratic steel industries, our sweatshops and our slums. We shall call that man un-American and no patriot who prates of liberty in Europe and resists it at home. A force is loose in America as well. Our own reactionaries will not assuage it with their Billy Sundays or control through lawyers and politicians of the Old Guard.

Herbert Hoover:
Introduction to Women of Belgium

Orphaned as a child in Iowa, raised by an uncle in Oregon, and educated at Stanford, Herbert Hoover pursued a highly successful international career as a mining engineer. A millionaire several times over by the time he was forty, he was living in England when the war broke out. In helping organize the safe return home of more than 100,000 Americans from Europe, Hoover realized he had left the private sector for public life. In November 1914, he founded the Commission for Relief in Belgium, an unprecedented philanthropic effort that lasted for the war's duration and helped feed four million people. With America's entry into the war, President Wilson appointed him United States Food Administrator, a position in which he supervised all American production, conservation, and distribution of food. In 1919 Hoover would establish the American Relief Administration, feeding seventeen million people in twenty-one countries and securing his reputation as "the Great Humanitarian."

BELGIUM, after centuries of intermittent misery and recuperation as the cockpit of Europe, had with a hundred years of the peaceful fruition of the intelligence, courage, thrift, and industry of its people, emerged as the beehive of the Continent. Its population of 8,000,000 upon an area of little less than Maryland was supported by the importation of raw materials, and by their manufacture and their exchange over-seas for two-thirds of the vital necessities of its daily life.

When in the summer of 1914 the people were again drawn into the European maelstrom, 600,000 of them became fugitives abroad, and the remainder were reduced to the state of a city which, captured by a hostile army, is in turn besieged from without. Thus, its boundaries were a wall of bayonets and a blockading fleet.

Under modern economic conditions, no importing nation carries more than a few weeks' reserve stock of food, depending as it does upon the daily arrivals of commerce; and the cessation of this inflow, together with the destruction and requisition of their meager stocks, threatened the Belgians with an even greater catastrophe—the loss of their very life.

With the stoppage of the industrial clock, their workpeople were idle, and destitution marched day and night into their slender savings, until to-day three and a half million people must be helped in charity.

The Belgians are a self-reliant people who had sought no favors of the world, and their first instinct and continuing endeavor has been to help themselves. Not only were all those who had resources insistent that they should either pay now or in the future for their food, but far beyond this, they have insisted upon caring for their own destitute to the fullest extent of those remaining resources—the charity of the poor toward the poor. They have themselves set up no cry for benevolence, but the American Relief Commission has insisted upon pleading to the world to help in a burden so far beyond their ability.

This Commission was created in order that by agreement with the belligerents on both sides, a door might be opened in the wall of steel, through which those who had resources could re-create the flow of supplies to themselves; that through the same channel, the world might come to the rescue of the destitute, and beyond this that it could guarantee the guardianship of these supplies to the sole use of the people.

Furthermore, due to the initial moral, social and economic disorganization of the country and the necessary restriction on movement and assembly, it was impossible for the Belgian people to project within themselves, without an assisting hand, the organization for the distribution of food supplies and the care of the impoverished. Therefore the Relief Organization has grown to a great economic engine that with its collateral agencies monopolizes the import food supply of a whole people, controlling directly and indirectly the largest part of the native products so as to eliminate all waste and to secure justice in distribution; and, above all, it is charged with the care of the destitute.

To visualize truly the mental and moral currents in the Belgian people during these two and a half years one must have lived with them and felt their misery. Overriding all physical suffering and all trial is the great cloud of mental depression, of repression and reserve in every act and word, a terror that is so real that it was little wonder to us when in the course of an investigation in one of the large cities we found the nursing period of mothers has been diminished by one-fourth. Every street corner and every crossroad is marked by a bayonet, and every night resounds with the march of armed men, the mark of national subjection. Belgium is a little country and the sound of the guns along a hundred miles of front strikes the senses hourly, and the hopes of the people rise and fall with the rise and fall in tones which follow the atmospheric changes and the daily rise and fall of battle. Not only do hope of deliverance and anxiety for one's loved ones fighting on the front vibrate with every change in volume of sound, but with every rumor which shivers through the population. At first the morale of a whole people was crusht: one saw it in every face, deadened and drawn by the whole gamut of emotions that had exhausted their souls, but slowly, and largely by the growth of the Relief Organization and the demand that it has made upon their exertion and their devotion, this morale has recovered to a fine flowering of national spirit and stoical resolution. The Relief Commission stands as an encouragement and protection to the endeavors of the Belgian people themselves and a shield to their despair. By degrees an army of 55,000 volunteer workers on Relief had grown up among the Belgian and French people, of a perfection and a patriotism without parallel in the existence of any country.

To find the finance of a nation's relief requiring eighteen million dollars monthly from economic cycles of exchange, from subsidies of different governments, from the world's public charity; to purchase 300,000,000 pounds of concentrated foodstuffs per month of a character appropriate to individual and class; to secure and operate a fleet of seventy cargo ships, to arrange their regular passages through blockades and war zones; to manage the reshipment by canal and rail and distribution to 140 terminals throughout Belgium and Northern France; to control the milling of wheat and the making of bread; to distribute with rigid efficiency and justice not only bread but milk, soup, potatoes, fats, rice, beans, corn, soap and other commodities; to create the machinery of public feeding

in cantines and soup-kitchens; to supply great clothing establishments; to give the necessary assurances that the occupying
army receives no benefit from the food supply; to maintain
checks and balances assuring efficiency and integrity—all these
things are a man's job. To this service the men of Belgium and
Northern France have given the most steadfast courage and
high intelligence.

Beyond all this, however, is the equally great and equally
important problem—the discrimination of the destitute from
those who can pay, the determination of their individual
needs—a service efficient, just and tender in its care of the
helpless.

To create a network of hundreds of cantines for expectant
mothers, growing babies, for orphans and debilitated children;
to provide the machinery for supplemental meals for the adolescent in the schools; to organize workrooms and to provide
stations for the distribution of clothing to the poor; to see that
all these reliefs cover the field, so that none fall by the wayside;
to investigate and counsel each and every case that no waste or
failure result; to search out and provide appropriate assistance
to those who would rather die than confess poverty; to direct
these stations, not from committee meetings after afternoon
tea, but by actual executive labor from early morning till late at
night—to go far beyond mere direction by giving themselves
to the actual manual labor of serving the lowly and helpless; to
do it with cheerfulness, sympathy and tenderness, not to hundreds but literally to millions, this is woman's work.

This service has been given, not by tens, but by thousands,
and it is a service that in turn has summoned a devotion, kindliness and tenderness in the Belgian and French women that
has welded all classes with a spiritual bond unknown in any
people before. It has implanted in the national heart and the
national character a quality which is in some measure a compensation for the calamities through which these people are
passing. The soul of Belgium received a grievous wound, but
the women of Belgium are staunching the flow—sustaining
and leading this stricken nation to greater strength and greater
life.

We of the Relief have been proud of the privilege to place
the tools in the hands of these women, and have watched their

skilful use and their improvement in method with hourly admiration. We have believed it to be so great an inspiration that we have daily wished it could be pictured by a sympathizing hand, and we confess to insisting that Mrs. Kellogg should spend some months with her husband during his administration of our Brussels office. She has done more than record in simple terms passing impressions of the varied facts of the great work of these women, for she spent months in loving sympathy with them.

We offer her little book as our, and Mrs. Kellogg's, tribute in admiration of them and the inspiration which they have contributed to this whole organization. This devotion and this service have now gone on for nearly 900 long days. Under unceasing difficulties the tools have been kept in the hands of these women, and they have accomplished their task. All of this time there have stood behind them our warehouses with from thirty to sixty days' supplies in advance, and tragedy has thus been that distance remote. Our share and the share of these women has therefore been a task of prevention, not a task of remedy. Our task and theirs has been to maintain the laughter of the children, not to dry their tears. The pathos of the long lines of expectant, chattering mites, each with a ticket of authority pinned to its chest or held in a grimy fist, never depresses the mind of childhood. Nor does fear ever enter their little heads lest the slender chain of finance, ships and direction which supports these warehouses should fail, for has the cantine ever failed in all these two and a half years? That the day shall not come when some Belgian woman amid her tears must stand before its gate to repeat: "*Mes petites, il n'y en a plus*," is simply a problem of labor and money. In this America has a duty, and the women of America a privilege.

From *Women of Belgium* (1917)

The New York Times: *German Airmen Kill 97, Hurt 437 in London Raid*

With each passing day of the conflict, any notions of chivalry in battle collided with the realities of modern warfare. The Italians first used aerial bombing in Libya, fighting the Ottomans in 1911. As airplanes increased in range and engine power, so too did their ability to destroy. World War I saw the first bombing of enemy cities far from any battlefield. Germany launched nighttime raids against England with Zeppelin airships in January 1915, executing its first raid on London during the night of May 31, 1915. Two years later, they initiated daytime raids, using Gothas, twin-engine biplane bombers based in Belgium. The unnamed correspondent who wrote this story for *The New York Times* witnessed the first Gotha raid on London, the most lethal air attack of the war, leaving 162 dead. Aerial raids on England would continue until May 1918, leaving a death toll of 1,413 (557 from Zeppelins and 856 from airplanes). During the war, Austro-Hungarian and German air raids killed 984 people in Italy, while British, French, and Italian bombing took 797 lives in Germany.

GERMAN AIRMEN KILL 97, HURT 437 IN LONDON RAID

Enemy Squadron Bombs East End and Business District at the Noon Hour.

120 CHILDREN VICTIMS

Ten Killed and 50 Injured in One School—
Harrowing Scenes in the Poor Quarter.

ONLY ONE PLANE DOWNED

Attackers Said to Number Fifteen,
Although Only Three Visited the Capital.

LONDON, Thursday, June 14.—There came to London yesterday the nearest vision of modern warfare that it has yet known. A squadron of enemy airplanes, variously estimated at from three to fifteen, bombed the East End and business districts of the city in daylight, killing 97 persons and injuring 437. Many of the victims are women and children, 120 of the latter being either killed or injured.

The Zeppelin raid which swept over the city in October, 1915, came in the darkness and mystery of night; it was in the late dusk of an Autumn evening that Londoners watched the monsters of the air dealing death upon the innocent. Yesterday it was different. In the gracious loveliness of a perfect Summer's day, when the sky was blue and gold and clear, enemy airplanes journeyed through the clouds like little silver birds, and their passage was watched by thousands of men and women who had but dimly seen the Zeppelins of other days.

It happened that I boarded a bus at Ludgate at 11:40. It was eastward bound. We had passed St. Paul's Cathedral, when there suddenly came in swift succession several tremendous crashes. The people on the bus jumped as people will at unexpected alarms, but there was no uneasiness.

WATCHING THE SKY DRAMA.

"Our guns are at it again," some one remarked; but the demeanor of the people in the streets suggested something else. From every office and warehouse and tea shop men and women strangely stood still, gazing up into the air. The conductor mounted the stairs to suggest that outside passengers should seek safety inside. Some of them did so.

"I'm not a religious man," remarked the conductor, "but what I say is, we are all in God's hands and if we are going to die we may as well die quiet."

But some inside passengers were determined that if they had to die quiet they might as well see something first and they climbed on top and with wonderstruck eyes watched the amazing drama of the skies. It was amazing because it was so beautiful. It was not easy to believe that those little silver specks far up in the heavens had the power to bring death and destruction and unendurable suffering to men and women, and little children living at peace.

Few people saw the entire fleet of Taubes at one and the same time. It seemed as if they were playing hide and seek in the clouds, for like little gleaming bits of quicksilver you could see one suddenly appear, only to vanish as quickly behind a filmy cloudmist, while another emerged to lose itself as swiftly in the shadows.

The bus went slowly on until some one stopped it, wishing to descend. Very soon, watching as we were from the top, the birds of war vanished altogether. One could see only the sharp white flame of bursting shrapnel, of its soft gray smoke. And still there was no panic. There came a moment, however, when some of us felt anxious. In the distance thick towers of smoke rose up from a certain point, which suggested gas bombs. There was something in the close, curious columns which seemed different from the smoke from fire, and we remembered how in the long ago we had been warned to use gas masks. I do not suppose one person in a thousand among the crowds possessed such a thing.

We came a little nearer to what seemed to be the real danger. Whiffs of smoke floated by, but they gave out no poisonous fumes and there was relief in our hearts as we realized our mistake. All along this eastward journey bombs were falling and guns were making great noises, but I saw no quick searching for shelter, no taking cover. If it had been an exhibition of flying at Hendon, the attitude of the people would not have been very different except in the immediately affected streets. Men and women and office clerks, little more than children, stood watching, vastly interested, a little excited, but not in the least frightened.

After minutes of tense interest and deafening noise the sudden silence was awful. The cessation of gunfire told that the raiders had been driven off, and, looking to the sun, one could see that peace had come once more to the air. Watching the light and movement in the sky drama had so fixed one's attention as to eliminate even a flashing thought of its meaning, but with silence came the swift running of ambulance cars, and pealing bells told of the ugliness of it all and its deep significance. And these ambulance cars darted out from all sorts of little side streets, joining together in one long stream that flowed eastward like a rapid stream. The special constables marched quickly about their business; fire engines came from nowhere, as it seemed. Where but a little while ago there had been stillness in the streets and great noises in the air there was now quiet above and queer noises and movements below.

It all happened in a quarter of an hour; all these things had been done in fifteen minutes that seemed like sixty when the time had come and gone. People went back to their shops and their offices and homes to carry on their normal way of living. They looked at their watches and thought they had stopped. When the regular lunch hour arrived they poured out into the streets once more, following the track of the raiders.

CHILDREN SLAIN IN SCHOOLROOM.

The terrible scenes at what Bonar Law, the Chancellor of the Exchequer, in making his statement in the House of Commons said was a London County Council school in the East End of London, were described by a soldier who assisted in rescuing uninjured children.

"Hearing what I thought was gun firing," the soldier said, "I stopped to speak to a policeman. Just then there was another explosion, and the policeman, pointing upward, said:

"'The raiders are out. Good heavens! They have got the school. Run round and give them all the help you can and I will get the police.'

"I looked up in the sky, and there could just see five tiny little things like gilded fish miles up, almost invisible. Looking round, I could see another three more to the south, and perhaps on the other side of the Thames. I dashed around to the school as the policeman advised, and there I found the class mistress, who had got the uninjured children into a passage where, if there came another bomb, they would be less likely to be hurt. She was all alone until I came. Then we both set to get out the uninjured. She brought down two or three from the upper room first, then we went into the classroom where the bomb had sunk into the earth when it exploded. The sight was a terrible one, and but for the excitement it would have been unbearable. Many of the little ones were lying across their desks, apparently dead, and with terrible wounds on heads and limbs, and scores of others were writhing with pain and moaning piteously in their terror and suffering.

"Many bodies were mutilated, but our first thought was to get at the injured and have them cared for. We took them gently in our arms and laid them out against a wall under a shed. I didn't count them, but I should think there were twenty or thirty. I was just wondering what we should do next when some more people came to help, including soldiers, naval cadets, police, and special constables. We were frantic for ambulances and it was impossible to carry them to the hospital, which was half a mile away. Just then two lorries drew up and the driver suggested that he should help. We packed the poor little souls on the lorries as gently as we could and he drove as if he was afraid of something giving away and so at last we got them to the hospital.

"While they were gone I put a sentry on the door, and I can tell you it was a tough job. The women were not in the slightest degree panicky, but they were selfish in their love at first and in their earnestness to get at their own babies endangered by others who were lying on the floor. Some mothers were almost insane with grief, and when they couldn't find their own children would rush through the bodies looking for them, and when you remember that there was a hole in the roof four feet deep and covering the whole area of the classroom it will be understood what that meant.

"The worst part of our task was the last—that of picking up the mutilated fragments of humanity."

Most of the victims were children in a school. Others were residents in a neighboring street; a baby, three days old, and the father who held it in his arms were killed, while the convalescent mother lay close by.

Eight enemy aircraft appeared to pass over in sight of the onlookers in this part of London. Apparently they were following the track of the Thames, one squadron of three on the south bank and another of five on the north, both undoubtedly searching for docks and aiming bombs with a view to the destruction of the shipping therein. Many bombs were heard to explode before the raiders reached this district, and hereabouts they dropped three more in an area of 200 yards, one killing several people in a side street and two others dropping in and close to the school. The bomb that did the most damage dropped in the outside rooms, where between sixty and seventy children were at class. Had it pierced the middle of the building the casualty list would have been three times as great.

No Panic in London.

Word of the approach of the raiders ran through London with incredible rapidity, but was received with the utmost calmness. A man riding down one street on top of a bus was attracted by the sight of dozens of clerks and typewriters gazing northeastward in the sky. In a square there were small crowds, all looking heavenward, but with nothing in sight. At last a faint, dull boom was heard in conjunction with a circular cloud of fleecy smoke.

"Wot cher, 're's another raid," remarked a passenger who had seen service in France. "But the Archies made twice as much noise over there."

All the streets and every window were now filled with people staring toward the sky. There was no panic, merely intelligent interest and curiosity.

"Observe the terrorized public," said a young officer, and his companion laughed. The chief emotion shown lay in the questions why nothing was done to stop this sort of thing in the third year of the war.

News of the damage done circulated remarkably quickly. Five minutes after one building was struck it was known throughout the city. A small bomb hit the roof, lifted a small section like a trap door, and wrecked the janitor's quarters on the top floor, leaving it like a place gutted by fire, except none of the ordinary blackening. The janitor's wife and her father stepped under cover two seconds before the bomb fell. The neighboring roofs were covered with splinters of glass. A man was repairing a flagpole on a building close by. "I heard an explosion, looked and saw something like a stick falling. I didn't want nothing else; never came off a roof quicker in my life," he said afterward.

Meanwhile managers had hard work to shepherd their girl clerks to the basement, as all were anxious to run to the roof to get just one look. Two men were wounded by this bomb, which seems to have fallen down an elevator shaft. One man ran out into the street, his clothes all awry and his gold watch chain curiously twisted. He was stone deaf for the moment, bleeding, and cut from glass. A woman hurried him into a saloon and gave him a stiff glass of brandy.

In a narrow thoroughfare, perhaps thirty feet wide, along one side of a strip of churchyard, a bomb fell among some ancient graves, dug a hole six feet across, shattered a wall on the other side of the street, but hurt no one. At one of the busiest corners in one section in the bombed area a bomb fell, smashing in a window of a large clothier's shop. A few were cut by falling glass, but it was curious to see in the window a dozen tailors' lay figures lying prostrate, their clothes and wigs disordered, gruesomely suggesting real persons injured.

The worst injury was done to a public elementary school, where ten children were killed and a number injured.

All the afternoon there were crowds of persons visiting the places where the bombs dropped, but business proceeded undisturbed and there were no signs of panic anywhere. Many large offices sent staffs to their lower floors for a brief period while the raid was in progress, but anger and curiosity were by far the most predominant emotions.

"They didn't come here; there are no infants' schools here," said a porter of one of the principal Government buildings. This fairly represents the general feeling.

HINT GERMANS SOUGHT PERSHING.

American medical officers who visited the scenes of the air raid today indulged in speculation on the reason for the attack. It was suggested that possibly the Germans planned the attack to coincide with the visit of General Pershing, not knowing that he left this morning for Paris.

One party considered it quite likely that some idea of the kind had actuated the enemy, for Pershing's visit to London, of course, was well known in Berlin. Others, however, were inclined to the belief that the Germans were probably well aware that Pershing and his staff would not long remain in England and that meteorological considerations, which it is possible to forecast, dictated the time of the raid. A thick heat haze hung over the east coast all morning, and although the London skies were blue in the main, there were frequent patches of vapor to help the raiders.

The officers who were Major Hugh Hampton Young, Captain

Montague L. Boyd, Captain Louis C. Lehr and Captain Howard Leo Cecil, all of the Medical Officers' Reserve Corps, U. S. A., visited under the guidance of THE NEW YORK TIMES correspondent a part of the area upon which bombs were dropped.

"The first lesson in kultur, gentlemen, the killing of women and children," called out a man in one crowd we passed through. The American officers, whose uniforms had caught the man's attention, thought his remark apt.

"Pretty good, that," said one of them.

The raid was indeed successful in the killing of women and children. On that point there was full agreement by the American officers, who were allowed to see everything there was to see, being most courteously conducted by the officials and police through places strictly barred to the public.

Major Young and his colleagues, by courtesy of an official of the railway company concerned, were taken over to the station mentioned in the communiqué. Here the chief victims were women and children. The military damage was negligible. Had the raid occurred in the evening, when hundreds of people would have been awaiting suburban trains, the loss of life would have been immeasurably greater. As it was, the station was not very full, but it was a very terrible scene. A train which was just about to start was bombed, and it immediately caught fire. Within twenty minutes of the attack the fire was well in hand. Three doctors in one carriage were injured, and one man at least in their company, who was pinned beneath the wreckage, was burned to death before their eyes.

The American medical men who listened to the story on indisputable authority set their jaws a little tighter. "I suppose the Germans will try it on New York one day," said one, suggesting that the Germans might one day manage to slip a vessel with airplanes aboard through the allied patrol. At another place where a bomb fell squarely on a roof of a block of offices in a purely commercial part of the raided area, one of the American Army men speculated as to the effect a bomb would have on one of New York's skyscrapers. Here the bomb had completely gutted a four-story building, leaving nothing but the walls standing. "I was standing looking up the street at the time," a witness told the American, "and the whole top of the building seemed to blow up and melt in the air. Then a thick cloud of dust and smoke obscured everything from view."

Dr. Hugh H. Young of Johns Hopkins Hospital, Major in the Medical Officers' Reserve Corps, U. S. A., when requested to make a statement by THE NEW YORK TIMES correspondent, said:

"The victims were injured not only by flying fragments and shrapnel, causing deep penetrating wounds and fractures, but also by severe burns from the incendiary character of the bombs, which were apparently about ten inches in diameter and evidently fell from a great height, as was shown by one which penetrated a concrete wall for a great depth without exploding.

"The psychological aspects of the incident were most interesting. The population showed no fear. As soon as the explosions and counter-bombardment were heard the people crowded the streets, verandas, windows, and roofs, and showed only contempt for the infernal methods of the Germans, who only succeeded in maiming and killing helpless women and children and some men, accomplishing nothing of a military value."

The New York Times, June 14, 1917

Woodrow Wilson:
Flag Day Address in Washington, D.C.

In May 1916 Wilson had issued a proclamation establishing June 14 as Flag Day, after which he delivered an address to mark the occasion. The President spoke at a time of mounting anxiety about the loyalty of "hyphenated Americans," European immigrants who were suspected of retaining allegiance to their country of origin. "There is disloyalty active in the United States, and it must be absolutely crushed," the President warned in 1916, calling on every citizen "to see to it that no man is tolerated who does not do honor" to the flag. Exactly one year later, at the new National Sylvan Theater near the Washington Monument, Wilson detailed both the external and internal threat posed by Germany. From the beginning of the war, German agents had engaged in espionage and sabotage in the United States, including the explosion that destroyed the "Black Tom" munitions depot in Jersey City in 1916 and plots to infect with anthrax horses and mules being sent to the Allied armies. On June 15, 1917, the day after his second Flag Day address, Wilson signed into law an Espionage Act that criminalized interference with the recruitment and enlistment practices of the armed forces as well as actual spying. The act would be used to prosecute outspoken opponents of the war.

---

14 June, 1917

My Fellow Citizens: We meet to celebrate Flag Day because this flag which we honor and under which we serve is the emblem of our unity, our power, our thought and purpose as a nation. It has no other character than that which we give it from generation to generation. The choices are ours. It floats in majestic silence above the hosts that execute those choices, whether in peace or in war. And yet, though silent, it speaks to us,—speaks to us of the past, of the men and women who went before us and of the records they wrote upon it. We celebrate the day of its birth; and from its birth until now it has witnessed a great history, has floated on high the symbol of great events, of a great plan of life worked out by a great people. We

are about to carry it into battle, to lift it where it will draw the
fire of our enemies. We are about to bid thousands, hundreds
of thousands, it may be millions, of our men, the young, the
strong, the capable men of the nation, to go forth and die beneath it on fields of blood far away,—for what? For some unac-
customed thing? For something for which it has never sought
the fire before? American armies were never before sent across
the seas. Why are they sent now? For some new purpose, for
which this great flag has never been carried before, or for some
old, familiar, heroic purpose for which it has seen men, its own
men, die on every battlefield upon which Americans have
borne arms since the Revolution?

These are questions which must be answered. We are Americans. We in our turn serve America, and can serve her with no
private purpose. We must use her flag as she has always used it.
We are accountable at the bar of history and must plead in
utter frankness what purpose it is we seek to serve.

It is plain enough how we were forced into the war. The
extraordinary insults and aggressions of the Imperial German
Government left us no self-respecting choice but to take up
arms in defense of our rights as a free people and of our honour as a sovereign government. The military masters of Germany denied us the right to be neutral. They filled our
unsuspecting communities with vicious spies and conspirators
and sought to corrupt the opinion of our people in their own
behalf. When they found that they could not do that, their
agents diligently spread sedition amongst us and sought to
draw our own citizens from their allegiance,—and some of those
agents were men connected with the official Embassy of the
German Government itself here in our own capital. They sought
by violence to destroy our industries and arrest our commerce.
They tried to incite Mexico to take up arms against us and to
draw Japan into a hostile alliance with her,—and that, not by
indirection, but by direct suggestion from the Foreign Office in
Berlin. They impudently denied us the use of the high seas and
repeatedly executed their threat that they would send to their
death any of our people who ventured to approach the coasts of
Europe. And many of our own people were corrupted. Men
began to look upon their own neighbours with suspicion and

to wonder in their hot resentment and surprise whether there was any community in which hostile intrigue did not lurk. What great nation in such circumstances would not have taken up arms? Much as we had desired peace, it was denied us, and not of our own choice. This flag under which we serve would have been dishonoured had we withheld our hand.

But that is only part of the story. We know now as clearly as we knew before we were ourselves engaged that we are not the enemies of the German people and that they are not our enemies. They did not originate or desire this hideous war or wish that we should be drawn into it; and we are vaguely conscious that we are fighting their cause, as they will some day see it, as well as our own. They are themselves in the grip of the same sinister power that has now at last stretched its ugly talons out and drawn blood from us. The whole world is at war because the whole world is in the grip of that power and is trying out the great battle which shall determine whether it is to be brought under its mastery or fling itself free.

The war was begun by the military masters of Germany, who proved to be also the masters of Austria-Hungary. These men have never regarded nations as peoples, men, women, and children of like blood and frame as themselves, for whom governments existed and in whom governments had their life. They have regarded them merely as serviceable organizations which they could by force or intrigue bend or corrupt to their own purpose. They have regarded the smaller states, in particular, and the peoples who could be overwhelmed by force, as their natural tools and instruments of domination. Their purpose has long been avowed. The statesmen of other nations, to whom that purpose was incredible, paid little attention; regarded what German professors expounded in their classrooms and German writers set forth to the world as the goal of German policy as rather the dream of minds detached from practical affairs, as preposterous private conceptions of German destiny, than as the actual plans of responsible rulers; but the rulers of Germany themselves knew all the while what concrete plans, what well advanced intrigues lay back of what the professors and the writers were saying, and were glad to go forward unmolested, filling the thrones of Balkan states with German princes, putting German officers at the service of

Turkey to drill her armies and make interest with her government, developing plans of sedition and rebellion in India and
Egypt, setting their fires in Persia. The demands made by
Austria upon Servia were a mere single step in a plan which
compassed Europe and Asia, from Berlin to Bagdad. They
hoped those demands might not arouse Europe, but they
meant to press them whether they did or not, for they thought
themselves ready for the final issue of arms.

Their plan was to throw a broad belt of German military
power and political control across the very centre of Europe
and beyond the Mediterranean into the heart of Asia; and
Austria-Hungary was to be as much their tool and pawn as
Servia or Bulgaria or Turkey or the ponderous states of the East.
Austria-Hungary, indeed, was to become part of the central
German Empire, absorbed and dominated by the same forces
and influences that had originally cemented the German states
themselves. The dream had its heart at Berlin. It could have
had a heart nowhere else! It rejected the idea of solidarity of
race entirely. The choice of peoples played no part in it at all. It
contemplated binding together racial and political units which
could be kept together only by force,—Czechs, Magyars, Croats, Serbs, Roumanians, Turks, Armenians,—the proud states of
Bohemia and Hungary, the stout little commonwealths of the
Balkans, the indomitable Turks, the subtile peoples of the East.
These peoples did not wish to be united. They ardently desired
to direct their own affairs, would be satisfied only by undis-
puted independence. They could be kept quiet only by the
presence or the constant threat of armed men. They would live
under a common power only by sheer compulsion and await
the day of revolution. But the German military statesmen had
reckoned with all that and were ready to deal with it in their
own way.

And they have actually carried the greater part of that amazing plan into execution! Look how things stand. Austria is at
their mercy. It has acted, not upon its own initiative or upon
the choice of its own people, but at Berlin's dictation ever since
the war began. Its people now desire peace, but cannot have it
until leave is granted from Berlin. The so-called Central Powers are in fact but a single Power. Servia is at its mercy, should
its hands be but for a moment freed. Bulgaria has consented to

its will, and Roumania is overrun. The Turkish armies, which Germans trained, are serving Germany, certainly not themselves, and the guns of German warships lying in the harbour at Constantinople remind Turkish statesmen every day that they have no choice but to take their orders from Berlin. From Hamburg to the Persian Gulf the net is spread.

Is it not easy to understand the eagerness for peace that has been manifested from Berlin ever since the snare was set and sprung? Peace, peace, peace has been the talk of her Foreign Office for now a year and more; not peace upon her own initiative, but upon the initiative of the nations over which she now deems herself to hold the advantage. A little of the talk has been public, but most of it has been private. Through all sorts of channels it has come to me, and in all sorts of guises, but never with the terms disclosed which the German Government would be willing to accept. That government has other valuable pawns in its hands besides those I have mentioned. It still holds a valuable part of France, though with slowly relaxing grasp, and practically the whole of Belgium. Its armies press close upon Russia and overrun Poland at their will. It cannot go further; it dare not go back. It wishes to close its bargain before it is too late and it has little left to offer for the pound of flesh it will demand.

The military masters under whom Germany is bleeding see very clearly to what point Fate has brought them. If they fall back or are forced back an inch, their power both abroad and at home will fall to pieces like a house of cards. It is their power at home they are thinking about now more than their power abroad. It is that power which is trembling under their very feet; and deep fear has entered their hearts. They have but one chance to perpetuate their military power or even their controlling political influence. If they can secure peace now with the immense advantages still in their hands which they have up to this point apparently gained, they will have justified themselves before the German people; they will have gained by force what they promised to gain by it; an immense expansion of German power, an immense enlargement of German industrial and commercial opportunities. Their prestige will be secure, and with their prestige their political power. If they fail, their people will thrust them aside; a government accountable to the people themselves will be set up in Germany, as it has been in England, in the United States, in France, and in all the great countries of the modern time except Germany. If they succeed they are safe and Germany and the world are undone; if they fail Germany is saved and the world will be at peace. If they succeed, America will fall within the menace. We and all the rest of the world must remain armed, as they will remain, and must make ready for the next step in their aggression; if they fail, the world may unite for peace and Germany may be of the union.

Do you not now understand the new intrigue, the intrigue for peace, and why the masters of Germany do not hesitate to use any agency that promises to effect their purpose, the deceit of the nations? Their present particular aim is to deceive all those who throughout the world stand for the rights of peoples and the self-government of nations; for they see what immense strength the forces of justice and of liberalism are gathering out of this war. They are employing liberals in their enterprise. They are using men, in Germany and without, as their spokesmen whom they have hitherto despised and oppressed, using them for their own destruction,—socialists, the leaders of labour, the thinkers they have hitherto sought to silence. Let them once succeed and these men, now their tools, will be ground to powder beneath the weight of the great military empire they will have set up; the revolutionists in Russia will be cut off from all succour or cooperation in western Europe and a counter revolution fostered and supported; Germany herself will lose her chance of freedom; and all Europe will arm for the next, the final struggle.

The sinister intrigue is being no less actively conducted in this country than in Russia and in every country in Europe to which the agents and dupes of the Imperial German Government can get access. That government has many spokesmen here, in places high and low. They have learned discretion. They keep within the law. It is opinion they utter now, not sedition. They proclaim the liberal purposes of their masters; declare this a foreign war which can touch America with no danger to either her lands or her institutions; set England at the centre of the stage and talk of her ambition to assert economic dominion throughout the world; appeal to our ancient tradition of isolation in the politics of the nations; and seek to undermine the government with false professions of loyalty to its principles.

But they will make no headway. The false betray themselves always in every accent. It is only friends and partisans of the German Government whom we have already identified who utter these thinly disguised disloyalties. The facts are patent to all the world, and nowhere are they more plainly seen than in the United States, where we are accustomed to deal with facts and not with sophistries; and the great fact that stands out above all the rest is that this is a Peoples' War, a war for freedom and justice and self-government amongst all the nations of the world, a war to make the world safe for the peoples who live upon it and have made it their own, the German people themselves included; and that with us rests the choice to break through all these hypocrisies and patent cheats and masks of brute force and help set the world free, or else stand aside and let it be dominated a long age through by sheer weight of arms and the arbitrary choices of self-constituted masters, by the nation which can maintain the biggest armies and the most irresistible armaments—a power to which the world has afforded no parallel and in the face of which political freedom must wither and perish.

For us there is but one choice. We have made it. Woe be to the man or group of men that seeks to stand in our way in this day of high resolution when every principle we hold dearest is to be vindicated and made secure for the salvation of the nations. We are ready to plead at the bar of history, and our flag shall wear a new lustre. Once more we shall make good with our lives and fortunes the great faith to which we were born, and a new glory shall shine in the face of our people.

Randolph Bourne:
The War and the Intellectuals

Born in Bloomfield, New Jersey, Randolph Bourne suffered from severe spinal tuberculosis in childhood. Educated at Columbia University, where he studied under John Dewey, Bourne published his first book, *Youth and Life*, in 1913 and became one of the outstanding spokesmen for progressivism, contributing social and political essays to *The New Republic*, *The Atlantic Monthly*, and other magazines. The American entry into the global conflict spurred him to write a series of impassioned antiwar articles for *The Seven Arts*, including this challenge to intellectual supporters of the war, as well as an unfinished essay in which he declared that "War is the health of the State." Bourne died from influenza in December 1918 at the age of thirty-two.

———————

TO THOSE OF US who still retain an irreconcilable animus against war, it has been a bitter experience to see the unanimity with which the American intellectuals have thrown their support to the use of war-technique in the crisis in which America found herself. Socialists, college professors, publicists, new-republicans, practitioners of literature, have vied with each other in confirming with their intellectual faith the collapse of neutrality and the riveting of the war-mind on a hundred million more of the world's people. And the intellectuals are not content with confirming our belligerent gesture. They are now complacently asserting that it was they who effectively willed it, against the hesitation and dim perceptions of the American democratic masses. A war made deliberately by the intellectuals! A calm moral verdict, arrived at after a penetrating study of inexorable facts! Sluggish masses, too remote from the world-conflict to be stirred, too lacking in intellect to perceive their danger! An alert intellectual class, saving the people in spite of themselves, biding their time with Fabian strategy until the nation could be moved into war without serious resistance! An intellectual class, gently guiding a nation through sheer force of ideas into what the other nations entered only through predatory craft or popular hysteria or militarist madness! A war free from any taint of self-seeking, a war that will secure the triumph of democracy and internationalize the world! This is the picture which the more self-conscious intellectuals have formed of themselves, and which they are slowly impressing upon a population which is being led no man knows whither by an indubitably intellectualized President. And they are right, in that the war certainly did not spring from either the ideals or the prejudices, from the national ambitions or hysterias, of the American people, however acquiescent the masses prove to be, and however clearly the intellectuals prove their putative intuition.

Those intellectuals who have felt themselves totally out of sympathy with this drag toward war will seek some explanation for this joyful leadership. They will want to understand this willingness of the American intellect to open the sluices and flood us with the sewage of the war spirit. We cannot forget the virtuous horror and stupefaction which filled our college professors when they read the famous manifesto of their ninety-three German colleagues in defence of their war. To the American academic mind of 1914 defence of war was inconceivable. From Bernhardi it recoiled as from a blasphemy, little dreaming that two years later would find it creating its own cleanly reasons for imposing military service on the country and for talking of the rough rude currents of health and regeneration that war would send through the American body politic. They would have thought anyone mad who talked of shipping American men by the hundreds of thousands—conscripts—to die on the fields of France. Such a spiritual change seems catastrophic when we shoot our minds back to those days when neutrality was a proud thing. But the intellectual progress has been so gradual that the country retains little sense of the irony. The war sentiment, begun so gradually but so perseveringly by the preparedness advocates who came from the ranks of big business, caught hold of one after another of the intellectual groups. With the aid of Roosevelt, the murmurs became a monotonous chant, and finally a chorus so mighty that to be out of it was at first to be disreputable and finally almost obscene. And slowly a strident rant was worked up against Germany which compared very creditably with the German fulminations against the greedy power of England. The nerve of the war-feeling centred, of course, in the richer and older classes of the Atlantic seaboard, and was keenest where there were French or English business and particularly social connections. The sentiment then spread over the country as a class-phenomenon, touching everywhere those upper-class elements in each section who identified themselves with this Eastern ruling group. It must never be forgotten that in every community it was the least liberal and least democratic elements among whom the preparedness and later the war sentiment was found. The farmers were apathetic, the small business men and workingmen are still apathetic towards the war. The election was a vote of confidence of these latter classes in a President who would keep the faith of neutrality. The intellectuals, in other words, have identified themselves with the least democratic forces in American life. They have assumed the leadership for war of those very classes whom the American democracy has been immemorially fighting. Only in a world where irony was dead could an intellectual class enter war at the head of such illiberal cohorts in the avowed cause of world-liberalism and world-democracy. No one is left to point out the undemocratic nature of this war-liberalism. In a time of faith, skepticism is the most intolerable of all insults.

Our intellectual class might have been occupied, during the last two years of war, in studying and clarifying the ideals and aspirations of the American democracy, in discovering a true Americanism which would not have been merely nebulous but might have federated the different ethnic groups and traditions. They might have spent the time in endeavoring to clear the public mind of the cant of war, to get rid of old mystical notions that clog our thinking. We might have used the time for a great wave of education, for setting our house in spiritual order. We could at least have set the problem before ourselves. If our intellectuals were going to lead the administration, they might conceivably have tried to find some way of securing peace by making neutrality effective. They might have turned their intellectual energy not to the problem of jockeying the nation into war, but to the problem of using our vast neutral power to attain democratic ends for the rest of the world and ourselves without the use of the malevolent technique of war. They might have failed. The point is that they scarcely tried. The time was spent not in clarification and education, but in a mulling over of nebulous ideals of democracy and liberalism and civilization which had never meant anything fruitful to those ruling classes who now so glibly used them, and in giving free rein to the elementary instinct of self-defence. The whole era has been spiritually wasted. The outstanding feature has been not its Americanism but its intense colonialism. The offence of our intellectuals was not so much that they were colonial —for what could we expect of a nation composed of so many national elements?—but that it was so one-sidedly and partisanly colonial. The official, reputable expression of the intellectual class has been that of the English colonial. Certain portions of it have been even more loyalist than the King, more British even than Australia. Other colonial attitudes have been vulgar. The colonialism of the other American stocks was denied a hearing from the start. America might have been made a meeting-ground for the different national attitudes. An intellectual class, cultural colonists of the different European nations, might have threshed out the issues here as they could not be threshed out in Europe. Instead of this, the English colonials in university and press took command at the start, and we became an intellectual Hungary where thought was subject to an effective process of Magyarization. The reputable opinion of the American intellectuals became more and more either what could be read pleasantly in London, or what was written in an earnest effort to put Englishmen straight on their war-aims and war-technique. This Magyarization of thought produced as a counter-reaction a peculiarly offensive and inept German apologetic, and the two partisans divided the field between them. The great masses, the other ethnic groups, were inarticulate. American public opinion was almost as little prepared for war in 1917 as it was in 1914.

The sterile results of such an intellectual policy are inevitable. During the war the American intellectual class has produced almost nothing in the way of original and illuminating interpretation. Veblen's "Imperial Germany;" Patten's "Culture and War," and addresses; Dewey's "German Philosophy and Politics;" a chapter or two in Weyl's "American Foreign

Policies;"—is there much else of creative value in the intellectual repercussion of the war? It is true that the shock of war put the American intellectual to an unusual strain. He had to sit idle and think as spectator not as actor. There was no government to which he could docilely and loyally tender his mind as did the Oxford professors to justify England in her own eyes. The American's training was such as to make the fact of war almost incredible. Both in his reading of history and in his lack of economic perspective he was badly prepared for it. He had to explain to himself something which was too colossal for the modern mind, which outran any language or terms which we had to interpret it in. He had to expand his sympathies to the breaking-point, while pulling the past and present into some sort of interpretative order. The intellectuals in the fighting countries had only to rationalize and justify what their country was already doing. Their task was easy. A neutral, however, had really to search out the truth. Perhaps perspective was too much to ask of any mind. Certainly the older colonials among our college professors let their prejudices at once dictate their thought. They have been comfortable ever since. The war has taught them nothing and will teach them nothing. And they have had the satisfaction, under the rigor of events, of seeing prejudice submerge the intellects of their younger colleagues. And they have lived to see almost their entire class, pacifists and democrats too, join them as apologists for the "gigantic irrelevance" of war.

We have had to watch, therefore, in this country the same process which so shocked us abroad,—the coalescence of the intellectual classes in support of the military programme. In this country, indeed, the socialist intellectuals did not even have the grace of their German brothers and wait for the declaration of war before they broke for cover. And when they declared for war they showed how thin was the intellectual veneer of their socialism. For they called us in terms that might have emanated from any bourgeois journal to defend democracy and civilization, just as if it was not exactly against those very bourgeois democracies and capitalist civilizations that socialists had been fighting for decades. But so subtle is the spiritual chemistry of the "inside" that all this intellectual cohesion—herd-instinct become herd-intellect—which seemed abroad so hysterical and so servile, comes to us here in highly rational terms. We go to war to save the world from subjugation! But the German intellectuals went to war to save their culture from barbarization! And the French went to war to save their beautiful France! And the English to save international honor! And Russia, most altruistic and self-sacrificing of all, to save a small State from destruction! Whence is our miraculous intuition of our moral spotlessness? Whence our confidence that history will not unravel huge economic and imperialist forces upon which our rationalizations float like bubbles? The Jew often marvels that his race alone should have been chosen as the true people of the cosmic God. Are not our intellectuals equally fatuous when they tell us that our war of all wars is stainless and thrillingly achieving for good?

An intellectual class that was wholly rational would have called insistently for peace and not for war. For months the crying need has been for a negotiated peace, in order to avoid the ruin of a deadlock. Would not the same amount of resolute statesmanship thrown into intervention have secured a peace that would have been a subjugation for neither side? Was the terrific bargaining power of a great neutral ever really used? Our war followed, as all wars follow, a monstrous failure of diplomacy. Shamefacedness should now be our intellectuals' attitude, because the American play for peace was made so little more than a polite play. The intellectuals have still to explain why, willing as they now are to use force to continue the war to absolute exhaustion, they were not willing to use force to coerce the world to a speedy peace.

Their forward vision is no more convincing than their past rationality. We go to war now to internationalize the world! But surely their League to Enforce Peace is only a palpable apocalyptic myth, like the syndicalists' myth of the "general strike." It is not a rational programme so much as a glowing symbol for the purpose of focusing belief, of setting enthusiasm on fire for international order. As far as it does this it has pragmatic value, but as far as it provides a certain radiant mirage of idealism for this war and for a world-order founded on mutual fear, it is dangerous and obnoxious. Idealism should be kept for what is ideal. It is depressing to think that the prospect of a world so strong that none dare challenge it should be the immediate ideal of the American intellectual. If the League is only a makeshift, a coalition into which we enter to restore order, then it is only a description of existing fact, and the idea should be treated as such. But if it is an actually prospective outcome of the settlement, the keystone of American policy, it is neither realizable nor desirable. For the programme of such a League contains no provision for dynamic national growth or for international economic justice. In a world which requires recognition of economic internationalism far more than of political internationalism, an idea is reactionary which proposes to petrify and federate the nations as political and economic units. Such a scheme for international order is a dubious justification for American policy. And if American policy had been sincere in its belief that our participation would achieve international beatitude, would we not have made our entrance into the war conditional upon a solemn general agreement to respect in the final settlement these principles of international order? Could we have afforded, if our war was to end war by the establishment of a league of honor, to risk the defeat of our vision and our betrayal in the settlement? Yet we are in the war, and no such solemn agreement was made, nor has it even been suggested.

The case of the intellectuals seems, therefore, only very speciously rational. They could have used their energy to force a just peace or at least to devise other means than war for carrying through American policy. They could have used their intellectual energy to ensure that our participation in the war meant the international order which they wish. Intellect was not so used. It was used to lead an apathetic nation into an irresponsible war, without guarantees from those belligerents whose cause we were saving. The American intellectual, therefore, has been rational neither in his hindsight nor his foresight. To explain him we must look beneath the intellectual reasons to the emotional disposition. It is not so much what they thought as how they felt that explains our intellectual class. Allowing for colonial sympathy, there was still the personal shock in a world-war which outraged all our preconceived notions of the way the world was tending. It reduced to rubbish most of the humanitarian internationalism and democratic nationalism which had been the emotional thread of our intellectuals' life. We had suddenly to make a new orientation. There were mental conflicts. Our latent colonialism strove with our longing for American unity. Our desire for peace strove with our desire for national responsibility in the world. That first lofty and remote and not altogether unsound feeling of our spiritual isolation from the conflict could not last. There was the itch to be in the great experience which the rest of the world was having. Numbers of intelligent people who had never been stirred by the horrors of capitalistic peace at home were shaken out of their slumber by the horrors of war in Belgium. Never having felt responsibility for labor wars and oppressed masses and excluded races at home, they had a large fund of idle emotional capital to invest in the oppressed nationalities and ravaged villages of Europe. Hearts that had felt only ugly contempt for democratic strivings at home beat in tune with the struggle for freedom abroad. All this was natural, but it tended to over-emphasize our responsibility. And it threw our thinking out of gear. The task of making our own country detailedly fit for peace was abandoned in favor of a feverish concern for the management of the war, advice to the fighting governments on all matters, military, social and political, and a gradual working up of the conviction that we were ordained as a nation to lead all erring brothers towards the light of liberty and democracy. The failure of the American intellectual class to erect a creative attitude toward the war can be explained by these sterile mental conflicts which the shock to our ideals sent raging through us.

Mental conflicts end either in a new and higher synthesis or adjustment, or else in a reversion to more primitive ideas which have been outgrown but to which we drop when jolted out of our attained position. The war caused in America a recrudescence of nebulous ideals which a younger generation was fast outgrowing because it had passed the wistful stage and was discovering concrete ways of getting them incarnated in actual institutions. The shock of the war threw us back from this pragmatic work into an emotional bath of these old ideals. There was even a somewhat rarefied revival of our primitive Yankee boastfulness, the reversion of senility to that republican childhood when we expected the whole world to copy our republican institutions. We amusingly ignored the fact that it was just that Imperial German regime, to whom we are to teach the art of self-government, which our own Federal structure, with its executive irresponsible in foreign policy and with its absence of parliamentary control, most resembles. And we are missing the exquisite irony of the unaffected homage paid by the American democratic intellectuals to the last and most detested of Britain's tory premiers as the representative of a "liberal" ally, as well as the irony of the selection of the best hated of America's bourbon "old guard" as the missionary of American democracy to Russia.

The intellectual state that could produce such things is one where reversion has taken place to more primitive ways of thinking. Simple syllogisms are substituted for analysis, things are known by their labels, our heart's desire dictates what we shall see. The American intellectual class, having failed to make the higher syntheses, regresses to ideas that can issue in quick, simplified action. Thought becomes any easy rationalization of what is actually going on or what is to happen inevitably to-morrow. It is true that certain groups did rationalize their colonialism and attach the doctrine of the inviolability of British sea-power to the doctrine of a League of Peace. But this agile resolution of the mental conflict did not become a higher synthesis, to be creatively developed. It gradually merged into a justification for our going to war. It petrified into a dogma to be propagated. Criticism flagged and emotional propaganda began. Most of the socialists, the college professors and the practitioners of literature, however, have not even reached this high-water mark of synthesis. Their mental conflicts have been resolved much more simply. War in the interests of democracy! This was almost the sum of their philosophy. The primitive idea to which they regressed became almost insensibly translated into a craving for action. War was seen as the crowning relief of their indecision. At last action, irresponsibility, the end of anxious and torturing attempts to reconcile peace-ideals with the drag of the world towards Hell. An end to the pain of trying to adjust the facts to what they ought to be! Let us consecrate the facts as ideal! Let us join the greased slide towards war! The momentum increased. Hesitations, ironies, consciences, considerations,—all were drowned in the elemental blare of doing something aggressive, colossal. The new-found Sabbath "peacefulness of being at war"! The thankfulness with which so many intellectuals lay down and floated with the current betrays the hesitation and suspense through which they had been. The American university is a brisk and happy place these days. Simple, unquestioning action has superseded the knots of thought. The thinker dances with reality.

With how many of the acceptors of war has it been mostly a dread of intellectual suspense? It is a mistake to suppose that intellectuality necessarily makes for suspended judgments. The intellect craves certitude. It takes effort to keep it supple and pliable. In a time of danger and disaster we jump desperately for some dogma to cling to. The time comes, if we try to hold out, when our nerves are sick with fatigue, and we seize in a great healing wave of release some doctrine that can be immediately translated into action. Neutrality meant suspense, and so it became the object of loathing to frayed nerves. The vital myth of the League of Peace provides a dogma to jump to. With war the world becomes motor again and speculation is brushed aside like cobwebs. The blessed emotion of self-defence intervenes too, which focused millions in Europe. A few keep up a critical pose after war is begun, but since they usually advise action which is in one-to-one correspondence with what the mass is already doing, their criticism is little more than a rationalization of the common emotional drive.

The results of war on the intellectual class are already apparent. Their thought becomes little more than a description and justification of what is going on. They turn upon any rash one who continues idly to speculate. Once the war is on, the conviction spreads that individual thought is helpless, that the only way one can count is as a cog in the great wheel. There is no good holding back. We are told to dry our unnoticed and ineffective tears and plunge into the great work. Not only is everyone forced into line, but the new certitude becomes idealized. It is a noble realism which opposes itself to futile obstruction and the cowardly refusal to face facts. This realistic boast is so loud and sonorous that one wonders whether realism is always a stern and intelligent grappling with realities. May it not be sometimes a mere surrender to the actual, an abdication of the ideal through a sheer fatigue from intellectual suspense? The pacifist is roundly scolded for refusing to face the facts, and for retiring into his own world of sentimental desire. But is the realist, who refuses to challenge or criticise facts, entitled to any more credit than that which comes from following the line of least resistance? The realist thinks he at least can control events by linking himself to the forces that are moving. Perhaps he can. But if it is a question of controlling war, it is difficult to see how the child on the back of a mad elephant is to be any more effective in stopping the beast than is the child who tries to stop him from the ground. The ex-humanitarian, turned realist, sneers at the snobbish neutrality, colossal conceit, crooked thinking, dazed sensibilities, of those who are still unable to find any balm of consolation for this war. We manufacture consolations here in America while there are probably not a dozen men fighting in Europe who did not long ago give up every reason for their being there except that nobody knew how to get them away.

But the intellectuals whom the crisis has crystallized into an acceptance of war have put themselves into a terrifyingly strategic position. It is only on the craft, in the stream, they say, that one has any chance of controlling the current forces for liberal purposes. If we obstruct, we surrender all power for influence. If we responsibly approve, we then retain our power for guiding. We will be listened to as responsible thinkers, while those who obstructed the coming of war have committed intellectual suicide and shall be cast into outer darkness. Criticism by the ruling powers will only be accepted from those intellectuals who are in sympathy with the general tendency of the war. Well, it is true that they may guide, but if their stream leads to disaster and the frustration of national life, is their guiding any more than a preference whether they shall go over the right-hand or the left-hand side of the precipice? Meanwhile, however, there is comfort on board. Be with us, they call, or be negligible, irrelevant. Dissenters are already excommunicated. Irreconcilable radicals, wringing their hands among the debris, become the most despicable and impotent of men. There seems no choice for the intellectual but to join the mass of acceptance. But again the terrible dilemma arises, —either support what is going on, in which case you count for nothing because you are swallowed in the mass and great incalculable forces bear you on; or remain aloof, passively resistant, in which case you count for nothing because you are outside the machinery of reality.

Is there no place left, then, for the intellectual who cannot yet crystallize, who does not dread suspense, and is not yet drugged with fatigue? The American intellectuals, in their preoccupation with reality, seem to have forgotten that the real enemy is War rather than imperial Germany. There is work to be done to prevent this war of ours from passing into popular mythology as a holy crusade. What shall we do with leaders who tell us that we go to war in moral spotlessness, or who make "democracy" synonymous with a republican form of government? There is work to be done in still shouting that all the revolutionary by-products will not justify the war, or make war anything else than the most noxious complex of all the evils that afflict men. There must be some to find no consolation whatever, and some to sneer at those who buy the cheap emotion of sacrifice. There must be some irreconcilables left who will not even accept the war with walrus tears. There must be some to call unceasingly for peace, and some to insist that the terms of settlement shall be not only liberal but democratic. There must be some intellectuals who are not willing to use the old discredited counters again and to support a peace which would leave all the old inflammable materials of armament lying about the world. There must still be opposition to any contemplated "liberal" world-order founded on military coalitions. The "irreconcilable" need not be disloyal. He need not even be "impossibilist." His apathy towards war should take the form of a heightened energy and enthusiasm for the education, the art, the interpretation that make for life in the midst of the world of death. The intellectual who retains his animus against war will push out more boldly than ever to make his case solid against it. The old ideals crumble; new ideals must be forged. His mind will continue to roam widely and ceaselessly. The thing he will fear most is premature crystallization. If the American intellectual class rivets itself to a "liberal" philosophy that perpetuates the old errors, there will then be need for "democrats" whose task will be to divide, confuse, disturb, keep the intellectual waters constantly in motion to prevent any such ice from ever forming.

Carlos F. Hurd to
the St. Louis Post-Dispatch

Wartime purchases of American food, raw materials, and manufac-
tured goods by the British and French had created an increased demand for labor in the Northeast and Midwest, while the war also
reduced the number of immigrants arriving from Europe. African
American migrants from the South filled some of the need for workers.
Between 1910 and 1917 the black population of East St. Louis, Illinois,
for example, had doubled; and in the spring of 1917, the hiring of
hundreds of black strikebreakers at a major metalworking factory
there exacerbated racial tensions. On the night of July 1, residents in a
black neighborhood mistook two white policemen for armed intrud-
ers and shot them to death. The next day white mobs attacked black
residents in the streets, beginning a reign of terror that continued
into July 3, 1917, resulting in the deaths of at least nine whites and
thirty-nine blacks. Carlos F. Hurd, a reporter for the *St. Louis Post-
Dispatch*, filed this eyewitness account of the rioting on July 2.

POST-DISPATCH MAN, AN EYE-WITNESS,
DESCRIBES MASSACRE OF NEGROES

Victims Driven from Home by Fire, Stoned, Beaten
and Hanged When Dying—Women Fight
Militiamen and Assist in Work

For an hour and a half last evening I saw the massacre of
helpless negroes at Broadway and Fourth street, in downtown
East St. Louis, where a black skin was a death warrant.

I have read of St. Bartholomew's night. I have heard stories
of the latter-day crimes of the Turks in Armenia, and I have
learned to loathe the German army for its barbarity in Belgium. But I do not believe that Moslem fanaticism or Prussian
frightfulness could perpetrate murders of more deliberate
brutality than those which I saw committed, in daylight by
citizens of the State of Abraham Lincoln.

I saw man after man, with hands raised, pleading for his life, surrounded by groups of men—men who had never seen him before and knew nothing about him except that he was black—and saw them administer the historic sentence of intolerance, death by stoning. I saw one of these men, almost dead from a savage shower of stones, hanged with a clothesline, and when it broke, hanged with a rope which held. Within a few paces of the pole from which he was suspended, four other negroes lay dead or dying, another having been removed, dead, a short time before. I saw the pockets of two of these negroes searched, without the finding of any weapon.

Rock Dropped on Negroes Neck.

I saw one of these men, covered with blood and half conscious, raise himself on his elbow, and look feebly about, when a young man, standing directly behind him, lifted a flat stone in both hands and hurled it upon his neck. This young man was much better dressed than most of the others. He walked away unmolested.

I saw negro women begging for mercy and pleading that they had harmed no one, set upon by white women of the baser sort, who laughed and answered the coarse sallies of men as they beat the negresses face and breasts with fists, stones and sticks. I saw one of the furies fling herself at a militiaman who was trying to protect a negress, and wrestle with for his bayonetted gun, while other women attacked the refugee.

What I saw, in the 90 minutes between 6:30 P.M. and the lurid coming of darkness, was but one local scene of the drama of death. I am satisfied that, in spirit and method, it typified the whole. And I cannot somehow speak of what I saw as mob violence. It was not my idea of a mob.

Crowd Mostly Workingmen.

A mob is passionate, a mob follows one man or a few men blindly; a mob sometimes takes chances. The East St. Louis affair, as I saw it, was a man hunt, conducted on a sporting basis, though with anything but the fair play which is the principle of sport. The East St. Louis men took no chances, except the chance from stray shots, which every spectator of their acts took.

They went in small groups, there was little leadership, and there was a horribly cool deliberateness and a spirit of fun about it. I cannot allow even the doubtful excuse of drink. No man whom I saw showed the effect of liquor.

It was no crowd of hot-headed youths. Young men were in the greater number, but there were the middle-aged, no less active in the task of destroying the life of every discoverable black man. It was a shirt-sleeve gathering, and the men were mostly workingmen, except for some who had the aspect of mere loafers. I have mentioned the peculiarly brutal crime committed by the only man there who had the appearance of being a business or professional man of any standing.

I would be more pessimistic about my fellow-Americans than I am today, if I could not say that there were other work-ingmen who protested against the senseless slaughter. I would be ashamed of myself if I could not say that I forgot my place as a professional observer and joined in such protests. But I do not think any verbal objection had the slightest effect. Only a volley of lead would have stopped those murderers.

"Get a nigger," was the slogan, and it was varied by the re-current cry, "Get another!" It was like nothing so much as the holiday crowd, with thumbs turned down, in the Roman Col-iseum, except that here the shouters were their own gladiators, and their own wild beasts.

When I got off a State street car on Broadway at 6:30, a fire apparatus was on its way to the blaze in the rear of Fourth street, south from Broadway. A moment's survey showed why this fire had been set, and what it was meant to accomplish.

FIRE DRIVES OUT NEGROES.

The sheds in the rear of negroes' houses, which were them-selves in the rear of the main buildings on Fourth street, had been ignited to drive out the negro occupants of the houses. And the slayers were waiting for them to come out.

It was stay in and be roasted, or come out and be slaugh-tered. A moment before I arrived, one negro had taken the desperate chance of coming out, and the rattle of revolver shots, which I heard as I approached the corner, was followed by the cry, "They've got him!"

And they had. He lay on the pavement, a bullet wound in his head and his skull bare in two places. At every movement of pain which showed that life remained, there came a terrific kick in the jaw or the nose, or a crashing stone, from some of the men who stood over him.

At the corner a few steps away, were a Sergeant and several guardsmen. The Sergeant approached the ring of men around the prostrate negro.

"This man is done for," he said. "You'd better get him away from here." No one made a move to lift the blood-covered form, and the Sergeant walked away, remarking, when I questioned him about an ambulance, that the ambulances had quit coming. However, an undertaker's ambulance did come 15 minutes later, and took away the lifeless negro, who had in the meantime been further kicked and stoned.

By that time, the fire in the rear of the negro houses had grown hotter, and men were standing in all the narrow spaces through which the negroes might come to the street. There was talk of a negro in one of the houses, who had a Winchester, and the opinion was expressed that he had no ammunition left but no one went too near, and the fire was depended on to drive him out. The firemen were at work on Broadway, some distance east, but the flames immediately in the rear of the negro houses burned without hindrance.

MILITIAMEN TRY TO CURB MOB.

A half-block to the south, there was a hue and cry at a railroad crossing, and a fusillade of shots was heard. More militiamen than I had seen elsewhere, up to that time, were standing on a platform and near a string of freight cars, and trying to keep back men who had started to pursue negroes along the track.

As I turned back toward Broadway, there was a shout at the alley, and a negro ran out, apparently hoping to find protection. He paid no attention to missiles thrown from behind, none of which had hurt him much, but he was stopped, in the middle of the street by a smashing blow in the jaw, struck by a man he had not seen.

"Don't do that," he appealed. "I haven't hurt nobody." The answer was a blow from one side, a piece of curbstone from the other side, and a push which sent him on the brick pavement. He did not rise again, and the battering and kicking of his skull continued until he lay still, his blood flowing halfway across the street. Before he had been booted to the opposite curb, another negro appeared, and the same deeds were repeated. I did not see any revolver shots fired at these men. Bullets and ammunition were saved for use at longer range. It was the last negro I have mentioned who was apparently finished by the stone hurled upon his neck by the noticeably well-dressed young man.

The butchering of the fire-trapped negroes went on so rapidly that, when I walked back to the alley a few minutes later, one was lying dead in the alley on the west side of Fourth street and another on the east side.

And now women began to appear. One frightened black girl, probably 20 years old, got so far as Broadway with no worse treatment than jeers and thrusts. At Broadway, in view of militiamen, the white women, several of whom had been watching the massacre of the negro men, pounced on the negress. I do not wish to be understood as saying that these women were representative of the womanhood of East St. Louis. Their faces showed, all too plainly, exactly who and what they were. But they were the heroines of the moment with that gathering of men, and when one man, sick of the brutality he had seen, seized one of the women by the arm to stop an impending blow, he was hustled away, with fists under his nose, and with more show of actual anger than had been bestowed on any of the negroes. He was a stocky, nervy chap, and he stood his ground until a diversion elsewhere drew the menacing ring of men away.

"Let the girls have her," was the shout as the women attacked the young negress. The victim's cry, "Please, please, I ain't done nothing," was stopped by a blow in the mouth with a broomstick, which one of the women swung like a baseball bat. Another woman seized the negress' hands, and the blow was repeated as she struggled helplessly. Finger nails clawed her hair, and the sleeves were torn from her waist, when some of the men called, "Now let her see how fast she can run." The women did not readily leave off beating her, but they stopped short of murder, and the crying, hysterical girl ran down the street.

An older negress, a few moments later, came along with two or three militiamen, and the same women made for her. When one of the soldiers held his gun as a barrier, the woman with the broomstick seized it with both hands, and struggled to wrest it from him, while the others, striking at the negress, in spite of the other militiamen, frightened her thoroughly and hurt her somewhat.

From negress baiting, the well-pleased procession turned to see a lynching. A negro, his head laid open by a great stone-cut, had been dragged to the mouth of the alley on Fourth street and a small rope was being put about his neck. There was joking comment on the weakness of the rope, and every-one was prepared for what happened when it was pulled over a projecting cable box, a short distance up the pole. It broke, letting the negro tumble back to his knees, and causing one of the men who was pulling on it to sprawl on the pavement.

Stouter Rope Obtained.

An old man, with a cap like those worn by street car conduc-tors, but showing no badge of car service, came out of his house to protest. "Don't you hang that man on this street," he shouted. "I dare you to." He was pushed angrily away, and a rope, obviously strong enough for its purpose, was brought.

Right here I saw the most sickening incident of the evening. To put the rope around the negro's neck, one of the lynchers stuck his fingers inside the gaping scalp and lifted the negro's head by it, literally bathing his hand in the man's blood.

"Get hold, and pull for East St. Louis!" called a man with a black coat and a new straw hat, as he seized the other end of the rope. The rope was long, but not too long for the number of hands that grasped it, and this time the negro was lifted to a height of about seven feet from the ground. The body was left hanging there.

While this lynching was in preparation I walked to Broad-way, found a Corporal's guard of militiamen, who had just come from where the firemen were working, and called their attention to what was going on. I do not know that they could have done anything to stop it. I know that they did not try to.

In the first hour that I was there I saw no sufficient body of militiamen anywhere, and no serious effort, on the part of the few who were about to prevent bloodshed. Most of the men in uniform were frankly fraternizing with the men in the street. But beginning at 7:30, I did see instances of what national guardsmen, in reasonable numbers, and led by worthy officers, can do.

RESCUE SOME NEGROES.

First, there came a hollow square of soldiers from the fire zone along Broadway. In the front row of the frightened group within the square was a mulatto boy, not more than 6 years old. Further within the group were other children with their mothers. The negro men were marching with their hands raised, and some of the women were also holding up their hands.

The natural point of attack was in the rear, and the soldiers, under sharp commands from an officer, repeatedly turned about and made room with their bayonets. The pitiful procession got safely around the corner and to the police station. Some smaller rescues of a similar kind were carried out in the next few minutes.

Following one of these rescue parties to the police station, I suddenly became aware that a new man, and a new spirit of soldiery, had entered into the situation. A man in a light suit and a straw hat, who had just come into town, was listening to a few details of what had happened in the neighborhood. He gave some quick commands, and in a moment, the first adequate body of guardsmen that I had seen was marching toward Broadway. The solders were from B company and other companies of the Fourth Illinois, and the apparent civilian in command was Col. Stephen O. Tripp of the Adjutant-General's office in Springfield.

As they turned into Broadway, double-quick was ordered, and it was none too quick, for another lynching was being prepared. This lynching was apparently to be on Broadway, and a negro, his head cut, but still conscious and struggling, was being dragged along the pavement with a rope around his neck.

"Get those men!" was the command, and a moment later several white men were in line on the south sidewalk, some of them with hands raised, while guardsmen faced them with bayonets. On the opposite sidewalk, the soldiers merely told the men to "move on," and this brought a sharp reprimand from Col. Tripp. "Don't let them get away," he ordered. "Make them prisoners." Most of these men were again lined up, and the two lines of prisoners, 25 or 30 men in all, were then marshaled in the car tracks, and the march to the station began, a guard being left behind to protect the negro, and to keep the street clear. I did not learn what became of this negro.

Temper Of Crowd Changes.

The temper of the men in the street showed a change after the first encounter with Tripp methods. It began to seem that the situation had found its master. But the most efficient Colonel cannot be everywhere at once, and while the uniformed line was busy keeping a crowd from forming about the police station, scattered shooting began in the neighborhood of the recent killings.

One negro ran the gauntlet on Broadway. Several shots were fired at him, in a reckless fashion that explains the number injured by stray bullets earlier in the day. But it appeared that he got away.

It was nearly dark, and the fire on Broadway was becoming more threatening. A half-hour before, some lines of hose, though apparently in insufficient number, had been in use, but now the use of water had ceased, and it was said that the hose had been cut. The fire was nearing the Mollman harness establishment, in which the mayor of East St. Louis is interested, and the big wooden horse on top of the building was silhouetted in the twilight.

As I returned from a look at the fire, I saw an ambulance drive into Fourth street, to get the bodies which had been lying there for nearly an hour. I saw one body placed in the ambulance. I heard it said, as I was leaving town, that the men in the street had prevented the removal of one of the bodies, saying that the negro was not dead, and must lie there until he died. I did not verify this, and I do not state it as a fact. Every thing which I have stated as a fact came under my own observation. And what I saw was, as I have said, but a small part of the whole.

I must add a word about the efficiency of the East St. Louis police. One of them kept me from going too near the fire. Absolutely the only thing that I saw policemen do was to keep that fire line. As the police detail marched to the fire, two of the men turned aside into Fourth street, apparently to see if two negroes, lying on the pavement, were dead. These policemen got a sharp call into line from their sergeant. They were not supposed to bother themselves about dead negroes.

In recording this, I do not forget that a policeman—by all accounts a fine and capable policeman—was killed by negroes the night before. I have not forgotten it in writing about the acts of the men in the street. Whether this crime excuses or palliates a massacre, which probably included none of the offenders, is something I will leave to apologists for last evening's occurrence, if there are any such, to explain.

July 3, 1917

Norman Thomas: War's Heretics, a Plea for the Conscientious Objector

A Princeton-educated Presbyterian minister who both preached and practiced the Social Gospel, Norman Thomas belonged to the Fellowship of Reconciliation, a Christian pacifist organization, and the American Union Against Militarism, a group founded in 1915 to oppose "preparedness." Exempt from the draft as a member of the clergy, in 1917 Thomas helped Roger Baldwin found the Civil Liberties Bureau, which assisted conscientious objectors. (Later renamed the National Civil Liberties Bureau, the organization would become the American Civil Liberties Union in 1920.) One of Thomas's brothers was a conscientious objector who was imprisoned in 1918 for refusing to perform alternative service, while two other brothers served in the army.

———————

ANY EFFORT to think intelligently about a war avowedly waged for human liberty brings one face to face with the problem of the conscientious objector. Undoubtedly he is an irritant to the whole-souled patriot. His very existence seems a piece of inconsiderate egotism and annoyingly interrupts us in the midst of our enthusiasms for a war fought "by no compulsion of the unwilling" "to make the world safe for democracy." So newspapers, orators and Colonel Roosevelt call him slacker, coward or pro-German; philosophers gravely pronounce him anti-social, and scientists like Dr. Paton analyze him from a study chair with a truly Teutonic subjectivity and heaviness. Meanwhile his defenders and comrades are a bit embarrassed because he is not of one type or philosophy, but of many. Even the name "conscientious objector" is most unwelcome to some moderns among them to whom the phrase has an "archaic flavor," an objective quality, "like a godly grandmother," which hardly fits into their scheme of life. They are not, then, overly sympathetic with the defense which is entirely satisfactory to the man to whom conscience is the real norm of life and "thou shalt not kill" a complete statement of its law.

Therefore, it is with some diffidence that I, a conscientious objector, undertake to speak for my brethren and to appeal even in the heat of war for some measure of understanding— not so much for our own sakes as in the interest of sound public policy and ultimately of democracy itself.

As a starting point we can define conscientious objectors as men who are absolutely persuaded that enforced participation in this war is so opposed to their deepest convictions of right and wrong for themselves or for society that they must refuse conscription at least for combatant service. If they know themselves they will hold this position whatever it may cost. This attitude springs from no insufferable priggishness. The objector does not primarily seek to judge others; he may heartily admire the heroism which leads his friends into battle, he may admit the idealism of their ends, only he cannot agree with them as to the method they use.

How many such folk there are in the United States no one knows. Naturally, the government will not permit an aggressive attempt to discover and organize all conscientious objectors. There are, however, many societies, local and national, whose members are avowed conscientious objectors, and there are many more unorganized individuals who hold such convictions. Again, it is uncertain how many of the thousands of objectors will be drawn in the first group called to report under the draft law.

It is natural to think of conscientious objectors as essentially religious, and the government showed a certain deference to religious liberty in exempting from combatant service members of well-recognized religious organizations whose creed or principles are opposed to war. Of course this is illogical in theory, for conscience is an individual and not a corporate matter. Not all conscientious objection is avowedly religious, nor is religious conscientious objection confined to the relatively small sects which have incorporated it in their creeds. Within the last generation there has been a wide growth of peace sentiment in the churches not all of which is as amenable to conversion to war as the average ecclesiastical organization or that erstwhile prophet of the Prince of Peace, William J. Bryan. You have to reckon with it. Then you have young idealists among the intellectuals to whom humanity is a reality never served by the stupid horrors of war, and the very much larger group of workingmen who have learned too well the doctrine of the solidarity of the working class to believe that the organized destruction of their brethren who march under a different national banner will hasten the dawn of real liberty and fraternity.

In short, conscientious objectors include Christians, Jews, agnostics and atheists; economic conservatists and radicals; philosophic anarchists and orthodox socialists.

It is not fair, therefore, to think of the conscientious objector simply as a man who with a somewhat dramatic gesture would save his own soul though liberty perish and his country be laid in ruins. I speak with personal knowledge when I say that such an attitude is rare. Rightly or wrongly, the conscientious objector believes that his religion or his social theory in the end can save what is precious in the world far better without than with this stupendously destructive war. He is a pacifist but not a passivist.

Even John Dewey seems to me to be dealing with only one phase of conscientious objection, and that not the most important, when, in a recent article on Conscience and Compulsion, he speaks critically of conscience "whose main concern is to maintain itself unspotted from within" or "whose search is for a fixed antecedent rule of justification." Doubtless this point of view exists; something of a case might be made for it; but it cannot be too strongly insisted that the majority of conscientious objectors, even of this type, believe that the same course of action which keeps one's self "unspotted from within" will ultimately prove the only safe means for establishing a worthy social system. They quite agree with Professor Dewey in the necessity of search for "the machinery for maintaining peace"; but they remember Edward T. Devine's sober and terrible indictment of war in his report at the recent Conference of Charities and Corrections, or they recall that a great Christian denomination in its very declaration of hearty support for the government's war policy declared war to be "irrational, inhuman and unchristian." So they feel that the burden of proof is decidedly on the shoulders of anyone who finds in the worldwide denials of humanity and democracy involved in this struggle a valuable part of that machinery of peace or the way for saving mankind.

We grant that our unity is to be found in our common denial of the righteousness or efficacy of our personal participation in the world war. Our positive philosophy, as I have already indicated, varies as does the philosophy of the larger pacifist movement, of which we are a part. At one extreme of our ranks is the Tolstoian non-resistant, at the other the man whose objection is to participation in *this* war.

Perhaps the extreme non-resistant gets the most understanding and respect for his consistency if not for his brains. The name "non-resistant," however, scarcely does justice to his convictions. He is persuaded that the supreme force in the world is Love and that Love can only win by its own weapons, which are never the weapons of violence. He is accused of ethical optimism, but he is too much of an ethical realist to preach to great armies the modern doctrine that they go out to kill each other with bayonets, bombs, big Berthas and poisonous gas in a spirit of love. He may believe in *dying* for one's country, or for ideals; but not in *killing* for them. And his objection is by no means only to killing, but to the essential autocracy, the lies, the contempt for personality, the stark barbarism of war which knows no crime but defeat. He is convinced that victory of those great ideals of democracy so eloquently phrased by the President will never be won, no matter what nation is victorious, till love is the animating principle of life.

THE RELIGIOUS OBJECTOR

Not all of this group are such extreme non-resistants as to deny the validity of police force. Such force can be organized and regulated, it can be applied to the real criminals and that for the purpose of their redemption in a way that is never true of the indiscriminate and all-inclusive violence of war.

The God of the religious conscientious objector, Jewish or Christian, is both stronger and more loving than the being recently discovered by H. G. Wells. He does not have to save

Himself and His causes by using the devil's means. Rather He waits for men to try His ways. We Christian conscientious objectors do not base our case on implicit obedience to one text even in that most revolutionary of documents, the Sermon on the Mount, but on the whole character and work of Jesus, who has conquered and is to conquer not by any might save Love and Truth. Churchmen nowadays say much of the "soldier's Calvary" and "salvation through suffering." If by sheer weight of agony the world is to be saved, long ago would salvation have come upon us. It is the spirit that counts, and the sublime sufferer on Calvary whose love and courage triumphed over shame and death did not receive His crown of martyrdom as an unfortunate incident in the attempt to kill as many of his enemies as possible. Singularly enough the world outside the church, despite the eloquent—and usually sincere—casuistry of her priests and ministers, appreciates the essential impossibility of denying that Jesus of Nazareth is the supreme inspiration to conscientious objection. Hence many an ardent pagan or worshiper at the shrine of the superman scorns him for his slave morality, and many an opportunist wistfully rejects him as an impossible idealist, but thousands of the humble hunger and thirst after him who find scant comfort in his church.

Because the phrase "religious liberty" has come to have meaning and value to mankind we religious conscientious objectors get a measure of consideration denied to our brothers who base their objection on grounds of humanity, respect for personality, economic considerations of the capitalistic exploitation at the root of all wars, whose guilt all great nations share, or "common sense" observation of that failure of war as an efficient means of progress to which this tragedy gives agonizing witness. Some of these objectors are more opposed to militarism than to war and their objection is to war's denials of democracy even more than to its inhumanity.

It is here that we find our point of contact with one distinct class of conscientious objectors—those who will not declare that no wars have ever been justified or that under no conceivable circumstances would they fight, but who feel that the ghastly horrors of this conflict will not win the liberty they seek. The public gives little sympathy to these men, yet there is no doubt that their sense of right and wrong forbids them to engage in the struggle as certainly as does the conscience of the objector to all war. The man who believes that we can win *now* by negotiation about as satisfactory a peace as in the indefinite future, and start on the long road of reconstruction without further ruin may have genuinely conscientious objection to engaging in this brutalizing war whose concrete ends he considers to be so ill-defined. Perhaps it is to this class that a great many radicals belong who are opposed to international wars but who in extreme cases would support violence in social revolution. I am not concerned to justify these men but only to argue that such a position can be conscientious. Among the possessing classes, especially if they are good churchmen, many men profess abhorrence of violence *per se* in labor struggles who are hearty believers in the violence of war. Now as a matter of fact, as radicals recognize, the violence of revolution is really less indiscriminate and more clearly directed to remedying specific injustice than modern international war. Furthermore, it is far less likely to perpetuate itself in great armies and a militaristic philosophy. The Russian revolution gives dramatic proof of this fact and of the impotence of autocracy buttressed by force and fear to withstand the might of great ideas.

Another group of objectors to participation in this war who might fairly be given generous consideration are certain Americans of German antecedents who, though in no sense disloyal to America, more on sentimental than on rational grounds, cannot bring themselves to join in the actual slaughter of their brethren. They might, on the other hand, be willing to render noncombatant service. They do not command popular sympathy, but it is fair to ask why a government which has consented to debarring *all* German-Americans from Red Cross work in France should insist on drafting some of them for the unspeakably bitter task of fighting in the trenches against their kin. Such methods may possibly conquer Prussia but never Prussianism.

Apart from these German-Americans—how numerous I do not know—whose feelings cannot be exorcised by coercion, conscientious objectors are overwhelmingly anti-Prussian. That system incarnates what they hate most. Their sin, if sin it be, is not in loving Prussianism but in the belief that Prussianism cannot be most effectually conquered in or out of Germany by Prussianizing America.

If the wide difference among conscientious objectors seems to discredit their cause it should be remembered that between no two of them is there a wider gulf fixed than, let us say, between William English Walling and the New York *Sun*, or those famous colonels, Bryan and Roosevelt, all of whom are backing the war. Indeed one argument for letting us objectors live is that liberals and radicals temporarily in another camp may find in our conviction that ideas are to be fought by ideas and not by jails or bullets, a strong tower of defense in the quarrels that will surely come between them and their present allies.

It is interesting to see how genuinely educational we find our comradeship in conscientious objection. Many a Christian pacifist is learning some profound lessons as to the economic roots of war and is coming to a sense of the futility of a doctrine of the power of good will and brotherhood which only functions in the sphere of international wars and does not cut down deep into the heart of social injustice; while certain economic radicals are learning a new respect for the "unscientific" idealist and occasionally find themselves speaking his language with real eloquence and perhaps some new emphasis on love rather than hate as the energizing force in the struggle for justice. Indeed it should be made clear that the division between conscientious objectors on religious or rational grounds is not absolute and exclusive. Many of us, for example, find our religious objections strongly confirmed by rational considerations.

THREE TYPES

Besides the underlying differences of philosophy which divide conscientious objectors, there is a fairly sharp practical division in their relation to national service. Along this line they fall in three classes:

1. Those whose objection is merely to personal participation in battle. Their objection is sincere but illogical and is based either on an emotional abhorrence of the ugly business of killing or a very narrowly literalistic interpretation of the command "Thou shalt not kill." Such men would accept almost any kind of *non-combatant* service.

2. Men who would not only reject combatant service but also most forms of non-combatant service which minister primarily and directly to military operations, such as making military roads or munitions. They might, however, accept *alternative* service in the reconstruction of devastated districts or in socially useful tasks, even though these like all useful work in war times indirectly add to the nation's war strength. They would prefer to show their devotion in voluntary work; they are fearful of the principle of conscription in war time, but so great is their desire to serve mankind that they might accept some tasks even under conscription, as thousands of sincere conscientious objectors have done in England.

3. The "absolutists," as they have been called in England, argue that any compulsory change of occupation in war time is war service, and that the highest social duty of the conscientious objector is to bear witness to his abhorrence of war and of the conscription principle. In England these men have proved their courage and sincerity by withstanding all sorts of brutality, imprisonment and the threat of death. It is important to remember that our present law, unlike the British, makes no provision for exemption for any of these classes.

I have dwelt on this statement of the types of conscientious objection and the philosophy behind them because in an understanding of these matters is the best answer to most of the uninformed criticism heaped upon us. It would be more amusing than profitable to point out how utterly contradictory are some of the charges brought against us. For example, in a recent amazing letter Prof. Stewart Paton accuses objectors of Hamlet's indecision of character and then calls them "rapturous sentimentalists," many of whom are ready to die for their convictions! As for cowardice, genuine conscientious objectors in America have already proved moral courage by their resistance both to the terrific social pressure of war time and to the organized appeal to fear which does so much to make war possible. If necessary they will prove their willingness to sacrifice comfort and liberty for their convictions as have thousands of their brethren in England.

I suppose we should, most of us, have to plead guilty to believing in principles rather than opportunism. Even the eloquent (and very romantic) "realism" of the *New Republic* seems to us to give elusive and unstable guidance in the present crisis. We have a feeling that certain of our ideals or principles are more satisfactory even from a pragmatic standpoint. Does this mean that we are a danger to democracy?

The charge that our position is essentially anti-social or parasitical deserves more extended answer. Very often it is put in a singularly inconsistent form by our critics. For instance, the other day an estimable gentleman assured some of us (1) that conscientious objection was a denial of democracy because "the people had spoken" and (2) that pacifists who advocated direct referendum on war or conscription were absurd or worse, because these were matters on which the people could not decide by direct vote!

Men and newspapers who are most concerned for the "anti-social" quality of conscientious objection are often violently opposed to what they call "conscription of wealth" even in so moderate a form as Amos Pinchot's proposal, because "business can't be run on patriotism." In order to defend our economic system they are rampant individualists and more tender in their treatment of money and profit, which have no conscience, than of the deepest convictions of men. As a matter of fact, conscription of wealth can be justified long before conscription of life, by any philosophy, social or individualistic. The most individualistic among us favor increased social control of property precisely because our present system of private property is a chief foe of the free development of personality. It makes both rich and poor slaves to *things* and denies to little children the chance for free development. These facts make us resent the charge of a selfish individualism from many of our critics as a peculiarly irritating piece of hypocrisy. Perhaps its most conclusive answer would be a challenge to find among an equal number of supporters of war more men and women who are rendering steady and unselfish service to society in philanthropy, education and the fighting of ancient abuses than there are among conscientious objectors. The records of the Quakers, of American abolitionists, of the newly formed Fellowship of Reconciliation, give conspicuous but not unique proof of this fact.

Yet sometimes the charge is brought by men who honestly

believe that these services cannot socially justify our refusal to yield to the state absolute obedience despite our personal judgment in time of war. Let them remember that we are conscientious objectors because to us war is supremely anti-social. It imperils for us far more than it can save. We have asked no man to defend us while we sat at ease; rather we advocated a different way whose risks we were willing to accept. Now that the nation has chosen the way of war we emphatically prefer her cause to Germany's. Our opposition to war is not on the plane of political obstruction or friendship for the Kaiser, but rather of supreme loyalty to certain convictions of right and wrong.

DEMOCRACY AND COMPULSION

We are lovers of America because we believe she still strives for democracy. It is the essence of democracy to believe that the state exists for the wellbeing of individuals; it is the essence of Prussianism to believe that individuals exist for the service of some unreal metaphysical entity called the state. True, the individual exists and finds his complete self-realization only in society—an immeasurably greater concept than the state. Democracy means, of course, mutual accommodation of individuals and social control. In proportion as the state is the effective agent of such control its power should grow but never should it grow to a control over men's convictions. It then becomes as dangerous to society as to the individual. When the state seeks to compel a man who believes that war is wrong, not merely to abstain from actual sedition, as is its right, but to participate in battle, it inevitably compels him, however deep his love of country, to raise once more the cry, "we ought to obey God rather than men." He acknowledges with Romain Rolland that he is the citizen of two fatherlands and his supreme loyalty is to the City of God of which he is a builder. Some conscientious objectors may substitute mankind or humanity for God, but their conviction remains the same; only the free spirit can finally determine for a man the highest service he can render. Compulsory service rendered against one's conscience is genuinely anti-social. The deep principles which guide a man's life are not formed or suddenly altered by any act of Congress whatsoever. There is a region in human life where the commandment of the state does not run. On this very issue Christianity long withstood the whole might of the Roman empire, and wherever she is strong it is because of her assertion of the responsibility of conscience to God. In the long run that state is most secure which recognizes this truth.

We are not now pleading that our critics recognize that conscientious objectors are right in their opposition to war. We are not claiming a monopoly of idealism for ourselves or denying that men may seek our name from unworthy motives. Our interest is deeper than securing justice for ourselves. We are pleading for recognition of the social value of heresy. Every movement worth while began with a minority. Democracy degenerates into mobocracy unless the rights of the minority are respected. The church of the Middle Ages made the sincerest, most magnificent effort in history to coerce the individual's conscience for the sake not only of the eternal welfare of his soul, but of the church universal. At last she recognized her failure, but not until she had done incalculable damage. Her own sons rejoice in that failure. Now the state, less universal in its outlook, less definite in its dogma, sets itself up as a secular deity and demands not the outward conformity which usually satisfied the church, but active participation in doing that which is to its heretic sons the supreme denial of their sense of righteousness. It deliberately thinks it can save democracy by this final act of autocracy. Gone is our belief in the power of ideas, in the might of right. America, founded by exiles for conscience's sake, their refuge in all generations, gives her sons the option of service in the trenches or imprisonment and thereby wounds her very soul as no outward victory of Prussian power can do. The heretic may be very irritating, he may be decidedly wrong, but the attempt to choke heresy or dissent from the dominant opinion by coercing the conscience is an incalculable danger to society. If war makes it necessary, it is the last count in the indictment against war.

I have chosen to dwell on the recognition of conscientious objection as a matter of democratic right rather than a matter of expediency or of sound public policy because this aspect is the more fundamental and because a nation that sees the

importance of the issue involved will discover the statesmanship to give justice expression in law.

In point of fact we might make a case on the question of
policy. The conscientious objector in prison adds no strength
to the nation, nor does he commend our brand of democracy to
the German people for whose freedom we are fighting. If the
conscientious objector is cowardly enough to be intimidated
into the ranks he is the last man to help win the war. This is no
time for the government to indulge in a petty fit of exaspera-
tion at the conscientious objector who oftentimes is quite
willing to give some real non-military service to his country.
The problem of giving effect to a policy of fair treatment for
conscientious objectors is not without its difficulties. Real
freedom of conscience is impossible under conscription partly
because of the practical difficulty of framing an exemption
clause and partly because some coercion upon the unformed
conscience inconsistent with genuine liberty is inevitable in
any system of conscription of young men. This is one of the
reasons why so many lovers of liberty were steadfast opponents
of the passage of the draft law.

But even under our present system exemption can be
granted on the basis of the individual, as in England, and he
can be at least allowed to take alternative service which may
not violate his conscience. It is entirely possible to copy the
general principles of the British system and avoid certain of its
stupid brutalities of administration.[1]

But behind any change in the law or its administration must
lie the far more fundamental matter of a public opinion not
swayed by false and prejudiced statements against conscientious objectors but informed as to their real position and attitude, and above all aroused to the desperate urgency that, in a
war for democracy, America shall not kill at home that "privilege of men everywhere to choose their way of life and obedience" which she seeks to secure for the world. If this is indeed

---

[1] The Civil Liberties Bureau has developed careful suggestions for the best
possible administration of the present law and for its amendment in accordance with the principles just indicated. Roger Baldwin, director of the bureau, 70 Fifth avenue, will welcome correspondence on this matter and on the
general subject of fair treatment for the objector.

a people's war for freedom the people can be trusted to see it through, without any coercion of conscience. To deny this is either to distrust democracy or to doubt the validity of war as its instrument. Justice to the conscientious objector secures, not imperils, the safety of the democratic state.

The Survey, August 4, 1917

Jessie Fauset to The Survey

Nearly 10,000 African Americans marched in silence down Fifth Avenue in New York City on July 28, 1917, to protest the violence in East St. Louis. Another response came from Jessie Fauset, a teacher at Paul Laurence Dunbar High School in Washington, D.C. Denied entrance to Bryn Mawr College because of her color, Fauset had graduated from Cornell University and began contributing articles, stories, and poems to *The Crisis* in 1912.

TO THE EDITOR: It was not labor masquerading under race prejudice, or even prejudice using the labor troubles as a pretence that caused the riots in East St. Louis; it was the absolute conviction on the part of the labor leaders that no Negro has a right to any position or privilege which the white man wants. Mr. Gompers, it may be remembered, in his reply to Colonel Roosevelt, complained that capitalists in East St. Louis had been "luring colored men" to that city. And a few days before the riots the secretary of the Central Trades and Labor Unions in East St. Louis had sent out a letter to this effect: "The southern Negro is being used to the detriment of our white citizens. The entire body of delegates to the central trades and labor unions will call upon the mayor and city council . . . and devise a way to get rid of a certain portion of those (Negroes) who are already here." The emphasis in both quotations is on color. Labor leaders are psychologists. They know that in this country the chances are more than even that any group of whites can attack a group of blacks, and not only get away with it, but probably have the protection of the laws. It was the connivance of the police and the militia which enabled the East St. Louis mob to expel from their homes 6,000 working men, burn down the dwellings of several thousands, and butcher and burn upwards of 200 helpless men, women and children.

How do we black Americans feel about all this? I asked an

unlettered southern "emigrant" the other day if he would be willing to go back South. "Miss," he told me, "if I had the money I would go South and dig up my father's and my mother's bones and bring them up to this country [Philadelphia]. I am forty-nine years old, and these six weeks I have spent here are the first weeks in my life of peace and comfort. And if I can't get along here I mean to keep on goin', but, no matter what happens, I'll never go back." Of course since then East St. Louis, Chester and Youngstown have shown him what he may expect—he is damned if he stays South and he is damned if he doesn't. But at least he has known a little respite, he has not died yearning vainly to see Carcassonne. Thus much for our untrained class.

As for the rest of us, being true democrats, we acknowledge only two classes, the trained and the untrained. We are becoming fatalists; we no longer expect any miraculous intervention of Providence. We are perfectly well aware that the outlook for us is not encouraging, but we know this, too, it is senseless to suppose that anarchy and autocracy can be confined to only one quarter of a nation. A people whose members would snatch a baby because it was black from its mother's arms, as was done in East St. Louis, and fling it into a blazing house while white furies held the mother until the men shot her to death—such a people is definitely approaching moral disintegration. Turkey has slaughtered its Armenians, Russia has held its pogroms, Belgium has tortured and maimed in the Congo, and today Turkey, Russia, Belgium are synonyms for anathema, demoralization and pauperdom. We, the American Negroes, are the acid test for occidental civilization. If we perish, we perish. But when we fall, we shall fall like Samson, dragging inevitably with us the pillars of a nation's democracy.

The Survey, August 18, 1917

John Dos Passos to Rumsey Marvin

A year after graduating from Harvard in 1916, John Dos Passos joined the Norton-Harjes Ambulance Corps, a volunteer organization run by the American Red Cross. He served at the Verdun front in August 1917, when the French were trying to recapture ground they had lost to the Germans the previous year. To a friend in the United States, he wrote about his first trip to the front.

———————

Aug 23

Dear Rummy

I've been meaning to write you again & again—but I've been so vastly bitter that I can produce nothing but gall and wormwood

The war is utter damn nonsense—a vast cancer fed by lies and self seeking malignity on the part of those who don't do the fighting.

Of all the things in this world a government is the thing least worth fighting for.

None of the poor devils whose mangled dirty bodies I take to the hospital in my ambulance really give a damn about any of the aims of this ridiculous affair—They fight because they are too cowardly & too unimaginative not to see which way they ought to turn their guns—

For God's sake, Rummy boy, put this in your pipe and smoke it—everything said & written & thought in America about the war is lies—God! They choke one like poison gas—

I am sitting, my gas mask over my shoulder, my tin helmet on my head—in a poste de secours—(down underground) near a battery of 220s which hit one over the head with their infernal barking as I write.

Apart from the utter bitterness I feel about the whole thing, I've been enjoying my work immensely—We've been for a week in what they say is the hottest sector an ambulance ever worked—All the time—ever since our section of twenty Fiat cars climbed down the long hill into the shot-to-hell valley back of this wood that most of our work is in, we've been under intermittent bombardment.

My first night of work I spent five hours in a poste de secours under poison gas—Of course we had our masks—but I can't imagine a more hellish experience. Every night we get gassed in this sector—which is right behind the two points where the great advance of the 21st of August was made—look it up & you'll see that we were kept busy—we evacuated from between the two *big hills.*

It's remarkable how many shells can explode round you without hitting you.

Our ambulance however is simply peppered with *holes*—how the old bus holds together is more than I can make out—

Do send news of yourself—and think about the war—and don't believe anything people tell you—'ceptin tis me—or anyone else whose really been here.

Incidentally Jane Addams account that the soldiers were fed *rum* & ether before attacks is true. No human being can stand the performance without constant stimulants—

It's queer how much happier I am here in the midst of it than in America, where the air was stinking with lies & hypocritical patriotic gibber—

The only German atrocity I've heard of was that they sent warning to a certain town three days before they dropped aero bombs on it so that the wounded might be evacuated from the hospitals—

Even French atrocities that you hear more of—slitting the throats of prisoners etc.—sort of fade away in reality—We've carried tons of wounded Germans and have found them very pleasant & grateful & given just as much care as the French. The prisoners & their captors laugh & chat & kid each other along at a great rate.

In fact there is less bitterness about the war—*at the front*—than there is over an ordinary Harvard-Yale baseball game.

It's damned remarkable how universally decent people are if you'll only leave them to themselves——

I could write on for hours, but I'm rather sleepy—so I think I'll take a nap among the friendly fleas——

Love
Jack

SS.Ane 60
7 Rue François I
Paris France
Here's another page—

You should have seen the dive I took out of the front seat of the car the other day when a shell exploded about twenty feet to one side of us—We were trying to turn on a narrow & much bombarded road——C'était rigolo, mon vieux! The brancardiers in the dugout are practicing their German on a prisoner——So long—Write at once.

1917

Martha Gruening:
Houston, an N.A.A.C.P. Investigation

Martha Gruening graduated from Smith College in 1909 and received a law degree from New York University five years later. A suffragist and opponent of conscription, she wrote for *The Dawn*, a pacifist magazine, and became an assistant secretary to the National Board of the NAACP. In July 1917 she went to East St. Louis with Du Bois to investigate the city's recent race riot. That summer the 24th Infantry Regiment, a black unit of the regular army, was posted to Houston. The soldiers resented the racist treatment they received from police and streetcar conductors there; and when the police beat a black soldier on August 23, more than 100 of his comrades rebelled, killing sixteen whites. Martha Gruening traveled to Houston to investigate the incident for *The Crisis*. After being court-martialed, thirteen black soldiers were hanged on December 11, 1917, and another six were executed in 1918.

THE PRIMARY cause of the Houston riot was the habitual brutality of the white police officers of Houston in their treatment of colored people. Contributing causes were (1) the mistake made in not arming members of the colored provost guard or military police, (2) lax discipline at Camp Logan which permitted promiscuous visiting at the camp and made drinking and immorality possible among the soldiers.

Houston is a hustling and progressive southern city having the commission form of government and, as southern cities go, a fairly liberal one. Its population before the Negro exodus, which has doubtless decreased it by many thousands, was estimated at 150,000. Harris County, in which it is situated, has never had a lynching, and there are other indications, such as the comparative restraint and self-control of the white citizens after the riot, that the colored people perhaps enjoy a greater degree of freedom with less danger than in many parts of the South. It is, however, a southern city, and the presence of the Negro troops inevitably stirred its Negrophobe element to protest. There was some feeling against the troops being there at all, but I could not find that it was universal. Most of the white people seem to have wanted the financial advantages to be derived from having the camp in the neighborhood. The sentiment I heard expressed most frequently by them was that they were willing to endure the colored soldiers if they could be "controlled." I was frequently told that Negroes in uniform were inevitably "insolent" and that members of the military police in particular were frequently "insolent" to the white police of Houston. It was almost universally conceded, however, that the members of the white police force habitually cursed, struck, and otherwise maltreated colored prisoners. One of the important results of the riot has been an attempt on the part of the Mayor and the Chief of Police of Houston to put a stop to this custom.

In deference to the southern feeling against the arming of Negroes and because of the expected co-operation of the city Police Department, members of the provost guard were not armed, thus creating a situation without precedent in the history of this guard. A few carried clubs, but none of them had guns, and most of them were without weapons of any kind. They were supposed to call on white police officers to make arrests. The feeling is strong among the colored people of Houston that this was the real cause of the riot. "You may have observed," one of them said to me, "that Southerners do not like to fight Negroes on equal terms. This is at the back of all the southern feeling against Negro soldiers. If Corporal Baltimore had been armed, they would never have dared to set upon him and we should not have had a riot." This was the general feeling I found among the colored people of Houston.

Several minor encounters took place between the military and civil police shortly after the troops arrived. As a result, Chief of Police Brock issued an order calling on his men to co-operate with the military police, to give them full assistance, and to refer to them as "colored" and not as "nigger" officers. Chief Brock is a northern man and though apparently sincere and well-meaning, does not seem to have the full confidence of all his men for this and other reasons. The order was obeyed in a few instances and more often disregarded.

On the afternoon of August 23, two policemen, Lee Sparks

and Rufe Daniels—the former known to the colored people as a brutal bully—entered the house of a respectable colored woman in an alleged search for a colored fugitive accused of crap-shooting. Failing to find him, they arrested the woman, striking and cursing her and forcing her out into the street only partly clad. While they were waiting for the patrol wagon a crowd gathered about the weeping woman who had become hysterical and was begging to know why she was being arrested. In this crowd was a colored soldier, Private Edwards. Edwards seems to have questioned the police officers or remonstrated with them. Accounts differ on this point, but they all agree that the officers immediately set upon him and beat him to the ground with the butts of their six-shooters, continuing to beat and kick him while he was on the ground, and arrested him. In the words of Sparks himself: "I beat that nigger until his heart got right. He was a good nigger when I got through with him." Later Corporal Baltimore, a member of the military police, approached the officers and inquired for Edwards, as it was his duty to do. Sparks immediately opened fire, and Baltimore, being unarmed, fled with the two policemen in pursuit shooting as they ran. Baltimore entered a house in the neighborhood and hid under a bed. They followed, dragged him out, beat him up and arrested him. It was this outrage which infuriated the men of the 24th Infantry to the point of revolt. Following is the story of the arrest as given by its victim, Mrs. Travers, and by eyewitnesses whose names are in the possession of the Association, but are withheld for their protection.

Mrs. Travers, an evidently respectable, hardworking colored woman, said:

"I was in my house ironing. I got five children. I heard shooting and I'd run out in my yard to see what was happening. Sparks he came into my house and said, 'Did you see a nigger jumping over that yard?' and I said, 'No, sir.' He came in the house and looked all around. Went in back. Then Daniels, the other policeman, he came around the corner on his horse. I called to Mrs. Williams, my friend that lives across the street, and asked her what was the matter. She said, 'I don't know; I think they were shooting at crap-shooters.'

"He (Sparks) came in again just then and said, 'You're a

God damn liar; I shot down in the ground.' I looked at her and she looked at me and he said, 'You all God damn nigger bitches. Since these God damn sons of bitches of nigger soldiers come here you are trying to take the town.' He came into the bedroom then and into the kitchen and I ask him what he want. He replied to me, 'Don't you ask an officer what he want in your house.' He say, 'I'm from Fort Ben and we don't allow niggers to talk back to us. We generally whip them down there.' Then he hauled off and slapped me. I hollered and the big one—this Daniels—he ran in, and then Sparks said to him, 'I slapped her and what shall we do about it?' Daniels says, 'Take and give her ninety days on the Pea Farm 'cause she's one of these biggety nigger women.' Then they both took me by the arm and commenced dragging me out. I asked them to let me put some clothes on and Sparks says, 'No, we'll take you just as you are. If you was naked we'd take you.' Then I take the baby in my arms and asked him to let me take it. He took it out of my arms and threw it down on the sidewalk. Took me with my arms behind my back and Daniels, he says, if I didn't come he'd break them. They took me out on Tempson Street. He rung up the Police Department. Whilst I was standing crowd began a-coming (all I had on was this old dress-skirt and a pair panties and a ol' raggedy waist. No shoes or nothing) —crowd and a colored soldier man came. [Private Edwards.] Sparks, he says to me, 'YOU STAND HERE,' and I did and a lady friend brought me shoes and a bonnet and apron and he (Sparks) says, 'Stay here,' and went over, and before the soldier could say a word he said, 'What you got to do with this,' and he raised his six-shooter and he beat him—beat him *good*. He didn't do a thing but just raise his hand to ward them off. Didn't even tell them to quit, nor nothing. Then another soldier, this Sergeant Somebody, came, and the first one called to him and the policeman said to him, 'If you come here, we'll give you the same.' Edwards said, 'Must I go with them?' and the second one says, 'Yes, go with them and we'll come along after you.' I hear they shot that second soldier but I didn't see it, for they took me away. They take me to the Police Department and locked me up for using 'abusive language'—but they dismissed the case today.

"I ain't never been before no court of inquiry, no ma'am.

Only just to the court when they dismissed the case against me, and there ain't no generals nor no one been out to see me or ask anything. I don't know why they don't come to me. They been to most everyone else around here, and I could tell them the truth. Seems like they might ask me, when I'm the one it happened to, and I'm not afraid to tell, even if Sparks do come back afterwards and do some more to me, but you're the only one yet that's come to ask me."

When interviewed a second time, Mrs. Travers added the following to her statement:

"I been down to the Prosecutor's office today. He asked me what did I know about the riot. I said, 'I don't know nothing about it. I was in bed with my children when it happened. Where else would I be at that time of night?' He said to me didn't I know beforehand that the soldiers were coming; didn't none of them tell me beforehand. I told him no, but I could tell him what happened before the riot to make it happen, and I started to tell him that Sparks came into my house and hit me. He say he didn't want to hear anything more about that and he sent me home. That's what I had to spend my carfare for."

One eye-witness said:

"I didn't see them arrest Mrs. Travers. I don't know what happened in the house, but I saw her afterwards and I know she said they slapped her in the house and pinched her arms and threw her baby under the bed. They had her right outside here waiting for the patrol wagon. She hadn't on but two pieces of clothes—and she was hollering and asking what she'd done to be arrested. Then Private Edwards came up and asked if he could take her. I heard the policeman say, 'Stand back,' and landed him on the head with his six-shooter. Then Baltimore he came and asked him about the other soldier. They beat him, too, and he ran and they shot after him. I saw Sparks fire after him three times, myself. Daniels shot, too, but I don't know if it was more than once. Baltimore ran away around the corner, with them firing after him, and his head was bloody. I thought he'd drop any time, but he didn't get hit. They said afterward they fired at the ground—but they didn't. They shot right straight at him and (they fired) into a street full of women and children. They haven't found any bullet holes in the sidewalk either, and it wasn't there that they fired. It was at Baltimore, and no mistake."

A second eye-witness said:

"I drive a butcher wagon. I make deliveries all about here and I saw a lot of what happened about here before the riot. When Sparks and Daniels came along that day I was driving past where three boys were shooting craps at the corner of Felipe and Bailey Streets. They fired a shot to scare the boys and they ran. Then the officers couldn't locate them. When I rode by again they had this woman, whose arrest was the cause of the riot, by the patrol box. She was insufficiently dressed to be out on the street and barefoot. There was a young soldier there (Private Edwards) who came up and asked the officers to let her put on shoes and clothes. The officers struck at him with their six-shooters. He put up his hand and blocked the first blow. The second hit him on the head and made him bloody. They followed that up and beat him to the ground. When he was down, one of them took the muzzle of his gun and punched him in the side, and Sparks said, 'That's the way we do things in the South. We're running things not the d—— niggers.'

"It was later—at the same spot—the policemen were still there when the military officer (Baltimore) came. I didn't hear what he said, but whatever was said between him and the police officers made him stop about half a block away and fold his arms, and at that one of the officers took out his revolver and commenced firing at him—right at him. He ran away around the corner of Mr. May's place. That's all I saw then."

When word of the outrage reached camp, feeling ran high. It was by no means the first incident of the kind that had occurred. A few days before a Negro had been beaten on a car by city detective Ed Stoermer, who, according to his own testimony before the Citizens Investigating Committee, cleared the car of its white passengers, telling them that he "might have to kill the nigger." I was reliably informed that on another occasion two colored soldiers were brutally beaten up by city detectives who boarded the car in which they sat from a Ford machine; that this machine drew up alongside of the car which was halted by the conductor long enough for the beating to take place, after which the detectives again got into the car and drove off.

Baltimore was popular among the men of the 24th Infantry, and for some time the rumor persisted that he had been killed. To quell the excitement Major Snow telephoned in to Police Headquarters to ascertain the facts and asked that Baltimore be returned to the camp immediately. At roll call that evening Snow addressed the men, telling them what had happened and stating that Sparks was to blame and would be punished. The men, however, were by that time beyond his control. In this connection it has been pointed out several times that Sparks has been suspended and is under indictment for the assault on Baltimore and for murder for the shooting of another Negro. There is no reason to believe that this indictment is anything but a bluff, the purpose of which is to show that there was no excuse for the soldiers taking the law into their hands. Chief Brock, who throughout has given evidence of good faith, did his duty in suspending Sparks, but there is no reason to believe that Sparks will receive any punishment at the hands of a white jury, and if he is acquitted, he probably cannot be kept off the police force. "Of course, Sparks will be let off with a fine. Our policemen have to beat the niggers when they are insolent. You can't expect them to let a nigger curse them," one white man told me. The same man, in reply to my question whether Sparks did not have a reputation as a bully, replied, "Oh, no; at least only among the colored people." The feeling of the colored people in regard to Sparks and the police in general is best illustrated by the statement of another colored man whose name I was unable to learn:

"It's like this, lady—I could talk all right, but I'm afeard. I know a lot, but I live here, and my family lives here, and all I got—all my savings of a lifetime is here—and there's prejudice here—and you see how 'tis. I made up my mind—I took like an oath to myself I wouldn't say nothing. I just made up my mind that I didn't *know* nothing. Only that my friend here says you're all right, I wouldn't say this much—but I got confidence in him.

"There's been a lot of dirty work here. I'm not saying nothing, but you find out who it was killed that colored man who was drafted into the army on Washington Street, and who shot that colored man, Williams, in the back, they say was killed in a crap game on Dallas Avenue. They can't find out that no one did it—but we *know* Sparks was in the gang that did the shooting. And that soldier man—the police shot him running—I saw *him* and he was hit in the back of the neck. And, what's more, I've seen three more colored men beat up without any cause by the police since the riot. There's a lot more I *could* say, only I'm afeard."

It is the Negro mentioned in this statement, Williams, for whose murder Sparks has been indicted. While I was in Houston the other Negro fugitive mentioned, who turned out to be an enlisted man under the selective draft law, was shot by a city detective simply for refusing to halt. The detective was "amicably" arrested by the Chief of Detectives and almost immediately released on a five hundred dollar bond. Sparks is also at liberty and although without the prestige given him by his position on the police force, was, at last report, using that liberty to further molest the colored people. About a week after the riot he entered the house of a respectable colored physician on Robbin Avenue early in the morning while the latter was in his bath and his wife partly dressed, on the pretext of looking for a fugitive, insulted and bullied them both when they protested, and threatened them with a drawn gun. On the same day he threatened a colored woman that he would "blow her damned head off" because he thought she had laughed at him. It was in pursuit of this woman that he entered several colored houses in this block, threatening and cursing the colored people.

When investigation made it apparent that the police were to blame for the beginning of the riot, a systematic attempt was made to shift the blame for this also on to the colored people. Strange stories began to be circulated in the papers and by word of mouth as to the real cause of the friction between the soldiers and the police. It was again the insolence of the Negro soldiers which in this case took the form of ignoring the "Jim Crow" regulations of Houston, particularly on the Houston Street cars. Testimony to this effect, which was obviously absurd, was given and reported apparently in all seriousness before the Citizen's Board of Inquiry. Several motormen and conductors were subpoenaed to testify to this effect, and one of them told a pathetic story of one occasion on which his car was boarded by a number of Negro soldiers (unarmed) who threw the "Jim Crow" screen out of the car window, over ran the car, forcing white passengers to get up and give them their seats, and who escaped unscathed to tell the tale. He was unable to give the names of any witnesses to this occurrence, although he stated that many of the white passengers left the car in great anger threatening that he would be reported and lose his job. The legend continued to the effect that white police officers were finally called in to deal with the Negro soldiers who were terrorizing the peaceable white citizens and demoralizing colored civilians, and that the former by merely doing their duty won the undying enmity of the colored soldiers.

Another outrageously false impression which was deliberately given by the white press was that Mrs. Travers was a woman of the underworld and that her arrest was the result of drunken and disorderly conduct. Mrs. Travers is unmistakably a hardworking, respectable woman. She had no connection with either Edwards or Baltimore, whom she had never seen before the day of the riot. The story, however, was never denied, and was still being circulated while I was in Houston, although so many white people who had employed her testified to her good character that it was necessary to acquit her at her trial for "using abusive language." She was also never called before the Citizen's Board of Inquiry.

Police brutality and bad discipline among the soldiers led up to the riot, which cost the city of Houston eighteen lives. Among them was that of Daniels, the policeman who had taken part in the beating of Baltimore and Edwards. There is abundant testimony from both white and colored people that there was excessive drinking and immorality among the soldiers at the camp, and there is testimony by white people to the effect that Edwards was drunk when he was arrested. While this may have been the case, it does not seem to materially effect the situation, as Baltimore, who was sober, received even worse treatment at the hands of the police officers. It is also very probable that some of the leaders were inflamed with drink at the time of the outbreak. That outbreak, acccording to a statement made by Major Snow before he received orders not to talk, was not an out and out mutiny, although the men were undoubtedly guilty of repeated disobedience to orders before they left the camp. If they did, as is alleged, shoot at their officers, they did not kill or wound any of them, though they did wound a colored soldier who was guarding the ammunition supply and who later died of his wounds. When the soldiers left the camp their slogan was, "On to the Police Station," where their idea was to punish the police for their attack on Edwards and Baltimore. Even the white people of Houston do not believe that their original intention was to shoot up the town. When on the way to the police station they met with opposition, they gave battle with terrible results. As in every riot, innocent bystanders were killed, one very pathetic case being that of a little white girl who was killed by a stray bullet which penetrated the room where she slept. The bitterness of the white people over this and other casualties is understandable, but the worst features of the Houston riot do not for one moment make it comparable with the massacre of East St. Louis. It was not a cold-blooded slaughter of innocents but the work of angry men whose endurance of wrong and injustice had been strained to the breaking point, and who in their turn committed injustices. There was no burning of women and children, no hanging, no torturing of innocent victims. The only atrocity reported being the bayoneting of Captain Mattes of the Illinois National Guard, spoken of by the Houston papers as the work of "black fiends," although bayoneting is not a practice discouraged by the United States Army.

All the men who are alleged to have taken part in the outbreak have been captured and are facing a court martial at El Paso. The one fact which admits of no uncertainty is that if they are found guilty they will be fully and sufficiently punished.

After the riot the white citizens of Houston behaved with unusual coolness and restraint and they have taken unto themselves full credit for so doing. The presence of United States troops undoubtedly assisted materially in keeping order. A half hour after the riot started Governor Ferguson had declared martial law which lasted for several days and order was restored without any lynching or other form of reprisal on the part of the white people. It was not to be expected that martial law or any other kind of law could be enforced impartially under the circumstances, and it was not so enforced. White citizens were given arms "to protect their homes" and the homes of Negro civilians were visited and their arms taken away from them. Many Negroes were also unjustly arrested, locked up for several days, and then dismissed without any charge having been made against them. That further disorder did not occur under such circumstances is one of the most remarkable things about the situation, and credit for it should be given to both races. The Houston *Post* and the white people generally explained it as another illustration of the well-known fact that "the South is the Negro's best friend"; that race riot and bloodshed are really indigenous to northern soil; and that the relations between black and white in the South are highly cordial. The colored people of Houston, however, are migrating North, and to this more than to any element in the case I attribute the new restraint in the attitude of white Houstonians. While I was in Houston, 130 colored people left in one day. In June, one labor agent exported more than nine hundred Negroes to points along the Pennsylvania Railroad. The Houston Chamber of Commerce became so alarmed over the Negro exodus that it telegraphed to the head of the railroad asking that this exportation be discontinued. The railroad complied with this request, but the colored people continued to leave. Colored men and women in every walk of life are still selling their homes and household goods at a loss and leaving because, as one of them, a physician, put it to me, "Having a home is all right, but not when you never know when you leave it in the morning if you will really be able to get back to it that night." White Houston, especially its business men, are beginning to realize this. For the first time they are showing some slight signs of seeking to make the South safe for the Negro. While the northern exodus of the Negroes, which began with the war, is largely responsible for this, occurrences such as the Houston riot must be admitted to quicken the sense of justice which has so long lain dormant in the white southern breast. However much the riot is to be condemned from the standpoint of justice, humanity, and military discipline, however badly it may be held to have stained the long and honorable record of Negro soldiers, however necessary it may be that the soldiers should be severely punished, it seems to me an undeniable fact that one of its results will be a new respect and consideration for the Negro in the South.

The Crisis, November 1917

Dorothy Canfield Fisher to Sarah Cleghorn

Born in 1879 in Lawrence, Kansas, the daughter of a humanities professor, Dorothy Canfield received a BA from Ohio State, studied at
the Sorbonne, and earned a PhD in French literature from Columbia
University before becoming a novelist, translator, and writer on education. In 1916 she went to France, where her husband, John Fisher,
was serving in the Norton-Harjes Ambulance Corps. She became active in war relief work, establishing a Braille press for blinded veterans
and a convalescent home for refugees. Her friend Sarah Cleghorn, a
poet and political radical, lived in Vermont.

———————

September 5
Crouy-sur-Ourcq

Dearest Sally:

Soldiers, hundreds of them are marching past my window as
I write . . . a strange accompaniment to a letter to you! The
regiment which has been quartered here at rest, is getting
ready to be sent back to the trenches, and are going through
preliminary exercises of marching etc. to get them into shape
for active service again. They look . . . curiously just like
anybody, just like the civilians-in-uniforms that they are. I am
all the time struck by the contrast between our regular army of
professional soldiers and these grocer's clerks and farm-hands
and college-professors, with their worn blue-gray clothes. The
strangest of all, though, to me, are the soldier-priests. A good
many of them wear their black soutanes just as usual, only a
good deal shorter, just about to the knee. With their chain and
cross hanging over their hearts and their big spurred cavalry
boots, and revolvers . . . don't they symbolize the world as it
is! Almost without exception they are strong broadly built
men, with serious, good faces and sad, earnest eyes. What *do*
they make of it, I wonder. I wonder so much that I want to go
up to them in the street and ask them! I can't tell you how

eagerly I read your Journal letters nor how deeply grateful I am to you for all the time you are taking to keep me close to what you are feeling and doing. I know that I'm not doing it for you . . . it's just from lack of time and strength! If I began I would never finish . . . and anyhow there is a wild incoherence about what I feel that I never could get on paper. It is mostly just pure suffering and horror. Here I come in contact with refugees, in close personal contact, and *feel* what the war means to them, as only personal contact can make you *feel* anything.

Don't children stump you! Jimmy said the other night as he was being dressed, "Me, I think that *le bon Dieu* is bad." "Oh why? Jimmy," "Because he made mosquitoes. If He isn't bad why did he make mosquitoes?"

And Sally, last evening, looking over some American newspapers, saw the cartoon in the *Post*, of the lynching of Little and the ironic heading "Montana's short-cut to law and order." Of course she wanted an explanation. I explained as best I could which was pretty badly, and ended, "I think of course that the men who hanged him were as bad as could be. He had a right to express his opinion about anything. That's what America should be like." Sally pondered and asked, "If he thought people ought to steal, would he have a right to try to get them to do it?" So I had to fall back on the fact, which even a child's abrupt reasoning can't disconcert, that no matter what anybody did, he should be treated according to the law. And a minute later, she was screaming with laughter over the antics of the new puppy, and had forgotten apparently the whole dark and terrible question . . . which is quite as disconcerting as anything else children do.

This is started as an answer to your letter of August 12, with its dreadful news of the suppression of the socialist-press and the general running-riot of Censorship and "Public Opinion." I've just thrown into the waste-paper basket, and now think I'll fish out to send you, a letter from Horace, Henry, my father's old friend on the Pacific Coast. I suppose that is quite genuinely and sincerely how the matter looks to him and others of his generation. My Godfather writes in the same strain, and says I ought to go home to "influence public opinion" to more active participation in the war and against the pro-

Germans etc., etc. If I went, it would be to make the biggest kind of protest against gagging anybody with a tongue in his head. If that is to be the system employed, there's no use bothering ourselves to fight Germany. She's won the war already, and infected us with her methods . . . because it was just such hideous and unnatural unanimity which made possible the German invasion of Belgium. But I'm sure of my country, and I feel certain that this is only the usual fervent American reaction to any stimulant . . . this is the way they "took up" the blue glass craze, and ping-pong and the Montessori system . . . to put together the most dissimilar examples I can think of. I mean not at all the serious earnest people on both sides, but this particular craze for unanimity I *know* it will give way to a more American way of thought. If I didn't think that . . . it would certainly be about the last blow necessary to convince me that the sooner this planet gets blown into star-dust, the better for everybody concerned.

The soldiers are coming back now, from where they have been drilling and look in on me wondering where I sit tapping on the typewriter . . . the only one Crouy has ever seen. They look a little tired, just agreeably so, and flushed and healthy with clear eyes and unconcerned expressions. As they pass one of the younger ones, while not losing step at all, manages to kick another one slyly in the leg. This makes the others laugh, and the young lieutenant look back at them sharply . . . and then that set passes out of sight and another files into view walking alertly, swinging their hands from one side to the other as French soldiers march, so vigorous, so *alive*. I send you this picture, taken as a snap-shot, to put in your war-Journal. They are so entirely human beings, like all others. Yesterday I saw a boche prisoner running a wheat-reaper, and noted with inexpressible interest, that he too looked just like anybody very calm and well-fed, much interested in running his machine right so the wheat would fall properly. I was on my way to send a package to a French prisoner in Germany to whom I have been sending food since the beginning of the war, and who is now working in the fields in Germany! I thought that very likely he is doing the work that his German-prisoner would be doing if he were at home . . . and found myself on the verge of that wild laughter which I imagine to fill madhouses. Thank heavens I have Jimmy and Sally.

Do write often, my dear, dear sister. And don't mind if I don't, nor regularly. Really I cannot!

Your loving
Dorothy

1917

James Weldon Johnson:
Experienced Men Wanted

A poet, lyricist, novelist, former U.S. consul in Venezuela and Nicaragua, field secretary of the NAACP, and editorial page editor of *The New York Age*, James Weldon Johnson proved himself one of the most eloquent civil rights advocates of his time. As the United States mobilized, Johnson examined the racial implications of War Department policies. African Americans, constituting 10 percent of the nation's population, would account for 13 percent of its army—serving in segregated units under predominantly white officers. Out of 200,000 wartime commissions, black officers received 1,200.

AN AGE reader at Jacksonville, Florida, sends us a circular which is being distributed in connection with the army recruiting stations at Jacksonville, Tampa, Miami, Pensacola and Tallahassee, and which reads as follows:

NON-COMMISSIONED OFFICERS WANTED
WHITE MEN
Married or Single

EXPERIENCED IN THE HANDLING
OF COLORED MEN

For Enlistment as Non-Commissioned
Officers in the Service,
Battalions, Engineer Corps
NATIONAL ARMY

"Experienced in the handling of colored men." That is about the most conspicuous example of grouping the Negro with the mule that has ever been brought to my attention. But aside from that, what kind of white non-commissioned officers does the War Department think it will get by allowing

recruiting stations to advertise in the South for white men "experienced in handling colored men?" Does the War Department have any idea of what it means in the South to have experience in handling Negroes? It generally means to have the qualifications of a slave driver, of a chain-gang guard, of an overseer of the roughest kind of labor. It means to be devoid of sympathetic understanding and human kindness. Of course, if it is absolutely necessary to have white non-commissioned officers over colored troops, the Department can find lots of white men in the South who make intelligent and sympathetic officers; but it will not find these men by advertising there for white men who are "*experienced in handling Negroes.*"

The War Department has adopted a policy of training Southern troops in the North and Northern troops in the South. In line with this policy, I would suggest, since the Department seems to deem it necessary that colored troops be commanded by white officers, that all white officers for colored troops be Northern men. It is true that the sort of Southern white man the Department would get by the above advertisement would have more "experience," but it would be experience of the wrong kind, it would be experience that would render him incapable of looking upon the men of his command as comrades in arms.

It is true that some of the finest and truest officers that the colored regiments of the regular army have are white men of Southern birth; but these men are entirely devoid of any "experience in handling Negroes" in the Southern sense. They went to West Point in their teens. Direct from West Point they went into the army and there have come to know the glorious traditions of the four crack colored regiments of the service, and to respect them and the men who made them. There is no plane of comparison between these officers and men taken out of civil life in the South and given command because of their "experience in handling Negroes."

Getting down to common sense and plain justice, since colored men must be in strictly colored regiments, *all non-commissioned officers of these regiments should be colored men: more, all line officers of those regiments should be colored men; and there is no good reason why, ultimately, all the field officers of those regiments should not be colored.*

But if it is decreed that white men must officer colored regiments, then at least let them be Northern white men who have had no "experience."

The New York Age, November 8, 1917

Carrie Chapman Catt: Votes for All

A graduate of Iowa State Agricultural College (now Iowa State University), Carrie Chapman Catt taught school before becoming a woman suffrage organizer in 1889. She succeeded Anna Howard Shaw as president of the National American Woman Suffrage Association in 1915 and formulated a strategy of pursuing suffrage on both a state-by-state basis and through a federal constitutional amendment. Then the struggle for enfranchisement became caught up in internecine battles. A founder of the Woman's Peace Party in 1915, Catt had broken with pacifists such as Jane Addams and supported American entry into the war, linking it with suffrage as part of a worldwide struggle for democracy. She also faced a challenge to her leadership from the more radical Alice Paul, who had broken away from NAWSA to found the National Woman's Party. While Catt and NAWSA used public lectures and petition drives to influence legislators, Paul and her "Silent Sentinels" picketed the White House. In a drive to widen support, Catt wrote this piece for *The Crisis* as part of a symposium in which she sought the support of black male voters for the November 1917 suffrage referendum in New York State. The measure passed.

––––––––––

OVER IN Europe the greatest war that history has ever known is shaking the foundations of kingdoms and empires. Millions of men have been blown to atoms in the Titanic struggle. Billions of dollars have been burned up in the smoke and fire of its battles. The whole world is locked in the struggle and the struggle is to the death.

What is it all about?

What is the idea underneath the horror and the heartache?

What is it for?

We all know the answer. Every soldier who straps on his knapsack and marches away to camp, bound later for "somewhere in France," every mother, every wife who weeps to see him go, every woman who steps forward to take his place in industry, even the little child who is lifted to kiss him good-by, knows the answer.

430

"For democracy,—for the right of those who submit to authority to have a voice in their own government."

In those nobly simple words of the President of the United States is set forth the whole story, the great ideal, the democratic faith that is sustaining alike the men of the Allied Armies on the battlefields of Europe, the women of the world waging their own double struggle to meet the new economic demands upon them while trying to secure a voice in their own government, and the Negro facing the selfsame problem and often refusing to see that through the Negro women his race is as vitally involved in the woman suffrage question as race can be.

For just as the world war is no white man's war but every man's war, so is the struggle for woman suffrage no white woman's struggle but every woman's struggle. Once long ago, the Negro man made the white man's mistake of deciding that the suffrage was the prerogative of men only. That was just after the Civil War. He had his chance then to stand by the woman's rights cause that stood by him. He did not do it. Like the white men around him, he could not and would not recognize that women were people, and that women, as well as men, must have a voice in their own government. Like the white man, he wanted democracy applied for himself, but not for woman. That is the crucial error of all men, white or black, in their efforts to apply democracy. It seems to be wholly a matter of sex, not at all of race or color. White man, black man, Mongolian, Malay, and Redskin are wonderfully alike when it comes to counting women out in any scheme for the political salvation of the world.

But however men have seen it, and may continue for a time to see it, women do count. Everybody counts in applying democracy. And there will never be a true democracy until every responsible and law-abiding adult in it, without regard to race, sex, color or creed has his or her own inalienable and unpurchasable voice in the government. That is the democratic goal toward which the world is striving today.

In our own country woman suffrage is but one, if acute, phase of the problem. The Negro question is but another. The enfranchisement of the foreign-born peoples who sweep into this country and forget to leave the hyphen at home is yet another.

How are we so to apply democracy that one and all of these problems may be fairly and squarely met by a voice in the government?

All along the line we fail of the right answer and the whole answer. Capital clashes with labor, class clashes with class, man-made laws are imposed on women who are denied all voice in the law-making, the individual sells his vote and pockets his dollar, race is arrayed against race, even to the perpetration of some such awful crime against common humanity as that against black people in the East St. Louis horror, and in woman's own struggle for democracy we hear some such retrograde outburst as emanated from the picket prisoners at being housed with Negro prisoners—not because they were prisoners, because they were black—a strangely and cruelly undemocratic protest!

Nowhere can we find the complete working basis for the democratic ideal. Yet everywhere that ideal rises again from the ashes of our wasted effort and again moves on ahead of us, a light that beckons.

Shall we shut our eyes and see it no more, remembering how hard it is to follow?

Shall we give up because we can't make a democracy work perfectly as yet?

Shall we cry quits because our patience wears out under the sorry failures and the long delay?

We could, of course, forswear democracy and herd together under an autocracy that would whip us into a grand machine, efficient as Germany's.

But who wants to be a Germany?

With all its failures, its delays, its harsh injustices, we will stick to democracy. We will not give up. We women, at least, will not even falter. We will press straightforward, knowing that the cure for the ills of democracy is more democracy.

As suffragists we have a profound belief that with the enfranchisement of all women will come improvement in our body politic. We believe that the vote will do woman good and that women will do politics good. If we did not believe it, if we held the franchise as a light thing, to be neglected, or idly cast, or bartered and sold, it would not be worth working for, and democracy would not be worth fighting for and dying for.

For centuries women have been trying to make their convictions, their feeling against oppression, carry without the franchise. And century by century, the need of the franchise has come steadily uppermost. For decades, since women have been working for the vote, they have been urged to condemn this, espouse that, and work for the other before they get the vote, or as a condition of their getting the vote. Such delaying, such conditioning are but added affronts to democracy. As suffragists women stand on but one plank today and that the plank of equal rights, for women as for men, without delay and without conditions. Standing on that plank alone they bespeak for and from America that broad application of democracy that knows no bias on the ground of race, color, creed, or sex. To the end that Americans may stand united, not as Irish-Americans, German-Americans, Negro-Americans, Slav-Americans and "the women," but, one and all, as Americans for America.

The Crisis, November 1917

Mary Borden: Unidentified

Mary Borden left the hospital at Bray-sur-Somme in February 1917. That spring she resumed her nursing duties in Mont-Notre-Dame during the failed French offensive on the Chemin des Dames and then returned to her original hospital at Rousbrugge in Belgium. Between August and December 1917, she published four poems and one sketch in *The English Review*. (All five pieces would be included in *The Forbidden Zone* in 1929.) *The English Review* featured "Unidentified" in December 1917, and it seems highly likely that William Butler Yeats read it. Two years later, he would write in "The Second Coming" that "Things fall apart; the centre cannot hold"—a sentiment Mary Borden's poem had expressed in similar language.

———————

LOOK well at this man. Look!
Come up out of your graves, philosophers,
And you who founded churches, and all you
Who for ten thousand years have talked of God.
Come up out of your silent, sheltering tombs
You scientists who died unsatisfied,
For you have something interesting to learn
By looking at this man.
Stand all about, you many legioned ghosts!
He will not notice you.
Fill up the desert with your shadowy forms,
And in this vast resounding waste of death
Be for him an unseen retinue,
For he is going to die.

Look at his ugliness.
See how he stands there, planted in the mud like some old
    battered image of a faith forgotten by its God.
Look at his grizzled head jammed up into that round, close
    hat of iron.
See how he hunches up his shoulders;
How his spine is bent under his clumsy coat like the hard
    bending of a taut strung bow;

434

And how he leans, gripping with grimy fists the muzzle of his
    gun that digs its butt end down into the mud between the
    solid columns of his legs.
Look close—come close, pale ghosts,
Come back out of the dim unfinished past,
Crowd up across the edges of the earth
Where the horizon like a red-hot wire writhes, smoking,
    underneath tremendous blows.
Come up, come up across the quaking ground that gapes in
    sudden holes beneath your feet—
Come fearlessly across the twisting field where bones of men
    stick through the tortured mud.
Ghosts have no need to fear,
Look close at this man—Look!

He waits for death—
He knows—
He watches it approach—
He hears it coming—
He can feel it underneath his feet—
Death bearing down on him from every side,
Violent death, death that tears the sky to shrieking pieces,
Death that suddenly explodes out of the dreadful bowels of
    the earth.
He hears it screaming through the frantic air,
He hears it burrowing underneath the ground,
He feels the impact of it on his back, his chest, his legs, his
    belly, and his arms,
He does not move.
In all the landscape there is just one thing that does not move,
The figure of the man.

The sky long since has fallen from its dome.
Terror let loose like a gigantic wind has torn it from the
    ceiling of the world
And it is flapping down in frantic shreds
The earth, ages ago, leaped screaming up; out of the fastness
    of its ancient laws,
There is no centre now to hold it down;
It rolls and writhes, a shifting, tortured thing, a floating mass
    of matter, set adrift.

And in between the flapping, suffering remnants of the sky
    and the convulsions of the maddened earth
The man stands solid.
Something holds him there.

What holds him, timid ghosts?
What do you say, you shuddering spirits dragged from secure
    vaults?
You who once died in kindly quiet rooms,
You who were companioned to the end by friends,
And closed your eyes in languor on a world
That you had fashioned for your peaceful selves?

Some of you scorned this man.
He was for you the ordinary man.
You thought him pitiable; contemptible or worse;
You gave him idols, temples, formulas of conduct, prisons,
    laws;
Some of you pitied him, and wept over his sins.
Some were horrified at what you called his passions, lust of
    women, food, drink, laughter, all such simple things.
And some of you were afraid;
Wanted to beat him down, break his spirit,
Muzzle his ideas, and bind with bands of hopelessness his
    energy.
None of you trusted him—
No! Not a single one of you trusted him.
Look at him now. Look well—look long.
Your giant—your brute—your ordinary man—
Your fornicator, drunkard, anarchist,
Your ruthless, seed-sowing male,
Your covetous and greedy egoist,
Come close and look into his haggard face.
It is too late to do him justice now.

But look!—look at the stillness of that face
Made up of little fragile bones and flesh,
Tissued of quivering muscles, fine as silk,
Exquisite nerve endings and scarlet blood
That travels smoothly through the tender veins;

One blow—one moment more—and that man's face will be a
    mass of matter, horrid slime—and little brittle bits—
He knows—
He waits—
His face remains quite still.
And underneath the bullet-spattered helmet on his head his
    steady eyes look out.
What is it that looks out?
What is there mirrored there in those deep, bloodshot eyes?
Terror? No!
Despair? Perhaps.
But what else?
Ah, poor ghosts—poor, blind, unseeing ghosts—
It is his self you see—His self that does remember what he
    loved and what he wanted, and what he never had—His
    self that can regret, that can reproach his own self now—
    His self that gave its self, let loose its hold of all but just its
    self—
Is that then nothing, just his naked self, inviolate; pinning
    down a shaking world like a single nail that holds;
A single rivet driven down to hold a universe together—

Go back, poor ghosts—go back into your graves.
He has no need of you, this nameless man.
You philosophers, you scientists, you men of God, leave this
    man alone.
Leave him the grandeur of obscurity,
Leave in darkness the dumb anguish of his soul.
Leave him the great loss of his identity.
Let the guns chant his death-song down the world;
Let the flare of cannon light his dying;
Let those remnants of men beneath his feet welcome him
    mutely when he falls beside them in the mud.
Take one last look and leave him standing there,
Unfriended—Unrecognised—Unrewarded and Unknown.

Charles J. Biddle:
from The Way of the Eagle

One hundred eighty American fighter pilots would fly with the French during the war, earning credit for the destruction of 199 German aircraft at a cost of fifty-one pilots killed in action. The scion of a long line of wealthy Philadelphians, and a graduate of Princeton and Harvard Law, Charles J. Biddle took leave of his legal practice for the French air service in March 1917. Assigned to Escadrille N. 73 in July, Biddle flew SPAD fighters over Flanders from an airfield at Bergues, six miles south of Dunkirk. In January 1918 he transferred to the recently formed American 103rd Aero Squadron. A major by the end of the war and credited with eight aerial victories, Biddle would publish a memoir, *The Way of the Eagle*. It drew from his wartime correspondence, which included this letter to his family in December 1917 that described his attacking a German reconnaissance plane.

BERGUES, December 8th, 1917.

You already know that from one cause or another, I have not been able to get out on the lines for some time, and when I finally did get out last Wednesday, it was exactly three weeks since I had last seen them; the same old lines, except a little more blown up, for there had been a great deal of artillery activity in part of the sector. On Wednesday I started out at nine in the morning on a patrol, with two Frenchmen, a lieutenant being the leader. We were on the lines for some time without seeing any Huns except well within their own lines, although once or twice I think I saw where some came on the lines, but the others evidently did not agree with me, and the Boches, if there were any, were too far off to justify my leaving the patrol and going to investigate. After a while however I noticed a two-seater of a type known as an Albatross which was flying up and down in his own lines. He was a long way off, but from the way he acted I thought he was just waiting for a clear path to slip across the lines, take his pictures or make some observa-

tions, and slip back again. I have had several encounters with
two-seaters in the same locality at about the same time of day,
and at about the same altitude, and accordingly kept my eye
on this fellow, to see what he would do. Sometimes he would
go way back into his own territory until he was just a speck in
the sky, and then again would come just above the lines, evidently see us, and turn back again.

Now a patrol has the duty of protecting a certain sector and
cannot go off and leave it, which is one reason why it does not
usually offer the same chance to get a shot at the Huns that a
voluntary chasse expedition does. If for instance I had been
there with another man just looking for Boches and with no
sector to protect, the thing to have done would obviously have
been to fly deep into our own lines as if we were leaving, then
climb up over that Hun's head and hang around with the sun
at our backs, in the hope that he would not notice us, and wait
for him to come into our territory. If he would not do this,
you could go to him, but it is always better to get them in your
own lines if possible, for you can then get a better shot without
having to spend half the time watching your own rear, and
ending up by being forced to retreat by the Boche's comrades
coming up in force. Once I left the patrol and started after this
Hun, but he evidently saw me at once and dove back into his
own lines; I saw that I could not get any kind of a shot at him,
so decided to wait a little longer. I rejoined the patrol, and we
made a tour of perhaps ten minutes.

When we got back to the same place again, the lieutenant
had gone down somewhat so that the Hun who was again just
coming to the lines, evidently saw us some 400 metres below
him instead of on the same level as before, thought he was
safe, and came on into our lines. My companions apparently
did not see him, so I turned to one side, flew directly under
the Boche, going in the opposite direction, and then put myself below and behind him by doing a renversement. He saw
me all the time, but I guess he thought he could do what he
wanted, and get out before I could climb up and catch him. I
must have followed him at least five minutes, first into our
lines, then back above the lines again and then back once
more. All the time he was manœuvring to keep me from getting behind his tail, where he could not see me, and doing it

well, for in order to try to stay behind him and to manœuvre
so as to give him only a long, hard, right-angle shot, I had to
fly further than he did, and accordingly could not catch him
quickly. I did get up to his level though (4,700 metres) and
when he finally started back for his own lines, I got directly
behind his tail and put after him as fast as my bus would travel.
When I got within 100 yards I tried to lay my sights on him,
but being directly behind him the back draught from his propeller made my machine unsteady so that accurate shooting
would have been impossible. I dove down 10 metres so as to
get out of this and tried again. After my sad experience with
the single-seater, which I wrote you about, and which I think
went down, but was not confirmed, I tried my best to shoot
most carefully this time.

All the time the Boche had not fired a shot, and from the
way he acted I think he must have lost track of me behind his
tail. Anyhow, I turned both my machine guns loose and
thought I saw my bullets going about right. My left hand gun
only fired about a dozen shots and then broke, the Boche at
the same time, giving a twist to the right to get me out from
under his tail. I kept on plugging away with my other gun,
shooting for the place where the pilot sits, and again I thought
I saw the bullets going into the right spot. After possibly thirty
shots however my right gun also broke, and left me with nothing, and at the same time the Hun started to join in the shooting, firing perhaps twenty shots. By this time we were I suppose
about 50 or 60 metres apart and I got under his tail quickly to
get out of the way, so that I could not see just where the Boche
was shooting, but am sure he came nowhere near me. There
never was a truer saying than that there is nothing which up-
sets a man's accuracy so much as having the other fellow putting them very close to him. That is I think one of the principal
reasons why accurate quick shooting is so important, not only
for the damage it does but because to come very close is one of
the best means of defense, even if you actually do not hit. At all
events, with two broken guns, close proximity to a Hun is not
a healthy locality, so I turned on my nose and dove out behind
my friend, at the same time watching him over my shoulder to
try to keep myself protected by his tail.

As I watched him he started diving until he was going down

vertically and I could see the silver color of his bottom and of the under sides of his wings, with the black maltese crosses on them. It was a good sized machine, and very pretty, with the shining silver paint underneath to make it less visible against the sky and the sides just by the tail a brilliant red, this last being probably the individual mark of his escadrille, for I have seen the same kind of a machine before, painted in this way. When he got in a vertical nose dive, instead of going on straight down, he kept on turning until from flying toward his own lines right side up he was flying back into ours, upside down, and diving slowly in this position. This is of course a sign that all is not well on board and usually means that the pilot has fallen forward over his control stick, thus forcing the machine into a nose dive and then onto its back. You will read in the Flying Magazines about flying upside down but it is not what it is cracked up to be. One often gets on one's back in certain manœuvres, but only for an instant, and with always sufficient centrifugal force to keep one securely in place. In learning to loop the loop however I have gotten upside down for longer than I intended because the loop was not done properly, and it is not pleasant. You start to fall out and even though your belt holds you pretty tight in your seat, there is a tendency to grab the side of the machine; then whatever dirt is in the bottom of the machine falls over you, the oil, etc., fizzles out of the top of its tank and the motor starts to splutter and wants to stop due to the gasoline not feeding properly. All this and everything being upside down, gives you a queer feeling in your middle, and although in some specially constructed machines I believe it is possible to fly upside down, it is not at all my idea of a good time.

Hence when I saw my friend the Hun flying into our lines with his wheels in the air I thought he must be pretty sick, but after my previous experience, was expecting every minute to see him come to and fly home, while I watched him helpless, with two guns that would not work. I accordingly dove after him, holding my controls, first with one hand, and then the other, and working with first the right and then the left gun, and trying each in the hope of getting one of them going, and taking a few more shots. At the same time, it is necessary to watch your own rear to see that no one is after you, so that between this and trying to keep close to the Boche I had little time to spare. Pretty soon some English machines came over my head, which relieved my mind very much as to the rear, and allowed me to concentrate on the Boche and my guns. I worked away and incidentally said some things I never learned in Sunday-school, but it is exasperating when you could get a good shot and your gun won't work and you have visions of what should be an easy victim escaping you. There was nothing to do though in this case, for upon returning to the field, I found both my guns not simply jammed but actually broken, one so that it had to be taken off the machine and replaced.

While trying to fix the guns in the air I kept glancing down at the Boche; sometimes he was on his back, sometimes on his nose, and again diving almost normally, which was what made me think he might come to life. The machine was however evidently completely uncontrolled; I chased him down almost 4000 metres, faster than I have ever come down before, so fast that when we reached 1000 metres he was not more than perhaps 400 metres ahead of me. A quick, great change of altitude like this is most unpleasant, as your ears get all stopped up and it gives you a headache, but in a fight you do not at the time notice it, and this time I was very anxious to see just where the Boche fell so as to get him confirmed if he did go down. At a thousand metres however I had to pull up and use my hand pump, for all the pressure had run out of my gas tank, due to the unusually long dive with the motor shut down. I lost sight of the Boche and did not see him hit the ground but after my motor was running nicely again I flew on down to 200 metres over the battle field and searched for him, for he had fallen several kilometres within our lines, so that it was possible to go down low and have a look. Pretty soon I spotted him lying on his back in the mud, his top plane was mashed into the soft ground, but the rest of the machine was apparently remarkably intact when you consider the height from which he had fallen. Probably the machine flopped over flat on its back, or right side up, just before striking, and in this way the force of the fall was broken.

Shortly after I got back to our field, the official confirmation came in from the lines. The pilot and observer were of course both dead. The pilot was I think killed by one of my shots, or at least completely knocked out, for there was nothing serious the matter with his machine, and it fell only because it was uncontrolled. The machine gunner was however alive after I had stopped shooting for I heard him shoot after I had finished. If he had been any kind of a decent man, or in fact any one but a Hun, one could not but have felt sorry for him in such a situation. Not much fun falling 4,700 metres, especially going down comparatively slowly, knowing all the while what is coming at the end, and with some little time to think it over. Particularly bad I should think with a good machine, which only needs someone to set the controls straight in order to right it. Much better to catch on fire, or have the machine break, and get it over with right away.

Also after having had experience with the same thing oneself, one cannot help thinking of the comrades of these men, standing around the aerodrome, and wondering why they don't come back, and again of the people at home, who after they get the report "Disparu," keep wondering and hoping for months whether perhaps they might not only have been taken prisoner. It is a brutal business at best, but when you stop to think for a moment of what these Huns have done, of the horrors they have committed, of the suffering they have brought on innocent people, and of the millions of men dead before their time, all because of them, you don't feel much sympathy for the individual but rather look forward to the time when you can perhaps bag another.

Bernice Evans: The Sayings of Patsy

From September 1917 to March 1918, the *New York Call*, a Socialist Party newspaper, published a series of thirteen unrhymed free-verse poems on its Sunday "Women's Sphere" page under the title "The Sayings of Patsy." Written by Bernice Evans, of whom little is known, the poems addressed the war, capitalism, the role of women in public life, food shortages, and the treatment of workers. Under the Espionage Act of 1917, which granted the authority to the government to withdraw second-class mailing privileges from publications deemed subversive, Postmaster General Albert S. Burleson banned the *New York Call* (and forty-three other periodicals, including *The Masses*). Not until May 31, 1921—when President Harding's postmaster general, Will H. Hays, lifted the ban—did the *Call* circulate outside New York City.

As Recorded by Bernice Evans
SAYS PATSY:
Sometimes,
These days,
I really don't know
Just where
My place is.
That certainly is
Confusing.
You see,
I'd always been
Solemnly assured
That it was
"In the home,"
But recently,
It's been pointed out
That, unquestionably,
My place is
Half way up

A step ladder
Cleaning windows,
So that
One more man
Can go to fight.
It really seems
That my place
Has been mislaid—
Not to say
Permanently lost.
And I begin
To suspect
That it is
Wherever
It's most convenient
For some folks
To place me.
We're getting
A lot of praise,
Just now,
For our "patriotism"
In taking
Men's jobs.
There's a
Horrible Grin,
Up on Oyster Bay,
Sometimes known as
The Battle Him
Of the Republic,
Who, in times past,
Never deigned
To notice us
At all,
But who writes
A whole column
About us now.
Indeed,
Praise
Is about all
We do get,

Considering that
Women are paid
Just about half
The regular wages
For their work,
Patriotism included.
But,
Be sure of this—
Women aren't going
To stay fooled
Very long.
It's a case of
"Timeo Danaos et dona ferentes,"
Which, being interpreted,
Readeth,
When interested folks
Wax eloquent
In their praises
Of your patriotism,
And nobility,
And self sacrifice,
And other virtues,
Carefully count
The contents
Of your pay envelope.
But, really,
They ought to be
Grateful to us,
Because
I honestly don't see
Whom they would do
Without us.

New York Call, December 30, 1917

Woodrow Wilson:
Address to Congress on War Aims

America's role in the global conflict expanded on December 7, 1917, after President Wilson described the Habsburg Empire as a "vassal of the German government" and Congress declared war on Austria-Hungary at his request. By the end of the year, the U-boat campaign had neither defeated Great Britain nor prevented the arrival of the first American troops in France. Nonetheless, the Central Powers found hope in Russia's exit from the war. A revolutionary uprising in Petrograd had forced Nicholas II to abdicate on March 15, and a Bolshevik coup on November 7 overthrew the Provisional Government that had replaced the Tsarist regime. Having promised the Russian masses an end to the war, the Bolsheviks arranged an armistice; and on December 22 they opened negotiations with Germany, Austria-Hungary, the Ottoman Empire, and Bulgaria at Brest-Litovsk (now Brest, Belarus). The Bolsheviks had also published diplomatic papers revealing Allied plans to divide the Ottoman Empire, to give Austrian territory to Italy, and to consider a French protectorate over the German Rhineland—plans to which the United States had never been a party. Wilson believed the world situation needed a clear statement of American war aims and peace terms. Drawing on a lengthy memorandum prepared by "the Inquiry," a group of confidential advisers that included Walter Lippmann, Wilson began writing an address on January 4, which he delivered to Congress four days later. "God was satisfied with Ten Commandments," jested French premier Georges Clemenceau. "Wilson gives us fourteen." The president would devote the rest of his life to realizing his Fourteen Points for international peace.

---

8 Jan'y, 1918

Gentlemen of the Congress: Once more, as repeatedly before, the spokesmen of the Central Empires have indicated their desire to discuss the objects of the war and the possible bases of a general peace. Parleys have been in progress at Brest-Litovsk between representatives of the Central Powers, to which the attention of all the belligerents has been invited for the purpose of ascertaining whether it may be possible to extend these parleys into a general conference with regard to terms of peace and settlement. The Russian representatives presented not only a perfectly definite statement of the principles upon which they would be willing to conclude peace, but also an equally definite programme of the concrete application of those principles. The representatives of the Central Powers, on their part, presented an outline of settlement which, if much less definite, seemed susceptible of liberal interpretation until their specific programme of practical terms was added. That programme proposed no concessions at all either to the sovereignty of Russia or to the preferences of the populations with whose fortunes it dealt, but meant, in a word, that the Central Empires were to keep every foot of territory their armed forces had occupied,—every province, every city, every point of vantage,—as a permanent addition to their territories and their power. It is a reasonable conjecture that the general principles of settlement which they at first suggested originated with the more liberal statesmen of Germany and Austria, the men who have begun to feel the force of their own peoples' thought and purpose, while the concrete terms of actual settlement came from the military leaders who have no thought but to keep what they have got. The negotiations have been broken off. The Russian representatives were sincere and in earnest. They cannot entertain such proposals of conquest and domination.

The whole incident is full of significance. It is also full of perplexity. With whom are the Russian representatives dealing? For whom are the representatives of the Central Empires speaking? Are they speaking for the majorities of their respective parliaments or for the minority parties, that military and imperialistic minority which has so far dominated their whole policy and controlled the affairs of Turkey and of the Balkan states which have felt obliged to become their associates in this war? The Russian representatives have insisted, very justly, very wisely, and in the true spirit of modern democracy, that the conferences they have been holding with the Teutonic and Turkish statesmen should be held within open, not closed doors, and all the world has been audience, as was desired. To whom have we been listening, then? To those who speak the

spirit and intention of the Resolutions of the German Reichstag of the ninth of July last, the spirit and intention of the
liberal leaders and parties of Germany, or to those who resist
and defy that spirit and intention and insist upon conquest and
subjugation? Or are we listening, in fact, to both, unreconciled
and in open and hopeless contradiction? These are very serious
and pregnant questions. Upon the answer to them depends
the peace of the world.

But, whatever the results of the parleys at Brest-Litovsk,
whatever the confusions of counsel and of purpose in the utterances of the spokesmen of the Central Empires, they have
again attempted to acquaint the world with their objects in the
war and have again challenged their adversaries to say what
their objects are and what sort of settlement they would deem
just and satisfactory. There is no good reason why that challenge should not be responded to, and responded to with the
utmost candor. We did not wait for it. Not once, but again and
again, we have laid our whole thought and purpose before the
world, not in general terms only, but each time with sufficient
definition to make it clear what sort of definitive terms of settlement must necessarily spring out of them. Within the last
week Mr. Lloyd George has spoken with admirable candor and
in admirable spirit for the people and Government of Great
Britain. There is no confusion of counsel among the adversaries of the Central Powers, no uncertainty of principle, no
vagueness of detail. The only secrecy of counsel, the only lack
of fearless frankness, the only failure to make definite statement
of the objects of the war, lies with Germany and her Allies. The
issues of life and death hang upon these definitions. No statesman who has the least conception of his responsibility ought for
a moment to permit himself to continue this tragical and appalling outpouring of blood and treasure unless he is sure beyond a
peradventure that the objects of the vital sacrifice are part and
parcel of the very life of Society and that the people for whom
he speaks think them right and imperative as he does.

There is, moreover, a voice calling for these definitions of
principle and of purpose which is, it seems to me, more thrilling and more compelling than any of the many moving voices
with which the troubled air of the world is filled. It is the voice
of the Russian people. They are prostrate and all but helpless,

it would seem, before the grim power of Germany, which has hitherto known no relenting and no pity. Their power, apparently, is shattered. And yet their soul is not subservient. They will not yield either in principle or in action. Their conception of what is right, of what is humane and honorable for them to accept, has been stated with a frankness, a largeness of view, a generosity of spirit, and a universal human sympathy which must challenge the admiration of every friend of mankind; and they have refused to compound their ideals or desert others that they themselves may be safe. They call to us to say what it is that we desire, in what, if in anything, our purpose and our spirit differ from theirs; and I believe that the people of the United States would wish me to respond, with utter simplicity and frankness. Whether their present leaders believe it or not, it is our heartfelt desire and hope that some way may be opened whereby we may be privileged to assist the people of Russia to attain their utmost hope of liberty and ordered peace.

It will be our wish and purpose that the processes of peace, when they are begun, shall be absolutely open and that they shall involve and permit henceforth no secret understandings of any kind. The day of conquest and aggrandizement is gone by; so is also the day of secret covenants entered into in the interest of particular governments and likely at some unlooked-for moment to upset the peace of the world. It is this happy fact, now clear to the view of every public man whose thoughts do not still linger in an age that is dead and gone, which makes it possible for every nation whose purposes are consistent with justice and the peace of the world to avow now or at any other time the objects it has in view.

We entered this war because violations of right had occurred which touched us to the quick and made the life of our own people impossible unless they were corrected and the world secured once for all against their recurrence. What we demand in this war, therefore, is nothing peculiar to ourselves. It is that the world be made fit and safe to live in; and particularly that it be made safe for every peace-loving nation which, like our own, wishes to live its own life, determine its own institutions, be assured of justice and fair dealing by the other peoples of the world as against force and selfish aggression. All the peoples of the world are in effect partners in this interest, and for our own part we see very clearly that unless justice be done to others it will not be done to us. The programme of the world's peace, therefore, is our programme; and that programme, the only possible programme, as we see it, is this:

I. Open covenants of peace, openly arrived at, after which there shall be no private international understandings of any kind but diplomacy shall proceed always frankly and in the public view.

II. Absolute freedom of navigation upon the seas, outside territorial waters, alike in peace and in war, except as the seas may be closed in whole or in part by international action for the enforcement of international covenants.

III. The removal, so far as possible, of all economic barriers and the establishment of an equality of trade conditions among all the nations consenting to the peace and associating themselves for its maintenance.

IV. Adequate guarantees given and taken that national armaments will be reduced to the lowest point consistent with domestic safety.

V. A free, open-minded, and absolutely impartial adjustment of all colonial claims, based upon a strict observance of the principle that in determining all such questions of sovereignty the interests of the populations concerned must have equal weight with the equitable claims of the government whose title is to be determined.

VI. The evacuation of all Russian territory and such a settlement of all questions affecting Russia as will secure the best and freest cooperation of the other nations of the world in obtaining for her an unhampered and unembarrassed opportunity for the independent determination of her own political development and national policy and assure her of a sincere welcome into the society of free nations under institutions of her own choosing; and, more than a welcome, assistance also of every kind that she may need and may herself desire. The treatment accorded Russia by her sister nations in the months to come will be the acid test of their good will, of their comprehension of her needs as distinguished from their own interests, and of their intelligent and unselfish sympathy.

VII. Belgium, the whole world will agree, must be evacuated

and restored, without any attempt to limit the sovereignty which she enjoys in common with all other free nations. No other single act will serve as this will serve to restore confidence among the nations in the laws which they have themselves set and determined for the government of their relations with one another. Without this healing act the whole structure and validity of international law is forever impaired.

VIII. All French territory should be freed and the invaded portions restored, and the wrong done to France by Prussia in 1871 in the matter of Alsace-Lorraine, which has unsettled the peace of the world for nearly fifty years, should be righted, in order that peace may once more be made secure in the interests of all.

IX. A readjustment of the frontiers of Italy should be effected along clearly recognizable lines of nationality.

X. The peoples of Austria-Hungary, whose place among the nations we wish to see safeguarded and assured, should be accorded the freest opportunity of autonomous development.

XI. Rumania, Serbia, and Montenegro should be evacuated; occupied territories restored; Serbia accorded free and secure access to the sea; and the relations of the several Balkan states to one another determined by friendly counsel along historically established lines of allegiance and nationality; and international guarantees of the political and economic independence and territorial integrity of the several Balkan states should be entered into.

XII. The Turkish portions of the present Ottoman Empire should be assured a secure sovereignty, but the other nationalities which are now under Turkish rule should be assured an undoubted security of life and an absolutely unmolested opportunity of autonomous development, and the Dardanelles should be permanently opened as a free passage to the ships and commerce of all nations under international guarantees.

XIII. An independent Polish state should be erected which should include the territories inhabited by indisputably Polish populations, which should be assured a free and secure access to the sea, and whose political and economic independence and territorial integrity should be guaranteed by international covenant.

XIV. A general association of nations must be formed under

specific covenants for the purpose of affording mutual guarantees of political independence and territorial integrity to great and small states alike.

In regard to these essential rectifications of wrong and assertions of right we feel ourselves to be intimate partners of all the governments and peoples associated together against the Imperialists. We cannot be separated in interest or divided in purpose. We stand together until the end.

For such arrangements and covenants we are willing to fight and to continue to fight until they are achieved; but only because we wish the right to prevail and desire a just and stable peace such as can be secured only by removing the chief provocations to war, which this programme does remove. We have no jealousy of German greatness, and there is nothing in this programme that impairs it. We grudge her no achievement or distinction of learning or of pacific enterprise such as have made her record very bright and very enviable. We do not wish to injure her or to block in any way her legitimate influence or power. We do not wish to fight her either with arms or with hostile arrangements of trade if she is willing to associate herself with us and the other peace-loving nations of the world in covenants of justice and law and fair dealing. We wish her only to accept a place of equality among the peoples of the world,— the new world in which we now live,—instead of a place of mastery.

Neither do we presume to suggest to her any alteration or modification of her institutions. But it is necessary, we must frankly say, and necessary as a preliminary to any intelligent dealings with her on our part, that we should know whom her spokesmen speak for when they speak to us, whether for the Reichstag majority or for the military party and the men whose creed is imperial domination.

We have spoken now, surely, in terms too concrete to admit of any further doubt or question. An evident principle runs through the whole programme I have outlined. It is the principle of justice to all peoples and nationalities, and their right to live on equal terms of liberty and safety with one another, whether they be strong or weak. Unless this principle be made its foundation no part of the structure of international justice can stand. The people of the United States could act upon no other principle; and to the vindication of this principle they are ready to devote their lives, their honor, and everything that they possess. The moral climax of this the culminating and final war for human liberty has come, and they are ready to put their own strength, their own highest purpose, their own integrity and devotion to the test.

Shirley Millard: from I Saw Them Die

On March 3, 1918, the Bolsheviks signed the Treaty of Brest-Litovsk, ceding Poland, the Baltic states, Finland, the Ukraine, and extensive territory in the southern Caucasus. The military collapse of Russia in late 1917 had allowed the Germans to shift troops away from the Eastern Front, giving them temporary numerical superiority in France and Belgium. Determined to deliver a decisive blow to the Allies before the Americans could arrive in full force, the Germans launched a major offensive on March 21, breaking through the British lines around St. Quentin and advancing more rapidly than had any army on the Western Front since 1914. Shirley Millard had volunteered to serve as a nurse with the American Red Cross, imagining herself "gliding silently among hospital cots, placing a cool hand on fevered brows, lifting bound heads to moisten pain-parched lips with water." Assigned to a French military hospital ten miles from Soissons, she arrived on March 24, in time to treat the waves of casualties from the spring offensive. In her memoir, *I Saw Them Die* (1936), excerpts from her wartime diary appeared in italics, while her recollections from the 1930s appeared in regular type.

––––––––––

French Evacuation Hospital, Château Gabriel
March 24th
As I scribble this we are in the dining hall waiting for coffee before going to work. They offered us food, but we are too excited to eat. However, it is cold and wet, and the coffee will warm us up. A French doctor came in and looked us over hurriedly. He seemed satisfied with what he saw; plenty of health and good nature. Ten American girls waiting for orders. Untrained, perhaps, some of us, but eager to help and ready for whatever comes our way.

March 28th
Terribly busy. It is all so different than I imagined. No time to write.

There was no need to write. The memory remains indelible. Thirty-five hundred cots filled with wounded men. And more pouring in all night from the procession of camouflaged ambulances without headlights crawling slowly along the muddy, shell-rutted roads.

The winter nights were pitch black and much of the way lay through dense woods. To make it more difficult for the ambulances the roads were crowded with troops, supply *camions* and ammunition *caissons*; all without lights . . . crawling through the mud on their way to the front. The grim, black, two-way serpentine seemed endless.

The ambulances could work only during the night for by daylight they would be seen and fired upon by the enemy. No matter at what time of day a man was wounded, he must lie in a second or third line trench dressing station until nightfall. Then the dark caravan began.

Arriving at the château, the men were deposited anywhere on the grounds, on stretchers, waiting their turn to be attended. Although cases that could be moved were evacuated constantly to hospitals farther back, hundreds of wounded men lay out there in the cold and rain, sometimes for three days and three nights, without blankets, before we could make room for them inside. From the black shadows under the trees came their moans, their cries and sobs. Some were unconscious from pain and fatigue.

These were the "sleeping men" we saw when our *camion* arrived. We had to step over them and through them when we were shown to our posts that night. We were distributed about the place where help was most needed and saw almost nothing of each other again for several days.

On the way to my barrack, number 42, at the other end of the grounds and some distance from the château itself, I saw my first airplane disaster. A rocket of red flame cut through the clouds almost directly above, and fell noiselessly through the blackness to blackness beyond. I saw many afterward, but the first had a special significance. It was, like the welcoming barrage and the tramp of marching men on the road below, part of my overture to war.

The door of the barrack was opened cautiously for me to slide quickly through. I went on duty.

Inside, all was confusion, disorder and excitement. Only dim flickers from candles illumined the chaos. Nurses, doctors, orderlies, beds everywhere; yet not nearly enough to take care of the influx of wounded. That is why they had hurried us through and put us to work at once.

The French hospital system had improved considerably since 1914 and was famed for its efficiency, but it was entirely demoralized during this greatest of all German drives. Hundreds upon hundreds of wounded poured in like a rushing torrent. No matter what we did, how hard we worked, it did not seem to be fast enough or hard enough. More came. It took me several days to steel my emotions against the stabbing cries of pain. The crowded, twisted bodies, the screams and groans, made one think of the old engravings in Dante's *Inferno*. More came, and still more.

Stretcher bearers perspired under their loads until the aisles of every ward were packed. And still the grounds outside were full to overflowing. In the darkness under the trees orderlies stumbled about, giving a hurried drink to parched lips that had cried for water for twenty-four hours. . . . Don't drink too much, pal, we haven't much left, and no time to boil more. . . . Here and there they pulled a blanket over a face. The covered men were carried out quickly to make room for others.

In the ward, orders flew at us. Do this! Do that! We did, as well as we could. No time for explanations or formalities. The preliminary instructions we were to have received from the hospital chief were never given. Our first lesson in nursing was to begin nursing, whether we knew how or not.

Someone thrust a huge hypodermic needle and a packet of something into my hands and told me hurriedly that every man who came in must have a shot against tetanus. The soil of the battlefields was impregnated with poisons from gas and explosives. After that I was to get them ready for the operating table. Hurry! Fast as you can. I looked about helplessly. How on earth did one give a hypodermic? I'd never even *had* one. And what did "get them ready" mean?

I watched another nurse snap the glass tube containing the antitoxin, fill the syringe, and jab the needle in. Taking a deep breath I filled my syringe, shut my eyes, and tried it. Unfortunately, my first attempt was on an Arab, and I was horrified to discover that I could not penetrate his flesh with the needle. I called to an orderly and showed him the bent needle; he assured me that it was because Arabs had skin as tough as leather. I attached a fresh needle and tried again. This time it worked. The second, third, fourth times are easier. Soon I am going like lightning.

But getting them ready is another matter. I watch my colleague closely to see what she does about that. She undresses them, removing all their clothing—boots, leggings, belts, gasmasks, kit bags. She washes their wounds as well as she can with the little tin basin of water and wraps them in a clean sheet to go in to the surgery. The clothes are left in a heap to stumble over in the aisles. I follow her example. It is not easy. My hands tremble as I pull at sodden boots and uniforms. The weather is cold and wet and most of their garments are caked with mud from head to foot, so that to get the things off without causing excruciating pain is almost impossible. "Leave me alone, will you!" they scream wildly and resist my ministrations. Many of them have nothing on their wounds but a strip of coat sleeve or an old muffler or a muddy legging wrapped on quickly by a comrade in the field. Some have only newspaper tied on with a bootlace. I remove blood- and mud-soaked bandages and find an arm hanging by a tendon. *Roses are blooming in Picardy* . . . the silly tune runs inanely through my head. I have a crazy impulse to run. But I stay.

Boom . . . Boom . . . Boom . . . Boom! The big guns roar. The line is only eight miles away. The earth trembles and the flimsy barracks shake with each report. It sounds like a bad thunder storm . . . a hundred bad thunder storms. Flashes from cannon fire light up the cracks around the shuttered windows. I am too busy to be frightened. The blood-soaked clothes and bandages begin to give more easily under my learning fingers.

As I work on one man, bathing the great hip cavity where a leg once was, a long row of others, their eyes fastened upon me, await their turn.

Gashes from bayonets. Flesh torn by shrapnel. Faces half shot away. Eyes seared by gas; one here with no eyes at all. I can see down into the back of his head. Here is a boy with a gray, set face. He is hanging on . . . too far gone to make a sound. His stomach is blown wide open, and only held together by a few bands of sopping gauze which I must pull away. I do so, as gently as I can. The odor is sickening; the gauze is a greenish yellow. Gangrene. He was wounded days ago and has been waiting on the grounds. He will die.

Every now and then the pit of my stomach sinks. I set my teeth and go on. A chest ripped open exposes lungs working feebly and slowing down under my very eyes. I stare fascinated . . . out, in . . . out and in . . . out . . . in . . . weaker and weaker. The next one is already dead; a young blond boy with a questioning look on his face; eyes wide open and cheeks streaked with mud that shows the trace of tears. I pull up the blanket.

My hands get firmer, faster. I can feel the hardness of emergency setting in. Perhaps after a while I won't mind. Here is an unconscious lad with his head completely bandaged. The gauze is stiff with blood and dirt. I cut carefully and remove it, glad he is unconscious; much easier to work when they cannot feel the pain. As the last band comes off, a sickening mass spills out of the wide gash at the side of his skull. Brains! I am stunned. I cannot think what to do. No time to ask questions. Everyone around me is occupied with similar problems. Boldly I wrap my hand in sterile gauze and thrust the slippery mass back as best I can, holding the wound closed while I awkwardly tie a clean bandage around the head. It does not occur to me until afterwards that he must have been dead.

On to the next. He is a short, powerfully built Breton. We used to go to Brittany for the summer . . . to Dinard. He reminds me of Ricou, the porter at the hotel, whom all the children adored. He is groaning with pain and screams deliriously as I begin undressing him. I distinguish in the unfamiliar patois a savage phrase: "I slit him open! Open, I tell you! God damn his soul!" He shakes with sobs. Is it delirium . . . or horror at what he has done?

John J. Pershing: Remarks to the Officers of the 1st Division

An 1886 West Point graduate, John J. Pershing served with the 6th Cavalry in campaigns against the Apaches and Lakota; during the Spanish-American War, he fought in Cuba with the 10th Cavalry, a regiment of African American "Buffalo Soldiers," which earned him the nickname "Black Jack"; he fought Moro insurgents in the southern Philippines and served as an observer in Manchuria during the Russo-Japanese War before commanding the American expedition into Mexico in 1916. On May 12, 1917, Wilson appointed Pershing as commander of the American Expeditionary Forces (AEF) in Europe. The President issued Pershing one main directive, with which the general wholeheartedly agreed: the AEF should maintain its national identity and fight as an independent army, not be broken up and "amalgamated" into the existing French and British armies. The U.S. 1st Division had arrived in France in June 1917 and spent the nine months either training behind the lines or holding quiet sectors of the front in Lorraine. On April 16, 1918, Pershing addressed the officers of the division at Chaumont-en-Vexin before their departure to the front in Picardy. There the division would win the first American offensive battle of the war when it captured the village of Cantigny on May 28.

General Bullard and Officers of the 1st Division:

It has not been convenient for me to meet the assembled officers of the 1st Division before, but I did not want you to enter into real participation in this war without my having said a word to you as a body.

You have now been on French soil ten months, and you have carried out a progressive system of instruction under varied circumstances. You have lived in billets according to the custom of European armies; you have served in different sections of the trenches as a part of your training and have taken on a military complexion akin to that of our Allies. Officers of the Allies, in passing judgment upon your work, have expressed themselves as completely satisfied. I, myself, having witnessed your maneuvers, and closely followed the progress of your work in the trenches and elsewhere, now express myself as well satisfied. I believe that you are well prepared to take your place along with the seasoned troops of our Allies.

But let us not for a moment forget that, while study and preparation are necessary, war itself is the real school where the art of war is learned. Whatever your previous instruction may have been, you must learn, in the actual experience of war, the practical application of the tactical principles that you have been taught during your preliminary training. Those principles are as absolute as they are immutable. Whatever may be the changing conditions of this war, those principles remain practically the same, and you should constantly bear them in mind. Now that you are going to take a place in the line of battle, you will be called upon to meet conditions that have never been presented to you before. When confronted with a new situation, do not try to recall examples given in any particular book on the subject; do not try to remember what your instructor has said in discussing some special problem; do not try to carry in your minds patterns of particular exercises or battles, thinking they will fit new cases, because no two sets of circumstances are alike; but bear in mind constantly, revolve in your thoughts frequently, and review at every opportunity, those well-established general principles, so that you may apply them when the time comes.

While it is necessary to know how to apply the general principles of military tactics to the problems of actual battle, yet the main reliance after all must be upon your own determination, upon the aggressiveness of your men, upon their stamina, upon their character and upon their will to win. It is this will to win, more than anything else, that will carry you over the trying periods that you are soon to meet.

You should always have the interests of the individual soldier at heart, for he is the principal part of the machine upon which you are to rely to carry you to success. His morale must be kept up to the highest pitch. That morale is affected by his confidence in his officers, by a realizing sense that they are his example. They should really be an example in everything that personifies the true soldier, in dress, in military bearing, in general conduct, and especially an example on the battlefield.

To get the best out of your men they must feel that you are their real leader and must know that they can depend upon you. They must have confidence in you. Do not hold yourself aloof from your men, but keep in close touch with them. Let them feel that you are doing the very best you can for them under all circumstances, not only in providing their personal wants, in looking forward to a regular supply of food, and clothing, but that, as their leader, you are directing them wisely in the trying conditions of battle. On the other hand, you should always endeavor to make them realize their own responsibility and that you, in turn, rely fully upon them, and that when the occasion demands it they must make the supreme sacrifice.

I did not come here to make a speech, I am not given to speech-making, so only a word more. I have every confidence in the 1st Division. You are about to enter this great battle of the greatest war in history, and in that battle you will represent the mightiest nation engaged. That thought itself must be to you a very appealing thought and one that should call forth the best and the noblest that is in you. Centuries of military tradition and of military and civil history are now looking toward this first contingent of the American Army as it enters this great battle. You have behind you your own national traditions that should make you the finest soldiers in Europe to-day. We come from a young and aggressive nation. We come from a nation that for one hundred and fifty years has stood before the world as the champion of the sacred principles of human liberty. We now return to Europe, the home of our ancestors, to help defend those same principles upon European soil. Could there be a more stimulating sentiment as you go from here to your commands, and from there to the battlefield?

Our people to-day are hanging expectant upon your deeds. Our future part in this conflict depends upon your action. You are going forward and your conduct will be an example for succeeding units of our army. I hope the standard you set will be high—I know it will be high. You are taking with you the sincerest good wishes and the highest hopes of the President and all of our people at home. I assure you in their behalf and in my own of our strong belief in your success and of our confidence in your courage and in your loyalty, with a feeling of certainty in our hearts that you are going to make a record of which your country will be proud.

Shirley Millard: from I Saw Them Die

In her diary and memoir, Millard wrote about the personal inter-actions, both welcome and unwelcome, that she and her fellow nurses experienced with French doctors. After the war, Millard returned home and married her American fiancé, who had served in France with the AEF.

———————

May 13th
One of the girls just brought up the mail and tossing me a letter, said: "Here's one from Romeo." It was postmarked Brest, but no hint of where he is going from there. It is thrilling to know he is so near but what good will it do? The war will have to last a long time for me to save up enough leave to make it worth while. Let's see—twelve hours every two months. With luck and good manage-ment I should be able to take off about three days by the fall.

It is still quiet here, but I have noticed a strange tension in the air and several things have happened that make me realize doc-tors are definitely human beings. Today as I was coming through the corridor in the officers' ward with a tray in my hands, I met Dr. Girard. I hardly know him; he has been in the theatre, as they call the surgery, almost constantly since I arrived. He stared at me in an odd sort of way and would not let me pass. Then he took the tray from my hands, set it on the window ledge and without further ado, grabbed me in his arms and kissed me vigorously. I struggled free with some difficulty, and he gravely handed me the tray again and began walking along beside me as if nothing had happened. I was quite upset because someone might have come along, but thank goodness no one did. I thought his behavior very undignified and silly and told him so. I tried to hurry away from him but he deliberately kept step with me and although he looked exactly as if we were discussing medical matters, he was calling me all sorts of French pet names and asking me when I would go to Paris with him. I said: "Absolument jamais!" and ducked into a ward. I don't think absolument jamais *is very good French but I hope he knew I meant it.*

Why doesn't Doctor Le Brun notice me once in a while? Yesterday I saw him in the ward sitting on the bed beside Hansen, a big gawky Swede from Minneapolis who has lost his right arm. Le B. was showing him how easy it is to write with the left hand. Le B. is left handed, does all his operating with his left hand. When he had gone I saw Hansen scribbling away, practicing cheerfully with his tongue tucked out of the corner of his mouth.

If Le B. asked me to go to Paris with him, I'm not so sure I would say Absolument jamais! *He is a dear. So good to all the men. Pats them and calls them* Mon Petit *and* Mon Vieux. *Not like the cold-blooded, goateed Moreau whom we all dislike, and who works like a mechanical man, without one spark of feeling. One of the surgery nurses told me he began operating the other day before the ether had taken effect.*

May 16th
Dr. Le Brun noticed me today. As I was coming out of the surgery with an armful of bottles he smiled at me and said: "Bien fait, bébé, bien fait." *Good work, baby, or words to that effect. It may not be exactly an impassioned speech but it is a lot coming from Dr. Le B. He isn't young, must be thirty-five, and he probably has a wife and children—or at least a fiancée down in Lyons. But I hope not.*

I seldom have time to think of Ted these days, but when I do get 'round to it, I love him dearly, and perhaps it is best to stick to one's own nationality. I must write to him tonight.

The little contretemps in the corridor with Dr. Girard was only one of the incidents which marked that period of comparative inactivity. Immediately after a big drive, everyone appeared to relax from accumulated fatigue. But after having rested a bit, our heroic doctors would begin looking about them, and it was natural that they should observe and admire the fresh vigor of the American unit. Nearly all of us had some similar adventure to report, and I am bound to confess that some of us were not above flirting outrageously with these not indifferent and altogether interesting males who were naturally somewhat woman-conscious after a long period of grim duty and military segregation. But apart from a normal amount of: "He said and I said . . ." and highly exaggerated accounts of being: "Scared to death, he looked so strange and wouldn't let me go . . ." I think we all emerged from our experiences none the worse, except for an increased opinion of our own seductiveness.

Remembering this period of slightly hysterical romanticism on the part of the hospital staff, I also recall Madame de R., one of the French nurses who had given her services to her country ever since the outbreak of the war. She had become, after the four long years of experience, head surgical assistant to one of the older doctors. She was by no means young herself, but very straight and brisk with hair dyed a reddish gold. She was the only nurse among the fifty odd who used cosmetics; her lipstick and *macquillage* were in the height of Parisian fashion; and her irregular features gave, by some trick of artifice, the impression of extreme attractiveness. I learned that she was a somewhat déclassée *vicomtesse* who had been for years the mistress of the surgeon she assisted. She went with him everywhere as his special nurse. At first we were inclined to resent her privileges and air of authority, but we soon found that she was a grand person, an understanding friend to all of us, and that she genuinely admired our spunk and appreciated our hard work.

Although she had lived a life of mondaine luxury until the war, no one was more efficient and tireless than this nearly middle-aged woman. We learned to love her devotedly. Her iron cot, with a shelf across the head for her belongings on which stood silver-framed photographs of her glamorous intimates, was the Mecca for all who needed a sympathetic ear in which to pour their troubles, real and imaginary.

There were still many details of duty which were not clear in my mind. Knowing she was thoroughly experienced and always glad to give the newcomers a lift, I sometimes went to her for advice. Should I change an uncomfortable dressing for the Canadian Captain without waiting for the doctor's orders? Could I ask an orderly to help me feed the bad cases so their food would not get cold? Was it all right to give an extra dose of morphine where the first had not given enough relief? She was so understanding and practical and never failed to make the humane decision which, during the first days, I hesitated to make for myself.

I recall the occasion of my first visit. She was propped up on her cot, against elaborately embroidered pillows, a fine lace boudoir cap on her red locks, wearing a sacque with lace frills at the throat and wrists. A rich silk comforter was thrown over the bed and her beautiful linen sheets were marked with a coronet and a monogram. I felt like a country mouse in my blue flannel dressing gown and knitted slippers, and sat quite awe-struck on the edge of the bed feeling as though I were having an intimate audience with the queen. In her relaxed moments Madame de R. was every inch the Parisian *vicomtesse*, and her splendor was a striking contrast to the gray bathrobes and drab army blankets on the other cots in the room.

May 18th

Took a long walk with Dr. Le Brun today. The woods were beautiful and I will never forget that walk. If I thought he was wonderful yesterday, I think he is much more so today. We talked and talked about so many things—partly in French and partly in English. He is shy about speaking English, although he really does very well. We fill in here and there with whichever word fits best and have a grand time. He has a delightful sense of humor. I discovered that today, and it is a dangerous thing to find out about someone you already like a lot. As we strolled along he surprised me by stopping suddenly and saying: "Ah, bon jour, Moreau!" I turned in dismay, expecting to greet the unpopular Dr. Moreau, but all I saw was a scraggy old goat, moving his chin whiskers up and down as he munched from the bushes. The resemblance was so ludicrous and my relief so intense that I laughed until I was weak.

Le B. asked me if I had ever been in love. I said: "No." I don't feel tonight as if I ever have been really in love. I wonder if Ted would mind if I shifted to somebody else, especially a Frenchman. I wouldn't be surprised if I completely forgot Ted, that is if Le B. shows any further signs of interest.

As we walked along, the roads were like bee-hives, with French troops moving forward although at the moment we are not very near the line. We had to step to the side to let them pass. Hundreds of poilus, singing Madelon as they swung along, their gray-blue overcoats pinned back at the knees.

Then a regiment of Americans, some marching, some in trucks and others astride the guns on the great cumbersome tractors. They were all grinning like pleased youngsters on the way to a picnic. One of them leaned down and shouted: "Hey, listen, where is all this trouble anyway?" That sticks in my mind for some odd reason. It seems to be the spirit of the entire A.E.F. They don't know what they are in for, and I do. Yet I am glad to see them marching up to the front. How can I be glad? It is all very puzzling. It must be because everything is so topsy-turvy these days.

Le B. remarked as they passed that one could see the difference in temperament between the French poilu and the American doughboy by the way they wear their helmets. The French plant theirs solidly on their heads, having learned from bitter experience that this is where they will do the most good. But our boys still wear theirs cocked jauntily over one ear.

Then Le B. and I had quite a heated argument as to whether it is better to be serious about life, or to take it all as a joke; but that didn't get us very far because we both had to agree that you are born one way or the other and that is the way you stay, whether you like it or not.

We found the most beautiful carpet of lilies of the valley growing wild under the trees. The stems grow eighteen inches high and the blossoms are enormous. A great bunch of them are beside me in my toothbrush glass as I scribble this and the fragrance is overpowering. We picked armfuls of the lovely things and on the way home stopped in the church-yard and put a few on some of the graves. With a few in my belt and a spray in his buttonhole, we strolled back through the high-walled lanes to supper, the inevitable prime ribs of horse, au jus.

From *I Saw Them Die* (1936)

Floyd Gibbons: Wounded—
How It Feels to Be Shot

Erich Ludendorff, the de facto commander of the German army since August 1916, halted the first stage of the German spring offensive on April 5, short of the crucial railroad junction at Amiens. He then attacked the British in Flanders, beginning a three-week battle that failed to capture either Ypres or the major Allied supply center at Hazebrouck. The third German offensive, launched against the French along the Aisne on May 27, proved unexpectedly successful and resulted in an advance south toward the Marne. American troops helped the French defend Château-Thierry, while American soldiers and Marines nearby fought a prolonged battle for possession of Belleau Wood. Floyd Gibbons of the *Chicago Tribune* was another of the war's star reporters, handsome and intrepid—on the ground in Mexico in 1916 when Pershing chased Pancho Villa and aboard the RMS *Laconia* in February 1917 when a U-boat off Ireland torpedoed it, killing twelve. On June 6, 1918, Gibbons entered Belleau Wood to report on the fighting; and in his efforts to rescue a wounded Marine officer, he was shot and lost an eye. In the years that followed, he would continue to cover wars and international crises wearing a signature white eye patch.

––––––––––––––

JUST HOW does it feel to be shot on the field of battle? Just what is the exact sensation when a bullet burns its way through your flesh or crashes through your bones?

I always wanted to know. As a police reporter I "covered" scores of shooting cases, but I could never learn from the victims what the precise feeling was as the piece of lead struck. For long years I had cherished an inordinate curiosity to know that sensation, if possible, without experiencing it. I was curious and eager for enlightenment just as I am still anxious to know how it is that some people willingly drink buttermilk when it isn't compulsory.

I am still in the dark concerning the inexplicable taste for the sour, clotted product of a sweet, well-meaning cow and the buttery, but I have found out how it feels to be shot. I know it now by experience.

470

Three German bullets that violated my person left me as many scars and at the same time completely satisfied my curiosity. I think now if I can ever muster up enough courage to drink a glass of buttermilk, I shall have bereft myself of my last inquisitiveness.

It happened on June 6th just to the northwest of Château-Thierry in the Bois de Belleau. On the morning of that day I left Paris by motor for a rush to the front. The Germans were on that day within forty miles of the capital of France. On the night before, the citizens of Paris, in their homes and hotels, had heard the roll of the guns drawing ever nearer. Many had left the city.

But American divisions were in the line between the enemy and their goal, and the operation of these divisions was my object in hustling to the front. On the broad, paved highway from Paris to Meaux, my car passed miles and miles of loaded motor trucks bound frontward. Long lines of these carried thousands of Americans. Other long lines were loaded down with shells and cartridge boxes. On the right side of the road, bound for Paris and points back of the line, was an endless stream of ambulances and other motor trucks bringing back wounded. Dense clouds of dust hung like a pall over the length of the road. The day was hot, the dust was stifling.

From Meaux we proceeded along the straight highway that borders the south banks of the Marne to LaFerte, at which place we crossed the river and turned north to Montreuil, which was the newly occupied headquarters of the Second United States Army Division, General Omar Bundy commanding. On the day before, the two infantry brigades of that division, one composed of the 5th and 6th U. S. Marines, under command of Brigadier General Harbord, the other composed of the 9th and 23rd U. S. Infantry, had been thrown into the line which was just four miles to the north and east.

The fight had been hot during the morning. The Marines on the left flank of the divisional sector had been pushing their lines forward through triangle woods and the village of Lucy-le-Bocage. The information of their advances was given to me by the Divisional Intelligence officer, who occupied a large room in the rear of the building that was used as Divisional Headquarters. The building was the village *Mairie*, which also included the village school-house. Now the desks of the school children were being used by our staff officers and the walls and blackboards were covered with maps.

I was accompanied by Lieutenant Oscar Hartzell, formerly of the *New York Times* staff. We learned that orders from the French High Command called for a continuation of the Marine advance during the afternoon and evening, and this information made it possible for us to make our plans. Although the Germans were shelling roads immediately behind the front, Lieutenant Hartzell and I agreed to proceed by motor from Montreuil a mile or so to a place called La Voie du Chatel, which was the headquarters of Colonel Neveille of the 5th Marines. Reaching that place around four o'clock, we turned a despatch over to the driver of our staff car with instructions that he proceed with all haste to Paris and there submit it to the U. S. Press Bureau.

Lieutenant Hartzell and I announced our intentions of proceeding at once to the front line to Colonel Neveille.

"Go wherever you like," said the regimental commander, looking up from the outspread maps on the kitchen table in the low-ceilinged stone farm-house that he had adopted as headquarters. "Go as far as you like, but I want to tell you it's damn hot up there."

An hour later found us in the woods to the west of the village of Lucy le Bocage, in which German shells were continually falling. To the west and north another nameless cluster of farm dwellings was in flames. Huge clouds of smoke rolled up like a smudge against the background of blue sky.

The ground under the trees in the wood was covered with small bits of white paper. I could not account for their presence until I examined several of them and found that these were letters from American mothers and wives and sweethearts— letters—whole packages of them, which the tired, dog-weary Marines had been forced to remove from their packs and destroy in order to ease the straps that cut into aching grooves in their shoulders. Circumstances also forced the abandonment of much other material and equipment.

Occasional shells were dropping in the woods, which were also within range from a long distance, indirect machine gun fire from the enemy. Bits of lead, wobbling in their flight at the end of their long trajectory, sung through the air above our heads and clipped leaves and twigs from the branches. On the edge of the woods we came upon a hastily dug out pit in which there were two American machine guns and their crews.

The field in front of the woods sloped gently down some two hundred yards to another cluster of trees. This cluster was almost as big as the one we were in. Part of it was occupied by the Germans. Our machine gunners maintained a continual fire into that part held by the enemy.

Five minutes before five o'clock, the order for the advance reached our pit. It was brought there by a second lieutenant, a platoon commander.

"What are you doing here?" he asked, looking at the green brassard and red "C" on my left arm.

"Looking for the big story," I said.

"If I were you I'd be about forty miles south of this place," said the Lieutenant, "but if you want to see the fun, stick around. We are going forward in five minutes."

That was the last I saw of him until days later, when both of us, wounded, met in the hospital. Of course, the first thing he said was, "I told you so."

We hurriedly finished the contents of the can of cold "Corned Willy" which one of the machine gunners and I were eating. The machine guns were taken down and the barrels, cradles and tripods were handed over to the members of the crew whose duties it was to carry them.

And then we went over. There are really no heroics about it. There is no bugle call, no sword waving, no dramatic enunciation of catchy commands, no theatricalism—it's just plain get up and go over. And it is done just the same as one would walk across a peaceful wheat field out in Iowa.

But with the appearance of our first line, as it stepped from the shelter of the woods into the open exposure of the flat field, the woods opposite began to cackle and rattle with the enemy machine gun fire. Our men advanced in open order, ten and twelve feet between men. Sometimes a squad would run forward fifty feet and drop. And as its members flattened on the ground for safety another squad would rise from the ground and make another rush.

They gained the woods. Then we could hear shouting. Then

we knew that work was being done with the bayonet. The machine gun fire continued in intensity and then died down completely. The wood had been won. Our men consolidated the position by moving forward in groups ever on the watch-out for snipers in the trees. A number of these were brought down by our crack pistol shots.

At different times during the advance runners had come through the woods inquiring for Major John Berry, the battalion commander. One of these runners attached himself to Lieutenant Hartzell and myself and together the three of us located the Major coming through the woods. He granted permission for Lieutenant Hartzell and me to accompany him and we started forward, in all a party of some fifteen, including ten runners attached to the battalion commander.

Owing to the continual evidences of German snipers in the trees, every one in our party carried a revolver ready in his hand, with the exception of myself. Correspondents, you will remember, are non-combatants and must be unarmed. I carried a notebook, but it was loaded. We made our way down the slope of the wooded hillside.

Midway down the slope, the hill was bisected by a sunken road which turned forward on the left. Lying in the road were a number of French bodies and several of our men who had been brought down but five minutes before. We crossed that road hurriedly knowing that it was covered from the left by German machine guns.

At the bottom of the slope there was a V-shaped field. The apex of the V was on the left. From left to right the field was some two hundred yards in width. The point where we came out of the woods was about one hundred yards from the apex. At that point the field was about one hundred yards across. It was perfectly flat and was covered with a young crop of oats between ten and fifteen inches high.

This V-shaped oat field was bordered on all sides by dense clusters of trees. In the trees on the side opposite the side on which we stood, were German machine guns. We could hear them. We could not see them but we knew that every leaf and piece of greenery there vibrated from their fire and the tops of the young oats waved and swayed with the streams of lead that swept across.

Major Berry gave orders for us to follow him at intervals of ten or fifteen yards. Then he started across the field alone at the head of the party. I followed. Behind me came Hartzell. Then the woods about us began to rattle fiercely. It was unusually close range. That lead travelled so fast that we could not hear it as it passed. We soon had visual demonstration of the hot place we were in when we began to see the dust puffs that the bullets kicked up in the dirt around our feet.

Major Berry had advanced well beyond the centre of the field when I saw him turn toward me and heard him shout:

"Get down everybody."

We all fell on our faces. And then it began to come hot and fast. Perfectly withering volleys of lead swept the tops of the oats just over us. For some reason it did not seem to be coming from the trees hardly a hundred yards in front of us. It was coming from a new direction—from the left.

I was busily engaged flattening myself on the ground. Then I heard a shout in front of me. It came from Major Berry. I lifted my head cautiously and looked forward. The Major was making an effort to get to his feet. With his right hand he was savagely grasping his left wrist.

"My hand's gone," he shouted. One of the streams of lead from the left had found him. A ball had entered his left arm at the elbow, had travelled down the side of the bone, tearing away muscles and nerves of the forearm and lodging itself in the palm of his hand. His pain was excruciating.

"Get down. Flatten out, Major," I shouted, and he dropped to the ground. I did not know the extent of his injuries at that time but I did know that he was courting death every minute he stood up.

"We've got to get out of here," said the Major. "We've got to get forward. They'll start shelling this open field in a few minutes."

I lifted my head for another cautious look.

I judged that I was lying about thirty yards from the edge of the trees in front of us. The Major was about ten yards in front of me.

"You are twenty yards from the trees," I shouted to the Major. "I am crawling over to you now. Wait until I get there and I'll help you. Then we'll get up and make a dash for it."

"All right," replied the Major, "hurry along."

I started forward, keeping as flat on the ground as it was possible to do so and at the same time move. As far as was feasible, I pushed forward by digging in with my toes and elbows extended in front of me. It was my object to make as little movement in the oats as possible. I was not mistaken about the intensity of fire that swept the field. It was terrific.

And then it happened. The lighted end of a cigarette touched me in the fleshy part of my upper left arm. That was all. It just felt like a sudden burn and nothing worse. The burned part did not seem to be any larger in area than that part which could be burned by the lighted end of a cigarette.

At the time there was no feeling within the arm, that is, no feeling as to aches or pain. There was nothing to indicate that the bullet, as I learned several days later, had gone through the bicep muscle of the upper arm and had come out on the other side. The only sensation perceptible at the time was the burning touch at the spot where the bullet entered.

I glanced down at the sleeve of my uniformed coat and could not even see the hole where the bullet had entered. Neither was there any sudden flow of blood. At the time there was no stiffness or discomfort in the arm and I continued to use it to work my way forward.

Then the second one hit. It nicked the top of my left shoulder. And again came the burning sensation, only this time the area affected seemed larger. Hitting as it did in the meaty cap of the shoulder, I feared that there would be no further use for the arm until it had received attention, but again I was surprised when I found upon experiment that I could still use it. The bone seemed to be affected in no way.

Again there was no sudden flow of blood, nor stiffness. It seemed hard for me to believe at the time, but I had been shot twice, penetrated through by two bullets and was experiencing not any more pain than I had experienced once when I dropped a lighted cigarette on the back of my hand. I am certain that the pain in no way approached that sensation which the dentist provides when he drills into a tooth with a live nerve in it.

So I continued to move toward the Major. Occasionally I would shout something to him, although, at this time, I am unable to remember what it was. I only wanted to let him know I was coming. I had fears, based on the one look that I had obtained of his pain-distorted face, that he had been mortally shot in the body.

And then the third one struck me. In order to keep as close to the ground as possible, I had swung my chin to the right so that I was pushing forward with my left cheek flat against the ground and in order to accommodate this position of the head, I had moved my steel helmet over so that it covered part of my face on the right.

Then there came a crash. It sounded to me like some one had dropped a glass bottle into a porcelain bathtub. A barrel of whitewash tipped over and it seemed that everything in the world turned white. That was the sensation. I did not recognise it because I have often been led to believe and often heard it said that when one receives a blow on the head everything turns black.

Maybe I am contrarily constructed, but in my case everything became pure white. I remember this distinctly because my years of newspaper training had been in but one direction —to sense and remember. So it was that, even without knowing it, my mind was making mental notes on every impression that my senses registered.

I did not know yet where I had been hit or what the bullet had done. I knew that I was still knowing things. I did not know whether I was alive or dead but I did know that my mind was still working. I was still mentally taking notes on every second.

The first recess in that note-taking came when I asked myself the following question:

"Am I dead?"

I didn't laugh or didn't even smile when I asked myself the question without putting it in words. I wanted to know. And wanting to know, I undertook to find out. I am not aware now that there was any appreciable passage of time during this mental progress. I feel certain, however, that I never lost consciousness.

How was I to find out if I was dead? The shock had lifted my head off the ground but I had immediately replaced it as close to the soil as possible. My twice punctured left arm was lying alongside my body. I decided to try and move my fingers on my left hand. I did so and they moved. I next moved my left foot. Then I knew I was alive.

Then I brought my right hand up toward my face and placed it to the left of my nose. My fingers rested on something soft and wet. I withdrew the hand and looked at it. It was covered with blood. As I looked at it, I was not aware that my entire vision was confined to my right eye, although there was considerable pain in the entire left side of my face.

This was sufficient to send me on another mental investigation. I closed my right eye and—all was dark. My first thought following this experiment was that my left eye was closed. So I again counselled with myself and tried to open my left eye—that is, tried to give the mental command that would cause the muscles of the left eye to open the lid and close it again.

I did this but could not feel or verify in any way whether the eyelid responded or not. I only knew that it remained dark on that side. This brought me to another conclusion and not a pessimistic one at that. I simply believed, in spite of the pain, that something had struck me in the eye and had closed it.

I did not know then, as I know now, that a bullet striking the ground immediately under my left cheek bone, had ricochetted upward, going completely through the left eye and then crashing out through my forehead, leaving the eyeball and upper eyelid completely halved, the lower eyelid torn away, and a compound fracture of the skull.

Further progress toward the Major was impossible. I must confess that I became so intensely interested in the weird sensations and subjective research, that I even neglected to call out and tell the wounded officer that I would not be able to continue to his assistance. I held this view in spite of the fact that my original intentions were strong. Lying there with my left cheek flat on the ground, I was able to observe some minutes later the wounded Major rise to his feet and in a perfect hail of lead rush forward and out of my line of vision.

It was several days later, in the hospital, that I learned that he reached the shelter of the woods beyond without being hit again, and in that place, although suffering intense pain, was able to shout back orders which resulted in the subsequent wiping out of the machine gun nest that had been our undoing. For this supreme effort, General Pershing decorated him with the Distinguished Service Cross.

I began to make plans to get out of the exposed position in

which I was lying. Whereas the field when I started across it had seemed perfectly flat, now it impressed me as being convex and I was further impressed with the belief that I was lying on the very uppermost and most exposed curvature of it. There is no doubt that the continued stream of machine gun lead that swept the field superinduced this belief. I got as close to the ground as a piece of paper on top of a table. I remember regretting sincerely that the war had reached the stage of open movement and one consequence of which was that there wasn't a shell hole anywhere to crawl into.

This did not, however, eliminate the dangerous possibility of shelling. With the fatalism that one acquires along the fronts, I was ready to take my chances with the casual German shell that one might have expected, but I devoted much thought to a consideration of the French and American artillery some miles behind me. I considered the possibility of word having been sent back that our advancing waves at this point had been cut down by enemy machine gunners who were still in position preventing all progress at this place. I knew that such information, if sent back, would immediately be forwarded to our guns and then a devastating concentration of shells would be directed toward the location of the machine gun nests.

I knew that I was lying one hundred yards from one of those nests and I knew that I was well within the fatal bursting radius of any shells our gunners might direct against that German target. My fear was that myself and other American wounded lying in that field would die by American guns. That is what would have happened if that information had reached our artillery and it is what should have happened.

The lives of the wounded in that field were as nothing compared with the importance of wiping out that machine gun nest on our left which was holding up the entire advance.

I wanted to see what time it was and my watch was attached to my left wrist. In endeavouring to get a look at it, I found out that my left arm was stiff and racked with pain. Hartzell, I knew, had a watch, but I did not know where he was lying, so I called out.

He answered me from some distance away but I could not tell how far or in what direction. I could see dimly but only at the expense of great pain. When he answered I shouted back to him:

"Are you hit?"

"No, are you?" he asked.

"Yes, what time is it?" I said.

"Are you hit badly?" he asked in reply.

"No, I don't think so," I said. "I think I'm all right."

"Where are you hit?" he asked.

"In the head," I said; "I think something hit my eye."

"In the head, you damn fool," he shouted louder with just a bit of anger and surprise in his voice. "How the hell can you be all right if you are hit in the head? Are you bleeding much?"

"No," I said. "What time is it, will you tell me?"

"I'm coming over to get you," shouted Hartzell.

"Don't move, you damn fool, you want to kill both of us?" I hastened to shout back. "If you start moving, don't move near me. I think they think I'm dead."

"Well you can't lie there and bleed to death," Hartzell replied. "We've got to do something to get to hell out of here. What'll we do?"

"Tell me what time it is and how long it will be before it's dark," I asked.

"It's six o'clock now," Hartzell said, "and it won't be dark 'til nine; this is June. Do you think you can stick it out?"

I told him that I thought I could and we were silent for some time. Both of us had the feeling that other ears—ears working in conjunction with eyes trained along the barrels of those machine guns a hundred yards on our left—would be aroused to better marksmanship if we continued to talk.

I began to take stock of my condition. During my year or more along the fronts I had been through many hospitals and from my observations in those institutions I had cultivated a keen distaste for one thing—gas gangrene. I had learned from doctors its fatal and horrible results and I also had learned from them that it was caused by germs which exist in large quantities in any ground that has been under artificial cultivation for a long period.

Such was the character of the very field I was lying in and I came to the realisation that the wound in the left side of my face and head was resting flatly on the soil. With my right hand

I drew up my British box respirator or gas mask and placed this under my head. Thus I rested with more confidence, although the machine gun lead continued to pass in sheets through the tops of the oats not two or three inches above my head.

All of it was coming from the left,—coming from the German nests located in the trees at the apex of the V-shaped field. Those guns were not a hundred yards away and they seemed to have an inexhaustible supply of ammunition. Twenty feet away on my left a wounded Marine was lying. Occasionally I would open my right eye for a painful look in his direction.

He was wounded and apparently unconscious. His pack, "the khaki doll," was still strapped between his shoulders. Unconsciously he was doing that which all wounded men do—that is, to assume the position that is the most comfortable. He was trying to roll over on his back.

But the pack was on his back and every time he would roll over on this it would elevate his body into full view of the German gunners. Then a withering hail of lead would sweep the field. It so happened that I was lying immediately in line between those German guns and this unconscious moving target. As the Marine would roll over on top of the pack his chest would be exposed to the fire.

I could see the buttons fly from his tunic and one of the shoulder straps of the back pack part as the sprays of lead struck him. He would limply roll off the pack over on his side. I found myself wishing that he would lie still, as every movement of his brought those streams of bullets closer and closer to my head. I even considered the thickness of the box respirator on which I had elevated my head off the ground. It was about two inches thick.

I remembered my French gas mask hanging from my shoulder and recalled immediately that it was much flatter, being hardly half an inch in thickness. I forthwith drew up the French mask to my head, extracted the British one and rested my cheek closer to the ground on the French one. Thus, I lowered my head about an inch and a half—an inch and a half that represented worlds of satisfaction and some optimism to me.

Sometimes there were lulls in the firing. During those periods of comparative quiet, I could hear the occasional moan of other wounded on that field. Very few of them cried out and it seemed to me that those who did were unconscious when they did it. One man in particular had a long, low groan. I could not see him, yet I felt he was lying somewhere close to me. In the quiet intervals, his unconscious expression of pain reminded me of the sound I had once heard made by a calf which had been tied by a short rope to a tree. The animal had strayed round and round the tree until its entanglements in the rope had left it a helpless prisoner. The groan of that unseen, unconscious wounded American who laid near me on the field that evening sounded exactly like the pitiful bawl of that calf.

Those three hours were long in passing. With the successive volleys that swept the field, I sometimes lost hope that I could ever survive it. It seemed to me that if three German bullets had found me within the space of fifteen minutes, I could hardly expect to spend three hours without receiving the fatal one. With such thoughts on my mind I reopened conversation with Hartzell.

"How's it coming, old man?" I shouted.

"They're coming damn close," he said; "how is it with you? Are you losing much blood?"

"No, I'm all right as far as that goes," I replied, "but I want you to communicate with my wife, if it's 'west' for me."

"What's her address?" said Hartzell.

"It's a long one," I said. "Are you ready to take it?"

"Shoot," said Hartzell.

"'Mrs. Floyd Gibbons, No. 12 Bis, Rue de la Chevalier de la Barre, Dijon, Côte d'Or, France.'" I said slowly.

"My God," said Hartzell, "say it again."

Back and forth we repeated the address correctly and incorrectly some ten or twelve times until Hartzell informed me that he knew it well enough to sing it. He also gave me his wife's address. Then just to make conversation he would shout over, every fifteen minutes, and tell me that there was just that much less time that we would have to lie there.

I thought that hour between seven and eight o'clock dragged the most, but the one between eight and nine seemed interminable. The hours were so long, particularly when we considered that a German machine gun could fire three hundred shots a minute. Dusk approached slowly. And finally Hartzell called over:

"I don't think they can see us now," he said; "let's start to crawl back."

"Which way shall we crawl?" I asked.

"Into the woods," said Hartzell.

"Which woods?" I asked.

"The woods we came out of, you damn fool," he replied.

"Which direction are they in?" I said, "I've been moving around and I don't know which way I am heading. Are you on my left, or on my right?"

"I can't tell whether I'm on your left or your right," he replied. "How are you lying, on your face or on your back?"

"On my face," I said, "and your voice sounds like it comes from in back of me and on the left."

"If that's the case," said Hartzell, "your head is lying toward the wrong woods. Work around in a half circle and you'll be facing the right direction."

I did so and then heard Hartzell's voice on my right. I started moving toward him. Against my better judgment and expressed wishes, he crawled out toward me and met me half way. His voice close in front of me surprised me.

"Hold your head up a little," he said, "I want to see where it hit you."

"I don't think it looks very nice," I replied, lifting my head. I wanted to know how it looked myself, so I painfully opened the right eye and looked through the oats eighteen inches into Hartzell's face. I saw the look of horror on it as he looked into mine.

Twenty minutes later, after crawling painfully through the interminable yards of young oats, we reached the edge of the woods and safety.

That's how it feels to be shot.

From *"And They Thought We Wouldn't Fight"* (1918)

Frederick A. Pottle: from Stretchers

Frederick A. Pottle graduated from Colby College in 1917 and enlisted in the army that December, only to be told that his poor eyesight would restrict his service to the medical corps. In May 1918 his evacuation hospital unit landed in France, and on June 8 he arrived in Juilly, northeast of Paris, where he worked as a surgical assistant treating casualties from Château-Thierry and Belleau Wood. Pottle describes the military medicine of the day—far advanced from that of the American Civil War, when sepsis control was unknown, but woefully lacking the antibiotics and blood plasma of future conflicts.

―――――――――――

NO QUARTERS have as yet been prepared for us, and it is imperative that we waste no time hunting for any. We drop our packs on the beautiful green lawn, where a line of our great brown ward tents is later to stand, and sit down on the grass to snatch a hasty dinner. Within thirty minutes of our arrival we are all at work. Our officers, indeed, who preceded us to town, have been in the operating rooms some time, having taken only time enough to scrub up. We are told off into details, pretty much at random, and assigned for duty in the receiving ward, the operating rooms, the surgical wards, to dig graves and bury the dead; in short, to perform all the multifarious tasks of a large evacuation hospital jammed with wounded.

Let us follow some of these men as they get their first impressions of war surgery. The separate glimpses will be confused, but the very confusion will make the picture more adequate. Our first man is assigned to Ward D. Ward D, he finds, is a detached building in the corner of the lawn, facing the great building with the statue of the Virgin at its peak. He goes up the steps, crosses a narrow entry, and looks in. What a strange room—large and bare, with the further end elevated like a stage. It *is* a stage. The place was evidently the theater of the school. Now it is filled with cots; not only the floor, but even the stage, from which all the scenery has been stripped.

The cots are lined up as thick as they will go, with only the narrowest alleys for walking between, and every cot has a wounded man on it. After all, the place looks a little more like a civilian hospital than he had expected. The beds are made up with sheets, covered, to be sure, with the inevitable army blankets, but the men have been completely undressed and clothed in various styles of Red Cross hospital shirts—short white gowns with loose sleeves, tying with strings at the back. It is in the only too obvious evidence of terrible wounds that one realizes that this is a war hospital. Here lies a fair-haired boy of eighteen or so, his eyes closed, his neck and shoulder exposed to show a great bulky wad of bandage over the stump of an arm amputated near the shoulder. Here is an older man, haggard, unshaven, and ugly, his knees drawn up over his distended stomach, a look of peculiar and characteristic agony on his face. He has a severe wound of the abdomen, and has not much longer to suffer. He struggles to repress the frequent coughing fits which tear him with pain. He is continually calling out something in a language that is not English. There are some French wounded here, but the card tied to the head of his cot shows that he is an American, an immigrant who enlisted before he had mastered the language of his adopted country. There is a black-haired youngster who has lost his leg above the knee. The majority of the others have suffered less severely, but there is not a man here who has not escaped death scores of times in the last week by the narrowest of margins. Some of them are babbling in delirium, some shouting and cursing as they fight their way out of the ether dream in which they are reënacting the horror of the trenches, some in their right minds, gaily talking and joking, but the most lie in a half-waking stupor, the inevitable reaction to days of hunger, fatigue, the nervous strain of incessant deadly peril, and, finally, the shock of severe wounds, ether, and surgical operations. They have been for days without food; they have lain for hours in shallow holes with shells bursting every moment within inches of them and inflicting sudden and awful death among their comrades; their ears have been deafened with noise which in itself would produce prostration; they have walked unprotected straight into the murderous hail of machine-gun bullets; they have fought hand-to-hand with bayonets, in duels where the only possible outcome was either victory or death. These are the wounded marines from Belleau Woods. One's first shock of surprise comes from finding them so young. Most of these wounded men are boys of the age of college freshmen or a little older, boys of magnificent physique, but preserving still in contour of limb and downy cheek the grace of boyhood. The beauty of their faces is only enhanced by suffering. They have not yet wasted away with weeks of torture. Their faces are smooth and round, though drained of all color, and their pallor makes their eyes stand out with extraordinary clearness. They are now touchingly brave, self-sacrificing, grateful. Weeks in hospital will sap their courage. They will become emaciated and fretful, calling out querulously, cringing at a touch. The hot room is pervaded with that indescribable but unforgettable atmosphere of an army hospital: fumes of ether, the heavy stench of gas gangrene and putrid infections, like the odor of decaying cabbage, and, strongest of all, the reek of chlorine from dressings wet with Dakin solution.

Some of this the new man has taken in as he stands in the door. He is not overcome with horror. He does not feel faint, even. Things are happening too fast for him to think of himself at all. He is moving in an existence apart from his own, like that of a dream. An army nurse, who was stooping over one of the patients, rises and comes to him. She is the first woman in uniform with whom he has ever had anything to do, and in the past months he has seen so little of women that her near proximity moves him strangely. He sees that she is ready to drop with fatigue. Her hair is escaping from under her cap, her face is gray and suffused with perspiration. She is so glad to see him that she nearly cries. During the last four days, this hospital has given surgical attention to nearly two thousand desperately wounded men. On June 2, it had only the personnel of a Red Cross base hospital of about 250 beds: two surgeons, twenty Red Cross nurses, a few civilian employees from the village, and, for transporting patients, half a dozen Annamite boys and a handful of French soldiers unfit for service at the front. The surgical force has been augmented by several hastily gathered teams, and day before yesterday these army nurses arrived. But the men available to lift and carry the wounded men (neither operating room is on the ground floor) were exhausted long ago, and there have been no proper replacements. Surgeons and nurses have been carrying litters in addition to their proper duties. For the last four days hardly anyone at Juilly has worked less than twenty hours a day.

There is no time now for chat. "Oh," says the nurse to our enlisted man, "will you please help me take care of a man who has just died?" He follows her to a cot well up the aisle on the right. The man who has just died bears no mark on his peaceful face. He looks as though he might be asleep. Under the direction of the nurse the new assistant takes off the shirt, which can be used again. The dead man has to be turned on his side to unfasten it; the flesh of his bare back is as warm as the hand which touches it. They wrap the long comely figure in the sheet, securing it with a strip or two of bandage. This man is so tall that the sheet will not cover him, and they pull a pillowcase on over his feet. Another enlisted man has meanwhile come in, and the two get the body on a stretcher and carry it to the morgue. From the driveway they pass into a wide cobbled court with buildings on all four sides, under a quaint old clock tower on the opposite side, into a corridor, and at last into a small bare whitewashed room. There has been no time to bury the dead, and a dozen long rigid white bundles lie here on stretchers, placed side by side on the floor. It will take many applications of chloride of lime and whitewash to remove the traces of the odor of mortal decay which assails one's nostrils long before he reaches the door of this room.

Or perhaps our man was sent instead to Ward E, the great room beneath the chapel, which is on the second floor under the statue of the Virgin and Child. This was of old the "Salle des Bustes," as we should say a memorial hall—a long, beautiful room with waxed floor, around the walls of which are ranged upon pedestals the busts of famous men. There are fine stained-glass windows and memorial tablets, including, in the most conspicuous position at the end of the room, a great marble slab to the memory of the graduates of the Collège who fell in the Franco-Prussian War. In the little alcove on the right lies a solitary patient, a French aviator who was burned in the crash of his plane. His body is not much marked, but his face is so charred that none of the features are distinguishable, and his hands are burned to mere stumps. Thin strips of gauze wet with some antiseptic solution cover his face, but not so completely that one cannot see the horror of his condition. His sense of hearing is acute, and as anyone comes up to his bed he begins to murmur in a faint, hoarse whisper, the hole where his lips should be puffing up the edges of the gauze. He is asking in French for something. It sounds like "morphine." Is it morphine? "Non! non!" says the whisper passionately, "pas morphine!" We cannot make him out, and try to tell him that we will call one of the French nuns.

Ward G is at the farthest distance from the operating rooms, above a fine cloister, up a steep and narrow flight of stairs. It was the children's dormitory and their little iron cots are still there. In the center of the room is a sort of trough, with running water, where they washed their faces of a morning. None of the beds are long enough for a six-foot marine; you must push their heads through the high open head of the cot until their feet clear, and then stick their feet out through the foot. It would be a laughable sight, were it not so pathetic, those rows of blanket-wrapped feet sticking out into the aisle, some motionless, some vigorously wiggling and getting uncovered.

Other men have gone to work in the operating rooms. To get there they enter the first great building by the gate, climb a broad stone stair, turn at a landing, and come out at the entrance of Ward B. Ward A is on the floor above. Beyond, on the corridor, are the X-ray rooms. Men in litters, undressed and wrapped in blankets, are lying on the floor waiting for their turns in the dark room. Ward B, which I suppose was formerly a recitation hall, is a long narrow room, divided down the center by a partition filled with arches. There is a double row of beds on each side of the partition, lined up with heads to the wall. Ward A is much the same kind of place. These are the best-equipped wards of all, and were probably the only ones in regular use from the time the Collège was overrun with French wounded in 1914 until Belleau Woods. Many of the beds are fitted with elaborate frameworks of wood ("Balkan frames") for the proper treatment of fractures. Men with broken thighs lie here for weeks—even months—flat on their backs, the broken limbs kept under constant tension by heavy weights. At the end of the ward is a little anteroom to the operating room. Evacuation Eight has not yet organized its receiving service so efficiently as it will later, when the men will come up to the operating room already undressed and with their wounds prepared for operation. The floor here is covered with litters on which lie the men just as they came from the ambulances, fully clothed with boots, puttees, breeches, shirt, and blouse, often with their steel helmets on their breasts and their gas masks beside them. Into one of the buttonholes of the blouse or shirt is tied a linen tag giving the man's name, his serial number and company, the treatment which he has thus far received, and from what medical unit. On their foreheads, standing out with startling distinctness on the white skin, are letters in iodine; always "T," and sometimes "M." These indicate the administration of morphine and antitetanic serum.

The first thing to do is to get their clothes off. Puttees come off first, then muddy shoes, tattered and bloody breeches, blouse, shirt, underwear. Much of it must be cut off to avoid bending wounded arms and legs. In spite of their pain the men make no outcry and do their best to help us. We put hospital shirts or pajamas on them, wrap them in blankets, and they are ready for the operating room. The stretcher bearers come out with a stretcher on which lies a wounded man just off the table, still deep under the ether, his face wet with perspiration, eyes closed, his breathing deep and heavy. Next! We pick up the stretcher nearest the door and carry it into the operating room.

There are three tables. Around two, busy and silent groups of white-gowned figures are bending over their work. The third is empty, and an attendant with a wet cloth is wiping off the blood which covers the lower portion in a shallow pool. We transfer our patient to the damp table, and at the same time get a mental picture of the room. It is not large, perhaps fifteen feet square, and very white and dazzling. The door is in one corner, and there are two high windows in the wall opposite. Against the wall on the left as you enter is a small oil cookstove, on which steams a highly polished copper tank for sterilizing the instruments. Against the wall facing you, between the windows, is a stout wooden table covered with a sheet, on which the sterilized instruments are laid out in shining rows, like silver in the drawers of a sideboard. Against the wall to the right are the lavatories where the surgeons scrub up. The three operating tables, white enamelled and covered with thin, oilcloth-covered mats, are lined up in the middle of the room, their heads toward the entrance, the feet toward the table with the sterilized instruments.

But we must get to work on our wounded man. The surgeons who have just finished with one man have stripped off their blood-stained gowns and gloves and are scrubbing their hands. Under their direction we fold back the blanket which covers the wounded man so as to expose the wound, let us say on the thigh. We fold another blanket to cover his feet and legs to the knee, and slip two stout straps around him, one just above the knees and one around the chest. The wound is still covered with the pack and bandages applied at the first-aid station or field hospital. We cut the bandage and expose it—a jagged aperture made by shrapnel, perhaps two inches long. With an ordinary razor we shave a considerable area around the wound. The surgeon has now finished scrubbing his hands. The nurse at the supply table opens for him a square parcel which contains a sterilized gown wrapped in a piece of muslin. He shakes it out gingerly by the neckband, careful not to touch the front. The attendant as gingerly ties the strings behind. The surgeon now rinses his hands with alcohol, and, when they have dried, pulls on a pair of rubber gloves, picking them up by their long, turned-back wrists, which, when the fingers are worked on, he turns up over the sleeves of his gown. His hands and the whole front of his body now present a perfectly sterilized surface, which nothing unsterilized has touched, and which must touch nothing unsterilized except the wound itself.

Meanwhile the anesthetist has been busy. She sits on a stool at the head of the table, at such a height that her elbows rest easily upon it on either side of the patient's head. Beside her is a little stand with her cans of ether, gauze, vaseline, a shallow basin shaped like a kidney, and clips for pulling forward the man's tongue if he should choke. The man has not cried out or in any way expressed his fear, but his eyes show that he is terrified by the array of glistening instruments, the solemn, white figures—worst of all, by the rapid play of scalpel and scissors which he can see by turning his head toward the tables on either side. His eyes in mute appeal seek those of the one familiar figure in the room, that of the enlisted man at his side. "Don't be frightened," I say, "the ether won't bother you at all, and it will all be over in a minute." (God forgive me, I have never taken ether in my life.) "Will you just take my hand, buddy," says the wounded man a trifle huskily, "I don't know much about this, and I'm afraid I may fight when the ether gets bad." "Sure!" I reply, "that's what I'm here for." The nurse smears a little vaseline around his eyes, and, holding the mask a few inches above his face, begins to pour the ether on it. "Breathe deep," she says, "and don't fight it." The mask comes lower, finally rests on his face, and a piece of gauze is wrapped around the edges to keep in the fumes. She pours on the ether faster. The man groans and struggles; he throws both his arms wide and tries to sit up. We have to tighten the straps and hold down his arms. Now he is limp, the moaning faint and dying away. The surgeon takes a long-handled clip which holds a swab, dips it in iodine, and paints a large area around the wound. One nurse stands all the time by the supply table, serving the surgeons at all three operating tables. She hands him four sterilized towels, which he lays around the wound, leaving exposed only a small rectangular patch of darkly stained skin with the wound in the center. How will he fasten his towels on? A little stand has been pushed up beside the foot of the table. The nurse covers it with a towel, and begins to lay out instruments on it. The surgeon picks up one that looks a little like a pair of manicure scissors, but, instead of cutting blades, it has two little sharp curved points that meet like a pair of pincers. With these he picks up the towels at the point where two of them overlap, and clips them together, pushing the points of the instrument down so that they meet in the skin underneath. The instrument has a catch which will hold it tightly shut until it is released. He puts on three more, one at each corner of the exposed patch. The uninitiated assistant gasps and flinches at this apparently cold-blooded process, and then derides his tenderness as he thinks how trivial these pin-pricks are in comparison with what is to come. The team is now ready: the chief, or operating, surgeon, his assistant (always a surgeon also, and an officer), and a nurse, who stands beside the little stand of instruments, ready to hand what is wanted. (This is in addition to the nurse at the large supply table of sterilized instruments.) These are all "scrubbed up," that is, provided with an elaborate surgical asepsis of sterilized gowns and gloves. The anesthetist and two enlisted men, who are not "scrubbed up," must look out for manipulating the patient, getting him on and off the table, bandaging, and bringing unsterilized equipment.

The surgeon takes a scalpel (a little knife with a rigid blade, no larger than a penknife), which he holds like a pen, and with firm, even pressure draws an incision on each side of the wound and considerably longer. The skin springs apart, showing the yellowish fatty layer beneath, and exposing the red of the muscle. This wound was made by a fragment of high explosive shell, which is still deeply embedded in the flesh. It has been located by the X-ray surgeon, who has made two marks with silver nitrate on the thigh, one on the top and one on the side. The foreign body lies at the point where perpendicular bisectors from those marks would intersect. The surgeon goes after it with scalpel and scissors, excising all the damaged tissue with what looks like reckless abandon. As he cuts into the muscle the blood spurts up like juice in a berry pie. The assistant mops it up with a gauze sponge, discovers the point where the blood vessel is severed, and the surgeon clips it with a haemostat, another variety of pincers with handles like manicure scissors. This is for small blood vessels; larger ones must be tied off at once. By the end of the operation the wound is full of these dangling haemostats. The surgeon probes with his finger between the muscle bundles for the shrapnel, and finally dislodges it, a jagged chunk of metal an inch square each way, with a great wad of cloth from the man's breeches clinging to it. He goes on, painstakingly removing every particle of clotted blood and tissue that has been damaged by the missile or resulting infection. Now, with the help of his assistant, he ties off the blood vessels still held by haemostats. During all this, the enlisted assistants at his direction have been turning the patient on the table, elevating or flexing the leg, or with a flashlight throwing light into some peculiarly inaccessible part of the wound. The operation is finished. What was a small jagged wound is now a gaping hole six inches long, two or three wide at the top, and perhaps four deep, perhaps extending through the entire thigh. The nurse places on the stand a bundle of little red rubber tubes, open at one end, the closed end punched full of holes. The surgeon pushes these into the wound, leaving the open ends out, inserting the closed ends into every crevice. He fills the cavity with gauze plentifully soaked with a solution smelling of chlorine, lays gauze strips soaked with yellow vaseline along the edges of the wound, and places a large absorbent pad over the orifice. His work is done. We bind on the pad with yards of bandage, roll the inert body onto a stretcher, and hurry it away to a ward. As he scrubs for the next case, the surgeon dictates to one of us a description of the case and the surgical treatment he has given it. All this may have taken half an hour; possibly an hour or more. We go on with the work, in twelve-hour shifts, night and day, as long as the supply of wounded holds out.

Remember that few of these enlisted men have ever been in an operating room before in their lives, and that as few of these surgeons have had actual previous experience in the technique of war surgery. Yet in that first afternoon they are called upon to perform the most dreadful as well as the most delicate operations. One could not plead inexperience as an excuse for delay. Amputations high in the thigh or upper arm, operations of the chest where the ribs must be sprung apart with retractors, and looking in with incredulous amazement we see the heart throbbing bare; wounds of the head and brain, wounds of the abdomen—in one day we performed more major operations than some civilian operating rooms see in six months. We work on without pause, undressing men, carrying them in, carrying them out, carrying them to the X-ray, carrying them to the wards. It is amazing how we form friendships in those few moments before the man goes onto the table. Late this evening, when we have gone off duty after twelve hours of such work, we shall stumble around to the wards to see how some of these boys are now, to wash their hands and faces, to sit quietly and talk with them. But we cannot sit long, for there is so much to be done in a ward, and wounded men naturally do not understand that you are not the regular ward orderly.

There are many, many other departments in this great organization. There is the division of trucking, all day on the road between Paris and Juilly bringing in surgical supplies, food, quartermaster's stores. An orderly is always bumping back and forth in a motorcycle with dispatches. In the great square flagged court (the "Cours d'Honneur") a tent has been erected to serve as receiving ward and personnel offices. The ambulances drive in unceasingly through the archway and unload their wounded before the tent. There are four litters in each ambulance, two above and two below, suspended from hooks. The ambulances are muddy, and frequently splashed with holes from the fragments of shells that have burst just beside them. The drivers are weary, but they hurry to unload their freight and hurry off again—a long, brown, almost unbroken line of ambulances filling the road from Château-Thierry to Juilly. The attendants in the receiving ward inspect the tag which comes tied to each wounded man, make other necessary records, check his few pathetic valuables and put them in a cotton-wool bag, and then send him to the operating room. Later, when things are better organized, the greater part of the work of preparing the patient for the table will be done here.

Every night we evacuate. Another long, brown, unbroken line of ambulances pulls out of the hospital, not empty, but filled with our wounded men who have undergone operation, bound for Paris. After operation, the wounded are sorted out according to the severity of their injuries, and the ward to which they are assigned indicates whether they may be immediately evacuated or not. For a large evacuation every man in the hospital not actually on night duty is expected to turn out and lend a hand, often extending the twelve hours of work he has already done by five or six more of carrying and lifting litters. Some wards are practically depleted at each evacuation. The ambulances pull up before the wards, the nurse indicates which men are to go, the orderlies and litter men transfer them gently to litters, lift and stow them away in the ambulances, call out a word of farewell, and they are off from Evacuation Eight forever.

One large detail has been at work all day on the grimmest task of all, that of digging graves and burying the dead. I shall describe the cemetery later, as it appeared after we had been at Juilly nearly two weeks. But today the grave detail finds the cemetery already well established. They dig the graves laboriously out of the stiff soil of a glorious field of wheat full of scarlet poppies, under a blazing sun; regulation graves, three feet wide, six feet and a half long, and six feet deep, and hastily lay in them the bodies of the dead. Later we had a burial party every afternoon about five. There would be five or six bodies, for which we then provided the luxury of unpainted wooden boxes. We piled them into a high two-wheeled French cart, drawn by a great patient work horse, and spread out an American flag over the ends of the boxes. The little procession started from the Cours d'Honneur, at the head the little crucifer from the parish church, then our Y.M.C.A. chaplain in plain khaki uniform, walking side by side with the village curé in his biretta, cassock, surplice, and stole. Behind trudged a French urchin, bearing the pail of holy water, a cotta over his breeches, but with an American trench cap on his head. Then came the lumbering cart driven by its stolid French owner, and, walking beside it, the men of the burial detail. At the cemetery we unloaded the coffins and lowered them down into the graves, jumping impatiently on the tops of the boxes if they happened to stick in the narrow space, and then stood uncovered, leaning on our spades, as the curé in his clear sonorous voice read the grand Latin of the Roman burial service over Catholic and Protestant, Jew and Gentile, and our chaplain followed with the familiar English words. One sprinkled with holy water, the other cast in a handful of earth. The bugler, facing the west and the golden lightning of the sunken sun, blew the long tender notes of taps, while far overhead an unseen lark poured forth its shrill delight.

From *Stretchers* (1929)

James Weldon Johnson:
"Why Should a Negro Fight?"

Johnson had helped organize the New York silent parade in July 1917 that protested the East St. Louis riot, and in February 1918 he led an NAACP delegation that petitioned President Wilson to review the sentences of sixteen black soldiers condemned to death for their role in the August 1917 riot in Houston. (Wilson eventually commuted ten of the sentences.) The delegation also asked him to condemn mob violence and lynchings publicly. While the President deliberated, Johnson addressed the question of how black Americans should view the war.

WHY SHOULD A NEGRO FIGHT?

THE ABOVE heading is the heading of an editorial in the Plainfield (N.J.) Courier-News of the 11th of this month. The Courier-News editorial was called forth by a letter written by some colored person to the editor asking reasons why the Negro should fight to protect the country. Two Age readers in Plainfield sent us the article and asked us to reply to it.

The letter which was sent to the editor of the Courier-News reads as follows:

> Plainfield Courier:
>
> Dear Sir: I am a buyer of your paper and I note in your column there are questions asked and answered. This is a question I should like you answer me. Why is it a Negro man should go to protect a country and public places when in it he can not even go in and drink a glass of ice cream soda nor even his female sex?
>
> E.R.

In the first place, this is a very lightweight letter. The person writing it picked out the weakest argument that could possibly be found. Of course, the denial of the privilege of drinking ice cream soda in certain places on account of race or color is a phase of the denial of full citizenship and common democracy; but it is trivial to single it out as a reason why the Negro should not do his part in this great war. If the duty of the Negro to fight was really a question in the mind of the writer of the letter, it seems that he should have backed up his inquiry with such arguments as the lynching and burning alive of Negroes, without any effort on the part of authorities to punish the perpetrators of these crimes; the disfranchisement and "Jim Crowing" of the race, even of those who are bearing arms and wearing the uniform; the shutting out of Negroes from many of the fields of occupation; the criminally unfair division of the public school funds in many states; the absence of even handed justice in the courts of many of the states, and other arguments that would carry weight.

In the second place, the letter contained a needless request for information. Any Negro outside of an insane asylum can by ten minutes of thought on the matter arrive at reasons why the race must do its full part in this war, which will outweigh any doubts there may have been in his mind.

America is the American Negro's country. He has been here three hundred years; that is, about two hundred years longer than most of the white people. He is a citizen of this country, declared so by the Constitution. Many of the rights and privileges of citizenship are still denied him, but the plain course before him is to continue to perform all of the duties of citizenship while he continually presses his demands for all of the rights and privileges. Both efforts must go together; to perform the duties and not demand the rights would be pusillanimous; and to demand the rights and not perform the duties would be futile.

It is a fact that the Negro is denied his full rights as a citizen, and that a good many people in the country are determined that he shall never have them; then the task before the Negro is to force the accordance of those rights, and that he cannot do by refusing to perform the duties. In fact, the moment he ceases to perform the duties of citizenship he abdicates the right to claim the full rights of citizenship.

As regards the present war, the central idea behind Germany is force; if that idea wins, it will be worse for the American

Negro and all the other groups belonging to submerged and oppressed peoples; so the American Negro should do all in his power to help defeat it.

Then, too, a German victory would mean the almost absolute destruction of France. France, the fountain of liberal ideas, the nation which more than any other in the world has freed itself from all kinds of prejudices, the nation which endeavors to practice as well as preach the brotherhood of man. The destruction of France would be the greatest blow to liberty that could now be dealt.

These are a few of the plain, logical reasons, based largely upon self-interest; besides there are other and more altruistic reasons; we leave the purely sentimental reasons out of consideration.

So much for the letter written to the Courier-News; now for the editorial written in answer to the letter. Here is the first sentence from it:

> A Negro should fight for this country because this nation freed him from the bonds of slavery.

Now if the editor of the Courier-News put up such an argument as that to a jackass he would get his brains kicked out. What was the slavery "from which this nation freed us?" It was the slavery into which this nation put us and held us for two hundred and fifty years. Can a man throw you into prison without cause in order to place you under a debt of gratitude to him for taking you out?

The editor of the Courier-News goes on to say:

> The Negro who tries to put himself on the level with white men socially is an enemy of the Negro race. The greatest men of that race have condemned those who are always finding fault because they cannot obtain service in hotels, restaurants and ice cream parlors patronized by the whites. It is the duty of these dissatisfied Negroes to open restaurants and ice cream parlors of their own and endeavor to conduct them better than any white man conducts his place of business.

We do not know from what part of the country the editor of the Courier-News hails, but his definition of "social equality" sounds very much as though it was made in Alabama or Mississippi. There is no more social equality in drinking ice cream soda in a public place than there is in riding in the same subway car. And where does this editor get his information that the greatest men of the race have condemned those who found fault because hotel and other public accommodations were refused to colored people?

His suggestion that Negroes should have their own hotels, theatres and other public places is impracticable. It would be impossible for the Negro or any other group in this country to duplicate the machinery of civilization. If a colored man is passing through Denver or Salt Lake City, is he to go without food and lodging because there are not enough Negroes in either of those cities to maintain a hotel or a restaurant? But even if the Negro could duplicate all of the machinery of civilization in the country and live his life separate and apart, would it be wise to have him do it? We are now trying to cut the hyphen out of our body politic, would it be wise to deliberately create another?

It is curious to note the amount of ego that goes with the attitude of the editor of the Courier-News on this question. He sits writing his little article shaming Negroes for wanting to associate with white people, not imagining for a moment that there are colored people who not only would not seek him for a social equal, but who probably might refuse to accept him as one. If he should be stopping at the Van-Astor hotel, and a colored man came in to register, the first thought to crop up in his mind would be, "Here is a Negro who wants to get into a hotel where I, a white man, and other white men are stopping," not knowing that what the Negro wants is something to eat and a place to sleep and that he is willing to pay for the best he can afford.

This ego is characteristic of all white people who talk like the editor of the Courier-News. They feel, when a Negro protests against discrimination and "Jim Crowism" that he is trying to get away from his race and associate with white people. When a self-respecting Negro so protests, the thought of merely associating with white people is the farthest from his mind; he is contending for a common democratic right which all other citizens of the country have, that of being accommodated in public places when he is clean, orderly and is able and willing to pay the price; or he is protesting against being forced to accept inferior service for the price of the best service, and he is especially resenting the badge of inferiority which being "Jim Crowed" places upon him.

This article of the Courier-News runs on for the length of a column, nearly all of it being a diatribe against Negroes who are seeking "social equality," meaning those who object to being "Jim Crowed" and shut out of theatres and hotels and restaurants and other public places where orderly conduct and the price are the only requisites exacted from other citizens. So it is not worth the while to quote any more of it.

We wish to say that there are many sound and solid reasons why the Negro should fight for his country, aside from the reasons that are altruistic and sentimental; but the editor of the Courier-News in using up a column of his more or less valuable space in answering the letter of E. R. failed to strike upon a single one.

The letter written to the Courier-News was lightweight, but the editor's article in answer to it did not weigh as much as the letter. His article is entirely apart from the mark.

The New York Age, June 29, 1918

W.E.B. Du Bois: Close Ranks

Since the spring of 1917, Du Bois had pronounced support for the war while continuing to denounce racial discrimination and violence. In June 1918 he met with his friend Joel Spingarn, a wealthy literary critic, educator, and the chairman of the NAACP board. Spingarn, then serving as a major in military intelligence, offered Du Bois a commission as an army captain and an assignment to a special intelligence bureau investigating racial problems. While considering the offer, Du Bois wrote this editorial, invoking black Americans to "forget our special grievances" for the duration of the war. His change of position and willingness to serve in the army drew intense criticism within the NAACP, and the offer of a military commission was withdrawn in late July.

———————

THIS IS the crisis of the world. For all the long years to come men will point to the year 1918 as the great Day of Decision, the day when the world decided whether it would submit to military despotism and an endless armed peace—if peace it could be called—or whether they would put down the menace of German militarism and inaugurate the United States of the World.

We of the colored race have no ordinary interest in the outcome. That which the German power represents today spells death to the aspirations of Negroes and all darker races for equality, freedom and democracy. Let us not hesitate. Let us, while this war lasts, forget our special grievances and close our ranks shoulder to shoulder with our own white fellow citizens and the allied nations that are fighting for democracy. We make no ordinary sacrifice, but we make it gladly and willingly with our eyes lifted to the hills.

The Crisis, July 1918

Hubert H. Harrison: Why Is the Red Cross?

Born in St. Croix in the Danish West Indies, Hubert Harrison moved to New York City in 1900. An accomplished writer and orator, he joined the Socialist Party but was suspended in 1914 for criticizing its policies toward black workers. In 1917 Harrison founded the Liberty League, an all-black political organization, and established its newspaper, *The Voice*, becoming a leading proponent of the militant "New Negro" movement.

THE RED CROSS, or Geneva Association, was the product of a Swiss infidel. He saw how cruel to man were those who loved God most—the Christians—and, out of his large humanity and loving kindness, he evolved an organization which should bring the charity of service to lessen the lurid horrors of Christian battlefields.

A love that rose above the love of country—the love of human kind: this was the proud principle of the Red Cross. Its nurses and its surgeons, stretcher-bearers and assistants were supposed to bring relief to those who were in pain, regardless of whether they were "friends" or "enemies." Discrimination was a word which did not exist for them: and it is not supposed to exist now even as against the wounded German aviator who has bombed a Red Cross hospital.

But, alack and alas! The splendid spirit of the Swiss infidel is seemingly too high for Christian race-prejudice to reach. Where he would not discriminate even against enemies, the American branch of his international society is discriminating against most loyal friends and willing helpers—when they are Negroes. Up to date the American Red Cross Society, which receives government aid and co-operation to help win the war, cannot cite the name of a single Negro woman as a nurse. True, it says that it has "enrolled" some. This we refuse to believe. But even if that were true, a nurse "enrolled" cannot save the life of any of our soldiers in France.

The Red Cross says that it wants to win the war. What war?

A white people's war, or America's and the world's? If this were a white people's war, as some seem to think, colored troops from Senegal, India, Egypt, America and the West Indies would have been kept out of it. But they were not, and we are driven to conclude that this is a world war. Then why doesn't the American Red Cross meet it in the spirit of the President—of world democracy? The cry goes up for nurses to save the lives of soldiers; yet here are thousands of Negro nurses whom the Red Cross won't accept. They must want to give Europe a "rotten" opinion of American democracy. For we may be sure that these things are known in Europe—even as our lynchings are. And anyone who would give Europe a "rotten" opinion of America at this time is no friend of America.

The American Red Cross must be compelled to do America's work in the spirit in which America has entered the war. There need be no biting of tongues: it must be compelled to forego Race Prejudice. If the N. A. A. C. P. were truly what it pretends instead of a National Association for the Advancement of Certain People, it would put its high-class lawyers on the job and bring the case into the United States courts. It would charge the American Red Cross with disloyalty to the war-aims of America. And if it does not (in spite of the money which it got from the "silent" protest parade and other moneys and legal talent at its disposal) then it will merit the name which one of its own members gave it—the National Association for the Acceptance of Color Proscription. Get busy, "friends of the colored people"! For we are not disposed to regard the camouflage of those who want nurses but do not want Negro nurses in any other light than that of Bret Harte's Truthful James:—

> Which I wish to remark—
>   And my language is plain—
> That for ways that are dark
>   And for tricks that are vain
> The Heathen Chinee is peculiar:
>   Which the same I am free to maintain.

The Voice, July 18, 1918

Ernest Hemingway to
His Family, July 21, 1918

After graduating from high school in 1917, in Oak Park, Illinois, Ernest Hemingway spent seven months writing for the *Kansas City Star*. Although the army rejected him because of defective vision, he wrote his sister Marcelline of the war, "I can't let a show like this go on without getting into it." Joining the Red Cross as an ambulance driver, Hemingway arrived in Italy in early June 1918 and volunteered to serve as a canteen worker, distributing chocolate and cigarettes to Italian soldiers on the front lines along the Piave River. On July 8, just thirteen days shy of his nineteenth birthday, he was severely wounded near Fossalta di Piave by shrapnel from an Austrian trench mortar projectile and was transported to the American Red Cross hospital in Milan.

———————

July 21.

Dear Folks—:

I suppose Brummy has written you all about my getting bunged up. So there isnt anything for me to say. I hope that the cable didnt worry you very much but Capt. Bates thought it was best that you hear from me first rather than the newspapers. You see I'm the first American wounded in Italy and I suppose the papers say something about it.

This is a peach of a hospital here and there are about 18 American nurses to take care of 4 patients. Everything is fine and I'm very comfortable and one of the best surgeons in Milan is looking after my wounds. There are a couple of pieces still in. One bullet in my knee that the X Ray showed. The surgeon, very wisely, after consultation, is going to wait for the wound in my right knee to become healed cleanly before operating. The bullet will then be rather encysted and he will make a clean cut and go in under the side of the knee cap. By allowing it to be completely healed first he thus avoids any danger of infection and stiff knee. That is wise dont you think Dad? He will also remove a bullet from my right foot at the same time. He will probably operate in about a week as the wound is healing cleanly and there is no infection. I had two shots of anti tetanus immediatley at the dressing station. All the other bullets and pieces of shell have been removed and all the wounds on my left leg are healing finely. My fingers are all cleared up and have the bandages off. There will be no permanent effects from any of the wounds as there are no bones shattered. Even in my knees. In both the left and right the bullets did not fracture the patella. One piece of shell about the size of a Timken roller bearing was in my left knee but it has been removed and the knee now moves perfectly and the wound is nearly healed. In the right knee the bullet went under the knee cap from the left side and didnt smash it a bit. By the time you get this letter the surgeon will have operated and It will be all healed. And I hope to be back driving in the mountains by the latter part of August. I have some fine photographs of the Piave and many other interesting pictures. Also a wonderful lot of souvenirs. I was all through the big battle and have Austrian carbines and ammunition, German and Austrian medals, officers automatic pistols, Boche helmets, about a dozen Bayonets, star shell pistols and knives and almost everything you can think of. The only limit to the amount of souvenirs I could have is what I could carry for there were so many dead Austrians and prisoners the ground was almost black with them. It was a great victory and showed the world what wonderful fighters the Italians.

I'll tell you all about everything when I get home for Christmas. It is awfully hot here now. I receive your letters regularly. Give my love to everybody and lots to all of you.

Ernie

Write to the Same address.

The medal that I have been recommended for and favourably voted on is a great honor of Italy and I am very proud to have been recommended for it. They were to present it to me at the other hospital in the field but I got away a day ahead of the time set for the presentation. Now they say it will occur in Milan.

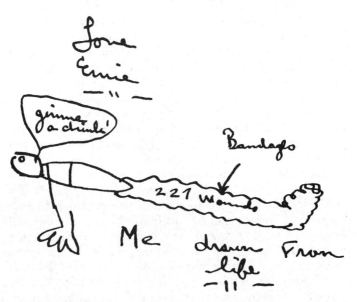

July 1918

Woodrow Wilson:
Statement on Lynching

Wilson considered improving race relations an evolutionary process. And so, while his administration had resegregated the federal workforce, he steadily welcomed black leaders throughout his two terms in the White House to discuss the plight of African Americans. In June 1918, four months after meeting with James Weldon Johnson and the NAACP delegation, he received a letter from Robert R. Moton, Booker T. Washington's successor as the principal of the Tuskegee Institute, who urged him to make a public statement against lynching. In light of the current situation, Wilson did so on July 26. The vast majority of the 373 lynching victims in the United States that the NAACP had recorded from 1913 to 1918 were black; but in 1918 a mob in Collinsville, Illinois, provided an exception when it hanged a white German American named Robert Prager for allegedly expressing opposition to the war.

––––––––––––

My Fellow Countrymen: I take the liberty of addressing you upon a subject which so vitally affects the honor of the Nation and the very character and integrity of our institutions that I trust you will think me justified in speaking very plainly about it.

I allude to the mob spirit which has recently here and there very frequently shown its head amongst us, not in any single region, but in many and widely separated parts of the country. There have been many lynchings, and every one of them has been a blow at the heart of ordered law and humane justice. No man who loves America, no man who really cares for her fame and honor and character, or who is truly loyal to her institutions, can justify mob action while the courts of justice are open and the governments of the States and the Nation are ready and able to do their duty. We are at this very moment fighting lawless passion. Germany has outlawed herself among the nations because she has disregarded the sacred obligations of law and has made lynchers of her armies. Lynchers emulate her disgraceful example. I, for my part, am anxious to see every community in America rise above that level with pride and a fixed resolution which no man or set of men can afford to despise.

We proudly claim to be the champions of democracy. If we really are, in deed and in truth, let us see to it that we do not discredit our own. I say plainly that every American who takes part in the action of a mob or gives it any sort of countenance is no true son of this great Democracy, but its betrayer, and does more to discredit her by that single disloyalty to her standards of law and of right than the words of her statesmen or the sacrifices of her heroic boys in the trenches can do to make suffering peoples believe her to be their savior. How shall we commend democracy to the acceptance of other peoples, if we disgrace our own by proving that it is, after all, no protection to the weak? Every mob contributes to German lies about the United States what her most gifted liars cannot improve upon by the way of calumny. They can at least say that such things cannot happen in Germany except in times of revolution, when law is swept away!

I therefore very earnestly and solemnly beg that the governors of all the States, the law officers of every community, and, above all, the men and women of every community in the United States, all who revere America and wish to keep her name without stain or reproach, will cooperate—not passively merely, but actively and watchfully—to make an end of this disgraceful evil. It cannot live where the community does not countenance it.

I have called upon the Nation to put its great energy into this war and it has responded—responded with a spirit and a genius for action that has thrilled the world. I now call upon it, upon its men and women everywhere, to see to it that its laws are kept inviolate, its fame untarnished. Let us show our utter contempt for the things that have made this war hideous among the wars of history by showing how those who love liberty and right and justice and are willing to lay down their lives for them upon foreign fields stand ready also to illustrate to all mankind their loyalty to the things at home which they wish to see established everywhere as a blessing and protection to the peoples who have never known the privileges of liberty and self-government. I can never accept any man as a champion of liberty either for ourselves or for the world who does not reverence and obey the laws of our own beloved land, whose laws we ourselves have made. He has adopted the standards of the enemies of his country, whom he affects to despise.

James Reese Europe:
On Patrol in No Man's Land

The composer, arranger, and conductor James Reese Europe pio-
neered early jazz and led his all-black Clef Club Orchestra in a
groundbreaking concert at Carnegie Hall in May 1912. Commissioned
as a first lieutenant in the 369th Infantry Regiment, a black National
Guard unit from New York known as the "Harlem Hellfighters,"
Europe served as both a company commander and the leader of the
regimental band. After being gassed in Champagne, he drew upon his
experiences of nighttime patrolling and composed this song in late
July 1918.

———————————

What's the time, nine, all in line,
Alright, boys, now take it slow
Are you ready? steady! very good, Eddy,
Over the top let's go
Quiet, sly it, else you'll start a riot,
Keep your proper distance, follow 'long
Cover, smother, and when you see me hover,
Obey my orders and you won't go wrong

There's a minnenwerfer coming, look out
Hear that roar, there's one more.
Stand fast, there's a Very Light
Don't gasp or they'll find you alright
Don't start to bombing with those hand grenades
There's a machine gun, Holy Spades
Alert, Gas, put on your masks
Adjust it correctly and hurry up fast
Drop, there's a rocket for the Boche Barrage,
Down hug the ground close as you can, don't stand,
Creep and crawl, follow me that's all
What do you hear, nothing near,
don't fear, all is clear,
That's the life of a stroll

when you take a patrol
Out in No Man's Land!
Ain't it grand?
Out in No Man's Land.

Shirley Millard: from I Saw Them Die

The Germans launched their last major offensive on July 15, attacking along the Marne east of Château-Thierry. This maneuver failed, and on July 18 the French and Americans took to the offensive, beginning an advance toward the Aisne that, within weeks, had cost the American forces 12,000 men killed, wounded, or missing. Shirley Millard wrote about the increase in American casualties.

———————

July 28th

Have not written for nearly two weeks. Today when I came up to our room to change my uniform, much soiled after working fourteen hours in the wards, I looked down from the big windows and could see the grounds—once more a sea of stretchers, a human carpet.

So many Americans. I hate to see them pouring in, yet I am proud of them. Such gallantry, such nerve, such pluck! Even the French nurses have remarked about it. Always: Thank you, for every little thing. And: How soon will I be able to go back to the line? And: Help him first, he has waited longer than I have.

I feel they are mine, every last one of them, and their downright grit makes me want to cry all over them. Now I know what real *nobility means.*

Am too sympathetic to make a good nurse. I want to explain to each man all about his wounds and reassure him, and tell him how fine the doctors are and that they will fix him up as good as new.

They seldom know what is the matter with them, but only that they are about to go under an anesthetic and that something is going to be done to them. Can't help thinking that if I were going to be operated on it would be an awfully important event and I would most certainly like to know something about it. So I try to tell them what the doctor will probably do, though more than half the time I don't know myself and I just make up something that sounds plausible and reassuring. They seem grateful and go into the surgery a little less bewildered.

Our efficient detachment of mind was shaken in those days. We were no longer compassionate sympathizers but active combatants. The war had come home to us.

Again the old excitement; the rush, the noise of guns and trembling of the earth from exploding shells. But this time it was different. This time the guns shook our blood; the shells exploded in our very hearts.

Here was a boy from Nebraska. I began unwrapping some sodden leggings from his stomach. He whispered weakly that he had been hit four days ago and nothing had been done to him as yet. In the huge wound was a seething mass of living writhing insects. I weakened for a moment. I thought I knew just about everything, but I had never seen this before. I beckoned to an orderly. He came and took one look.

"Maggots," he said. "I'll get you a can of ether. That kills them." At first I thought I couldn't do it, but I did. The orderly explained that this was a natural, even a healthy symptom. I watched the squirming mass wither and die under the ether. When I removed them I saw that the wound was clean and fresh. These strange little organisms, it appears, eat away the decay and prevent infection of the blood stream. I soon learned to welcome the uncovering of these horrifying creatures, for often the removal of bandages revealed the hideous and hopeless color of gangrene.

A boy from Idaho, a big broad boy, had his head all bound up and the tag around his neck, put on at a dressing station, said: "Eyes shot away and both feet gone." I talked to him and patted him on the shoulder, assuring him that everything would be all right now. He moaned through the bandages that his head was splitting with pain. I gave him morphine. Suddenly aware of the fact that he had other wounds, he asked: "Sa-ay! what's the matter with my legs?" Reaching down to feel his legs before I could stop him, he uttered a heartbreaking scream. I held his hands firmly until the drug I had given him took effect.

From *I Saw Them Die* (1936)

Hervey Allen: *from* Toward the Flame

A 1915 graduate of the University of Pennsylvania, Lieutenant Hervey Allen served in the 111th Infantry Regiment, 28th Division. His memoir *Toward the Flame*, published in 1926, described his regiment's actions from early July to mid-August 1918 as it advanced from the Marne to the Vesle. In his preface, Allen explained that the book developed from wartime letters and recollections written in 1919 "when memories were so strong as to be almost photographic." The final five chapters record his experiences on the Vesle in Fismes and Fismette from August 7 to 14, culminating in what Allen called "a picture of war, broken off when the film burned out."

CHAPTER XIV

INTO THE PIT

LATE THAT NIGHT the captain wakened me and told me to get the company ready, as we were going to move. The platoon leaders went down the trench, wakening the men with the help of the sergeants, and in a few moments the dark masses of the platoons could be dimly made out standing on the gleaming white road. Each platoon was provided with its own rockets, which, for the most part, none of us had the slightest idea how to use. No instruction was provided. That a red rocket was at that time the call for a barrage was the extent of our knowledge. It was pitch black, but in the velvet darkness the battalion began to move down the hill toward Fismes.

The road fell away quite rapidly from the plateau with a high bank on our left, screening us from the Germans and the valley, on the far side of which they lay. There were shelter holes and dugouts in places along the bank, but at the bottom we emerged into a deep side valley with a railroad track. A stream ran down this through Fismes and emptied into the Vesle beyond. The town itself lay on the flat between the hills and the river.

As we emerged onto the flat, we could look back at the

heights and see the machine guns spitting fire from the woods at the Germans on the other side of the river. There were shots coming back too. At one place, just off the road in a wood, the enemy's shells had fallen into the ammunition dump of our machine guns, and the ammunition was burning fiercely, making a bright glow and exploding like a lot of firecrackers. I think we must have been observed as we passed this fire, for they started to shell the road so as to make it very lively. Just at the foot of the hill, where the little stream flowed into the Vesle and emerged onto a flat, our engineers were repairing a bridge. "Fritz" had been gunning steadily for this, arousing with each shell a violent chattering from the nests of machine guns on our side of the valley. The engineers had not yet finished repairing the bridge, so there was only a narrow footpath over it as yet, and here the battalion halted in the dark. The major turned aside into a roofless ruin for a while. The whole place was redolent of gas.

By the light of the burning ammunition I saw a man's legs lying by the road, buttocks up. The whole upper part of the body had been taken off by a shell, and the two naked legs looked exactly like a giant frog's. Things started to happen here. I was talking to Charley Wright, the company artificer, when a spent rifle bullet hit him on the helmet right above the eyes. It glanced off after tearing the front rim from his helmet, and then bounced off mine. Just then the enemy started gunning for the woods in dead earnest.

A large number of shells passed right over our heads and burst immediately beyond—a few yards lower, and they would have cleaned the highway. Everybody at first lay flat. We crawled forward a few yards and gained the shelter of some stone piles and logs just off the road. The gas seemed like a fog, and we put on our masks. I lay there for several minutes. The explosion and red glare were terrific, but after a while I saw that no shells fell on the road. Taking heart at this, Sergeant Griffin and I got up and ran along it for a short distance. Small pieces of iron fragments rattled off us several times. A little way along the road I met Lieutenant Horner of "C" company.

"We must tell the major we can't lie here," I shouted.

"We're supposed to go into Fismes and relieve the 112th

Infantry," he replied. This was the first time I had heard what our mission was.

I told the captain I would go ahead and try to find our way and some shelter. None of us had any idea what lay on the other side of the little bridge. I ran along the road with Sergeant Griffin and found Lieutenant Horner again, who said he would go with us, so we headed for the bridge.

I must say that road was terrific. Four or five shells a minute were coming. There was always one in the air. These burst with an earth-rocking smash on the other side of the road, just on the far side of the railway embankment. On the "safe" side of the road were the prone figures of the men hugging the ground. Branches, stones, iron fragments, and all manner of débris was hurtling about us; trees were crashing, and over our heads the machine guns were firing in a frenzy of chattering rage.

We found the engineers working frantically at their bridge, an old stone approach that they were trying to repair with planks. I questioned the engineer officer in a series of shouts, and he gave us a guide to take us to the dugout of the major of the 112th, whose battalion was occupying the town. We crossed the bridge on one plank, which was all that was ready, and found ourselves immediately among the houses and on the paved street of a good-sized town.

Behind us was the pandemonium of the barrage and the hammers of the engineers working feverishly at the bridge, all of which echoed up the empty street, mingled with the crackle of roof slates, and the tiles and bricks over which we stumbled. Pressing on for about two blocks, we turned suddenly into the main street of the town.

The fronts of large and handsome houses, built wall to wall, looked blindly across at each other with rows of open doors and yawning windows, as far as the eye could reach. It was a city of the dead, only wakened by the noise of firing, the glare of strange lights, and the flicks of rifle fire here and there.

At our backs the street ran out into the country onto the usual white tree-lined road, down which, a few hundred yards beyond, a furious rifle fight was in progress. Some of our men were sniping diligently from a house near by. There were strange lulls at times when an appalling silence would settle down over everything.

We turned up another side street. At a place where it cut through a little hill between two walls of rock, the guide turned aside. Lifting up a blanket that revealed a gleam of light, we entered what had once been a big wine cellar, a cave in the rock, now being used as a command post dugout. By the yellow light of several guttering candles and a carefully shaded lantern a group of officers were dozing about a table on which lay a map and the remnants of a meal. Back in the shadows could be dimly seen the forms of the sleeping runners and scouts who were always so numerous at any headquarters. Everybody, of course, who had the slightest excuse, and some slackers, invariably crowded into such a place of safety. Among the crowd of runners and orderlies it was indeed hard to separate the sheep from the goats. Consequently the air in there was fetid, and so tainted with gas that everybody felt drowsy.

I reported myself to a captain of the 112th Infantry, who, it turned out, was commanding the battalion in Fismes at that time; told him where we were, and asked him what he wanted us to do.

I learned from him that the situation was something like this: Part of the 112th Infantry were in a little town across the river called Fismette, where they were directly in touch with the enemy, fighting day and night. Fismes itself was for the most part ours. Germans were thought still to be in some of the houses sniping, or scattered along the railroad near the river. Most of the captain's battalion was scattered through Fismes in the cellars, and there was a part of the 109th Machine Gun Battalion near the town hall. During the day, a more or less stealthy man hunt went on from house to house, with occasional brisk fights, while the enemy shelled the town constantly from the heights across the river, throwing shells down into Fismes, sometimes in a barrage and sometimes intermittently. There was scarcely any time when you could not hear one bursting somewhere, followed by the slide and crumbling-sound of brick and plaster or the tinkle of glass. Having occupied the town for so long himself, "Fritz" was disgustingly familiar with it, and knew all the best places to shell.

The captain told me our best plan would be to find some more or less safe cellars, bring our men in, and leave them there for the night; after which he would move out when he could. The men over the river in Fismette would have to be relieved the next night, as it was too late to attempt it now, only a few hours before dawn.

Lieutenant Horner and I both left on the run and began to hunt for some convenient places. Up the street a house was burning, and as it flared up from time to time, I could see the tower of the town hall stand out, and the fronts of whole lines of empty houses up the street. Then the shadows would swoop down and engulf all.

I crossed the street and ran through what was evidently the gate of a big house. There was a large garden stretching several hundred yards down to the river in which a wrecked automobile was standing, and in the rear of the house I came across a dome-shaped structure made of large cut stones, cement, and railroad rails; this I knew was a dugout. Over the door was a board with a four-leaf clover on it and "*Villa Bremen*" in German letters. This I saw next day. A flight of carefully winding stone steps led down into the dark cement cavern, into which opened a wooden door. Holding up a lighted match, I discovered numerous old mattresses lying around and the dim outline of a door beyond that led into the depths of a large cellar, judging by the cold draft. Place number one—this would do! Running out, I met Horner hurrying up the street. He had found a big cellar vault under a seminary for his men, and was in luck.

There was no time to lose. No time to consider whether or not some enemy might not still be lurking about. Our men were out there by the bridge under fire, and every minute might mean lives. The next place I hit was a big club or hotel with a huge white, wooden gate that swung in. One look there was enough to assure me that there was room for an army, and best of all, a spigot was running in the court, gushing freely. That would be a godsend. Horner and I came out of our second places about the same time, and meeting up with the rest of the party, we raced down the littered street toward the bridge, where I was relieved to see that the barrage had lifted. So many stray shells were falling here and there that it was not till we got quite near that we could be sure of this.

Just on the other side of the bridge I met Captain Law. "I have a fine place, captain," I cried. "Thank God!" he said fervently, and the men near by scrambled to their feet expectant of the move. It must have been ticklish work lying there doing nothing. Horner ran back to his company. I sent a runner to inform the major, and we moved off in single file over the bridge, cautioning the men to be as silent as they could. As it was, the ring of the iron hobnails on the littered stone pavement seemed to make enough noise to alarm all the Germans between Fismes and Berlin.

I showed the captain the dugout I had found, and while he posted one platoon there, in the cellar, I went up the street with the others to put them to bed in the big club which, as I expected, had an ample cave-like vaulted cellar underneath. Sometimes I think the cellars of France did as much to win the war as the generals.

We certainly felt elated on having got the men into Fismes with so little loss. A few of the men were wounded by the barrage along the road, which, had it fallen a little to the left, would have landed on the highway with results appalling to think of. Such are the fortunes of war. A few feet one way or another is the difference between life and death. Getting such snug and safe places for the night, we also considered fortunate.

When I returned to the "*Villa Bremen*," I found everybody preparing to turn in. One dim little candle was burning in the place, which was like a nice family tomb paved with mattresses. Beyond, in the dark cellar, the men could be heard stirring and clinking around from time to time, but most of them slept. It was very quiet down there. Even the sound of shells breaking in the street near by came only as dull thuds, shocks felt more than heard.

Our fortunate escape from the barrage, and the successful hunt for billets through the dark town, had so elated me that I remember boasting like a Turk about not seeing much to be afraid of in shell fire. I must really have made quite a cad of myself, as I remember some of the others, the poor captain particularly, who had had to lie still through all that rain of shells, looking at me rather disgustedly. My excitement and fatigue were beginning to tell. I actually plumped down on a mattress in the best corner, and when I accidentally put my feet on the captain, who had stretched out on the floor, I took his quiet remonstrance without feeling it. I had the best bed, too.

A few hours later, I woke up after a sound sleep and, seeing him so uncomfortable on the floor, insisted on his coming over onto the mattress, with an excess of remorse for my callousness that nearly overcame me. He shook me by the hand. I shall never get over putting my feet on him that night. He was not to live very long.

Next morning it was quite late when I got up. Of course, no light penetrated the dugout, and in the cellar the worn-out men slumbered on night and day.

A little salmon and bread for breakfast—food was getting scarce—then I sallied out into the intense sunlight and the ruined town of Fismes.

It was nearly quiet at the time, only once in a while the long drone of a shell would pass overhead followed by a smash far off among the labyrinth of deserted houses. Now and then from over the river came the crack of a rifle. Crossing a street warily, I descended several flights of stone steps into a subcellar where I found Lieutenant Horner with his company. We decided to take a little walk about the town, and find out where we were.

Walking up the street, we were very wary and hugged the houses closely. The first place we dropped into was the clubhouse where I had billeted two of our platoons in the cellar the night before. Not a soul was to be seen when I pushed in the big, white gate that led into the court. The hydrant was still gushing away, but a hail brought some of the men out, blinking in the sunlight. They had been rummaging and showed us the house.

It had been the home of some club or society. Fismes was a large and rich town, and the "club" was luxuriously furnished. The Germans had been living here. Sofas and chairs sat around in vacant-looking groups. Tapestries and dirty, torn hangings flapped from the walls, where all the mirrors were cracked. The clocks and frescoes were defaced and names and vile pictures scribbled on the walls. Plaster dust was stamped all over the carpets that were covered with torn books and trash and ripped up in some places. The rear of the clubhouse opened onto a garden. Instead of a porch there was a partly demolished sun parlor with little iron tables and chairs like a French café. These sat around looking most forlorn. There were some empty bottles and glasses on them, dusty and full of flies. At the foot of the garden was a barn. Through the cracks in the rear door of it there was the vista of a path leading down through the interior of a partly demolished and abandoned steel mill.

Beyond that lay the railroad, coal piles, and the sparkling river, then in flood. I established an observation post, and remembered that here was a short cut down this path to the river.

Across the street was a Roman Catholic seminary, a big building with wide, sweeping stairs and high ceilings. Here, too, had been a German billet. There was a hodgepodge of cast-off clothes and junk in the dormitories, where the Germans had slept in the rows of iron beds. We went up into the garret to get a view of the town. From the front windows we had a view of the handsome *Hôtel de Ville* with its clock tower, and the main square, very badly wrecked. The other windows showed us nothing but acres of slate roofs, with a cone-shaped hill in the distance. But the garret was quite interesting on account of its contents. Horner went down and left me alone for a while.

There was a poor little foot-organ that had been played to death, boxes of tinsel cards, plaster images of the saints, a portable altar, prayer books, school texts, vestments, a little English-French dictionary, which I took, and queer pious pictures. Some German soldier had come up there and changed his shoes, leaving the old worn-out boots with no toes standing side by side as mute witnesses of his visit. In one corner we found a small print shop with type already set, and the proof sheets of some strange little religious journal scattered about. How utterly futile it all seemed. The Virgin's heart, it seems, was yearning over the boys in the seminary who said their prayers to her. I added a footnote in penciled English about Mars. I wonder who read it:

> "*The Virgin is plucking asphodels in Heaven with*
> *little Saint John and the angels;*
> *Mars is walking the meadows of France, cutting*
> *the throats of God's sheep;*
> *The laughter of children has departed from this*
> *town. It is bereft forever.*"

A German printer had come in and set something in German. The grinning, inked type stood fixed like tiny black teeth in the sheet which would never be finished. There were also piles and piles of wreaths of tinsel and paper flowers. Then I came downstairs and found some of our men stamping about. One platoon of "C" company was in the cellar.

While the place was so quiet, I felt determined to see the town, partly from curiosity and partly from a desire to know my way about the place in case of future necessity. I left Horner standing on the corner near the town hall, and made toward the cone-shaped hill I had seen from the garret windows of the seminary.

Imagine your own home town without a single soul in it, wrecked after a great storm, and partly burned, with all the evidences of the familiar activities of everyday life about, but that life and movement cut off suddenly, turned off like a light, and you will have a little idea of Fismes.

The looted stores stood gaping vacantly around the main square, where I met part of the machine gun battalion. They had their gun set up about halfway down a long hall that commanded a view of the street leading to the bridge. Rocks and earth were piled up as a sort of breastwork on the floor before it, and the ammunition was in the library. A corporal here warned me about the streets. One corner was bad for snipers. I could see it from the window upstairs and there was a dead runner lying there with the red band on his arm.

We dodged across the street to the town hall. This was a lovely white stone *Hôtel de Ville* with a mansard roof. There was a big wooden sign over the door in German, proclaiming it the Zone Kommandator's headquarters. The inside was badly wrecked. A mess of German and French town records lay all over the place. I found a chart there showing a German plan of defense for Fismes and several maps of the town which I rolled up for our major. There were also several recent issues of German magazines.* *Die Woche*, and others. There was indeed a great deal of interesting German material. Among other things I picked up a postcard with the King of Saxony peering out between draped flags up in one corner, and below H. M., a rural scene with two little children hand in hand looking at a field full of cows. Underneath it said, "Little ones, do without milk so we can keep our colonies." How that must have appealed to the children!

I did not linger around the town hall very long as they were shelling that region pretty often, but headed back into some of

---

*July, 1918, and a few months earlier.

the smaller streets, and edged over toward the hill, not so far off as I had thought.

Passing through the utterly empty streets was an eery experience. At one corner a German gunner lay dead by his machine gun. I think he had been hit by a big shell fragment, for his head was kicked in like a rotten pumpkin. He was short and thickset, a Bavarian, I think, with warts on his hands. Beside him was a gummy piece of bread made out of brown bran. Near by lay a number of empty cartridges, probably the last he had fired. The tremendously heavy boots and the iron helmet always lent the Germans a peculiarly brutal aspect. This man had turned the same dull gray as his coat, he had been dead so long. Poor devil, his interest in colonies had lapsed.

I felt pretty certain that that part of Fismes was no longer occupied by the enemy as it was too far back from the river, so I took a good many short cuts through the little lanes and finally, after crossing a spur of the railroad, I came out directly behind my little hill where there were several coal piles. The "Boche" had some curious shallow trenches dug on this elevation and there were several enormous shell craters near the top. This must at one time have been an observation station. I crawled when I got near the summit and, lying on my stomach, had an excellent view over the town. Its roofs stretched away from me to the bridge, beyond which lay the hillside and country on the other side of the Vesle. That was "Hunland" I was looking at over there.

A railroad ran along the river's edge, and there was a badly damaged stone bridge over the Vesle, with a hamlet on the far side stretching along a road paralleling the stream. Above all this rose the steep hillside occupied by the enemy, with draws here and there leading back to a sort of tableland behind, green with orchards and farms, but crossed now and then by a road. There was not a soul to be seen. Only now and then came a "boom," and a great geyser of mud and water shot up into the air beside the bridge.

I lay and examined the hill carefully and after a while saw a man walking across a field. He came out of a clump of bushes, passed on down a path, moved over a field till he struck a road—up this he walked and disappeared. He was a German and looked like a pigmy over there on the great lone hill. That was all I saw of the enemy, although I watched for nearly an hour.

On the way back I noticed several very deep dugouts. The door of the house instead of opening into the hall had been made to open directly down a steep stairway that descended some thirty or forty feet. I think these had been built by the French inhabitants, as Fismes had been more or less under fire since the early days of the war. Alan Seeger speaks about that in his letters in 1914.

I found the major sheltered in the house right across the street from the "*Villa Bremen*," and it was not long before a dressing station was established in the house above our dugout. The major looked over my town maps, but said he had a better one. By that time it was getting on toward noon, and the Germans began to shell the town violently, as they must have seen a lot of our men moving about the streets. The engineers had repaired the little bridge and an ambulance drove into the town and stopped before the door of the dressing station as if it were driving up to a house at home. Then two or three big shells went off in the house across the road and another fell directly into the street with a tremendous detonation. The major went into the cellar and I dodged across into the "*Villa Bremen*." I found that the Germans shelled our garden pretty often on account of the broken automobile there and because the ambulances could be seen coming up to "our door."

I found our cellar next to the dugout full of cases of potato-masher bombs and barrels of signal-lights which "Fritz" had left. These made us very uncomfortable. If a shell had come through the roof into that cellar, we would all have gone to glory in a burst of fireworks. During the lulls the men therefore set these out in the garden, or shoved them into the street through the cellar windows. I went upstairs to take a shave while this was being done.

The house had evidently belonged to a well-to-do man, who had conducted some kind of an agricultural league or society, as near as I could make out. It was pitiable to see the desks and beautifully kept records and accounts all forced open and wasted around. In the office was a set of maps showing the growth of Paris from Roman times to the Third Empire. It was made from old prints and quaintly interesting. Private letters lay around in piles or strewn on the floor. To dip into these was always like tasting forbidden sweets or peeping in over a

stranger's transom. "Before the war letters"—what a serene
world that seemed now, to be sure: "*Cher Adolph: Le printemps
est venu ici, nous*" . . . ri*dic*ulous!

I tried to shave at the kitchen sink; the water still ran in Fismes although somewhat feebly. There was the remains of the
last meal the German orderly had prepared, yellow mayonnaise
dressing and lettuce leaves in a pile of dirty plates. Outside was
a glimpse of the old broken automobile in the yard, and the
men carrying crates of bombs out of the cellar. Beyond was a
vista down to the river bank.

I was only halfway through the shave when I heard a shell
that I knew was coming very near. It burst in the yard and
started the bombs going. There was a frightful series of explosions, during which I returned to the cellar, lather and all. Our
dugout was proof against even a direct hit. I spent most of the
rest of the day in it, or in the cellar with the men. Food was
already very scarce. The road into the town was being shelled
so skillfully as to make it difficult for mess details to get in or
out. We sent one detail, but it was impossible to spare a good
leader at the time, so it came back. I could not spare the sergeants for mess details. The 112th had left that morning, all
but the men across the river in Fismette, whom we found it
impossible to relieve that day.

Intense firing could be heard over there from time to time.

The rumor here was that when we drove the enemy over the
hill on the other side of the Vesle, we were to go back for a
rest. "The general had said so"—as usual just what general was
not specified. At any rate we were to make an attack, and the
captain was going with the major next morning to make a reconnaissance. We went to sleep early with very little supper. It
seemed already as if we had been in Fismes a great many days.

CHAPTER XV

A WILD DAY

AFTER THE *strafing* of the day before, the major moved his
headquarters to the cave where I had first found the captain of
the 112th on the night we entered Fismes. I found a short cut
to it from our own hole in the ground through several

connecting gardens and down a little pair of steps. In the largest of these gardens there were one or two graves of men of the 110th U. S. Infantry. The short cut kept us off the streets away from snipers and shells.

That morning the major and the captain, with some of the other company commanders, left on the reconnaissance, going down the river to an old tannery a mile or so away. A lot of the men were ordered out on detail to carry wounded back from Fismette. This left me, with the mess details that were already out, about thirty men altogether. Some were billeted in the "*Villa Bremen*," and some in the cellar at the "club." There was a great deal of firing all morning over in Fismette, and enemy planes came over Fismes several times, after which a bombardment more or less intense would follow.

The German artillery back among the hills must have had a good time shelling their old homes. Our house was gunned for persistently on account of the dressing station being there, and about one o'clock they made a direct hit on the dugout. Several of us were sitting around smoking on the mattresses, when there was a noise and a skull-cracking jar that almost stunned us. It was hard to think for a minute or so afterwards. Our ears were so numbed that everything seemed very silent for some time. Everybody cowered down; there was the trickle of dirt on us from the ceiling, and dust in the air. But the tremendously thick stone, cement, and iron rails still held. Only a few of the outer layers were dislodged although it was a 6-inch shell.

We kept pretty "close" after that for some time. I opened a precious tin of beef, and we were just going to eat it when some one opened the door and called down. It was very silent in the dugout, but as soon as any one opened the door there came down the stairs a tremendous din of firing, machine guns chattering, the crack of rifles, and the smash of shells booming among the houses. It was the major at the door.

"The Germans are making a counter attack!" cried he, "get the men out, and in line!" I left the top sergeant tumbling the men out of our cellar, while I ran up the street to the "club," where part of another platoon was billeted. Both the major and the adjutant kept begging me, almost beseeching me, to hurry. I supposed, of course, that the Germans had penetrated the town again.

A very few moments sufficed to get the men together at the "club." The sergeants exerted themselves to the utmost, hauling men out of the dark cellars and getting the equipment on them like harnessing fire horses. As soon as we were sure we had the cellar clear, we started on a run for the "*Villa Bremen*," where I found the rest of the men waiting in the garden. These were tag ends of all the platoons, as the mess details, the men detailed to carry wounded, and those detached to battalion headquarters had left us with a very small remnant of our three-platoon company, already small to begin with.

With what non-coms I had, we formed the men rapidly into squads and made on a run for the lower part of the garden. There we crawled through a fence and went into skirmish line, deploying in a field that led straight down to the river and the railroad track. On our right was the old steel mill and the rear of the houses that faced on the street going down to the bridge. On our left, near the river, was a big factory of some kind. I took all this in at a glance. The excitement photographed it forever on my retina. Danger makes one live intensely.

It was our intention to take up a position along the river, using the railway embankment as a trench to resist the enemy should they attempt to cross the stream. I instructed the first sergeant, who had about half the men, to move over into the factory on the left as we advanced. After taking a few seconds to get the automatic rifle teams* and the skirmish line properly disposed, we started forward on the double.

The sergeant led his men off to the left, while we made straight for the river, a stretch of about two hundred yards. About halfway the enemy turned his machine guns on us. The air suddenly seemed to be alive with a swarm of vicious wasps and I saw the dust cut up all about our feet. There were one or two cries, but we were moving too fast to find out who it was that had been hit. I thought the fire was coming from behind a huge coal pile directly in front of us and led the way straight for it. We were all greatly bewildered and the men bunched. There was a dreadful second or two when I could not get them started toward the pile. Then Sergeant Griffin jumped out and started with me, and the rest closed in with

*These men were armed with the French *Chauchat* automatic rifle.

their bayonets. We came onto the pile with a fierce rush. There was nothing there!

I got the platoon sheltered behind it and looked about me. About fifty yards back were three or four quiet bundles that had been men a few seconds before. I watched them from time to time, but there was no more movement. They were dead, not wounded. That coal pile was about thirty feet high, made of brickets and slack which stopped shells excellently. It stretched along the railroad track for some seventy-five feet or so. Just behind us was a very deep hole, a little railroad switchman's house, the upper part of which was glass, and a long, low dugout, like an Eskimo's igloo, that was capable of sheltering twenty or thirty men.

The air was still full of the vicious *ttt-ang* of bullets over our heads, and, of course, the Germans had seen us take shelter behind the coal. The machine gun fire which had caught us came from guns across the river, high up on the hillside almost a mile away. There was no attack on at all. Everything was quieting down, but we were in such a position that we would have to wait till dark to get back to the town. To move back in any numbers meant to be shot up again.

I sent a runner back to the captain with a sketch of our position and got one of the men to crawl over to Sergeant Davidson in the factory telling him where we were and our plans. About an hour later the runner to the captain returned, having crept through the steel mill and along the railroad track. The enemy sniped at us continually. To put one's helmet over the top of the pile was to draw bullets instantly. We saw some of our men attacking a house on the other side of the river. Several of them were brought down and Sergeant Griffin located a German sniper who was standing back in a room out of our fellows' line of sight calmly firing at them. Griffin took a rifle and after long and careful aim from the side of the coal pile brought the German down. He hung down out of the window. Our men on the other side instantly closed in on the house which was near the bridgehead in Fismette.

Our own position was absurd. The river in front of us was too deep to be crossed in force, and the little footbridge was nearly wrecked. There was no counter attack. If there ever had been any, it was across the river in Fismette, and it had now subsided. We were simply caught in the open space between the town and the river and had to wait till dark, keeping behind the coal pile. In the meantime I shifted all the men I could move back into the dugout on the other side of the ditch, and put the rest of the men in the ditch where I crawled myself. This was simply a rather deep cut worn by the rainwater where it had run down to a little drainage culvert under the tracks. It was well we moved there.

All the activity the Germans had seen on our side of the river, crossing the fields in skirmish order, etc., had alarmed them. I think they must have thought an attack was preparing on *our* part, for just about twilight they poured a barrage along the river front and into the town. In the waning light we sat huddled in the ditch while the wailing shells came over.

An experience of that kind can never be described. Death is very near. There is a constant howling shuddering the air, and shells were dropping everywhere about us. I expected a direct hit every minute, but the coal pile saved us. It mercifully cut off the shells just in the angle of their drop. Then some shrapnel came over. One of our men, a big Montenegrin, who had been wounded by a machine gun bullet in the arm during the futile rush on the coal pile, was hit by shrapnel fragments in the other arm, while several of the men got other wounds in various places. Slivers and rocks rattled off our tin hats constantly. Finally one lad, who had crawled halfway into the drain partly to shelter his body, got a sickening shrapnel cut in the leg. We had a hard time to stop the hemorrhage, the blood spurted all over us; naturally enough, he was terrorized. Jack, the Montenegrin, was as brave as he could be and sat with set jaw. He must have been in extreme pain.

The roar of the explosions about us was almost continuous. The air was full of peculiar black smoke, dust, débris, and the stifling odor of high explosive, luckily no gas. During one of the short lulls we saw some of our men running along the railroad track like figures in a fog. These were some of the lads the first sergeant had led to the factory. They had been shelled out of that, and came scudding through the haze and dust like birds in a storm, plunging down into our little ditch and filling it to the point of crowding. I had to take stern measures here to make place for all. Some of them we shouted to, or they would never have seen us. I shall never forget how weird and weak our voices sounded in that great uproar. One or two of those who had been in the factory were wounded too. They lay quiet and shook through the rest of the barrage which followed. About dark it let up with an occasional shell howling now and then, but these finally died away, leaving a heavy silence. I waited till I was sure that it was over and then sent the men back by twos and threes, getting the wounded out first. Through the darkness, shaking and quivering, we sneaked back to the ghostly, white town.

The men who had been killed had had their lives wasted after a certain manner. Boys playing Indian would have known enough to stick to the houses if there *had been* an attack. But there is an aphorism about the reticence of dead men who are the only competent witnesses to this kind of fooling.

CHAPTER XVI

OVER THE BRIDGE

ONE CAN well imagine that after the experience of the afternoon we were pretty well fagged out mentally and physically, so that when the captain told me we were to cross the bridge that night into Fismette, relieve the 112th there, and make an attack, I was not exactly enthusiastic.

Nothing was said to the men. There is no use worrying soldiers in advance. Somehow, I could not fully realize that after the miracle of coming through unharmed that afternoon, the whole process would have to be repeated. One always felt subconsciously, "Surely, surely, this is enough!" Then we were tired, very tired, so I lay down on one of the mattresses and slept—more than slept—I died for a few hours.

About two o'clock I wakened to find the captain shaking me in the dim yellow light of one candle burning without a flicker in the calm and silence of the dugout. The feeling that we were going into battle was so distasteful and so strong that it was like mental indigestion. One felt weak, and I realized that the only thing to do was to get moving and doing something quickly. The captain was telling me the plans.

We were to cross the bridge into Fismette, march down the

river about a mile to an old Tannery, where we were to join
hands with our second battalion, and then move up the hill in
attack.

"Get the men ready," said the captain. "Issue extra ammunition and bombs."

There was no ration to issue. Our mess detail had failed to
get through to the ration dump that afternoon for the second
time. We knew that there was still some of the emergency, or
"iron ration," as it was called, left among the men, although
many must have eaten much of this during the hungry time of
the last three or four days.

The emergency ration consisted of two or three little red
cans full of corned beef, known as "monkey meat," and hard
crackers in long pasteboard boxes, the hard bread, or "hardtack," of fame. Sometimes we got the French hard bread that
was like a round rusk and was issued loose. All this the men
were not supposed to eat without a direct order, but under
actual conditions, with the companies scattered about in cellars, very hungry, and in no fear of inspections, it was almost
impossible to prevent nibbling. One can scarcely court-martial
a man on the firing line for eating a cracker after having gone
without food for many hours. It takes a professional martinet
to punish a man for that.

I went into the adjoining cellar and wakened the top sergeant, who in a few minutes had the men stirring. They were
to come up the street to the "club" and rendezvous with the
rest of the platoons there. I learned that the captain would
really be in charge of the battalion, as the major did not intend
to accompany us in the attack. He was to remain in his command post in Fismes.

As I ran up the street to the club, I could hear the din of the
firing in Fismette, and see the white glare made by the German
flares. Getting the men out of the huge, dark cellar was not
easy. They were all worn out and kept dropping off to sleep
again. At last we got them lined up in the court and started to
issue ammunition and grenades. The excitement now swept
me along so I was going strong. Getting the grenades open
was difficult as they were in wooden boxes tightly screwed
down. We split these with our bayonets and found inside the
deadly pear-shaped objects. These were French *citron grenades*

with a tin cylinder at one end which you pulled off, exposing a spring and plunger. The plunger, when struck on your helmet or any convenient object, set off the grenade, the explosion following five or six seconds later. The men had been taught in grenade school, but I made sure they all knew how to operate these.

Then we took our precious rockets, now much the worse for wear, looking like a leftover from last Fourth of July. I begged the ammunition officer for some rifle grenades, but none were issued. Most of the men had thrown away their *tromblones** anyway. I found this often happened in other commands. In the darkness the court seemed to swarm with the men. As they filed out the gate the seeming confusion died down and each man received his grenade. That seemed to sober them. It looked like business. At the last, two or three stragglers ran up the steps from the cellar followed by the sergeants, who had done their best to turn everybody out. Despite this, a few remained, some asleep, and some slackers, well-hidden in the long vaulted cellar. There was no time to hunt through this. Some men of the machine gun battalions were also sleeping down there. Our little three-platoon company was down to one hundred and twenty men that night. We led the column.

I found the captain waiting in the street until the platoons came out of the gate. He was impatient at the time we had taken to fall in, which doubtless seemed long to him waiting there in suspense. We moved off down the street in single file, hugging the side of the houses to avoid being seen when the flares went up. I could hear the shuffle and crackle of the men's feet among the loose slate and débris, while the long caterpillar of "the relief" wound around the corner at the city hall and started down toward the bridge. As we got near the bridge, where flares went up from time to time, the whole stealthy line would stop, lost in the waning, flickering, monstrous shadows cast by the Véry lights that floated in a string of little parachutes for a few seconds and then drifted to earth, to quench themselves in a sea of ink. Then darkness shut down like a lid. There were no orders needed when to halt; the men did it by

---

*Funnel-shaped caps fitted on the end of a rifle from which the grenade was thrown by shooting the gun.

instinct, the old instinct that keeps the rabbit still even when the hound comes sniffing near. The Germans were very close.

There was a halt for a minute or two at the bridge before we left the shelter of the last house. This, in order to see that the column was well "closed up." Then we started over, making a tremendous noise it seemed.

At the end of the town there was the flash and crackle of rifle fire. The Germans had been bursting shells on the bridge for several days and the stone above the arch had in one place been blown through, making an oval dip about the middle of the bridge with half of the roadway blown away, showing the river underneath. Big stones from the coping lay scattered about on the top of the bridge itself, and in one place only was there a section about two feet wide on which to cross. The river below was a tangle of débris, a snarl of old wire. The mud banks were splashed and pitted with shell-holes where the mud geysers had spouted over everything when the shells lit. Over this bridge we started, hoping fervently the enemy machine gunners would not see us. About fifty yards up the road, on the other side, some of our men in a ruin were fighting the Germans across the street in another house. The firing through windows and from between cracks in the walls lit the night fitfully.

The captain crossed first, and turned to the left on the other side followed by the men in file. We went through a gutted house and out into the village street beyond. I stood at the bridge, keeping the men closed up until our last platoon was over, and I saw "A" company following. As the captain turned to the left, I heard two or three rifle cracks but paid no attention to them at the time. As soon as the company was over I hastened to catch up with him again.

But when I turned the corner into the single lonely street of Fismette, I found three or four of our lads gathered about the body of one of our own men. It was Charley Wright, from whose helmet the spent bullet had glanced when we came into Fismes. He had been shot by one of our own men, having for some reason or other stepped out into the street between the houses where the fighting had been going on. He was certainly dead. It seemed tremendously futile.

I ran on down the street past our own men, now halted and

hugging the houses closely, till I came to the head of the column. The captain was standing shouting at an officer of the 112th. The din ahead was tremendous. About a square away a trench mortar shell was falling every fifteen seconds.

We were, as you may remember, supposed to move on down the river a mile and join hands with the second battalion at the Tannery, to make an attack. The orders, of course, had been written by some one looking at a map, and typed in a comfortable billet some twenty or thirty kilometers in the rear.

I heard the lieutenant of the 112th roar, "Mile! nothing! You can only go another block. We have only half the town; 'Fritz' owns the rest. The Prussian Guard is right across the street." His remarks were punctuated by the rocking explosions of the trench mortar shells. In the gray light I looked about me.

We were in a straight village street packed solid with houses on either side. The back doors of one line of houses opened out onto a field that stretched on a gentle slope about two hundred yards down to the river. From the back yards of the buildings on the other side of the street rose a steep hill. The Germans were up there somewhere. Ahead was a cross street where there was the almost constant flash of mortar shells. A whole battery was playing on it from the heights above. There was only one thing to do, occupy all the town that we could, and hold it. The 112th man was too impatient to leave to give us much information. I didn't blame him. I wished he were relieving us.

The captain and I went with him along the street for another block, and at the end of this, a little way back from the street crossing, was a low half breastwork, half barricade of barrels, furniture, and big stones across the street. Several of the 112th were lying behind this, firing up the street. I caught a glimpse of some skulking gray figures up there in the doorways. We turned aside into a house, went upstairs and looked out of the rear windows.

It was very early dawn, almost dark yet, and in the dust drifting back from the shell bursts we could see very little. Right below our window there was the beginning of a thin line of our men that stretched at right angles to the village street almost down to the river. Some were in shell-holes, and others in little pits that they had dug. In the obscurity there was only

the dim outline of the prone figures, but from them, and beyond into the darkness, sprang out the stabbing jets from the
rifles and the flash, flash, flash from the automatics.

We could see nothing of the Germans, but by now there was
the constant shuddering of shells passing overhead and the
crash where they burst in great columns of water and mud
down at the bridge. The red flash of one would light up the
spurts of those already exploding. By this time, though, our
men were all over the bridge. We stood there only a few seconds watching, awed by the tremendousness of the spectacle,
but, I remember, quite calm. That it was impossible to push
on to the Tannery was too evident to be even discussed.

"What do you think we had better do?" I asked the captain.
I was thinking of an attack by the Germans from the rear hillside and pointed this possibility out to him.

He ordered me to lead the first two platoons up the hill,
back of the houses on the other side of the street, and take the
best position I could find. I was also to relieve the men of the
112th that we saw from the window with our third platoon, all
that we had in Company "B." This meant simply that at the
barricade two platoons turned to the right up the hill on one
side of the street, and one platoon to the left down toward the
river. The captain himself went back to instruct the other
company commanders of the change in plans.

I lost no time, but dodged across the street and through one
of the half-ruined houses on the other side. There was a long
hall, but the back door opened on a garden with high walls
and a barn between it and the cross street, so we were hidden.
The garden was very steep, going up the hill about fifty yards
to a wall with some scraggly trees along it that seemed to extend along all the back yards of the village, parallel with the
street. To jump back into the street and beckon the men
toward me was the work of a few seconds only.

Glendenning led the way, a tower of strength in time of
need as usual. I scarcely had to say anything to him. He took in
the plan of taking up position behind the wall at a glance. I
had to stay in the doorway to turn the third platoon the opposite way when it came up. It was in charge of a young lieutenant
of the 77th Division who had just joined us. I forget his name.
He was a little chap, but one of the bravest, gamest, little

fellows that ever lived, and he handled his men like a veteran. I told him what his position was to be and saw some of our men lie down beside the 112th at the barricade across the street. Just then the captain joined me. As we went down the long hall to the garden, I saw a picture on the wall by the flash of a shell that lit in the garden ahead. A lot of plaster fell behind us.

We ran up the garden as fast as we could, for the shell had knocked part of a barn down. The ascent was very steep at the back. The last of the men were just scrambling up this when another shell lit in the barn again right behind us. After that they continued to fall there for some time.

It was a very near thing. The Germans must have seen us passing there. They evidently had wonderful *liaison* with their trench mortars to switch the fire so quickly. The captain went right up to the wall and told me to work down to the right and see if we were connecting with "C" company there. It was the last time I ever saw him.

The wall was only about knee-high in places, sometimes only a few stones for quite a stretch. Behind this our men lay firing at nothing. From somewhere was coming a perfect hail of machine gun bullets, mostly over our heads, but the worst of it was that some of it was coming from the flanks. We were beautifully enfiladed, probably by some guns away up on the hills above us a mile away. In the darkness this could not have been foreseen. It was plain right away that to keep the men in line along that wall was suicidal, but, of course, I could do nothing as I was not in command. I tried to stop the men from firing at nothing as I went along, but control was out of the question. One had to hug the ground close, backing down the slope a little in order to crawl toward the right. In a little hollow I came across a group. Lieutenant Glendenning and one or two sergeants were stooping over Lieutenant Larned, another of the 77th officers. He had been shot in the throat and was choking in his own blood. He lay quiet but was still alive. There was nothing we could do. I spoke to him, but he shook his head. Then I told Glendenning where I was going, and crawled on. It was the last time I ever saw *him* alive.

When I finally reached the left flank of our company line I found the wall had gaps in it here and there. Through these the machine gun barrage poured, striking the roofs of the houses at the bottom of the garden. The slate slithered off like scales. Behind one clump of rocks and stones was a squad of our men firing at a haystack, while in a sort of hollow of the hill, and just rising above its crest, was the roof mass of another hamlet. I felt sure some of the fire must be coming from there. The men said there was a machine gun in the haystack. Away to the left was a half-burnt house. There was barbed wire about it. The rest was just orchards and fields. Not a sign of any living thing. Out of this apparent void was coming the deadly hail that was killing us. Here and there along the wall I saw men tearing open their first-aid packages. That something must be done was evident. A change of position would have to be made, or there would be no one to change.

Just then I saw the men getting up from the left all along the line, waver a minute and then move forward.

I motioned forward to the line ahead of me and jumped up with them leading out into the fields up the hill. The machine guns were like a hundred riveters going all at once, such a chattering I never heard. Just where we were there was a little draw in the hill which seems to have saved us. At that part of the line we advanced about fifty yards, I judged. Looking back, I saw the rest of the line returning. There was absolutely no place to advance to. It was a brave but senseless attack. Some of the men lay down and fired where they were. I think I took about six men back with me behind the wall in my section of the line. Most of those who lay out in the fields were killed, but a few crawled back that night. The captain was killed in this attack, but I did not know that until hours later. He had ordered it.

It was so evident that another position would have to be taken up quickly that I determined to find Lieutenant Horner of "C" company and make arrangements with him, captain or no captain. It was no longer a question of waiting for orders but of holding the town. Accordingly, I told one of the sergeants of "C" company where I was going, and gave him strict orders to hold until he got word to move. I then crawled down a path between the houses to the street. If it was bad by the wall, it was worse in the street. A stream of machine gun bullets was racing past. It sounded like sawing. I crawled along close to the houses where Lieutenant Glendenning was afterwards killed, and got across the street by a rain ditch. By this time crawling like a turtle seemed to be the most natural form of movement in the world. Any other method I could not even think of. I met Horner with one runner moving along in the rear of the houses evidently trying to pick a new and more sheltered position. We held a very hasty but very serious consultation.

Comparing notes, it was perfectly evident that there could no longer be any question of attack, and that if we did not receive reënforcements *and ammunition* and get the help of a barrage on the hillside to clean the enemy out, we should not long be able to hold the town. Both of us felt that a message could not explain the situation which had already been so utterly misunderstood on the other side of the river. If an officer could get across, it might be made clear and the coördinates could be given for the barrage. It would not do to trust that to an enlisted man. Horner could not swim, so it was up to me.

I left a message for the captain, telling him what I was going to try to do. Horner shook hands, wished me good luck, and I started.

CHAPTER XVII

OVER THE RIVER AGAIN

IT HAD been my intention at first to cross by the bridge, but one look at the barrage falling there marked it off the slate of possibilities. There was a barrage all along the river front, but especially heavy at the bridge. The shells arriving there and along the stream were very large ones, throwing up immense fountains of liquid mud and exploding in the water with a peculiar muffled crack and roar. As I watched them I nearly turned back; it seemed such a futile task. Only a fool would have dashed out.

A little study showed that away from the bridge there were considerable intervals of time between shells, and that they were pretty well scattered. I also noted a small drainage ditch across the field running down to the river. Along this was the path which led to the ruined wooden footbridge, now floating level with the water and partly shot away. I could see the tangle of it from Fismette. Through the barrage haze Fismes looked miles away, the white houses standing out more plainly in the sun.

The ditch was the only thing that could enable one to reach the river. My body lay in the hollow, so the machine gun barrage went over me. . . .

It took me about half an hour to crawl to the river. I had to put my mask on at the last, as the mustard gas was strong in the little hollow in which I lay. My hands were smarting. Some of the shells brought my heart into my mouth; lying there waiting for them was intolerable. I was sure I was going to be blown to pieces. The river was very nearly in flood and so there was no bank, the field gradually getting soggy and swampy till it sloped out into the water. There was a lot of submerged barbed wire that made going ahead very painful and slow. I had, of course, to throw away my mask as it got full of water. My pistol went also. It was too heavy to risk.

Once in the water, I worked under the single board of the footbridge, shifting along hand over hand, which took me halfway across. There I struck out, plunging in a few strokes to the other side and working through the wire.* Swimming with shoes was not so difficult as I had thought, but the cold water seemed to take all my courage, which was what I needed more than ever. Our own machine guns were playing along the railroad track on our side of the river. After getting across, it seemed for a while that I would be caught between the two fires.

I lay there in the river for a minute and gave up. When you do that something dies inside.

Then I saw the culvert under the track leading into the hole where we had lain during the barrage of the night before. I crawled through this and into the dugout at its edge, taking great care not to show myself for fear some of our own snipers might pick me up.

The luxury of that place was immense. I was safe there, safe, for a few minutes! I forgot everything but my own escape. The river had washed most of the mustard gas off, too. Only my

---

*It should be remembered that the Vesle is not a "river" in the American sense of the word; it is really a "creek" across which one could shy a stone.

eyes still smarted. A very few minutes, however, brought on a
nausea that made me afraid I should not be able to cover the
rest of my trip. I crawled out of the dugout very warily, still
afraid of our own machine guns and the guns across the river
that had picked us up the day before, and finally made way
through the ruined steel mill which kept me out of sight most
of the distance. It had a long shed. Then I took the little path
straight up to the barn behind the "club" which we had occupied, and shoving the door aside, stepped into the courtyard
and sat down.

Some of the machine gun men there jumped up rather
startled, and then came over to give me a lift, but I was able to
go on all right after a few minutes' breathing, and made my
own way to the major's dugout.

They must have been shelling Fismes very heavily that
morning, for the little lane leading to the wine cave was literally strewn with dead runners. The air was heavy with gas, the
effect of which I could now plainly feel, a sort of tightening
across the lungs and a burning rawness. Not having a mask
worried me greatly. There was an old blanket over the door to
keep out the gas, and as I went in I noticed a big unexploded
air bomb just on the bank above. How it got there I do not
know. I lifted the blanket and stepped inside.

The major was telephoning to the colonel as I came in, using
the line which the signal corps had established with great difficulty. The different telephones had queer names in order to
give no information in case the enemy listened in. I remember
the major was talking to "Hindu" something. He was telling the
colonel that the attack was so far going well and that we were
taking prisoners. I believe some Germans had been taken somewhere, which gave him the impression that we were having a
great success. It did not take me very long to give him the real
situation, and a very different story went over the wire than had
been started. The gravity of affairs was at once apparent.

That dugout was absolutely packed. All the battalion scouts,
the runners from all the different organizations in *liaison* with
us,* a good many wounded, and some simply taking shelter
filled the place to the stifling point. In addition there were a

---

*Runners were interchanged.

good many officers—the captain of our machine gun company, which had just moved into Fismes, our battalion scout officer, and several others from the third battalion that was just then entering the town. Runners were coming and going.

The major and his adjutant sat at a table with a map on which we were soon drawing the lines for the barrage with an artillery *liaison* officer superintending the job. We drew them in a horseshoe curve well above the town to avoid the possibility of "shorts" among our own men. Pretty soon the artillery lieutenant was telephoning to the batteries, but the line was cut about this time and there was a maddening delay. I asked for a gas mask and one was taken from a dead man near the door. There were no extras about.

Things began to get pretty hazy for me about this time. I remember giving a book of notes and poems to our scout officer. It was soaked with water but not ruined. Some of the men helped me out of my pack. The river water I had swallowed was the last touch.

Major Donnely, the commanding officer of the third battalion, came in now. He grew very angry at the crowded condition of the dugout and made some of the men move out to other shelter, ordering them to keep away from the door where they cut off what little air there was. Shells were falling outside every few minutes. Between them Godfrey Wyke skipped in, neat, lively, and the same as ever. He and the other company commanders of the third battalion were called in for a little council, and it was decided that after dark an attempt would be made to reënforce the first battalion in Fismette. About this time a runner came in from the other side of the river. He had gotten across the bridge in a lull. The intensity of the barrage after our attack had now relaxed greatly. The message told us that Captain Law of my company had been killed, that the captain of "A" company was wounded, and that the men had been safely withdrawn to the town, but needed reënforcements and ammunition. I said I would guide the reënforcing companies back that night. There was some good news, though. A platoon of the 109th machine gun battalion had crossed the river higher up and worked into Fismette.

After an hour or two the nausea passed off, and the major gave me some cornbeef hash, but I was not quite able to get away with it. After sitting around an hour, I got up and went out with our ammunition officer to see if we could get down to the river and "ferry" some boxes across, near to the little footbridge.

We moved very carefully, cutting across the road just behind an ambulance that drove by at reckless speed. Another was loading just across the street from the house above the "*Villa Bremen*." The lieutenant and I went up to the "club" and took a peep at the river from the barn. The whole bank was still being torn up by the shells, a lot of which were also falling in the fields and through the town.

As soon as I saw that hell-hole, I knew absolutely that I didn't have the courage to try it again. Whether we ever could have carried ammunition boxes through that gantlet and then floated them across the river on planks I do not know. But I do know I didn't have the courage then to head the gang that was going to try it. The ammunition officer said nothing one way or the other. I was so tired I didn't care what he thought. While we stood there looking, our own barrage fell around Fismette.

Imagine that little white town up on the hillside, and just above and around it in a semi-horseshoe a great waving cloud of black dust, spurting earth fountains, smoke and flying dirt as though giants were throwing wagonloads of it into the air. There was a howling and whistling overhead and a steady roar from the other side of the river. This kept up for about a half hour, after which there was a dead silence for a long time. I hated to tell the major that I couldn't get the ammunition across, so I went over to the "*Villa Bremen*" and slept. The quiet, the coolness, the sense of isolation in the dugout was grateful. One of the medical men was there. Now and then we could hear the dull thud of a shell. It seemed far away. "Doc" got me a little cornbeef hash. I slept till four o'clock, it being impossible to stay awake any longer.

When I woke I seemed to have slept off most of the dizzy feeling of the morning. I had pretty well breathed myself clear of the sick gas feeling and was able to think clearly again. I went over to the major's dugout and found two engineer officers there with the two majors. We talked over the possibility of rebuilding the little footbridge across the river. I thought that it might be possible to slip down at night and reconstruct this bridge out of the material lying around near by, light trusses from the near by steel mill and heavy fence planks. It was a very short span. Things had quieted down now, and I took the two engineer officers, a major and a captain to look at the footbridge. We tried to get as near as possible without being seen.

The landscape about Fismes and Fismette that mellow summer afternoon about the middle of August is indelibly printed on my memory. We went down through the "club" again. A shell had broken all the glass out of the little sun parlor. It lay about in great sword-like splinters sparkling and twinkling on the iron wine tables and chairs. Then we cut out through the barn and down the path through the steel mill towards the railroad. Here I could point out the wreck of the little plank suspension bridge floating on the turbid, muddy current rolling by so rapidly. Across there was the little town of Fismette, just then so quiet, so white on the green vacant hillside, and the ruined buildings and back lots of Fismes with the railroad stretching along the river. Almost any moment one could expect a train to come puffing around the curve. It seemed so peaceful. But there was a caution, a fear that kept us from showing ourselves, that made us glide quietly, quickly by open spaces between buildings, an expectancy, a breathlessness, an unnatural calm that meant war.

We went back to the command post. The engineers were to try that night to build the bridge, but we could not wait for that, and it was decided to attempt the reënforcement of Fismette by sending over "L" and "M" companies of the third battalion, with part of "I" company equipped with stretchers, to bring out the wounded as soon as it was thoroughly dark. We were going to try to cross by the ruined stone bridge, hoping we could sneak in. I was to guide them, since I had been over once and knew the ropes.

Supper was very intense that night. Ten or twelve men of our own battalion who had remained behind the night before, for one reason or another, were to go over with us also, and they were not very cheerful. The ration was very scarce. Some salmon and half-raw canned sweet potatoes. I took leave of "*Villa Bremen*" again with regret, and went across the street to

find Captain Keel of "L" company with his outfit. He was lin-
ing them up in the courtyard of the seminary ready to march.
In the fast-failing light they looked tremendously grim and
business-like. "L" company was about the finest body of men I
ever saw. A few houses up the street "M" company was waiting
under Captain Thompson, a fiery, determined little soldier; to
talk to him for a few minutes in the street gave one renewed
nerve. He had an intrepid personality. With him in charge, we
were halfway over already.

He gave the word and the two companies came filing out of
the houses in single file, just as we had moved the night
before.

We started to make stealthily for the bridge. The men had all
been warned, and this time moved with great care. As we got
near the river the flares began to stop us. Again and again came
the green-white light, and again and again we froze into silence
and stillness. One saw the skeleton houses, windows agape, the
rows on rows of slate roofs, the tense, silent line of white faces
under the helmets—swoop came the shadows, blackness and
night—then we moved on again.

About a block from the bridge one of the platoon on guard
there came back to tell us that the German machine guns
played on it whenever the slightest noise was made by any one
crossing. He told us an encouraging tale of several runners
who had been killed that afternoon trying to get across. The
story completely sickened me. I lost for a moment all the resolution I had. "No more machine guns, no more!" I kept saying
to myself against my will. Just then a flare went up, and we
halted. I told the news to Captain Thompson, who kept the
men halted and ordered them to sit down. Captain Keel came
up and suggested sending a message back to the major to apprise him of the situation. This gave some excuse to ourselves
for a delay. At least we needed a little time to con the affair
over. To be stopped at the bridge would be to bring down a
barrage that would make the reënforcement of Fismette impossible. Captain Thompson wanted to get some information
from the machine gun outfit who had been near the bridge all
day. So one of the machine gun company stationed near here
led us into a big house. The outer doors were closed fast after
we entered. Then we went through a hall and another door

was closed. After this a light was lit and we descended into a big cellar. The whole machine gun company seemed to be there, and very comfortable. Lieutenant Dan Brooks, a light-hearted, generous youth, was in charge. We drank some white wine, of which there were several barrels about. It was the last time I ever saw Dan Brooks. He laughed, gave us some information, wished us good luck, and shook hands. Thompson and I looked at each other—there was no excuse for any further delay. Now was as good as any other time.

We left Brooks in the cheerful candlelight and sallied out through the big door of the house and down the steps to our men sitting silently along the sides of the houses as we had left them. Thompson gave the word, and in a moment we were under way again, making rapidly but carefully for the bridge. At the bridge we halted sheltering behind the last houses.

Keel, who was leading "L" company, and I went first. I remembered passing two of our snipers at the bridgehead, lying behind a stone with their rifles ready. They were going to fire at the flash if a gun spoke. One of them whispered to me, "Don't stoop down, lieutenant, they are shooting low when they cut loose." Then we went out onto the bridge.

It was much more damaged than the night before, big stones blown loose all over it, holes in the middle, the pit of the night before much enlarged. As we descended into this a flare went up. That was undoubtedly the most intense moment I ever knew. For me, it was the great moment of the war. I was sure we must be seen. We stood rigid. The flare rose, drifted to the ground, and went out—not a shot! The last half we made in a silent but brief scramble.

There was not a soul on the other side, but I am afraid to say how many dead lay around the house at the head of the bridge. I threw a stone back, which was the signal agreed upon, and the men began to come over, three at a time and very quietly, crouching so that they looked like the big stones when a flare went up. After about twenty were over I started into the town by the back way, leading the file through several houses and twists and turns to a barricade across the street. At every corner a man was left to keep saying, "This way, this way." It was essential not to lose contact here. The line kept feeding across without a hitch, man after man crouching down to cross the village street behind the barrels filled with stone that led over into the doorway of a big barn. It was a combination barn and house around a big central court. At the upper end of it was a wine cave that went into the almost perpendicular hill.

Out of this came Captain Haller, who was in charge of what was left of the first battalion in Fismette. He was rather startled at first at seeing so many silent figures in the courtyard, but his welcome was more than hearty. In a few minutes the new men were being stationed. Some were sent up on the line to relieve the tired watchers there, others to sleep in lofts, a cellar or a house, but all ready for instant call. We brought in with us several bags of ammunition, grenades, and litters to carry out the wounded, whose evacuation was started immediately.

It was half an hour before the Germans "got wise" and started to gun for the bridge. In the meantime the town had been reënforced.

"Fritz" was very near here. From a little hamlet, the cluster of roofs just up the hill back of our barn and cave, he shot flares right down into the court. Captain Haller came out and put up a red rocket. I remember him standing in that court with the stars above, and now and then the green glare of the German flare freezing us all into statues, then the sudden spurt of his match, and the hiss of the rocket soaring up over the roofs. A few minutes later our own barrage came down about our own ears. The shells came perilously close. That morning they had caught some of our own men falling short, I was told. Under cover of the fire from our batteries the evacuation of the wounded went on.

CHAPTER XVIII

LAST HOURS IN FISMETTE

IN THAT great time there was never any rest or let-up until the body was killed, or it sank exhausted.

That night we set to work immediately to try to get Captain Williams of "A" company across the river before daylight. He had been struck by a machine gun bullet in the attack that morning. The bullet had travelled around his ribs and, lodging under the spine, had paralyzed him.

He lay in another little dugout—a wine cave, too—about ten houses up the street from the big cave in the court. I made my way up to him through the houses and tried to cheer him by telling him we had come to get him. He was so cheerful and kindly and glad to see us, it would have brought the tears to our eyes—at any other time. Getting him out was not such an easy task.

It was impossible even to appear in the street. Lieutenant Glendenning lay dead there, shot through the heart, fine brave heart, I couldn't help crying when I heard of that—and we would have to knock holes through the walls of the houses to get Captain Williams' stretcher through from house to house.

We picked some strong Italians and started working through the big court, battering away with logs and picks, dislodging rocks from the mud plaster and working like mad in a race against time—for if it was morning before we reached the captain, he would have to stay another day in Fismette—and that might be fatal. We could use no lights. I can still see those dark figures battering away, then crawling through, choosing the space in the next wall for the tunneling, and going on and on. At last towards morning the passageway was ready and we carried the captain down as far as the court, lifting him through the holes in the wall with great care, sliding the stretcher from room to room, but it was too late. We had to stay in the big cave with Captain Haller's command post, where they brought a great many other wounded.

In there was a dressing station. One of the hospital corps worked night and day, poor lad! He was almost all in. The place had rows of wounded in it, moaning, and he had little with which to help them. Bandages were running out. In the cave there was a light, and hay on the floor. It ran far back into the hill. Some of us crawled in there and towards morning got some sleep. The last thing I heard was Captain Williams cheering some of the wounded, especially one Italian lad who was in great pain.

That night, and part of the next day, was fairly quiet. There was nothing to eat. Yes—something—one of my own men, who had heard that I had got back, brought me some fish, about half a cupful, and asked me to share it. He was so much in earnest about it, that I ate it with him like a sacrament.

Next morning not a shot could be heard, and it was warm and sunny. I got up and walked up the line of houses between the street and the hill, working from back yard to back yard. The little dugout where Captain Williams had been the night before, I determined to make my headquarters, and as a sign of authority carried my officer's raincoat there. There were one or two men sleeping in it and some wounded. Up above it on the hillside was a house which overlooked the fields beyond. There we had an observation post. A garret in one of the houses along the street sheltered one of our invaluable machine guns and its valiant crew. A few of our lads were still lying along the wall as sentries. The rest were down in the houses. The wall and the space in front of it for many yards had dead men lying every here and there.

Farther along near the cross street, I found some of our men in a house which had a spring in it. Here one of our wounded sergeants, Davidson, lay near the water. A fine chap and very glad to see me. He had heard I had been killed. We moved him down to the big cave and got him across the river later. Lieutenant Horner was holding this end of the line. The men were sitting around in the rooms of the little deserted houses, waiting for anything that might happen, and hoping that nothing would. Night was the time we all dreaded. The days seemed easy in comparison.

As we could not use the street, I felt the need of quick communication up and down the line and set some of the men to completing the knocking of holes between houses. In the barn by the court, I started, with Captain Haller's sanction, a number of men digging a tunnel under the narrow street so we could cross into the houses on the other side and occupy them also. Captain Thompson and I went up a few houses and tried to "fish" Lieutenant Glendenning's body from the street where it was lying face downward, by making a loop, getting it around him, and then dragging him in through the window, but we could not make it. It was impossible to show oneself even for a minute in the street and the rope we had was a miserable stiff piece of old hemp that forever slipped. We had to give it up. I went back to see how the tunnel was coming on.

The men were digging, standing in one room of the barn while some of us stood talking in the next, when, without any warning but a swift whistle, a trench mortar shell fell through the roof and exploded in the room where the men were working, killing and wounding about eight or nine. A lot of fragments came through the door into our room and one struck me on the knee. It seemed nothing at the time with so many killed. One or two of the poor lads who had been digging were carried into the cave, one fellow had his face blown full of dirt and stones, and was frightfully shell shocked, jerking and crying out pitifully.

There is certainly such a thing as shell shock, and a very terrible thing it is, not to be explained away by doctors who write articles for the library table magazines. The rest of the poor, black, dust-covered bodies were buried in the pit they had dug for themselves, or in the hole the shell had made. All those dead faces were covered with an ashen-gray dust, and there was a hellish scent of high explosive in the air. That was about noon.

About three o'clock Major Donnely appeared among us, having crossed the bridge, like the brave man he was, in daylight. He had orders to make another attack. That is, his battalion was to attack while what was left of ours was to hold the town.

It was a frightful order, murder. All of us knew that. I tried to explain the situation to the major, thinking he did not know that he was flinging three companies against the German army, but I left off, seeing that he did know and was only carrying out what he had been ordered to do.*

The companies that had come into town the night before were to make the attack. I talked to Fletcher, who came up looking very grave and sad over it. I remember he looked at me significantly as the men filed out. Captain Thompson led. That was the last time I ever saw either him or Fletcher.

We of the first battalion left in Fismette got our men sheltered as well as we could for the barrage which we knew was sure to follow, and at the same time kept up a sharp watch.

*The orders for this attack and for the whole Fismette fiasco, it now appears, had come from the French Army Commander through the 3rd Corps headquarters. The tactical reason seems to have been that the Fismes-Fismette bridgehead was worth all that it might cost. See Major General Bullard's Memoirs and his letter to General Pershing of August 28, 1918.

The other companies marched out of the town to the left and made an attack up the hill. It was not hard to tell when the battle was on.

I took my station in the observation house above the little dugout. One of our scouts was there. "Look here, lieutenant," said he, and between the cracks in the roof pointed out a haystack about fifty yards away. I looked at it carefully through his glass. From it poked the ugly nose of a machine gun from which went up a faint blue haze. Oh! if we had only had rifle grenades then!

The whole hill seemed to be alive with machine guns and artillery. Such a barrage fell on Fismette that we were instantly driven from our posts into the dugout. In the yard beside us shell after shell smashed. We closed the iron door to our cave to keep out the fragments, but the choking gas and the smell of high explosives came in. Above all the roar suddenly sounded, seemingly right above our heads, the sharp bark of our own single machine gun. Brave lads, they were still sticking to it in the garret. We knew they had only one box of ammunition left. Houses along the street were blown up and disappeared inwardly in a cloud of dust and a sliding noise. I hopped out once to see Major Donnely at the big cave.

"Hang on," he said.

After what seemed an eternity, some one came and said our men were coming back—then our own barrage fell. It was the greatest we had thrown around there. The hillside was tossed about for an hour and the German shells had ceased. As always, when it lifted, there followed the silence of the dead. We were all breathing in relief when what was left of the other companies returned. It was a miserable remnant. The loss had been terrific. Some of the companies were down to a few men. The gain had been nothing and we had exposed the smallness of our force to the Germans. A German plane came down so close it seemed to glide along the roofs. All was silent in the courts and houses till it passed. The aviator could have counted our buttons. No one was fool enough to shoot at him. As usual at that time, the Germans owned the air.

Captain Thompson had been killed, hit by a shell, some of his men said, while he was shouting to them to rally for the third time. The survivors were all in no shape to stand any further strain, having borne all that flesh and blood could, and more. The town was choked with dead and wounded. Even my own little dugout was full of them by this time.

About nightfall the little lieutenant,* who had our third platoon on the left flank, came up to tell me there was nobody left there. He was badly wounded and half out of his head. The story of his platoon is an heroic one. All alone on the left flank, they held on and on, the little groups at the barricade and in the shell-holes gradually becoming less and less, till *no one* was left. My fine little Italian striker, Nick de Saza, had his head taken off by a shell, working his *Chauchat* automatic to the last. I sent the lieutenant over with some of the other wounded. They got back that night into Fismes. He was too young to die miserably of gas after being wounded.

That night—unforgettable—darkness settled down on a despairing but determined little group of survivors in Fismette. Every now and then one of our machine guns barked from the roof, and, as ever at dark, the German flares began. There were very few of us left to hold the line. We got instructions from the major about dusk, and some hope of relief, but I knew that it was only to hearten us. On the other side of the river no one knew what was going on. I tried to string my men out along the wall, but there were so few, I felt it was better to keep most in shelter and some sentries along the wall. We could at least rush out then and make a stand. The last of our remaining officers in "B" company, Lieutenant Gerald, came up and joined me with a remnant of men. He was all in, almost out of his head with fatigue and two days on the line without sleep or food, but still wonderfully game. The dugout filled up with wounded and gassed men, two layers deep. It was a crazy house in there.

I went up in the little house on the hill just above, where we had been observing. A shell fell in the garden, and by its red flash I saw a picture of Christ on the wall. The thorn-crowned face leaped suddenly out of the frame at each devil's candle. Simple-hearted Catholic peasants had lived there once. I saw that picture by the same light a good many times that night. It was a real piece of melodrama.

---

*Lieutenant Francis Welton, I have since learned.

We arranged a regular system of reliefs, the men taking turns on the line and then in the dugout. To crawl out onto that line among the dead men by the wall in the tense darkness, shells whistling and falling, and now and then a flare of a corpse-like light, was a terrific test for a man. It grew harder and harder to get the men to leave the dugout as the shelling kept up.

Towards morning the shelling stopped. I began to realize that all the men by the wall were dead. One young Italian whose turn it was to go on post whimpered and begged—he was sick, he said. God knows, we all were! I was numbly trying to think what I could do with him, when the barrage fell. All that were still outside made for the dugout. We crawled in over the wounded and sat shaking. I knew when it lifted that we must meet an attack.

In all that awful uproar I heard some one at the door. The men next to it did not want to open it. It took me some time to give orders to let him in. I was getting very hazy. The poor devil came in shaking and crying. It seemed as though the place was afire outside. We slammed the door again—"gas!" "gas!"—on went the masks. It was real this time. The wounded begged piteously to be helped into theirs and everybody did what they could. A shell-shocked man was shouting and jumping about. Some one held him down, cursing him. Then came the direct hit—a great stunning blow on the top of the dugout; everybody was quieted by that, and the smell of explosive was intense! Gradually I heard the faint stir in the darkness again and the voices through the gas masks. The cave had held. "Open the door!" cried somebody, "and beat out the gas." We did so and I saw that it was quiet again outside.

That meant only one thing. I felt—an attack—but I seemed to know it without being able to do anything about it. It was a long time seemingly before I moved myself with great effort. Then I tried to get the men up on the line again. We were all choking with gas. I heard Gerald pleading and remonstrating; he was trying to be very logical. "Don't you see?" I heard him say. "All right, I'll go then," and he started up in the darkness after a few of the others who had gone already to man the line. I stood trying to get the men out of the dugout, half wondering what I was trying to do at times and then remembering. It was strangely quiet.

Some one came and said, "They are all dead up there along the wall, lieutenant, and there's no one between us and 'C' company. The machine gun is knocked out." I tried to think this out.

Suddenly along the top of the hill there was a puff, a rolling cloud of smoke, and then a great burst of dirty, yellow flame. By its glare I could see Gerald standing halfway up the hill with his pistol drawn. It was the *Flammenwerfer*, the flame throwers; the men along the crest curled up like leaves to save themselves as the flame and smoke rolled clear over them. There was another flash between the houses. One of the men stood up, turning around outlined against the flame—"Oh! my God!" he cried. "Oh! God!"

Here ends this narrative.

Ernest Hemingway to His Family

Hemingway reported on his recovery seven weeks after being wounded.

_____

American Red X
Hospital,
Milano
Aug 18

Dear Folks—;

That includes Grandma and Grandpa and Aunt Grace. Thanks very much for the 40 lire! It was appreciated very much. Gee Family but there certainly has been a lot of burble about my getting shot up! The Oak Leaves and the opposition came today and I have begun to think, family, that maybe you didn't appreciate me when I used to reside in the bosom. It's the next best thing to getting killed and reading your own obituary.

You know they say there isn't anything funny about this war. And there isn't. I wouldn't say it was hell, because that's been a bit overworked since Gen. Sherman's time, but there have been about 8 times when I would have welcomed Hell. Just on a chance that it couldn't come up to the phase of war I was experiencing. F'rexample. In the trenches during an attack when a shell makes a direct hit in a group where you're standing. Shells aren't bad except direct hits. You just take chances on the fragments of the bursts. But when there is a direct hit your pals get spattered all over you. Spattered is literal.

During the six days I was up in the Front line trenches, only 50 yds from the Austrians I got the rep of having a charmed life. The rep of having one doesn't mean much but having one does! I hope I have one. That knocking sound is my knuckles striking the wooden bed tray.

It's too hard to write on two sides of the paper so Ill skip—

Well I can now hold up my hand and say I've been shelled by high explosive, shrapnel and gas. Shot at by trench mortars, snipers and machine guns. And as an added attraction an aeroplane machine gunning the lines. I've never had a hand grenade thrown at me, but a rifle grenade struck rather close. Maybe I'll get a hand grenade later. Now out of all that mess to only be struck by a trench mortar and a machine gun bullet while advancing toward the rear, as the Irish say, was fairly lucky. What Family?

The 227 wounds I got from the trench mortar didn't hurt a bit at the time, only my feet felt like I had rubber boots full of water on. Hot water. And my knee cap was acting queer. The machine gun bullet just felt like a sharp smack on my leg with an icy snow ball. However it spilled me. But I got up again and got my wounded into the dug out. I kind of collapsed at the dug out. The Italian I had with me had bled all over my coat and my pants looked like somebody had made current jelly in them and then punched holes to let the pulp out. Well the Captain who was a great pal of mine, it was his dug out, said "Poor Hem he'll be R.I.P. soon." Rest In Peace, that is. You see they thought I was shot through the chest on account of my bloody coat. But I made them take my coat and shirt off. I wasn't wearing any under shirt, and the old torso was intact. Then they said I'd probably live. That cheered me up any amount. I told him in Italian that I wanted to see my legs, though I was afraid to look at them. So we took off my trousers and the old limbs were still there but gee they were a mess. They couldn't figure out how I had walked 150 yards with a load with both knees shot through and my right shoe punctured two big places. Also over 200 flesh wounds. "Oh," says I in Italian, "My Captain. It is of nothing. In America they all do it! It is thought well not to allow the enemy to percieve that they have captured our goats!"

The goat speech required some masterful lingual ability but I got it across and then went to sleep for a couple of minutes.

After I came to they carried me on a stretcher three kilometers back to a dressing station. The stretcher bearers had to go over lots because the road was having the "entrails" shelled out of it. Whenever a big one would come, wheeeee whoosh—

Boom—they'd lay me down and get flat. My wounds were now hurting like 227 little devils were driving nails into the raw. The dressing station had been evacuated during the attack so I lay for two hours in a stable, with the roof shot off, waiting for an ambulance. When it came I ordered it down the road to get the soldiers that had been wounded first. It came back with a load and then they lifted me in. The shelling was still pretty thick and our batteries were going off all the time way back of us and the big 250s and 350's going over head for Austria with a noise like a railway train. Then we'd hear the bursts back of the lines. Then shreek would come a big Austrian shell and then the crash of the burst. But we were giving them more and bigger stuff than they sent. Then a battery of field guns would go off just back of the shed boom, boom, boom, boom. And the Seventy Fives or 149s would go whimpering over to the Austrian lines and the Star shells going up all the time and the machine going like rivetters. Tat a tat, tat a tat.

After a ride of a couple of Kilomets in an Italian ambulance, they unloaded me at the dressing station where I had a lot of pals among the medical officers. They gave me a shot of morphine and an anti tetanus injection and shaved my legs and took out about twenty 8 shell fragments varying from to about in size out of my legs. Then they did a fine job of bandaging and all shook hands with me and would have kissed me but I kidded them along. Then I stayed 5 days in a field hospital and was then evacuated to the Base Hospital here.

I sent you that cable so you wouldn't worry. I've been in the Hospital a month and 12 days and hope to be out in another month. The Italian Surgeon did a peach of a job on my right knee joint and right foot. Took 28 stitches and assures me that I will be able to walk as well as ever. The wounds all healed up clean and there was no infection. He has my right leg in a plaster splint now so that the joint will be all right. I have some snappy souvenirs that he took out at the last operation.

I wouldn't really be comfortable now unless I had some pain. The Surgeon is going to take the plaster off in a week now and will allow me on crutches in 10 days.

I'll have to learn to walk again.

You ask about Art Newburn. He was in our section but has

been transferred to II. Brummy is in our section now. Dont weep if I tell you that back in my youth I learned to play poker. Art Newburn held some delusions that he was a poker player. I won't go into the sad details but I convinced him otherwise. Without holding anything I stood pat. Doubled his [   ] sweetened openers and bluffed him out of a 50 lire pot. He held three aces and was afraid to call. Tell that to somebody that knows the game Pop. I think Art said in a letter home to the Oak Parker that he was going to take care of me. Now Pop as man to man was that taking care of me? Nay not so. So you see that while war isn't funny a lot of funny things happen in war. But Art won the championship of Italy pitching horse shoes.

This is the longest letter I've ever written to anybody and it says the least. Give my love to everybody that asked about me and as Ma Pettengill says, "Leave us keep the home fires burning!"

Good night and love to all.

Ernie

I got a letter today from the Helmles addressed Private Ernest H— what I am is S. Ten. or Soto Tenenente Ernest Hemingway.

That is my rank in the Italian Army and it means 2nd Lieut. I hope to be a Tenente or 1st Lieut. soon.

Dear Pop—; Yours of July 23rd Rece'd. Thanks very much. But you need the Kale worse than I do. If I ever get really broke I'll cable. Send any money that others send me Pop, but dont *you* give me any unless I cable for it. I'll cable if I need it.

Love

Ernie.

1918

Frederick Trevenen Edwards to Frederick Edwards

On August 8 the British launched a successful counteroffensive east of Amiens. As the Germans retreated from the territory they had captured earlier in the year, Marshal Ferdinand Foch allowed Pershing to conduct an independent American operation against the St. Mihiel salient, which the Germans had held since 1914. (Army orders indicate that it was the first American operation to use the terms "D-Day" and "H-Hour" for planning purposes.) From September 12 to 16, American troops captured the salient and 15,000 German prisoners, with 7,000 of their own killed, wounded, or missing. Frederick Trevenen Edwards had left the Episcopal General Theological Seminary in New York City in May 1917 to enlist in the army. A first lieutenant in the 118th Field Artillery Regiment, 3rd Division, he served in the regimental headquarters during the Marne-Aisne campaign in July. Wounded by German shellfire at Montfaucon during the Meuse-Argonne offensive, Edwards died on October 6, 1918.

AMERICAN EXPEDITIONARY FORCES, FRANCE
September 12, 1918.

Dear Dad,—It's nearly night; that time after supper when we light our candles and pull the blankets over the windows. I am in a farmhouse in a village just back of the lines. A long street winds away over the hill towards the Front. As the darkness comes on, the noise of the street grows more turbulent; swelling with the dark until it becomes a roaring turmoil; the thunder of heavy trucks; the rattle of guns and wagons; the steady tramp, tramp of marching Infantry; all punctuated by the whistle of the Military Police on the corner, regulating the traffic. His is a mighty job. A New York traffic Cop would be lost; for here no light can be shown. Every night it has rained a downpour; it is so black one cannot see a hand before his face; and still he has to stand on a muddy, desolate crossroads, that is apt to be shelled at any minute, and direct traffic heavier than the streets in New York.

Last night I sat here in this damp old house waiting for the battle to begin. What a queer experience it was! Outside, the rumble of the street, the shouts, the whistles, the steady downpour of the rain on the roof, that trickled and splashed on the floor inside. There I sat at one end of a table with a candle on either side of me and a map in front. The map was dotted with German batteries and jagged trenches, marked with lines which showed where our attack would be, how far it would progress by such and such a time. On the other side of the table sat the Colonel. Between us was a telephone with a spidery wire going out through the dark in every direction.

It was a wild stormy night, when one would like to pull a comfortable chair in front of the fire, with a good book to read. But this was very different; the room was cold, wet and cheerless. I took a chance on the smoke showing from the chimney, broke up some old furniture and built a little fire to warm us.

There we sat; not much to say; now and then a dripping messenger would rap, stand stiffly at attention and present a message. Again, the telephone would jangle and over the wire we would get a weird garble of letters. There would be a conning of the code book and an answer to code and send back. Then it would be quiet again. Just over the hill were the trenches. Ever since the war began, they had not been changed; year after year there had been no attack on either side; yet night after night now we had been piling up troops and guns behind that line waiting for the hour when they would go over. The night had come.

The little fire snapped cheerily, the rain drummed on the old tiles; and the steady roar of the Infantry went on outside. I thought about the Germans just across the way; poor devils; there they were oblivious to it all; probably snug in their dugouts out of the rain. How many of them would die there in the mud in to-morrow's grey dawn? And the poor chaps were probably sitting there playing pinocle and thinking of home.

Outside, the Infantry were tramping by, thousands of them; every road was choked with them. All over the hills the guns were waiting, thousands of them, where before there had only been hundreds. As yet they had not spoken; they had been dragged into position on dark nights, and there they sat, with the rain dripping off the shining muzzles that were all pointing over the hill.

It was one of the longest nights I have ever spent. Then, five minutes before the hour, I went to the window and pulled off the blanket. The rain had stopped; it was cold and clammy, a fog was spreading over the valley.

How still it was! A cricket in the chimney place began to chirp; my watch ticked loudly as I watched the hand drag on. There it was, finally, over the dot, and, as if the thing had automatically touched the world off, the sky was torn asunder with a mighty flash and thunder. The attack was on; every gun all over those long hills was roaring at the German lines; the sky quaked with flames. The roar and rumble was of a thousand thunder storms. It was the most magnificient and terrifying sight that I have ever seen. Then the rockets began going up from the enemies' trenches, white ones, red ones, ones like fountains of stars; crawling across the sky singly, in pairs, agitatedly tumbling. The telephone jangled and the pleading voice over the wire called for an ambulance.

I went back to the window fascinated. Hour after hour the thing went on; just as the light began to creep up out of the east it magically stopped. I could not see; but I knew how the Infantry were climbing up the ladders out of the trenches, slipping over the muddy tops and through the wire. I knew the hundreds of tanks, whippets that I had seen crawling up the road night after night, were now going over; crawling out from under the trees and squirming through the fog of No Man's Land. Faintly I could hear the German machine guns trying to stop them. Then the artillery began again; I could see the barrage creeping up just in front of the Infantry. After that the telephone kept me so busy that I forgot the Battle.

It was nine o'clock before I could lie down for a moment's sleep, the first in three nights. I crawled into a haymow, thinking how warm and cosy my blankets would be; but I found that the roof had leaked over them and wet them through. I was quite discouraged, but buried myself in the hay and fell asleep. When I awoke, I heard the tramp of feet on the echoing road again; this time going the other way, and through the big barn door I found myself watching a long column of grey clad prisoners going to the rear. All day long they have been shuffling by, boys most of them, with here and there old men; most of them smiling broadly as though they were glad that it was all over. They were a muddy lot, dirty, unshaven and poor-looking. We have advanced steadily all day and must have demoralized the Germans because we have taken thousands of prisoners. Hour after hour the guns and things move up, harassing the enemy, who retreats as fast as he can out of this deadly rain of shell.

It's night again; the same kind of program probably ahead of us. I must stop and and go back to my work. All my love, TREVENEN.

P.S. I forgot to tell you—I'm a First Lieutenant now. I began to think it never would come, for I have been recommended three times by the Colonel and nothing seemed to come of it. There are two Adjutants now in every Regiment and I am one of them. I have charge of the Personnel.

Eugene V. Debs: Speech to the Court

Eugene V. Debs, the four-time Socialist candidate for president, delivered a speech in Canton, Ohio, on June 16, 1918, in which he endorsed the antiwar platform adopted by his party in St. Louis in 1917.
He told his listeners they were "fit for something better than slavery
and cannon fodder." Tried under the Espionage Act of 1917 for inciting disloyalty in the armed forces and obstructing military recruiting,
Debs was convicted on September 13 and sentenced the next day to
ten years' imprisonment. On March 10, 1919, the U.S. Supreme Court
upheld his conviction in a 9–0 decision written by Justice Oliver
Wendell Holmes. Even after the war, President Wilson considered
Debs a "traitor to his country" and refused to pardon him. In 1920
Debs would run for President from his prison cell in Atlanta and win
close to a million votes. At Christmas in 1921, President Warren G.
Harding would commute his sentence.

Your Honor, years ago I recognized my kinship with all living beings, and I made up my mind that I was not one bit
better than the meanest of earth. I said then, I say now, that
while there is a lower class I am in it; while there is a criminal
element, I am of it; while there is a soul in prison, I am not
free.

If the law under which I have been convicted is a good law,
then there is no reason why sentence should not be pronounced upon me. I listened to all that was said in this court in
support and justification of this law, but my mind remains unchanged. I look upon it as a despotic enactment in flagrant
conflict with democratic principles and with the spirit of free
institutions.

I have no fault to find with this court or with the trial. Everything in connection with this case has been conducted
upon a dignified plane, and in a respectful and decent spirit—
with just one exception. Your Honor, my sainted mother inspired me with a reverence for womanhood that amounts to
worship. I can think with disrespect of no woman, and I can
think with respect of no man who can. I resent the manner in

which the names of two noble women were bandied with in this court. The levity and the wantonness in this instance were absolutely inexcusable. When I think of what was said in this connection, I feel that when I pass a woman, even though it be a sister of the street, I should take off my hat and apologize to her for being a man.

Your Honor, I have stated in this court that I am opposed to the form of our present government; that I am opposed to the social system in which we live; that I believed in the change of both—but by perfectly peaceable and orderly means.

Let me call your attention to the fact this morning that in this system five per cent of our people own and control two-thirds of our wealth; sixty-five per cent. of the people, embracing the working class who produce all wealth, have but five per cent to show for it.

Standing here this morning, I recall my boyhood. At fourteen, I went to work in the railroad shops; at sixteen, I was firing a freight engine on a railroad. I remember all the hardships, all the privations, of that earlier day, and from that time until now, my heart has been with the working class. I could have been in Congress long ago. I have preferred to go to prison. The choice has been deliberately made. I could not have done otherwise. I have no regret.

In the struggle—the unceasing struggle—between the toilers and producers and their exploiters, I have tried, as best I might, to serve those among whom I was born, with whom I expect to share my lot until the end of my days.

I am thinking this morning of the men in the mills and factories; I am thinking of the women who, for a paltry wage, are compelled to work out their lives; of the little children who, in this system, are robbed of their childhood, and in their early, tender years, are seized in the remorseless grasp of Mammon, and forced into the industrial dungeons, there to feed the machines while they themselves are being starved body and soul. I can see them dwarfed, diseased, stunted, their little lives broken, and their hopes blasted, because in this high noon of our twentieth century civilization money is still so much more important than human life. Gold is god and rules in the affairs of men.

The little girls, and there are a million of them in this country—this the most favored land beneath the bending skies,

a land in which we have vast areas of rich and fertile soil, material resources in inexhaustible abundance, the most marvelous
productive machinery on earth, millions of eager workers ready
to apply their labor to that machinery to produce an abundance for every man, woman and child—and if there are still
many millions of our people who are the victims of poverty,
whose life is a ceaseless struggle all the way from youth to age,
until at last death comes to their rescue and stills the aching
heart, and lulls the victim to dreamless sleep, it is not the fault
of the Almighty, it can't be charged to nature; it is due entirely
to an outgrown social system that ought to be abolished not
only in the interest of the working class, but in a higher interest
of all humanity.

When I think of these little children—the girls that are in
the textile mills of all description in the East, in the cotton
factories of the South—when I think of them at work in a viti-
ated atmosphere, when I think of them at work when they
ought to be at play or at school, when I think that when they do
grow up, if they live long enough to approach the marriage
state, they are unfit for it. Their nerves are worn out, their tissue is exhausted, their vitality is spent. They have been fed to
industry. Their lives have been coined into gold. Their off-
spring are born tired. That is why there are so many failures in
our modern life.

Your Honor, the five per cent of the people that I have made
reference to constitute that element that absolutely rules our
country. They privately own all our public necessities. They
wear no crowns; they wield no scepters; they sit upon no
thrones; and yet they are our economic masters and our political rulers. They control this government and all of its institutions. They control the courts.

And, Your Honor, if you will permit me, I wish to make just
one correction. It was stated here that I had charged that all
federal judges were crooks. The charge is absolutely untrue. I
did say that all federal judges are appointed through the influence and power of the capitalist class and not the working class.
If that statement is not true, I am more than willing to retract it.

The five per cent of our people who own and control all the
sources of wealth, all of the nation's industries, all of the means
of our common life, it is they who declare war; it is they who

make peace; it is they who control our destiny. And so long as this is true, we can make no just claim to being a democratic government—a self-governing people.

I believe, Your Honor, in common with all Socialists, that this nation ought to own and control its industries. I believe, as all Socialists do, that all things that are jointly needed and used ought to be jointly owned—that industry, the basis of life, instead of being the private property of the few and operated for their enrichment, ought to be the common property of all, democratically administered in the interest of all.

John D. Rockefeller has to-day an income of sixty million dollars a year, five million dollars a month, two hundred thousand dollars a day. He does not produce a penny of it. I make no attack upon Mr. Rockefeller personally. I do not in the least dislike him. If he were in need and it were in my power to serve him, I should serve him as gladly as I would any other human being. I have no quarrel with Mr. Rockefeller personally, nor with any other capitalist. I am simply opposing a social order in which it is possible for one man who does absolutely nothing that is useful to amass a fortune of hundreds of millions of dollars, while millions of men and women who work all of the days of their lives secure barely enough for an existence.

This order of things cannot always endure. I have registered my protest against it. I recognize the feebleness of my effort, but, fortunately, I am not alone. There are multiplied thousands of others who, like myself, have come to realize that before we may truly enjoy the blessings of civilized life, we must reorganize society upon a mutual and coöperative basis; and to this end we have organized a great economic and political movement that is spread over the face of all the earth.

There are to-day upwards of sixty million Socialists, loyal, devoted, adherents to this cause, regardless of nationality, race, creed, color or sex. They are all making common cause. They are all spreading the propaganda of the new social order. They are waiting, watching and working through all the weary hours of the day and night. They are still in the minority. They have learned how to be patient and abide their time. They feel—they know, indeed,—that the time is coming, in spite of all opposition, all persecution, when this emancipating gospel will spread among all the peoples, and when this minority will become the triumphant majority, and sweeping into power, inaugurate the greatest change in history.

In that day we will have the universal commonwealth—not the destruction of the nation, but, on the contrary, the harmonious coöperation of every nation with every other nation on earth. In that day war will curse this earth no more.

I have been accused, Your Honor, of being an enemy of the soldier. I hope I am laying no flattering unction to my soul when I say that I don't believe the soldier has a more sympathetic friend than I am. If I had my way there would be no soldiers. But I realize the sacrifices they are making, Your Honor. I can think of them. I can feel for them. I can sympathize with them. That is one of the reasons why I have been doing what little has been in my power to bring about a condition of affairs in this country worthy of the sacrifices they have made and that they are now making in its behalf.

Your Honor, in a local paper yesterday there was some editorial exultation about my prospective imprisonment. I do not resent it in the least. I can understand it perfectly. In the same paper there appears an editorial this morning that has in it a hint of the wrong to which I have been trying to call attention."

Reading: 'A senator of the United States receives a salary of $7500—$45,000 for the six years for which he is elected. One of the candidates for senator from a state adjoining Ohio is reported to have spent through his committee $150,000 to secure the nomination. For advertising he spent $35,000; for printing $30,000; for traveling expenses $10,000 and the rest in ways known to political managers.

'The theory is that public office is as open to a poor man as to a rich man. One may easily imagine, however, how slight a chance one of ordinary resources would have in a contest against this man who was willing to spend more than three times his six years' salary merely to secure a nomination. Were these conditions to hold in every state, the senate would soon become again what it was once held to be—a rich men's club.

'Campaign expenditures have been the subject of much restrictive legislation in recent years, but it has not always reached the mark. The authors of primary reform have accomplished some of the things they set out to do, but they have not yet taken the bank roll out of politics.'

They never will take it out of politics, they never can take it out of politics in this system.

Your Honor, I wish to make acknowledgment of my thanks to the counsel for the defense. They have not only defended me with exceptional legal ability, but with a personal attachment and devotion of which I am deeply sensible, and which I can never forget.

Your Honor, I ask no mercy, I plead for no immunity. I realize that finally the right must prevail. I never more clearly comprehended than now the great struggle between the powers of greed on the one hand and upon the other the rising hosts of freedom. I can see the dawn of a better day of humanity. The people are awakening. In due course of time they will come into their own.

When the mariner, sailing over tropic seas, looks for relief from his weary watch, he turns his eyes toward the Southern Cross, burning luridly above the tempest-vexed ocean. As the midnight approaches, the Southern Cross begins to bend, and the whirling worlds change their places, and with starry finger-points the Almighty marks the passage of Time upon the dial of the universe; and though no bell may beat the glad tidings, the look-out knows that the midnight is passing—that relief and rest are close at hand.

Let the people take heart and hope everywhere, for the cross is bending, the midnight is passing, and joy cometh with the morning.

> 'He is true to God who is true to man.
> Wherever wrong is done
> To the humblest and the weakest
> 'Neath the all-beholding sun,
> That wrong is also done to us,
> And they are slaves most base
> Whose love of right is for themselves
> And not for all the race.'

Your Honor, I thank you, and I thank all of this court for their courtesy, for their kindness, which I shall remember always.

I am prepared to receive your sentence."

September 14, 1918

Willa Cather:
Roll Call on the Prairies

Although she was born in Virginia and spent most of her life in New York City, Willa Cather had spent much of her early years in Nebraska and set some of her most powerful fiction on its prairies. Her cousin G. P. Cather was killed at Cantigny in May 1918. That summer, Cather returned to the family home in Red Cloud, where she read his letters and began plotting her novel *One of Ours*, published in 1922. Her essay about the effect of the war on the American heartland appeared in *The Red Cross Magazine*.

———————

NO ONE remembers now that the "fighting spirit" of the West was ever questioned; but at the time the United States entered the war, people along the Atlantic seaboard felt concern as to how the Middle West and the prairie states would respond. Again and again I heard New York business men and journalists say that the West wouldn't know there was a war until it was in the next county: the West was too busy making money and spending it.

Myself, I scarcely realized what being "in the war" meant until I went back to Nebraska and Colorado in the summer of 1917. In New York the war was one of many subjects people talked about; but in Omaha, Lincoln, in my own town, and the other towns along the Republican Valley, and over in the north of Kansas, there was nothing but the war. Everywhere the Red Cross was fully organized and at work, the first Liberty Loan was over-subscribed, many of the young men I knew had not waited for the draft but were already in training camps. In the afternoons one saw white things gleaming in the sun off through the trees; boys in their shirts and trousers, drilling in the schoolhouse yard or in the Court House Square.

Early the next summer, when we had still to prove whether we were a fighting nation or not, the First Division, so largely made up of Western men, made our début at Cantigny; and when the casualty lists began to appear in the New York papers, morning after morning I saw the names of little towns I knew in Nebraska, Kansas, Wyoming, Colorado—little country towns, happy and prosperous, where nothing so terrible or so wonderful had ever happened as to drag them into the New York newspapers, towns hidden away in miles of cornfields or tracts of sand and sage; and now their names came out one after another with the name of some boy who brought his home town into the light once and gloriously. It was like a long roll call, and all the little prairie towns were answering that they were there.

When I went West again in the summer of 1918, soon after Cantigny and Belleau Wood, I saw the working out of all that had been begun the summer before. Everyone supposed that the war would go on for another year, perhaps for two or three years, and everyone was living in the war and for the war. The women were "in the war" even more than the men. Not only in their thoughts, because they had sons and brothers in France, but in almost every detail of their daily lives.

In the first place, diet and cookery, the foundation of life, were revolutionized (city people could never realize what this means in the country and in little towns). All the neighbor women began to tell me how to make bread without white flour, cakes without eggs, cakes out of oatmeal, how to sweeten ice cream and puddings with honey or molasses. When my father absentmindedly took a second piece of sugar at breakfast, he felt the stony eyes of his women-folk and put it back with a sigh. My old friends could talk to me all day about the number of hot breads they could make without wheat flour, about rice bread, and oatmeal loafs, and rye loafs. All winter long they had experimented with breadstuffs. In New York we merely took a new kind of bread from the baker—hoping it wouldn't be worse than the last—and grumbled at the grocer because he wouldn't give us more sugar. But in the little towns, Hooverizing was creative and a test of character as well.

Out in the big grass counties of western Nebraska, where the ranches are a long way from town and it is the custom to lay in large supplies during the summer against the chance of bad roads in winter, many of the ranchers had bought their usual amount of sugar before the injunction about saving sugar was issued. They, at least, were "well fixed," as we say, and had a liberal supply for the winter in their own store rooms. But what they did was to haul that sugar back over the long roads and deliver it to the merchants. (Again, city people wouldn't know what that meant!)

"Who is Hoover? What is he? That all our wives obey him?" I doubt if the name of mortal man was ever uttered by so many women, so many times a day, as was his. He became a moral law. Every caution and injunction he uttered was published in the little county papers in Nebraska, Kansas, Colorado—everywhere else, probably, but I know about those states—and the women no more questioned any mandate he issued than they would the revealed Word. In cities we took what was sold to us; but there the housewives had all the raw materials of their old liberal dietary, and they could be underhanded and use them if they chose. All the new cookery was more difficult and troublesome than the old, partly because it was new, and the results were not so satisfactory. When a woman had plenty of butter and eggs, when her husband's general merchandise store was stocked with flour and sugar, why should she skimp and scrape and invent to save all these?

Hoover was the answer. No wonder he got results, with every woman in every kitchen from the Missouri River to the Rocky Mountains watching her flour barrel and her sugar box as a cat watches its kittens. An old German farmer-woman told me, "I chust Hoovered and Hoovered so long I loss my appetite. I don't eat no more."

There wasn't a church sociable in our town all winter and spring. Late in the summer the first church supper of the year was given in the basement dining room of the Methodist Church. It was an unusually good one—lots of fried chicken with cream gravy, mashed potatoes and scalloped potatoes, half a dozen kinds of salad, white biscuit, coffee with all the sugar you wanted, ice cream, and cakes and cakes. One old lady who had "partaken" until she was quite red in the face, turned to me and said it seemed like old times to sit down to a Methodist supper once again, adding, with a twinkle in her eye, "And I don't believe he'd begrudge it to us, this once, do you?"

"He? Who?"

"Hoover."

*

Not only was the cookery changed in my town and in all other little towns like it, but the whole routine of housekeeping was different from what it used to be. When a woman worked three afternoons a week at the Red Cross rooms, and knitted socks and sweaters in the evening, her domestic schedule had to be considerably altered. When I first got home I wondered why some of my old friends did not come to see me as they used to. How could they? When they were not at the Red Cross rooms, they were at home trying to catch up with their housework. One got used to such telephone messages as this:

"I will be at Surgical Dressings, in the basement of the Court House, until five. Can't you come over and walk home with me?"

That was the best one could do for a visit. The afternoon whist club had become a Red Cross sewing circle, and there were no parties but war parties. There were no town band concerts any more, because the band was in France; no football, no baseball, no skating rink. The merchants and bankers went out into the country after business hours and worked late into the night, helping the farmers, whose sons were gone, to save their grain.

Wherever I went out in the country, among the farms, the women met at least once a week at some appointed farmhouse to cut out garments, get their Red Cross instructions and materials, and then take the garments home to sew on them whenever they could. It went on in every farmhouse—American women, Swedish women, Germans, Norwegians, Bohemians, Canadian-French women, sewing and knitting. An old Danish grandmother, well along in her nineties, was knitting socks; her memory was failing and half the time she thought she was knitting for some other war, long ago. A bedridden woman who lived down by the depot begged the young girls who went canvassing to bring garments to her, so that she could work buttonholes, lying on her back. One Sunday at the Catholic church I saw an old woman crippled with rheumatism and palsy who had not risen during the service for years. But when the choir sang "The Star Spangled Banner" at the close of the mass she got to her feet and, using the shoulder of her little grandson for a crutch, stood, her head trembling and wobbling, until the last note died away.

From memory I cannot say how many hundreds of sweaters, drawers, bed jackets, women's blouses, mufflers, socks came out of our county. Before the day of shipment they were all brought to town and piled up in the show-windows of the shoe store—more than any one could believe, and next month there would be just as many. I used to walk slowly by, looking at them. Their presence there was taken as a matter of course, and I didn't wish to seem eccentric. Bales of heavy, queer-shaped chemises and blouses made for the homeless women of northern France, by the women on these big, safe, prosperous farms where there was plenty of everything but sons. When a people really speaks to a people, I felt, it doesn't speak by oratory or cablegrams; it speaks by things like these.

Up in the French settlement, in the north part of our county, the boys had been snatched away early—not to training camps or to way-stations, but rushed through to France. They all spoke a little household French, which was just what the American college boy who had been reading Racine and Victor Hugo could not do. So our French boys were given a few weeks of instruction and scattered among the American Expeditionary Force at the front wherever they were most needed.

Sarka Herbkova, Professor of Slavonic Languages at the University of Nebraska, did invaluable work in organizing not only the women of her own people, but all the women of Nebraska, American born and foreign born. She went about over the state a great deal for the Women's Council for National Defense and saw what sacrifices some of the farmers' wives made. She told a story of a Bohemian woman, living in one of the far western counties, who had saved fifty dollars of her egg money to buy a new winter dress and a warm coat. A Liberty Bond canvasser rode up to her door and presented her arguments. She heard the canvasser through, then brought her fifty dollars and put it down on the table and took the bond, remarking, "I guess I help fight Austria in my same clothes anyhow!"

Letters from the front usually reached our town on Saturday nights. The "foreign mail" had become a feature of life in

Kansas and Nebraska. The letters came in bunches; if one mother heard from her son, so did half a dozen others. One could hear them chatting to each other about what Vernon thought of Bordeaux, or what Roy had to say about the farming country along the Oise, or how much Elmer had enjoyed his rest leave in Paris. To me, knowing the boys, nearly all of these letters were remarkable. The most amusing were those which made severe strictures upon American manners; the boys were afraid the French would think us all farmers! One complained that his comrades talked and pushed chairs about in the Y hut while the singers who came to entertain them were on the platform. "And in this country, too, the Home of Politeness! Some yaps have no pride," he wrote bitterly. I can say for the boys from our town that they wanted to make a good impression.

A serious young man who had just come out of severe action wrote that he thought the Lord must have spared him for a purpose; but he was later killed in one of the advances before Château-Thiérry. A lively boy, the town favorite, who was dying of his wounds in a hospital on the Place de la Concorde, wrote only gay letters, telling about the charm of Paris, the kindness of everyone, and the pretty French girls who came to hold his hand and talk to him while his dressings were being changed. One happy-go-lucky lad, a third generation German, wrote often and was always having the time of his life; he had been buying laces for his mother in Paris, or recuperating in villas at Nice and Aix-les-Bains. He was coming home to Red Cloud all right, but he was coming by way of Vienna and Berlin. The butcher's son happened to be in London, and his letters were a curious mixture of information about Zeppelin raids and London monuments, and his burning curiosity to know more about the electric meat-chopper that had been put in the shop at home since he went away.

While I was at home the fourth Lovemann boy was drafted —his three brothers were already at the front. The father was a farmer, and a farmer's sons are his arms and hands; he can't work the land without them. The oldest son wrote in mournful anxiety from Paris, "If John goes, who will get the corn in this fall?" It seemed to me unfair that all the Lovemann boys should have to go. I asked a German girl, a neighbor of the

Lovemanns', why they didn't try to get exemption for John. "His sister says if they got exemption, John would run away!" she declared proudly.

Early in the summer of 1917, I stopped in the eastern part of the state and went to see a fine German farmer woman whom I had always known. She looked so aged and broken that I asked her if she had been ill.

"Oh, no; it's this terrible war. I have so many sons and grandsons. I am making black dresses."

"But why? The draft is not called yet. Your men may not even go. Why get ready to bury them?"

She shook her head. "I come from a war country. I know."

The next summer she was wearing her black dresses.

When I was a child, on the farm, we had many German neighbors, and the mothers and grandmothers told me such interesting things about farm-life and customs in the old country—beautiful things which I can never forget—that I used to ask them why they had left such a lovely land for our raw prairies. The answer was always the same—to escape military service. That I could not understand. What could be more romantic than to be a soldier? Some of our farmers had served in the German Army in their youth, and their wives had photographs of them in their uniforms; certainly they looked more jaunty and attractive than in their shirts and overalls as I saw them every day. The women, and even the children, used to tell me stories of the brutality of officers; how their father had been spat upon and struck in the face, and made to do repulsive things. Out in Wyoming I knew a clergyman who had been an officer in the German Army and had run away while he wore the uniform, escaping from the port of Antwerp after almost incredible dangers. He was a mild, genial man, and I could not understand why he should have run such chances. He explained that his colonel, a stupid and disgusting young count who hated University men, had selected him as the butt of his ridicule, and had so abused and humiliated him that he had not the least fear of death.

These people had left their country to get away from war, and now they were caught up in the wheels of it again. No one who read the casualty lists can doubt the loyalty of the foreign peoples in our country.

*

In "The Education of Henry Adams," a book which everyone has been reading, Mr. Adams says, in speaking of his student life in Germany: "I loved, or thought I loved, the people, but the Germany I loved was the eighteenth-century which the Germans were ashamed of, and were destroying as fast as they could." Our Germans in the West are nearly all people of that old-fashioned type who came away because they could not bear conditions at home. Two rich German farmers who lived on their broad acres near Beatrice, Nebraska, did say bitter things when America entered the war. They were summoned before a magistrate in Lincoln, who fined them lightly and administered to them a rebuke which was so wise and temperate and fair-minded that I cut the printed report of it out of the newspaper and put it in my scrap-book. "No man," he said, "can ask you to cease from loving the country of your birth." Sentences are commonplace or memorable according to the circumstances in which they are spoken; I thought that sentence, uttered by a magistrate at such a heated time to two blustery old men, a very remarkable one.

I heard much at home about an efficient woman in Omaha who was at the head of the Red Cross work in the state and who kept on her desk a map with colored pins stuck in the dots which indicate the little towns, and these pins in some way told her how many pairs of socks and how many sweaters Riverton, or Guide Rock, or Blue Hill, had delivered up to date. The finished garments which I saw piled in the shoe store, and in the farm houses, gave me a better idea of the magnitude of what was going on than did all the figures I read in the newspapers. Shiploads of food, shiploads of clothes—what do they mean, unless you know the fields that grew the grain and the hands that made the clothes?

Nothing brought the wonders of this war home to me so much as the work I saw being done on what were called "refugee garments"—chemises and blouses for the destitute women of Belgium and northern France, and underdrawers and shirts for the old men. These garments were all made according to very minute instructions from Headquarters, and they were exactly like the clothes these people had been accustomed to wear. Anything more clumsy and out-of-date according to American standards could hardly be imagined. In the Red Cross rooms under the court house and in the basement of the town library, out in the farmhouses all over our great rich county, women sat day after day and made underdrawers with from ten to fifteen buttons, and worked the buttonholes.

I am sure there is not a woman in our town who makes her husband's underclothes. American women, especially Western women, have a natural intolerance of slow, old-fashioned ways; they economize in effort and in time, eliminate involved processes. Yet the women in our town made hundreds of pairs of these drawers and an equal number of other garments just as clumsy. Why did they do it? Why didn't they send the old men X.Y.Z. underclothes, such as their own husbands wore? Or explain to the Belgians that they didn't need buttonholes, and that Belgium would get on better if she adopted modern methods? Americans are never slow to give advice of that kind.

I believe, in this case, the answer is that our women simply admired Belgium too much; they had no suggestions to offer to such a people. Their one wish was that those old men and women should have the kind of clothes they had always lived in, with no feeling of strangeness. The every-day ways of a very foreign people had come through to us, who are always so sure that our own are best. A great deal of verse has been written to Belgium in this country; but when I saw our smart, capable Western women patiently making drawers with fifteen button-holes and smiling with a kind of pride in their work, I thought that was poetry. I knew how many old feelings must have been rooted out and new feelings born, to make them *want* to do it, love to do it, in that tedious way that was against the tempo of their whole lives.

The Red Cross Magazine, July 1919

Ashby Williams:
from Experiences of the Great War

After the victory at St. Mihiel, Pershing wanted to advance eastward toward Metz but was overruled by Foch, who was planning a coordinated general offensive by the Belgian, British, French, and American armies. He directed Pershing to attack north from Verdun, along a front extending from the Argonne Forest to the Meuse River toward the vital railway line at Sedan. A lawyer from Roanoke, Virginia, Major Ashby Williams had commanded the First Battalion, 320th Infantry Regiment, 80th Division at St. Mihiel. While advancing to their jumping-off position on the night of September 25, Williams and his men came under artillery fire.

———————

A HORRIBLE EXPERIENCE

AFTER THE MEN had had their coffee—I remember I drank a good swig of it, too—I gave directions that the men should get in shape to move out of the woods. Then followed one of the most horrible experiences of my whole life in the war, and one which I hope never to have to go through again. The Boche began to shell the woods. When the first one came over I was sitting under the canvas that had been still spread over the cart shafts. It fell on the up side of the woods. As I came out another one fell closer. I was glad it was dark because I was afraid my knees were shaking. I was afraid of my voice, too, and I remember I spoke in a loud voice so it would not tremble, and gave orders that Commanders should take their units to the dugouts which were less than a hundred yards away until the shelling was over, as I did not think it necessary to sacrifice any lives under the circumstances. Notwithstanding my precautions, some of the shells fell among the cooks and others who remained about the kitchens, killing some of them and wounding others.

In about twenty minutes I ordered the companies to fall in

577

on the road by our area preparatory to marching out of the woods. They got into a column of squads in perfect order, and we had proceeded perhaps a hundred yards along the road in the woods when we came on to one of the companies of the Second Battalion which we were to follow that night. We were held there perhaps forty-five minutes while the Second Battalion ahead of us got in shape to move out. One cannot imagine the horrible suspense and experience of that wait. The Boche began to shell the woods again. There was no turning back now, no passing around the companies ahead of us, we could only wait and trust to the Grace of God.

We could hear the explosion as the shell left the muzzle of the Boche gun, then the noise of the shell as it came toward us, faint at first, then louder and louder until the shell struck and shook the earth with its explosion. One can only feel, one cannot describe the horror that fills the heart and mind during this short interval of time. You know he is aiming the gun at you and wants to kill you. In your mind you see him swab out the hot barrel, you see him thrust in the deadly shell and place the bundle of explosives in the breach; you see the gunner throw all his weight against the trigger; you hear the explosion like the single bark of a great dog in the distance, and you hear the deadly missile singing as it comes towards you, faintly at first, then distinctly, then louder and louder until it seems so loud that everything else has died, and then the earth shakes and the eardrums ring, and dirt and iron reverberate through the woods and fall about you.

This is what you hear, but no man can tell what surges through the heart and mind as you lie with your face upon the ground listening to the growing sound of the hellish thing as it comes towards you. You do not think, sorrow only fills the heart, and you only hope and pray. And when the doubly-damned thing hits the ground, you take a breath and feel relieved, and think how good God has been to you again. And God was good to us that night—to those of us who escaped unhurt. And for the ones who were killed, poor fellows, some blown to fragments that could not be recognized, and the men who were hurt, we said a prayer in our hearts.

Such was my experience and the experience of my men that night in the Bois de Borrus, but their conduct was fine. I think, indeed, their conduct was the more splendid because they knew they were not free to shift for themselves and find shelter, but must obey orders, and obey they did in the spirit of fine soldiers to the last man. After that experience I knew that men like these would never turn back, and they never did.

From *Experiences of the Great War* (1919)

Edward C. Lukens:
from A Blue Ridge Memoir

Edward C. Lukens had left the University of Pennsylvania law school
to serve as a lieutenant in the Third Battalion, 320th Infantry, 80th
Division. In *A Blue Ridge Memoir*, written in February–March 1919
and published in 1922, Lukens would recall the opening hours of the
Meuse-Argonne offensive. The attack on September 26, 1918, ignited
forty-seven days of fighting in which 26,000 Americans were killed
and 95,000 wounded.

WE DEPLOYED in an open field in front of Dead Man's Hill,
guiding the moppers-up on the support companies of the
battalion ahead. We had about six squads, which we placed at
intervals with the corporal in charge of each one, while Lieutenant Titus and I each took the command of three squads.
Less than an hour remained after we had completed our dispositions until the advance should begin. Titus and I sat down
together for a few minutes and shared a jelly sandwich that I
had carried with me for the last two days and shook hands to
our mutual luck; then we went to our own sections, and I attached myself to the middle squad of the three, as it was too
dark to hope to see them all. Meanwhile our barrage had been
going on in great intensity, lighting up the sky in back of us
and creating a tremendous racket as it burst only a few hundred yards in front. Combined with the smoke which the artillery put down in addition to their H.E.'s was a considerable
natural fog, and a few minutes before "H Hour" it became so
thick that one could hardly see five yards ahead of him. We
looked at our watches frequently and awaited 5.30.

"Going over the top" is an expression that has lasted from
the trench days when the British troops climbed out of the
trenches by ladders on the appointed minute, and there was a
sharp and sudden break from the security of the trench to the
exposure on top of the parapet. With us it was a misnomer.

There was no "top" to go over. We were already deployed in an open field with only a few scattered shell holes in it. The outposts had been withdrawn to avoid our own barrage; the boundaries of "No Man's Land" were not clearly defined. In fact, in one sense we really deployed in No Man's Land, under the protection of our artillery. "H Hour" was chiefly remarkable for its failure to be dramatic or intense.

Five-thirty came. I could see just eight men and could not tell whether the rest of the outfit was starting or not. We started forward as a "combat group" (single file) depending on my compass, for we were as much cut off from the others as if we had been alone at sea. We kept walking forward at a moderate pace, constantly wondering whether the other groups were going faster or slower. Soon some of our shells began to hit too close in front of us, and we slowed down a little. We did not know whether they were exceptionally short, or on the normal barrage line, for the air was too thick to see where the rest were bursting. The first living thing that I saw was a rabbit, coming through the smoke from the Boche lines like greased lightning. All kinds of game birds were also started, and flew about bewildered. Then we saw a Boche coming toward us with his hands high in air and the most terrified look in his face that I have ever seen in mortal man, running almost as fast as the rabbit. We let him go on by, laughing at him as we passed, and we knew that the companies up ahead had begun to do business.

We came to a gully about ankle deep in water, and crossed it at a leap. We didn't know that this was Forges Brook, which we had been told was deep enough to require bridges, and kept on wondering when we would come to it. Some of the Engineers made the same mistake, for we had gone several hundred yards beyond it when there loomed up out of the fog, going diagonally, a crowd of about twenty men carrying a bulky wooden structure which they told us was a bridge for Forges Brook. Soon we began to meet parts of other outfits, generally striking on slightly different angles from our own, for very slight compass errors make a big difference when a little distance has passed. It became apparent that the different companies had already become pretty badly intermixed, and as for the moppers-up, I didn't have the slightest idea where any of my other squads were. The smoke and fog were fatal to any hope of keeping organizations in their proper place and formation, but in spite of that it was a tremendous life-saver, for the front waves had gone over and flanked the first row of machine gun nests before the Boche gunners had hardly a chance to fire a shot, and our casualties were almost nothing as long as we were hidden. I began to run into other officers that I knew, and we exchanged "good mornings" and cigarettes as though we were meeting on a city street. I could not make head nor tail of where I was with reference to the companies, for I kept getting mixed up with the Second Battalion, whom I was supposed to follow, and then whenever we would be delayed a little we would find ourselves crowded on by L Company whom we were supposed to keep ahead of.

Meanwhile there was the "mopping-up" to do, although the assault companies had pretty well finished the job themselves. We were supposed to work from left to right on our sector, but this beautiful theory didn't work in practice, for the rest of the detachment was now entirely out of my control, and I had to trust to them to take care of the ground in front of them while my squad confined themselves to what was in our sight. To have attempted to go much to the flank with such a small group would have left us hopelessly behind, and spoiled any chance of our making the way clear for our battalion. So we ran along the top of the trenches, heaving bombs into all dugouts that might contain hidden gunners or snipers, looking at scattered wounded Germans to assure ourselves that they were safely out of action, ready to kill them if they should show any signs of treachery, and making the prisoners who were not badly hurt run faster to the rear. The old-fashioned way of "mopping-up" was to kill everything, and there is no possible doubt but that it was necessary in the days of closer personal combat and greater danger of treachery, but in the new open style of fighting, and with the Boche's general willingness to get safely to the rear as fast as he could, it was unnecessary and almost impracticable. Furthermore, we had been ordered to take prisoners whenever possible, because the Boche will stop shooting sooner to go to the rear than when he knows he is in for sure death. One of our companies that morning had the experience of opening fire on a group of Boche coming forward to surrender, and having them return to their guns and hit several of our men before they were again subdued. But it was often hard to tell just when a Boche was safely out of action and we heard later of a case in our sector where one had slipped back to a buzzer station after being wounded, to be found and killed a few minutes later, so it is probable that if anything, we should have been even rougher than we were.

The first dead Yank I saw was lying directly in front of a machine gun in a shallow trench, not more than two yards in front of the muzzle, and the Boche behind the gun was also dead. They must have got each other at almost the same instant. We lost comparatively few men in this first stage of the drive, and had hardly any shelling at first because the sharpness of the attack kept the Boche busy moving his guns back. Company H almost ran into a gun as it was being moved, and shot the horses and drivers before they could escape.

One of our men's faults was their curiosity and their craze for souvenirs. I came upon a whole group of them gathered around a few prisoners, accepting presents of iron crosses and buttons which the frightened Boche offered doubtless as bribes for their lives, our men apparently forgetting that there were more enemies close at hand. By this time I had lost all my original men, as they would be delayed at some little job and be absorbed into the companies in rear, so I broke up the souvenir party and thereby recruited a dozen or so new moppers-up. I saw a lone American lying on the ground shooting his Chauchat, so ran over to see what the fuss was, and had no sooner dropped down beside him than he curled up with a bullet in the stomach. I took his gun while another fellow picked up a few magazines. The wounded boy did not seem to be suffering, but talked in the voice of a sleepy child protesting against my taking his gun away, and I had to humor him as you would a child, and tell him I would give it back in a minute, in order to get it out of his grasp. We crawled rapidly around the flank of the hostile nest, but by the time we got to it someone had already crippled the single Hun with a shot from the other flank. By this time we were too far onward for me to leave my job and go back to the wounded man and I don't know whether he lived or not, but I believe he soon went painlessly to sleep still murmuring about the loss of his beloved gun.

Our soldiers in this drive walked ahead for the most part as nonchalantly as though they were on a route march. Only when something was actually encountered was the atmosphere in the least intense. In fact sometimes they were too easy-going, apparently too innocent to realize what sudden crises might arise. They were all hungry by this time, and out came the bread and hardtack, though we did not stop. I think this attitude "got the German's goat" even more than intense ferocity, which they better understood. One Boche officer who was captured said he had seen many kinds of soldiers in many kinds of fighting, but he had never before seen soldiers advancing against the enemy with their rifles slung over their shoulders and bread and jam in their hands. I have been asked whether it was true that the Yanks went forward shouting "Lusitania!" They did not, in our outfit. They went forward eating, smoking cigarettes, chewing tobacco, and when they did holler at the Boche it was invariably a less romantic and more vulgar word that they yelled.

By about eleven o'clock we had reached our preliminary objective, where we were to reform our lines and wait thirty-five minutes while the barrage was again laid down ahead of us. Our artillery this time was weaker and less accurate, either because of the more extreme range or because some of it was moving up, and we also got a little desultory shelling from "Jerry." My own company came up, and I found most of my detachment had already rejoined them, so as the mopping-up job was about over, I decided to go back to I Company and try to get my own platoon into shape.

A large group of prisoners came over the hill on our left, and as we didn't see any guards with them, some officers thought it was a counter-attack coming, so I Company started over to meet them, and narrowly averted shooting them up by suddenly seeing some Americans with them. This move had put us too far over to the left, and when we started forward again, I and K Companies were separated from the rest of the regiment. However, as there had been a gap between us and the 4th Division, it probably was just as well in the end.

We advanced by ourselves in a double skirmish line over the next hill, with apparently no sign of trouble, and the right flank of the company was approaching a small patch of woods, when a burst of machine gun fire suddenly splattered the ground about our feet, slightly wounding one man in the leg. We dropped instantly, and hugged the ground close until some men from the other end of the company, who were not in direct range, had time to work into the woods from the flank, for it is an inevitable cause of needless casualties to advance frontally on a machine gun nest if it can possibly be flanked. Then we crawled around until we could also get into the woods, and a regular man-hunt developed. The woods was grown thick with laurel, penetrated by many intersecting paths, and two or three men would sneak up each fork to hunt out the prey. About eight of us, keeping on the main path, came to a small clearing which contained two small wooden shanties. We approached cautiously, watching the trees for snipers, and glancing sharply around on all sides. We found the buildings deserted, and then saw near one of them the entrance of a dugout. I peered down, and saw something moving down in the darkness, so I pulled a bomb out of my pocket and struck the cap against my tin hat. At the sound of the hissing fuse, there came from the dugout the most unholy conglomeration of yells that I ever heard from human throats—screams of terror and abject pleading. But six seconds is too short a time to negotiate a surrender; they had kept hidden too long and could not possibly claim to be regarded as prisoners. The fuse was already going and down the hole went the bomb. I jumped back from the mouth and in an instant there was a terrific explosion and a cloud of dust and smoke came up. Why it didn't kill them all, we couldn't imagine, but no sooner had the smoke cleared than the cries started again, and we could distinguish the words "No more" in English. This time we waited with our guns ready, and out piled eight Boche, apparently without a scratch, but as scared as men could well be. There was something ludicrous and at the same time contemptible in the way they screamed for mercy. A short five minutes ago, they had almost killed us, and now they were yelping "Kamerad," and giving us their pistols and even offering their personal belongings with the attitude of whipped curs. We didn't kill them, but we didn't want any of their "Kamerad" stuff either, and we scarcely knew how to express our disgust at their offer to shake hands with us for sparing their lives. It was this same feeling of loathing that kept me from wanting anything they had as souvenirs, though two of the men got beautiful Luger revolvers and various other articles. Most of the men were souvenir-crazy, but in fairness it must be remembered that whatever they took was purely as souvenirs, and I don't believe any of the prisoners' stuff was ever taken for its money value. I contented myself with a small wooden sign on the shanty, which proved that we had captured a battalion headquarters, and I lost that soon afterwards. We also found a whole bag full of maps and documents, which we sent back to the Intelligence Officer, though I never heard whether they proved of any value. The eight prisoners were started back over the hill and sent running to the rear with an "Allez!" and perhaps a kick, and after searching the woods a few minutes more, we rejoined the company.

Horace Pippin:
from "Autobiography, First World War"

A manual laborer with a love of drawing and little formal education, Horace Pippin had lived a hardscrabble life in upstate New York and New Jersey before enlisting in the 369th Infantry Regiment in 1917. During the Meuse-Argonne offensive, the "Harlem Hellfighters" were attached to the French 161st Division, and they fought in Champagne, apart from the main American army. On September 30, 1918, Pippin was shot in the shoulder, permanently disabling his right arm. After the war he learned to guide his wounded limb with his left hand and eventually became a widely exhibited painter. Pippin's unpublished manuscript from the 1920s includes this narrative of the fighting around Séchault.

AT ONE o clock the artillery were in thir Position and Began to fire. The Germens air plaines were after us good and strong the end of this Day we got 14 machine guns 500 prisners and a town. Then we hel the line for the artillery to move up. Prisners were comeing throu our line. Goeine Back and every one were happy. That they were out of it. For they knew that, they would see home a gan some time. We onley hell the line that night. The machine guns were thick they keeped spiteing Bullets a cross our line on till the artillery came up, then that morneing. I got in, with Co I. I had notheing to eait for 3 Days. The Germens line were strong. And shells dropeing every where. Yet we were advancing sloley. I were in shell holes that were smokeing, and they were hot, the machine guns were in trees as well as in Bushess and in Housess and any thing they could get a machine gun in. They had it there. Wimens as well as men, ueseing a machine gun we were faceing a nother hill. The snipers were thick all so, I seen a machine gun nest I got him. My Budy and I were after a nother one. Both of us were in the same shell hole. I were lookeing for a nother hole that would put me in [   ] of him. After I seen one. I said to my comrad, you go one way, and Ill go the other, and one of us can get him. For we could not see him, from where we were at. For he were Back of a Rock. Now it were to get him in sight and to do that we hat to take a chance of one to get it. Both of us left the shell hole, at the same time, I got near the shell hole that I had pecked out. When he let me have it. I went Down in the shell hole. He cliped my neck and got me throu my shoulder and right arm. Yet I had notheing to eait yet and I onley had a little water in my canteen. I Began to plug up my wounds when my Budy came to me and did what he could for me. Then he tole me that he got the Germen and the gun. I were leyeing on my Back. I thought I could get up But I could not do so. I shook hands with him and I never seen him cents. Now the shells were comeing close to me. Piceses of shell would come in near me some times. Then the Germen sniper kepted after me all Day. His Bullets would clep the shell hole that hell me this were 8 o clock in the morning. Some time that after noon some French swipers came By. They look for Germen that is left Back so he seen me layeing there. When he did so. He stoped to say sometheing to me. But he never got it out for just then a Bullet past throu his head. And he sank on me. I seen him comeing on But I could not move. I were just that weeke. So I hat to take him. I were glad to get his water and all so Bread. I took my left hand and I got some coffee. After some hird time geteing it from him, after that I felt good and I trided to get up a gan. But I were to week to do so. Night were comeing on. And it Began to Rain. Then I tried to get the Blanked from my Dead comrad. That I could not do. And I could not get him of off me. The Rain came more and more ontill I were in water yet I were groweing weeker and weeker all the time and I went to sleep. I cant say how long I slep. But two Boyes came and I woke up. They took the French men of off me and then took me out of the shell hole for some Distens where there were more wonded ones. I were left there the Rest of the night. Every time I would get in a sleep I would Be woken up By the French troops goeing to the line. On tell near morning four French took me in to a Dugout and then to a nother on till they found a Dr. Then he did somtheing, I do not no aney more that night. When I woke up, it were Day. Then I were caryed out of the Dugout I seen then that it were full of shot up men like my self some wirst then I. I layed out there for some time in the Rain waiteing for my tirn to be taken Down to the Road to the amblance. Over the hell came some Germen prisners with a French officer and they took me to the Road. It were all they could do, were to stand up under me goeing Down the hell. They had me over thir heads. And I thought that I would Roal of. A shell or two came close to us. But they made the Road. I seen the artillery were Hobe to Hobe and all at work. I were shoved in the amblance with 5 others made 6 in all and shells foloed us ontell we got to the feel Hospital. When I got there it were all I could do, to tell them ho I were. So I pointed to my shirt I had Riten down like this 101127 Horace Pippin Co. K. 369. Inf, I new no more. On tell I were taken to the table to see what were Rong with me. They gave me some dop and that did put me a way for good. I cant say how long I were in it. After I came out of it I were not there long. They took me to a nother Hospital Bace 1 in leeon.

Ernest W. Gibson:
from History of First Vermont and 57th Pioneer Infantry

In March 1918 a virulent strain of the influenza virus appeared at Camp Funston, an army training facility in northeastern Kansas. The virus spread across the United States and into Europe and Asia over the next six months. A much deadlier wave of the disease began to ravage the United States that fall. The 1918–19 influenza pandemic killed between thirty and fifty million people worldwide, including 675,000 Americans. Even though medical authorities realized that packed troopships cultured an environment that spread the disease, the constant requirement to deliver more men to France during the fall offensive outweighed concerns about infection. In an address given at Montpelier, Vermont, on October 23, 1919, Captain Ernest W. Gibson, a company commander in the 57th Pioneer Infantry Regiment, recalled how his regiment left Camp Merritt in northern New Jersey on September 29, 1918, and prepared to cross the Atlantic on the troopship *Leviathan* (formerly the German ocean liner *Vaterland*).

———————

The first battalion assigned to guard duty aboard the troopship moved out from Camp about one o'clock in the morning of the 28th of September. The 2nd and 3rd battalions marched out from their barracks about one A.M. on the morning of the 29th of September.

We had proceeded but a short distance when it was discovered that the men were falling out of ranks, unable to keep up. The attention of the commanding officer was called to the situation. The column was halted and the camp surgeon was summoned. The examination showed that the dreaded Influenza had hit us. Although many men had fallen out we were ordered to resume the march. We went forward up and up over that winding moonlit road leading to Alpine Landing on the Hudson, where ferry boats were waiting to take us to Hoboken.

The victims of the epidemic fell on either side of the road unable to carry their heavy packs. Some threw their equipment away and with determination tried to keep up with their comrades. Army trucks and ambulances following picked up those who had fallen and took them back to the camp hospital. How many men or how much equipment was lost on that march has never been determined.

On board the transport men continued to be stricken and 100 of these were taken off and returned to shore before sailing. On Sunday afternoon the 29th tugs pulled the great ship into mid stream, turned her prow in the direction of the open ocean, the great propellers began to turn and we were off to the Great Adventure. We had on board 9033 officers and men and about 200 army nurses on their way to hospitals in France. The presence of the nurses was very fortunate as it afterwards turned out. The ship was packed, conditions were such that the Influenza bacillus could breed and multiply with extraordinary swiftness. We were much of the way without convoy. The U-boat menace made it necessary to keep every port hole closed at night, and the air below decks where the men slept was hot and heavy. The number of sick increased rapidly. Washington was appraised of the situation, but the call for men for the allied armies was so great that we must go on at any cost. The sick bay became overcrowded and it became necessary to evacuate the greater portion of deck E and turn that into sick quarters. Doctors and nurses were stricken. Every available doctor and nurse was utilized to the limit of endurance.

The official government report now on file with the Navy Department has this to say in regard to the conditions on board the Leviathan: "The conditions during the night cannot be visualized by anyone who has not actually seen them. Pools of blood from severe nasal hemorrhages of many patients were scattered throughout the compartments, and the attendants were powerless to escape tracking through the mess, because of the narrow passages between the bunks. The decks became wet and slippery, groans and cries of the terrified added to the confusion of the applicants clamoring for treatment, and altogether a true inferno reigned supreme."

We landed at Brest October 7th, and all who were able to march were moved to the mud flats beyond the Pontanezzan Barracks, where we remained until October 11th. Several hundred of the men never reached camp or their organizations. They were picked up by Y. M. C. A. and K. C. men or by army ambulances and taken to hospitals as soon as they were unable to walk. Official records show that within a few days after landing 123 of the men died at Kehruon Hospital, about forty at Base Hospital Number 33, several at Naval Base Hospital number 5 and at the hospital at Landernau.

Nearly two hundred of the regiment were buried in the American cemetery at Lambezellec. This cemetery is well located on a hill, from which one, looking to the West towards the Land of Liberty, gets a beautiful view in the distance of the waters of the great ocean separating the sleepers from their homeland. One of my last acts before leaving France was to visit the cemetery, pick out the graves of our Vermont men, pay honor to their sacrifice, and say a word of farewell to the heroes who sleep in the soil of our Sister Republic.

Henry A. May:
from History of the U.S.S. Leviathan

Lieutenant Commander Henry A. May, a senior medical officer assigned to the troopship USS *Leviathan* during the crossing of September 29–October 7, 1918 (the same voyage that brought Gibson and his regiment to France), recorded the progress of the disease as it spread among the passengers and crew. An estimated 46,000 members of the U.S. armed forces died of influenza in 1918–19.

COURSE OF THE EPIDEMIC

THIS WAS influenced materially by these main factors:

First, the widespread infection of several organizations before they embarked, and their assignment to many different parts of the ship.

Second, the type of men comprising the most heavily infected group. These men were particularly liable to infection.

Third, the absolute lassitude of those becoming ill caused them to lie in their bunks without complaint until their infection had become profound and pneumonia had begun. The severe epistaxis which ushered in the disease in a very large proportion of the cases, caused a lowering of resisting powers which was added to by fright, by the confined space, and the motion of the ship. Where pneumonia set in, not one man was in condition to make a fight for life.

As noted above, the sick bay was filled a few hours after leaving Hoboken. All pneumonia cases were placed in one isolation ward at the beginning, and another isolation unit was set aside for measles and mumps, both of which diseases were present among the troops. The other isolation units were first filled with influenza cases and later with pneumonias. Until the fifth day of the voyage, few patients could be sent to duty because of great weakness following the drop in temperature as they grew better. Only the worst cases in E-deck ward were

sent to sick bay at any time, and all were potentially pneumonias. The E-deck ward was more than full all the time and
there were many ill men in various troop spaces in other parts
of the ship.

There are no means of knowing the actual number of sick at
any one time, but it is estimated that fully 700 cases had developed by the night of September 30th. They were brought to
the sick bay from all parts of the ship, in a continuous stream,
only to be turned away because all beds were occupied. Most
of them then lay down on the decks, inside and out, and made
no effort to reach the compartment where they belonged. In
fact practically no one had the slightest idea where he did belong, and he left his blankets, clothing, kit, and all his possessions to be salvaged at the end of the voyage.

During October 1st, every effort was made to increase hospital space below, as noted above. The heretofore satisfactory
arrangements for army sick call were not adhered to by the
army medical officers, and hundreds of men applied for treatment at the E-deck ward instead of going to the twelve outlying sick call stations. On this day, Colonel Decker, the Chief
Army Surgeon, became ill. As he was the only army medical
officer who had had army experience in administrative matters
there was now no competent head to the army organization.
Two other medical officers also became ill and remained in
their rooms to the end of the voyage.

Late in the evening of this day the E-deck ward was opened
on the starboard side and was filled before morning. Twenty
army nurses were detailed for duty during the night. When
patients were brought up, their mates carefully left their blankets and clothing below and scouting parties had to be sent
through the compartments to gather up all loose blankets for
use of the sick. Fortunately we had about 100 army blankets in
the medical storeroom which had been salvaged on other
voyages. These were used while they lasted.

HORRORS OF WAR

The conditions during this night cannot be visualized by any
one who has not actually seen them.

The morning of October 2nd brought no relief. Things seemed to grow worse instead of better. Cleaning details were demanded of the army, but few men responded. Those who came would stay awhile and wander away, never to be seen again. No N.C.O.'s were sent, and there was no organization for control. The nurses made a valiant effort to clean up and the navy hospital corpsmen did marvels of work, but always against tremendous odds. Only by constant patrolling between the bunks could any impression be made upon the litter and finally our own sailors were put on the job. They took hold like veterans and the place was kept respectably clean thereafter.

The first death from pneumonia occurred on this day, and the body was promptly embalmed and encased in a navy standard casket.

When evening came no impression had been made upon the great number of sick men about the decks and in their own bunks. So arrangements were made to enlarge the hospital space by including the port side of E.R.S. 2. On October 3rd this was accomplished and from that time to the end of the voyage we had enough bunks to accommodate practically all the worst cases. Three deaths occurred this day and all were embalmed and encased. After going through the hospital and troop spaces that night it was estimated that there were about 900 cases of influenza in the ship. In the wards we sent back to bunks below all men whose temperature reached 99 and kept all bunks filled with cases of higher fever.

October 4th, seven deaths during the day. The sea was rough and the ship rolled heavily. Hundreds of men were thoroughly miserable from seasickness and other hundreds who had been off the farm but a few weeks, were miserable from terror of the strange surroundings and the ravages of the epidemic. Dozens of these men applied at the wards for treatment and the inexperience of army doctors in the recognition of seasickness caused a great many needless admissions to the hospital.

Many officers and nurses were ill in their rooms, and required the constant attention of a corps of well nurses, and an army medical officer to attend them.

Each succeeding day of the voyage was like those preceding, a nightmare of weariness and anxiety on the part of nurses, doctors, and hospital corpsmen. No one thought of bed for himself and all hands worked day and night. On the 5th there were 10 deaths, on the 6th there were 24, and on the 7th, the day of arrival at our destination, the toll was 31. The army ambulance boat was promptly alongside, and debarkation of the sick began about noon. The sick bay was cleared first and we at once began to clean up in preparation for the wounded to be carried westbound. E-deck was then evacuated, but all the sick could not be handled before night, about 200 remaining on board.

On the 8th these were taken off by the army, but not before fourteen more deaths had occurred. Although on this day almost the entire personnel (army) had gone, the nurses remained until the last sick man was taken off.

PNEUMONIA

It is the opinion of myself and the other medical officers attached to the ship that there were fully 2,000 cases of influenza on board. How many developed pneumonia there are no means of knowing. Over 75 cases of the latter disease were admitted to the sick bay, most of them moribund. Of these, 3 improved so much that they went back to their compartments, 29 were transferred to hospital ashore, and about 40 died. As the records required to transfer patients from the army to the navy medical officers were furnished in but few cases, and as my records embrace all the dead, I had no means of knowing how many died in the sick bay and how many in the E-deck ward. Cases of pneumonia were found dying in various parts of the ship and many died in the E-deck ward a few minutes after admission. Owing to the public character of that ward, men passing would see a vacant bunk and lie down in it without applying to a medical officer at all. Records were impossible, and even identification of patients was extremely difficult because hundreds of men had blank tags tied about their necks. Many were either delirious or too ill to know their own names. Nine hundred and sixty-six patients were removed by the army hospital authorities in France.

DEATHS

Ninety-one deaths occurred among the army personnel, of whom one was an officer, as follows:

October	2 1	death
"	3 3	deaths
"	4 7	deaths
"	5 10	deaths
"	6 24	deaths
"	7 31	deaths
"	8 14	deaths
"	10 1	death

The sick officer was treated in the open air on B deck, had a special army nurse during the day, and a navy hospital corpsman at night.

HOSPITAL CORPS

I cannot speak in terms of sufficient commendation of the work of the hospital corps of this ship. Every man was called upon to exert himself to the limit of endurance during the entire round trip. No one complained, every man was on the job. Many of them worked twenty-four hours at a stretch amid conditions that can never be understood by one ashore or on a man-of-war. Some of the embalming detail, worked at their gruesome task forty-eight hours at a stretch without complaint, and at the end I had to drive them away to a bath and bed.

I have learned that the following named men of the Commissary Department voluntarily remained on duty with the sick on E-deck during the entire voyage.

George Willis	CCS
H. L. Ringrose	SC-2
A. Barbel	SC-4
R. Steinman	SC-4

Had we been in the midst of smallpox or plague they would doubtless have done the same. The actual danger to all hands was extremely great and all these men deserve the highest commendation for their actions.

From *History of the U.S.S. Leviathan* (1919)

Woodrow Wilson: Address to the Senate on Woman Suffrage

The 1916 Democratic platform had endorsed the adoption of woman suffrage on a state-by-state basis but did not propose the passage of a federal constitutional amendment. Upon his nation's entering the war, President Wilson's interest in the passage of a suffrage amendment steadily increased; and on January 9, 1918, he publicly embraced the idea. The next day the House of Representatives approved the amendment without a vote to spare, 274–136. When the amendment came before the Senate in the fall of 1918, Carrie Chapman Catt anticipated that it would fall short of the requisite two-thirds majority and asked the President himself to intervene. Wilson addressed the Senate on September 30; but the next day, the measure failed as predicted, 62–34. Rejected by one vote in February 1919, the amendment would finally pass the Senate, 56–25, on June 4, 1919. Ratification by three-fourths of the states would follow on August 18, 1920.

Speaking Copy 30 Sept., 1918.

GENTLEMEN OF THE SENATE: The unusual circumstances of a world war in which we stand and are judged in the view not only of our own people and our own consciences but also in the view of all nations and peoples will, I hope, justify in your thought, as it does in mine, the message I have come to bring you. I regard the concurrence of the Senate in the constitutional amendment proposing the extension of the suffrage to women as vitally essential to the successful prosecution of the great war of humanity in which we are engaged. I have come to urge upon you the considerations which have led me to that conclusion. It is not only my privilege, it is also my duty to apprise you of every circumstance and element involved in this momentous struggle which seems to me to affect its very processes and its outcome. It is my duty to win the war and to ask you to remove every obstacle that stands in the way of winning it.

I had assumed that the Senate would concur in the amendment because no disputable principle is involved but only a question of the method by which the suffrage is to be extended to women. There is and can be no party issue involved in it. Both of our great national parties are pledged, explicitly pledged, to equality of suffrage for the women of the country. Neither party, therefore, it seems to me, can justify hesitation as to the method of obtaining it, can rightfully hesitate to substitute federal initiative for state initiative, if the early adoption of the measure is necessary to the successful prosecution of the war and if the method of state action proposed in the party platforms of 1916 is impracticable within any reasonable length of time, if practicable at all. And its adoption is, in my judgment, clearly necessary to the successful prosecution of the war and the successful realization of the objects for which the war is being fought.

That judgment I take the liberty of urging upon you with solemn earnestness for reasons which I shall state very frankly and which I shall hope will seem as conclusive to you as they seem to me.

This is a peoples' war and the peoples' thinking constitutes its atmosphere and morale, not the predilections of the drawing room or the political considerations of the caucus. If we be indeed democrats and wish to lead the world to democracy, we can ask other peoples to accept in proof of our sincerity and our ability to lead them whither they wish to be led nothing less persuasive and convincing than our actions. Our professions will not suffice. Verification must be forthcoming when verification is asked for. And in this case verification is asked for,—asked for in this particular matter. You ask by whom? Not through diplomatic channels; not by Foreign Ministers. Not by the intimations of parliaments. It is asked for by the anxious, expectant, suffering peoples with whom we are dealing and who are willing to put their destinies in some measure in our hands, if they are sure that we wish the same things that they do. I do not speak by conjecture. It is not alone the voices of statesmen and of newspapers that reach me, and the voices of foolish and intemperate agitators do not reach me at all. Through many, many channels I have been made aware what the plain, struggling, workaday folk are thinking upon whom the chief terror and suffering of this tragic war falls. They are looking to the great, powerful, famous Democracy of the West to lead them to the new day for which they have so long waited; and they think, in their logical simplicity, that democracy means that women shall play their part in affairs alongside men and upon an equal footing with them. If we reject measures like this, in ignorance or defiance of what a new age has brought forth, of what they have seen but we have not, they will cease to believe in us; they will cease to follow or to trust us. They have seen their own governments accept this interpretation of democracy,—seen old governments like that of Great Britain, which did not profess to be democratic, promise readily and as of course this justice to women, though they had before refused it, the strange revelations of this war having made many things new and plain, to governments as well as to peoples.

Are we alone to refuse to learn the lesson? Are we alone to ask and take the utmost that our women can give,—service and sacrifice of every kind,—and still say we do not see what title that gives them to stand by our sides in the guidance of the affairs of their nation and ours? We have made partners of the women in this war; shall we admit them only to a partnership of suffering and sacrifice and toil and not to a partnership of privilege and right? This war could not have been fought, either by the other nations engaged or by America, if it had not been for the services of the women,—services rendered in every sphere,—not merely in the fields of effort in which we have been accustomed to see them work, but wherever men have worked and upon the very skirts and edges of the battle itself. We shall not only be distrusted but shall deserve to be distrusted if we do not enfranchise them with the fullest possible enfranchisement, as it is now certain that the other great free nations will enfranchise them. We cannot isolate our thought or our action in such a matter from the thought of the rest of the world. We must either conform or deliberately reject what they propose and resign the leadership of liberal minds to others.

The women of America are too noble and too intelligent and too devoted to be slackers whether you give or withhold this thing that is mere justice; but I know the magic it will work in their thoughts and spirits if you give it them. I propose it as I would propose to admit soldiers to the suffrage, the men fighting in the field for our liberties and the liberties of the world, were they excluded. The tasks of the women lie at the very heart of the war, and I know how much stronger that heart will beat if you do this just thing and show our women that you trust them as much as you in fact and of necessity depend upon them.

Have I said that the passage of this amendment is a vitally necessary war measure, and do you need further proof? Do you stand in need of the trust of other peoples and of the trust of our own women? Is that trust an asset or is it not? I tell you plainly, as the commander-in-chief of our armies and of the gallant men in our fleets, as the present spokesman of this people in our dealings with the men and women throughout the world who are now our partners, as the responsible head of a great government which stands and is questioned day by day as to its purposes, its principles, its hopes, whether they be serviceable to men everywhere or only to itself, and who must himself answer these questionings or be shamed, as the guide and director of forces caught in the grip of war and by the same token in need of every material and spiritual resource this great nation possesses,—I tell you plainly that this measure which I urge upon you is vital to the winning of the war and to the energies alike of preparation and of battle.

And not to the winning of the war only. It is vital to the right solution of the great problems which we must settle, and settle immediately, when the war is over. We shall need then in our vision of affairs, as we have never needed them before, the sympathy and insight and clear moral instinct of the women of the world. The problems of that time will strike to the roots of many things that we have not hitherto questioned, and I for one believe that our safety in those questioning days, as well as our comprehension of matters that touch society to the quick, will depend upon the direct and authoritative participation of women in our counsels. We shall need their moral sense to preserve what is right and fine and worthy in our system of life as well as to discover just what it is that ought to be purified and reformed. Without their counsellings we shall be only half wise.

That is my case. This is my appeal. Many may deny its validity, if they choose, but no one can brush aside or answer the arguments upon which it is based. The executive tasks of this war rest upon me. I ask that you lighten them and place in my hands instruments, spiritual instruments, which I do not now possess, which I sorely need, and which I have daily to apologise for not being able to employ.

Ashby Williams:
from Experiences of the Great War

The Meuse-Argonne presented a succession of severe challenges for the AEF: many of its divisions were fighting their first major battle; inexperienced leaders struggled to control poorly trained troops while under intense artillery and machine-gun fire; crowded roads and poor communications increased the trials of fighting over rugged terrain full of steep ravines, dense woods, and thick underbrush. Major Ashby Williams fought with the 80th Division on the eastern flank of the battlefield near the Meuse.

IT WAS a hazardous move looked at from any point of view, but the triangle of wood in my left front was practically impregnable as the situation stood, protected as it was by its own defensive weapons and by the mutually supporting positions on its flank, but, if I could take the system of trenches somewhat to the rear and to the right of it, either the enemy would be compelled to withdraw from the triangle of woods because of the threat against his flank or rear or I would then be in a position to attack him from three sides without being subjected to the enemy supporting fire from the positions in the 319th sector in my left. It was indeed a beautiful game, just like a game of checkers. I remember, at the same time that I sent Lieutenant Caulkins out on this mission on the right flank, I sent a message to Captain Little who was occupying the trenches on my right front, advising him of the move that was being made and telling him of the purpose and mission of the move, and that he would receive further orders telling him of the success of the mission.

It was now between three and four o'clock in the afternoon. Having made my new disposition I moved back to my temporary headquarters in the edge of the Malaumont Woods south of the Cunel-Brieulles Road which was near the center of my sector. Here I sat, together with Major Emory, in a little rifle pit, and I remember how we went over the mission together, and I wrote a message to regimental headquarters advising them of the move that I had made. As I said, Major Emory and I were sitting in the little rifle pit which was about three feet deep, two feet wide and five feet long, he in one end and I in the other so, as we were sitting, our knees touched and the tops of our helmets were slightly above the level of the ground. I remember an officer of the 5th Division came up after a little while and sat on the edge of the rifle pit and said that his Division was to relieve us, which relief, he said, was to take place that night. There were a number of other officers and a number of men immediately around the place. I remember Lieutenant France was sitting on the edge of the pit on one side and Lieutenant Preston on the other. Captain Sumner and Lieutenant Vermule were in a little pit about twenty feet away and some wounded machine gunners and other men were seated in rifle pits or lying upon the ground. I remember as we sat in this rifle pit one of the companies from the 319th Infantry sector on our left came in battle formation across the open space that separated our wood from their sector and poured a great volume of fire into our wood, under the impression, the officer in charge said, that enemy fire was coming from our woods. I remember Lieutenant Ben Temple, who was also close by, rushed out to the edge of the woods, held up his hands and said:

"For God's sake, men, stop shooting us up!"

The bullets did not do us any harm, but the Boche saw the movement of the troops into our woods and communicated this fact to his artillery, and in about twenty minutes the Boche began to pour steel into the woods in the area in which we were, and they were falling fast and furious about us. It was during this bombardment that I had perhaps the narrowest escape of my life. Indeed, as narrow an escape, perhaps, as any man ever had who came out alive. Without the slightest warning of any sort I suddenly found myself under the ground as if by magic, with a ringing in my ears as of many bells. There was a sense of great bewilderment—for the act was quicker than thought, and I remember my first thought was:

"I am not dead, I am thinking."

After a bewildered moment or two I worked my helmet and my head through the surface of the earth and looked around. Major Emory was just then doing the same thing, and I remember the dazed and bewildered look in his eye as he gazed around the place. I think he spoke, because his lips moved, but I was too deaf to hear whether he said anything. I tried to get my arms loose, but could not, so tight had they been packed in by the impact of the shell. Presently two men (I think Captain Wilson was one of them) took hold of me and pulled me out. And I remember as I scrambled out of the dirt I took hold of an unexploded portion of a six-inch high explosive shell that had stopped within a few inches of my face, and it was so hot I had to let it go. This shell had struck about two feet from the edge of the rifle pit in which we were sitting. How Major Emory and I escaped being blown to pieces is almost incredible. The shell had struck and exploded with its full force against the body of the 5th Division Officer who was talking to us, blowing him into a thousand pieces. Lieutenant France, with his head crushed in, was blown across the rifle pit and killed, two machine gunners were killed outright and four others were wounded. Lieutenant Preston was struck in the side and in the neck with pieces of steel but was able, with some assistance, to move to the first aid station. Captain Sumner was shell-shocked.

I remember as I got out of the hole my legs had been cramped with the impact of the earth and were very shaky and my ear drums were ringing so that I could not hear a person speak. In that condition of mind and body I determined to go back to my headquarters at once where I could collect my scattered thoughts and rest my shattered nerves for a time; so I got my stick (which I never forsook under any circumstances at the front) and started out of the woods in the direction of my headquarters. I remember as I passed along the beaten path a few feet from the edge of the woods, a man's liver was scattered along the path, and twenty feet out in the open I saw a leg and part of a stomach, still warm with the blood of life so recently departed. It was a horrible sight that I shall never forget. I passed along the hollow that leads by the Ville aux

Bois, and I remember the shells were bursting in the woods and they sounded in my ears like the ringing of many bells. As I passed along also I recollected that I had left a pair of Boche gloves in the hole where I was buried but I decided that if the Boche wanted them that bad he could have them.

From *Experiences of the Great War* (1919)

Damon Runyon: Runyon
Sees Return of Lost New York Battalion

On October 2, 1918, six companies from the 308th Infantry Regiment, 77th Division, found themselves trapped behind the German lines near Charlevaux Mill in the Argonne Forest. By the time the "Lost Battalion" was relieved on October 7, only 194 of the 554 surrounded men remained alive and unwounded. Damon Runyon, a former sports reporter and columnist then covering the war for the *New York American*, filed a story that emphasized the New York City origins of many of the besieged soldiers.

RUNYON SEES RETURN OF
LOST NEW YORK BATTALION

Universal Service Correspondent Looks On as
Whittlesey's Famous Heroes, Polyglots a Seige of
Their Captivity in Argonne Forest.

AT THE AMERICAN ARGONNE FRONT, Oct. 12.—Out of the fog of fighting that hangs over the Forest of Argonne came limping to-day Whittlesey's battered battalion which made the epic defense in the dark glades beyond.

They are men of New York's own Seventy-seventh Division —most of them from the big town itself.

ONCE BAND OF STRAGGLERS.

A little over a year ago this writer reported the parade of these same men, when they marched in straggling columns down Fifth avenue between walls of cheering people. Nearly all of them wore vintage straw hats that day. Some of them were in crumpled Palm Beach suits.

Some of them were in overalls, having come direct from their jobs to appear in the first parade of drafted men on Manhattan Island.

Some were late of the Hudson Dusters. Some of them once trained with the Gophers. Some of them were from ornate houses on Park and Madison or the upper reaches of the Seventies and Eighties.

More were from the lower East Side. Broad and Harlem, Broadway and the Bronx shuffled down the avenue in that strange procession that day, while the bands bawled "Over There!"

Later the writer saw them tumble off the trains at Yaphank carrying scarred suit cases and big bundles, saw them form into irregular lines and march to their new barracks.

Many of them had been celebrating their departure for camp the night before, and looked it. Hester street quarrelled with Greenwich village—not the Greenwich village of long-haired fame, but the hardier, close-cropped region around the docks.

A couple of fist fights occurred at the landing place between querulous parties from the vicinity of Erie Basin, Brooklyn. Nervous young officers, fresh from Plattsburg, fluttered about trying to get a semblance of order.

Their commands brought small alert replies from the new recruits.

Three were Chinamen from Mott street. Also, there were Japs and Italians, all jabbering in their own language at once.

Hopeless enough as military material they seemed then. But some of the same faces I saw at Yaphank that day were under biscuit-shaped steel helmets in the muddy columns that tramped out of the Argonne Forest to-day.

BIG TOWN'S POLYGLOTS.

The big town's polyglot population sent heroes of one of the Homeric fights of the war.

For four days and four nights the one-time counter jumpers, brokers' clerks, gangsters, newsboys, truck drivers, collegians, peddlars and what not held the positions which they had been ordered to take and hold while several times their number of Germans were busily engaged shoveling a variety of hell upon them.

They served as the anchor catch for the whole advance. Totally cut off from their main command, without food and with very little water, the boys from the big town hung on.

They fought under a man who only a short time ago was a New York lawyer. Charles Whittlesey is a tall, lean-flanked fellow, around forty years old. He has a funny little smile.

He smiled this funny little smile when one of his men who had been taken prisoner was sent back to him by the Germans with a neatly typewritten note requesting his surrender.

It would make this story more dramatic to say that Whittlesey sent back some stirring phrase in answer to the Germans. But as a matter of fact he merely smiled his funny little smile after reading the note, and tucked the paper away in his pocket.

Bullet Gives Reply.

The Germans got their real reply the next time a Boche poked his head up. It was in the form of a bullet.

They are telling in some quarters that Whittlesey's reply to the demand for his surrender was "Go to hell!"

Whittlesey says he did not say it, but that it covered his thoughts at the time, anyway.

Not all men in his command are New Yorkers. Some time ago the Seventy-seventh Division had to take on replacements. Many new recruits came from Oregon and other parts of the Northwest. One in the first bunch out of the forest, however, was a little chap who used to sell newspapers around Times Square.

He was covered with mud. His eyes were heavy with battle sleep, but he was grinning broadly.

The commander of the beleaguered force was a captain when he led his men into battle. He has since been recommended for Lieutenant-Colonel. He had six companies with him, three from the first and three from the second battalions of his regiment.

One battalion was commanded by Captain George G. McMurtry, a former New York broker. As hour after hour and day after day went by, there was no sign of a relieving column. The officers in command commenced to believe their case was hopeless.

On the fourth day a soldier told McMurtry that Captain Whittlesey was talking to some officers of another regiment of the division over in the woods.

McMurtry doubted the story, but investigated. He found

Whittlesey conversing with officers of a relieving force which had just got up. Whittlesey was eating a sandwich as he talked.

On Two Days' Rations.

McMurtry walked over to him. His first and only words were:

"For God's sake give me a bite of that!"

The men greeted the members of the relieving column with requests for food and water. They had gone into the fight with the usual two days' rations. For two days they had absolutely no food.

There was a little spring near where they took up their position, but the Germans sniped them whenever they tried to go for water. First they went only at night. Finally they got so desperate from thirst they took chances in broad daylight. The officers posted a guard near the spring to keep the men from exposing themselves.

Whittlesey had been ordered to advance to a certain position. He advanced there. The Germans slipped in behind him through an old trench. Presently Whittlesey realized he was cut off and surrounded. A torrent of shell and machine gun fire and grenades came over.

Men Told to Dig In.

The Americans were on sloping ground. Whittlesey ordered his men to dig in. They quickly burrowed into the ground like moles. They had machine guns and returned the German fire with these and with their rifles. Fortunately, they had plenty of ammunition.

They could constantly hear the Germans in the wood. The Germans talking and shouting to each other as they tried to advance on the devoted little band. Sometimes they got as near as thirty yards. The Americans let them come on as far as they would, then opening fire on them. At night Whittlesey kept out patrols who maintained contact with the enemy.

Just as soon as they were certain they were completely cut off, the officers made it plain to all men that they were expected to hold the position at all hazards.

The announcement was received with grim nods.

Time and time again the best men in the command were

picked and sent out as runners, in the hope they might get through the German lines.

Of nine men thus sent out, four were killed, four wounded, and the ninth was captured. It was this man who was sent back by the Germans with the note demanding surrender. He was taken before the German commander and closely interrogated, but declined to give any information whatsoever. The German commander mentioned this fact in the note to Whittlesey. Then the American was blindfolded and given the message.

The Argonne forest in which the Seventy-seventh Division is fighting is a maze of trees. They are not big trees, but stand close together like stalks in a wheat field. Woven through them in the undergrowth are vines.

It is impossible for a man to walk through the woods straight for any distance in any direction. It is impossible even to see through them to any great depth.

It is said the French lost 60,000 men trying to take these woods since the outbreak of the war. The Germans must have lost many more in holding them.

Trapped in Forest.

It was in a particularly deep section of this modern wilderness that the little command of New Yorkers was trapped. Before the war Central Park probably was the largest forest ever seen by most of these men.

About forty men were killed as they lay there. The fellows buried their dead as best they could, usually under fire. Rarely did the Germans cease pounding them with shell. Minenwarfers (from mine throwers) came through the trees in bunches.

The wounded men were given the best attention possible. In his note demanding surrender the German commander appealed to Whittlesey on the ground of humanity, saying the Germans could hear the cries of the American wounded.

The soldiers say that as a matter of fact our men were peculiarly stoical and made little outcry, while, on the other hand, they could hear Germans squalling in the woods after every volley.

In a couple of days Whittlesey's men had exhausted every vestige of food. Cold rain came on and drenched them day and night. Only a few of them had their overcoats. It gets bitter in the Argonne wood at night, whatever the season of the year.

They could get little sleep on account of the terrific din of the gun fire. They say they never saw any sign of food. Other supplies were dropped into the woods by American airplanes. Neither did they ever find the box of carrier pigeons flung into the trees from aloft.

The rain soon made bog walls out of their little trenches. They couldn't get warm and began to suffer intensely from the exposure and lack of food. Some of them were very weak when they reached the rear at last.

But the men came out of that hellish wood singing the praises of their officers, especially of Whittlesey.

"You are certainly a great anchor man for the division," said the general commanding that front to the New Yorker. "You held on where you were caught!"

Whittlesey merely smiled his funny little smile.

The battalions were sent back for rest. As soon as they have got warmed up and washed up they will be back in the line. They are less excited about their amazing exploit than any one else in the army, that speculated on nothing else for days but their probable fate.

New York American, October 13, 1918

Woodrow Wilson: Second and Third Peace Notes to Germany

By the end of September, General Erich Ludendorff had shown signs of breaking down under the strain of defeat. On September 29, Bulgaria signed an armistice that allowed the Allies to block Romania as a source of food and oil for Germany; and the next day the moderate Prince Max of Baden became the new German chancellor. Hoping a temporary truce might allow his troops to regroup, Ludendorff recommended seeking a cease-fire. On October 4 Prince Max sent a note to Wilson requesting an armistice on the basis of the Fourteen Points. Without consulting the British or French, Wilson replied on October 8, demanding a German commitment to evacuate occupied Belgian and French territory. In the United States many Republicans and some Democrats demanded unconditional surrender, prompting the President to express surprise at "how war mad our people have become." When a U-boat sank the British passenger ship *Leinster* on October 10, with the loss of 501 lives, Wilson lost his patience: his note of October 14 (signed by Robert Lansing) demanded an immediate end to submarine attacks on civilian ships. When the Germans agreed, he pressed them on October 23 to make constitutional changes in their government. Finally, the Germans had to accept that the Allied commanders in France would set the military terms of the Armistice.

The Secretary of State to the Swiss Chargé (Oederlin)

No. 285   WASHINGTON, *October 14, 1918.*

SIR: In reply to the communication of the German Government, dated the 12th instant, which you handed me to-day, I have the honor to request you to transmit the following answer:

The unqualified acceptance by the present German Government and by a large majority of the German Reichstag of the terms laid down by the President of the United States of America in his address to the Congress of the United States on the 8th of January, 1918, and in his subsequent addresses, justifies the President in making a frank and direct statement of his decision with regard to the communications of the German Government of the 8th [*6th*] and 12th of October, 1918.

It must be clearly understood that the process of evacuation and the conditions of an armistice are matters which must be left to the judgment and advice of the military advisers of the Government of the United States and the Allied Governments, and the President feels it his duty to say that no arrangement can be accepted by the Government of the United States which does not provide absolutely satisfactory safeguards and guarantees of the maintenance of the present military supremacy of the armies of the United States and of the Allies in the field. He feels confident that he can safely assume that this will also be the judgment and decision of the Allied Governments.

The President feels that it is also his duty to add that neither the Government of the United States nor, he is quite sure, the Governments with which the Government of the United States is associated as a belligerent will consent to consider an armistice so long as the armed forces of Germany continue the illegal and inhumane practices which they still persist in. At the very time that the German Government approaches the Government of the United States with proposals of peace its submarines are engaged in sinking passenger ships at sea, and not the ships alone but the very boats in which their passengers and crews seek to make their way to safety; and in their present enforced withdrawal from Flanders and France the German armies are pursuing a course of wanton destruction which has always been regarded as in direct violation of the rules and practices of civilized warfare. Cities and villages, if not destroyed, are being stripped of all they contain not only but often of their very inhabitants. The nations associated against Germany cannot be expected to agree to a cessation of arms while acts of inhumanity, spoliation, and desolation are being continued which they justly look upon with horror and with burning hearts.

It is necessary, also, in order that there may be no possibility of misunderstanding, that the President should very solemnly call the attention of the Government of Germany to the language and plain intent of one of the terms of peace which the German Government has now accepted. It is contained in the address of the President delivered at Mount Vernon on the Fourth of July last. It is as follows: "The destruction of every arbitrary power anywhere that can separately, secretly, and of its single choice disturb the peace of the world; or, if it cannot be presently destroyed, at least its reduction to virtual impotency." The power which has hitherto controlled the German Nation is of the sort here described. It is within the choice of the German Nation to alter it. The President's words just quoted naturally constitute a condition precedent to peace, if peace is to come by the action of the German people themselves. The President feels bound to say that the whole process of peace will, in his judgment, depend upon the definiteness and the satisfactory character of the guarantees which can be given in this fundamental matter. It is indispensable that the Governments associated against Germany should know beyond a peradventure with whom they are dealing.

The President will make a separate reply to the Royal and Imperial Government of Austria-Hungary.

Accept [etc.]   ROBERT LANSING

The Secretary of State to the Swiss Chargé (Oederlin)

WASHINGTON, *October 23, 1918.*

SIR: I have the honor to acknowledge the receipt of your note of the 22d transmitting a communication under date of the 20th from the German Government and to advise you that the President has instructed me to reply thereto as follows:

Having received the solemn and explicit assurance of the German Government that it unreservedly accepts the terms of peace laid down in his address to the Congress of the United States on the 8th of January, 1918, and the principles of settlement enunciated in his subsequent addresses, particularly the address of the 27th of September, and that it desires to discuss the details of their application, and that this wish and purpose emanate, not from those who have hitherto dictated German policy and conducted the present war on Germany's behalf, but from Ministers who speak for the Majority of the Reichstag and for an overwhelming majority of the German people; and having received also the explicit promise of the present German Government that the humane rules of civilized warfare will be observed both on land and sea by the German armed forces, the President of the United States feels that he cannot decline to take up with the Governments with which the Government of the United States is associated the question of an armistice.

He deems it his duty to say again, however, that the only armistice he would feel justified in submitting for consideration would be one which should leave the United States and the powers associated with her in a position to enforce any arrangements that may be entered into and to make a renewal of hostilities on the part of Germany impossible. The President has, therefore, transmitted his correspondence with the present German authorities to the Governments with which the Government of the United States is associated as a belligerent, with the suggestion that, if those Governments are disposed to effect peace upon the terms and principles indicated, their military advisers and the military advisers of the United States be asked to submit to the Governments associated against Germany the necessary terms of such an armistice as will fully protect the interests of the peoples involved and ensure to the Associated Governments the unrestricted power to safeguard and enforce the details of the peace to which the German Government has agreed, provided they deem such an armistice possible from the military point of view. Should such terms of armistice be suggested, their acceptance by Germany will afford the best concrete evidence of her unequivocal acceptance of the terms and principles of peace from which the whole action proceeds.

The President would deem himself lacking in candour did he not point out in the frankest possible terms the reason why extraordinary safeguards must be demanded. Significant and important as the constitutional changes seem to be which are spoken of by the German Foreign Secretary in his note of the 20th of October, it does not appear that the principle of a Government responsible to the German people has yet been fully worked out or that any guarantees either exist or are in contemplation that the alterations of principle and of practice now partially agreed upon will be permanent. Moreover, it does not appear that the heart of the present difficulty has been reached. It may be that future wars have been brought under the control of the German people, but the present war has not been; and it is with the present war that we are dealing. It is evident that the German people have no means of commanding the acquiescence of the military authorities of the Empire in the popular will; that the power of the King of Prussia to control the policy of the Empire is unimpaired; that the determining initiative still remains with those who have hitherto been the masters of Germany. Feeling that the whole peace of the world depends now on plain speaking and straightforward action, the President deems it his duty to say, without any attempt to soften what may seem harsh words, that the nations of the world do not and cannot trust the word of those who have hitherto been the masters of German policy, and to point out once more that in concluding peace and attempting to undo the infinite injuries and injustices of this war the Government of the United States cannot deal with any but veritable representatives of the German people who have been assured of a genuine constitutional standing as the real rulers of Germany. If it must deal with the military masters and the monarchical autocrats of Germany now, or if it is likely to have to deal with them later in regard to the international obligations of the German Empire, it must demand, not peace negotiations, but surrender. Nothing can be gained by leaving this essential thing unsaid.

Accept [etc.] ROBERT LANSING

John J. Pershing to the Supreme War Council

After Ludendorff attempted to reject Wilson's latest demands, the government of Chancellor Max forced the Kaiser to dismiss him on October 26. As the German armies slowly retreated from France and Belgium, General Pershing expressed his optimism regarding the current military situation to the Allied heads of government. They did not pursue his recommendation that the Allies insist on unconditional surrender.

Paris, October 30, 1918.

To the Allied Supreme War Council,
Paris.

GENTLEMEN:

In considering the question of whether or not Germany's request for an armistice should be granted, the following expresses my opinion from the military point of view:

1. Judging by their excellent conduct during the past three months, the British, French, Belgian and American Armies appear capable of continuing the offensive indefinitely. Their morale is high and the prospects of certain victory should keep it so.

2. The American Army is constantly increasing in strength and experience, and should be able to take an increasingly important part in the Allied offensive. Its growth both in personnel and matériel, with such reserves as the Allies may furnish, not counting the Italian Army, should be more than equal to the combined losses of the Allied armies.

3. German manpower is constantly diminishing and her armies have lost over 300,000 prisoners and over one-third of their artillery during the past three months in their effort to extricate themselves from a difficult situation and avoid disaster.

4. The estimated strength of the Allies on the Western Front, not counting Italy, and of Germany, in rifles is:

Allies 1,563,000
Germany. 1,134,000
An advantage in favor of the Allies of 37 per cent.

In guns:

Allies 22,413
Germany. 16,495
An advantage of 35 per cent in favor of the Allies.

If Italy's forces should be added to the Western Front we should have a still greater advantage.

5. Germany's morale is undoubtedly low, her Allies have deserted her one by one and she can no longer hope to win. Therefore we should take full advantage of the situation and continue the offensive until we compel her unconditional surrender.

6. An armistice would revivify the low spirits of the German Army and enable it to reorganize and resist later on, and would deprive the Allies of the full measure of victory by failing to press their present advantage to its complete military end.

7. As the apparent humility of German leaders in talking of peace may be feigned, the Allies should distrust their sincerity and their motives. The appeal for an armistice is undoubtedly to enable the withdrawal from a critical situation to one more advantageous.

8. On the other hand, the internal political conditions of Germany, if correctly reported, are such that she is practically forced to ask for an armistice to save the overthrow of her present Government, a consummation which should be sought by the Allies as precedent to permanent peace.

9. A cessation of hostilities short of capitulation postpones, if it does not render impossible, the imposition of satisfactory peace terms, because it would allow Germany to withdraw her army with its present strength, ready to resume hostilities if terms were not satisfactory to her.

10. An armistice would lead the Allied armies to believe this the end of fighting and it would be difficult, if not impossible, to resume hostilities with our present advantage in morale in the event of failure to secure at a peace conference what we have fought for.

11. By agreeing to an armistice under the present favorable military situation of the Allies and accepting the principle of a negotiated peace rather than a dictated peace the Allies would jeopardize the moral position they now hold and possibly lose the chance actually to secure world peace on terms that would insure its permanence.

12. It is the experience of history that victorious armies are prone to overestimate the enemy's strength and too eagerly seek an opportunity for peace. This mistake is likely to be made now on account of the reputation Germany has gained through her victories of the last four years.

13. Finally, I believe the complete victory can only be obtained by continuing the war until we force unconditional surrender from Germany, but if the Allied Governments decide to grant an armistice, the terms should be so rigid that under no circumstances could Germany again take up arms.

Respectfully submitted:

JOHN J. PERSHING,
COMMANDER-IN-CHIEF, A.E.F.

Harry S. Truman to Bess Wallace

To compensate for his poor vision, Harry S. Truman of Independence, Missouri, had allegedly memorized the eye chart so that he
could join the National Guard in 1905. He left the Guard in 1911 but
rejoined when America entered the war. Commissioned as a captain,
he commanded a battery of 188 men in the 129th Field Artillery
Regiment, 35th Infantry Division, and saw action in the Vosges, St.
Mihiel, and in the Meuse-Argonne campaign. While Marshal Foch
waited in a railroad car in the forest of Compiègne for the German
delegation to sign the Armistice, Truman wrote to Bess Wallace, his
fiancée in Missouri. On June 28, 1919, seven weeks after his discharge
from the army, they would marry.

———————

Nov 10, 1918

Dear Bess:—

I got a letter today from Boxley and one from Joe Bielsford
who was our auditor in Morgan and Company and none from
you. I am disappointed as a kid who didn't get any candy but I
know that Uncle Sam's mail and not you are to blame and
maybe I'll get one or two or three tomorrow. I am still holding
down a place in a quiet sector and I'm getting fat on it. Also
that helmet is *not* going to make me bald headed, at least I
don't think so.

The Hun is yelling for peace like a stuck hog and I hope old
daddy Foch makes him yell louder yet or throttles him one.
Throttling would be too easy. When you see some of the
things those birds did and then hear them put up the talk they
do for peace it doesn't impress you at all. A complete and
thorough thrashing is all they've got coming and take my
word they are getting it and getting it right.

This has been a beautiful Sunday. The sun shining and as
warm as summer. It sure made me wish for Lizzie and five
gallons of gas with her nose pointed down Blue Ridge Blvd.
and me stepping on the throttle to get there quickly. I wonder

how long it will be before we do any riding down that road.
Easter? Maybe if not sooner. Heine seems to be about finished.
Just to make the day interesting one of thier planes came over
and shot down one of our sausage balloons and came near
getting shot down him self. I shot away about 500 rounds of
high explosive shells my self. Not at the plane but at some
Hun machine guns about seven miles away. I don't know if
I hit them but I have hopes as I laid the guns very carefully. A
Hun plane dropped some bomb not far from my back yard last
night and sort of shook things up. They made him run home
in a hurry too. There is a big railroad gun about a kilometer
behind me that shoots about every fifteen minutes and I heard
one of the boys remark that "There goes another rolling
kitchen over to pulverize Jerry." The projectile makes a noise
like a wagon going down the road when it goes through the
air so the remark was very good.

I have been censoring letters today and it is some job. I had
no idea that there were so many accomplished liars in any organization on earth as I have in mine. They are eternally trying
to get by the censor with some big talk of thier heroism and
accomplishments in this war and they do it too sometimes,
especially if they put in something nice about thier commanding officer and the part he took in the tale. Usually though I
have to tear 'em up or send them back when they tell too much or
stretch the truth even beyond literary licence. Some of them write
very good and very interesting letters and some of them do not.
It is a job to censor them and when my Lts get too far behind
I help them out.

I hope the base censor doesn't laugh at mine as I sometimes
have to at thiers.

Hope I get that letter tomorrow. Also Hope the Hun signs
the peace agreement. Write as often as you can to one who
thinks of you

Always
Harry.

Harry S Truman
Capt 129 FA
American E.F.

Nov. 11, 1918

Dear Bess:—

I know Uncle Samuel was holding out on me when your letter came not with Boxley's and Bielsford's. Two came this morning and I am of course very happy. We are all wondering what the Hun is going to do about Marshal Foch's proposition to him. We don't care what he does. He's licked either way he goes. For my part I'd as soon be Provost-Marshall of Cologne or Metz or Munich or Berlin as have any other job I know of now. It is a shame we can't go in and devatate Germany and cut off a few of the Dutch kids hands and feet and scalp a few of thier old men but I guess it will be better to make them work for France and Belgium for fifty years.

Thier time for acceptance will be up in 30 minutes. There is a great big 155 battery right behind me across the road that seems to want to get rid of all of its ammunition before the time is up. It has been banging away almost as fast as a 75 battery for the last two hours. Every time one of the guns goes off it shakes my house like an earth quake.

I just got official notice that hostilities would cease at 11 o'clock. Everyone is about to have a fit. I fired 164 rounds at him before he quit this morning, anyway. It seems that everyone was just about to blow up wondering if Heine would come in. I knew that Germany could not stand the gaff. For all thier preparedness and swashbuckling talk they cannot stand adversity. France was whipped for four years and never gave up and one good licking suffices for Germany. What pleases me most is the fact that I was lucky enough to take a battery through the last drive. The battery has shot something over 10000 rounds at the Hun and I am sure they had a slight effect.

I am returning the enclosure from the K.C. Post. It is a good thing I didn't censor Bill's letter or I probably would have thrown it out. It was evidently not quoted correctly even as it is. He was promoted for bravery by me but he was not mentioned in orders. Of course the remark about his Captain is pleasing but there are no vacant sergeancies now so he won't get promoted for that.

It is pleasant also to hear that Mrs. Wells has adopted me as a real nephew and I shall certainly be more than pleased to call her Auntie Maud and I hope it won't be long before I can do it.

You evidently did some very excellent work as a Liberty Bond saleswoman because I saw in the "Stars & Stripes" where some 22000000 people bought them and that they were over-subscribed by $1000 000 000 which is some stunt for you to have helped pull off. I know that it had as much to do with breaking the German morale as our cannon shots had and we owe you as much for an early home comming as we do the fighters.

Here's hoping to see you soon

Yours always
Harry

Harry S. Truman
Capt FAUSA

Robert J. Casey:
from The Cannoneers Have Hairy Ears

Under the terms of the Armistice, Germany would withdraw to its 1914 borders in both the east and west, evacuate Alsace-Lorraine, and surrender 5,000 artillery guns, 3,000 mortars, 25,000 machine guns, 1,700 aircraft, sixteen battleships and battle cruisers, and all of its U-boats. Until a peace treaty was signed, the Allied blockade of Germany would continue, and the Allies would occupy the western bank of the Rhine and three bridgeheads on its eastern bank. An experienced journalist in Chicago before the war, Robert J. Casey joined the army in 1917 and commanded Battery C, 124th Field Artillery Regiment, 33rd Division, in the St. Mihiel and Meuse-Argonne campaigns. In 1927 Casey published an anonymous memoir of his service as an artilleryman, in which he captured the moments leading up to "the eleventh hour of the eleventh day of the eleventh month" of 1918.

THE END OF THE ROAD

GAUDRON FERME, *November 11, Eight o'clock* A.M. —And this is the end of it. In three hours the war will be over. It seems incredible even as I write it. I suppose I ought to be thrilled and cheering. Instead I am merely apathetic and incredulous.

We got the word about 5:30 this morning amid a scene of great anticlimax.

The little wooden shack was silent—or at least as silent as it could be with shells, friendly and hostile, just clearing the roof. The hillside along the east wall cut off most of the light of the dawn and the tenants, undisturbed by daylight, were sleeping like dead men.

A telephone switchboard had been installed at one end of the old brick stove. Before it an operator was fighting to keep awake. Near by the adjutant lay in a chicken wire cot. Beyond the board partition four lieutenants of the regimental staff lay draped on tables that had once been part of the Boche officers' mess.

The officers did not stir in their sleep as the 77s cracked down on to the road or even when the shells of the 11th F.A.'s 155s started over toward the roads behind Pouilly with a detonation that jarred the choking dust from the rafters and the shingles from the roof. . . .

Then the big scene:

The telephone clicks.

The adjutant snores.

The operator hesitates.

A second click.

The operator plugs in:

"Hello, yes, hello, radio!"

I sat up. . . .

"He's asleep. I'll take the message. . . ."

Delay . . . Rustling of paper.

"Ready now . . . Shoot . . . I get you . . . I'll repeat:

"'An armistice has been signed and becomes effective on the eleventh November at 11 o'clock.'"

I rolled out of my blankets.

"'At that hour hostilities and advance are to cease. Hold the line attained and give exact information as to the line attained at that hour. No communication nor fraternizing will take place with the enemy. . . . Signed . . . Pershing'"

"That all? . . . Sure, of course it's enough. . . . Finie la guerre!"

I jumped over and grabbed the message.

The adjutant sat up in his cot.

"What's that?"

"Armistice signed," I reported. "Cease firing at 11 o'clock. . . . Radio from Eiffel."

The adjutant: "Good! Now all we have to do is keep alive until eleven o'clock. I know where there's a culvert half a kilo down the road. You'll find me under it if I'm wanted." Rolls up his blankets.

"Wish they could have decided this thing before we had to dope out that barrage." He goes out in a hurry.

The Operations Officer: "It's probably the bunk."

The Radio Officer: "Picked it up by radio from Eiffel. My men are always on the job."

I—just aware of a remarkably pleasant thought: "Slipped one over on 'em. I won't have to string that wire to the O.P."

The Medical Officer: "Quit the noise and let a fellow sleep."

The medical officer seemed to have the right idea. We all crawled back into our blankets again and stayed there until the smell of frying bacon awakened us.

Nine A.M.—Heinie has some ammunition to dispose of. He's dropping 150s on the Laneuville-Beaumont road. Not hitting anything so far.

Nine-fifteen A.M.—Order from Gen. Hall to lessen rate of fire and cease firing in thirty minutes. Runners start out to spread the glad tidings to the batteries.

Nine-forty-five A.M.—Sporadic shots. Distant shelling and machine gun chatter. Ambulances still going forward. Nobody on road who doesn't have to be there.

Ten A.M.—Whiz-bang just burst at the bridge over the creek north of here. From doorway of the regimental P.C. one can count seven bodies in a stack at the side of the road.

Ten-thirty-seven A.M.—Heavies far back of Pouilly are dumping everything they've got. G.I. cans are tearing up the road. The sector has become another Romagne. . . .

A shell just lit in the old sawmill. Men are out in the road running madly about. Other men are staggering out of the wreck and dropping as they emerge. Ambulances have been stopped and litter bearers are on their way across the clearing.

There is a tinkling note, somehow familiar and yet like something out of a life we can barely remember having lived; moisture is dripping from the eaves.

The pontoon engineers are swinging down the road to the crossing singing:

"And we'll all go back 'cause it's over, over here." Maybe they're right.

There is some cheering across the river—occasional bursts of it as the news is carried to the advanced lines. For the most part, though, we are in silence. The air is full of half-forgotten sounds: the rustling of dead leaves, the organ tone of wind in the tree tops, whispers through the underbrush, lazy echoes of voices in the road.

With all is a feeling that it can't be true. For months we have slept under the guns. For months the smash of the 75, the boom of the 155, the trembling roar of Heinie's bursting G.I. cans, have been a part of our lives. We cannot comprehend the stillness.

A doughboy at the gate is wiping his eyes with his sleeve, his mud-caked rifle caught up under his other arm. Nobody has noticed him. We all would feel like doing the same thing if we felt like doing anything at all.

I am going back to sleep.

Elizabeth Shepley Sergeant:
from Shadow-Shapes

In 1917 *The New Republic* sent one of its original contributors, Bryn Mawr graduate Elizabeth Shepley Sergeant, to cover the war. While touring the Mont-Bligny battlefield near Reims in October 1918, a woman in her party unwittingly detonated a hand grenade, seriously wounding Sergeant in both legs. She recuperated in a Paris hospital as the opening of the peace conference approached and delegations from dozens of countries and constituencies descended upon the city, all hoping to influence the final agreements. The four primary participants—France, Great Britain, Italy, and the United States—did not invite Bolshevik Russia, and they would summon Germany only after they had agreed on the terms of the peace. When President Wilson arrived in Paris on December 14, he was hailed as the savior of the world.

December 6

THE BOUNDARIES of my narrow world are beginning to bulge and crack. I have had my first afternoon out of bed. They lifted me on to the *chaise longue* and wrapped me up and I stayed with the doors wide open for two hours—the idea is to get strength and confidence enough to try crutches on Christmas Day—watching the little garden cosmos of tents, and wounded doughboys, and hurrying nurses. How easily and effectively it turns on its own axis—so indifferent to one's wretched private miseries. But how damp and forlorn the tents are. . . . I had almost forgotten. . . .

I was accosted from the garden door by a mutilated Blue Devil from the Grand Palais who had a collection of hideous "souvenirs" made out of copper shell-cases to sell. He had only one leg and part of a jaw, and told me he was going to "manifest" for Wilson and the *Société des Nations* with the *Fédération Ouvrière des Mutilés* and the C.G.T. He had the *Populaire* in his pocket, and pointed out with a bitter twist of his cheek this passage: "A man is coming who has kept in the terrible drama a pitiful heart, a right conscience, a clear brain. We salute him and we say: 'Be faithful to yourself. You have wanted to win to be just. Be just.'"

December 13

Impossible to think of anything but the George Washington, drawing nearer and nearer to the coast of France. The French working class, the Socialists, the "people" as distinguished from official France, seem determined to give Wilson a mandate in their cause. Politics are mixed up in it, but the *cri de cœur* is unmistakably there too. The *Journal du Peuple* says: "No man since Jesus, not even Jaurès, has so strongly embodied the hope of the world. For the peasant, as for the man of letters, for the workman and the artist this name represents divine Wisdom."

December 14

Guns! That means ten o'clock. Wilson is arriving at the little station in the avenue du Bois. More guns! He is embracing M. Clemenceau and M. Poincaré. More guns! He is starting to drive down the Champs Élysées through the soldiers and the enormous crowds, and the flags. . . .

How can I bear to be here? Scarcely a patch of white cloud on the blue garden sky. The hospital feels lonely and deserted, as on Armistice day. I sent Miss O. to try to see the President. I miss her awfully. I wish she would hurry and get back.

At least the postman goes his rounds. Louise, the concierge, whose rotund, competent countenance now sometimes appears at my door, brings a letter from Rick—raging and champing at Brest, waiting for a transport—to describe yesterday's landing. He saw it from the dock-side where he got a military job for that purpose, and writes of salutes, of Breton peasants by the thousands—"silent, not very interested save when a bit drunk"—of German prisoners throwing down their work to run and stare across the dirty water at the man in the silk hat and fine clothes who is so greatly to influence their destiny.

"The President himself very fine. I wondered just what

thrill he had seeing his ugly army men, long straight lines of them down every street, (Americans being the ugliest race on earth, but a great lot, a great and wonderful lot.) He was stirred—obviously. I did not think it possible to show such emotion as he showed with such a fine restraint and dignity. His silk hat, waved only slightly, was more moving and more moved than a whole body's gesture of a Bernhardt. Was he seeing the French as well, or only us? Us, I am certain—just as I could 'hear' his wife's trite comments on the quaint Breton cap.

"We've been dancing—the peasants and some drunken quarter-masters—on the bandstand in the square—now *place Président Wilson*—all evening. Even Brest, hole that it is, is gay. Peasants in gorgeous gala still parade the streets in automobiles, passing the hat as they go—alas—in honor of the President!"

* * *

My nurse is here, breathless and dazed and happy to have been squashed in the crowd, and trampled on by soldiers. She managed to rent a stool for a large sum from one of the "prof-iteers" and saw the President's smile. Every one is talking of his smile—as if the poor man had been expected to weep. But Paris is so little given to heroics, so prompt to ridicule the least pompousness in a celebrity, that Wilson's bearing must have been perfect to arouse this extraordinary enthusiasm.

A visit from Lippmann, Merz, R. Hayes, just at supper-time. They were in hilarious spirits, laughing at my efforts to eat my dull meal and also swallow the far more important gist of their remarks. W. L. fairly uplifted. He says the popular feeling came incredibly out of the depths, that Wilson seemed to meet it just as it was given, as if he did realize it was not offered to him as a man, but to the ideas for which he stands. . . . To the promise of reorganization for the poor old European world.

The day has been strangely mild and sweet, something like a breath of spring coming in the night windows still. France was the first to say in 1914, "we are making the war against war." They had practically stopped believing it, but now . . . there are thousands of people in Paris to-night who almost again believe the war has been fought for something bigger than national preservation. . . .

December 16

The press continues to jubilate over Wilson and he to be fêted in the streets.

But I have heard one dissenting voice at last and that in an unexpected quarter: Tom's. He came out late this afternoon to bring me a book and said the President's hash was settled for him. No, he hadn't seen any of the festivities, hadn't (scornfully) cared to, but *happened* to be in an office on the rue de Rivoli when Wilson went by from the Hôtel de Ville. He was kissing his *gloved* hand to the crowds! "A terrible omen," said Tom, with a disgusted laugh and a critical gleam.

As if divining my query at his scepticism, he reminded me of the summer evening during the air-raid period, when we had explored the working-class region beyond the place de la Nation. Every house, every shop, was closed and empty in the quarters of the well-to-do—who had fled to safer regions; but here life seethed and teemed, unquenchable and voluble and unafraid. Men, women, and children thronging everywhere. "*Bistros*" full of gesticulating customers. Family groups seated on the sidewalks. In one street, badly hit by a raid two nights earlier, a friendly baker indicated a warehouse burnt down, three houses smashed in, a wall under which seven people were crushed, a sidewalk from which they had had to dig a woman, embedded like a fly in amber.

Yet only one local shop had closed up, and some wit, voicing the general sense of mankind, had written on the shutters in chalk: "*Fermée par cause de frousse*"—in similar American argot: "He got cold feet."

"*Fermée par cause de frousse!*" Tom chuckled again at the recollection. If the Germans had marched into Paris, these were the only Parisians who wouldn't have budged. And now it was these people who were the great backers of Wilson against powers and potentates they completely mistrusted. Let the President beware of kidglove sentiment! Let him beware of giving a sign of *la frousse*!

Tom is desperately restless and abstracted—just as much so as Rick was, really—and wants more than ever to get away from Paris which, he says, is losing its wistful, war-time charm without regaining its peace-time glamour. You can no longer see the town from end to end in one doting glance—as last summer, when it was empty as Pisa—because a hybrid mass of foreigners obstruct the vistas. Turks in turbans on the steps of the Madeleine! Generals of every hue and nation! And—worse—smooth, opulent, possessive, elderly civilians with decorations in their button-holes who wave bunches of twenty-franc notes like so many carrots before the noses of the already baulky taxi-drivers. Hard to hold down a job . . .

"Where do you want to go?"

"Russia! Germany! Any old revolutionary place! Life here is too much like a book. Interesting but unreal. And it'll be more and more so when the diplomats get going. (You'll see, the Peace Conference will be true to the form of all Peace Conferences!) I want to get into the mess itself. Up to the *ears*. . . . I want to wander over the face of Europe—for about fifteen years. . . . That might be enough. . . ." (He has forgotten all about his listener now and his keen, sandy gaze is far-away.) "What interests me is just simply—the world! The divers ways in which men live, produce, eat, think, play, and create. . . . That's where everything leads you. . . . New Republic, politics, problem of Middle Europe, science of economics. . . .

"I want a big job to tackle. . . . There ought to be some for a young man, especially if the old order is gone. . . . Well, I'll be sure to tell you whether it is or not," he added with a smile and a flash of mending spirits. "We're not going to let you miss anything just because you have a few broken bones! . . ."

Tom has been a great support through the thick and thin of war Paris. I shall miss him badly. His warm human curiosity, his almost novelist's sense for life, his frankness and his irony. He is changing—something steely and detached is replacing his boyish faiths. Yet I trust his intelligence and his heart. His personal reactions are somehow involved with the bed-rock of the universe. As the universe is now disrupted, he has to go and look down the cracks. Of course. All the more that (through no fault of his own) he missed the great experience of the war—the fighting. Though he doesn't believe in war as a solution for the world's troubles, and knows he has, in his humane food-office, been more closely in touch with its issues—trade, economic balance in Europe—than our common friend Rick, floating high over No Man's Land, he still feels a little cheated, a little reproached by his immunity from danger. He needs "to get into the mess." Hoover ought to manage it.

December 19

The King of Italy is now being welcomed, in a dismal rain, with—the *femme de ménage* assures me—a very skimpy number of salutes. She listened jealously as they were going off, concerned for America's honor, and nodded with satisfaction when it was over: Wilson wins!

December 20

This morning she hastened to report the opinion of her daughter, the postal clerk, who went to the station to see the King arrive. Most inferior exhibition. Only one row of soldiers! *"'Je t'assure, maman,' qu'elle m'a dit, 'c'était quelconque, il n'y avait pas deux haies.'"*

My eyes turn only in two directions to-day: towards a pair of crutches standing in the corner; towards the window which reveals lame doughboys walloping along the garden paths as if crutches were no possible impediment. . . . I shall be leaving the hospital soon, after all. . . .

Cessation from pain is a very positive emotion. The psychology of the New Testament miracles is sound. The God who restores you to these common functions—usually so unthankfully taken for granted—of sight, hearing, locomotion, is really the Saviour of the world. This is what gives doctors their position of almost divine arbitration. There is nothing I would not do for mine, or my nurse, so patient and so homesick as Christmas approaches. (She read me a letter from the Dakota farm to-day about the fall butchering.)

Joffre was yesterday received into the French Academy, and M.'s account of it, and the report of his speech in the *Débats*, has set the Franco-American chord to twanging, clear and far. All the way to Boston Common where I first saw the bluff, serene old soldier—who in so many ways recalls our own Grant —lifted on the tide of America's violent devotion to France. How remote that exalted spring of 1917 already feels. . . . "It seemed to the American people that by sheer force of love they would instantly accomplish something great and comforting for the relief of the allied armies." (In French the prose has the noblest classic ring.) "And they were right: this love was to allow France, overwhelmed by the hard trials of the Spring of 1917, to keep her confidence and her courage intact."

It used to seem to me, a year ago, when the early detachments of the A.E.F. and the A.R.C. were arriving in France, that the two countries were exactly in the position of two lovers who had become engaged by correspondence and were meeting for the first time in the flesh. Feelings were brimming over, but fashions of dressing and conducting the business of life were mutually strange and disconcerting.

Theoretically the French themselves desired to be converted to the new American fashion. Our confident youth, our fertility of invention, our vast material prosperity, our efficiency and our scientific method became as lyric a theme as "Wilsonism" is now. But let us hope some lover of the *comédie humaine* made notes of the actual encounter between the French manufacturer who pointed with pride to a factory unchanged since his grandfather's day and the American capitalist who asked when he was going to tear it down; between the New York business man, accustomed in five minutes' telephone conversation to start a train of events to culminate within a week, and the French administrative official who had not abandoned his habit of long-hand letters, long, polite conversations, and long-deferred decisions; between the French peasant who made his toilet in the barnyard, kept his gold in a stocking, and lived frugally on vegetable soup in a house inherited from a revolutionary ancestor, and the sergeant from Ohio, with a cheque-book in his pocket, brought up in an apartment on enamelled bathtubs and beefsteak; between the *poilu*, with his *pinard*, and his resignation, and his pay of five sous a day, and the American private who found his dollars scarcely sufficient to storm the biggest town near his camp on a Saturday night, and drive French Colonels from their accustomed chairs to make way for his fizzing champagne.

The question is, as the Conference draws near, how much understanding have we achieved through these various contacts and trials? How much even by dying side by side? The first outburst of love between America and France, as Joffre recalls, brought us into war. The second, whose magnetic waves have been radiating from Wilson's smile into the remotest French countryside, is to bring us into peace. But when it comes to the application of Wilson's doctrine, such cheerful remarks as M. Gauvain's in the *Débats* leave one gasping:

"The better we know him the more do we realize that his mind, *though different in formation from ours*, is close to ours. There is reason to hope that our methods, *apparently divergent*, will adjust themselves to our common purposes. . . ."

Christmas Night

If I were Amy Lowell I should write a free-verse poem about Christmas Day in the American Hospital. All pictures.

Little French nurses flitting in and out, like pigeons on blue wing. *"Heureux Noël!"* Dakota sails more leisurely, plump and white and starched, from mistletoe to holly. Roses and mimosa and heaps of ribboned bundles. A pair of silver earrings, and crutches in the corner.

"Now for it," says the Head Nurse. She stands by, a little mocking, critical, and earnest. Now for it. Can I? Good. A bit wobbly. "Get her foot up again." The cast weighs a thousand pounds. A million fierce prickles run up my leg like ants, and bite and seethe and bicker in a red-hot ankle.

The doctor makes a fine salute, and eyes the Christmas bottle. *Vieux Marc*, with a doggerel Christmas rhyme about its neck. He listens, till his eyes grow moist. Grabs it, and hurries out.

"Merry Christmas and cheers from Brest, now and forever apparently. Gawd damn." Classic voice of the A.E.F. Merry Christmas from Dijon and Ernest in an equally loud Western voice that fills my room to brimming. Flowers, chocolates, and enormous boots, stowed anywhere at all. Christmas dinner sits lightly on a tray. "Take half my turkey. All my plum-pudding." (Nothing fills him up. His eyes stay hungry.) "*I miss them too. Horribly*. Let's talk about Nancy." But visitors come streaming in, with sherry, and cigarettes, and chocolates.

"*Encore du chocolat?*" comments the little *chasseur* with scorn. "Will President Wilson feed it to the Germans?"

The door ajar on Christmas plants, set in a row. Holly rustling. Doughboys snoring in their tents, under their comfort bags. My mood flows out to meet and share their dreams of home.

On into Paris. On and on to the confines of the earth. And then still on, drawing strength and goodness from some bottomless world-reservoir.

December 30

I am beginning to be worried by Wilson's apparent unawareness of the complete divergence between his views and those of Clemenceau. Is it unawareness or deliberate ignoring? The President told our troops on Christmas Day that he did not find in the hearts of the great leaders with whom he was associated any difference of principle or fundamental purpose. And now that he is in London, fêted and adored and acclaimed again, he seems to have mounted—above the Guildhall—to the crest of a still rosier cloud, whence he waves his silk hat and speaks even more nebulous humanities. It is a strange thing to see Clemenceau craning a stiff neck to this cloud, from the firm soil of *la patrie* and responding with chiselled particularities. The dialogue may be thus abridged from the morning papers:

Wilson: "Our soldiers fought to do away with the old order and establish a new one which will bring honor and justice to the world."

Clemenceau: "From most ancient times peoples have rushed at one another's throats to satisfy appetites or interests."

Wilson: "The centre of the old order was the 'balance of power,' maintained by jealous watchfulness. We must now have, not one group set against another, but a single overwhelming group of nations, trustees of the peace of the world."

Clemenceau: "There was an old system, which appears to be condemned to-day by very high authorities, but to which I am not ashamed to say I remain partially faithful: the balance of power. The guiding principle of the Conference is that nothing should happen, after the war, to break up the alliance of the four powers which together won the victory."

Wilson: "The foundations are laid. We have accepted the same great body of principles. Their application should afford no fundamental difficulty."

Clemenceau: "With old materials you cannot build a new edifice. America is far from the German frontier. Never shall I cease to have my gaze fixed on the immediate satisfaction of the claims to which France is entitled."

Wilson: "It was this incomparably great object that brought me overseas . . . to lend my counsel to this great—may I not say final?—enterprise of humanity."

Clemenceau: "I may make mistakes, but I can say, without self-flattery, that I am a patriot. France is in an especially difficult situation. *La question de la paix est une question terrible.*"

What is "France" to this powerful, little old sceptic? An ancient, intricate, delicately adjusted toy that he holds in his wrinkled hands? Rather, a mistress, whom he clutches to his passionate old heart. His accent, when he speaks of her—again and again through this speech in the *Chambre*—makes Wilson seem, by comparison, to be holding "humanity" at arm's length.

There is a rumor that Lloyd George has won a complete victory for England against the Fourteen Points on the question of freedom of the seas. And the Ebert Government is tottering. . . .

Sam M. Lewis and Joe Young: How 'Ya Gonna Keep 'Em Down on the Farm?

A hit on the vaudeville stage as sung by Sophie Tucker and by Eddie Cantor, and as part of James Reese Europe's repertoire when his 369th Infantry band returned from the war, this ditty playfully suggested that the war had irrevocably changed American society.

———————————

"Reuben, Reuben, I've been thinking,"
Said his wifey dear;
"Now that all is peaceful and calm,
The boys will soon be back on the farm;"
Mister Reuben, started winking,
And slowly rubbed his chin;
He pulled his chair up close to mother,
And he asked her with a grin:

How 'ya gonna keep 'em, down on the farm,
After they've seen Paree?
How 'ya gonna keep 'em away from Broadway;
Jazzin' a'roun', and paintin' the town?
How 'ya gonna keep 'em away from harm?
That's a mystery;
They'll never want to see a rake or plow,
And who the deuce can parleyvous a cow?
How 'ya gonna keep 'em down on the farm,
After they've seen Paree?

How ya gonna keep 'em, down on the farm,
After they've seen Paree?
How 'ya gonna keep 'em away from Broadway;
Jazzin' a'roun', and paintin' the town?
How 'ya gonna keep 'em away from harm?
That's a mystery;
Imagine Reuben when he meets his pa,

He'll kiss his cheek and holler "oo-la-la!"
How 'ya gonna keep 'em down on the farm,
After they've seen Paree?

"Reuben, Reuben, You're mistaken,"
Said his wifey dear;
"Once a farmer, always a jay,
And farmers always stick to the hay;"
"Mother Reuben, I'm not fakin',
Tho' you may think it strange;
But wine and women play the mischief,
With a boy who's loose with change:"

How 'ya gonna keep 'em, down on the farm,
After they've seen Paree?
How 'ya gonna keep 'em away from Broadway;
Jazzin' a'roun', And paintin' the town?
How 'ya gonna keep 'em away from harm?
That's a mystery;
They'll never want to see a rake or plow,
And who the deuce can parleyvous a cow?
How 'ya gonna keep 'em down on the farm,
After they've seen Paree?

How 'ya gonna keep 'em, down on the farm,
After they've seen Paree?
How 'ya gonna keep 'em away from Broadway;
Jazzin' a'roun', And paintin' the town?
How 'ya gonna keep 'em away from harm?
That's a mystery;
Imagine Reuben when he meets his pa,
He'll kiss his cheek and holler "oo-la-la!"
How 'ya gonna keep 'em down on the farm,
After they've seen Paree?

Oliver Wendell Holmes:
Opinion in Schenck v. United States

No previous case had challenged the constitutionality of the 1798 Sedition Act or any of the restrictive measures taken by the Lincoln administration during the Civil War, making *Schenck v. United States* the first major Supreme Court case to determine the boundaries of free speech under the First Amendment. After hearing arguments in January 1919, the Court ruled 9–0 on March 3 to uphold the constitutionality of the 1917 Espionage Act. In time of war, it decided, Congress could regulate free speech if it caused a "clear and present danger" to national interests. Oliver Wendell Holmes, who had been appointed to the Supreme Court by Theodore Roosevelt in 1902, wrote the opinion. A week after the Court handed down the *Schenck* decision, Holmes furthered his argument in upholding the conviction of Eugene V. Debs under the Espionage Act in another unanimous decision.

MR. JUSTICE HOLMES delivered the opinion of the court.

This is an indictment in three counts. The first charges a conspiracy to violate the Espionage Act of June 15, 1917, c. 30, § 3, 40 Stat. 217, 219, by causing and attempting to cause insubordination, &c., in the military and naval forces of the United States, and to obstruct the recruiting and enlistment service of the United States, when the United States was at war with the German Empire, to-wit, that the defendants wilfully conspired to have printed and circulated to men who had been called and accepted for military service under the Act of May 18, 1917, a document set forth and alleged to be calculated to cause such insubordination and obstruction. The count alleges overt acts in pursuance of the conspiracy, ending in the distribution of the document set forth. The second count alleges a conspiracy to commit an offence against the United States, to-wit, to use the mails for the transmission of matter declared to be non-mailable by Title XII, § 2 of the Act of June 15, 1917, to-wit, the above mentioned document, with an averment of the same overt acts. The third count charges an unlawful use of the mails for the transmission of the same matter and otherwise as above. The defendants were found guilty on all the counts. They set up the First Amendment to the Constitution forbidding Congress to make any law abridging the freedom of speech, or of the press, and bringing the case here on that ground have argued some other points also of which we must dispose.

It is argued that the evidence, if admissible, was not sufficient to prove that the defendant Schenck was concerned in sending the documents. According to the testimony Schenck said he was general secretary of the Socialist party and had charge of the Socialist headquarters from which the documents were sent. He identified a book found there as the minutes of the Executive Committee of the party. The book showed a resolution of August 13, 1917, that 15,000 leaflets should be printed on the other side of one of them in use, to be mailed to men who had passed exemption boards, and for distribution. Schenck personally attended to the printing. On August 20 the general secretary's report said "Obtained new leaflets from printer and started work addressing envelopes" &c.; and there was a resolve that Comrade Schenck be allowed $125 for sending leaflets through the mail. He said that he had about fifteen or sixteen thousand printed. There were files of the circular in question in the inner office which he said were printed on the other side of the one sided circular and were there for distribution. Other copies were proved to have been sent through the mails to drafted men. Without going into confirmatory details that were proved, no reasonable man could doubt that the defendant Schenck was largely instrumental in sending the circulars about. As to the defendant Baer there was evidence that she was a member of the Executive Board and that the minutes of its transactions were hers. The argument as to the sufficiency of the evidence that the defendants conspired to send the documents only impairs the seriousness of the real defence.

It is objected that the documentary evidence was not admissible because obtained upon a search warrant, valid so far as appears. The contrary is established. *Adams* v. *New York*, 192

U. S. 585; *Weeks* v. *United States*, 232 U. S. 383, 395, 396. The search warrant did not issue against the defendant but against the Socialist headquarters at 1326 Arch Street and it would seem that the documents technically were not even in the defendants' possession. See *Johnson* v. *United States*, 228 U. S. 457. Notwithstanding some protest in argument the notion that evidence even directly proceeding from the defendant in a criminal proceeding is excluded in all cases by the Fifth Amendment is plainly unsound. *Holt* v. *United States*, 218 U. S. 245, 252, 253.

The document in question upon its first printed side recited the first section of the Thirteenth Amendment, said that the idea embodied in it was violated by the Conscription Act and that a conscript is little better than a convict. In impassioned language it intimated that conscription was despotism in its worst form and a monstrous wrong against humanity in the interest of Wall Street's chosen few. It said "Do not submit to intimidation," but in form at least confined itself to peaceful measures such as a petition for the repeal of the act. The other and later printed side of the sheet was headed "Assert Your Rights." It stated reasons for alleging that any one violated the Constitution when he refused to recognize "your right to assert your opposition to the draft," and went on "If you do not assert and support your rights, you are helping to deny or disparage rights which it is the solemn duty of all citizens and residents of the United States to retain." It described the arguments on the other side as coming from cunning politicians and a mercenary capitalist press, and even silent consent to the conscription law as helping to support an infamous conspiracy. It denied the power to send our citizens away to foreign shores to shoot up the people of other lands, and added that words could not express the condemnation such cold-blooded ruthlessness deserves, &c., &c., winding up "You must do your share to maintain, support and uphold the rights of the people of this country." Of course the document would not have been sent unless it had been intended to have some effect, and we do not see what effect it could be expected to have upon persons subject to the draft except to influence them to obstruct the carrying of it out. The defendants do not deny that the jury might find against them on this point.

But it is said, suppose that that was the tendency of this

circular, it is protected by the First Amendment to the Constitution. Two of the strongest expressions are said to be quoted respectively from well-known public men. It well may be that the prohibition of laws abridging the freedom of speech is not confined to previous restraints, although to prevent them may have been the main purpose, as intimated in *Patterson* v. *Colorado*, 205 U. S. 454, 462. We admit that in many places and in ordinary times the defendants in saying all that was said in the circular would have been within their constitutional rights. But the character of every act depends upon the circumstances in which it is done. *Aikens* v. *Wisconsin*, 195 U. S. 194, 205, 206. The most stringent protection of free speech would not protect a man in falsely shouting fire in a theatre and causing a panic. It does not even protect a man from an injunction against uttering words that may have all the effect of force. *Gompers* v. *Bucks Stove & Range Co.*, 221 U. S. 418, 439. The question in every case is whether the words used are used in such circumstances and are of such a nature as to create a clear and present danger that they will bring about the substantive evils that Congress has a right to prevent. It is a question of proximity and degree. When a nation is at war many things that might be said in time of peace are such a hindrance to its effort that their utterance will not be endured so long as men fight and that no Court could regard them as protected by any constitutional right. It seems to be admitted that if an actual obstruction of the recruiting service were proved, liability for words that produced that effect might be enforced. The statute of 1917 in § 4 punishes conspiracies to obstruct as well as actual obstruction. If the act, (speaking, or circulating a paper,) its tendency and the intent with which it is done are the same, we perceive no ground for saying that success alone warrants making the act a crime. *Goldman* v. *United States*, 245 U. S. 474, 477. Indeed that case might be said to dispose of the present contention if the precedent covers all *media concludendi*. But as the right to free speech was not referred to specially, we have thought fit to add a few words.

It was not argued that a conspiracy to obstruct the draft was not within the words of the Act of 1917. The words are "obstruct the recruiting or enlistment service," and it might be suggested that they refer only to making it hard to get volunteers. Recruiting heretofore usually having been accomplished by getting volunteers the word is apt to call up that method only in our minds. But recruiting is gaining fresh supplies for the forces, as well by draft as otherwise. It is put as an alternative to enlistment or voluntary enrollment in this act. The fact that the Act of 1917 was enlarged by the amending Act of May 16, 1918, c. 75, 40 Stat. 553, of course, does not affect the present indictment and would not, even if the former act had been repealed. Rev. Stats., § 13.

Judgments affirmed.

March 3, 1919

Ray Stannard Baker:
Diary, March 8, April 3–5, and April 7, 1919

Except for nine days when he returned for the closing of the 65th Congress, February 24–March 5, 1919, the President of the United States spent the months from December 4, 1918, to July 8, 1919, outside the country, mostly in Paris. During the period before his return home in February, Wilson had persuaded the peace conference to accept the draft covenant he had proposed for the League of Nations; but upon his return to France in March, he discovered that his trusted adviser Colonel House had, in fact, compromised many of his positions regarding the financial and territorial terms of the peace. In the meantime, the presence of another figure had grown in Wilson's life—Ray Stannard Baker, yet another stellar journalist who had begun his career as a "muck-raker." A supporter of Wilson since 1912, Baker had sent confidential political reports to Washington from Europe in 1918. The President called upon him to serve as press secretary to the American delegation to the peace conference and came to trust him implicitly. Only Wilson's wife, Edith, and his personal physician, Cary T. Grayson, had greater access to the President at this time.

At Sea, March 8

I had quite an interesting talk, in company with Attorney General Gregory, with the President today. At the Metropolitan meeting the other night he looked much worn, his face gray and drawn, showing the strain of his heavy work at Washington —a really terrific week—but a little rest has put him in good condition again. His physical endurance is remarkable. I asked him about his interview the other night after the Metropolitan meeting with the Irish committee. No question has more dynamite in it now than the Irish question and the Irish-Americans have been trying to "smoke out" the President upon it. They want him, quite candidly, to come out for the independence of Ireland. He said he told the committee in language so plain and loud that it could be heard by the Tammany policemen who stood about that he regarded Judge Daniel Cohalan as a traitor and refused to meet him. The Representatives withdrew and finally they reappeared without Cohalan.

"They were so insistent," said the President, "that I had hard work keeping my temper."

He believes that the Irish question is now a domestic affair of the British Empire and that neither he nor any other foreign leader has any right to interfere. He said he did not tell them so, but he believed that when the League of Nations Covenant was adopted and the League came into being, a foreign nation —America if you like—might suggest, under one of its provisions, that the Irish question might become a cause of war and that therefore it became the concern of the League—but that time had not yet arrived.

The President has a good deal of the red Indian in him—and his dislikes of certain men (like Cohalan) are implacable. Once, in Paris last month, he refused to receive a group of newspaper men because of one of them whom he would not, under any circumstances, meet.

In amplification of the memorandum I gave the President on public opinion in America regarding the League of Nations, I argued that it was necessary to explain more fully the problems presented to the committee (the President's committee) that drew up the League's Covenant—my idea being that the average American would come to the same conclusions embodied in the Covenant if he had access to the same facts. What was needed now, I argued, was not so much to convince our people of the necessity for *a* League, the great majority being already convinced, but to assure them that *the* League of the Paris Covenant is the best obtainable. The President said that this specific knowledge would be valuable in most cases, but not in all. He gave this example. In his original draft of the Covenant (a copy of which he gave me) there was a provision (article VI of the Supplementary Agreements) that provided that all new states must bind themselves to accord "to all racial or national minorities within their separate jurisdiction exactly the same treatment and security, both in law and in fact, that is accorded the racial or national majority of their people." This was a valuable provision, making for more democracy in the world; but it was violently opposed by Dmowski, the Polish leader, who is bitterly anti-Semitic and who feared the Jewish issue in Poland; and it also brought up, acutely, the Japanese question, the Japanese standing for what the President called "an absurdly mild" recognition of the racial equality of the Japanese—but this was opposed by the British, on account of their colonies, particularly Australia. Therefore the whole provision was left out. He considered that publicity upon such an acute issue as this would do more harm than good, and make the adoption of the best obtainable Covenant more difficult.

I cannot feel myself in agreement here. I believe the President's initial proposal was sound and right and that with real publicity at every step he could have carried it before the court of the world's conscience. It is probably right now that the Covenant is before us in black and white not to raise the issue— for the important thing now is to *get peace*, get something started instantly, and a welter of new discussion can only make for delay. It is an odd thing that while the President stands for "pitiless publicity" and "open covenants openly arrived at"—a true position if ever there was one—it is so difficult for him to practice it. He is really so fearful of it. No man ever wanted greater publicity than he for the *general* statements of his position. He speaks to the masses in terms of the new diplomacy, but he deals with the leaders by the methods of the old.

This may be greater wisdom of comprise; it may be the only present method, considering the immense ignorance of the masses of mankind, to get constructive results. What he does is to get the crowd upon the general principles—and I supposed no man ever lived who could do it better—and then to dicker remorselessly with the leaders in the practical application of those principles. Could it be done differently? I think so. I have greater faith in the general sense of humankind and would trust them more fully, even if it took longer to reach a decision. But the President is a very wise and a very great man—and in the long run he will be guided by results rather than by methods.

If only there were more time, if the world was not literally dissolving in anarchy while the discussions at Paris are going on, I believe it would be far better to trust the people more fully, even if it took longer to reach a decision. But how to educate men while their coat-tails are afire!

The President is a good hater, and how he does hate those obstructive senators at Washington. He is inclined now to stand by the Covenant word for word as drawn, accepting no amendments, so that the thirty-seven of the round robin will be utterly vanquished, will have no chance of saying afterwards:

"Well, we forced the amendments, didn't we?" This would enable them to withdraw from their present ugly position and come to the support of the Covenant.

Dr. Grayson told me today that the President was partially blind in one eye, the result of the rupture of a blood vessel some years ago—the kind of a rupture which, if it had been in his brain, would have killed him. Grayson is one of the men who ought to have credit for a League of Nations, if ever it is established, for he has done a wonderful service in preserving the precious life of the President. When the President came to the White House in 1913 he was far from being a well man. His digestion was poor, and he had serious neuritis in his shoulder. It was the opinion of so good a doctor as Weir Mitchell that he could not live a year. Today he is in practically perfect health and can stand no end of work and strain, and this is due, in no small degree, to the daily care of Dr. Grayson, who watches him like a hawk. It is also due, of course, to the remarkable self-discipline of the President himself—his complete command of both body and mind. He rests when he rests, completely, and works when he works, utterly.

The President and Mrs. Wilson have attended the moving picture shows every evening both going and coming on these voyages—many of which bore me to death—and today they were at the shows both afternoon and evening. Some of them are so utterly trashy that it is hard to understand how a man of Wilson's intellect can bear them at all. They do not, he says, hurt his eyes, and he finds them restful. Possibly he is like another accomplished friend of mine who goes to the "movies," as he says, to relax. He is often not conscious of what the pictures are all about; the hypnotic flicker puts him to sleep.

It is very curious, the play of the President's mind. He likes a pun, he loves limericks. He quoted one today about sea sickness—and sometimes he apparently finds amusement in the most childish anagrams and puzzles. Grayson showed me the other day, to see if I could solve it, the following verbal puzzle, supposed to have been used as the address on a letter, which the President had set down for him:

    Wood
    John
    Mass.

It was in the President's handwriting. You are to read it off: "John Underwood, Andover, Mass." Surely these are about the lowest and most childish forays of humor or wit and yet the President relaxes in that way.

Mrs. Wilson has been reading aloud to the President a good deal during the voyage. He has enjoyed A. G. Gardiner's books of sketches of public men: *Prophets, Priests and Kings*, and *War Lords*. Admiral Grayson also said that he had read to the President several essays by an author named David Grayson!

The President told me today that he had never been seasick but once—crossing the English channel.

For a public man he sees very few people and seems to have almost no really intimate friends. There is no man in the world who better understands the democratic spirit in its broad manifestations—and few with less of the easy democracy of personal friendship and the give and take of intimacy. The voice of humanity reaches him with wonderful clearness and makes him an almost infallible judge of the great groundswells of public opinion. How he gets it is the secret of his genius; at any rate he seems not to want to get it from innumerable visitors (as Theodore Roosevelt did) and it is apparently a strain upon him to have people argue with him about anything whatsoever. He receives delegations but keeps them at arm's length and does most of the talking himself. He does it as a duty without, I think, any particular enjoyment. Neither in Washington nor in Paris has he ever entertained much. Yet he is most dependent upon Mrs. Wilson and Admiral Grayson; and with a few people around him whom he likes, he is altogether delightful.

My luncheon today with the President and Mrs. Wilson was altogether a charming occasion. The President was full of good stories, interesting comments on affairs in Paris—witty and genial. I enjoyed it greatly. Mrs. Wilson is a good woman and of enormous service to the President; but the man himself lives the lonely life of the mind and it is in his public addresses that he is most self-revealing. He is the type, par excellence, of the *public man* and, in order to do the great service he is called upon to do, he has reduced his private life to the utmost simplicity. To many of those who know the true riches of friendship, to those who wish to enjoy the world as they go through it, it will seem a poverty-stricken private life. It may be the price he has to pay.

The President, as one would anyway know, is an extremely temperate man. He smokes not at all, and infrequently, coming in wet or cold, takes a small drink of Scotch whiskey. Dr. Grayson tells me that not one of the three Presidents he has known so intimately was a smoker. Roosevelt took some wine with his meals and liked champagne with big dinners, but was never intemperate in this respect, though he was often charged with being. Taft was and is a total abstainer. Roosevelt was not, however, a temperate man by nature, but was given to many extremes and excesses—very different in temperament from Wilson. Though not an excessive user of alcohol, he sometimes drank an inordinate amount of tea—six or eight or even ten cups at a sitting. This stimulated him violently, so that he sometimes talked and acted almost as though intoxicated. Afterwards he could not sleep and would get up the next morning fagged and worn. But he would not give up. In order to clear his head and put himself in order again he would send for his horse and invite some long-suffering diplomat or army officer to go with him for a pounding ride in the country. He would do all sorts of "stunts," such as jumping fences or riding through streams and getting himself wet through, perspire tremendously—and come back feeling "bully." In the long run it was probably these excesses that killed him. He developed rheumatism and a kind of eczema, his heart finally gave out and he died too young. Yet, if he had not had this determination and will power—even this extreme temperament—he probably never would have developed himself, in his earlier years, from a weakling youth into a manhood of unexampled robustity.

Wilson is given to no excesses whatever. He has perfect control of himself—including a hot temper. Under the most bitter and provocative attacks by Roosevelt he has never once responded, never even referred to Roosevelt, treated Roosevelt and his whole campaign of opposition as though they did not exist. Nothing could have been better calculated to infuriate a man of Roosevelt's temperament more than this. It drove him wild!

Mr. Wilson made a very significant remark to me yesterday. "A high degree of education," he said, "tends, I think, to weaken a man's human sympathies."

It is remarkable and satisfactory that all three of our latest Presidents have been irreproachable in their private lives, loving their families and children. All three have been active in their religious observances, and strong in their religious convictions —Roosevelt of the Dutch Reformed Church, Taft, Unitarian, and Wilson, Presbyterian. The Puritan tradition is strong in all three.

April 3

The President fell ill today just after the Council of Four meeting and Admiral Grayson put him to bed. He has a severe cold with fever.

The Four had up the Adriatic problems this afternoon, and Signor Orlando refused to be present when the Jugo-Slavs (represented by Ante Trumbić) set forth their case. The Four jumps about from question to question and decides nothing. There is unlimited greedy bargaining, especially by the French and Italians, with only the President, growing grayer and grimmer all the time, standing upon principles of justice and right. He will probably be beaten. I only hope he goes down fighting for his principles.

The King of the Belgians flew down from Brussels and came in this afternoon to see the President. He is a tall, blond, youthful-looking man—handsome and engaging. I saw him this morning. All agree that he is frank and honest—and much more moderate in his demands than some of the Belgian delegates.

Italian friends of mine rushed around this evening with the story that Orlando and the entire delegation were going to leave the conference if they were not given Fiume. They were all wildly excited—in the Italian way—and indeed Orlando's government will probably fall unless they do get Fiume. The Italians already have won back their unredeemed provinces with over 1 million Italians and yet they are willing to endanger everything for twenty-five thousand Italians in the wholly doubtful city of Fiume, which, even in the pact of London, they never claimed. The worst of all the imperialists are the weaker, newer nations—Italy, Poland, Czecho-Slovakia, Jugo-Slavia.

I had a long talk this evening with Colonel House, who was sitting on his lounge with a figured blanket over his chilly legs—quite serenely dictating his diary to Miss Denton. More and more he impresses me as the dilettante—the lover of the game—the eager secretary without profound responsibility. He stands, in the midst of great events, to lose nothing. He gains experiences to put in his diary, makes great acquaintances, and plays at getting important men together for the sheer joy of using his presumptive power. He is an excellent conciliator, but with the faults of his virtue, for he conciliates over the border of minor disagreements into the solid flesh of principle. I found him tonight quite cheerful—quite optimistic. He told me that if *he* had it to do he could make peace in an hour! Were the Italians going home—well and good, let them go. Was Lloyd George going to issue a defense (as I intimated to him) that might compromise the President—all right, let him issue it. I told him of the President's illness (of which I had just been talking with Grayson) and said that Grayson told me that the President had probably contracted his cold from contact with Clemenceau, who coughs fearfully. "I hope," said the Colonel genially, "that Clemenceau will pass on the germ to Lloyd George."

Thus, a bright, lively, little man, optimistic in the presence of tragic events—while the great serious man of the conference —gray, grim, lonely, there on the hill—fights a losing battle against heavy odds. The President can escape no responsibility and must go to punishment not only for his own mistakes and weaknesses of temperament, but for the fear and the greed of the world. I do not love him—but beyond any other man I admire and respect him. He is *real*. He is the only great man here. Clemenceau is serious, but serious for smaller causes, immediate gains. Lloyd George is a poor third, and yet he too is a serious man—who lives for the moment, is pleased with every new compromise, pledges reckless future benefits for each present gain. Orlando is an amiable southern Italian without depth or vision, playing little games of local politics while the world is afire.

In the meantime Germany drifts always nearer bolshevism.

April 4

If it were not for the feeling that *peace must be made*, that the peace conference *cannot be allowed to fail*, I should say that everything was going to smash. The President was in bed all day, the Italians are threatening to go home, news comes from northern Russia that the Bolsheviks are threatening the extermination of the Allied troops that have been sent up there. The Four met today, with Colonel House taking the President's place. The Colonel prefers to work with Clemenceau rather than Lloyd George. He told me today that Lloyd George said to him: "You and I do not agree as well as the President and I agree." The Colonel is still optimistic! He would make peace quickly by giving the greedy ones all they want.

The other members of the Commission, Secretary Lansing and Mr. White, know next to nothing of what is going on. I usually tell them at the morning conference more than they get through their own sources.

The Colonel sides with the group that desires a swift peace on any terms. The President struggles almost alone to secure some constructive and idealistic result out of the general ruin. If these old leaders only knew it, Wilson is the only strong bulwark left to the old order against Leninism. He would save the present democratic system by making it just, decent, honest. What they are doing with their greedy demands and selfish interests is to give new arguments, new forces, to Lenin, and his following. They can't see this—and plunge on to their doom.

Wilson is really the supreme champion of the old order, the old nationalism, and would save it. I think he does not even see the new social revolution as a reality. Colonel House sees it and would, as usual, conciliate it. So does Lloyd George see it and would temporize with it. So does Clemenceau see it—and would fight it.

April 5

I have felt this fine spring day like going off alone to the quiet woods, and sitting down by some stream-side and railing at a mad world. It seems to me that I never before was so impressed with the crazy futility of human endeavor, or the greater need for the sanity of the quiet life and simple things.

There is some slight evidence today that peace will be made because peace must be made—a peace written on paper and signed by a few old men, none of whom will believe in what he is doing—but it will solve nothing.

Wilson is still in bed. Colonel House is still chirping hopefully —and has fixed another date for the conclusion of negotiations (while Bavaria is setting up a Soviet Republic). The only sane man I saw today was Dr. Nansen, the Norwegian, who has a plan for feeding the starving Russians.

The only hope left for this conference is that Wilson will come out with a last terrific blast for his principles, and their *specific application*, and go down in the ruin. *I fear he won't*. And that is complete failure. For what good will be a League of Nations unless the settlements upon which it rests are just? A League the only purpose of which is to guarantee "grabs" of land by France, Italy, Poland, etc., etc., is doomed to speedy failure. I have been here mostly because I saw a chance to help along the reconstructive movement, with the organization of a League of Nations, to keep the peace of the world. It now looks as though the League would be so weak, its foundations so insecure, that I could not myself support it. It will make very little difference now what peace is signed, for nothing essential will be settled.

April 7

This has been a great day—and we are now upon the very crisis of events. We shall soon know whether the peace conference is going to pieces or not. This morning Admiral Grayson sent me word that the President has ordered the *George Washington* to sail immediately for Brest. She is in dry dock and was not expected out until the 14th, so that the order has peculiar significance. In giving it out to the press I took pains to make no interpretations—stating the fact and leaving the correspondents to place upon it such interpretation as they chose. The implication, however, is perfectly clear—that the President has grown tired of the delay and is determined to make an end of it.

I went up to see Mr. Wilson at six-thirty—the first time since he fell ill—and had a long talk. I found him fully dressed, in his study, looking thin and pale. A slight hollowness of the eyes emphasized a characteristic I have often noted before—the size and luminosity of his eyes. They are extraordinarily clear, and he looks at one with a piercing intentness.

What he said put new courage into me. He is going to fight to the end. He has reached the point where he will give no further. When I talk with Colonel House (he was as smoothly optimistic today as ever), I am half persuaded that he could win a peace—by giving everything away; but when I talk with this man—this grim, rocklike man—I think he could bring down the world around him before giving over his convictions, and everything that is strong and sure within me rejoices. This is *victory*!

I had suggested to Grayson a day or so ago that I was confused by the diverse counsels I got from House and Lansing and when I came in the President said: "What about this difference between Lansing and House?"

"They do not agree at all," I said, "as to the present situation in the conference. Colonel House is strongly optimistic, Mr. Lansing is pessimistic."

"Lansing is much nearer right," said the President.

In passing, Close told me that only half an hour before I saw the President, Colonel House, coming over from the meeting of the Big Four at Lloyd George's, had talked with the President and had then come rushing out, saying that everything was going to pieces, that there was no agreement anywhere. Yet half an hour later, on his return to the Crillon, he was giving the correspondents the usual soothing dose of hopefulness, saying that there were only differences in details, etc., etc. In a time like this, what matters but the truth?

I told the President about the effect of his announcement regarding the *George Washington*.

"Well, the time has come to bring this thing to a head," he said. "House was just here and told me that Clemenceau and Klotz have talked away another day. They brought in a report which Clemenceau said he had not seen. There is the best of evidence that he had seen it. The unspeakable Klotz was called to explain it. One mass of tergiversations! I will not discuss anything with them anymore."

I then urged, as I have done before, that a statement be issued at once setting forth the specific applications of his principles. This we discussed, he being doubtful about too detailed a statement upon the specific issues. He said if he had not fallen ill, the time for meeting the situation would have been today. He proposed to stand upon his principles.

"Then Italy will not get Fiume?"

"Absolutely not—so long as I am here," he said sharply.

"Nor France the Saar?"

"No. We agreed among ourselves, and we agreed with Germany upon certain general principles. The whole course of the conference has been made up of a series of attempts, especially by France, to break over this agreement, to get territory, to impose crushing indemnities. The only real interest of France in Poland is to weaken Germany by giving Poland territory to which she has no right."

He said that a League of Nations founded upon an unjust peace could have no future. I told him of the remark of the Italian who came to see me the other day. When I asked him whether or not he was for the League of Nations, he replied naively: "Yes, but we want Fiume first."

I observed that this seemed typical of the position of all the Allies—that they wanted first to be sure of their "grabs" and "indemnities" and then to have a League of Nations to protect them in their possession. I told him how I had answered two Italians who came to see me today, and declared they were going home if they did not get Fiume.

"That is interesting," I said. "It would relieve us of a great responsibility."

"How is that," they said.

"Well, we are now stabilizing your lira at 6:32. Of course if you withdraw from the conference, you cannot expect us to go forward doing that."

Their faces fell.

"And," I said, "our merchants are now shipping much wheat and other food to Italy. I presume they will not care to do this unless they are well assured of their pay."

The two Italians (who are aides of Orlando's) went off, I think, with a new angle of the situation in mind.

"That was exactly what you should have said," the President remarked.

We had some talk of Lloyd George's position and the clear intimation that he is preparing to throw the blame for delay upon Wilson.

"Well," said the President sadly, "I suppose I shall have to stand alone."

I told him I believed the great masses of people were still strongly with him, but were confused and puzzled by hearing every case in the world but ours, and that they would rally again strongly to his support if he told them exactly what the situation was and the nature of his opposition.

"I believe so too," he said.

I asked him what I could say to the correspondents, and he told me to tell them to read again our agreements on the basis of the peace with the other Allies and with Germany, and to assure them that he would not surrender on these principles—which I did, gladly.

He is not "bluffing" in ordering the *George Washington*—he is not the kind of man who bluffs.

When I got back, Colonel House sent for me and said that some of the correspondents told him that I was putting a dark interpretation on the situation, and he expostulated. He had actually not known until evening that the President had sent for the *George Washington*, nor did he know that I had seen the President until I told him.

"The President does not seem cheerful," I said.

"No," he admitted.

"And if he wants to show that his patience is exhausted," I argued, "by so extreme a step as the ordering of the *George Washington*, I do not see why we should try to smooth over the situation and imply that everything is all right."

"We are all together on everything but certain small details."

"Have you decided the question of Fiume?"

"Not yet."

"Or that of Poland?"

"No."

And there you are!

Details, of course, cause all the trouble. In settling an estate it is often not the money nor the old home over which the heirs quarrel, but the family *Bible* and grandmother's alpaca shawl.

So much of the trouble in the world comes from trying to apply excellent general principles to difficult specific cases— whether the general principles are the Fourteen Points, or the Ten Commandments, or the Golden Rule. One was crucified for trying to apply the latter.

Wilson will get something out of it, but will disappoint most of the world, now dreaming of ideal results, and doubtful whether Wilsonism or bolshevism is the true remedy.

Vernon E. Kniptash:
Diary, March 30–April 1, and April 18–19, 1919

An architectural draftsman from Indianapolis, Vernon Kniptash served as a radio operator in the 150th Field Artillery Regiment, 42nd (Rainbow) Division, and had seen action in Champagne and the Meuse-Argonne. The spring of 1919 found him on occupation duty at Bad Neuenahr in the Rhineland, waiting to go home.

———————

Mar. 30, 1919 Sunday and baked 'em all day. Got restless after dinner, and Skinner and I walked around town. Had the blues pretty bad. Monotony gets me going. Played solitaire this evening. Such is Sunday in the A. of O.

Mar. 31, 1919 We got 'em. Had 'em all day. Can't shake 'em. Damn Blues.

April 1, 1919 Had a parade this morning. Gen. Gatley pinned a ribbon on our standard, and then we Passed in Review before him. Col. Bob then made a speech. He talked to us once before at St. Nazaire in 1917. Made a fairly good speech this time. Told us what a Hell of a good regiment we were, etc., etc. He's trying pretty hard to get back on speaking terms with the boys. Not much of a job after a month under that Heth. He's a welcomed visitor, believe me. He said during his speech that the Regiment had taken part in eleven different battles; two of them were major operations, and nine were minor. It's quite a record, and one that few Regiments can boast.—There's an indescribable restlessness springing up among the American soldiers and the German people now. When we first came here they treated us like Kings, and we couldn't understand it. We were too glad to leave the cave man life and get back to civilization to try to dope out their friendliness. I savvy it now. It's their damn propaganda again. They had hopes that Wilson would make things easy for them at the peace table, and treated us accordingly. Now that Wilson is sitting on them as hard as the rest they are getting ugly. They are poor losers in the first place, and then to lose their final bet is too much for them. They're forgetting who came out on the short end of this war, and are trying to order us around. See where they killed an American soldier in Coblenz. They better watch their step and not carry things too far. I've lost patience with them, and I venture to say I'm not the only one. Damn Dutch square-heads. I loathe every last one of them. Everything they do is underhanded and sneaking. Dirtiest fighters in the world, and they have lost none of their habits since they've gotten back into civil life. Lord, how I hate this race. I don't want any Kaiser lover in the States to get sassy with me. Might lose my temper and get mad. Germany will never be the same again, I'm afraid. Too many Americans have seen her the way she really is. Sure be glad when we leave here. Am sick of it all.

April 18, 1919   Slept like a log last night and had breakfast at 9:00. We're supposed to pull out this afternoon. The confusion has cleared up, and things are running pretty smoothly now. There's fellows from several different Divisions on board. Most of them are wounded men. Men with legs off, blinded, and 75 cases of shell shock. They're in a bad way.—Well, we're on our way. Just finished our supper and heard the engines start up. Choked the meal down and hustled on deck. At 5:30 P.M., the boat got into motion, and at 7:00 P.M. there was no more France. Nothing but water now. The boys did not cheer. They are all happy, but they regret to leave France just a little bit. Just 18 months ago today we left New York harbor. Coincidence. Quite a little difference between the two take-offs. The other one left me with an empty feeling in the pit of my stomach while this one . . . well . . . I don't know just how it does make me feel. I don't feel like yelling and raising Hell, and yet I'm not a bit sorry I'm leaving France. Curious. I didn't get sick on the other trip. Wonder if I will on this one? Don't see why I should. This boat won't ride near as rough as the Lincoln did. We'll see.

April 19, 1919   Slept like a log again last night. The ventilation is perfect. This is sure some boat. Had breakfast, and then went up and listened to a band concert. Then went thru a cootie inspection. This damn Army just can't do without inspections.— Watched the shell shocked boys for awhile. They are caged in on all sides. At times they act perfectly sane, and then again they're hog wild. One of them thinks he owns a white horse, and he spends the biggest part of the day grooming him. Another ties and unties knots in a rope for hours at a time. The worst case of them all is the one that walks back and forth with his head sunk on his chest and his hands clasped in front of him. He never says a word and never gets off his path. It's a shame to see these big huskies in such a condition. It would be far better to lose an arm or a leg. They say that they will be alright in two to three years. I sincerely hope so.—The ship is just naturally leaving this place. Doing its best, and that's 24 knots an hour (27 miles). It makes the Lincoln look like a tub. Haven't had any inkling of seasickness yet. I've seen only one boy sick as yet. The sea is like glass, and you'd never know it was moving. Don't imagine choppy waves would have much effect on this baby.—Had supper at 4 o'clock and laid around on deck till bedtime. Sure was a wonderful day. Tomorrow is Easter Sunday, and all's I got in the way of new clothes is a shirt that fits me around the neck.

Elmer W. Sherwood: Diary, April 18–21, 1919

Another Hoosier, Corporal Elmer Sherwood also served with the
150th Field Artillery Regiment in the 42nd Division. During his voyage home on the *Leviathan*, he reflected on the war and the changes
it had brought.

————————————

April 18

Rain. Loaded at about nine our ferry boat looked like a
speck beside the Leviathan. We walked up the gang plank from
the midget to the monster and taken to our compartments.

This ship is the largest in world.
Standard speed—16 knots
Emergency speed—23 knots
Speed being made on this trip—20 knots
length—950 feet
Beam—100 feet
Displacement—68,000 tons
Keel to top of mast—297 feet
Horsepower—65,000
Engines—4 turbine
Decks—13, besides bridge
Crew—2,083
three stacks including dummy

Marsh and I travelled the boat from top to bottom. It is not
only big but magnificent. It rocks very little and is fitted out
like a great hotel. Swimming pool is a big tile one. Dining
room is big and fine. Rest rooms libraries etc—elevators.

Left Brest 5 P.M. while band played Home, sweet Home and
Smiles.—Every body happy? hell yes. The Aquitania sister ship of
Lusitania sailor told us, led us out of Brest, a port filled with ships
flying the American flag. Some French battlships there too.

This sure is the day of days we are just as anxious to go

home as we were to come across. It has been a great experience and of course a necessary task but we hope it wont have to be repeated. The bunks are more comfortable and less crowded than on the Lincoln. We stayed on deck until land disappeared.

April 19

I am on a baggage detail. We are taking baggage to state-rooms etc. among baggage handled was some for Ambassador Sharp who has resigned position to White, Maj Gen G. W. Read Maj Gen S. D. Sturgis of 80th div; Brig Gen Douglass MacArthur 84 Brigade, Ex secty Treas O. T. Crosby Ex-postmaster gen Hitchcock and three congressmen.

Army units on board:

149th F. A.	Casual details St. Aignan detach.
150th F. A.	Cas. Co. 704
166th Inf	Brest cas. det.
168th Inf	sick and wounded #184 to #192
117 gas train	
117 T.H. and MP	Total 11505 officers and men
42 div Hq troop	
Hq det. 84 Brigade	
at 8:00 am	Brest 281 mi
	New York 2878 mi

The sad sight on ship are the one legged men over two hundred of them. The war never will be over for them but they are much better off than the "nuts" of whom there are a number in a caged compartments. Shell shock nervousness etc have contributed to make them lose their minds.

The food aboard is fine tho only two meals a day. Same system in great dining hall as in the camps.

April 20

Easter sunday—excellent turkey dinner. In evening picture show in dining room.

April 21

"A sweet young thing" member of one of the parties aboard, was heard to remark yesterday that she would like to see the cattle feed. So this morning every doughboy aboard has heard of it and tho none of us can help but feel insulted there are many jokes about it, for instance as we were going to mess this morning the mooing of cows was initiated. Of course the girl should be spanked or if too old punished in another way for such a brainless and unpatriotic expression. It would not have been resented had a soldier said it, for of course the way we feed isn't much different than the way animals are fed. But having fought for such as her we deserve more than sneers. However we have learned much about snobbishness and caste since going to war.

In the crowds packed in the mess hall many men with an arm or a leg gone are to be seen. Any reasonable person would think that a bed in a stateroom, such as the officers have, would be nothing too much to give them; but they have the same uncomfortable canvas bunks as we.

No doubt the American soldier will be a force in American life and politics. We should be and the principle which we now desire to uphold is equality. I saw a picture in "Life" yesterday of an Irish laborer in shirt sleeves riding home from work in an automobile. That is funny now but I hope that it is not a joke long because the man who works hard thru the day deserves a motor car as much as any one in the world. High wages are right, if a man is a worker he deserves a better living than he has had in the past. Of course no one should be paid for work he doesnt do. A good worker is a rare find so a man should be paid in proportion to what he accomplishes. The piece work system is right. And high wages for labor is right. We cannot do away with snobbishness but we can change the money status upon which the American caste system is built and the political system is made corrupt.

The army has been a frightful example to us of the least work getting the highest reward of favoritism, money value, caste and snobbishness. It hasn't been wholly bad of course but we have learned that we don't want the same system in the govt. of the nation.

The A.L.A. has distributed a bunch of magazines so we have plenty to read. Band concerts are a regular event and movies are given in the big mess hall, so our time is passed fairly pleasantly.

Clyde D. Eoff to Josephine Eoff

Sergeant Clyde Eoff served in the 314th Mobile Ordnance Repair Shop of the 89th Division. His fondness for his unit's trucks reflects the increasing mechanization of the U.S. Army and the need for soldiers with mechanical skills and affinities.

Bitburg Germany
April. 28 1919

My Dear Sister:—

I have before me your letter of April 4th, 1919 and am answering it on the eve of my birthday. I have passed another milestone and am still an old bachelor. I don't feel a bit older than I did a year ago, although I have a few more grey hairs than I had at that time. This has been one birthday that will linger in my memory for many years to come. I spent the day making out a list of the men who will sail for America in a short time. Men of my company who I have played with and drilled with and slept with and shared all the hardships of the days gone by.

We had a heavy snow fall today and everything is white this evening. It seems as if we are doomed to have our winter now, as it failed to come at the proper time. During the winter months it just rained and the weather was chilly most of the time. I have lived in Germany for almost five months and I haven't been able to figure out this weather yet. You can start out in the morning and feel comfortable in your shirt sleeves, and by noon you will need an overcoat to keep from freezing to death. But the snow that fell today is certainly beautiful. It was a wet snow and heavy, and it is piled up on the trees and the wires and looks like a picture in a story book.

We turned in all of our motor equipment yesterday, and finished packing the balance of the stock today. It was just like bidding goodbye to an old friend to have to part with the old Veteran Trucks. They had won a place in our heart, and even the joy of going home failed to make the parting a pleasant one. It may sound foolish to you but the men for several days have been putting in their spare time dolling them up and petting them as if they were a living creature and could understand what was going on.

The old Kelley was our main stay and all through the war it never failed us once. It was the first truck we were issued. It was turned over to us at Is-sur-Tille, France last August and has not been out of service for one day, due to any defect. It has been shot at by the Germans, and stuck in the mud, and driven over shell torn roads at night with no lights, at breakneck speed, and you can imagine how a man will drive with a battery of German artillery trying to knock you off the road, and the shells falling within ten feet of the truck and covering you with dirt.

While I had the Advance Station located at Romagne, on the edge of the Bantheville Woods, the only road leading to it was under observation by the Germans and they seemed to take great pleasure in trying to hit anyone who tried to reach the town with any sort of conveyance. And I must say they showed some excellent marksmanship at times. During the two weeks previous to the drive of November 1st they made five direct hits on trucks on this road. Now for the old Kelley. Lee Fleming, formerly a motorcycle cop on the Omaha police force was leaving the Advance Station one day, after bringing up some supplies. Well the Huns seen him pull out and opened fire. About that time Lee decided that it was his move. Just as he pulled out I heard a shell screaming overhead and I knew they were after him for it was the only truck on the road at that time. Well the first one lit about 15 feet behind him and from where I was I thought they had got him. But when the dirt quit flying I saw he was still on the move and driving like H——. Well they raised their range and fired at him till he disappeared over the hill about a mile away. Two days later I went back to the Shop on business and Lee told me about the wild ride.

He said there was some engineers working on the road at the top of the hill, and when he drove up they stopped him and asked him if he had seen that truck at the bottom of the hill. They thought it had been hit as the road turned at the foot of the hill and they could not see it after that. Lee said

"That was me they were shooting at" and they just looked at him and laughed. They said "Why you couldn't get up here since we saw that truck at the bottom of the hill." Well there is no use of me tiring you out with that ancient history, but I just wanted to recall one of the many little episodes in which the old Kelley took part.

Now to get back to the present time. The snow is still on the trees and it is still my Birthday and I am still in Bitburg Germany. A few more days will see us all ready for the word to start on our way, and we will not shed any tears of sorrow. America seems just like a dream and home is a word that we hardly realize the meaning of. I will have to get acquainted with my own family all over again. But I won't remain a stranger very long. Oh, No.

So Dad tried to scare you did he! Well you might know that would be the way he would break the news. But I am all right now and none the worse for the experience. I will have to jump on his neck when I get back. And the thumb is about well too although it is still a little sore.

Speaking of the old Hudson I have a suggestion to make. Suppose we just wait till I get back and look around and see some of the new cars that have come out since I left the States. I noticed an ad in a magazine the other day that interested me very much. It was a new car called the "Spitandkick" Twin Eight. The ad said: Just throttle the car down and see the old men with canes whiz by. And it rides like a pond lily on a quiet lake. The ad says they quit making windshields in 1914 owing to the fact they could find no glass to withstand the wind pressure when the car was driven at high speed. They inserted a letter from the prominent film star, Douglas Chapbanks saying: "My car is a wonder. I lash the steering wheel with a rope and climb out on the hood and play my banjo. It runs better in a cornfield than it does in the road." Some car, what you think?

I read in the *World Herald* the other day that another cyclone visited your fair city. On Sunday evening again and almost the same time of year that the other one passed over. Well Dundee got the brunt of it this time and it was not as wild as the other one. Omaha seems to be a regular stopping point for these whirl winds.

Recently I have taken some 75 exposures with different kodacs, and up to time of going to press I have had "rotten luck" soda speak. I am convinced that the fault lies between the poor films, the lack of knowledge in developing, the poor print paper and the ignorance of the workman. Anyway I will bring the films back and let your trained eye rove over the result. I think with the proper care we could get a few good prints off of some of them. By the way, was there anything on the roll I sent you some time ago. Judging from the other films that I exposed with the same kodac, there was very little on them.

No I remember no girl by the name of Dessie Moore, and further more I have no desire for her acquaintance. If she is married that is her hard luck, for she ought to have known better. If she lived next to Tillie she had a good neighbor. I wonder if my likeness still adorns the Struppith household. I ceased corresponding with the fair maiden several months ago, and she straightway got peeved and announced her intention to refrain from writing until she heard from me. So far she has proved to be truthful little girl, which is something to be proud of. I trust that her aching heart has found solace in some other companion who will appreciate her worth. "Gas Alarm" Masks on.

Expect to be in the States about the middle of May, unless unforeseen happens. Will write again before we leave Bitburg.

3,000,000 barrels of LOVE to be divided among the family and my Old Pal, Teddy. Be sure to get your share.

                                        Brother Clyde.

Sgt. Clyde Eoff
314 M.O.R.S.
A.P.O. 761

W.E.B. Du Bois: Returning Soldiers

Du Bois had traveled to France in December 1918 to investigate for the NAACP the treatment of black soldiers. While in Paris he helped organize a pan-African Congress, held in February 1919, which called on the peace conference to protect the rights of Africans living under colonial rule. He returned to the United States in April with material for "An Essay Toward a History of the Black Man in the Great War," published in *The Crisis* in June, and with documentation of the attempts by the U.S. military to prevent black soldiers from fraternizing with French civilians. "Documents of the War" appeared in the May number along with the editorial "Returning Soldiers." Postmaster General Burleson considered withholding mailing privileges from the magazine, but he relented. The May 1919 *Crisis* sold 106,000 copies, its highest circulation ever.

WE ARE returning from war! *The Crisis* and tens of thousands of black men were drafted into a great struggle. For bleeding France and what she means and has meant and will mean to us and humanity and against the threat of German race arrogance, we fought gladly and to the last drop of blood; for America and her highest ideals, we fought in far-off hope; for the dominant southern oligarchy entrenched in Washington, we fought in bitter resignation. For the America that represents and gloats in lynching, disfranchisement, caste, brutality and devilish insult—for this, in the hateful upturning and mixing of things, we were forced by vindictive fate to fight, also.

But today we return! We return from the slavery of uniform which the world's madness demanded us to don to the freedom of civil garb. We stand again to look America squarely in the face and call a spade a spade. We sing: This country of ours, despite all its better souls have done and dreamed, is yet a shameful land.

It *lynches*.

And lynching is barbarism of a degree of contemptible

nastiness unparalleled in human history. Yet for fifty years we have lynched two Negroes a week, and we have kept this up right through the war.

It *disfranchises* its own citizens.

Disfranchisement is the deliberate theft and robbery of the only protection of poor against rich and black against white. The land that disfranchises its citizens and calls itself a democracy lies and knows it lies.

It encourages *ignorance.*

It has never really tried to educate the Negro. A dominant minority does not want Negroes educated. It wants servants, dogs, whores and monkeys. And when this land allows a reactionary group by its stolen political power to force as many black folk into these categories as it possibly can, it cries in contemptible hypocrisy: "They threaten us with degeneracy; they cannot be educated."

It *steals* from us.

It organizes industry to cheat us. It cheats us out of our land; it cheats us out of our labor. It confiscates our savings. It reduces our wages. It raises our rent. It steals our profit. It taxes us without representation. It keeps us consistently and universally poor, and then feeds us on charity and derides our poverty.

It *insults* us.

It has organized a nation-wide and latterly a world-wide propaganda of deliberate and continuous insult and defamation of black blood wherever found. It decrees that it shall not be possible in travel nor residence, work nor play, education nor instruction for a black man to exist without tacit or open acknowledgment of his inferiority to the dirtiest white dog. And it looks upon any attempt to question or even discuss this dogma as arrogance, unwarranted assumption and treason.

This is the country to which we Soldiers of Democracy return. This is the fatherland for which we fought! But it is *our* fatherland. It was right for us to fight. The faults of *our* country are *our* faults. Under similar circumstances, we would fight again. But by the God of Heaven, we are cowards and jackasses if now that that war is over, we do not marshal every ounce of our brain and brawn to fight a sterner, longer, more unbending battle against the forces of hell in our own land.

We *return*.
We *return from fighting*.
We *return fighting*.

Make way for Democracy! We saved it in France, and by the Great Jehovah, we will save it in the United States of America, or know the reason why.

Charles R. Isum to W.E.B. Du Bois

A bookbinder from Los Angeles, Sergeant Charles Isum served with the medical detachment of the 365th Infantry Regiment, 92nd Division, in the Meuse-Argonne and in the Marbache Sector, where he treated wounded and gassed men under artillery fire during the final days of the war. Isum himself was gassed the day before the Armistice but remained in the field. In his letter to Du Bois he related his experiences with the army anti-fraternization policies described in the May number of *The Crisis*. In 1922 Charles and Zellee Isum had a daughter, Rachel, who later became a nurse; in 1946 she would marry the baseball player Jackie Robinson.

————————

1343 Lawerence Street,
Los Angeles, California,
May 17, 1919.

Hon. W.E.B. DuBois,
Editor of *The Crisis*,
70 Fifth Avenue, N.Y.

Dear Sir:

I have just finished reading the May issue of *The Crisis* and have enjoyed it immensely. I am indeed pleased to note that someone has the nerve and backbone to tell the public the unvarnished facts concerning the injustice, discrimination and southern prejudices practiced by the white Americans against the black Americans in France.

I am a recently discharged Sergeant of the Medical Detachment, 365th. Infantry, 92nd. Division, and I take this opportunity to relate one of my personal experiences with the southern rednecks who were in command of my division, brigade and regiment.

On or about December 26, 1918 General Order No. 40 was issued from the headquarters of the 92nd. Division. I cannot recall the exact wording of the part of the order which was of a discriminating nature, but it read something to this effect, "Military Police will see that soldiers do not address, carry-on conversation with or accompany the female inhabitants of this area." At the time this order was issued we were billeted in the village of Ambrieres, Mayenne. There were white soldiers also billeted in the same village but they did not belong to the 92nd. Division and the order did not affect them, hence it was an order for Colored soldiers only. It was not an A.E.F. order. It was a divisional order for Colored soldiers. We were living in the same houses with the French people and under the terms of this order we were forbidden to even speak to the people with whom we lived, while the white soldiers of the 325th. Baking Co. and the Subsupply Depot #10 were allowed to address, visit or accompany these same people where and whenever they desired.

On Jan. 21, 1919 Mademoiselle Marie Meziere, the eldest daughter of Monsieur Charles Meziere, a merchant tailor of Ambeieres was married to Monsieur Mauriece Barbe, a French soldier. I was invited to be a guest at the wine party, to accompany the bridal party on the marrige promonade and to be a guest at the supper, which was to take place at 8:30 P.M. I attended the wine party with four other Colored soldiers from the Medical Detachment. No whites were invited but Capt. Willis (white) of the Supply Company "butted in". He spoke miserable french and the members of the party called on the Colored soldiers to interpet for him. Willis became enraged and turned his back on the Colored boys and told the French people that it was improper for them to associate with the black soldiers. The French people paid no attention to what he said and we all left him sitting in the cafe alone. His temperature at this time was at about 104 degrees. The other Colored soldiers returned to the Infirmary and I accompanied the bridal party on the promanade out on the boulevard. There were seven persons in the party; the bride and groom, the bride's sister, the groom's brother and sister, a French soldier and myself. I was the only American. As we reached town on returning from the stroll Colonel George McMaster, Commanding Officer of our regiment accosted me and demanded, "Who are you. What are you doing with these people" I told him and he called a Military Police and ordered me taken to the Adjutant with orders for the Adjutant to prefer charges against me for accompanying white people. On arriving at the Adjutant's hotel we found Capt. Willis there evidently waiting for me to be brought in. The Adjutant asked only two questions, "Was he with a girl?", "What is your name and to what company do you belong?". Then he said, "Put him in the guard house."

The following afternoon I was ordered to appear for trial. At 1:15 P.M. I was taken through the streets to the Town Major's office by an armed guard who was a private soldier—my rank was not respected. I was called into the room and was suprised to find there was no one present but Major Paul Murry. He read the charges which had me charged with violating the 96th. Article of War and with disobeying General Order No. 40. After reading the charges he asked for my plea. I told him that I did not care to plea that I would exercise my right as a non-commissioned officer to refuse trial in a Summary Court. This was a complete suprise to him. He had no idea that I was aware of my rights. He looked it up in the Manual of Army Court Martials and said that it was my right but I was very foolish to use it. I told him that from the appearance of things there had been no intention of giving me a fair trial. The prosecuting witness was not present, the members of the board were absent and I had not been given an opportunity to call witnesses or secure counsel. At first he tried to frighten and intimidate me by saying that if I were given a General Court Martial trial I would be left in France awaiting trial after my regiment had gone home. He also said that I might get six month in Leavenworth if I should be found guilty. (Can you imagine it—six months for walking on the street with white people). After he saw that he could not intimidate me he assumed the air of comradship and used all his presusavive powers to entice me to submit to a speedy quiet trial in his kangaroo court but I stood pat. He said that I was trying to play martyr and was trying to make a big fuss out of a little incident, but I claimed that I was standing for a principle, that I had been unjustly treated, that the G.O. was unconstitutional, undemocratic and in direct opposition to principles for which we had fought. I asked that General Pershing be given a copy of the General Order and also a copy of the charges against me. He laughed at this request and said that the General was too busy for such small matters. He gave me a half an hour to think the matter over and stated that I might get some advice from the officers present. There were only two present. They had come in during the argument. One was Capt. Willis and the other Capt. Benj. Thomas. I took the matter up with Capt. Thomas and in the meantime my Detachment Commander, Major E.B. Simmons (white), of Massachusetts came in and I told him my story. He became indignant and told me to fight it to the last ditch and he would do all in his power to help me. I returned to the court room, and demanded a General Court Martial Trial and a release from the guard house pending trial. Major Murry said that I was making a great mistake and reluctantly gave me a release from the guard house.

That night I visited some of my French friends and found that the whole town was in an uproar over my case. M. Meziere had been to prevail on the Town Mayor in my behalf and was informed that nothing couldn be done as the Americans had charge of the town. M. Meziere had also called on Brig. Gen Gehardt our Brigade Commander, another Negro-hater of the meanest type. He refused to even give M. Meziere a civil audience. M. Meziere then went to the Town Mayor and swore to an affidavit that my character was of the best, that I was a respected friend of the family and was their invited guest. Mme. Emil Harmon, my landlady also made an affidavit of character in my behalf. I now have both affidavits in my possesion.

The following day I was rearrested at my billet and placed in the guard house, contrary to military rules. The Manual of Army Court Martials states that a non-commissioned officer shall not be confined in a guard house with privates but no attention was paid to that rule. No charges were given and no explaination made except that it was Colonel McMaster's orders. I was released that night and sent to my Detachment under "arrest in quarters" Nothing more has been said about the case to this day except at New York when I asked Major Murry when I was going have my trial and he said that the best thing to do was to keep quiet about it.

On March 22, 1919 I was given an honorable discharge from the army, with character grade Excellent and rank of Sergeant M.D. No mention of the case was made on my Service Record.

If I had comitted an offense sufficient to cause me to be arrested twice and placed in the guard house, why was I given an honorable discharge with and Excellent grade character and a non-commissioned officer's rank?

If space would permit I could quote other instances where our boys were shamefully mistreated by the white Americans while in France.

Respectfully yours,
Charles R. Isum
Fromerly Sergeant Medical Detachment, 365th. Inf.

P.S. If you should desire a copy of G.O. #40 write to Sergeant-Major Clarence Lee, 3426 Vernon Ave., Chicago, Ill.

Will Rogers: from Rogers-isms: The Cowboy Philosopher on the Peace Conference

A part-Cherokee cowboy from Oklahoma, Will Rogers had become a star on the vaudeville circuit by telling topical jokes about the news of the day while performing rope tricks. In his preface to *Rogers-isms: The Cowboy Philosopher on the Peace Conference*, Rogers wrote: "In the Five times I have appeared before president Wilson I have used dozens of these same jokes, about him, And he has the best sense of humor and is the best audience I ever played too . . ." In addition to perfecting the art of stand-up political satire, Rogers would become one of America's most popular newspaper columnists, radio personalities, and movie stars.

I was going to write a Book on the War, But I heard some fellow had already done it,

In fact I figure that the fellow who dont write on the war will be a novelty, There is so many Books on the War that no two people will have to read the same Book.

Then the War was too serious a subject I could not write on it, But the Peace Feast, That seemed to offer a better field for Humor provided you stick to the *facts*,

I have some inside facts procured from the most reliable source, And as I dont want to see the World grow up in ignorance on this historical subject I would really feel selfish and mean too withold it,

Heres how I got it, There is a fellow I know, Who had a friend, And this friends Sister had a sweetheart and he was a Soldier in France and his cousins pal was a Bunkie of Col Houses Chouffer, The Col told his Chouffer So you see my information comes from the same place Pres Wilsons does,

---

We are handicapped at this meeting, England and France both have their Prime Ministers there while *BILLY SUNDAY* dident go for us,

---

Germany couldent figure out how America could get troops over there and get them trained so quick they dident know that in our manual there is nothing about RETREATING and when you only got to teach an Army to go one way you can do it in half the time,

I feel pretty proud over that last little gag, As I used it before Pres Wilson in Washington and he repeated it in his Boston speech, Saying "as one of our AMERICAN HUMORISTS says," Up to then I had only been an ordinary Rope thrower,

Pretty tough when the Pres cops your act,

America dident know till they got over there that those European Nations have had a disease for years called the Gimmes.

England and Japan had a secret Treaty where England was to get everything south of the equator and Japan everything North, Guess they were going to leave the equator for Ireland,

---

They agreed on one of the 14 points that was that America went in for *nothing* and *expects nothing* they are all UNANIMOUS WE GET IT,

Wanted to put the LEAGUE of nations in with Peace Treaty,

thats like a fellow going into a store and the Merchant wont
sell him a Suit unless he uses a Gillette Razor,

————————

Italy left the Conference and got what she wanted, Japan
threatened to leave and got what she wanted, If Pres Wilson
had left some Republican Senators would have gotten what
they wanted,

————————

Well they finally handed Germany the Peace terms 80 thousand words only thing ever written longer than a Lafollette
Speech,

HAD TO BE THAT LONG TO TELL THE GERMANS WHAT THEY
THOUGHT OF THEM

Imagine what a document for Lawers to pick flaws in,

Could have settled the whole thing in one sentence, "IF
YOU BIRDS START ANYTHING AGAIN WE WILL GIVE
YOU THE OTHER BARREL,"

From *Rogers-isms: The Cowboy Philosopher on the Peace Conference* (1919)

Woodrow Wilson:
Memorial Day Address at Suresnes

With the peace talks in Paris drawing to a close, Woodrow Wilson left the morning session on Memorial Day for the four-mile drive to Suresnes, where the French government had dedicated a few acres as a final resting place for 1,500 doughboys. Local women had decorated each grave with a small American flag and wreath. A visibly moved President—whose hair had turned white over the last few months— delivered one of the most heartrending speeches of his life.

––––––––

May 30, 1919.

Mr. Ambassador, ladies and gentlemen, fellow countrymen: No one with a heart in his breast, no American, no lover of humanity, can stand in the presence of these graves without the most profound emotion. These men who lie here are men of unique breed. Their like has not been seen since the far days of the Crusades. Never before have men crossed the seas to a foreign land to fight for a cause which they did not pretend was peculiarly their own, but knew was the cause of humanity and of mankind. And when they came, they found fit comrades for their courage and their devotion. They found armies of liberty already in the field—men who, though they had gone through three years of fiery trial, seemed only to be just discovering, not for a moment losing, the high temper of the great affair, men seasoned in the bloody service of liberty. Joining hands with these, the men of America gave that greatest of all gifts, the gift of life and the gift of spirit.

It will always be a treasured memory on the part of those who knew and loved these men that the testimony of everybody who saw them in the field of action was of their unflinching courage, their ardor to the point of audacity, their full consciousness of the high cause they had come to serve, and their constant vision of the issue. It is delightful to learn from those who saw these men fight and saw them waiting in the trenches for the summons to the fight that they had a touch of the high spirit of religion, that they knew they were exhibiting a spiritual as well as a physical might, and those of us who know and love America know they were discovering to the whole world the true spirit and devotion of their motherland. It was America who came in the person of these men and who will forever be grateful that she was so represented.

And it is the more delightful to entertain these thoughts because we know that these men, though buried in a foreign, are not buried in an alien soil. They are at home, sleeping with the spirits of those who thought the same thoughts and entertained the same aspirations. The noble women of Suresnes have given evidence of the loving sense with which they received these dead as their own, for they have cared for their graves, they have made it their interest, their loving interest, to see that there was no hour of neglect, and that constantly through all the months that have gone by the mothers at home should know that there were mothers here who remembered and honored their dead.

You have just heard in the beautiful letter from Monsieur Clemenceau what I believe to be the real message of France to us on a day like this, a message of genuine comradeship, a message of genuine sympathy, and I have no doubt that if our British comrades were here, they would speak in the same spirit and in the same language. For the beauty of this war is that it has brought a new partnership and a new comradeship and a new understanding into the field of the effort of the nations.

But it would be no profit to us to eulogize these illustrious dead if we did not take to heart the lesson which they have taught us. They are dead; they have done their utmost to show their devotion to a great cause; and they have left us to see to it that that cause shall not be betrayed, whether in war or in peace. It is our privilege and our high duty to consecrate ourselves afresh on a day like this to the objects for which they fought. It is not necessary that I should rehearse to you what those objects were. These men did not come across the sea merely to defeat Germany and her associated powers in the war. They came to defeat forever the things for which the Central Powers stood, the sort of power they meant to assert in the world, the arrogant, selfish dominance which they meant to establish; and they came, moreover, to see to it that there should never be a war like this again. It is for us, particularly for us who are civilians, to use our proper weapons of counsel and agreement to see to it that there never is such a war again. The nation that should now fling out of this common concord of counsel would betray the human race.

So it is our duty to take and maintain the safeguards which will see to it that the mothers of America and the mothers of France and England and Italy and Belgium and all the other suffering nations should never be called upon for this sacrifice again. This can be done. It must be done. And it will be done. The thing that these men left us, though they did not in their counsels conceive it, is the great instrument which we have just erected in the League of Nations. The League of Nations is the covenant of governments that these men shall not have died in vain. I like to think that the dust of those sons of America who were privileged to be buried in their mother country will mingle with the dust of the men who fought for the preservation of the Union, and that as those men gave their lives in order that America might be united, these men have given their lives in order that the world might be united. Those men gave their lives in order to secure the freedom of a nation. These men have given theirs in order to secure the freedom of mankind; and I look forward to an age when it will be just as impossible to regret the results of their labor as it is now impossible to regret the result of the labor of those who fought for the union of the states. I look for the time when every man who now puts his counsel against the united service of mankind under the League of Nations will be just as ashamed of it as if he now regretted the union of the states.

You are aware, as I am aware, that the airs of an older day are beginning to stir again, that the standards of an old order are trying to assert themselves again. There is here and there an attempt to insert into the counsel of statesmen the old reckonings of selfishness and bargaining and national advantage which were the roots of this war, and any man who counsels these things advocates the renewal of the sacrifice which these men have made; for if this is not the final battle for right, there will be another that will be final. Let these gentlemen not suppose that it is possible for them to accomplish this return to an order of which we are ashamed and that we are ready to forget. They cannot accomplish it. The peoples of the world are awake, and the peoples of the world are in the saddle. Private counsels of statesmen cannot now and cannot hereafter determine the destinies of nations. If we are not the servants of the opinion of mankind, we are of all men the littlest, the most contemptible, the least gifted with vision. If we do not know our age, we cannot accomplish our purpose, and this age is an age which looks forward, not backward; which rejects the standards of national selfishness that once governed the counsels of nations and demands that they shall give way to a new order of things in which the only questions will be: "Is it right?" "Is it just?" "Is it in the interest of mankind?"

This is a challenge that no previous generation ever dared to give ear to. So many things have happened, and they have happened so fast, in the last four years, that I do not think many of us realize what it is that has happened. Think how impossible it would have been to get a body of responsible statesmen seriously to entertain the idea of the organization of a League of Nations four years ago. And think of the change that has taken place! I was told before I came to France that there would be confusion of counsel about this thing, and I found unity of counsel. I was told that there would be opposition, and I found union of action. I found the statesmen with whom I was about to deal united in the idea that we must have a League of Nations, that we could not merely make a peace settlement and then leave it to make itself effectual, but that we must conceive some common organization by which we should give our common faith that this peace would be maintained and the conclusions at which we had arrived should be made as secure as the united counsels of all the great nations that fought against Germany could make them. We have listened to the challenge, and that is the proof that there shall never be a war like this again.

Ladies and gentlemen, we all believe, I hope, that the spirits of these men are not buried with their bodies. Their spirits live. I hope—I believe—that their spirits are present with us at this hour. I hope that I feel the compulsion of their presence. I hope that I realize the significance of their presence. Think, soldiers, of those comrades of yours who are gone. If they were here, what would they say? They would not remember what you are talking about today. They would remember America which they left with their high hope and purpose. They would remember the terrible field of battle. They would remember what they constantly recalled in times of danger, what they had come for and how worthwhile it was to give their lives for it. And they would say, "Forget all the little circumstances of the day. Be ashamed of the jealousies that divide you. We command you in the name of those who, like ourselves, have died to bring the counsels of men together, and we remind you what America said she was born for. She was born, she said, to show mankind the way to liberty. She was born to make this great gift a common gift. She was born to show men the way of experience by which they might realize this gift and maintain it, and we adjure you in the name of all the great traditions of America to make yourselves soldiers now once for all in this common cause, where we need wear no uniform except the uniform of the heart, clothing ourselves with the principles of right and saying to men everywhere, 'You are our brothers, and we invite you into the comradeship of liberty and of peace.'"

Let us go away hearing these unspoken mandates of our dead comrades.

If I may speak a personal word, I beg you to realize the compulsion that I myself feel that I am under. By the Constitution of our great country I was the Commander in Chief of these men. I advised the Congress to declare that a state of war existed. I sent these lads over here to die. Shall I—can I—ever speak a word of counsel which is inconsistent with the assurances I gave them when they came over? It is inconceivable. There is something better, if possible, that a man can give than his life, and that is his living spirit to a service that is not easy, to resist counsels that are hard to resist, to stand against purposes that are difficult to stand against, and to say, "Here stand I, consecrated in spirit to the men who were once my comrades and who are now gone, and who have left me under eternal bonds of fidelity."

Claude McKay: The Little Peoples

Born in Jamaica, Claude McKay came to America to study at Tuskegee Institute but found both the racial prejudice in Alabama and the strict regimen on campus intolerable enough to leave for Kansas State University. He moved to New York City in 1917 and became friends with Hubert Harrison, founder of the Liberty League and editor of *The Voice*, and with Max Eastman, publisher of the radical magazine *The Liberator*. In July 1919 *The Liberator* published seven of McKay's poems, including "If We Must Die" and "The Little Peoples." Anti-colonialists' hopes that the peace conference might lead to self-determination for African peoples dimmed as the former German colonies became spoils divided among the victors in the form of League of Nations mandates.

———————————

The little peoples of the troubled earth,
The little nations that are weak and white;—
For them the glory of another birth,
For them the lifting of the veil of night.
The big men of the world in concert met,
Have sent forth in their power a new decree:
Upon the old harsh wrongs the sun must set,
Henceforth the little peoples must be free!

But we, the blacks, less than the trampled dust,
Who walk the new ways with the old dim eyes,—
We to the ancient gods of greed and lust
Must still be offered up as sacrifice:
Oh, we who deign to live but will not dare,
The white world's burden must forever bear!

George Creel: The "Second Lines"

After earning his stripes as a reform-minded journalist in Kansas City and Denver, George Creel had worked on Wilson's reelection campaign in 1916; and upon America's entry into the war, Wilson appointed Creel as the chairman of the Committee on Public Information, a controversial organization created by executive order to spread the "Gospel of Americanism" to all corners of the country and the world. Creel considered his work "propaganda" only in the sense of the propagation of faith. The CPI kindled support for the war and then fanned the flames through articles, pamphlets, speakers ("Four Minute Men"), motion pictures, and posters. While Creel insisted that the CPI existed to share information, not impose censorship, all of the agency's actions fell somewhere between morale-building and manipulation. One of Creel's subordinates, Edward Bernays, a nephew of Sigmund Freud, would later become a pioneer in the field of public relations.

———————————

As SECRETARY BAKER points out, the war was not fought in France alone. Back of the firing-line, back of armies and navies, back of the great supply-depots, another struggle waged with the same intensity and with almost equal significance attaching to its victories and defeats. It was the fight for the *minds* of men, for the "conquest of their convictions," and the battle-line ran through every home in every country.

It was in this recognition of Public Opinion as a major force that the Great War differed most essentially from all previous conflicts. The trial of strength was not only between massed bodies of armed men, but between opposed ideals, and moral verdicts took on all the value of military decisions. Other wars went no deeper than the physical aspects, but German *Kultur* raised issues that had to be fought out in the hearts and minds of people as well as on the actual firing-line. The approval of the world meant the steady flow of inspiration into the trenches; it meant the strengthened resolve and the renewed determination of the civilian population that is a nation's second line. The condemnation of the world meant the destruction of morale

687

and the surrender of that conviction of justice which is the very heart of courage.

The Committee on Public Information was called into existence to make this fight for the "verdict of mankind," the voice created to plead the justice of America's cause before the jury of Public Opinion. The fantastic legend that associated gags and muzzles with its work may be likened only to those trees which are evolved out of the air by Hindu magicians and which rise, grow, and flourish in gay disregard of such usual necessities as roots, sap, and sustenance. *In no degree was the Committee an agency of censorship, a machinery of concealment or repression. Its emphasis throughout was on the open and the positive. At no point did it seek or exercise authorities under those war laws that limited the freedom of speech and press.* In all things, from first to last, without halt or change, it was a plain publicity proposition, a vast enterprise in salesmanship, the world's greatest adventure in advertising.

Under the pressure of tremendous necessities an organization grew that not only reached deep into every American community, but that carried to every corner of the civilized globe the full message of America's idealism, unselfishness, and indomitable purpose. We fought prejudice, indifference, and disaffection at home and we fought ignorance and falsehood abroad. We strove for the maintenance of our own morale and the Allied morale by every process of stimulation; every possible expedient was employed to break through the barrage of lies that kept the people of the Central Powers in darkness and delusion; we sought the friendship and support of the neutral nations by continuous presentation of facts. We did not call it propaganda, for that word, in German hands, had come to be associated with deceit and corruption. Our effort was educational and informative throughout, for we had such confidence in our case as to feel that no other argument was needed than the simple, straightforward presentation of facts.

There was no part of the great war machinery that we did not touch, no medium of appeal that we did not employ. The printed word, the spoken word, the motion picture, the telegraph, the cable, the wireless, the poster, the sign-board—all these were used in our campaign to make our own people and all other peoples understand the causes that compelled America to take arms. All that was fine and ardent in the civilian population came at our call until more than one hundred and fifty thousand men and women were devoting highly specialized abilities to the work of the Committee, as faithful and devoted in their service as though they wore the khaki.

While America's summons was answered without question by the citizenship as a whole, it is to be remembered that during the three and a half years of our neutrality the land had been torn by a thousand divisive prejudices, stunned by the voices of anger and confusion, and muddled by the pull and haul of opposed interests. These were conditions that could not be permitted to endure. What we had to have was no mere surface unity, but a passionate belief in the justice of America's cause that should weld the people of the United States into one white-hot mass instinct with fraternity, devotion, courage, and deathless determination. The *war-will*, the will-to-win, of a democracy depends upon the degree to which each one of all the people of that democracy can concentrate and consecrate body and soul and spirit in the supreme effort of service and sacrifice. What had to be driven home was that all business was the nation's business, and every task a common task for a single purpose.

Starting with the initial conviction that the war was not the war of an administration, but the war of one hundred million people, and believing that public support was a matter of public understanding, we opened up the activities of government to the inspection of the citizenship. A voluntary censorship agreement safeguarded military information of obvious value to the enemy, but in all else the rights of the press were recognized and furthered. Trained men, at the center of effort in every one of the war-making branches of government, reported on progress and achievement, and in no other belligerent nation was there such absolute frankness with respect to every detail of the national war endeavor.

As swiftly as might be, there were put into pamphlet form America's reasons for entering the war, the meaning of America, the nature of our free institutions, our war aims, likewise analyses of the Prussian system, the purposes of the imperial German government, and full exposure of the enemy's misrepresentations, aggressions, and barbarities. Written by the country's foremost publicists, scholars, and historians, and distinguished for their conciseness, accuracy, and simplicity, these pamphlets blew as a great wind against the clouds of confusion and misrepresentation. Money could not have purchased the volunteer aid that was given freely, the various universities lending their best men and the National Board of Historical Service placing its three thousand members at the complete disposal of the Committee. Some thirty-odd booklets, covering every phase of America's ideals, purposes, and aims, were printed in many languages other than English. Seventy-five millions reached the people of America, and other millions went to every corner of the world, carrying our defense and our attack.

The importance of the spoken word was not underestimated. A speaking division toured great groups like the Blue Devils, Pershing's Veterans, and the Belgians, arranged massmeetings in the communities, conducted forty-five war conferences from coast to coast, co-ordinated the entire speaking activities of the nation, and assured consideration to the crossroads hamlet as well as to the city.

The Four Minute Men, an organization that will live in history by reason of its originality and effectiveness, commanded the volunteer services of 75,000 speakers, operating in 5,200 communities, and making a total of 755,190 speeches, every one having the carry of shrapnel.

With the aid of a volunteer staff of several hundred translators, the Committee kept in direct touch with the foreign-language press, supplying selected articles designed to combat ignorance and disaffection. It organized and directed twenty-three societies and leagues designed to appeal to certain classes and particular foreign-language groups, each body carrying a specific message of unity and enthusiasm to its section of America's adopted peoples.

It planned war exhibits for the state fairs of the United States, also a great series of interallied war expositions that brought home to our millions the exact nature of the struggle that was being waged in France. In Chicago alone two million people attended in two weeks, and in nineteen cities the receipts aggregated $1,432,261.36.

The Committee mobilized the advertising forces of the country—press, periodical, car, and outdoor—for the patriotic campaign that gave millions of dollars' worth of free space to the national service.

It assembled the artists of America on a volunteer basis for the production of posters, window-cards, and similar material of pictorial publicity for the use of various government departments and patriotic societies. A total of 1,438 drawings was used.

It issued an official daily newspaper, serving every department of government, with a circulation of one hundred thousand copies a day. For official use only, its value was such that private citizens ignored the supposedly prohibitive subscription price, subscribing to the amount of $77,622.58.

It organized a bureau of information for all persons who sought direction in volunteer war-work, in acquiring knowledge of any administrative activities, or in approaching business dealings with the government. In the ten months of its existence it gave answers to eighty-six thousand requests for specific information.

It gathered together the leading novelists, essayists, and publicists of the land, and these men and women, without payment, worked faithfully in the production of brilliant, comprehensive articles that went to the press as syndicate features.

One division paid particular attention to the rural press and the plate-matter service. Others looked after the specialized needs of the labor press, the religious press, and the periodical press. The Division of Women's War Work prepared and issued the information of peculiar interest to the women of the United States, also aiding in the task of organizing and directing.

Through the medium of the motion picture, America's war progress, as well as the meanings and purposes of democracy, were carried to every community in the United States and to every corner of the world. "Pershing's Crusaders," "America's Answer," and "Under Four Flags" were types of feature films by which we drove home America's resources and determinations, while other pictures, showing our social and industrial life, made our free institutions vivid to foreign peoples. From the domestic showings alone, under a fair plan of distribution, the sum of $878,215 was gained, which went to support the cost of the campaigns in foreign countries where the exhibitions were necessarily free.

Another division prepared and distributed still photographs and stereopticon slides to the press and public. Over two hundred thousand of the latter were issued at cost. This division also conceived the idea of the "permit system," that opened up our military and naval activities to civilian camera men, and operated it successfully. It handled, also, the voluntary censorship of still and motion pictures in order that there might be no disclosure of information valuable to the enemy. The number of pictures reviewed averaged seven hundred a day.

Turning away from the United States to the world beyond our borders, a triple task confronted us. First, there were the peoples of the Allied nations that had to be fired by the magnitude of the American effort and the certainty of speedy and effective aid, in order to relieve the war-weariness of the civilian population and also to fan the enthusiasm of the firing-line to new flame. Second, we had to carry the truth to the neutral nations, poisoned by German lies; and third, we had to get the ideals of America, the determination of America, and the invincibility of America into the Central Powers.

Unlike other countries, the United States had no subsidized press service with which to meet the emergency. As a matter of bitter fact, we had few direct news contacts of our own with the outside world, owing to a scheme of contracts that turned the foreign distribution of American news over to European agencies. The volume of information that went out from our shores was small, and, what was worse, it was concerned only with the violent and unusual in our national life. It was news of strikes and lynchings, riots, murder cases, graft prosecutions, sensational divorces, the bizarre extravagance of "sudden millionaires." Naturally enough, we were looked upon as a race of dollar-mad materialists, a land of cruel monopolists, our real rulers the corporations and our democracy a "fake."

Looking about for some way in which to remedy this evil situation, we saw the government wireless lying comparatively idle, and through the close and generous cooperation of the navy we worked out a news machinery that soon began to pour a steady stream of American information into international channels of communication. Opening an office in every capital of the world outside the Central Powers, a daily service went out from Tuckerton to the Eiffel Tower for use in France and then for relay to our representatives in Berne, Rome, Madrid, and Lisbon. From Tuckerton the service flashed to England, and from England there was relay to Holland, the Scandinavian countries, and Russia. We went into Mexico by cable and land wires; from Darien we sent a service in Spanish to Central and South-American countries for distribution by our representatives; the Orient was served by telegraph from New York to San Diego, and by wireless leaps to Cavite and Shanghai. From Shanghai the news went to Tokio and Peking, and from Peking on to Vladivostok for Siberia. Australia, India, Egypt, and the Balkans were also reached, completing the world chain.

For the first time in history the speeches of a national executive were given universal circulation. The official addresses of President Wilson, setting forth the position of America, were put on the wireless always at the very moment of their delivery, and within twenty-four hours were in every language in every country in the world. Carried in the newspapers initially, they were also printed by the Committee's agents on native presses and circulated by the millions. The swift rush of our war progress, the tremendous resources of the United States, the Acts of Congress, our official deeds and utterances, the laws that showed our devotion to justice, instances of our enthusiasm and unity—all were put on the wireless for the information of the world, Teheran and Tokio getting them as completely as Paris or Rome or London or Madrid.

Through the press of Switzerland, Denmark, and Holland we filtered an enormous amount of truth to the German people, and from our headquarters in Paris went out a direct attack upon Hun censorship. Mortar-guns, loaded with "paper bullets," and airplanes, carrying pamphlet matter, bombarded the German front, and at the time of the armistice balloons with a cruising radius of five hundred miles were ready to reach far into the Central Powers with America's message.

This daily news service by wire and radio was supplemented by a mail service of special articles and illustrations that went into foreign newspapers and magazines and technical journals and periodicals of special appeal. We aimed to give in this way a true picture of the American democracy, not only in its war activities, but also in its devotion to the interests of peace. There were, too, series of illustrated articles on our education, our trade and industry, our finance, our labor conditions, our religions, our work in medicine, our agriculture, our women's work, our government, and our ideals.

Reading-rooms were opened in foreign countries and furnished with American books, periodicals, and newspapers. Schools and public libraries were similarly supplied. Photographs were sent for display on easels in shop windows abroad. Window-hangers and news-display sheets went out in English, French, Italian, Swedish, Portuguese, Spanish, Danish, Norwegian, and Dutch; and display-sheets went to Russia, China, Japan, Korea, parts of India and the Orient, to be supplemented with printed reading-matter by the Committee's agents there.

To our representatives in foreign capitals went, also, the feature films that showed our military effort—cantonments, shipyards, training-stations, war-ships, and marching thousands —together with other motion pictures expressing our social and industrial progress, all to be retitled in the language of the land, and shown either in theaters, public squares, or open fields. Likewise we supplied pamphlets for translation and distribution, and sent speakers, selected in the United States from among our foreign-born, to lecture in the universities and schools, or else to go about among the farmers, to the labor unions, to the merchants, etc.

Every conceivable means was used to reach the foreign mind with America's message, and in addition to our direct approach we hit upon the idea of inviting the foremost newspaper men of other nations to come to the United States to see with their own eyes, to hear with their own ears, in order that they might report truly to their people as to American unity, resolve, and invincibility. The visits of the editors of Mexico, Italy, Switzerland, Denmark, Sweden, and Norway were remarkable in their effect upon these countries, and no less successful were the trips made to the American front in France under our guidance by the newspaper men of Holland and Spain.

Before this flood of publicity the German misrepresentations were swept away in Switzerland, the Scandinavian countries, Italy, Spain, the Far East, Mexico, and Central and South America. From being the most misunderstood nation, America became the most popular. A world that was either inimical, contemptuous, or indifferent was changed into a world of friends and well-wishers. Our policies, America's unselfish aims in the war, the services by which these policies were explained and these aims supported, and the flood of news items and articles about our normal life and our commonplace activities —these combined to give a true picture of the United States to foreign eyes. It is a picture that will be of incalculable value in our future dealings with the world, political and commercial. It was a bit of press-agenting that money could not buy, done out of patriotism by men and women whose services no money could have bought.

In no other belligerent nation was there any such degree of centralization as marked our duties. In England and France, for instance, five to ten organizations were intrusted with the tasks that the Committee discharged in the United States. And in one country, in one year, many of the warring nations spent more money than the total expenditure of the Committee on Public Information during the eighteen months of its existence in its varied activities that reached to every community in America and to every corner of the civilized world. From the President's fund we received $5,600,000, and Congress granted us an appropriation of $1,250,000, a total working capital of $6,850,000. From our films, war expositions, and minor sources we earned $2,825,670.23, and at the end were able to return $2,937,447 to the Treasury. Deduct this amount from the original appropriations, and it is seen that the Committee on Public Information cost the taxpayers of the United States just $4,912,553! These figures might well be put in bronze to stand as an enduring monument to the sacrifice and devotion of the one hundred and fifty thousand men and women who were responsible for the results. A world-fight for the verdict of mankind—a fight that was won against terrific odds—and all for less than five millions—less than half what Germany spent in Spain alone!

It is the pride of the Committee, as it should be the pride of America, that every activity was at all times open to the sun. No dollar was ever sent on a furtive errand, no paper subsidized, no official bought. From a thousand sources we were told of the wonders of German propaganda, but our original determinations never altered. Always did we try to find out what the Germans were doing and then we *did not do it*.

There is pride, also, in the record of stainless patriotism and unspotted Americanism. In June, 1918, after one year of operation —a year clamorous with ugly attack—the Committee submitted itself to the searching examination of the House Committee on Appropriations. Every charge of partizanship, dishonesty, inaccuracy, and inefficiency was investigated, the expenditure of every dollar scrutinized, and the Congressmen even went back as far as 1912 to study my writings and my political thought. At the end of the inquiry the appropriation was voted unanimously, and on the floor of the House the Republican members supported the recommendation as strongly as did the Democrats. Mr. Gillett of Massachusetts, then acting leader of the Republican minority, and now Speaker, made this declaration in the course of the debate:

> But after examining Mr. Creel and the other members of his bureau I came to the conclusion that as far as any evidence that we could discover it had not been conducted in a partizan spirit.

Mr. Mondel of Wyoming, after expressing his disapproval of Initiative and Referendum editorials written by me in 1912, spoke as follows:

> Having said this much about Mr. Creel and his past utterances, I now want to say that I believe Mr. Creel has endeavored to patriotically do his duty at the head of this bureau. I am of the opinion that, whatever his opinions may have been or may be now, so far as his activities in connection with this work are concerned, they have been, in the main, judicious, and that the work has been carried on for the most part in a businesslike, thoroughgoing, effective, and patriotic way. Mr. Creel has called to his assistance and placed in positions of responsibility men of a variety of political views, some of them Republicans of recognized standing. I do not believe that Mr. Creel has endeavored to influence their activities and I do not believe there have been any activities of the bureau consciously and intentionally partizan. A great work has been done. A great work has been done by the Four Minute Men, forty thousand of them speaking continuously to audiences, ready-made, all over the country. A great work has been done and will be done through the medium of the picture-film. A great work

has been done through the medium of the publications of the bureau, which I believe can be commended and approved by every good citizen. Much remains to be done, and I believe the committee has not granted any too much money for this work.

From *How We Advertised America* (1920)

Woodrow Wilson:
Address to the Senate on the League of Nations

In early March, Senator Henry Cabot Lodge had issued a statement signed by thirty-nine Republican senators pledging their opposition to the draft covenant. Nonetheless, on June 28 the peace treaty with Germany—complete with the League covenant—was signed in the Hall of Mirrors in the Palace of Versailles. "As no one is satisfied," Wilson said of the treaty to Edith, "it makes me hope we have made a just peace." The Wilsons landed in New Jersey on July 8, and two days later, the President entered the Senate chamber carrying the treaty. He received a standing ovation from everyone on the floor and in the public galleries, though the Republicans withheld their applause. Wilson realized Senate passage of the treaty would be an uphill battle, of which this speech was the opening salvo.

Gentlemen of the Senate: The treaty of peace with Germany was signed at Versailles on the twenty-eighth of June. I avail myself of the earliest opportunity to lay the treaty before you for ratification and to inform you with regard to the work of the Conference by which that treaty was formulated.

The treaty constitutes nothing less than a world settlement. It would not be possible for me either to summarize or to construe its manifold provisions in an address which must of necessity be something less than a treatise. My services and all the information I possess will be at your disposal and at the disposal of your Committee on Foreign Relations at any time, either informally or in session, as you may prefer; and I hope that you will not hesitate to make use of them. I shall at this time, prior to your own study of the document, attempt only a general characterization of its scope and purpose.

In one sense, no doubt, there is no need that I should report to you what was attempted and done at Paris. You have been daily cognizant of what was going on there,—of the problems with which the Peace Conference had to deal and of the difficulty of laying down straight lines of settlement anywhere on a

field on which the old lines of international relationship, and
the new alike, followed so intricate a pattern and were for the
most part cut so deep by historical circumstances which dominated action even where it would have been best to ignore or
reverse them. The cross currents of politics and of interest
must have been evident to you. It would be presuming in me
to attempt to explain the questions which arose or the many
diverse elements that entered into them. I shall attempt something less ambitious than that and more clearly suggested by
my duty to report to the Congress the part it seemed necessary
for my colleagues and me to play as the representatives of the
Government of the United States.

That part was dictated by the role America had played in the
war and by the expectations that had been created in the minds
of the peoples with whom we had associated ourselves in that
great struggle.

The United States entered the war upon a different footing
from every other nation except our associates on this side of
the sea. We entered it, not because our material interests were
directly threatened or because any special treaty obligations to
which we were parties had been violated, but only because we
saw the supremacy, and even the validity, of right everywhere
put in jeopardy and free government likely to be everywhere
imperiled by the intolerable aggression of a power which respected neither right nor obligation and whose very system of
government flouted the rights of the citizens as against the
autocratic authority of his governors. And in the settlements of
the peace we have sought no special reparation for ourselves,
but only the restoration of right and the assurance of liberty
everywhere that the effects of the settlement were to be felt.
We entered the war as the disinterested champions of right and
we interested ourselves in the terms of the peace in no other
capacity.

The hopes of the nations allied against the central powers
were at a very low ebb when our soldiers began to pour across
the sea. There was everywhere amongst them, except in their
stoutest spirits, a sombre foreboding of disaster. The war
ended in November, eight months ago, but you have only to
recall what was feared in midsummer last, four short months
before the armistice, to realize what it was that our timely aid

accomplished alike for their morale and their physical safety. That first, never-to-be-forgotten action at Château-Thierry had already taken place. Our redoubtable soldiers and marines had already closed the gap the enemy had succeeded in opening for their advance upon Paris,—had already turned the tide of battle back towards the frontiers of France and begun the rout that was to save Europe and the world. Thereafter the Germans were to be always forced back, back, were never to thrust successfully forward again. And yet there was no confident hope. Anxious men and women, leading spirits of France, attended the celebration of the fourth of July last year in Paris out of generous courtesy,—with no heart for festivity, little zest for hope. But they came away with something new at their hearts: they have themselves told us so. The mere sight of our men,—of their vigour, of the confidence that showed itself in every movement of their stalwart figures and every turn of their swinging march, in their steady comprehending eyes and easy discipline, in the indomitable air that added spirit to everything they did,—made everyone who saw them that memorable day realize that something had happened that was much more than a mere incident in the fighting, something very different from the mere arrival of fresh troops. A great moral force had flung itself into the struggle. The fine physical force of those spirited men spoke of something more than bodily vigour. They carried the great ideals of a free people at their hearts and with that vision were unconquerable. Their very presence brought reassurance; their fighting made victory certain.

They were recognized as crusaders, and as their thousands swelled to millions their strength was seen to mean salvation. And they were fit men to carry such a hope and make good the assurance it forecast. Finer men never went into battle; and their officers were worthy of them. This is not the occasion upon which to utter a eulogy of the armies America sent to France, but perhaps, since I am speaking of their mission, I may speak also of the pride I shared with every American who saw or dealt with them there. They were the sort of men America would wish to be represented by, the sort of men every American would wish to claim as fellow countrymen and comrades in a great cause. They were terrible in battle, and gentle and helpful out of it, remembering the mothers and the sisters, the wives and the little children at home. They were free men under arms, not forgetting their ideals of duty in the midst of tasks of violence. I am proud to have had the privilege of being associated with them and of calling myself their leader.

But I speak now of what they meant to the men by whose sides they fought and to the people with whom they mingled with such utter simplicity, as friends who asked only to be of service. They were for all the visible embodiment of America. What they did made America and all that she stood for a living reality in the thoughts not only of the people of France but also of tens of millions of men and women throughout all the toiling nations of a world standing everywhere in peril of its freedom and of the loss of everything it held dear, in deadly fear that its bonds were never to be loosed, its hopes forever to be mocked and disappointed.

And the compulsion of what they stood for was upon us who represented America at the peace table. It was our duty to see to it that every decision we took part in contributed, so far as we were able to influence it, to quiet the fears and realize the hopes of the peoples who had been living in that shadow, the nations that had come by our assistance to their freedom. It was our duty to do everything that it was within our power to do to make the triumph of freedom and of right a lasting triumph in the assurance of which men might everywhere live without fear.

Old entanglements of every kind stood in the way,—promises which Governments had made to one another in the days when might and right were confused and the power of the victor was without restraint. Engagements which contemplated any dispositions of territory, any extensions of sovereignty that might seem to be to the interest of those who had the power to insist upon them, had been entered into without thought of what the peoples concerned might wish or profit by; and these could not always be honourably brushed aside. It was not easy to graft the new order of ideas on the old, and some of the fruits of the grafting may, I fear, for a time be bitter. But, with very few exceptions, the men who sat with us at the peace table desired as sincerely as we did to get away from the bad influences, the illegitimate purposes, the demoralizing ambitions, the international counsels and expedients out of which the sinister designs of Germany had sprung as a natural growth.

It had been our privilege to formulate the principles which were accepted as the basis of the peace, but they had been accepted, not because we had come in to hasten and assure the victory and insisted upon them, but because they were readily acceded to as the principles to which honourable and enlightened minds everywhere had been bred. They spoke the conscience of the world as well as the conscience of America, and I am happy to pay my tribute of respect and gratitude to the able, forward-looking men with whom it was my privilege to cooperate for their unfailing spirit of cooperation, their constant effort to accommodate the interests they represented to the principles we were all agreed upon. The difficulties, which were many, lay in the circumstances, not often in the men. Almost without exception the men who led had caught the true and full vision of the problem of peace as an indivisible whole, a problem, not of mere adjustments of interest, but of justice and right action.

The atmosphere in which the Conference worked seemed created, not by the ambitions of strong governments, but by the hopes and aspirations of small nations and of peoples hitherto under bondage to the power that victory had shattered and destroyed. Two great empires had been forced into political bankruptcy, and we were the receivers. Our task was not only to make peace with the central empires and remedy the wrongs their armies had done. The central empires had lived in open violation of many of the very rights for which the war had been fought, dominating alien peoples over whom they had no natural right to rule, enforcing, not obedience, but veritable bondage, exploiting those who were weak for the benefit of those who were masters and overlords only by force of arms. There could be no peace until the whole order of central Europe was set right.

That meant that new nations were to be created,—Poland, Czecho-Slovakia, Hungary itself. No part of ancient Poland had ever in any true sense become a part of Germany, or of Austria, or of Russia. Bohemia was alien in every thought and hope to the monarchy of which she had so long been an artificial part; and the uneasy partnership between Austria and

Hungary had been one rather of interest than of kinship or sympathy. The Slavs whom Austria had chosen to force into her empire on the south were kept to their obedience by nothing but fear. Their hearts were with their kinsmen in the Balkans. These were all arrangements of power, not arrangements of natural union or association. It was the imperative task of those who would make peace and make it intelligently to establish a new order which would rest upon the free choice of peoples rather than upon the arbitrary authority of Hapsburgs or Hohenzollerns.

More than that, great populations bound by sympathy and actual kin to Rumania were also linked against their will to the conglomerate Austro-Hungarian monarchy or to other alien sovereignties, and it was part of the task of peace to make a new Rumania as well as a new Slavic state clustering about Serbia.

And no natural frontiers could be found to these new fields of adjustment and redemption. It was necessary to look constantly forward to other related tasks. The German colonies were to be disposed of. They had not been governed; they had been exploited merely, without thought of the interest or even the ordinary human rights of their inhabitants.

The Turkish Empire, moreover, had fallen apart, as the Austro-Hungarian had. It had never had any real unity. It had been held together only by pitiless, inhuman force. Its people cried aloud for release, for succour from unspeakable distress, for all that the new day of hope seemed at last to bring within its dawn. Peoples hitherto in utter darkness were to be led out into the same light and given at last a helping hand. Undeveloped peoples and peoples ready for recognition but not yet ready to assume the full responsibilities of statehood were to be given adequate guarantees of friendly protection, guidance, and assistance.

And out of the execution of these great enterprises of liberty sprang opportunities to attempt what statesmen had never found the way before to do; an opportunity to throw safeguards about the rights of racial, national, and religious minorities by solemn international covenant; an opportunity to limit and regulate military establishments where they were most likely to be mischievous; an opportunity to effect a complete and systematic internationalization of waterways and railways which were necessary to the free economic life of more than one nation and to clear many of the normal channels of commerce of unfair obstructions of law or of privilege; and the very welcome opportunity to secure for labour the concerted protection of definite international pledges of principle and practice.

These were not tasks which the Conference looked about it to find and went out of its way to perform. They were thrust upon it by circumstances which could not be overlooked. The war had created them. In all quarters of the world old established relationships had been disturbed or broken and affairs were at loose ends, needing to be mended or united again, but could not be made what they were before. They had to be set right by applying some uniform principle of justice or enlightened expediency. And they could not be adjusted by merely prescribing in a treaty what should be done. New states were to be set up which could not hope to live through their first period of weakness without assured support by the great nations that had consented to their creation and won for them their independence. Ill governed colonies could not be put in the hands of governments which were to act as trustees for their people and not as their masters if there was to be no common authority among the nations to which they were to be responsible in the execution of their trust. Future international conventions with regard to the control of waterways, with regard to illicit traffic of many kinds, in arms or in deadly drugs, or with regard to the adjustment of many varying international administrative arrangements could not be assured if the treaty were to provide no permanent common international agency, if its execution in such matters was to be left to the slow and uncertain processes of cooperation by ordinary methods of negotiation. If the Peace Conference itself was to be the end of cooperative authority and common counsel among the governments to which the world was looking to enforce justice and give pledges of an enduring settlement, regions like the Saar basin could not be put under a temporary administrative regime which did not involve a transfer of political sovereignty and which contemplated a final determination of its political connections by popular vote to be taken at a distant date; no free city like Dantzig could be created which was, under elaborate international guarantees, to accept exceptional obligations with regard to the use of its port and exceptional relations with a State of which it was not to form a part; properly safeguarded plebiscites could not be provided for where populations were at some future date to make choice what sovereignty they would live under; no certain and uniform method of arbitration could be secured for the settlement of anticipated difficulties of final decision with regard to many matters dealt with in the treaty itself; the long-continued supervision of the task of reparation which Germany was to undertake to complete within the next generation might entirely break down; the reconsideration and revision of administrative arrangements and restrictions which the treaty prescribed but which it was recognized might not prove of lasting advantage or entirely fair if too long enforced would be impracticable. The promises governments were making to one another about the way in which labour was to be dealt with, by law not only but in fact as well, would remain a mere humane thesis if there was to be no common tribunal of opinion and judgment to which liberal statesmen could resort for the influences which alone might secure their redemption. A league of free nations had become a practical necessity. Examine the treaty of peace and you will find that everywhere throughout its manifold provisions its framers have felt obliged to turn to the League of Nations as an indispensable instrumentality for the maintenance of the new order it has been their purpose to set up in the world,— the world of civilized men.

That there should be a league of nations to steady the counsels and maintain the peaceful understandings of the world, to make, not treaties alone, but the accepted principles of international law as well, the actual rule of conduct among the governments of the world, had been one of the agreements accepted from the first as the basis of peace with the central powers. The statesmen of all the belligerent countries were agreed that such a league must be created to sustain the settlements that were to be effected. But at first I think there was a feeling among some of them that, while it must be attempted, the formulation of such a league was perhaps a counsel of perfection which practical men, long experienced in the world of affairs, must agree to very cautiously and with many misgivings. It was only as the difficult work of arranging an all but universal adjustment of the world's affairs advanced from day to day from one stage of conference to another that it became evident to them that what they were seeking would be little more than something written upon paper, to be interpreted and applied by such methods as the chances of politics might make available if they did not provide a means of common counsel which all were obliged to accept, a common authority whose decisions would be recognized as decisions which all must respect.

And so the most practical, the most skeptical among them turned more and more to the League as the authority through which international action was to be secured, the authority without which, as they had come to see it, it would be difficult to give assured effect either to this treaty or to any other international understanding upon which they were to depend for the maintenance of peace. The fact that the Covenant of the League was the first substantive part of the treaty to be worked out and agreed upon, while all else was in solution, helped to make the formulation of the rest easier. The Conference was, after all, not to be ephemeral. The concert of nations was to continue, under a definite Covenant which had been agreed upon and which all were convinced was workable. They could go forward with confidence to make arrangements intended to be permanent. The most practical of the conferees were at last the most ready to refer to the League of Nations the superintendence of all interests which did not admit of immediate determination, of all administrative problems which were to require a continuing oversight. What had seemed a counsel of perfection had come to seem a plain counsel of necessity. The League of Nations was the practical statesman's hope of success in many of the most difficult things he was attempting.

And it had validated itself in the thought of every member of the Conference as something much bigger, much greater every way, than a mere instrument for carrying out the provisions of a particular treaty. It was universally recognized that all the peoples of the world demanded of the Conference that it should create such a continuing concert of free nations as would make wars of aggression and spoliation such as this that has just ended forever impossible. A cry had gone out from every home in every stricken land from which sons and brothers and fathers had gone forth to the great sacrifice that such a sacrifice should never again be exacted. It was manifest why it had been exacted. It had been exacted because one nation desired dominion and other nations had known no means of defence except armaments and alliances. War had lain at the heart of every arrangement of the Europe,—of every arrangement of the world,—that preceded the war. Restive peoples had been told that fleets and armies, which they toiled to sustain, meant peace; and they now knew that they had been lied to: that fleets and armies had been maintained to promote national ambitions and meant war. They knew that no old policy meant anything else but force, force,—always force. And they knew that it was intolerable. Every true heart in the world, and every enlightened judgment demanded that, at whatever cost of independent action, every government that took thought for its people or for justice or for ordered freedom should lend itself to a new purpose and utterly destroy the old order of international politics. Statesmen might see difficulties, but the people could see none and could brook no denial. A war in which they had been bled white to beat the terror that lay concealed in every Balance of Power must not end in a mere victory of arms and a new balance. The monster that had resorted to arms must be put in chains that could not be broken. The united power of free nations must put a stop to aggression, and the world must be given peace. If there was not the will or the intelligence to accomplish that now, there must be another and a final war and the world must be swept clean of every power that could renew the terror. The League of Nations was not merely an instrument to adjust and remedy old wrongs under a new treaty of peace; it was the only hope for mankind. Again and again had the demon of war been cast out of the house of the peoples and the house swept clean by a treaty of peace; only to prepare a time when he would enter in again with spirits worse than himself. The house must now be given a tenant who could hold it against all such. Convenient, indeed indispensable, as statesmen found the newly planned League of Nations to be for the execution of present plans of peace and reparation, they saw it in a new aspect before their work was finished. They saw it as the main object of the peace, as the only thing that could complete it or make it worth while. They saw it as the hope of the world, and that hope they did not dare to disappoint. Shall we or any other free people hesitate to accept this great duty? Dare we reject it and break the heart of the world?

And so the result of the Conference of Peace, so far as Germany is concerned, stands complete. The difficulties encountered were very many. Sometimes they seemed insuperable. It was impossible to accommodate the interests of so great a body of nations,—interests which directly or indirectly affected almost every nation in the world,—without many minor compromises. The treaty, as a result, is not exactly what we would have written. It is probably not what any one of the national delegations would have written. But results were worked out which on the whole bear test. I think that it will be found that the compromises which were accepted as inevitable nowhere cut to the heart of any principle. The work of the Conference squares, as a whole, with the principles agreed upon as the basis of the peace as well as with the practical possibilities of the international situations which had to be faced and dealt with as facts.

I shall presently have occasion to lay before you a special treaty with France, whose object is the temporary protection of France from unprovoked aggression by the Power with whom this treaty of peace has been negotiated. Its terms link it with this treaty. I take the liberty, however, of reserving it for special explication on another occasion.

The rôle which America was to play in the Conference seemed determined, as I have said, before my colleagues and I got to Paris,—determined by the universal expectations of the nations whose representatives, drawn from all quarters of the globe, we were to deal with. It was universally recognized that America had entered the war to promote no private or peculiar interest of her own but only as the champion of rights which she was glad to share with free men and lovers of justice everywhere. We had formulated the principles upon which the settlement was to be made,—the principles upon which the armistice had been agreed to and the parleys of peace undertaken,—and no one doubted that our desire was to see the treaty of peace formulated along the actual lines of those principles,—and desired nothing else. We were welcomed as disinterested friends. We were resorted to as arbiters in many a difficult matter. It was recognized that our material aid would be indispensable in the days to come, when industry and credit would have to be brought back to their normal operation again and communities beaten to the ground assisted to their feet once more, and it was taken for granted, I am proud to say, that we would play the helpful friend in these things as in all others without prejudice or favour. We were generously accepted as the unaffected champions of what was right. It was a very responsible rôle to play; but I am happy to report that the fine group of Americans who helped with their expert advice in each part of the varied settlements sought in every translation to justify the high confidence reposed in them.

And that confidence, it seems to me, is the measure of our opportunity and of our duty in the days to come, in which the new hope of the peoples of the world is to be fulfilled or disappointed. The fact that America is the friend of the nations, whether they be rivals or associates, is no new fact: it is only the discovery of it by the rest of the world that is new.

America may be said to have just reached her majority as a world power. It was almost exactly twenty-one years ago that the results of the war with Spain put us unexpectedly in possession of rich islands on the other side of the world and brought us into association with other governments in the control of the West Indies. It was regarded as a sinister and ominous thing by the statesmen of more than one European chancellery that we should have extended our power beyond the confines of our continental dominions. They were accustomed to think of new neighbours as a new menace, of rivals as watchful enemies. There were persons amongst us at home who looked with deep disapproval and avowed anxiety on such extensions of our national authority over distant islands and over peoples whom they feared we might exploit, not serve and assist. But we have not exploited them. And our dominion has been a menace to no other nation. We redeemed our honour to the utmost in our dealings with Cuba. She is weak but absolutely free; and it is her trust in us that makes her free. Weak peoples everywhere stand ready to give us any authority among them that will assure them a like friendly oversight and direction. They know that there is no ground for fear in receiving us as their mentors and guides. Our isolation was ended twenty years ago; and now fear of us is ended also, our counsel and association sought after and desired. There can be no question of our ceasing to be a world power. The only question is whether we can refuse the moral leadership that is offered us, whether we shall accept or reject the confidence of the world.

The war and the Conference of Peace now sitting in Paris seem to me to have answered that question. Our participation in the war established our position among the nations and nothing but our own mistaken action can alter it. It was not an accident or a matter of sudden choice that we are no longer isolated and devoted to a policy which has only our own interest and advantage for its object. It was our duty to go in, if we were indeed the champions of liberty and of right. We answered to the call of duty in a way so spirited, so utterly without thought of what we spent of blood or treasure, so effective, so worthy of the admiration of true men everywhere, so wrought out of the stuff of all that was heroic, that the whole world saw at last, in the flesh, in noble action, a great ideal asserted and vindicated, by a nation they had deemed material and now found to be compact of the spiritual forces that must free men of every nation from every unworthy bondage. It is thus that a new role and a new responsibility have come to this great nation that we honour and which we would all wish to lift to yet higher levels of service and achievement.

The stage is set, the destiny disclosed. It has come about by no plan of our conceiving, but by the hand of God who led us into this way. We cannot turn back. We can only go forward, with lifted eyes and freshened spirit, to follow the vision. It was of this that we dreamed at our birth. America shall in truth show the way. The light streams upon the path ahead, and nowhere else.

July 10, 1919

Newton D. Baker and Woodrow Wilson: An Exchange

The war that had just been fought and won needed to be named; but how to label such a catastrophe, and how do wars even get named in the first place? When Lindley M. Garrison, his first secretary of war, resigned in 1916, Wilson had appointed Newton D. Baker, the former mayor of Cleveland, as his successor. While debate over the peace clangored, Wilson and Baker quietly chose a name for the war.

My dear Mr. President: Washington. July 23, 1919.

We are called upon in all manner of official documents and communications to give a name to the war. We have always named our wars, as "The American Revolution," "The Mexican War," "The Civil War," and "The Spanish-American War." Present usage with regard to this war is unsettled, and various names have been suggested, as, for instance, "The Great War," "The World War," "The War of 1917," and "The War Against Teutonic Aggression."

I am told that the Navy has more or less adopted the name "The War Against Teutonic Aggression."

The commanders of the Allied Armies in devising the Victory Medal put upon its reverse side, "The Great War for Civilization."

Some of these titles seem too long to be descriptive. Great Britain is reported to have officially named the war, so far as she is concerned, "The War of 1914–1918." My own preference is for the phrase "The World War." "The Great War" would be equally descriptive, as this was the greatest war in history.

As Commander-in-Chief of the Army and Navy, would you be willing to give us your judgment so that we can all adopt it and establish the name by official sanction?

Respectfully yours,   Newton D. Baker

My dear Mr. Secretary: 31 July, 1919.

It is hard to find a satisfactory "official" name for the war, but the best, I think, that has been suggested is "The World War," and I hope that your judgment will concur.

I know you will understand the brevity of this note.

Cordially and faithfully yours,   Woodrow Wilson

Henry Cabot Lodge: Speech in the U.S. Senate on the League of Nations

Few political rivalries in American politics can match the enmity between Woodrow Wilson and Henry Cabot Lodge. The Constitution required that the treaty receive two-thirds approval of the Senate; and Lodge—Boston patrician, intimate of the recently deceased Theodore Roosevelt, chairman of the Republican Senate conference and of the Senate Foreign Relations Committee—was hell-bent on defeating it. He hung most of his arguments on Article X, which established a collective security arrangement among members of the League. Lodge asserted that Article X would impinge upon Congress's constitutional power to declare war; and for the next few months, he would place every political obstacle that he could in the way of the treaty's passage. He would eventually offer a series of amendments and reservations, knowing full well that his idealistic adversary would never offer a single significant concession.

Mr. President, in the Essays of Elia, one of the most delightful is that entitled "Popular Fallacies." There is one very popular fallacy, however, which Lamb did not include in his list, and that is the common saying that history repeats itself. Universal negatives are always dangerous, but if there is anything which is fairly certain, it is that history never exactly repeats itself. Popular fallacies, nevertheless, generally have some basis, and this saying springs from the undoubted truth that mankind from generation to generation is constantly repeating itself. We have an excellent illustration of this fact in the proposed experiment now before us, of making arrangements to secure the permanent peace of the world. To assure the peace of the world by a combination of the nations is no new idea. Leaving out the leagues of antiquity and of mediæval times and going back no further than the treaty of Utrecht, at the beginning of the eighteenth century, we find that at that period a project of a treaty to establish perpetual peace was brought forward in

1713 by the Abbé de Saint-Pierre. The treaty of Utrecht was to
be the basis of an international system. A European league or
Christian republic was to be set up, under which the members
were to renounce the right of making war against each other
and submit their disputes for arbitration to a central tribunal of
the allies, the decisions of which were to be enforced by a
common armament. I need not point out the resemblance
between this theory and that which underlies the present
league of nations. It was widely discussed during the eighteenth century, receiving much support in public opinion; and
Voltaire said that the nations of Europe, united by ties of religion, institutions, and culture, were really but a single family.
The idea remained in an academic condition until 1791, when
under the pressure of the French Revolution Count Kaunitz
sent out a circular letter in the name of Leopold, of Austria,
urging that it was the duty of all the powers to make common
cause for the purpose of "preserving public peace, tranquillity
of States, the inviolability of possession, and the faith of treaties," which has a very familiar sound. Napoleon had a scheme
of his own for consolidating the Great European peoples and
establishing a central assembly, but the Napoleonic idea differed from that of the eighteenth century, as one would expect.
A single great personality dominated and hovered over all. In
1804 the Emperor Alexander took up the question and urged
a general treaty for the formation of a European confederation.
"Why could one not submit to it," the Emperor asked, "the
positive rights of nations, assure the privilege of neutrality, insert the obligation of never beginning war until all the resources which the mediation of a third party could offer have
been exhausted, until the grievances have by this means been
brought to light, and an effort to remove them has been made?
On principles such as these one could proceed to a general
pacification, and give birth to a league of which the stipulations
would form, so to speak, a new code of the law of nations,
while those who should try to infringe it would risk bringing
upon themselves the forces of the new union."

The Emperor, moved by more immediately alluring visions,
put aside this scheme at the treaty of Tilsit and then decided
that peace could best be restored to the world by having two
all-powerful emperors, one of the east and one of the west.

After the Moscow campaign, however, he returned to his early dream. Under the influence of the Baroness von Krudener he became a devotee of a certain mystic pietism which for some time guided his public acts, and I think it may be fairly said that his liberal and popular ideas of that period, however vague and uncertain, were sufficiently genuine. Based upon the treaties of alliance against France, those of Chaumont and of Vienna, was the final treaty of Paris, of November 20, 1815. In the preamble the signatories, who were Great Britain, Austria, Russia, and Prussia, stated that it is the purpose of the ensuing treaty and their desire "to employ all their means to prevent the general tranquillity—the object of the wishes of mankind and the constant end of their efforts—from being again disturbed; desirous, moreover, to draw closer the ties which unite them for the common interests of their people, have resolved to give to the principles solemnly laid down in the treaties of Chaumont of March 1, 1814, and of Vienna of March 25, 1815, the application the most analogous to the present state of affairs, and to fix beforehand by a solemn treaty the principles which they propose to follow, in order to guarantee Europe from dangers by which she may still be menaced."

Then follow five articles which are devoted to an agreement to hold France in control and checks, based largely on other more detailed agreements. But in article 6 it is said:

> "To facilitate and to secure the execution of the present treaty, and to consolidate the connections which at the present moment so closely unite the four sovereigns for the happiness of the world, the high contracting parties have agreed to renew their meeting at fixed periods, either under the immediate auspices of the sovereigns themselves, or by their respective ministers, for the purpose of consulting upon their common interests, and for the consideration of the measures which at each of those periods shall be considered the most salutary for the repose and prosperity of nations and for the maintenance of the peace of Europe."

Certainly nothing could be more ingenuous or more praiseworthy than the purposes of the alliance then formed, and yet it was this very combination of powers which was destined to grow into what has been known, and we might add cursed, throughout history as the Holy Alliance.

As early as 1818 it had become apparent that upon this innocent statement might be built an alliance which was to be used to suppress the rights of nationalities and every attempt of any oppressed people to secure their freedom. Lord Castlereagh was a Tory of the Tories, but at that time, only three years after the treaty of Paris, when the representatives of the alliance met at Aix-la-Chapelle, he began to suspect that this new European system was wholly inconsistent with the liberties to which Englishmen of all types were devoted. At the succeeding meetings, at Troppau and Laibach, his suspicion was confirmed, and England began to draw away from her partners. He had indeed determined to break with the alliance before the Congress of Verona, but his death threw the question into the hands of George Canning, who stands forth as the man who separated Great Britain from the combination of the continental powers. The attitude of England, which was defined in a memorandum where it was said that nothing could be more injurious to the idea of government generally than the belief that their force was collectively to be prostituted to the support of an established power without any consideration of the extent to which it was to be abused, led to a compromise in 1818 in which it was declared that it was the intention of the five powers, France being invited to adhere, "to maintain the intimate union, strengthened by the ties of Christian brotherhood, contracted by the sovereigns; to pronounce the object of this union to be the preservation of peace on the basis of respect for treaties." Admirable and gentle words these, setting forth purposes which all men must approve.

In 1820 the British Government stated that they were prepared to fulfill all treaty obligations, but that if it was desired "to extend the alliance, so as to include all objects, present and future, foreseen and unforeseen, it would change its character to such an extent and carry us so far that we should see in it an additional motive for adhering to our course at the risk of seeing the alliance move away from us, without our having quitted it." The Czar Alexander abandoned his Liberal theories and threw himself into the arms of Metternich, as mean a tyrant as history can show, whose sinister designs probably caused as much misery and oppression in the years which followed as have ever been evolved by one man of second-rate abilities. The three powers, Russia, Austria, and Prussia, then put out a famous protocol in which it was said that the "States which have undergone a change of government due to revolution, the results of which threaten other States, *ipso facto* cease to be members of the European alliance and remain excluded from it until their situation gives guaranties for legal order and stability. If, owing to such alterations, immediate danger threatens other States, the powers bind themselves, by peaceful means, or, if need be, by arms, to bring back the guilty State into the bosom of the great alliance." To this point had the innocent and laudable declaration of the treaty of Paris already developed. In 1822 England broke away, and Canning made no secret of his pleasure at the breach. In a letter to the British minister at St. Petersburg he said:

> "So things are getting back to a wholesome state again. Every nation for itself, and God for us all. The time for Areopagus, and the like of that, is gone by."

He also said, in the same year, 1823:

> "What is the influence we have had in the counsels of the alliance, and which Prince Metternich exhorts us to be so careful not to throw away? We protested at Laibach; we remonstrated at Verona. Our protest was treated as waste paper; our remonstrances mingled with the air. Our influence, if it is to be maintained abroad, must be secured in the source of strength at home; and the sources of that strength are in sympathy between the people and the Government; in the union of the public sentiment with the public counsels; in the reciprocal confidence and cooperation of the House of Commons and the Crown."

These words of Canning are as applicable and as weighty now as when they were uttered and as worthy of consideration.

The Holy Alliance, thus developed by the three continental powers and accepted by France under the Bourbons, proceeded to restore the inquisition in Spain, to establish the Neapolitan Bourbons, who for 40 years were to subject the people of southern Italy to one of the most detestable tyrannies ever known, and proposed further to interfere against the colonies in South America which had revolted from Spain and to have their case submitted to a congress of the powers. It was then that Canning made his famous statement, "We have called a new world into existence to redress the balance of the old." It was at this point also that the United States intervened. The famous message of Monroe, sent to Congress on December 2, 1823, put an end to any danger of European influence in the American Continents. A distinguished English historian, Mr. William Alison Phillips, says:

> "The attitude of the United States effectually prevented the attempt to extend the dictatorship of the alliance beyond the bounds of Europe, in itself a great service to mankind."

In 1825 Great Britain recognized the South American Republics. So far as the New World was concerned the Holy Alliance had failed. It was deprived of the support of France by the revolution of 1830, but it continued to exist under the guidance of Metternich and its last exploit was in 1849, when the Emperor Nicholas sent a Russian army into Hungary to crush out the struggle of Kossuth for freedom and independence.

I have taken the trouble to trace in the merest outline the development of the Holy Alliance, so hostile and dangerous to human freedom, because I think it carries with it a lesson for us at the present moment, showing as it does what may come from general propositions and declarations of purposes in which all the world agrees. Turn to the preamble of the covenant of the league of nations now before us, which states the object of the league. It is formed "in order to promote international cooperation and to achieve international peace and security by the acceptance of obligations not to resort to war, by the prescription of open, just, and honorable relations between nations, by the firm establishment of the understandings of international laws as the actual rule of conduct among governments and by the maintenance of justice and a scrupulous respect for all treaty obligations in the dealings of organized peoples with one another."

No one would contest the loftiness or the benevolence of these purposes. Brave words, indeed! They do not differ essentially from the preamble of the treaty of Paris, from which sprang the Holy Alliance. But the covenant of this league contains a provision which I do not find in the treaty of Paris, and which is as follows:

> "The assembly may deal at its meetings with any matter within the sphere of action of the league or affecting the peace of the world."

There is no such sweeping or far-reaching provision as that in the treaty of Paris, and yet able men developed from that treaty the Holy Alliance, which England, and later France were forced to abandon and which, for 35 years, was an unmitigated curse to the world. England broke from the Holy Alliance and the breach began three years after it was formed, because English statesmen saw that it was intended to turn the alliance—and this league is an alliance—into a means of repressing internal revolutions or insurrections. There was nothing in the treaty of Paris which warranted such action, but in this covenant of the league of nations the authority is clearly given in the third paragraph of article 3, where it is said:

> "The assembly may deal at its meetings with any matter within the sphere of action of the league or affecting the peace of the world."

No revolutionary movement, no internal conflict of any magnitude can fail to affect the peace of the world. The French Revolution, which was wholly internal at the beginning, affected the peace of the world to such an extent that it brought on a world war which lasted some 25 years. Can anyone say that our Civil War did not affect the peace of the world? At this very moment, who would deny that the condition of Russia, with internal conflicts raging in all parts of that great Empire, does not affect the peace of the world and therefore come properly within the jurisdiction of the league. "Any matter affecting the peace of the world" is a very broad statement which could be made to justify almost any interference on the part of the league with the internal affairs of other countries. That this fair and obvious interpretation is the one given to it abroad is made perfectly apparent in the direct and vigorous statement of M. Clemenceau in his letter to Mr. Paderewski, in which he takes the ground in behalf of the Jews and other nationalities in Poland that they should be protected, and where he says that the associated powers would feel themselves bound to secure guaranties in Poland "of certain essential rights which will afford to the inhabitants the necessary protection, whatever changes may take place in the internal constitution of the Polish Republic." He contemplates and defends interference with the internal affairs of Poland—among other things—in behalf of a complete religious freedom, a purpose with which we all deeply sympathize. These promises of the French prime minister are embodied in effective clauses in the treaties with Germany and with Poland and deal with the internal affairs of nations, and their execution is intrusted to the "principal allied and associated powers"; that is, to the United States, Great Britain, France, Italy, and Japan. This is a practical demonstration of what can be done under article 3 and under article 11 of the league covenant, and the authority which permits interference in behalf of religious freedom, an admirable object, is easily extended to the repression of internal disturbances which may well prove a less admirable purpose. If Europe desires such an alliance or league with a power of this kind, so be it. I have no objection, provided they do not interfere with the American Continents or force us against our will but bound by a moral obligation into all the quarrels of Europe. If England, abandoning the policy of Canning, desires to be a member of a league which has such powers as this, I have not a word to say. But I object in the strongest possible way to having the United States agree, directly or indirectly, to be controlled by a league which may at any time, and perfectly lawfully and in accordance with the terms of the covenant, be drawn in to deal with internal conflicts in other countries, no matter what those conflicts may be. We should never permit the United States to be involved in any internal conflict in another country, except by the will of her people expressed through the Congress which represents them.

With regard to wars of external aggression on a member of the league the case is perfectly clear. There can be no genuine dispute whatever about the meaning of the first clause of article 10. In the first place, it differs from every other obligation in being individual and placed upon each nation without the intervention of the league. Each nation for itself promises to respect and preserve as against external aggression the boundaries and the political independence of every member of the league. Of the right of the United States to give such a guaranty I have never had the slightest doubt, and the elaborate arguments which have been made here and the learning which has been displayed about our treaty with Granada, now Colombia, and with Panama, were not necessary for me, because, I repeat, there can be no doubt of our right to give a guaranty to another nation that we will protect its boundaries and independence. The point I wish to make is that the pledge is an individual pledge. We have, for example, given guaranties to Panama and for obvious and sufficient reasons. The application of that guaranty would not be in the slightest degree affected by 10 or 20 other nations giving the same pledge if Panama, when in danger, appealed to us to fulfill our obligation. We should be bound to do so without the slightest reference to the other guarantors. In article 10 the United States is bound on the appeal of any member of the league not only to respect but to preserve its independence and its boundaries, and that pledge if we give it, must be fulfilled.

There is to me no distinction whatever in a treaty between what some persons are pleased to call legal and moral obligations. A treaty rests and must rest, except where it is imposed under duress and securities and hostages are taken for its fulfillment, upon moral obligations. No doubt a great power impossible of coercion can cast aside a moral obligation if it sees fit and escape from the performance of the duty which it promises. The pathway of dishonor is always open. I, for one, however, cannot conceive of voting for a clause of which I disapprove because I know it can be escaped in that way. Whatever the United States agrees to, by that agreement she must abide. Nothing could so surely destroy all prospects of the world's peace as to have any powerful nation refuse to carry out an obligation, direct or indirect, because it rests only on moral grounds. Whatever we promise we must carry out to the full, "without mental reservation or purpose of evasion." To me any other attitude is inconceivable. Without the most absolute and minute good faith in carrying out a treaty to which we have agreed, without ever resorting to doubtful interpretations or to the plea that it is only a moral obligation, treaties are worthless. The greatest foundation of peace is the scrupulous observance of every promise, express or implied, of every pledge, whether it can be described as legal or moral. No vote should be given to any clause in any treaty or to any treaty except in this spirit and with this understanding.

I return, then, to the first clause of article 10. It is, I repeat, an individual obligation. It requires no action on the part of the league, except that in the second sentence the authorities of the league are to have the power to advise as to the means to be employed in order to fulfill the purpose of the first sentence. But that is a detail of execution, and I consider that we are morally and in honor bound to accept and act upon that advice. The broad fact remains that if any member of the league suffering from external aggression should appeal directly to the United States for support the United States would be bound to give that support in its own capacity and without reference to the action of other powers because the United States itself is bound, and I hope the day will never come when the United States will not carry out its promises. If that day should come, and the United States or any other great country should refuse, no matter how specious the reasons, to fulfill both in letter and spirit every obligation in this covenant, the United States would be dishonored and the league would crumble into dust, leaving behind it a legacy of wars. If China should rise up and attack Japan in an effort to undo the great wrong of the cession of the control of Shantung to that power, we should be bound under the terms of article 10 to sustain Japan against China, and a guaranty of that sort is never involved except when the question has passed beyond the stage of negotiation and has become a question for the application of force. I do not like the prospect. It shall not come into existence by any vote of mine.

Article 11 carries this danger still further, for it says:

> "Any war or threat of war, whether immediately affecting any of the members of the league or not, is hereby declared a matter of concern to the whole league, and the league shall take any action that shall be deemed wise and effectual to safeguard the peace of nations."

"Any war or threat of war"—that means both external aggression and internal disturbance, as I have already pointed out in dealing with article 3. "Any action" covers military action, because it covers action of any sort or kind. Let me take an example, not an imaginary case, but one which may have been overlooked because most people have not the slightest idea where or what a King of the Hedjaz is. The following dispatch appeared recently in the newspapers:

"HEDJAZ AGAINST BEDOUINS.
"The forces of Emir Abdullah recently suffered a grave defeat, the Wahabis attacking and capturing Kurma, east of Mecca. Ibn Savond is believed to be working in harmony with the Wahabis. A squadron of the royal air force was ordered recently to go to the assistance of King Hussein."

Hussein I take to be the Sultan of Hedjaz. He is being attacked by the Bedouins, as they are known to us, although I fancy the general knowledge about the Wahabis and Ibn Savond and Emir Abdullah is slight and the names mean but little to the American people. Nevertheless, here is a case of a member of the league—for the King of Hedjaz is such a member in good and regular standing and signed the treaty by his representatives, Mr. Rustem Haidar and Mr. Abdul Havi Aouni.

Under article 10, if King Hussein appealed to us for aid and protection against external aggression affecting his independence and the boundaries of his Kingdom, we should be bound to give that aid and protection and to send American soldiers to Arabia. It is not relevant to say that this is unlikely to occur; that Great Britain is quite able to take care of King Hussein, who is her fair creation, reminding one a little of the Mosquito King, a monarch once developed by Great Britain on the Mosquito Coast of Central America. The fact that we should not be called upon does not alter the right which the King of Hedjaz possesses to demand the sending of American troops to Arabia in order to preserve his independence against the assaults of the Wahabis or Bedouins. I am unwilling to give that right to King Hussein, and this illustrates the point which is to me the most objectionable in the league as it stands; the right of other powers to call out American troops and American ships to go to any part of the world, an obligation we are bound to fulfill under the terms of this treaty. I know the answer well—that of course they could not be sent without action by Congress. Congress would have no choice if acting in good faith, and if under article 10 any member of the league summoned us, or if under article 11 the league itself summoned us, we should be bound in honor and morally to obey. There would be no escape except by a breach of faith, and legislation by Congress under those circumstances would be a mockery of independent action. Is it too much to ask that provision should be made that American troops and American ships should never be sent anywhere or ordered to take part in any conflict except after the deliberate action of the American people, expressed according to the Constitution through their chosen representatives in Congress?

Let me now briefly point out the insuperable difficulty which I find in article 15. It begins: "If there should arise between members of the league any dispute likely to lead to a rupture." "Any dispute" covers every possible dispute. It therefore covers a dispute over tariff duties and over immigration. Suppose we have a dispute with Japan or with some European country as to immigration. I put aside tariff duties as less important than immigration. This is not an imaginary case. Of late years there has probably been more international discussion and negotiation about questions growing out of immigration laws than any other one subject. It comes within the definition of "any dispute" at the beginning of article 15. In the eighth paragraph of that article it is said that "if the dispute between the parties is claimed by one of them, and is found by the council to arise out of a matter which, by international law, is solely within the domestic jurisdiction of that party, the council shall so report and shall make no recommendation as to its settlement." That is one of the statements, of which there are several in this treaty, where words are used which it is difficult to believe their authors could have written down in seriousness. They seem to have been put in for the same purpose as what is known in natural history as protective coloring. Protective coloring is intended so to merge the animal, the bird, or the insect in its background that it will be indistinguishable from its surroundings and difficult, if not impossible, to find the elusive and hidden bird, animal, or insect. Protective coloring here is used in the form of words to give an impression that we are perfectly safe upon immigration and tariffs, for example, because questions which international law holds to be solely within domestic jurisdiction are not to have any recommendation from the council, but the dangers are there just the same, like the cunningly colored insect on the tree or the young bird crouching motionless upon the sand. The words and the coloring are alike intended to deceive. I wish somebody would point out to me those provisions of international law which make a list of questions which are hard and fast within the domestic jurisdiction. No such distinction can be applied to tariff duties or immigration, nor indeed finally and conclusively to any subject. Have we not seen the school laws of California, most domestic of subjects, rise to the dignity of a grave international dispute? No doubt both import duties and immigration are primarily domestic questions, but they both constantly involve and will continue to involve international effects. Like the protective coloration, this paragraph is wholly worthless unless it is successful in screening from the observer the existence of the animal, insect, or bird which it is desired to conceal. It fails to do so and the real object is detected. But even if this bit of deception was omitted—and so far as the question of immigration or tariff questions are concerned it might as well be—the ninth paragraph brings the important point clearly to the front. Immigration, which is the example I took, cannot escape the action of the league by any claim of domestic jurisdiction; it has too many international aspects.

Article 9 says:

> "The council may, in any case under this article, refer the dispute to the assembly."

We have our dispute as to immigration with Japan or with one of the Balkan States, let us say. The council has the power to refer the dispute to the assembly. Moreover the dispute shall be so referred at the request of either party to the dispute, provided that such request be made within 14 days after the submission of the dispute to the council. So that Japan or the Balkan States, for example, with which we may easily have the dispute, ask that it be referred to the assembly and the immigration question between the United States and Jugoslavia or Japan as the case may be, goes to the assembly. The United States and Japan or Jugoslavia are excluded from voting and the provision of article 12, relating to the action and powers of the council apply to the action and powers of the assembly provided, as set forth in article 15, that a report made by the assembly "if concurred in by the representatives of those members of the league represented on the council and of a majority of the other members of the league, exclusive in each case of the representatives of the parties to the dispute, shall have the same force as a report by the council concurred in by all the members thereof other than the representatives of one or more of the parties to the dispute." This course of procedure having been pursued, we find the question of immigration between the United States and Japan is before the assembly for decision. The representatives of the council, except the delegates of the United States and of Japan or Jugoslavia, must all vote unanimously upon it as I understand it, but a majority of the entire assembly, where the council will have only seven votes, will decide. Can anyone say beforehand what the decision of that assembly will be, in which the United States and Jugoslavia or Japan will have no vote? The question in one case may affect immigration from every country in Europe, although the dispute exists only for one, and in the other the whole matter of Asiatic immigration is involved. Is it too fanciful to think that it might be decided against us? For my purpose it matters not whether it is decided for or against us. An immigration dispute or a dispute over tariff duties, met by the procedure set forth in article 15, comes before the assembly of delegates for a decision by what is practically a majority vote of the entire assembly. That is something to which I do not find myself able to give my assent. So far as immigration is concerned, and also so far as tariff duties, although less important, are concerned, I deny the jurisdiction. There should be no possibility of other nations deciding who shall come into the United States, or under what conditions they shall enter. The right to say who shall come into a country is one of the very highest attributes of sovereignty. If a nation cannot say without appeal who shall come within its gates and become a part of its citizenship it has ceased to be a sovereign nation. It has become a tributary and a subject nation, and it makes no difference whether it is subject to a league or to a conqueror.

If other nations are willing to subject themselves to such a domination, the United States, to which many immigrants have come and many more will come, ought never to submit to it for a moment. They tell us that so far as Asiatic emigration is concerned there is not the slightest danger that that will ever be forced upon us by the league, because Australia and Canada and New Zealand are equally opposed to it. I think it highly improbable that it would be forced upon us under those conditions, but it is by no means impossible. It is true the United States has one vote and that England, if you count the King of the Hedjaz, has seven—in all eight—votes; yet it might not be impossible for Japan and China and Siam to rally enough other votes to defeat us; but whether we are protected in that way or not does not matter. The very offering of that explanation accepts the jurisdiction of the league, and personally, I cannot consent to putting the protection of my country and of her workingmen against undesirable immigration, out of our own hands. We and we alone must say who shall come into the United States and become citizens of this Republic, and no one else should have any power to utter one word in regard to it.

Article 21 says:

> "Nothing in this covenant shall be deemed to affect the validity of international engagements, such as treaties of arbitration or regional understandings like the Monroe doctrine for securing the maintenance of peace."

The provision did not appear in the first draft of the covenant, and when the President explained the second draft of the convention in the peace conference he said:

> "Article 21 is new."

And that was all he said. No one can question the truth of the remark, but I trust I shall not be considered disrespectful if I say that it was not an illuminating statement. The article was new, but the fact of its novelty, which the President declared, was known to everyone who had taken the trouble to read the two documents. We were not left, however, without a fitting explanation. The British delegation took it upon themselves to explain article 21 at some length, and this is what they said:

> "Article 21 makes it clear that the covenant is not intended to abrogate or weaken any other agreements, so long as they are consistent with its own terms, into which members of the league may have entered or may hereafter enter for the assurance of

peace. Such agreements would include special treaties for compulsory arbitration and military conventions that are genuinely defensive.

"The Monroe doctrine and similar understandings are put in the same category. They have shown themselves in history to be not instruments of national ambition, but guarantees of peace. The origin of the Monroe doctrine is well known. It was proclaimed in 1823 to prevent America from becoming a theater for intrigues of European absolutism. At first a principle of American foreign policy, it has become an international understanding, and it is not illegitimate for the people of the United States to say that the covenant should recognize that fact.

"In its essence it is consistent with the spirit of the covenant, and, indeed, the principles of the league, as expressed in article 10, represent the extension to the whole world of the principles of the doctrine, while, should any dispute as to the meaning of the latter ever arise between the American and European powers, the league is there to settle it."

The explanation of Great Britain received the assent of France.

"It seems to me monumentally paradoxical and a trifle infantile—"

Says M. Lausanne, editor of the *Matin* and a chief spokesman for M. Clemenceau—

"to pretend the contrary.

"When the executive council of the league of nations fixes the 'reasonable limits of the armament of Peru'; when it shall demand information concerning the naval program of Brazil (art. 7 of the covenant); when it shall tell Argentina what shall be the measure of the 'contribution to the armed forces to protect the signature of the social covenant' (art. 16); when it shall demand the immediate registration of the treaty between the United States and Canada at the seat of the league, it will control, whether it wills or not, the destinies of America.

"And when the American States shall be obliged to take a hand in every war or menace of war in Europe (art. 11) they will necessarily fall afoul of the fundamental principle laid down by Monroe.

"*   *   * If the league takes in the world, then Europe must mix in the affairs of America; if only Europe is included, then America will violate of necessity her own doctrine by intermixing in the affairs of Europe."

It has seemed to me that the British delegation traveled a little out of the precincts of the peace conference when they undertook to explain the Monroe doctrine and tell the United States what it was and what it was not proposed to do with it under the new article. That, however, is merely a matter of taste and judgment. Their statement that the Monroe doctrine under this article, if any question arose in regard to it, would be passed upon and interpreted by the league of nations is absolutely correct. There is no doubt that this is what the article means. Great Britain so stated it, and no American authority, whether friendly or unfriendly to the league, has dared to question it. I have wondered a little why it was left to the British delegation to explain this article, which so nearly concerns the United States, but that was merely a fugitive thought upon which I will not dwell. The statement of M. Lausanne is equally explicit and truthful, but he makes one mistake. He says, in substance, that if we are to meddle in Europe, Europe cannot be excluded from the Americas. He overlooks the fact that the Monroe doctrine also says:

> "Our policy in regard to Europe, which was adopted at an early stage of the wars which have so long agitated that quarter of the globe, nevertheless remains the same, which is not to interfere in the internal concerns of any of the powers."

The Monroe doctrine was the corollary of Washington's neutrality policy and of his injunction against permanent alliances. It reiterates and reaffirms the principle. We do not seek to meddle in the affairs of Europe and keep Europe out of the Americas. It is as important to keep the United States out of European affairs as to keep Europe out of the American Continents. Let us maintain the Monroe doctrine, then, in its entirety, and not only preserve our own safety, but in this way best promote the real peace of the world. Whenever the preservation of freedom and civilization and the overthrow of a menacing world conqueror summon us we shall respond fully and nobly, as we did in 1917. He who doubts that we could do so has little faith in America. But let it be our own act and not done reluctantly by the coercion of other nations, at the bidding or by the permission of other countries.

Let me now deal with the article itself. We have here some

protective coloration again. The Monroe doctrine is described as a "regional understanding" whatever that may mean. The boundaries between the States of the Union, I suppose, are "regional understandings," if anyone chooses to apply to them that somewhat swollen phraseology. But the Monroe doctrine is no more a regional understanding than it is an "international engagement." The Monroe doctrine was a policy declared by President Monroe. Its immediate purpose was to shut out Europe from interfering with the South American Republics, which the Holy Alliance designed to do. It was stated broadly, however, as we all know, and went much further than that. It was, as I have just said, the corollary of Washington's declaration against our interfering in European questions. It was so regarded by Jefferson at the time and by John Quincy Adams, who formulated it, and by President Monroe, who declared it. It rested firmly on the great law of self-preservation, which is the basic principle of every independent State.

It is not necessary to trace its history or to point out the extensions which it has received or its universal acceptance by all American statesmen without regard to party. All Americans have always been for it. They may not have known its details or read all the many discussions in regard to it, but they knew that it was an American doctrine and that, broadly stated, it meant the exclusion of Europe from interference with American affairs and from any attempt to colonize or set up new States within the boundaries of the American Continent. I repeat it was purely an American doctrine, a purely American policy, designed and wisely designed for our defense. It has never been an "international engagement." No nation has ever formally recognized it. It has been the subject of reservation at international conventions by American delegates. It has never been a "regional understanding" or an understanding of any kind with anybody. It was the declaration of the United States of America, in their own behalf, supported by their own power. They brought it into being, and its life was predicated on the force which the United States could place behind it. Unless the United States could sustain it it would die. The United States has supported it. It has lived—strong, efficient, respected. It is now proposed to kill it by a provision in a treaty for a league of nations.

The instant that the United States, who declared, interpreted, and sustained the doctrine, ceases to be the sole judge of what it means, that instant the Monroe doctrine ceases and disappears from history and from the face of the earth. I think it is just as undesirable to have Europe interfere in American affairs now as Mr. Monroe thought it was in 1823, and equally undesirable that we should be compelled to involve ourselves in all the wars and brawls of Europe. The Monroe doctrine has made for peace. Without the Monroe doctrine we should have had many a struggle with European powers to save ourselves from possible assault and certainly from the necessity of becoming a great military power, always under arms and always ready to resist invasion from States in our near neighborhood. In the interests of the peace of the world it is now proposed to wipe away this American policy, which has been a bulwark and a barrier for peace. With one exception it has always been successful, and then success was only delayed. When we were torn by civil war France saw fit to enter Mexico and endeavored to establish an empire there. When our hands were once free the empire perished, and with it the unhappy tool of the third Napoleon. If the United States had not been rent by civil war no such attempt would have been made, and nothing better illustrates the value to the cause of peace of the Monroe doctrine. Why, in the name of peace, should we extinguish it? Why, in the name of peace, should we be called upon to leave the interpretation of the Monroe doctrine to other nations? It is an American policy. It is our own. It has guarded us well, and I, for one, can never find consent in my heart to destroy it by a clause in a treaty and hand over its body for dissection to the nations of Europe. If we need authority to demonstrate what the Monroe doctrine has meant to the United States we cannot do better than quote the words of Grover Cleveland, who directed Mr. Olney to notify the world that "to-day the United States is practically sovereign on this continent, and its fiat is law to which it confines its interposition." Theodore Roosevelt, in the last article written before his death, warned us, his countrymen, that we are "in honor bound to keep ourselves so prepared that the Monroe doctrine shall be accepted as immutable international law." Grover Cleveland was a Democrat and Theodore Roosevelt was a Republican, but they were both Americans, and it is the American spirit which has carried this country always to victory and which should govern us to-day, and not the international spirit which would in the name of peace hand the United States over bound hand and foot to obey the fiat of other powers.

Another point in this covenant where change must be made in order to protect the safety of the United States in the future is in article I, where withdrawal is provided for. This provision was an attempt to meet the very general objection to the first draft of the league, that there was no means of getting out of it without denouncing the treaty; that is, there was no arrangement for the withdrawal of any nation. As it now stands it reads that—

> "Any member of the league may, after two years' notice of its intention to do so, withdraw from the league, provided that all its international obligations, and all its obligations under this covenant shall have been fulfilled at the time of its withdrawal."

The right of withdrawal is given by this clause, although the time for notice, two years, is altogether too long. Six months or a year would be found, I think, in most treaties to be the normal period fixed for notice of withdrawal. But whatever virtue there may be in the right thus conferred is completely nullified by the proviso. The right of withdrawal cannot be exercised until all the international obligations and all the obligations of the withdrawing nations have been fulfilled. The league alone can decide whether "all international obligations and all obligations under this covenant" have been fulfilled, and this would require, under the provisions of the league, a unanimous vote so that any nation desiring to withdraw could not do so, even on the two years' notice, if one nation voted that the obligations had not been fulfilled. Remember that this gives the league not only power to review all our obligations under the covenant but all our treaties with all nations for every one of those is an "international obligation."

Are we deliberately to put ourselves in fetters and be examined by the league of nations as to whether we have kept faith with Cuba or Panama before we can be permitted to leave the league? This seems to me humiliating to say the least. The right of withdrawal, if it is to be of any value whatever, must be absolute, because otherwise a nation desiring to withdraw could be held in the league by objections from other nations until the very act which induces the nation to withdraw had been completed; until the withdrawing nation had been forced to send troops to take part in a war with which it had no concern and upon which it did not desire to enter. It seems to me vital to the safety of the United States not only that this provision should be eliminated and the right to withdraw made absolute but that the period of withdrawal should be much reduced. As it stands it is practically no better in this respect than the first league draft which contained no provision for withdrawal at all, because the proviso here inserted so incumbers it that every nation to all intents and purposes must remain a member of the league indefinitely unless all the other members are willing that it should retire. Such a provision as this, ostensibly framed to meet the objection, has the defect which other similar gestures to give an impression of meeting objections have, that it apparently keeps the promise to the ear but most certainly breaks it to the hope.

I have dwelt only upon those points which seem to me most dangerous. There are, of course, many others, but these points, in the interest not only of the safety of the United States but of the maintenance of the treaty and the peace of the world, should be dealt with here before it is too late. Once in the league the chance of amendment is so slight that it is not worth considering. Any analysis of the provisions of this league covenant, however, brings out in startling relief one great fact. Whatever may be said, it is not a league of peace; it is an alliance, dominated at the present moment by five great powers, really by three, and it has all the marks of an alliance. The development of international law is neglected. The court which is to decide disputes brought before it fills but a small place. The conditions for which this league really provides with the utmost care are political conditions, not judicial questions, to be reached by the executive council and the assembly, purely political bodies without any trace of a judicial character about them. Such being its machinery, the control being in the hands of political appointees whose votes will be controlled by interest and expedience, it exhibits that most marked characteristic of an alliance—that its decisions are to be carried out by force. Those

articles upon which the whole structure rests are articles which
provide for the use of force; that is, for war. This league to
enforce peace does a great deal for enforcement and very little
for peace. It makes more essential provisions looking to war
than to peace, for the settlement of disputes.

Article 10 I have already discussed. There is no question that
the preservation of a State against external aggression can
contemplate nothing but war. In article 11, again, the league is
authorized to take any action which may be necessary to safeguard the peace of the world. "Any action" includes war. We
also have specific provisions for a boycott, which is a form of
economic warfare. The use of troops might be avoided but the
enforcement of a boycott would require blockades in all probability, and certainly a boycott in its essence is simply an effort
to starve a people into submission, to ruin their trade, and, in
the case of nations which are not self-supporting, to cut off their
food supply. The misery and suffering caused by such a measure
as this may easily rival that caused by actual war. Article 16
embodies the boycott and also, in the last paragraph, provides
explicitly for war. We are told that the word "recommends"
has no binding force; it constitutes a moral obligation, that is
all. But it means that if we, for example, should refuse to accept
the recommendation, we should nullify the operation of article
16 and, to that extent, of the league. It seems to me that to
attempt to relieve us of clearly imposed duties by saying that
the word "recommend" is not binding is an escape of which
no nation regarding the sanctity of treaties and its own honor
would care to avail itself. The provisions of article 16 are extended to States outside the league who refuse to obey its
command to come in and submit themselves to its jurisdiction;
another provision for war.

Taken altogether, these provisions for war present what to
my mind is the gravest objection to this league in its present
form. We are told that of course nothing will be done in the
way of warlike acts without the assent of Congress. If that is
true, let us say so in the covenant. But as it stands there is no
doubt whatever in my mind that American troops and American ships may be ordered to any part of the world by nations
other than the United States, and that is a proposition to
which I for one can never assent. It must be made perfectly

clear that no American soldiers, not even a corporal's guard, that no American sailors, not even the crew of a submarine, can ever be engaged in war or ordered anywhere except by the constitutional authorities of the United States. To Congress is granted by the Constitution the right to declare war, and nothing that would take the troops out of the country at the bidding or demand of other nations should ever be permitted except through congressional action. The lives of Americans must never be sacrificed except by the will of the American people expressed through their chosen Representatives in Congress. This is a point upon which no doubt can be permitted. American soldiers and American sailors have never failed the country when the country called upon them. They went in their hundreds of thousands into the war just closed. They went to die for the great cause of freedom and of civilization. They went at their country's bidding and because their country summoned them to service. We were late in entering the war. We made no preparation as we ought to have done, for the ordeal which was clearly coming upon us; but we went and we turned the wavering scale. It was done by the American soldier, the American sailor, and the spirit and energy of the American people. They overrode all obstacles and all shortcomings on the part of the administration or of Congress, and gave to their country a great place in the great victory. It was the first time we had been called upon to rescue the civilized world. Did we fail? On the contrary, we succeeded, we succeeded largely and nobly, and we did it without any command from any league of nations. When the emergency came we met it and we were able to meet it because we had built up on this continent the greatest and most powerful nation in the world, built it up under our own policies, in our own way, and one great element of our strength was the fact that we had held aloof and had not thrust ourselves into European quarrels; that we had no selfish interest to serve. We made great sacrifices. We have done splendid work. I believe that we do not require to be told by foreign nations when we shall do work which freedom and civilization require. I think we can move to victory much better under our own command than under the command of others. Let us unite with the world to promote the peaceable settlement of all international disputes. Let us try to develop international law. Let us associate ourselves with the other nations for these purposes. But let us retain in our own hands and in our own control the lives of the youth of the land. Let no American be sent into battle except by the constituted authorities of his own country and by the will of the people of the United States.

Those of us, Mr. President, who are either wholly opposed to the league or who are trying to preserve the independence and the safety of the United States by changing the terms of the league and who are endeavoring to make the league, if we are to be a member of it, less certain to promote war instead of peace, have been reproached with selfishness in our outlook and with a desire to keep our country in a state of isolation. So far as the question of isolation goes, it is impossible to isolate the United States. I well remember the time, 20 years ago, when eminent Senators and other distinguished gentlemen who were opposing the Philippines and shrieking about imperialism, sneered at the statement made by some of us, that the United States had become a world power. I think no one now would question that the Spanish War marked the entrance of the United States into world affairs to a degree which had never obtained before. It was both an inevitable and an irrevocable step, and our entrance into the war with Germany certainly showed once and for all that the United States was not unmindful of its world responsibilities. We may set aside all this empty talk about isolation. Nobody expects to isolate the United States or to make it a hermit Nation, which is a sheer absurdity. But there is a wide difference between taking a suitable part and bearing a due responsibility in world affairs and plunging the United States into every controversy and conflict on the face of the globe. By meddling in all the differences which may arise among any portion or fragment of humankind we simply fritter away our influence and injure ourselves to no good purpose. We shall be of far more value to the world and its peace by occupying, so far as possible, the situation which we have occupied for the last 20 years and by adhering to the policy of Washington and Hamilton, of Jefferson and Monroe, under which we have risen to our present greatness and prosperity. The fact that we have been separated by our geographical situation and by our consistent policy from the broils of

Europe has made us more than any one thing capable of performing the great work which we performed in the war against Germany, and our disinterestedness is of far more value to the world than our eternal meddling in every possible dispute could ever be.

Now, as to our selfishness. I have no desire to boast that we are better than our neighbors, but the fact remains that this Nation in making peace with Germany had not a single selfish or individual interest to serve. All we asked was that Germany should be rendered incapable of again breaking forth, with all the horrors incident to German warfare, upon an unoffending world, and that demand was shared by every free nation and indeed by humanity itself. For ourselves we asked absolutely nothing. We have not asked any government or governments to guarantee our boundaries or our political independence. We have no fear in regard to either. We have sought no territory, no privileges, no advantages, for ourselves. That is the fact. It is apparent on the face of the treaty. I do not mean to reflect upon a single one of the powers with which we have been associated in the war against Germany, but there is not one of them which has not sought individual advantages for their own national benefit. I do not criticize their desires at all. The services and sacrifices of England and France and Belgium and Italy are beyond estimate and beyond praise. I am glad they should have what they desire for their own welfare and safety. But they all receive under the peace territorial and commercial benefits. We are asked to give, and we in no way seek to take. Surely it is not too much to insist that when we are offered nothing but the opportunity to give and to aid others we should have the right to say what sacrifices we shall make and what the magnitude of our gifts shall be. In the prosecution of the war we gave unstintedly American lives and American treasure. When the war closed we had 3,000,000 men under arms. We were turning the country into a vast workshop for war. We advanced ten billions to our allies. We refused no assistance that we could possibly render. All the great energy and power of the Republic were put at the service of the good cause. We have not been ungenerous. We have been devoted to the cause of freedom, humanity, and civilization everywhere. Now we are asked, in the making of peace, to sacrifice our sovereignty in important respects, to involve ourselves almost without limit in the affairs of other nations, and to yield up policies and rights which we have maintained throughout our history. We are asked to incur liabilities to an unlimited extent and furnish assets at the same time which no man can measure. I think it is not only our right but our duty to determine how far we shall go. Not only must we look carefully to see where we are being led into endless disputes and entanglements, but we must not forget that we have in this country millions of people of foreign birth and parentage.

Our one great object is to make all these people Americans so that we may call on them to place America first and serve America as they have done in the war just closed. We cannot Americanize them if we are continually thrusting them back into the quarrels and difficulties of the countries from which they came to us. We shall fill this land with political disputes about the troubles and quarrels of other countries. We shall have a large portion of our people voting not on American questions and not on what concerns the United States but dividing on issues which concern foreign countries alone. That is an unwholesome and perilous condition to force upon this country. We must avoid it. We ought to reduce to the lowest possible point the foreign questions in which we involve ourselves. Never forget that this league is primarily—I might say overwhelmingly—a political organization, and I object strongly to having the politics of the United States turn upon disputes where deep feeling is aroused but in which we have no direct interest. It will all tend to delay the Americanization of our great population, and it is more important not only to the United States but to the peace of the world to make all these people good Americans than it is to determine that some piece of territory should belong to one European country rather than to another. For this reason I wish to limit strictly our interference in the affairs of Europe and of Africa. We have interests of our own in Asia and in the Pacific which we must guard upon our own account, but the less we undertake to play the part of umpire and thrust ourselves into European conflicts the better for the United States and for the world.

It has been reiterated here on this floor, and reiterated to the point of weariness, that in every treaty there is some sacrifice of sovereignty. That is not a universal truth by any means, but it is true of some treaties and it is a platitude which does not require reiteration. The question and the only question before us here is how much of our sovereignty we are justified in sacrificing. In what I have already said about other nations putting us into war I have covered one point of sovereignty which ought never to be yielded, the power to send American soldiers and sailors everywhere, which ought never to be taken from the American people or impaired in the slightest degree. Let us beware how we palter with our independence. We have not reached the great position from which we were able to come down into the field of battle and help to save the world from tyranny by being guided by others. Our vast power has all been built up and gathered together by ourselves alone. We forced our way upward from the days of the Revolution, through a world often hostile and always indifferent. We owe no debt to anyone except to France in that Revolution, and those policies and those rights on which our power has been founded should never be lessened or weakened. It will be no service to the world to do so and it will be of intolerable injury to the United States. We will do our share. We are ready and anxious to help in all ways to preserve the world's peace. But we can do it best by not crippling ourselves.

I am as anxious as any human being can be to have the United States render every possible service to the civilization and the peace of mankind, but I am certain we can do it best by not putting ourselves in leading strings or subjecting our policies and our sovereignty to other nations. The independence of the United States is not only more precious to ourselves but to the world than any single possession. Look at the United States to-day. We have made mistakes in the past. We have had shortcomings. We shall make mistakes in the future and fall short of our own best hopes. But none the less is there any country to-day on the face of the earth which can compare with this in ordered liberty, in peace, and in the largest freedom? I feel that I can say this without being accused of undue boastfulness, for it is the simple fact, and in making this treaty and taking on these obligations all that we do is in a spirit of unselfishness and in a desire for the good of mankind. But it is well to remember that we are dealing with nations every one of which has a direct individual interest to serve and there is grave danger in an unshared idealism. Contrast the United States with any country on the face of the earth to-day and ask yourself whether the situation of the United States is not the best to be found. I will go as far as anyone in world service, but the first step to world service is the maintenance of the United States. You may call me selfish if you will, conservative or reactionary, or use any other harsh adjective you see fit to apply, but an American I was born, an American I have remained all my life. I can never be anything else but an American, and I must think of the United States first, and when I think of the United States first in an arrangement like this I am thinking of what is best for the world, for if the United States fails the best hopes of mankind fail with it. I have never had but one allegiance—I cannot divide it now. I have loved but one flag and I cannot share that devotion and give affection to the mongrel banner invented for a league. Internationalism, illustrated by the Bolshevik and by the men to whom all countries are alike provided they can make money out of them, is to me repulsive. National I must remain, and in that way I, like all other Americans, can render the amplest service to the world. The United States is the world's best hope, but if you fetter her in the interests and quarrels of other nations, if you tangle her in the intrigues of Europe, you will destroy her power for good and endanger her very existence. Leave her to march freely through the centuries to come as in the years that have gone. Strong, generous, and confident, she has nobly served mankind. Beware how you trifle with your marvelous inheritance, this great land of ordered liberty, for if we stumble and fall, freedom and civilization everywhere will go down in ruin.

We are told that we shall "break the heart of the world" if we do not take this league just as it stands. I fear that the hearts of the vast majority of mankind would beat on strongly and steadily and without any quickening if the league were to perish altogether. If it should be effectively and beneficently changed the people who would lie awake in sorrow for a single night could be easily gathered in one not very large room, but those who would draw a long breath of relief would reach to millions.

We hear much of visions and I trust we shall continue to have visions and dream dreams of a fairer future for the race. But visions are one thing and visionaries are another, and the mechanical appliances of the rhetorician designed to give a picture of a present which does not exist and of a future which no man can predict are as unreal and shortlived as the steam or canvas clouds, the angels suspended on wires, and the artificial lights of the stage. They pass with the moment of effect and are shabby and tawdry in the daylight. Let us at least be real. Washington's entire honesty of mind and his fearless look into the face of all facts are qualities which can never go out of fashion and which we should all do well to imitate.

Ideals have been thrust upon us as an argument for the league until the healthy mind, which rejects cant, revolts from them. Are ideals confined to this deformed experiment upon a noble purpose, tainted as it is with bargains, and tied to a peace treaty which might have been disposed of long ago to the great benefit of the world if it had not been compelled to carry this rider on its back? "*Post equitem sedet atra cura*," Horace tells us, but no blacker care ever sat behind any rider than we shall find in this covenant of doubtful and disputed interpretation as it now perches upon the treaty of peace.

No doubt many excellent and patriotic people see a coming fulfillment of noble ideals in the words "league for peace." We all respect and share these aspirations and desires, but some of us see no hope, but rather defeat, for them in this murky covenant. For we, too, have our ideals, even if we differ from those who have tried to establish a monopoly of idealism. Our first ideal is our country, and we see her in the future, as in the past, giving service to all her people and to the world. Our ideal of the future is that she should continue to render that service of her own free will. She has great problems of her own to solve, very grim and perilous problems, and a right solution, if we can attain to it, would largely benefit mankind. We would have our country strong to resist a peril from the West, as she has flung back the German menace from the East. We would not have our politics distracted and embittered by the dissensions of other lands. We would not have our country's vigor exhausted or her moral force abated by everlasting meddling and muddling in every quarrel, great and small, which afflicts the world. Our ideal is to make her ever stronger and better and finer, because in that way alone, as we believe, can she be of the greatest service to the world's peace and to the welfare of mankind. [Prolonged applause in the galleries.]

August 12, 1919

W. A. Domingo and Claude McKay: "If We Must Die"

Dozens of race riots and lynchings erupted across the country in the summer of 1919, moving James Weldon Johnson to christen the season the "Red Summer." At least seven people were killed in late July in Washington, D.C., and a riot in Chicago claimed thirty-eight lives a few days later. In many cases, the determination with which black Americans fought back shocked the white population. W. A. Domingo, Jamaican by birth, was a former associate of Marcus Garvey who wrote for A. Philip Randolph's socialist magazine *The Messenger*. Concluding his essay with Claude McKay's powerful poem (originally printed in *The Liberator*), Domingo defined the militant spirit of the "New Negro."

――――――――――

AMERICA WON the war that was alleged to be fought for the purpose of making the world safe for democracy, but in the light of recent happenings in Washington, the Capital city, and Chicago, it would seem as though the United States is not a part of the world. In order to win the war President Wilson employed "force, unstinted force," and those who expect to bring any similar desirable termination to a just cause can do no less than follow the splendid example set them by the reputed spokesman of humanity. That the lesson did not take long to penetrate the minds of Negroes is demonstrated by the change that has taken place in their demeanor and tactics. No longer are Negroes willing to be shot down or hunted from place to place like wild beasts; no longer will they flee from their homes and leave their property to the tender mercies of the howling and cowardly mob. They have changed, and now they intend to give men's account of themselves. If death is to be their portion, New Negroes are determined to make their dying a costly investment for all concerned. If they must die they are determined that they shall not travel through the valley of the shadow of death alone, but that some of their oppressors shall be their companions.

This new spirit is but a reflex of the great war, and it is largely due to the insistent and vigorous agitation carried on by younger men of the race. The demand is uncompromisingly made for either liberty or death, and since death is likely to be a two-edged sword it will be to the advantage of those in a position to do so to give the race its long-denied liberty.

The new spirit animating Negroes is not confined to the United States, where it is most acutely manifested, but is simmering beneath the surface in every country where the race is oppressed. The Washington and Chicago outbreaks should be regarded as symptoms of a great pandemic, and the Negroes as courageous surgeons who performed the necessary though painful operation. That the remedy is efficacious is beyond question. It has brought results, for as a consequence the eyes of the entire world are focused upon the racial situation in the United States. The world knows now that the New Negroes arc determined to observe the primal law of self-preservation whenever civil laws break down; to assist the authorities to preserve order and prevent themselves and families from being murdered in cold blood. Surely, no one can sincerely object to this new and laudable determination. Justification for this course is not lacking, for it is the white man's own Bible that says "Those who live by the sword shall perish by the sword," and since white men believe in force, Negroes who have mimicked them for nearly three centuries must copy them in that respect. Since fire must be fought with hell fire, and diamond alone can cut diamond, Negroes realize that force alone is an effective medium to counteract force. Counter irritants are useful in curing diseases, and Negroes are being driven by their white fellow citizens to investigate the curative values inherent in mass action, revolvers and other lethal devices when applied to social diseases.

The New Negro has arrived with stiffened back bone, dauntless manhood, defiant eye, steady hand and a will of iron. His creed is admirably summed up in the poem of Claude McKay, the black Jamaican poet, who is carving out for himself a niche in the Hall of Fame:

IF WE MUST DIE

If we must die, let it not be like hogs
   Hunted and penned in an inglorious spot,

While round us bark the mad and hungry dogs,
   Making their mock at our accursed lot.
If we must die, oh, let us nobly die,
   So that our precious blood may not be shed
In vain; then even the monsters we defy
   Shall be constrained to honor us, though dead!

Oh, kinsmen! We must meet the common foe;
   Though far outnumbered, let us still be brave,
And for their thousand blows deal one death-blow!
   What though before us lies the open grave?
Like men we'll face the murderous, cowardly pack,
   Pressed to the wall, dying, but—fighting back!

The Messenger, September 1919

Woodrow Wilson: Speech at Pueblo, Colorado

When President Wilson realized that Senator Lodge had effectively blocked approval of the League treaty, he decided to take his cause to the people. Exhausted and afflicted with arteriosclerosis, the President embarked on a quixotic four-week tour across the country to rally public support for his covenant of peace. Rallying audiences several times a day, he sometimes delivered his hour-long appeals to thousands of people without benefit of modern amplification systems and often while suffering blinding headaches. When the whistle-stop tour reached Pueblo, Colorado, he entered the city's new Memorial Hall looking tired; and, for the first time, his weak voice occasionally stumbled on a line. After the speech, the presidential train left for Kansas City, but Wilson complained of an intense headache; his face twitched, he was nauseous, and he suffered an asthmatic attack. By morning, Dr. Grayson insisted that the tour come to an end. Undergoing a nervous breakdown, Wilson was too weak to argue. On his fourth day back at the White House, he collapsed on the bathroom floor, suffering an ischemic stroke—a clot in an artery of the brain. Although he could still think and speak, his left side was paralyzed, and he would be confined to his bed for weeks. For the rest of his presidency, he was hardly seen or heard again in public, and no one revealed the extent of his condition to the nation. While the President languished that November, the Senate killed his treaty.

September 25, 1919.

Mr. Chairman and fellow citizens: It is with a great deal of genuine pleasure that I find myself in Pueblo, and I feel it a compliment that I should be permitted to be the first speaker in this beautiful hall. One of the advantages of this hall, as I look about, is that you are not too far away from me, because there is nothing so reassuring to men who are trying to express the public sentiment as getting into real personal contact with their fellow citizens.

I have gained a renewed impression as I have crossed the continent this time of the homogeneity of this great people to whom we belong. They come from many stocks, but they are all of one kind. They come from many origins, but they are all shot through with the same principles and desire the same righteous and honest things. So I have received a more inspiring impression this time of the public opinion of the United States than it was ever my privilege to receive before.

The chief pleasure of my trip has been that it has nothing to do with my personal fortunes, that it has nothing to do with my personal reputation, that it has nothing to do with anything except the great principles uttered by Americans of all sorts and of all parties which we are now trying to realize at this crisis of the affairs of the world.

But there have been unpleasant impressions as well as pleasant impressions, my fellow citizens, as I have crossed the continent. I have perceived more and more that men have been busy creating an absolutely false impression of what the treaty of peace and the Covenant of the League of Nations contain and mean. I find, moreover, that there is an organized propaganda against the League of Nations and against the treaty proceeding from exactly the same sources that the organized propaganda proceeded from which threatened this country here and there with disloyalty. And I want to say—I cannot say it too often—any man who carries a hyphen about with him carries a dagger that he is ready to plunge into the vitals of this republic whenever he gets the chance. (applause) If I can catch any man with a hyphen in this great contest, I will know that I have caught an enemy of the republic. My fellow citizens, it is only certain bodies of foreign sympathies, certain bodies of sympathy with foreign nations that are organized against this great document, which the American representatives have brought back from Paris. Therefore, it is in order to clear away the mists, in order to remove misapprehensions, in order to do away with false impressions that have clustered around this great subject, that I want to tell you a few simple things about these essential things—the treaty and the Covenant of the League of Nations.

Don't think of this treaty of peace as merely a settlement with Germany. It is that. It is a very severe settlement with Germany, but there is not anything in it that she did not earn. (applause) Indeed, she earned more than she can ever be able to pay for, and the punishment exacted of her is not a punishment greater than she can bear. And it is absolutely necessary in order that no other nation may ever plot such a thing against humanity and civilization.

But the treaty is so much more than that. It is not merely a settlement with Germany; it is a readjustment of those great injustices which underlay the whole structure of European and Asiatic societies. Of course this is only the first of several treaties. They are all constructed on the same plan. The Austrian treaty follows the same lines. The treaty with Hungary follows the same lines. The treaty with Bulgaria follows the same lines. The treaty with Turkey, when it is formulated, will follow the same lines.

What are those lines? They are based on the principle that every government dealt with in this great settlement is put in the hands of the people and taken out of the hands of coteries and sovereigns who had no right to rule over the people. (applause) It is a people's treaty, that accomplishes by a great sweep of practical justice the liberation of men who never could have liberated themselves. And the power of the most powerful nations has been devoted, not to their aggrandizement, but to the liberation of people whom they could have put under their control if they had chosen to do so. Not one foot of territory is demanded by the conquerors, not one single item of submission to their authority is demanded by them. The men who sat around that table in Paris knew that the time had come when the people were no longer going to consent to live under masters, but were going to live their lives as they chose to live and under such governments as they chose to erect. That is the fundamental principle of this great settlement.

And we did not stop with that. We added a great international charter for the rights of labor. (applause) Reject this treaty, impair it, and this is the consequence to the laboring men of the world—there is no international tribunal which can bring the moral judgments of the world to bear upon the great labor questions of the day. What we need to do with regard to the labor questions of the day, my fellow countrymen, is to lift them into the light, is to lift them out of the haze and distraction of passion, of hostility, into the calm spaces where men look at things without passion. The more men you get into a great discussion the more you exclude passion. Just so soon as the calm judgment of the world is directed upon the question of justice to labor, labor is going to have a forum such as it never was supplied with before. And men everywhere are going to see that the problem of labor is nothing more nor less than the problem of the elevation of humanity. (applause) We must see that all the questions which have disturbed the world, all the questions which have eaten into the confidence of men toward their governments, all the questions which have disturbed the processes of industry, shall be brought out where men of all points of view, men of all attitudes of mind, men of all kinds of experience, may contribute their part to the settlement of the great questions which we must settle and cannot ignore.

But at the front of this great treaty is put the Covenant of the League of Nations. It will also be at the front of the Austrian treaty and the Hungarian treaty and the Bulgarian treaty and the treaty with Turkey. Every one of them will contain the Covenant of the League of Nations, because you cannot work any of them without the Covenant of the League of Nations. Unless you get the united, concerted purpose and power of the great governments of the world behind this settlement, it will fall down like a house of cards.

There is only one power to put behind the liberation of mankind, and that is the power of mankind. It is the power of the united moral forces of the world. And in the Covenant of the League of Nations, the moral forces of the world are mobilized. For what purpose? Reflect, my fellow citizens, that the membership of this great League is going to include all the great fighting nations of the world, as well as the weak ones. It is not for the present going to include Germany, but for the time being Germany is not a great fighting country. (applause) But all the nations that have power that can be mobilized are going to be members of this League, including the United States. And what do they unite for? They enter into a solemn promise to one another that they will never use their power against one another for aggression; that they never will impair the territorial integrity of a neighbor; that they will never interfere with the political independence of a neighbor; that they will abide by the principle that great populations are entitled to determine their own destiny and that they will not interfere with that destiny; and that, no matter what differences arise amongst them, they will never resort to war without first having done one or other of two things—either submitting the matter of controversy to arbitration, in which case they agree to abide by the result without question, or, having submitted it to the consideration of the Council of the League of Nations, laying before that Council all the documents, all the facts, agreeing that the Council can publish the documents and the facts to the whole world. You understand that there are six months allowed for the mature consideration of these facts by the Council, and, at the expiration of these six months, even if they are not then ready to accept the advice of the Council with regard to the settlement of the dispute, they will still not go to war for another three months.

In other words, they consent, no matter what happens, to submit every matter of difference between them to the judgment of mankind. And, just so certainly as they do that, my fellow citizens, war will be in the far background, war will be pushed out of that foreground of terror in which it has kept the world for generation after generation, and men will know that there will be a calm time of deliberate counsel.

The most dangerous thing for a bad cause is to expose it to the opinion of the world. The most certain way that you can prove that a man is mistaken is by letting all his neighbors know what he thinks, by letting all his neighbors discuss what he thinks, and, if he is in the wrong, you will notice that he will stay at home, he will not walk on the streets. He will be afraid of the eyes of his neighbors. He will be afraid of their judgment of his character. He will know that his cause is lost unless he can sustain it by the arguments of right and of justice. The same law that applies to individuals applies to nations.

But you say, "We have heard that we might be at a disadvantage in the League of Nations." Well, whoever told you that either was deliberately falsifying or he had not read the Covenant of the League of Nations. I leave him the choice. I want to give you a very simple account of the organization of the League of Nations and let you judge for yourselves. It is a very simple organization. The power of the League, or rather the activities of the League, lie in two bodies. There is the Council, which consists of one representative from each of the Principal

Allied and Associated Powers—that is to say, the United States, Great Britain, France, Italy, and Japan, along with four other representatives of the smaller powers chosen out of the general body of the membership of the League. The Council is the source of every active policy of the League, and no active policy of the League can be adopted without a unanimous vote of the Council. That is explicitly stated in the Covenant itself.

Does it not evidently follow that the League of Nations can adopt no policy whatever without the consent of the United States? The affirmative vote of the representative of the United States is necessary in every case.

Now, you have heard of six votes belonging to the British Empire. Those six votes are not in the Council. They are in the Assembly, and the interesting thing is that the Assembly does not vote. (applause) I must qualify that statement a little, but essentially it is absolutely true. In every matter in which the Assembly is given a vote—and there are only four or five—its vote does not count unless concurred in by the representatives of all the nations represented on the Council. So that there is no validity to any vote of the Assembly unless in that vote also the representative of the United States concurs. That one vote of the United States is as big as the six votes of the British Empire. (applause) I am not jealous for advantage, my fellow citizens, but I think that is a perfectly safe situation. There isn't validity in a vote, either by the Council or the Assembly, in which we do not concur. So much for the statements about the six votes of the British Empire.

Look at it in another aspect. The Assembly is the talking body. The Assembly was created in order that anybody that purposed anything wrong would be subjected to the awkward circumstance that everybody could talk about it. This is the great assembly in which all the things that are likely to disturb the peace of the world or the good understanding between nations are to be exposed to the general view. And I want to ask you if you think it was unjust, unjust to the United States, that speaking parts should be assigned to the several portions of the British Empire? Do you think it unjust that there should be some spokesman in debate for that fine little stout republic down in the Pacific, New Zealand? Do you think it unjust that Australia should be allowed to stand up and take part in the debate—Australia, from which we have learned some of the most useful progressive policies of modern time, a little nation only five million in a great continent, but counting for several times five in its activities and in its interest in liberal reform.

Do you think it unjust that that little republic down in South Africa, whose gallant resistance to being subjected to any outside authority at all we admired for so many months, and whose fortunes we followed with such interest, should have a speaking part? Great Britain obliged South Africa to submit to her sovereignty, but she immediately after that felt that it was convenient and right to hand the whole self-government of that colony over to the very men whom she had beaten.

The representatives of South Africa in Paris were two of the most distinguished generals of the Boer army, two of the most intelligent men I ever met, two men that could talk sober counsel and wise advice along with the best statesmen in Europe. To exclude General Botha and General Smuts from the right to stand up in the parliament of the world and say something concerning the affairs of mankind would be absurd.

And what about Canada? Is not Canada a good neighbor? I ask you, is not Canada more likely to agree with the United States than with Great Britain? Canada has a speaking part. And then, for the first time in the history of the world, that great voiceless multitude, that throng hundreds of millions strong in India, has a voice among the nations of the world. And I want to testify that some of the wisest and most dignified figures in the peace conference at Paris came from India, men who seemed to carry in their minds an older wisdom than the rest of us had, whose traditions ran back into so many of the unhappy fortunes of mankind that they seemed very useful counselors as to how some ray of hope and some prospect of happiness could be opened to its people. I, for my part, have no jealousy whatever of those five speaking parts in the Assembly. Those speaking parts cannot translate themselves into five votes that can in any matter override the voice and purpose of the United States.

Let us sweep aside all this language of jealousy. Let us be big enough to know the facts and to welcome the facts, because the facts are based upon the principle that America has always fought for, namely, the equality of self-governing peoples, whether they were big or little—not counting men, but counting rights, not counting representation, but counting the purpose of that representation.

When you hear an opinion quoted you do not count the number of persons who hold it; you ask, "Who said that?" You weigh opinions, you do not count them. And the beauty of all democracies is that every voice can be heard, every voice can have its effect, every voice can contribute to the general judgment that is finally arrived at. That is the object of democracy. Let us accept what America has always fought for, and accept it with pride—that America showed the way and made the proposal. I do not mean that America made the proposal in this particular instance. I mean that the principle was an American principle, proposed by America.

When you come to the heart of the Covenant, my fellow citizens, you will find it in Article X, and I am very much interested to know that the other things have been blown away like bubbles. There is nothing in the other contentions with regard to the League of Nations, but there is something in Article X that you ought to realize and ought to accept or reject. Article X is the heart of the whole matter.

What is Article X? I never am certain that I can from memory give a literal repetition of its language, but I am sure that I can give an exact interpretation of its meaning. Article X provides that every member of the League covenants to respect and preserve the territorial integrity and existing political independence of every other member of the League as against external aggression.

Not against internal disturbance. There was not a man at that table who did not admit the sacredness of the right of self-determination, the sacredness of the right of any body of people to say that they would not continue to live under the government they were then living under. And under Article XI of the Covenant, they are given the privilege to say whether they will live under it or not. For following Article X is Article XI, which makes it the right of any member of the League at any time to call attention to anything, anywhere, that is likely to disturb the peace of the world or the good understanding between nations upon which the peace of the world depends. I want to give you an illustration of what that would mean.

You have heard a great deal—something that was true and a great deal that was false—about that provision of the treaty which hands over to Japan the rights which Germany enjoyed in the province of Shantung in China. In the first place, Germany did not enjoy any rights there that other nations had not already claimed. For my part, my judgment, my moral judgment, is against the whole set of concessions. They were all of them unjust to China, they ought never to have been exacted, they were all exacted by duress from a great body of thoughtful and ancient and helpless people. There never was any right in any of them. Thank God, America never asked for any, never dreamed of asking for any.

But when Germany got this concession in 1898, the government of the United States made no protest whatsoever. That was not because the government of the United States was not in the hands of high-minded and conscientious men. It was. William McKinley was President and John Hay was Secretary of State—as safe hands to leave the honor of the United States in as any that you can cite. They made no protest because the state of international law at that time was that it was none of their business unless they could show that the interests of the United States were affected, and the only thing that they could show with regard to the interests of the United States was that Germany might close the doors of Shantung Province against the trade of the United States. They, therefore, demanded and obtained promises that we could continue to sell merchandise in Shantung. And what good that would be for the independence of China, it is very difficult to see.

Immediately following that concession to Germany, there was a concession to Russia of the same sort—of Port Arthur, and Port Arthur was handed over subsequently to Japan on the very territory of the United States. Don't you remember that, when Russia and Japan got into war with one another, the war was brought to a conclusion by a treaty written at Portsmouth, New Hampshire? And in that treaty, without the slightest intimation from any authoritative sources in America that the government of the United States had any objection, Port Arthur, Chinese territory, was turned over to Japan.

I want you distinctly to understand that there is no thought of criticism in my mind. I am expounding to you a state of international law. Now, read Article X and XI. You will see that international law is revolutionized by putting morals into it. Article X says that no member of the League, and that includes all these nations that have done these things unjustly to China, shall impair the territorial integrity or the political independence of any other member of the League. China is going to be a member of the League. Article XI says that any member of the League can call attention to anything that is likely to disturb the peace of the world or the good understanding between nations, and China is for the first time in the history of mankind afforded a standing before the jury of the world.

I, for my part, have a profound sympathy for China, and I am proud to have taken part in an arrangement which promises the protection of the world to the rights of China. The whole atmosphere of the world is changed by a thing like that, my fellow citizens. The whole international practice of the world is revolutionized.

But, you will say, "What is the second sentence of Article X? That is what gives very disturbing thoughts." The second sentence is that the Council of the League shall advise what steps, if any, are necessary to carry out the guarantee of the first sentence, namely, that the members will respect and preserve the territorial integrity and political independence of the other members. I do not know any other meaning for the word "advise" except "advise." The Council advises, and it cannot advise without the vote of the United States. Why gentlemen should fear that the Congress of the United States would be advised to do something that it did not want to do, I frankly cannot imagine, because they cannot even be advised to do anything unless their own representative has participated in the advice.

It may be that that will impair somewhat the vigor of the League, but, nevertheless, the fact is so—that we are not obliged to take any advice except our own, which to any man who wants to go his own course is a very satisfactory state of affairs. Every man regards his own advice as best, and I dare say every man mixes his own advice with some thought of his own interest. Whether we use it wisely or unwisely, we can use the vote of the United States to make impossible drawing the United States into any enterprise that she does not care to be drawn into.

Yet Article X strikes at the taproot of war. Article X is a statement that the very things that have always been sought in imperialistic wars are henceforth forgone by every ambitious nation in the world.

I would have felt very lonely, my fellow countrymen, and I would have felt very much disturbed if, sitting at the peace table in Paris, I had supposed that I was expounding my own ideas. Whether you believe it or not, I know the relative size of my own ideas; I know how they stand related in bulk and proportion to the moral judgments of my fellow countrymen. And I proposed nothing whatever at the peace table at Paris that I had not sufficiently certain knowledge embodied the moral judgment of the citizens of the United States. I had gone over there with, so to say, explicit instructions.

Don't you remember that we laid down fourteen points which should contain the principles of the settlement? They were not my points. In every one of them I was conscientiously trying to read the thought of the people of the United States. And, after I uttered those points, I had every assurance given me that could be given me that they did speak the moral judgment of the United States and not my single judgment. Then, when it came to that critical period just a little less than a year ago, when it was evident that the war was coming to its critical end, all the nations engaged in the war accepted those fourteen principles explicitly as the basis of the Armistice and the basis of the peace.

In those circumstances, I crossed the ocean under bond to my own people and to the other governments with which I was dealing. The whole specification of the method of settlement was written down and accepted beforehand, and we were architects building on those specifications. It reassures me and fortifies my position to find how, before I went over, men whose judgment the United States has often trusted were of exactly the same opinion that I went abroad to express. Here is something I want to read from Theodore Roosevelt:

"The one effective move for obtaining peace is by an agreement among all the great powers in which each should pledge itself not only to abide by the decisions of a common tribunal, but to back its decisions by force. The great civilized nations should combine by solemn agreement in a great world league for the peace of righteousness; a court should be established. A changed and amplified Hague Court would meet the requirements, composed of representatives from each nation, whose representatives are sworn to act as judges in each case and not in a representative capacity." Now, there is Article X. He goes on and says this: "The nations should agree on certain rights that should not be questioned, such as territorial integrity, their right to deal with their domestic affairs, and with such matters as whom they should admit to citizenship. All such guarantee each of their number in possession of these rights."

Now, the other specification is in the Covenant. The Covenant in another portion guarantees to the members the independent control of their domestic question. There is not a leg for these gentlemen to stand on when they say that the interests of the United States are not safeguarded in the very points where we are most sensitive. You do not need to be told again that the Covenant expressly says that nothing in this Covenant shall be construed as affecting the validity of the Monroe Doctrine, for example. You could not be more explicit than that.

And every point of interest is covered, partly for one very interesting reason. This is not the first time that the Foreign Relations Committee of the Senate of the United States has read and considered this Covenant. I brought it to this country in March last in a tentative, provisional form, in practically the form that it now has, with the exception of certain additions which I shall mention immediately. I asked the foreign relations committees of both houses to come to the White House, and we spent a long evening in the frankest discussion of every portion that they wished to discuss. They made certain specific suggestions as to what should be contained in this document when it was to be revised. I carried those suggestions to Paris, and every one of them was adopted.

What more could I have done? What more could have been obtained? The very matters upon which these gentlemen were most concerned were the right of withdrawal, which is now expressly stated; the safeguarding of the Monroe Doctrine, which is now accomplished; the exclusion from action by the League of domestic questions, which is now accomplished. All along the line, every suggestion of the United States was adopted after the Covenant had been drawn up in its first form and had been published for the criticism of the world. There is a very true sense in which I can say this is a tested American document.

I am dwelling upon these points, my fellow citizens, in spite of the fact that I dare say to most of you they are perfectly well known, because, in order to meet the present situation, we have got to know what we are dealing with. We are not dealing with the kind of document which this is represented by some gentlemen to be. And, inasmuch as we are dealing with a document simon-pure in respect of the very principles we have professed and lived up to, we have got to do one or other of two things—we have got to adopt it or reject it. There is no middle course. You cannot go in on a special-privilege basis of your own. I take it that you are too proud to ask to be exempted from responsibilities which the other members of the League will carry. We go in upon equal terms or we do not go in at all. And if we do not go in, my fellow citizens, think of the tragedy of that result—the only sufficient guarantee of the peace of the world withheld! Ourselves drawn apart with that dangerous pride, which means that we shall be ready to take care of ourselves. And that means that we shall maintain great standing armies and an irresistible navy; that means we shall have the organization of a military nation; that means we shall have a general staff, with the kind of power that the General Staff of Germany had, to mobilize this great manhood of the nation when it pleases, all the energy of our young men drawn into the thought and preparation for war.

What of our pledges to the men that lie dead in France? We said that they went over there, not to prove the prowess of America or her readiness for another war, but to see to it that there never was such a war again.

It always seems to make it difficult for me to say anything, my fellow citizens, when I think of my clients in this case. My clients are the children; my clients are the next generation. They do not know what promises and bonds I undertook when I ordered the armies of the United States to the soil of France, but I know. And I intend to redeem my pledges to the children; they shall not be sent upon a similar errand.

Again and again, my fellow citizens, mothers who lost their sons in France have come to me and, taking my hand, have shed tears upon it, not only that, but they have added, "God bless you, Mr. President!" Why, my fellow citizens, should they pray God to bless me? I advised the Congress of the United States to create the situation that led to the death of their sons. I ordered their sons overseas. I consented to their sons being put in the most difficult parts of the battle line, where death was certain, as in the impenetrable difficulties of the forest of Argonne.

Why should they weep upon my hand and call down the blessings of God upon me? Because they believe that their boys died for something that vastly transcends any of the immediate and palpable objects of the war. They believe, and they rightly believe, that their sons saved the liberty of the world. They believe that, wrapped up with the liberty of the world, is the continuous protection of that liberty by the concerted powers of all civilized people. They believe that this sacrifice was made in order that other sons should not be called upon for a similar gift—the gift of life, the gift of all that died.

And, if we did not see this thing through, if we fulfilled the dearest present wish of Germany and now dissociated ourselves from those alongside whom we fought in the war, would not something of the halo go away from the gun over the mantelpiece, or the sword? Would not the old uniform lose something of its significance? These men were crusaders. They were not going forth to prove the might of the United States. They were going forth to prove the might of justice and right. And all the world accepted them as crusaders, and their transcendent achievement has made all the world believe in America as it believes in no other nation organized in the modern world. There seems to me to stand between us and the rejection or qualification of this treaty the serried ranks of those boys in khaki—not only those boys who came home, but those dear ghosts that still deploy upon the fields of France.

My friends, on last Decoration Day, I went to a beautiful hillside near Paris, where was located the cemetery of Suresnes, a cemetery given over to the burial of the American dead. Behind me on the slopes was rank upon rank of living American soldiers. And, lying before me upon the levels of the plain, was rank upon rank of departed American soldiers. Right by the side of the stand where I spoke, there was a little group of

French women who had adopted these boys—they were mothers to these dear boys—putting flowers every day upon those graves, taking them as their own sons, their own beloved, because they had died to save France. France was free, and the world was free because America had come! I wish that some men in public life who are now opposing the settlement for which these men died could visit such a spot as that. I wish that that feeling which came to me could penetrate their hearts. I wish that they could feel the moral obligation that rests upon us not to go back on those boys, but to see the thing through, to see it through to the end and make good their redemption of the world. For nothing less depends upon us, nothing less than the liberation and salvation of the world.

You will say, "Is the League an absolute guarantee against war?" No, I do not know any absolute guarantee against the errors of human judgment or the violence of human passion. But I tell you this: with a cooling space of nine months for human passion, not much of it will keep hot.

I had a couple of friends who were in the habit of losing their tempers, and, when they lost their tempers, they were in the habit of using very unparliamentary language. Some of their friends induced them to make a promise that they never swear inside the town limits. When the impulse next came upon them, they took a streetcar to go out of town to swear, and by the time they got out of town, they did not want to swear. They came back convinced that they were just what they were—a couple of unspeakable fools, and the habit of losing their tempers and of swearing suffered great inroads upon it by that experience.

Now, illustrating the great by the small, that is true of the passions of nations. It is true of the passions of men, however you combine them. Give them space to cool off. I ask you this: if this is not an absolute insurance against war, do you want no insurance at all? Do you want nothing? Do you want not only no probability that war will not recur, but the probability that it will recur? The arrangements of justice do not stand of themselves, my fellow citizens. The arrangements of this treaty are just, but they need the support of the combined power of the great nations of the world. (applause) And they will have that support.

Now that the mists of this great question have cleared away, I believe that men will see the truth, eye to eye and face to face. There is one thing that the American people always rise to and extend their hand to, and that is the truth of justice and of liberty and of peace. We have accepted that truth, and we are going to be led by it, and it is going to lead us, and, through us, the world, out into pastures of quietness and peace such as the world never dreamed of before. (applause)

Oliver Wendell Holmes:
Dissenting Opinion in Abrams v. United States

In his article "Freedom of Speech in War Time," published in June 1919, Harvard Law School professor and First Amendment scholar Zechariah Chafee, Jr., criticized Justice Holmes for having done "nothing to emphasize the social interest behind free speech, and show the need of balancing even in war time" in his *Schenck* decision of three months prior. In November the Court upheld the convictions of several radicals prosecuted under the 1918 Sedition Act in *Abrams v. United States*; but this time Holmes dissented, joined by Justice Louis Brandeis, whom President Wilson had appointed in 1916.

Mr. Justice Holmes dissenting.

This indictment is founded wholly upon the publication of two leaflets which I shall describe in a moment. The first count charges a conspiracy pending the war with Germany to publish abusive language about the form of government of the United States, laying the preparation and publishing of the first leaflet as overt acts. The second count charges a conspiracy pending the war to publish language intended to bring the form of government into contempt, laying the preparation and publishing of the two leaflets as overt acts. The third count alleges a conspiracy to encourage resistance to the United States in the same war and to attempt to effectuate the purpose by publishing the same leaflets. The fourth count lays a conspiracy to incite curtailment of production of things necessary to the prosecution of the war and to attempt to accomplish it by publishing the second leaflet to which I have referred.

The first of these leaflets says that the President's cowardly silence about the intervention in Russia reveals the hypocrisy of the plutocratic gang in Washington. It intimates that "German militarism combined with allied capitalism to crush the

762

Russian revolution"—goes on that the tyrants of the world fight each other until they see a common enemy—working class enlightenment, when they combine to crush it; and that now militarism and capitalism combined, though not openly, to crush the Russian revolution. It says that there is only one enemy of the workers of the world and that is capitalism; that it is a crime for workers of America, &c., to fight the workers' republic of Russia, and ends "Awake! Awake, you Workers of the World! Revolutionists." A note adds "It is absurd to call us pro-German. We hate and despise German militarism more than do you hypocritical tyrants. We have more reasons for denouncing German militarism than has the coward of the White House."

The other leaflet, headed "Workers—Wake Up," with abusive language says that America together with the Allies will march for Russia to help the Czecho-Slovaks in their struggle against the Bolsheviki, and that this time the hypocrites shall not fool the Russian emigrants and friends of Russia in America. It tells the Russian emigrants that they now must spit in the face of the false military propaganda by which their sympathy and help to the prosecution of the war have been called forth and says that with the money they have lent or are going to lend "they will make bullets not only for the Germans but also for the Workers Soviets of Russia," and further, "Workers in the ammunition factories, you are producing bullets, bayonets, cannon, to murder not only the Germans, but also your dearest, best, who are in Russia and are fighting for freedom." It then appeals to the same Russian emigrants at some length not to consent to the "inquisitionary expedition to Russia," and says that the destruction of the Russian revolution is "the politics of the march to Russia." The leaflet winds up by saying "Workers, our reply to this barbaric intervention has to be a general strike!," and after a few words on the spirit of revolution, exhortations not to be afraid, and some usual tall talk ends "Woe unto those who will be in the way of progress. Let solidarity live! The Rebels."

No argument seems to me necessary to show that these pronunciamentos in no way attack the form of government of the United States, or that they do not support either of the first two counts. What little I have to say about the third count may be postponed until I have considered the fourth. With regard to that it seems too plain to be denied that the suggestion to workers in the ammunition factories that they are producing bullets to murder their dearest, and the further advocacy of a general strike, both in the second leaflet, do urge curtailment of production of things necessary to the prosecution of the war within the meaning of the Act of May 16, 1918, c. 75, 40 Stat. 553, amending § 3 of the earlier Act of 1917. But to make the conduct criminal that statute requires that it should be "with intent by such curtailment to cripple or hinder the United States in the prosecution of the war." It seems to me that no such intent is proved.

I am aware of course that the word intent as vaguely used in ordinary legal discussion means no more than knowledge at the time of the act that the consequences said to be intended will ensue. Even less than that will satisfy the general principle of civil and criminal liability. A man may have to pay damages, may be sent to prison, at common law might be hanged, if at the time of his act he knew facts from which common experience showed that the consequences would follow, whether he individually could foresee them or not. But, when words are used exactly, a deed is not done with intent to produce a consequence unless that consequence is the aim of the deed. It may be obvious, and obvious to the actor, that the consequence will follow, and he may be liable for it even if he regrets it, but he does not do the act with intent to produce it unless the aim to produce it is the proximate motive of the specific act, although there may be some deeper motive behind.

It seems to me that this statute must be taken to use its words in a strict and accurate sense. They would be absurd in any other. A patriot might think that we were wasting money on aeroplanes, or making more cannon of a certain kind than we needed, and might advocate curtailment with success, yet even if it turned out that the curtailment hindered and was thought by other minds to have been obviously likely to hinder the United States in the prosecution of the war, no one would hold such conduct a crime. I admit that my illustration does not answer all that might be said but it is enough to show what I think and to let me pass to a more important aspect of the case. I refer to the First Amendment to the Constitution that Congress shall make no law abridging the freedom of speech.

I never have seen any reason to doubt that the questions of law that alone were before this Court in the cases of *Schenck*, *Frohwerk* and *Debs*, 249 U. S. 47, 204, 211, were rightly decided. I do not doubt for a moment that by the same reasoning that would justify punishing persuasion to murder, the United States constitutionally may punish speech that produces or is intended to produce a clear and imminent danger that it will bring about forthwith certain substantive evils that the United States constitutionally may seek to prevent. The power undoubtedly is greater in time of war than in time of peace because war opens dangers that do not exist at other times.

But as against dangers peculiar to war, as against others, the principle of the right to free speech is always the same. It is only the present danger of immediate evil or an intent to bring it about that warrants Congress in setting a limit to the expression of opinion where private rights are not concerned. Congress certainly cannot forbid all effort to change the mind of the country. Now nobody can suppose that the surreptitious publishing of a silly leaflet by an unknown man, without more, would present any immediate danger that its opinions would hinder the success of the government arms or have any appreciable tendency to do so. Publishing those opinions for the very purpose of obstructing however, might indicate a greater danger and at any rate would have the quality of an attempt. So I assume that the second leaflet if published for the purposes alleged in the fourth count might be punishable. But it seems pretty clear to me that nothing less than that would bring these papers within the scope of this law. An actual intent in the sense that I have explained is necessary to constitute an attempt, where a further act of the same individual is required to complete the substantive crime, for reasons given in *Swift & Co.* v. *United States*, 196 U. S. 375, 396. It is necessary where the success of the attempt depends upon others because if that intent is not present the actor's aim may be accomplished without bringing about the evils sought to be checked. An intent to prevent interference with the revolution in Russia might have been satisfied without any hindrance to carrying on the war in which we were engaged.

I do not see how anyone can find the intent required by the statute in any of the defendants' words. The second leaflet is the only one that affords even a foundation for the charge, and there, without invoking the hatred of German militarism expressed in the former one, it is evident from the beginning to the end that the only object of the paper is to help Russia and stop American intervention there against the popular government —not to impede the United States in the war that it was carrying on. To say that two phrases taken literally might import a suggestion of conduct that would have interference with the war as an indirect and probably undesired effect seems to me by no means enough to show an attempt to produce that effect.

I return for a moment to the third count. That charges an intent to provoke resistance to the United States in its war with Germany. Taking the clause in the statute that deals with that in connection with the other elaborate provisions of the act, I think that resistance to the United States means some forcible act of opposition to some proceeding of the United States in pursuance of the war. I think the intent must be the specific intent that I have described and for the reasons that I have given I think that no such intent was proved or existed in fact. I also think that there is no hint at resistance to the United States as I construe the phrase.

In this case sentences of twenty years imprisonment have been imposed for the publishing of two leaflets that I believe the defendants had as much right to publish as the Government has to publish the Constitution of the United States now vainly invoked by them. Even if I am technically wrong and enough can be squeezed from these poor and puny anonymities to turn the color of legal litmus paper; I will add, even if what I think the necessary intent were shown; the most nominal punishment seems to me all that possibly could be inflicted, unless the defendants are to be made to suffer not for what the indictment alleges but for the creed that they avow—a creed that I believe to be the creed of ignorance and immaturity when honestly held, as I see no reason to doubt that it was held here, but which, although made the subject of examination at the trial, no one has a right even to consider in dealing with the charges before the Court.

Persecution for the expression of opinions seems to me perfectly logical. If you have no doubt of your premises or your power and want a certain result with all your heart you naturally express your wishes in law and sweep away all opposition. To allow opposition by speech seems to indicate that you think the speech impotent, as when a man says that he has squared the circle, or that you do not care whole-heartedly for the result, or that you doubt either your power or your premises. But when men have realized that time has upset many fighting faiths, they may come to believe even more than they believe the very foundations of their own conduct that the ultimate good desired is better reached by free trade in ideas— that the best test of truth is the power of the thought to get itself accepted in the competition of the market, and that truth is the only ground upon which their wishes safely can be carried out. That at any rate is the theory of our Constitution. It is an experiment, as all life is an experiment. Every year if not every day we have to wager our salvation upon some prophecy based upon imperfect knowledge. While that experiment is part of our system I think that we should be eternally vigilant against attempts to check the expression of opinions that we loathe and believe to be fraught with death, unless they so imminently threaten immediate interference with the lawful and pressing purposes of the law that an immediate check is required to save the country. I wholly disagree with the argument of the Government that the First Amendment left the common law as to seditious libel in force. History seems to me against the notion. I had conceived that the United States through many years had shown its repentance for the Sedition Act of 1798, by repaying fines that it imposed. Only the emergency that makes it immediately dangerous to leave the correction of evil counsels to time warrants making any exception to the sweeping command, "Congress shall make no law . . . abridging the freedom of speech." Of course I am speaking only of expressions of opinion and exhortations, which were all that were uttered here, but I regret that I cannot put into more impressive words my belief that in their conviction upon this indictment the defendants were deprived of their rights under the Constitution of the United States.

Mr. Justice Brandeis concurs with the foregoing opinion.

November 10, 1919

William N. Vaile:
Before the Buford Sailed

In March 1919 former Pennsylvania congressman A. Mitchell Palmer succeeded Thomas Gregory as attorney general. Three months later an anarchist bombed his house, converting him overnight into an obsessive defender of national security and an enemy of lawlessness and Bolshevism. J. Edgar Hoover, the twenty-four-year-old assistant to the attorney general, who headed the Justice Department's General Intelligence Division, would assist him in his mission. Palmer and Hoover launched a series of raids on suspected subversives and arranged for the deportation of the foreign-born among them. Their efforts led to the departure of the "Soviet Ark" from New York harbor in December 1919, carrying Emma Goldman and her longtime companion, Alexander Berkman, into Russian exile. William N. Vaile, a Republican congressman from Colorado, described the scene.

The following description of the actual deportation of 246 alien undesirables, headed by Alexander Berkman and Emma Goldman, is from the Congressional Record, but was not delivered as a speech in the House.

By WILLIAM N. VAILE,
Representative from Colorado.

As there were no newspaper men present, this story of the deportation of these people for their beloved Soviet Russia may possess some historical interest as the version of an eye-witness of that departure.

The night was clear and starry and rather cold, though the air did not have a real cutting edge and there was no wind to sharpen it.

At midnight at the Barge Office there were a good many people, mostly men. Mr. Hoover, that slender bundle of high-charged electric wire, the prosecutor of the Department of Justice, told us that these were mostly agents of his department, brought here for this particular job. There were perhaps thirty of them at the Barge Office waiting for the boat that was to take them on the first stage, the eighteen-minute stage, of their eighteen-day journey across the Atlantic and through the Baltic. The others were people who worked and lived at Ellis Island, who had been spending the evening in town, and were availing themselves of the unusual opportunity of a late boat back.

That boat shortly drew up at the pier and was seen to be transformed by the snow and frost from the dingy, grimy, little tug of a month ago into a beautiful dream boat. Viewed thus, she might have represented, according to the mood or the age of the observer, a fairy ship from a child's picture book or the frosted cake of a bride's confection. To me she seemed more emblematic of the cold, sharp cleanliness of the undertaking on which we were engaged, and suggested the spotless apron of the surgeon.

A keen-eyed special agent of the Department of Justice and an immigration inspector looked sharply at each of us as we boarded. There were to be "none but Americans on guard" this night.

Just as the boat had suggested the surgeon's apron, so Ellis Island, white in the moonlight with her light covering of fresh snow, suggested the operating table. A little later we inspected the cancerous growth about to be cut out of the American body politic.

Two hundred and forty-six anarchists were gathered in the great wardroom. Alexander Berkman, the obvious leader, dressed as for a sporting trip, in soldier's puttees, a soldier's khaki flannel shirt, a flowing cravat, and a pair of gray breeches of military cut, was writing letters and conferring with his three principal associates—Peter Blanky, President of the Russian Workers' Union, who had attempted to blow up Ohio factories, and Oredowsky and Schnebel, lately officers of the Seattle I. W. W. These were organizers and promoters of the general strike, described by I. W. W. literature as "a social revolution of the world; an entire new organization; a demolition of the entire old system of all governments."

Faces Stupid and Brutal.

Most of the 246 seemed to me to have rather stupid faces. I tried to make allowance for the fact that the hour was long after midnight, that the men were tired and naturally anxious and worried; that they were seen under such circumstances as to create the least favorable impression in the beholder. And yet, with the exception of the leaders mentioned and a very few others, the faces did not look to me like those of intellectual men, but like those of degraded and brutalized men.

One exception was a lean-faced, rather crafty faced, young Jew, who told me he had not had a chance to get cashed his last pay check from the silk mills, and that consequently he had been unable to buy tobacco. I gave him a package of cigarettes, for which he very courteously thanked me. This man said that he had a mother and sisters here and that as he had lived in this country for nearly twenty years and had come here in his teens, he did not know any one in Russia, nor had he, as far as he knew, any relatives there. He did not contend that his mother and sister needed his support. I asked him if he had not considered deportation as among the probable consequences of his conduct before he was arrested. He contended very bitterly that he had done nothing which would justify deportation from a "free country." He believed in "free speech" and "free press," and capitalism had suppressed them. The Government was merely run in the interests of capitalism and should be abolished, by force if necessary.

I might refer here to a popular misunderstanding of the deportation law. Deportation is not a punishment for crime, though certain kinds of criminal aliens may be deported following conviction. Deportation is merely the act of ridding ourselves of foreigners who are not eligible for residence here under our laws and who would be excluded if they were subject to, and were known to be subject to, the disqualifications of the law when they first sought admission. It must, I think, be conceded that a nation has the right to refuse its privileges and protection to any class of aliens whom it may consider undesirable residents. For this reason we refuse admission to certain classes who are not criminals but who are deemed detrimental to us for economic or social reasons, as, for instance, illiterates, persons suffering from certain diseases, persons likely to become a public charge, and Chinese.

Now, if you are an American citizen, you cannot be deprived of the right of residence in the United States, even though you may be illiterate or a public charge. We have many—too many—of both classes, but deportation is not the way in which the country deals with Americans who fall in these categories. And so, if you are an American, you may still advocate the overthrow of the Government by force and violence, and so long as you do not yourself commit an overt act you may do this without yourself being thrown in jail—for a short time only, because there will soon be a law to fit your case. But for reasons which have appeared sufficient to us we have exercised our national prerogative to declare that just as we will not admit aliens who are illiterate or likely to become a public charge or who are suffering from a contagious disease, so we will not admit or keep "aliens who are anarchists, aliens who believe in or advocate the overthrow by force or violence of the Government of the United States; * * * aliens who are opposed to all organized government; aliens who advocate or teach the assassination of public officials; aliens who advocate or teach the unlawful destruction of property," and so forth.

And the House of Representatives in the last few days has amended this by passing a bill prepared by our committee so as to catch aliens who "advise" or who belong to or are affiliated with or contribute money to any organization which advises, advocates or teaches these things or which publishes or circulates literature which does so.

In other words, the alien who comes here or who stays here must do so on our terms, and it is not a question of whether he actually commits a crime. It is a question of whether he is qualified to be here under our rules. Personally, I think those rules are about the minimum that we can impose for our own protection and safety, and that they furnish no ground of complaint whatsoever to a person who comes here because he did not like the conditions in the land which produced him.

Free Anarchistic Literature!

One remarkable youth—Bukhanob, I believe his name is—was looking forward to the trip as a great lark. This lad is only 17 years old, but has been a teacher for two years in an anarchist school in New York. He said that he had started in at 10 as a Socialist, but had become an anarchist through reading anarchist literature at the New York public libraries. Investigation by reporters disclosed that there was plenty of such to be found there, "Kropotkin's Memories of a Revolutionist," for example, being kept there in nine different languages. It was difficult to get a copy of this work because all copies were generally "out." However, the young man told us that he was a nephew of Peter Blanky, so we can hardly lay all blame for his perverted education to the free public fountain of knowledge. He told us he was going to write two books, and when we asked him what he was going to say in the second one he replied: "All that I didn't say in the first."

And there were quite a number of others who were not stupid—one a young giant with flaming red hair. He got another package of cigarettes from me. I had a dozen packs in my pocket. I feel a smoker's sympathy for another smoker who may be without tobacco and had intended to distribute these small offerings of good will to individuals. I had come to the island with a firm determination to be charitable and to distinguish between the individual and his views. I found it impossible to do so. As I listened to the conversation of these men and noticed their bitter sneers I became filled with loathing for them and decided that the rest of my tobacco should go to Americans.

All together, try as I might in the interest of fairness, to avoid first-hand impressions, these men seemed, on the average, though with the exceptions noted, to be a very poor lot, both as to physique and mentality. They certainly would compare unfavorably with any equal number of American workingmen.

Berkman went out of the room once, by permission of the guards, to get a package which he had overlooked and on his return the others all arose and remained standing until he had taken his seat, a curious demonstration of the fact that even in an anarchist society there is some authority or leadership which is respected.

Of course, no such personal respect would be paid to individual representatives of the hated "capitalistic" Government of America, though some confidence seemed to be imposed in its stability, notwithstanding the necessity of its immediate overthrow. This was shown by the fact that a great many thousands of dollars of their money was in postal savings certificates. All together they had about $200,000. The major part of it was in cash. Some of it was in uncertified checks of former employers. Of course, to have had Liberty bonds would have been unspeakable, and none were discovered. In respect to this large sum of money, they enjoyed a privilege not granted to the rest of us, for no effort was made by the internal revenue office to collect the tax paid by other people on money taken out of the country.

A Fake Hunger Strike.

Some 70 of the 246 had been detained for some time at Ellis Island and had participated in a hunger strike as a protest against being allowed to see their relatives only through a screen. The screen had been erected on account of one or two attempts to pass weapons. We had seen the men during this hunger strike, and they did not seem to be suffering much, though they were accumulating plenty of venom. Blanky had told Chairman Johnson of the Immigration Committee, in my presence, that they were going to stop destroying buildings. Hereafter they were going to break heads and use the buildings. "Meaning my head, I suppose," said Chairman Johnson. "Yes," replied Blanky, "your head and other heads like it." Possibly some of them may yet reach the conclusion that even heads are worth preserving. I hope so.

As a matter of fact, however, the hunger strike was not real. It only lasted until they had consumed the supply of food which they had cached in preparation for it.

At 3:30 A.M., of the 21st of December, they were marched out of the building in single file, between two rows of guards, to the gangplank of the tug. A coast guard at the shore end of the gangplank counted them off by tens, making a little pause between each ten. A frank-faced American youth, Lieutenant Cunningham of the Thirteenth Infantry, with an automatic pistol on his hip, stood at one side of the ship end of the gangplank. Opposite him was a soldier of his company with a rifle lying in his elbow. Two other soldiers stood, rifles in hand, on the upper deck of the tug, immediately over the gangplank deck. Nothing was said during the boarding except Lieutenant Cunningham's occasional warning to "mind your head" on account of the low-hanging upper deck.

The women came separately—Emma Goldman in a gray

and black fur coat reaching below her knees, the two young women, Dora Lipkin and Ethel Bernstein, in heavy woolen coats. They were sent immediately into the kitchen of the tug, which served as their cabin for the two hours' journey out to the transport lying beyond the "Narrows" at Gravesend. A soldier stood at the door of the kitchen, but paid no particular attention to the women, who conversed freely but not eagerly with us. Miss Goldman took off her fur coat and sat with her gray sweater unbuttoned, morose and bitter, occasionally heaving a silent sigh. Dora Lipkin was sad and very quiet.

Ethel Bernstein had a single rose, which she held to her lips occasionally. It was sent to her, she said, by one of her "good friends." Miss Goldman had a few sprigs of holly, which lay beside her Corona typewriter case on the tug's kitchen table. That typewriter case was rather worn from hard usage, but I am sure that the keys are in perfect working order.

Coming and Going.

The little tug was pretty crowded, though the officers told us she had often carried as many as a hundred more than were then aboard. This necessitated some of the passengers remaining on deck for the two hours' trip down the bay, and resulted in a curious incident. Just after passing the Liberty Statue the tug met an incoming immigrant vessel. Some of the newly arriving ones were crowding to the rail of the inbound steamship, eager for the first glimpse of the promised land. They cheered us, not knowing who we were, but because we were a small boat of the new country evidently engaged on its local business, and, I believe, because the Star-Spangled Banner floating over us was just "catching the gleam of the morning's first beam."

It was a brave little cheer, just a bit quavery, a sort of timid, inquiring little cheer like the cry of children hoping for a welcome from the grownups. The answer was a throaty "Yah-ah-ah!" from our upper deck, a jeering, raucous, sarcastic, bitter yell, scalding with hatred, spite and bitter jest, long drawn out, venomous. As it died away the tug gave a couple of reassuring little friendly toots, and some one from the upper deck—I believe it was one of the Arizona Rangers of the border patrol—shouted, "Mornin', folks!"

In company with Mr. Hoover, I talked a little with Miss Goldman on the trip across the bay. This, she said, was the beginning of the end of the United States. Time was when this country had professed to welcome the downtrodden of other lands. At that time Russia was deporting men and women to Siberia for their political beliefs. Now it was reversed. A free Russia had arisen. As the old Russia had fallen, so the new United States would fall, and for the same reasons. Oh, yes; she would be back and give us another job, though it would not be an official job. Our days of official authority would be over before her return, early though that would be. Our days of official authority were numbered and the number was getting low.

Shortly thereafter we were lashed to the Buford, an old Spanish War transport, an excellent and comfortable boat, according to all who have traveled in her; and we of the Congressional party, being certain that the country will some day be flooded with horrible stories of the shocking brutalities attendant upon this forced exodus, were very particular to observe the accommodations provided for the unwilling passengers.

The women were to travel substantially first class. There was one large stateroom of four beds provided for the three of them, with a bathroom for their exclusive use. They are to eat in the same cabin as the ship's officers, though, of course, at a separate table.

The men have the same quarters as those used by our soldiers during the Spanish War. These were much more commodious than those of the transports used by our men during the recent war, and on the Buford they are certainly ample. The beds are in double tiers, three high, but the top tier of each set is reserved for baggage. There are 50 or more lavatories, and there are a number of shower baths. The beds are all provided with plenty of warm blankets and with white linen. The anarchists eat in a large dining hall at tables with clean linen, not as our soldiers did, standing, and out of their mess kits.

Our soldiers on the transport—there are fifty picked men from the 18th Infantry—told us that the anarchists' quarters were much better in every way than those which they themselves had

had in their recent trips to and from the war zone. They are, in fact, somewhat better than the quarters now used by our guards on this vessel, and the soldiers use their own blankets, without bed linen.

The New York Times, January 14, 1920

Ezra Pound:
from Hugh Selwyn Mauberley

Ezra Pound, born in Idaho but an expatriate for most of his life, lived in England throughout the war. Deeply affected by the death of sculptor Henri Gaudier-Brzeska, a friend who was killed near Arras in June 1915, he took to railing against the war and its relation to "usury." His poem *Hugh Selwyn Mauberley* gave expression to the disillusionment many experienced in the aftermath of the war.

IV.

These fought, in any case,
and some believing, pro domo, in any case . . .
Some quick to arm,
some for adventure,
some from fear of weakness,
some from fear of censure,
some for love of slaughter, in imagination,
learning later . . .

some in fear, learning love of slaughter;
Died some pro patria, non dulce non et decor" . . .

walked eye-deep in hell
believing in old men's lies, then unbelieving
came home, home to a lie,
home to many deceits,
home to old lies and new infamy;

usury age-old and age-thick
and liars in public places.

Daring as never before, wastage as never before.
Young blood and high blood,
Fair cheeks, and fine bodies;

fortitude as never before

frankness as never before,
disillusions as never told in the old days,
hysterias, trench confessions,
laughter out of dead bellies.

V.

There died a myriad,
And of the best, among them,
For an old bitch gone in the teeth,
For a botched civilization,

Charm, smiling at the good mouth,
Quick eyes gone under earth's lid,

For two gross of broken statues,
For a few thousand battered books.

From *Hugh Selwyn Mauberley* (1920)

Norman Fenton:
from Shell Shock and Its Aftermath

Psychologist Norman Fenton served in the army medical corps at Base Hospital 117, an American facility established in 1918 in the foothills of the Vosges to treat soldiers suffering from "war neuroses" —mostly cases that would later be labeled "post-traumatic stress disorder." In 1919–20 and 1924–25, Fenton performed follow-up studies to see how former Base Hospital 117 patients had adjusted to the postwar world.

EXPLANATION OF THE CATEGORIES FOR
PRESENT CONDITION OF THE WAR NEUROTIC GROUP:

1. "Normal:" Back on the Job.—The first category to be used in discussing these cases is "Normal." Under this come those men who upon return home went back to work and readjusted themselves to civilian life and have been able to support themselves and their families. Many of them note certain novel tendencies in themselves, such as tendencies to become angry or excited easily, some little nervousness, restlessness, forgetfulness, and occasional slight headaches or dizziness (seldom sufficient to incapacitate them from work) and other like mild neurotic symptoms. A typical answer from this type of man was the following one: "Health excellent with the exception that loud noises, such as a band, a blast, a factory whistle, a passing train, and particularly a thunderstorm, will set my nerves aquiver for periods ranging from five minutes to three hours. Am trying to gradually get control of myself and I think I will." Another wrote: "Any excitement or anything which causes anger leaves me kind of weak. Outside of that I do not notice anything wrong with me." Somewhat in the same vein was this note: "I have not as much patience as I originally had and am inclined to be snappish and say something quick that I regret a week afterwards." Yet the general health of these men is good; they are able to be self-supporting and are normally happy.

2. "Neurotic:" Work Full-time but Nervous.—The second group called "neurotic," consists of those who made practical readjustments to their old way of living, yet continued to suffer from one or more rather severe nervous difficulties. Most of these men were under a physician's care, or else had at least consulted one about their condition. They were able to work fairly well, but their own personal lives were unhappy because of these neurotic troubles. Some of these men were assigned to lighter and easier work in their old places and were very sensitive about their lowered status. One finds among them the residue of symptoms shown in France—occasionally fine tremors and tics, more often speech defects, weakness, insomnia, jumpiness, distressing inability to concentrate, memory disorders, and "spells" of all sorts. One case, that of a man with combined concussion and gas neurosis, working as an express helper, fainted away in a railroad station when a nearby locomotive puffed suddenly. The following are sentences taken at random from the replies of this group: "I make mistakes I ordinarily would not make." "Sometimes I find myself between here and France." "It looks to me as if I had lost some of my sense." One man who was formerly a chauffeur returned to his old position and now finds that when he gets into a crowded part of the city where there are many other vehicles about he loses his head—so far he has had two accidents, fortunately not serious ones. Another patient returned to his old work as printer. Several dizzy spells at this work interfered with the quality of his product; the last spell led to a serious injury to one of his fingers.[1] A great many minor injuries are reported by men in this group as the result of their nervous condition, and several serious accidents. This group tended also to lose considerable in weight upon working hard, especially during the summer. In all men who carried over symptoms to civilian life there was a marked reaction to changes of weather, especially damp weather, which called out moods and depression, seriously handicapping them. In this "neurotic" group there were many men who upon return home tried their former work in machine shops or factories but could not control themselves and became nervous and tired. As

[1] This man was referred to Federal Board for Vocational Education and given a course in salesmanship.

one man put it: "I used to work a pneumatic drill but I cannot any longer; the constancy of action is so much like a machine-gun. I tried my best but could not stick it out. I had a semi-breakdown." In the cases of some of the men when gas or ideas of gas were involved, indoor work was difficult. Many of these men, especially during the warm summer months, took positions as salesmen, farmers, sailors, laborers—any position which would give them outdoor work. This change in many cases was the basis of cure, for some later wrote that their new work agreed with them and they were gradually getting back to themselves. With difficulty in standing indoor work came the same inability to remain in noisy places, especially machine shops or factories. Also some men who were in school or college reported that they found it very difficult to concentrate upon their work and that their memories were bad.

3. *"Fatigued:" Work about Half-time.*—Third comes the group called "fatigued." Most of these men cannot work regularly without suffering and being confined to bed. The symptoms here are ready fatiguability, severe headaches, lack of ambition and depression (general neurasthenic coloring.) Whereas the "neurotic group" are able to work, though with much discomfort, this group can only work on the average above one-half of the time. Some of them are fortunate in having easy jobs or considerate employers and so manage to support themselves after a fashion. In some cases where the men are married, their wives are also working to meet the expenses of living.

4. *"Disabled:" No Work.*—The fourth group consists of those at this time actually rehospitalized for psychoneurosis or reporting a "nervous breakdown" or some incapacitating medical disease, such as tuberculosis. One would anticipate many physical disorders occurring as an aftermath of the conditions to which the men were exposed in France, and indeed, many of the men have had some difficulty or other as a result of these experiences. There may also be some men in the "fatigued" group outlined above who have disabilities of an organic nature. A study like the one reported here made by correspondence naturally cannot make adequate clinical differentiations. Intensive neurological and physical examinations of these cases would unquestionably bring to light many interesting clinical facts.

The question might be raised—why include organic conditions in a discussion of neurosis aftermath? It is not suggested, of course, that the tuberculosis or heart trouble is a direct outworking of neurosis; yet it is to the point in considering the relationship of organic conditions to neurosis to recall that an "anxiety" case at the hospital was greatly improved when a tapeworm was removed, and that a splendid young officer with a supposedly hysterical condition diagnosed as astasia-abasia in France turned out to have a spinal cord lesion. Likewise another unfortunate man (never a patient at Base Hospital 117), whose life has been ruined by inadequacy of diagnosis, and who was paraded around at clinics as an interesting example of hysterical gait, proved to have a displaced hip-bone. Southard[2] well makes the point "What needs emphasis is that just because we have concluded that the statistical majority of the cases of the so-called Shell Shock belongs in the division of the neuroses, we should *not feel too cock-sure* that a given case of alleged *Shell Shock appearing* in the war zone or behind it is *necessarily* a case of *neurosis*."

Likewise, it should be noted that a corollary fact makes this inclusion advisable. Because one of the former patients of Base Hospital 117, who was discharged as a psychoneurotic, is now said to have tuberculosis (only 4 of the cases reached in 1919–20 were so defined and 6 in 1924–25) does not necessarily mean that the neurotic factors are no longer prominent. Quite on the contrary, the principal disabling factor may indeed still be the neurotic rather than the tuberculous elements. In fact, one expert of the Veteran's Bureau who has had considerable experience with this type of patient has stated that: "The tuberculosis patient on discharge from hospital is almost without exception a mental case because of worry over his condition . . . At least four months of training passes before this condition is overcome."[3] If this is true of the ordinary case, how much more significant in the case of the practiced neurotic. Southard[4] has defined another aspect

[2] Shattuck Lecture, 1918, p. 55.
[3] Report U. S. Veterans' Bureau, Washington, U. S. Govt. Printing Office, 1923, p. 934.
[4] Shell Shock, W. M. Leonard, Boston, 1919, p. 873, and elsewhere in the book.

of this problem under the concept of "periorganic" symptoms. A slight wound, not serious in itself, may serve as the focus about which are grouped seriously disabling conditions, for instance, paralysis, contracture, etc. There are so few patients (one per cent) who have reported themselves as disabled from organic disease that their inclusion will be permissible since we have no definite assurance of the insignificance or nonactivity of neurotic factors even in those cases.

5. "Psychotics."—Fifth is the psychotic group, including such conditions as dementia precox, psychopathic personality, epilepsy, etc. An interesting commentary of theoretic interest is the infrequency of psychotic outworkings among the former patients of Base Hospital 117 as a group. In the 1919–20 study, only one suicide was reported—this a man of poor stock and make-up, never at the front, who entered the hospital after the Armistice and was evacuated with the diagnosis neurasthenia. Otherwise there were relatively few men (ten, or about 1 per cent) whose condition had changed by 1920 from the psychoneurosis diagnosed at the hospital to a psychosis. By 1925 there were four deaths reported as suicides. Twelve others were definitely psychotic, another fourteen were returned as either "in hospital; parents uncertain of address" or "lost" with a fugue or psychopathic coloring attaching to their disappearance. For instance, one boy enlisted in the navy under his brother's name causing the family considerable trouble when he later deserted. The outside total of possible psychotics was 28 cases, diagnosed psychoneurotic in France or 3.4 per cent of the group. This is striking evidence favoring the psychological conception of war neurosis, for the mere possibility of insanity developing in 830 men over a period of seven years would probably not be less than this total.[5]

From *Shell Shock and Its Aftermath* (1926)

[5] "Few physicians are aware that one person in ten in this state (New York) who reaches adult life is admitted to a mental hospital before he dies, or that the number of beds in public hospitals for the insane in this country equals those occupied by all other sick persons combined." Salmon, T. W.: Mind and Medicine, New York, Columbia Univ. Press, 1924, pp. 4–5. The Mental Hygiene Bulletin, January, 1926, p. 4, gives the probability of insane hospital admission for school and college students as "about 4 per cent" "at some period in their lives."

Frederick Palmer:
from The Folly of Nations

War correspondent Frederick Palmer had covered the Greco-Turkish War of 1897, the Boxer Rebellion, the Boer War, the Russo-Japanese War, the Balkan War in 1912, and the American occupation of Veracruz in 1914. Three years later he accepted a request from General Pershing to serve as a press censor for the AEF. Writing after the war, he recalled a revealing incident from November 1917.

WE MUST WIN the war; and war requires deception of self and others. My atomic self was in the vise with the millions of other atoms. I was held to my part by my own illusion as others were held to their parts by their illusions. My illusion was that we were fighting a war to end war; that we were fighting for a new world. Others might smile at my illusion as I smiled at theirs. They might see me as a self-deceived pawn just as I saw them as self-deceived pawns.

Though the dream which I nursed does not come true, it justified for me as their illusions justified for others the means to the end; it gave me heart for my task in the period when I served as censor after I was commissioned in our army. Each of us must make that sacrifice which would be the fullest contribution in his power to the cause. I was to stand between the allied publics and that little band of pioneers under Pershing in the troublous days of 1917 when it was thought that a confession of our weakness would be fatal. The atom was offering his all as a stop-gap. If my inclination ran toward cynicism I should have material for irony without end at my command.

I had ceased to be a writer. I was in uniform. I was no longer a spectator on the "outside," but on the "inside" of things. All the allied suspicions and jealousies came naked to the censor's office to be clothed into brotherly love to walk abroad. There, in obedience to regulations, one must suffer agony as he strangled the truth and squirm with nausea as he allowed propaganda to pass. One must keep up all the illusions that made men fight; stifle all the information which would interfere with the illusions.

Enlightening and enjoyable discrimination about the qualities of an Englishman, a Frenchman, an Italian, or an American as a human being and a unit of a great race ceased. Publicly, an ally had no faults. All his soldiers were undaunted warriors of spotless character and all his women saintly and beautiful; but the enemy's soldiers were all barbarous fiends and his women slatternly and unmoral. There was inter-allied lying as well as anti-enemy lying. Lying became a fine art. Their natural fitness for lying enabled some men to achieve honors "in organizing victory in the rear" while the one man who was not facing a lie was the Allied soldier or German soldier who fought a brave antagonist.

How the single minded forthright nobility of the fighting men and of the women who were knitting, sewing and scrubbing and urging their men on to death contrasted with the banal mouthings of the Greek Deputy type and of other types of slacking intriguers and with the petty selfishness of some leaders who saw the war as a source of glory, promotion and profit and whom the regulations of the censorship had to protect! I commend all to the censor's office who would like to taste the distilled broth of the folly of nations. It revealed humanity magnificent in sacrifice and betrayed by its own emotions to self-destruction.

I should not mention the incident of the censorship service if it had not been for the first prisoner taken by the Americans, a German boy of nineteen who was in the Landstürm with the middle aged reservists because he was a physical defective incapable of serving with men of his years. The sector, where our pioneer division was to receive its first trench experience, was inactive and lightly held by the enemy. Our men had been drilled at a training camp for many months. One of their exercises was thrusting the bayonet into a stuffed bag which was supposed to be a German. The thing was to thrust promptly and thrust hard; you must overcome all your natural and civilized feeling against killing your own kind. You must want to kill that imaginary German and kill him instantly. He was pictured as a diabolically savage trickster who gave no quarter. The vise of war required that you must be as ferocious as he was. If you did not kill him he would kill you. So, kill him! Thrust in hate, thrust in joy, thrust in vengeance, thrust for your comrades' and civilization's sake!

That boy of nineteen was a mail carrier who lost his way in his lines and wandered behind our lines in the dark. His illusion was that, though a weakling among his fellows, he might still be of some use in saving German "kultur" from us barbarians. When two of our soldiers saw him, both fired at him. One bullet passed through his forearm making a painful wound. He fell with an outcry.

Here was a real German. All the drills in thrusting at the stuffed bag called for a thrust at him; and a stab in his abdomen after he had yielded himself was the eventual cause of his death. There was no second stab because instinctive human mercy, due to generations of training in peace time, checked the killing instinct that had been developed at the training camp. Other soldiers came up and began cutting buttons off the uniform of the bleeding captive for souvenirs. Then officers and the fully recovered sense of decency, bred in peace, intervened, and the boy was treated with the utmost kindness and gentleness. Free the two soldiers and the German of their illusions and they might be friendly neighbors. The two were no more brutal by nature than other men, perhaps much less brutal than the average man. We say that wars must come because we cannot change human nature when we have to brutalize modern human nature back to primitive savagery in order that we shall have sufficient brutality to be efficient soldiers.

The taking of our first prisoner was an important bit of news. Our correspondents wanted to describe the event in detail. Ethically, right was on their side. The value of a free press is in holding up the mirror to our excesses of passion as well as our better moments. My own feeling was to allow the "story" to go in full; but I had to consider the "nice discrimination" in profit and loss on the ledger of slaughter!

What more telling propagandic item could the German desire for inspiriting their own men to fight to the death than a copied account from an American newspaper showing how the wild western savages had bayoneted a weakling youth of the Landstürm and then submitted him to gross indignities in defiance of the canons of civilized warfare while America was boasting that she was fighting to save civilization! So I elided the apparent features of the correspondents' accounts. And what right had I to say what should be published? What right was there in any form of censorship?

A few days later the Germans made a night raid upon our trenches under cover of a box barrage. After it was over the correspondents were told that the Germans had wantonly cut the throats of our men who had already expired. Experience warned me that the Germans were too hurried on such occasions to pause to mutilate dead men in the dark in a dug-out even though it suited their inclinations. At close quarters the trench knife was a supple weapon and the rifle a clumsy one. Slashing the carotid artery or jugular vein which causes instant death, was no more barbarous to my mind than eviscerating a man by the burst of a high explosive shell or making him cough to death from poison gas. I called up the divisional operations officer who confirmed my hypothesis from personal observation with an emphasis reflecting not only his professional fondness for accuracy but his sense of professional chivalry. So I did not permit the reports to say that the Germans had mutilated our dead when official eye witnesses said that they had received no other wounds except those inflicted by the knife.

At the time that I made this decision I had on my desk a memorandum by a high staff officer in which he said that "Hate was a most important factor in promoting morale." Personally, he enormously admired the Germans. He thought that they had "the greatest army in all history." I think he even admired them for their "hymn of hate." From his point of view I was soft-minded and culpable, especially as at that time the United States had more than two million men in training in our camps. I had prevented their reading a piece of news which would "blood" them against the enemy and make their thrusts against the dummy bag more savage. It had seemed to me that if we were really making an idealistic war to end war the inculcation of hate to fester in the minds of future generations was a poor way of attaining our object.

What mattered my compunctions? What mattered one lie more or less when all our lies were a means to a noble end? I

had allowed my personal illusion to influence me in performing my official duty which was to encourage the war spirit in
every one else through strengthening the illusion which most
appealed to him.

The thing was to teach the public to rejoice in the brutality
of our own soldiers, applaud them for not taking prisoners and
incite them to all the bad practices which we hailed as atrocious
in the enemy and as justifying our own excesses. We brutalized
the public at the same time that we brutalized our soldiers,
while we protested that we were not making war on the German people whom we would deliver from bondage into better
ways. If the Germans exhibited chivalry or kindness, if we
found their doctors in German thoroughness of detail gently
caring for our wounded when a counter charge swept over lost
ground, these facts must be censored out lest they weaken the
war lust necessary to keep our determination steeled to our
task. Logically, we should have rejoiced over these individual
exceptions to German depravity as encouraging the Germans
to mend their ways and as proof of our faith in a new Germany
once her people were freed from the blight of Kaiserism.

The German censors were taking the same attitude on their
side of the line as we on ours. They were dealing in the brutality of a blockade that was starving their babies as an incentive
for their soldiers to fight to the death; not in the brutality of
submarines stabbing passenger or hospital ships or planes
bombing women and children in Paris and London.

"What a lot you will have to tell when the war is over!"
friends used to say when I was in the censorship. They made
the same remark after the excruciating misery of the assignment was over and I was back at the front and still "on the inside of things."

From *The Folly of Nations* (1921)

Ludwig Lewisohn: Myth and Blood

Born in Berlin and raised in South Carolina, Ludwig Lewisohn spent the war teaching German at Ohio State University, which he calls "Central City" in his memoir *Up Stream*. Looking back, he recalls the pervasive anti-German sentiment during the war and the effect those years had on intellectual freedom.

I

IN AUGUST the grass on the campus looked singed, the trees and bushes stale. In the halls the graduate students, registered for summer school, raised a clatter that was somehow drained of energy. They went through all the motions of intense life, but the inner principle was lacking. White skirts, filmy bodices, filmier stockings. Firm bodies that throbbed. But the outer mind, carefully trained in the mimicry of self-preservation, pursued points of pedagogical technique with a bitter eagerness. A few were old and quiet. There was also one small, consumptive-looking Chinaman with a cold, remorseless appetite for knowledge. He seemed to gnaw at my brain. The dusty class-rooms pulsed with the hot air and the bodies of the young women. "When one is young"—I was discussing Schnitzler in my seminar that summer of 1914—"life is full of windows and beyond every window the world begins." That saying seemed a ferocious irony in Central City. We moved in a cruel hush behind black bars. Our windows were all prison windows.

There were no signs in the heavens. There never are. Only I remember one dry, blazing noon looking intently at the stripped and wilted lilac bushes and saying to myself: "Little Servia." It must have been July. In August it would have been: "Little Belgium." Those phrases are cheap and ugly and tattered to-day. They are like the styles of a decade ago. No one is saying: "Little Hayti." They are out of fashion but lacking in the dignity of age; they are ugly without quaintness, like shoulder-of-mutton sleeves.

Some day they will flame once more for that small community of spirits which remembers and records the vicissitudes of mankind. Then it will be written down how huge populations devoid of gallantry or mercy, aching themselves through their emissaries to dabble in the blood of any at their feet—in Amritsar or Balbriggan, Hayti or North Africa, Jewish villages in Poland or black belt towns in Georgia—took up the cry of "Hun" and poisoned the minds of young people and little children on three continents not against the fierce competitions that end in hate and blood, but against the soul of the German people. It will be written down in the history books. But to the man and woman on the street historic truth is pragmatic. Truth is what prevails. That is one reason why I think this Christian-capitalistic civilization will be overturned. At its core festers a cancerous lie. It feeds on spiritual tissue. The superstructure will decay. . . .

I shall not fight the war over. A mind that does not see it to-day as universal guilt or else universal blundering and fatality and does not mourn over every portion of mankind with an intensity measured purely by that portion's acuteness of suffering, is beyond the reach of reason and humanity. I find a good many people admitting that now, but often with a shadow of mental reservation. Aren't we, their eyes seem to plead, a little, oh, just a little better than the Germans—just we and the British? That plea, that look, is fatal. Only by giving up self-righteousness to the last shred, only by an utter and universal brotherhood in self-abasement can anything be saved from the wreckage. For those with that look in their eyes and also to steady and keep true the drift of this story which is not only a story but a symbol I recall and record:

The German militarists commanded the fighting to be done with merciless severity.

British troops before going into action were habitually given the following instructions: "The second bayonet man kills the wounded. You cannot afford to be encumbered by wounded enemies lying about your feet. Don't be squeamish. The army provides you with a good pair of boots; you know how to use them." (Stephen Graham: A Private of the Guards.)

From 1917 on the German High Command used wildly desperate and brutal measures to win the war.

From the autumn of 1917 on, the hunger blockade, which the government of the United States called "illegal and

indefensible" in 1914, produced rachitis, a change and softening of the bony structure among the civilian population of
Germany. The chief sufferers were children under five, adoles-
cents between fourteen and eighteen and women over forty.
The little children became crippled and could not walk; the
girls and boys crumpled up in the streets; the women died.

The Germans had lost the ancient tradition of a chivalrous
respect for one's foes.

It was during their final retreat in 1918. "'I must admit that
the boche is a tenacious brute,' said a young French lieutenant
just back from the firing line. 'This Grand Division has been
smashed to pieces, yet the remnant fights just as hard. Cor-
nered rats, I suppose. Anyway, it shows that their discipline is
still strong, that men will sell their lives thus without hope!'"
(The New York Times, July 31, 1918.)

The armies of the allies went forth to defeat a menacing
militarism. They believed what they were told.

The Germans "were men fighting blindly to guard an ideal,
the Heimat, some patch of mother earth. . . . This everything that meant home to them they were told was in danger,
and this they went out to save." (Evelyn, Princess Blücher: An
English Wife in Berlin.)

Lissauer wrote a Song of Hate, Regnier wrote Serment, our
population went to a propaganda film: The Beast of Berlin.

Thackeray recalls the wars against Napoleon in his lecture on
George III. "We prided ourselves on our prejudices; we blus-
tered and bragged with absurd vainglory; we dealt to our
enemy a monstrous injustice of contempt and scorn; we fought
them with all weapons, mean as well as heroic. There was no
lie we would not believe, no charge of crime which our furious
prejudice would not credit. I thought at one time of making a
collection of the lies which the French had written against us
and we had published against them during the war: it would
be a strange memorial of popular falsehood."

A universal brotherhood of self-abasement!

II

In Central City invisible pulses began to beat all about me in
the air. I wrote: All the few hard-won virtues of the free

personality are going down to disaster. The individual was merciful; the tribe is callous. The individual was reasonable; the tribe is in the grip of dark, irrational instincts. Thus public passions, however generous their apparent origin, degenerate into wild unreason and bestiality. A public passion of religion sees miracles; a public passion of hatred sees atrocities. Both are well attested in all countries and in all ages of a religious or a war-like mood. Immemorial savage impulses which the individual dare not express are vented under the supposed righteousness of a tribal sanction and decent men become persecutors, lynchers and murderers. Such, from any civilized point of view, is the basic tragedy of war. The merging of the individual into the tribe wipes out all the difficult gains of the cultural process. It hurls us back into the red, primordial mists of hate and cruelty and self-righteousness. The imaginative vision comes to see and hear in the tense atmosphere of still peaceful cities symbolical scenes of a forgotten age—the flashing cymbals, the foaming devotees, the shrill scream of the human sacrifice in the storm-shaken grove. . . .

The great myth crystalized with a suddenness that took one's breath away. A quick, thunderous passion for a living sacrifice flared up. I am persuaded that any other object would have served equally well. Nearly all my colleagues in Central City owed the sounder part of their intellectual equipment to German sources; many had endearing memories of the German land and its people. These potent subjective realities were submerged at once. The flood, then, was one that had always been pounding in the darkness against the dykes of the mind. Historic accident or fatality made a breach. The waters swirled.

They all led—the great, decent, American middle-classes, business and professional—rigid and unnatural lives. They led and still lead unreal lives. In France, in Germany, in Italy, the same official codes and forms prevail. But there the forms are large-meshed nets; here they are cages of concrete and steel. The respectable American unless he is quite rich cannot take a moral holiday. Even when he takes it, his nature is so inhibited and corrupted by an unreal morality that his holiday becomes a debauch. He usually marries rather early and marries a woman nearly or quite his own age. Three or four children are born. When the man is forty, his wife has no freshness left. She is a little wrinkled and without emotional resilience. It is tragic for the women, more tragic than for the men. But they refuse compassion or cure by refusing to admit the reality of the tragic facts. They insist on what they call equal marriages and as they fade demand more stonily the rigidness of the home as due to their cooperation, their social worth, the sacred service of their motherhood. It is very astute of them. They deny out of existence the wildness of nature. The churches aid them. The men, who are not thinkers, are deceived into hideous repressions or ugly debauches and either become insensitive or battle with a foolish sense of sin.

It will be thought degraded to attribute the outburst of so-called patriotic passion that swept this country in any degree to the sex-repressions practised by our middle-classes. But it was not due to terror and revengefulness as in France, nor to terror and ambition as in Germany. Nor were there historic hatreds or old feuds or national memories involved. Many elements unquestionably contributed to it. But its peculiarly unmotivated ferocity, its hectic heat had in it something unmistakably religious, orgiastic and hence obscurely sexual. Upon Germany, the vicarious sacrifice, was heaped all secret horror and shame and corruption, to her were transferred all hidden sins and rebellions and perversities. The nation became a lynching party. Its mood expressed itself spontaneously through sex-symbolism. The rape of Belgium! In propaganda films and plays, the German villain was always represented as seeking the defloration of American virgins. Faith, blood, sadism—an old trinity. If this is ignoble it is because human nature is so. Or, rather, because man through a pathetic delusion insists that what in him is natural is ignoble. The fact remains. Neither proletarians nor plutocrats were as hectic, were as sick in soul with the war fever as the intelligent, moral, thoughtful bourgeoisie. The campus in Central City became like an infected place. The young students were quite cool and sane. The middle-aged professors with homely and withered wives and strong moral opinions shouted and flared up and wreaked themselves on William II—and Kant and Nietzsche and Wagner and even Eucken. When they saw me their eyes glowed strangely or turned fiercely cold. I would not join the lynching-party. I had a weakness for the lynchee. . . . I was regarded as good, loyal Southerners—guardians of Christianity, morality, democracy—regard a "nigger-lover." The parallel is exact.

III

Yet my weakness for the lynchee was wholly un-political in character. It included neither Prussian pastors nor Prussian soldiers nor Bavarian priests and ultramontanes, even as my sympathies cannot include England's Black and Tan constabulary or vulgar imperialists or the fierce parsons of our own Protestant churches. If, as I freely admitted, I did not wish to see the empire stricken and abased, it was because it happened to be the temporary vessel, however imperfect, however riddled with flaws, of a spirit of civilization which seemed to me then and seems to me now of a sovereign preciousness both in itself and also for all mankind. I can illustrate my meaning best from the present moment. The year is 1921. The reparations committee is sitting in Paris seeking to reconcile the extortion of an incalculable indemnity from the German people with a permanent crippling of that people's industries, shipping, power and wealth. The republic that signed the peace of Versailles is discredited at home and abroad; the lost provinces writhe under a tyranny compared to which the stupid Polish policy of the empire was merciful and enlightened; the cities and industrial districts of what was, seven years ago, the most orderly and the healthiest country in recorded history are gaunt with hunger and rotten with disease. In Berlin, the profiteers celebrate a witches' sabbath of wild and desperate debauchery. The bureaucratic classes who lived with dignity and security under the old order are in a state of suicidal reactionary fervor; the workers are too hungry and enfeebled to revolt. Fallen from a position of boundless power and respect and intellectual preeminence in the world, this nation is humbled as none has been in modern times. She is in the dust and every demagogue and fool the world over can void his venom on her. Old poets spoke of the terrors of the thing they called Mutability and celebrated the tragic circumstances of the fall of even the weakest and vilest princes. Who, among men, can withhold from a proud and gifted people a sombre and remorseful sympathy? And yet. . . . A strange thrill of life is running through all those stricken German lands. Matthew Arnold called that minority which reflects and transcends the passions and lives creatively the saving remnant. In Germany the saving remnant has always been large and it is large to-day. Fools and mere tribesmen crowd the cities and citadels, but each of these places can be saved not by one righteous man but by a thousand. It seems ironic enough to use the word righteous; for righteous in a rigid sense and according to standards that antedate experience is precisely what these people are not. What they have done is to rend inner veils and to substitute for the moral nominalism which is the ultimate source of the world's sickness a vision that discerns men and things and actions in their real and unique and incomparable nature. They have offered defiance to that gigantic Beast which Dante saw passing mountains, breaking through walls and weapons, polluting the whole world—that uncleanly image of Fraud whose face is the face of a just man, so mild is its aspect, but whose body is the body of a foul serpent.

> La faccia sua era faccia d'uom giusto,
> tanto benigna avea di fuor la pelle;
> e d'un serpente tutto l'altro fusto.

Life is far deeper and more intricate than most people permit themselves to know. They make it shallow and simple by formulations: a man can love but one woman; guilt must be punished; we must be unselfish. Out of these formulations and others like them they build bridges over the abyss of the soul. But the bridges are bridges of ice which only a careful chill can preserve. A day comes on which the deeps begin to glow and the bridge bursts and there is chaos. The Germans of whom I was thinking had gone on quests into those deeps. They are going on those quests now. They were careless of the character of the polity in which they lived before the war; I am not sure that they are building their new one with a very practical wisdom. But polities crumble and one form of the state succeeds another and so far man has invented none that is not irrational and tyrannical at its core. The best we can achieve is an inner freedom, moral and intellectual liberty, the power of standing above the state, face to face with essential things. It is not only the poets and the thinkers of Germany who have done that, but undistinguished and unrecorded men by the million—teachers and traders and waiters and workingmen. When they talk they talk about life, not about dead formulae, about the feelings and the thoughts that are, not about those they would have others entertain. In 1916 a very humble German said to me: "Life is curious. I was a socialist in the old country and I've got no use for the government. No, and I don't believe in conscription. So I didn't think I'd have any trouble at all. But when people talk to me about the war, they and I talk about different things altogether. They talk about militarism and Prussianism and they don't mean anything, good or bad, that really exists. They mean something they've made up out of their own minds. And when I tell them facts—mixed facts—because the world isn't a simple place, is it?—they're mad at me because I know something definite and real and they call me a damned Hun." And another very plain man who came to me said: "I'm in trouble with my boss, an American gentleman, because I had a love affair with a girl in the shop. 'But you're a married man,' he said to me. 'I know it,' I answered. 'Then what right did you have to approach this girl?' 'I don't know,' I said, 'but I've been married twenty years and my wife is a stringy woman with a bitter temper. And this girl liked me and it was spring. And I said to myself: here's this war and the world's gone cruel crazy and pretty soon we'll all be dead and rotten. There was a lilac bush in the garden and it was twilight and so I kissed her a few times. And I almost thought I was young again and back in the old country and life was just beginning and there was peace and a little hope and beauty in the world.' The boss looked at me as if I was crazy. 'I'll have no immorality around here,' he shouted. 'You're fired!' Now what sort of a man is this? He called this immorality and I heard him tell some young fellows about the immorality of going to a street full of bawdy houses. He didn't pay any attention to things, you see. He just had a word—immorality—and it made him angry at others and satisfied with himself."

A word—and it made him angry at others and satisfied with himself. . . . Poor Benecke! He could get no more work in Central City. A Hun and probably, like all Huns, immoral to boot. He drifted away. But he had given me another definition

of the evil malignity that lies at the root of moralistic general-
izations and a fresh sense of what I knew to be the saving and
triumphant virtue of the people to whom he belonged.

IV

Thus, too, to-day, poets and thinkers and publicists and
millions of men and women are striving in Germany to re-un-
derstand and re-create a world in chaos. Once more in 1921 as
in 1914 Germany leads the world in the production of books.
There is trash enough—morbid rather than empty, as among
us. But there are philosophies and visions so packed with
thought and experience that the many thousands of people
who buy and read them, as the editions show, must be admitted to possess a culture and a discipline of the mind and a
knowledge of their own souls unheard of in any other age or
land. Likewise the imaginative literature—novels and plays and
especially the books of the new lyrical movement—is drawn
from sources of perception and reflection which the average
cultured reader in other countries has not yet reached within
himself. I do not expect this thing which, for the sake of my
own mind's integrity, I must assert, to be believed. Nothing is
so deep-rooted in us as a sense of our ultimate superiority. We
may appear to yield on this point or that. At the core of the self
is a granite-hard conviction of the betterness of that self and its
friends and its group. Such is the spiritual malady of the race.
If once we could stop working with the concepts "better" and
"worse" which we identify with higher and lower and so, in a
primitive and subconscious way, with above and below in physical modes of being—master, slave, slayer, slain: if we could bring
ourselves to think in terms of fruitful co-existent qualities in
the psychical world, we would not struggle against such cogni-
tions as I am trying to convey; we would have a much larger
chance of deriving our self-respect from serenity and justice
rather than from wilful ignorance and rage.

In Central City I once spoke to a colleague, a professor of
political science, of the literature and art and thought of the
Germans and of the wide dissemination of these things among
the people and made a plea for an, at least, inquiring attitude
toward such a nation. He replied that what I told him was

doubtless true, but that it did not to his mind constitute a claim to high national culture which resided rather in political vigilance and political activity. I did not point out to him—he would have regarded it as presumptuous—the actual political supineness of Americans; their extreme suggestibility and their utter carelessness as to the quarters whence their winds of doctrine blow. I saw so clearly that he and I were shouting across a gulf. Literature and art and philosophy were to him not expressions and therefore forms of life, not the spiritual organs by which men understand and intercommunicate experience; they were to him decorative additions to life, like tin cornices on a shop front. And it would have been useless to tell him that the aesthetic and philosophical saturation of great masses of the German people had naturally led them to esteem political action lightly. For all such action implies hard limitation. To choose such action at all means a devotion to narrowly defined policies of whose insufficiency and mere opportunism the reflective mind is at once aware. Thus in every day life the unreflective man who is also the energetic one has the philosopher at his mercy. To know little is to dare easily, to have looked upon all sides of all mortal questions is to come near paralysis. Rude men in primitive communities pass judgment and execute sentences in matters that would have left Jesus dumb and Socrates puzzled. Then they ride off, these posses and lynchers, and eat their dinners in peace.

Yet the young poets in Germany who are listened to by thousands and thousands—Franz Werfel and Walter Hasenclever and many others—are crying out for more inwardness, not less, for a spiritualization and conquest and absorption into the mind of all things and all men; for a suspension of all moral judgment, all strife and for the remoulding of the world through love. They do not heed the traders and chafferers and diplomats—Stinnes no more than Morgan, Simon no more than Lloyd George. They are bent upon another business and men and women who lack bread and meat buy the books of these poets and creators of higher realities and go home and read and transcend hunger and cold, embargoes and reparations and the loss of mines. And they lift their heads from their books, these readers, and hear that Lloyd George reaffirms the single and absolute guilt of Germany in the war and for a moment they remember a world which is still ruled by such hollow and such savage fictions. But it is only for a moment. Their bluish lids are lowered. They read on. They are rebuilding the broken universe in their souls.

V

What could I do with this vision and this knowledge and this protest of mine in Central City? Men talked such arrant nonsense that I committed a hundred indiscretions, overstated and misstated the intimate truths that I possessed and even, on the great principle of John Stuart Mill that no truth, however partial, needs so sorely to be emphasized as that which a particular hour in history derides or disregards, joined certain friends and colleagues in explaining to a technically neutral country the political and military actions of the German government. I did not count the consequences nor, at bottom, greatly fear them. Others were dependent on me and I did not dare to fling away the meager sustenance which the university doled out to me. But I knew very firmly, though I did not always permit that knowledge to reach my consciousness, that life could not permanently be bounded for me by that campus and that town. If by defending my mind's integrity, a catastrophe came . . . well, I almost awaited it as one awaits rain and thunder on a day of unbearable sultriness.

When America entered the war the president of the university sent for me. A tall, thick, old man with a hoarse, monotonous voice and a large, determined, self-righteous mouth. A mouth like William Jennings Bryan's—half business man's, half fanatic's. The intellectual equipment of a Presbyterian elder in a small town; the economic views of a professional strikebreaker tempered by a willingness to be charitable to the subservient poor; the aesthetic and philosophic vision of the Saturday Evening Post. He talked to me like a war editorial in the New York Evening Telegram and tried to make that talk persuasive to me. He who believed, let us say, in the virgin birth of Christ, tried to convince me that the countrymen of Dehmel and Hauptmann and Strauss and Einstein had mediaeval minds. A perverse imp leapt up in me. I translated some observations of Goethe and Shelley and John Stuart Mill and

Whitman into his vernacular and spoke. His eyes grew a little hard and forbidding and shifted to the blotter on his desk. But he thought me more unpractical idealist—his euphemism for fool—than knave and promised, quite sincerely, that he would guard my interests unless his hand were forced. He made a virtue of this moral opportunism. Personally, he assured me, again sincerely, that he was willing to be tolerant; if the herd stampeded he would trample with the best. Such was the notion of democracy held by this essentially good and honest man.

I expected no more. But my friend, the professor of philosophy, failed me. Not personally. They were all kind enough. But intellectually. And that was worse. He who had always protested against the notion that truth could be discovered by committees now made the war-psychosis of the crowd his criterion of conduct and opinion. "How about the splendor of being in a minority, of resisting the mass, of suffering for an unpopular conviction?" I asked him. He stultified and denied himself, his intellectual past, his moral character. He thundered against the ninety-three German intellectuals who had believed what their government had told them and himself accepted as gospel the reports of the capitalistic and jingo press. The German intellectuals are dead or have recanted either explicitly in words or implicitly by supporting the revolution. My friend has not been heard from. He still teaches philosophy.

The crash came in a curious and, rightly looked upon, an amusing way. In 1916 I had published a little book on the modern movement in German literature. It was an unpolitical little book. It tried to convey a spirit, an atmosphere, a mood . . . to show that the best living writers were liberals, radicals, cultivators of a Goethean freedom. I said, among other things, that Nietzsche was indisputably one of the great masters of prose. The book fell into the hands of a real-estate broker. One must savor that fact. One must visualize the pudgy gentleman at his golden oak roll-top desk in his private office. He has been reading the editorial in his paper; he is fired to do his duty as a man and an American. There is something wonderful in the supreme innocence and directness of his mental processes. What, shall a man be supported by the people's money who glorifies that which our sons are going out to destroy at the cost of their blood? He summons his secretary who pats her sleek hair with brilliantly manicured fingers and shifts her chewing-gum to the other cheek. He dictates and a glow fills his bosom. The letter goes to the president and the deans of the university, to the governor of the state, to the trustees, to senators. The real estate broker—like Dwight Deacon in Zona Gale's excellent story—goes virtuously home and, at the head of his domestic board, impresses an admiring family with his patriotic vigor, his acumen, his importance. He looks instructively over his glasses, then for a moment glumly: "Vera, did I hear you giggle? You may leave the table. Upon my word! Well, as I was saying: these disloyalists . . . seditious talk . . . undermine morale . . . contaminate the young . . . dooty of every wide awake citizen. . . ." It goes on and on, the talk of the eternal real estate broker, it goes on in peace as well as in war: Be like me, be like me, think and feel as I do, or I will drive you out, burn you, hang, draw and quarter you and lick my lips at the trickle of your blood. . . . And I, in my own small and dusty way, was the eternal outcast, rebel, the other-thinking one—guilty before the herd, guiltless in the dwelling-places of the permanent, breaker of taboos, creator of new values, doomed to defeat on this day in this little grimy corner of the universe, invincible and inextinguishable as a type. Shall I ever conquer the real estate broker? Shall I ever absorb him into myself? And if I ever absorb him into myself shall I not be *he* again? That is the question at the core of human history. And it is fathomless.

VI

The president balked a little at the real estate broker. Not for any deep reason. Only he had a dumb feeling that the real estate broker was attacking the thing from a wrong angle and interfering with his own paternalistic and, upon the whole, humane and kindly management of faculty affairs. Yet he was gradually being saved the nuisance of a final decision. The matter was being taken out of his hands.

The campus had been turned into a training-camp and swarmed with youths in khaki. They studied, slept, ate, drilled, talked in mechanically formed groups. A slow, stinging horror seized my flesh and crept into my bones. They were being trained to kill and be killed, to mutilate and to be mutilated.

They were very cheerful. Each, at the innermost point of consciousness, carried the invincible, mystical assurance that he would come out unscathed. Each, like all of us, was unable to imagine his own death. For the universe is unimaginable to the individual without his consciousness of it: his perception of it creates and upholds it. Since he believes in its permanence, he believes, despite reason and experience, in his own. Such is the mystical and fatal delusion which, disguised under the names of patriotism, courage, sacrifice, makes conscription and modern war possible. If we could rip that delusion asunder, unswathe the consciousness of common men from these sticky layers, the enslaving state would crumble. The sight of those cheery, healthy boys turned me sick. I saw them blinded, waving bloody stumps, rotten with gangrene in trenches under fire. I rebelled against that place of irony and horror; I refused to take any precautions. A leprous sun seemed to burn over Central City. Middle-aged men and women roared and wheezed and sweated with hatred and patriotism and urged these young bodies to hasten to hurl themselves into blood and ooze and ordure.

An oily voice, a sleek, voluble voice with a hard contradictory snicker in it came to me over the telephone. My presence was required on such a day at such an hour in the office of the district attorney. The voice purred reassuringly and then repeated the order with a sudden, lustfully cruel bark.

It was the owner of that voice who received me—white-haired, ruddy, cold-eyed but with a set, wheedling smile fixed under a thick, heavy, dogged nose. He took me into the district attorney's office, a large, square, ordinary lawyer's room with shabby desks and swivel chairs and rusty calf-skin volumes with red labels. Sharp sunshine poured in through the tall windows; a pigeon sped past; a bough tapped against the stonework. The district attorney sat back in his chair, a big, dark, bald man, not fat but fleshy; cold, meanly sensual, a careless begetter of children, a good "provider," a family man, a politician, a "handshaker." . . . He shook hands with me. I looked at his enormous cheeks, his small, official eyes. A huge expanse of shirt extended from his long chin to his belt. There was something monumental about the man, but also something obscene. I felt both the impenetrability of him and the raw, voracious appetites. He was, of all things, jovial! "Well, professor, I thought we'd better have a talk." His pretense that we were good fellows together was odious. "What have you against me?" I asked. He leaned forward. "A stack of evidence this high." "Let me see the evidence and confront me with the persons who provided it." "We don't do that," he snapped. "Then how can I tell what you're talking about?" He sat back comfortably and drawled: "Didn't you say that if America entered the war. . . ." I had, as a matter of fact, said none of the things he repeated. In the privacy of my office at the university I had made remarks that malice had twisted, broadened, coarsened and then communicated to him. I at once suspected the stupid woman who had probably written him anonymous letters. I pointed out to him that the evidence was garbled, not of a character that would be admitted in any American court of law and that it referred exclusively to the period of American neutrality during which, from the narrowest and most autocratic point of view, I had been free to say what I chose. Instead of replying he suddenly sprang up and roared. "What have you ever done to show your patriotism? What have you ever done for this country?" "I have taught and written. . . ." He roared me down. "You liked to do that! What've you ever done for your country, I ask you!" The thing went on for an hour. I tried to reach his reason. He didn't want that to happen. At the end of the session he shook his head gloomily. He would see. . . .

Upon the whole he evidently thought me small game. Several influential members of the faculty wrote him in my behalf; the president sent him a message; he consented to my remaining in the service of the state. But I did not remain. The colleagues who pleaded for me did so not because they believed in freedom, but because they had a personal kindness for me and some respect for my character; the president protected me because he knew that I was poor and a good teacher and because he did not consider my wrongheadedness grave enough to warrant Mary's being exposed to material suffering. The tacit understanding was that I could buy a continued tenure of my job by silence, conformity, slavish submission. I asked for a sabbatical year that was due me and was granted the favor.

I fared very well and I am not insensitive to kindness. But

what I had hoped for came from no quarter—a recognition, however faint, of the tenableness of my intellectual position. A German colleague, an exquisitely lovable, gifted, gentle soul, was fired without mercy. He was ill in body and had a frail wife—an American woman—and three small children. A poet and a philosopher, he wandered about selling books, tortured by the dull surfaces of an unfeeling world. He finally took a small position in Mexico. There, at the age of thirty-five, he died the other day. Hardship had undermined his strength; the process begun in Central City reached a fatal conclusion. Yet the men there knew the beauty of his mind, his complete political harmlessness, the fact that he had not come to us an immigrant but had been summoned as an exchange teacher to a great American University. But they were utterly callous to his fate. They had studied and philosophized with him and broken bread with him. They cast him out to die. . . .

Why did they relent to me? Because of the native tongue in my head, the things I had written, the fact that in all fundamental senses I am an American. A blind, half-conscious feeling of solidarity with me guided them, neither the idea of justice nor that of freedom. Yet this was a university and there they taught then and there they teach now Plato and Kant, Montaigne and Voltaire, Goethe and Shelley and even Walt Whitman who "beat the gong of revolt and stopped with them that plot and conspire."

From Up Stream (1922)

Warren G. Harding: Address at the Burial of an Unknown American Soldier

Warren G. Harding's election resoundingly repudiated Woodrow Wilson's idealistic vision of the League of Nations. The United States and Germany signed a separate peace treaty in August 1921, officially concluding the state of war that had lasted four years. In his final minutes in office, Wilson had authorized the exhumation of an unidentified American soldier from a cemetery in France and his entombment in a new marble sarcophagus at the National Cemetery, where he would represent all of the soldiers whose remains could not be identified. On November 11, 1921, the third anniversary of the Armistice, a great procession accompanied the casket of the Unknown Soldier from the Capitol to Arlington. The physically disabled Wilson rode with Edith in the parade only as far as the White House before returning to their new home nearby, while the rest of the cortege proceeded to the vast graveyard across the Potomac. Thousands gathered to hear the President's speech, Marshal Foch and Medal of Honor winners among them; and hundreds of thousands more heard his message, as it was carried on telephone lines to public-address speakers in cities around the country. With these remarks, the curtain descended on the World War.

Mr. Secretary of War and Ladies and Gentlemen: We are met to-day to pay the impersonal tribute. The name of him whose body lies before us took flight with his imperishable soul. We know not whence he came, but only that his death marks him with the everlasting glory of an American dying for his country.

He might have come from any one of millions of American homes. Some mother gave him in her love and tenderness, and with him her most cherished hopes. Hundreds of mothers are wondering to-day, finding a touch of solace in the possibility that the Nation bows in grief over the body of one she bore to live and die, if need be, for the Republic. If we give rein to fancy, a score of sympathetic chords are touched, for in this body there once glowed the soul of an American, with the aspirations and ambitions of a citizen who cherished life and its opportunities. He may have been a native or an adopted son; that matters little, because they glorified the same loyalty, they sacrificed alike.

We do not know his station in life, because from every station came the patriotic response of the five millions. I recall the days of creating armies, and the departing of caravels which braved the murderous seas to reach the battle lines for maintained nationality and preserved civilization. The service flag marked mansion and cottage alike, and riches were common to all homes in the consciousness of service to country.

We do not know the eminence of his birth, but we do know the glory of his death. He died for his country, and greater devotion hath no man than this. He died unquestioning, uncomplaining, with faith in his heart and hope on his lips, that his country should triumph and its civilization survive. As a typical soldier of this representative democracy, he fought and died, believing in the indisputable justice of his country's cause. Conscious of the world's upheaval, appraising the magnitude of a war the like of which had never horrified humanity before, perhaps he believed his to be a service destined to change the tide of human affairs.

In the death gloom of gas, the bursting of shells and rain of bullets, men face more intimately the great God over all, their souls are aflame, and consciousness expands and hearts are searched. With the din of battle, the glow of conflict, and the supreme trial of courage, come involuntarily the hurried appraisal of life and the contemplation of death's great mystery. On the threshhold of eternity, many a soldier, I can well believe, wondered how his ebbing blood would color the stream of human life, flowing on after his sacrifice. His patriotism was none less if he craved more than triumph of country; rather, it was greater if he hoped for a victory for all human kind. Indeed, I revere that citizen whose confidence in the righteousness of his country inspired belief that its triumph is the victory of humanity.

This American soldier went forth to battle with no hatred for any people in the world, but hating war and hating the purpose of every war for conquest. He cherished our national rights, and abhorred the threat of armed domination; and in the maelstrom of destruction and suffering and death he fired his shot for liberation of the captive conscience of the world. In advancing toward his objective was somewhere a thought of a world awakened; and we are here to testify undying gratitude and reverence for that thought of a wider freedom.

On such an occasion as this, amid such a scene, our thoughts alternate between defenders living and defenders dead. A grateful Republic will be worthy of them both. Our part is to atone for the losses of heroic dead by making a better Republic for the living.

Sleeping in these hallowed grounds are thousands of Americans who have given their blood for the baptism of freedom and its maintenance, armed exponents of the Nation's conscience. It is better and nobler for their deeds. Burial here is rather more than a sign of the Government's favor, it is a suggestion of a tomb in the heart of the Nation, sorrowing for its noble dead.

To-day's ceremonies proclaim that the hero unknown is not unhonored. We gather him to the Nation's breast, within the shadow of the Capitol, of the towering shaft that honors Washington, the great father, and of the exquisite monument to Lincoln, the martyred savior. Here the inspirations of yesterday and the conscience of to-day forever unite to make the Republic worthy of his death for flag and country.

Ours are lofty resolutions to-day, as with tribute to the dead we consecrate ourselves to a better order for the living. With all my heart, I wish we might say to the defenders who survive, to mothers who sorrow, to widows and children who mourn, that no such sacrifice shall be asked again.

It was my fortune recently to see a demonstration of modern warfare. It is no longer a conflict in chivalry, no more a test of militant manhood. It is only cruel, deliberate, scientific destruction. There was no contending enemy, only the theoretical defense of a hypothetic objective. But the attack was made with all the relentless methods of modern destruction. There was the rain of ruin from the aircraft, the thunder of artillery, followed by the unspeakable devastation wrought by bursting shells; there were mortars belching their bombs of desolation; machine guns concentrating their leaden storms; there was the infantry, advancing, firing, and falling—like men with souls sacrificing for the decision. The flying missiles were revealed by illuminating tracers, so that we could note their flight and appraise their deadliness. The air was streaked with tiny flames marking the flight of massed destruction; while the effectiveness of the theoretical defense was impressed by the simulation of dead and wounded among those going forward, undaunted and unheeding. As this panorama of unutterable destruction visualized the horrors of modern conflict, there grew on me the sense of the failure of a civilization which can leave its problems to such cruel arbitrament. Surely no one in authority, with human attributes and a full appraisal of the patriotic loyalty of his countrymen, could ask the manhood of kingdom, empire, or republic to make such sacrifice until all reason had failed, until appeal to justice through understanding had been denied, until every effort of love and consideration for fellow men had been exhausted, until freedom itself and inviolate honor had been brutally threatened.

I speak not as a pacifist fearing war, but as one who loves justice and hates war. I speak as one who believes the highest function of government is to give its citizens the security of peace, the opportunity to achieve, and the pursuit of happiness.

The loftiest tribute we can bestow to-day—the heroically earned tribute—fashioned in deliberate conviction, out of unclouded thought, neither shadowed by remorse nor made vain by fancies, is the commitment of this Republic to an advancement never made before. If American achievement is a cherished pride at home, if our unselfishness among nations is all we wish it to be, and ours is a helpful example in the world, then let us give of our influence and strength, yea, of our aspirations and convictions, to put mankind on a little higher plane, exulting and exalting, with war's distressing and depressing tragedies barred from the stage of righteous civilization.

There have been a thousand defenses justly and patriotically made; a thousand offenses which reason and righteousness ought to have stayed. Let us beseech all men to join us in seeking the rule under which reason and righteousness shall prevail.

Standing to-day on hallowed ground, conscious that all America has halted to share in the tribute of heart and mind and soul to this fellow American, and knowing that the world is noting this expression of the Republic's mindfulness, it is fitting to say that his sacrifice, and that of the millions dead, shall not be in vain. There must be, there shall be, the commanding voice of a conscious civilization against armed warfare.

As we return this poor clay to its mother soil, garlanded by love and covered with the decorations that only nations can bestow, I can sense the prayers of our people, of all peoples, that this Armistice Day shall mark the beginning of a new and lasting era of peace on earth, good will among men. Let me join in that prayer.

Our Father who art in heaven, hallowed be Thy name. Thy kingdom come, Thy will be done on earth, as it is in heaven. Give us this day our daily bread, and forgive us our trespasses as we forgive those who trespass against us. And lead us not into temptation, but deliver us from evil, for Thine is the kingdom, and the power, and the glory, forever. Amen.

CODA

Ernest Hemingway: Soldier's Home

Nowhere were the changes in American life seen more vividly than in its fiction, not in just the substance but also in the style; and nobody epitomized that literary readjustment—with his stark staccato sentences—more than Hemingway. After recovering from his wounds in Italy, he returned home in early 1919. That summer he visited Michigan's Upper Peninsula, which, coupled with his remembrances of war, would inspire several of the works included in *In Our Time* (1925), his first collection of short stories. A job with the *Toronto Star* allowed him to return to Europe in 1921 and become part of the expatriate literary world in Paris. Over the next decade, the war permeated his writing, most especially his novel *A Farewell to Arms* (1929), which his experiences in Italy inspired.

KREBS WENT to the war from a Methodist college in Kansas. There is a picture which shows him among his fraternity brothers, all of them wearing exactly the same height and style collar. He enlisted in the Marines in 1917 and did not return to the United States until the second division returned from the Rhine in the summer of 1919.

There is a picture which shows him on the Rhine with two German girls and another corporal. Krebs and the corporal look too big for their uniforms. The German girls are not beautiful. The Rhine does not show in the picture.

By the time Krebs returned to his home town in Oklahoma the greeting of heroes was over. He came back much too late. The men from the town who had been drafted had all been welcomed elaborately on their return. There had been a great deal of hysteria. Now the reaction had set in. People seemed to think it was rather ridiculous for Krebs to be getting back so late, years after the war was over.

At first Krebs, who had been at Belleau Wood, Soissons, the Champagne, St. Mihiel and in the Argonne did not want to talk about the war at all. Later he felt the need to talk but no one wanted to hear about it. His town had heard too many atrocity stories to be thrilled by actualities. Krebs found that to be listened to at all he had to lie, and after he had done this twice he, too, had a reaction against the war and against talking about it. A distaste for everything that had happened to him in the war set in because of the lies he had told. All of the times that had been able to make him feel cool and clear inside himself when he thought of them; the times so long back when he had done the one thing, the only thing for a man to do, easily and naturally, when he might have done something else, now lost their cool, valuable quality and then were lost themselves.

His lies were quite unimportant lies and consisted in attributing to himself things other men had seen, done or heard of, and stating as facts certain apocryphal incidents familiar to all soldiers. Even his lies were not sensational at the pool room. His acquaintances, who had heard detailed accounts of German women found chained to machine guns in the Argonne forest and who could not comprehend, or were barred by their patriotism from interest in, any German machine gunners who were not chained, were not thrilled by his stories.

Krebs acquired the nausea in regard to experience that is the result of untruth or exaggeration, and when he occasionally met another man who had really been a soldier and they talked a few minutes in the dressing room at a dance he fell into the easy pose of the old soldier among other soldiers: that he had been badly, sickeningly frightened all the time. In this way he lost everything.

During this time, it was late summer, he was sleeping late in bed, getting up to walk down town to the library to get a book, eating lunch at home, reading on the front porch until he became bored and then walking down through the town to spend the hottest hours of the day in the cool dark of the pool room. He loved to play pool.

In the evening he practiced on his clarinet, strolled down town, read and went to bed. He was still a hero to his two young sisters. His mother would have given him breakfast in bed if he had wanted it. She often came in when he was in bed and asked him to tell her about the war, but her attention always wandered. His father was non-committal.

Before Krebs went away to the war he had never been allowed to drive the family motor car. His father was in the real estate business and always wanted the car to be at his command when he required it to take clients out into the country to show them a piece of farm property. The car always stood outside the First National Bank building where his father had an office on the second floor. Now, after the war, it was still the same car.

Nothing was changed in the town except that the young girls had grown up. But they lived in such a complicated world of already defined alliances and shifting feuds that Krebs did not feel the energy or the courage to break into it. He liked to look at them, though. There were so many good-looking young girls. Most of them had their hair cut short. When he went away only little girls wore their hair like that or girls that were fast. They all wore sweaters and shirt waists with round Dutch collars. It was a pattern. He liked to look at them from the front porch as they walked on the other side of the street. He liked to watch them walking under the shade of the trees. He liked the round Dutch collars above their sweaters. He liked their silk stockings and flat shoes. He liked their bobbed hair and the way they walked.

When he was in town their appeal to him was not very strong. He did not like them when he saw them in the Greek's ice cream parlor. He did not want them themselves really. They were too complicated. There was something else. Vaguely he wanted a girl but he did not want to have to work to get her. He would have liked to have a girl but he did not want to have to spend a long time getting her. He did not want to get into the intrigue and the politics. He did not want to have to do any courting. He did not want to tell any more lies. It wasn't worth it.

He did not want any consequences. He did not want any consequences ever again. He wanted to live along without consequences. Besides he did not really need a girl. The army had taught him that. It was all right to pose as though you had to have a girl. Nearly everybody did that. But it wasn't true. You did not need a girl. That was the funny thing. First a fellow boasted how girls mean nothing to him, that he never thought of them, that they could not touch him. Then a fellow boasted that he could not get along without girls, that he had to have them all the time, that he could not go to sleep without them.

That was all a lie. It was all a lie both ways. You did not need a girl unless you thought about them. He learned that in the army. Then sooner or later you always got one. When you were really ripe for a girl you always got one. You did not have to think about it. Sooner or later it would come. He had learned that in the army.

Now he would have liked a girl if she had come to him and not wanted to talk. But here at home it was all too complicated. He knew he could never get through it all again. It was not worth the trouble. That was the thing about French girls and German girls. There was not all this talking. You couldn't talk much and you did not need to talk. It was simple and you were friends. He thought about France and then he began to think about Germany. On the whole he had liked Germany better. He did not want to leave Germany. He did not want to come home. Still, he had come home. He sat on the front porch.

He liked the girls that were walking along the other side of the street. He liked the look of them much better than the French girls or the German girls. But the world they were in was not the world he was in. He would like to have one of them. But it was not worth it. They were such a nice pattern. He liked the pattern. It was exciting. But he would not go through all the talking. He did not want one badly enough. He liked to look at them all, though. It was not worth it. Not now when things were getting good again.

He sat there on the porch reading a book on the war. It was a history and he was reading about all the engagements he had been in. It was the most interesting reading he had ever done. He wished there were more maps. He looked forward with a good feeling to reading all the really good histories when they would come out with good detail maps. Now he was really learning about the war. He had been a good soldier. That made a difference.

One morning after he had been home about a month his mother came into his bedroom and sat on the bed. She smoothed her apron.

"I had a talk with your father last night, Harold," she said, "and he is willing for you to take the car out in the evenings."

"Yeah?" said Krebs, who was not fully awake. "Take the car out? Yeah?"

"Yes. Your father has felt for some time that you should be

able to take the car out in the evenings whenever you wished but we only talked it over last night."

"I'll bet you made him," Krebs said.

"No. It was your father's suggestion that we talk the matter over."

"Yeah. I'll bet you made him," Krebs sat up in bed.

"Will you come down to breakfast, Harold?" his mother said.

"As soon as I get my clothes on," Krebs said.

His mother went out of the room and he could hear her frying something downstairs while he washed, shaved and dressed to go down into the dining-room for breakfast. While he was eating breakfast his sister brought in the mail.

"Well, Hare," she said. "You old sleepyhead. What do you ever get up for?"

Krebs looked at her. He liked her. She was his best sister.

"Have you got the paper?" he asked.

She handed him the Kansas City *Star* and he shucked off its brown wrapper and opened it to the sporting page. He folded the *Star* open and propped it against the water pitcher with his cereal dish to steady it, so he could read while he ate.

"Harold," his mother stood in the kitchen doorway, "Harold, please don't muss up the paper. Your father can't read his *Star* if it's been mussed."

"I won't muss it," Krebs said.

His sister sat down at the table and watched him while he read.

"We're playing indoor over at school this afternoon," she said. "I'm going to pitch."

"Good," said Krebs. "How's the old wing?"

"I can pitch better than lots of the boys. I tell them all you taught me. The other girls aren't much good."

"Yeah?" said Krebs.

"I tell them all you're my beau. Aren't you my beau, Hare?"

"You bet."

"Couldn't your brother really be your beau just because he's your brother?"

"I don't know."

"Sure you know. Couldn't you be my beau, Hare, if I was old enough and if you wanted to?"

"Sure. You're my girl now."

"Am I really your girl?"

"Sure."

"Do you love me?"

"Uh, huh."

"Will you love me always?"

"Sure."

"Will you come over and watch me play indoor?"

"Maybe."

"Aw, Hare, you don't love me. If you loved me, you'd want to come over and watch me play indoor."

Krebs's mother came into the dining-room from the kitchen. She carried a plate with two fried eggs and some crisp bacon on it and a plate of buckwheat cakes.

"You run along, Helen," she said. "I want to talk to Harold."

She put the eggs and bacon down in front of him and brought in a jug of maple syrup for the buckwheat cakes. Then she sat down across the table from Krebs.

"I wish you'd put down the paper a minute, Harold," she said.

Krebs took down the paper and folded it.

"Have you decided what you are going to do yet, Harold?" his mother said, taking off her glasses.

"No," said Krebs.

"Don't you think it's about time?" His mother did not say this in a mean way. She seemed worried.

"I hadn't thought about it," Krebs said.

"God has some work for everyone to do," his mother said. "There can be no idle hands in His Kingdom."

"I'm not in His Kingdom," Krebs said.

"We are all of us in His Kingdom."

Krebs felt embarrassed and resentful as always.

"I've worried about you so much, Harold," his mother went on. "I know the temptations you must have been exposed to. I know how weak men are. I know what your own dear grandfather, my own father, told us about the Civil War and I have prayed for you. I pray for you all day long, Harold."

Krebs looked at the bacon fat hardening on his plate.

"Your father is worried, too," his mother went on. "He thinks you have lost your ambition, that you haven't got a definite aim in life. Charley Simmons, who is just your age, has a good job and is going to be married. The boys are all settling down; they're all determined to get somewhere; you can see that boys like Charley Simmons are on their way to being really a credit to the community."

Krebs said nothing.

"Don't look that way, Harold," his mother said. "You know we love you and I want to tell you for your own good how matters stand. Your father does not want to hamper your freedom. He thinks you should be allowed to drive the car. If you want to take some of the nice girls out riding with you, we are only too pleased. We want you to enjoy yourself. But you are going to have to settle down to work, Harold. Your father doesn't care what you start in at. All work is honorable as he says. But you've got to make a start at something. He asked me to speak to you this morning and then you can stop in and see him at his office."

"Is that all?" Krebs said.

"Yes. Don't you love your mother, dear boy?"

"No," Krebs said.

His mother looked at him across the table. Her eyes were shiny. She started crying.

"I don't love anybody," Krebs said.

It wasn't any good. He couldn't tell her, he couldn't make her see it. It was silly to have said it. He had only hurt her. He went over and took hold of her arm. She was crying with her head in her hands.

"I didn't mean it," he said. "I was just angry at something. I didn't mean I didn't love you."

His mother went on crying. Krebs put his arm on her shoulder.

"Can't you believe me, mother?"

His mother shook her head.

"Please, please, mother. Please believe me."

"All right," his mother said chokily. She looked up at him. "I believe you, Harold."

Krebs kissed her hair. She put her face up to him.

"I'm your mother," she said. "I held you next to my heart when you were a tiny baby."

Krebs felt sick and vaguely nauseated.

"I know, Mummy," he said. "I'll try and be a good boy for you."

"Would you kneel and pray with me, Harold?" his mother asked.

They knelt down beside the dining-room table and Krebs's mother prayed.

"Now, you pray, Harold," she said.

"I can't," Krebs said.

"Try, Harold."

"I can't."

"Do you want me to pray for you?"

"Yes."

So his mother prayed for him and then they stood up and Krebs kissed his mother and went out of the house. He had tried so to keep his life from being complicated. Still, none of it had touched him. He had felt sorry for his mother and she had made him lie. He would go to Kansas City and get a job and she would feel all right about it. There would be one more scene maybe before he got away. He would not go down to his father's office. He would miss that one. He wanted his life to go smoothly. It had just gotten going that way. Well, that was all over now, anyway. He would go over to the schoolyard and watch Helen play indoor baseball.

From *In Our Time* (1925)

E. E. Cummings: *my sweet old etcetera*

The son of a Harvard professor, Edward Estlin Cummings joined the Norton-Harjes Ambulance Corps in 1917 and served in France. Antiwar sentiments in his letters home as well as unruly behavior while he was serving abroad drew the attention of French authorities, who arrested him and his friend William Slater Brown on suspicion of sedition. They were held in a military detention camp in Normandy for more than three months. This incarceration would provide the material for Cummings's first book, *The Enormous Room*, a fictionalized memoir published in 1922. Hundreds of poems would follow, many of which expressed his disillusioned view of the war and the rhetoric that accompanied it.

———————

my sweet old etcetera
aunt lucy during the recent

war could and what
is more did tell you just
what everybody was fighting

for,
my sister

isabel created hundreds
(and
hundreds)of socks not to
mention shirts fleaproof earwarmers

etcetera wristers etcetera,my

mother hoped that

i would die etcetera
bravely of course my father used
to become hoarse talking about how it was
a privilege and if only he
could meanwhile my

self etcetera lay quietly
in the deep mud et

cetera
(dreaming,
et
   cetera,of
Your smile
eyes knees and of your Etcetera)

From *is 5* (1926)

John Dos Passos:
The Body of an American

Shortly after his ambulance corps service, Dos Passos began his literary career with two starkly realistic novels about the war: *One Man's Initiation: 1917* (1920) and *Three Soldiers* (1921). His masterpiece, *U. S. A.* —a trilogy of novels published from 1930 to 1936—follows the lives of a dozen characters from the dawn of 1900 to the twilight of 1929. Dos Passos employed an ambitious "montage" technique in these books, alternating between traditional narrative chapters and more unorthodox storytelling devices: "Newsreels," filled with headlines and song fragments; "Camera Eye" musings written in stream of consciousness; and thumbnail "Biographies" of influential figures of the day. The cynicism and antiheroism that imbue this particular passage would have seemed so foreign to the world just a generation earlier, when a Europe at peace with itself and full of hope greeted the twentieth century. These words close the central volume of the trilogy, *1919*, providing the novel's final words on the war and the people who lived it.

———————

Whereasthe Congressoftheunitedstates byaconcurrentresolutionadoptedon the4thdayofmarch lastauthorizedthe Secretaryofwar to cause to be brought to theunitedstatesthe body of an Americanwhowasamemberoftheamericanexpeditionaryforcesineurope wholosthislifeduringtheworldwarandwhoseidentityhasnotbeenestablished for burial inthememorialamphitheatreofthe nationalcemeteryatarlingtonvirginia

In the tarpaper morgue at Chalons-sur-Marne in the reek of chloride of lime and the dead, they picked out the pine box that held all that was left of
enie menie minie moe plenty other pine boxes stacked up there containing what they'd scraped up of Richard Roe
and other person or persons unknown. Only one can go. How did they pick John Doe?
Make sure he aint a dinge, boys,
make sure he aint a guinea or a kike,
how can you tell a guy's a hunredpercent when all you've

823

got's a gunnysack full of bones, bronze buttons stamped with the screaming eagle and a pair of roll puttees?

. . . and the gagging chloride and the puky dirt-stench of the yearold dead . . .

> The day withal was too meaningful and tragic for applause. Silence, tears, songs and prayer, muffled drums and soft music were the instrumentalities today of national approbation.

John Doe was born (thudding din of blood in love into the shuddering soar of a man and a woman alone indeed together lurching into

and ninemonths sick drowse waking into scared agony and the pain and blood and mess of birth). John Doe was born

and raised in Brooklyn, in Memphis, near the lakefront in Cleveland, Ohio, in the stench of the stockyards in Chi, on Beacon Hill, in an old brick house in Alexandria Virginia, on Telegraph Hill, in a halftimbered Tudor cottage in Portland the city of roses,

in the Lying-In Hospital old Morgan endowed on Stuyvesant Square,

across the railroad tracks, out near the country club, in a shack cabin tenement apartmenthouse exclusive residential suburb;

scion of one of the best families in the social register, won first prize in the baby parade at Coronado Beach, was marbles champion of the Little Rock grammarschools, crack basketballplayer at the Booneville High, quarterback at the State Reformatory, having saved the sheriff's kid from drowning in the Little Missouri River was invited to Washington to be photographed shaking hands with the President on the White House steps;—

> though this was a time of mourning, such an assemblage necessarily has about it a touch of color. In the boxes are seen the court uniforms of foreign diplomats, the gold braid of our own and foreign fleets and armies, the black of the conventional morning dress of American statesmen, the varicolored furs and outdoor wrapping garments of mothers and sisters come to mourn, the drab and blue of soldiers and sailors, the glitter of musical instruments and the white and black of a vested choir

—busboy harveststiff hogcaller boyscout champeen cornshucker of Western Kansas bellhop at the United States Hotel at Saratoga Springs office boy callboy fruiter telephone lineman longshoreman lumberjack plumber's helper,

worked for an exterminating company in Union City, filled pipes in an opium joint in Trenton, N. J.

Y.M.C.A. secretary, express agent, truckdriver, fordmechanic, sold books in Denver Colorado: Madam would you be willing to help a young man work his way through college?

President Harding, with a reverence seemingly more significant because of his high temporal station, concluded his speech:

We are met today to pay the impersonal tribute;
the name of him whose body lies before us took flight with his imperishable soul . . .
as a typical soldier of this representative democracy he fought and died believing in the indisputable justice of his country's cause . . .

by raising his right hand and asking the thousands within the sound of his voice to join in the prayer:

Our Father which art in heaven hallowed be thy name . . .

Naked he went into the army;

they weighed you, measured you, looked for flat feet, squeezed your penis to see if you had clap, looked up your anus to see if you had piles, counted your teeth, made you cough, listened to your heart and lungs, made you read the letters on the card, charted your urine and your intelligence,

gave you a service record for a future (imperishable soul)

and an identification tag stamped with your serial number to hang around your neck, issued O D regulation equipment, a condiment can and a copy of the articles of war.

Atten'SHUN suck in your gut you c——r wipe that smile off your face eyes right wattja tink dis is a choirch-social? For-war-D'ARCH.

John Doe

and Richard Roe and other person or persons unknown

drilled hiked, manual of arms, ate slum, learned to salute, to soldier, to loaf in the latrines, forbidden to smoke on deck, overseas guard duty, forty men and eight horses, shortarm inspection and the ping of shrapnel and the shrill bullets

combing the air and the sorehead woodpeckers the machine-
guns mud cooties gasmasks and the itch.

Say feller tell me how I can get back to my outfit.

John Doe had a head
for twentyodd years intensely the nerves of the eyes the ears
the palate the tongue the fingers the toes the armpits, the
nerves warmfeeling under the skin charged the coiled brain
with hurt sweet warm cold mine must dont sayings print
headlines:

Thou shalt not the multiplication table long division, Now
is the time for all good men knocks but once at a young man's
door, It's a great life if Ish gebibbel, The first five years'll be the
Safety First, Suppose a hun tried to rape your my country right
or wrong, Catch 'em young, What he dont know wont treat
'em rough, Tell 'em nothin, He got what was coming to him
he got his, This is a white man's country, Kick the bucket,
Gone west, If you dont like it you can croaked him

Say buddy cant you tell me how I can get back to my outfit?

Cant help jumpin when them things go off, give me the
trots them things do. I lost my identification tag swimmin in
the Marne, roughhousin with a guy while we was waitin to be
deloused, in bed with a girl named Jeanne (Love moving picture wet French postcard dream began with saltpeter in the
coffee and ended at the propho station);—

*Say soldier for chrissake cant you tell me how I can get back to
my outfit?*

John Doe's
heart pumped blood:
alive thudding silence of blood in your ears
down in the clearing in the Oregon forest where the punkins
were punkincolor pouring into the blood through the eyes
and the fallcolored trees and the bronze hoopers were hopping
through the dry grass, where tiny striped snails hung on the
underside of the blades and the flies hummed, wasps droned,
bumblebees buzzed, and the woods smelt of wine and mush-
rooms and apples, homey smell of fall pouring into the blood,

and I dropped the tin hat and the sweaty pack and lay flat with the dogday sun licking my throat and adamsapple and the tight skin over the breastbone.

The shell had his number on it.

The blood ran into the ground.

The service record dropped out of the filing cabinet when the quartermaster sergeant got blotto that time they had to pack up and leave the billets in a hurry.
The identification tag was in the bottom of the Marne.

The blood ran into the ground, the brains oozed out of the cracked skull and were licked up by the trenchrats, the belly swelled and raised a generation of bluebottle flies,
and the incorruptible skeleton,
and the scraps of dried viscera and skin bundled in khaki

they took to Chalons-sur-Marne
and laid it out neat in a pine coffin
and took it home to God's Country on a battleship
and buried it in a sarcophagus in the Memorial Amphitheatre in the Arlington National Cemetery
and draped the Old Glory over it
and the bugler played taps
and Mr. Harding prayed to God and the diplomats and the generals and the admirals and the brasshats and the politicians and the handsomely dressed ladies out of the society column of the *Washington Post* stood up solemn
and thought how beautiful sad Old Glory God's Country it was to have the bugler play taps and the three volleys made their ears ring.

Where his chest ought to have been they pinned
the Congressional Medal, the D.S.C., the Medaille Militaire, the Belgian Croix de Guerre, the Italian gold medal, the Vitutea Militara sent by Queen Marie of Rumania, the Czechoslovak war cross, the Virtuti Militari of the Poles, a wreath sent by

Hamilton Fish, Jr., of New York, and a little wampum presented by a deputation of Arizona redskins in warpaint and
feathers. All the Washingtonians brought flowers.

Woodrow Wilson brought a bouquet of poppies.

From *1919* (1932)

CHRONOLOGY

BIOGRAPHICAL NOTES

NOTE ON THE TEXTS

NOTES

INDEX

1914   Archduke Franz Ferdinand, heir to the throne of Austria-
        Hungary, and his wife Sophie are shot to death in Sarajevo,
        Bosnia-Herzegovina, on June 28 by Gavrilo Princip, a
        young Bosnian Serb. Germany assures Austria-Hungary of
        its support if possible military action against Serbia leads
        to confrontation with Russia, July 5–6. Investigators in-
        form Austro-Hungarian government on July 13 that Princip
        and his fellow conspirators received weapons and training
        from a Serbian army major, but that no evidence connects
        the Serbian government to the assassination. (The assassi-
        nation was organized by the chief of Serbian military intel-
        ligence; it is unclear whether the civilian leadership of
        Serbia was aware of the plot.) Austria-Hungary presents
        ultimatum to Serbia on July 23, demanding the suppres-
        sion of anti-Austrian agitation in Serbia and an Austro-
        Hungarian role in the investigation and punishment of
        Serbian nationals implicated in the assassination. Russia
        decides on July 24 to support Serbia against Austria-
        Hungary. Serbia rejects ultimatum, July 25. Austria-Hungary
        declares war on Serbia, July 28. Russia orders partial mili-
        tary mobilization, July 29, and full mobilization, July 30.
        Austria-Hungary orders full mobilization, July 31.
            Germany orders full mobilization and declares war on
        Russia, August 1. France orders full mobilization, August
        1. Germans invade Luxembourg and demand free passage
        for its troops through neutral Belgium, August 2. (Ger-
        man war plan anticipates fighting on two fronts, and calls
        for decisive offensive against France while defending
        against Russia. Plan requires German forces to advance
        through southern Belgium and Luxembourg and outflank
        French troops deployed along the French-German bor-
        der.) Germany declares war on France, August 3. Germans
        invade Belgium, August 4. Britain declares war on Ger-
        many, August 4. (Declaration brings British dominions of
        Canada, Newfoundland, South Africa, Australia, and New
        Zealand into the conflict.) President Woodrow Wilson
        proclaims American neutrality on August 4. Montenegro

declares war on Austria-Hungary, August 5. Austria-Hungary
declares war on Russia, August 6. France and Great Britain
declare war on Austria-Hungary, August 12. Japan declares
war on Germany, August 23. (Alliance of Germany and
Austria-Hungary becomes known as the Central Powers,
and alliance of France, Russia, and Britain as the Entente
or the Allies.)

German troops in Belgium lay siege to fortresses surrounding Liège, August 5–16. Germans occupy Brussels,
August 20. French and British are defeated in series of
battles fought along the French frontiers, August 20–24.
(French army loses 75,000 men killed in August, including 27,000 on August 22 alone.)

Germans defeat Russians in East Prussia in battle of
Tannenberg, August 24–31, capturing 92,000 prisoners.

Austro-Hungarian forces advance into southern Poland,
August 23. Russians begin offensive in eastern Galicia,
August 26.

Austro-Hungarians invade northwest Serbia, August 12,
but are defeated and retreat across border, August 23.

British sink three German light cruisers and one destroyer in battle of the Heligoland Bight, August 28. Main
body of German surface fleet remains in harbor, unwilling
to risk battle with numerically superior British forces.
Germans begin war with twenty-four U-boats (submarines) in commission, and initially use them against merchant shipping in accordance with international rules that
require the crew of a ship to be in lifeboats before it is
sunk. German surface raiders, mines, and U-boats sink
360,000 tons of merchant shipping, August 1914–January
1915, while five U-boats are lost in 1914. British begin naval
blockade of Germany.

German troops in Togoland surrender to British and
French forces, August 26. New Zealand forces occupy
German Samoa, August 30.

French and British halt German advance in battle of the
Marne, fought west of Paris, September 5–9. Germans
withdrawn from the Marne to the Aisne River. Both sides
move troops north toward the Channel coast.

Russians capture Lemberg (Lviv) in Austrian Galicia,
September 3, and begin siege of Przemyśl, September 24.

Germans defeat Russians in East Prussia in battle of the
Masurian Lakes, September 7–13.

Austro-Hungarians launch second invasion of northwest

Serbia, September 8. Fighting becomes stalemated in late September.

German authorities in New Guinea and the Bismarck and Solomon islands surrender to Australian forces, September 17. British and French capture Douala, capital of Cameroon, September 27. (Last German garrison in the interior of Cameroon surrenders February 18, 1916.)

Germans begin series of attacks on Allied forces defending Belgian town of Ypres, October 19, in attempt to break through to Channel ports of Dunkirk and Calais. Belgian army retreats to west bank of Yser River and floods lowlands between Nieuport and Dixmude.

Austro-Hungarian forces in Galicia relieve siege of Przemyśl, October 9.

Japanese complete occupation of German-held Northern Mariana, Marshall, and Caroline islands in the Pacific, October 14.

Ottoman Empire enters war on October 29 as Turkish fleet bombards Russian ports in Black Sea.

Battle of Ypres ends November 22 as Germans fail to break through Allied defenses. Both sides entrench along Western Front, which runs for 475 miles from Nieuport south to Noyon, east to Verdun, and then southeast to the Swiss border. (Front will remain essentially unchanged until spring 1918, with most of the fighting taking place between Verdun and the sea.)

Siege of Przemyśl resumes on November 6 as Austro-Hungarian armies in Galicia withdraw to the Carpathians.

German East Asiatic Squadron sinks two obsolete British armored cruisers off coast of Chile in battle of Coronel, November 1. British declare entire North Sea a military zone, November 2, in effort to restrict neutral trade with Germany.

British landing at Tanga in German East Africa (Tanzania) is repulsed, November 2–5. Garrison at Tsingtao (Qingdao), German concession port in northern China, surrenders to Japanese, November 7, after six-week-long siege.

Austro-Hungarian forces begin major offensive in Serbia, November 6. Serbs evacuate Belgrade, November 29.

British forces occupy oil fields in southwestern Persia (Iran), November 1. Fighting begins between Russians and Turks in the Caucasus, November 6. Ottoman Sultan Mehmed V declares jihad against the Allies, November 14, in unsuccessful attempt to foment rebellion among the Muslim populations of the British, French, and Russian empires. British and Indian troops occupy Basra in Mesopotamia, November 22.

French launch unsuccessful offensives in the Artois, December 17, 1914–January 13, 1915, and in Champagne, December 20, 1914–March 20, 1915, aimed at the flanks of the Noyon salient.

Germans occupy Łódź in western Poland, December 6. Austro-Hungarian forces defeat Russians in battle of Limanowa-Lapanow, fought southeast of Cracow, December 3–12. Fighting continues in Carpathians during winter.

Serbs launch counteroffensive, December 3–6, that recaptures Belgrade on December 15 as Austro-Hungarian forces are driven from Serbia.

British battle cruiser squadron defeats German East Asiatic Squadron in battle of the Falkland Islands, December 8, sinking two armored cruisers and two light cruisers.

Turks launch offensive in Caucasus, December 22, and are defeated at Sarikamish, December 29–30.

1915   Turkish troops occupy Tabriz in northwestern Persia (Iran), January 8. Sarikamish campaign ends, January 15, after Turks lose 75,000 men killed or captured. Russians occupy Tabriz, January 30. (Although Persia remains officially neutral throughout the war, in 1915–16 inconclusive fighting continues in northwestern Persia between Russians and Turks, while the British extend their occupation of oil-producing areas in the south.)

German navy begins 1915 with twenty-nine U-boats in commission. British sink German armored cruiser in battle of the Dogger Bank, fought in the North Sea on January 24. Unable to break blockade of the North Sea, Germans announce on February 4 that Allied merchant ships in war zone around Great Britain and Ireland will be sunk without warning and that neutral shipping should avoid entering the zone. United States warns Germany on February 10 that sinking American ships, or ships carrying American passengers, would be considered "an indefensible violation of neutral rights" and that the U.S. will hold Germany to "a strict accountability" for its naval actions. Unrestricted U-boat campaign begins on February 18.

Germans defeat Russians in second battle of the Masurian Lakes, February 7–22.

British repulse Turkish attempt to cross the Suez Canal on February 3. Anglo-French naval force begins bombarding Turkish fortifications in the Dardanelles, February 19.

Russians capture 120,000 prisoners when garrison of Przemyśl surrenders on March 22.

British impose total blockade on Germany, including all food imports, March 11.

Russia, Britain, and France reach secret agreement, March 4–April 10, giving Russia control of Istanbul and the Dardanelles following defeat of the Ottoman Empire. Anglo-French fleet loses three obsolete battleships to mines in unsuccessful attempt to force passage of the Dardanelles, March 18.

Germans launch offensive at Ypres, April 22, using poisonous chlorine gas released from cylinders. Battle continues until May 25 as Germans gain ground but fail to capture Ypres. (British begin using chlorine gas in September 1915.)

Turkish police arrest more than two hundred prominent Armenians in Istanbul, April 24. (Evidence indicates that in March 1915 the leadership of the Committee of Union and Progress, which had ruled the Ottoman Empire since 1913, decided to remove the Armenian population of Anatolia by deportation and mass murder.) British, Australian, New Zealand, and French troops land on Gallipoli peninsula, April 25, beginning land campaign to open the Dardanelles. Allies are unable to seize high ground from Turkish defenders. Campaign becomes stalemated, with Allied forces confined to shallow beachheads.

Italy signs secret treaty with Russia, Britain, and France, April 26, agreeing to join the Allies in return for Austrian territory in South Tyrol and on the Adriatic coast. French launch new offensive in the Artois, May 9–June 18, supported by British attacks at Aubers Ridge, May 9, and Festubert, May 15–25.

Germans and Austro-Hungarians break through Russian lines between Gorlice and Tarnow in southeast Poland, May 2–4, and recapture Przemyśl, June 3, and Lemberg, June 22, as Russians retreat from Galicia.

Italy declares war on Austria-Hungary, May 23. Italian troops cross the Austrian border and advance to the Isonzo River with objective of seizing Trieste. In the first battle of the Isonzo, June 23–July 7, Italians fail to capture high ground east of the river. (Italians will launch four additional offensives in the Isonzo valley, July 1915–March 1916, that fail to break through Austro-Hungarian defenses.)

Ottoman authorities begin deportation of Armenians from Anatolia into the Syrian desert in May as mass killings are carried out by Kurdish tribesmen and criminal gangs recruited by the Special Organization, paramilitary group controlled by the Committee of Union and Progress. (By the summer of 1916 an estimated 800,000 to one million Armenians are killed, or die from hunger and disease, in the massacres and deportations, along with at least 150,000 Assyrian Christians.)

U-boat sinks British ocean liner *Lusitania* off the coast of Ireland on May 7, killing 1,198 people, including 128 Americans. United States protests sinking on May 13 as an "unlawful and inhumane act." Germany responds on May 28 with note defending sinking. Secretary of State William Jennings Bryan resigns on June 9, fearing that Wilson's continued defense of the right of Americans to travel on belligerent ships will lead to war.

German air service deploys first fighter aircraft with forward-firing machine gun in July. (British and French will introduce equivalent aircraft into service by early 1916. From the beginning of the war all of the major powers use aircraft for reconnaissance and bombing raids; Germans also use Zeppelins for bombing and maritime reconnaissance.)

German forces in South-West Africa (Namibia) surrender, July 9.

Germans and Austro-Hungarians launch new offensive, July 13, that forces Russians to retreat from Poland. German forces capture Warsaw, August 5. Austro-Hungarians capture Brest-Litovsk, August 26.

United States warns Germany on July 21 that any further violation of American neutral rights will be regarded as "deliberately unfriendly." U-boat sinks British liner *Arabic* off Ireland, August 19, killing two Americans. Seeking to avoid American entry into war, Germans suspend unrestricted U-boat campaign, August 27, and pledge on September 1 not to sink passenger ships without warning. Germans sink 740,000 tons of merchant shipping, February–August 1915.

British troops land at Suvla Bay, August 6, as part of new attempt to break stalemate at Gallipoli. Offensive ends on August 15 with Turks still holding high ground and the Allies confined to their beachheads. French renew offensive against the Noyon salient, attacking in Champagne, September 25–November 6, and the Artois, September 25–October 16. Attack in the Artois is supported by British offensive at Loos, September 25–October 19. Despite increased use of heavy artillery, none of the Allied offensives succeed in breaking through German defenses. (By the fall of 1915 Germans have built defenses in depth on the Western Front involving multiple trench lines protected by barbed wire and defended by artillery and machine guns. Allied attacks that succeed in capturing forward German positions are vulnerable to counterattack and are limited by unreliable battlefield communications and the need to bring artillery forward before renewing the offensive. In 1916–17, Allies will continue to launch offensives intended to break through German defenses while also pursuing attritional strategy of "wearing down" German army.)

Germans capture Vilna, September 18. Russian retreat ends in late September along line running from Gulf of Riga south to the Romanian border near Czernowitz (Chernivtsi).

British and Indian troops in Mesopotamia advance up Tigris and capture Kut, September 28.

French and British troops begin landing at Salonika, Greece, on October 5 in effort to aid Serbs. German and Austro-Hungarian forces invade Serbia from the north, October 7, and capture Belgrade, October 9. Bulgaria invades Serbia from east, October 14. Serbian army begins winter retreat across mountains into Montenegro and Albania, November 24. (Survivors are evacuated from the Adriatic coast by Allies, January–April 1916, and later join Allied forces at Salonika.)

Germans use phosgene gas, a more lethal agent than chlorine, in attack on French near Reims, October 19. (Allies will begin using phosgene in February 1916, and in 1916 both sides will begin using poison gas in artillery shells.)

British authorities in Egypt write to Sharif Hussein ibn Ali, emir of Mecca, on October 24, pledging support for creation of an independent Arab state in the Middle East in return for Arab participation in the war against the Ottoman Empire. (Pledge is made with stated reservations concerning French ambitions in Syria and recent British conquests in Mesopotamia, as well as prewar British relationships with Arab sheikdoms in the Persian Gulf.) British begin advance up Tigris toward Baghdad, November 19, but fail to breakthrough Turkish defenses at Ctesiphon (Salman Pak), November 22–25, and retreat to Kut. Turks begin siege of Kut, December 7. Allies begin evacuation of Gallipoli in mid-December.

Wilson calls for expanding the size of the U.S. Army and Navy in his State of the Union address, December 7.

1916   German navy begins year with fifty-four U-boats in commission; nineteen U-boats were lost in 1915.

Allied evacuation of Gallipoli is completed, January 8. Austro-Hungarians invade Montenegro, January 5, and complete occupation of the country, January 25. Russians begin offensive in the Caucasus, January 10, and capture Erzurum, February 16.

Wilson makes speaking tour in New York and the Midwest, January 27–February 3, to build public support for military "preparedness."

Germans begin offensive at Verdun, February 21, and capture Fort Douaumont, key French position, February 25, but are unable to break through inner defensive line. Fighting extends to left (west) bank of the Meuse, March 6, as Germans continue offensive intended to exhaust French army in battle of attrition. (Verdun becomes first battle in which opposing sides both use fighter aircraft in attempt to gain air superiority over battlefield, as aerial artillery spotting and photography become increasingly important in determining course of land fighting.)

Germany declares war on Portugal, March 9, after the Portuguese government seizes interned German ships.

Mexican revolutionary Pancho Villa raids Columbus, New Mexico, on March 9, killing eighteen Americans. Wilson sends military expedition led by General John J. Pershing into Mexico in pursuit of Villa, March 15 (expedition ends in early February 1917 without Villa being captured).

U-boat torpedoes French passenger ship *Sussex* in the English Channel, March 24, injuring several Americans. Wilson warns Germany on April 18 that the U.S. will break diplomatic relations if attacks on passenger ships continue. German government pledges on May 4 that it will abide by established rules of naval warfare. U-boats sink one million tons of merchant shipping, September 1915–April 1916.

Allied forces begin offensive in German East Africa, April 3. Despite numerical superiority, Allies become involved in protracted campaign due to losses from disease, supply difficulties, and mobility of German-led African troops. (Fighting extends into Portuguese East Africa and Northern Rhodesia in 1917–18 before last German forces surrender on November 25, 1918.)

Irish republicans begin Easter Uprising in Dublin, April 24. Insurrection is suppressed by British troops, April 29.

Russians capture Trabzon, Turkish Black Sea port, on April 18. British garrison at Kut surrenders, April 29.

American volunteer pilots fly first patrol with Escadrille N. 124, French fighter squadron later known as the Lafayette Escadrille, May 13.

Sykes-Picot agreement, ratified May 16, divides postwar Middle East into zones of British and French direct control and indirect influence while envisioning international zone in Palestine under British, French, and Russian administration. (The borders established in Middle East during the 1920s do not follow boundaries outlined in Sykes-Picot agreement.)

Austro-Hungarians begin offensive in the Trentino, May 15, and capture Asiago, May 28. Offensive is halted on June 10.

German fleet sails into North Sea on May 31 in attempt to engage British fleet on favorable terms. In battle of Jutland, May 31–June 1, British lose three battle cruisers, three armored cruisers, eight destroyers, and 6,000 men killed, while Germans lose one battle cruiser, one obsolete battleship, four light cruisers, five destroyers, and 2,500 men killed. British retain control of North Sea and continue blockade.

Russian offensive in Galicia, June 4, breaks through Austro-Hungarian lines and captures 200,000 prisoners by June 12. Germans make final attempt to capture Verdun, June 23.

Arab revolt against Ottoman rule begins in the Hejaz, June 10.

Wilson signs National Defense Act, June 3, authorizing five-year expansion of the army to 175,000 men and the National Guard to 400,000 men; law also authorizes the president to deploy the Guard overseas.

British and French begin offensive along Somme River, July 1, after weeklong preliminary bombardment. British suffer 57,000 casualties, including 19,000 killed, on first day.

British repel Turkish attack on Suez Canal, August 3–5.

In sixth battle of the Isonzo, August 6–17, Italians succeed in capturing Gorizia. (Italians will launch another four offensives along the Isonzo, September 1916–June 1917, that make limited gains in the high ground east of the river.) Italy declares war on Germany, August 28.

Romania declares war on Austria-Hungary, August 27, and invades Transylvania. German, Bulgarian, and Turkish forces invade southern Romania, September 2. Germans and Austro-Hungarians begin counteroffensive in Transylvania, September 25.

British use tanks for the first time with limited success on the Somme, September 15. Russian offensive in Galicia ends, September 20. French counteroffensive at Verdun recaptures Fort Douaumont, October 24.

Wilson wins reelection on November 7, defeating Republican Charles Evans Hughes with 277 electoral votes and 49 percent of the popular vote; Hughes receives 254 electoral votes.

Battle of the Somme ends, November 18, with a maximum Allied advance of seven miles. British lose 420,000 men killed, wounded, or missing, while French casualties total 200,000; German casualties are estimated at 430,000.

Franz Joseph, emperor of Austria since 1848, dies on November 21 and is succeeded by his nephew Karl.

Herbert Henry Asquith, prime minister of Great Britain since 1908, resigns on December 5, and is succeeded by David Lloyd George. Germans capture Bucharest, December 6, as Romanian army retreats north into Moldavia. French counteroffensive at Verdun, December 15–18, regains much of the ground lost earlier in the year. French lose 377,000 men killed, wounded, or missing in battle, while German casualties total 337,000.

Wilson sends note to belligerents asking them to state peace terms, December 18; Germany and Austria-Hungary refuse.

1917   German navy begins year with 133 U-boats in commission. Germans sink 2.1 million tons of merchant shipping, May 1916–January 1917, and lose twenty-two U-boats in 1916. Decision by German military and naval leadership to resume unrestricted U-boat warfare is endorsed by Kaiser Wilhelm II on January 9.

Wilson calls for "peace without victory" in address to the Senate, January 22.

Unrestricted U-boat warfare resumes, February 1. United States breaks diplomatic relations with Germany, February 3. Decoded text of Zimmerman telegram, diplomatic message proposing a German-Mexican alliance against the United States, is published on March 1. Three American merchant ships are torpedoed without warning on March 18 and fifteen Americans killed. Cabinet unanimously recommends that Wilson ask Congress for a declaration of war, March 20.

Germans shorten their line in France by withdrawing from Noyon salient to "Hindenburg Line," strongly fortified position twelve to twenty-five miles to the rear, March 16–18.

British retake Kut, February 25, and occupy Baghdad, March 11.

Food riots in Petrograd (St. Petersburg), March 8–12, result in mutiny by city garrison. Tsar Nicholas II abdicates, March 15, as provisional government is established with Prince Lvov as prime minister.

Wilson asks Congress on April 2 to declare war against Germany. War resolution is approved by the Senate, 82–6, on April 4 and by the House, 373–50, on April 6. (U.S. Army has 127,000 officers and men, with another 80,000 men in the National Guard on federal service.) Wilson establishes Committee on Public Information, April 13, government propaganda agency intended to promote support for the war domestically and to publicize American war aims internationally.

British begin offensive at Arras on April 9. Canadian troops capture Vimy Ridge, April 9–12. The ridge was the scene of intense fighting during the 1915 French offensives in the Artois. Battle continues until May 16 as British are unable to exploit initial success; British casualties total 150,000 killed, wounded, or missing.

French launch offensive against Chemin des Dames, high ground north of the Aisne, on April 16 that fails to achieve breakthrough. Offensive ends on May 16 after French lose 130,000 men killed, wounded, or missing. Failure of attack causes widespread protests and unrest in French army, with many soldiers refusing to engage in further attacks. French commanders restore order by improving leave conditions and avoiding costly attacks.

General Pershing is appointed commander of the American Expeditionary Forces (AEF), May 10. Wilson signs Selective Service Act, May 18, making men twenty-one to thirty eligible for the draft (registration is extended in September 1918 to men eighteen to forty-five).

British capture Messines ridge south of Ypres, June 7–14.

Wilson signs Espionage Act, June 15. Legislation provides penalties for disclosure of "national defence" information to foreign powers while also making it a crime to attempt to cause "insubordination, disloyalty, mutiny" in the armed forces, or to "obstruct the recruiting or enlistment service of the United States."

White mobs attack black residents of East St. Louis, Illinois, July 2–3, during rioting in which at least thirty-nine African Americans and nine whites are killed.

Greece declares war on Central Powers, July 2. Arab insurgents capture Aqaba, July 6.

Russians launch offensive in Galicia, July 1–16. Demoralized Russian forces collapse when Germans counterattack, July 19. Alexander Kerensky becomes prime minister of Russian provisional government, July 21.

Germans begin using mustard gas, a liquid blistering agent, in Flanders, July 12. (Allies will begin using mustard gas in June 1918. Poison gas causes death of an estimated 90,000 soldiers on all sides, 1915–18.)

British launch offensive at Ypres, July 31, after fifteen-day preliminary bombardment.

U-boats sink almost 4.4 million tons of shipping, February–August 1917. Sinkings begin to decline as British gradually adopt convoy system, aided by increasing numbers of U.S. destroyers made available for escort duty.

Italians capture Bainsizza plateau northeast of Gorizia in eleventh battle of the Isonzo, August 19–September 12.

Germans capture Riga, September 3.

Germans and Austro-Hungarians launch offensive at Caporetto on the upper Isonzo, October 24, and force the Italians to retreat sixty miles to the Paive River. Italians lose 280,000 men taken prisoner, while another 350,000 men become stragglers or desert.

Third battle of Ypres (also known as battle of Passchendaele) ends, November 10, with maximum Allied advance of four miles; British lose 244,000 killed, wounded, or missing, the Germans 215,000. Georges Clemenceau becomes premier of France, November 16. British break through Hindenburg Line at Cambrai, November 20, in surprise attack using more than 300 tanks. German counteroffensive on November 30 recovers much of the lost ground.

British break through Turkish defenses at Gaza, November 1–6, and advance into Palestine. Foreign Secretary Arthur Balfour issues declaration on November 2 committing British government to "the establishment in Palestine of a national home for the Jewish people." British occupy Jerusalem, December 9.

Bolshevik coup in Petrograd overthrows provisional government, November 7, and establishes Soviet regime led by Vladimir Lenin. Romania signs armistice, December 9. Bolsheviks sign armistice, December 15.

U.S. declares war on Austria-Hungary, December 7. Congress proposes Eighteenth Amendment, establishing prohibition, to the states, December 18.

1918   German navy begins year with 142 U-boats in commission; sixty-three U-boats were lost in 1917. American troops in Europe total 184,000.

Wilson outlines terms of peace settlement in Fourteen Points address to Congress, January 8.

Bolsheviks sign peace treaty with Central Powers at Brest-Litovsk, March 3.

Outbreak of Spanish influenza in Kansas in early March spreads across the United States and travels overseas.

Germans launch offensive against British at St. Quentin, March 21–April 5, and advance up to forty miles. Attack is most successful on Western Front since 1914, but fails to capture railroad junction at Amiens; German ability to exploit breakthrough is limited by shortage of trucks and transport horses. Allies lose 255,000 men killed, wounded, or captured, the Germans 240,000. French general Ferdinand Foch becomes first Allied supreme commander on the Western Front, April 3. Germans break through British defenses along Lys River south of Ypres, April 9–29, but fail to capture supply center at Hazebrouck. (German offensives in spring of 1918 achieve initial success using short, intense artillery bombardments employing mixture of high-explosive and gas shells, and specially trained infantry units equipped with light machine guns and mortars.)

Romania signs peace treaty with Central Powers at Bucharest, May 7.

Wilson signs Sedition Act (an amendment to the Espionage Act), May 16, making it a crime during wartime to utter or print "disloyal, profane, scurrilous, or abusive language about the form of government of the United States," to "use any language" intended to bring form of government "into contempt, scorn, contumely, or disrepute," or "by word or act oppose the cause of the United States" in the war. (The Wilson administration will prosecute 2,168 individuals under the Espionage and Sedition acts for their speeches or writings and obtain 1,055 convictions; forty-one defendants are sentenced to terms of ten, fifteen, or twenty years.)

Germans launch third spring offensive, May 27–June 4, breaking through French lines along the Aisne River and advancing to the Marne. American troops join French in defense of Marne crossing at Château-Thierry, June 1–3, and drive Germans from Belleau Wood, June 6–25.

Italians defeat Austro-Hungarian offensive along Piave, June 15–23. American troops in Europe total 897,000 by June 30.

During final German offensive, July 15–18, Americans fight with the French along the Marne, then join counteroffensive that advances to Aisne and Vesle rivers in early August.

British launch offensive at Amiens, August 8–12, that captures 12,000 prisoners in its first day. (French and British offensives in summer and fall of 1918 employ improved artillery and infantry tactics and increasing numbers of tanks and aircraft; by November 1918 the Allies have 7,000 aircraft on the Western Front, the Germans 2,200.)

American troops land at Russian Pacific port of Vladivostok, August 16, and Arctic port of Archangel, September 4. (Troops are sent to guard military supplies and railroads and to assist Czechoslovak forces that seek to leave Russia and fight with the Allies.)

New and more virulent strain of Spanish influenza arrives in United States in late August. (Influenza pandemic of 1918–19 kills an estimated 675,000 Americans and at least thirty million people worldwide.)

In its first operation as an independent army under Pershing's command, the AEF eliminates the St. Mihiel salient southeast of Verdun, September 12–16, capturing 13,000 prisoners. Allies begin general offensive, September 26–29, attacking in Flanders, Picardy, and Champagne. AEF launches Meuse-Argonne offensive, September 26.

French, British, Serbian, and Greek forces begin offensive in Macedonia, September 15, and advance up the Vardar valley. Bulgaria signs armistice, September 29. British forces in Palestine defeat Turks in battle of Megiddo, September 19–25, and capture Damascus, October 1.

Eugene V. Debs, four-time Socialist candidate for president, is tried in Cleveland under the Espionage Act of 1917 for having made an antiwar speech in June 1918. Convicted on September 13, he is sentenced to ten years' imprisonment.

British break through Hindenburg Line, September 29–October 5. Prince Max of Baden, the newly appointed German chancellor, sends note to Wilson on October 5 asking for an armistice and peace negotiations on basis of the Fourteen Points. Americans break through main defensive line in the Meuse-Argonne, October 14–17. German navy orders U-boats to end attacks on civilian ships, October 21. (Germans sink 4.1 million tons of merchant shipping, September 1917–October 1918; sixty-nine U-boats are lost at sea in 1918.) American troops in Europe total 2,057,000.

Ottoman Empire signs armistice, October 30. Italian victory in battle of Vittorio Veneto, October 24–November 3, brings about collapse of Austro-Hungarian army. Austria-Hungary signs armistice, November 3. Allies launch series of attacks along the Western Front, October 31–November 4. Wilhelm II abdicates his throne, November 9, as German republic is proclaimed in Berlin. Germans sign armistice, which goes into effect on November 11 at 11 A.M.

Czechoslovak republic proclaimed in Prague, November 14. Independent Polish state proclaimed in Warsaw, November 16.

Kingdom of Serbs, Croats, and Slovenes proclaimed in Belgrade, December 1. American occupation forces enter Germany, December 1, and cross the Rhine, December 13. Wilson sails for France on December 5 to attend peace conference.

1919   Ratification of Eighteenth Amendment completed, January 16 (Prohibition goes into effect on January 17, 1920).

Paris peace conference opens, January 18, and adopts draft of the Covenant of the League of Nations, February 14. Wilson returns to United States, February 24, to sign legislation and meet with congressional leaders. Republican Senator Henry Cabot Lodge announces that thirty-seven senators and senators-elect are opposed to the draft covenant, March 4. Wilson sails for France, March 5. Treaty of Versailles is presented to German delegation, May 17. American troops leave North Russia, June 3–August 5. Congress proposes Nineteenth Amendment, giving women the right to vote, to the states on June 4. Treaty of Versailles is signed on June 28. Wilson returns to the United States, July 8, and presents the treaty to the Senate, July 10. Twenty-three African Americans and fifteen whites are killed during race riots in Chicago, July 27–31. Senate Foreign Relations Committee, chaired by Lodge, begins hearings on the treaty, July 31. Wilson appears before committee in special session held at the White House, August 19. In attempt to rally support for the League of Nations, Wilson begins national speaking tour, September 3. Peace treaty with Austria is signed at St. Germain, September 10. Wilson has nervous breakdown in Pueblo, Colorado, on September 25 and returns to the White House. Suffers ischemic stroke that leaves him paralyzed on his left side, October 2. White mobs and U.S. troops kill more than one hundred African Americans in Phillips County, Arkansas, September 30–October 4, in response to false reports of an uprising by black sharecroppers. Lodge presents fourteen reservations to treaty, October 24. Wilson sends letter on November 18 rejecting the Lodge reservations as a "nullification" of the Treaty. On November 19 Senate rejects ratification with reservations, 39–55, and unconditional ratification, 38–53. (In first vote, thirty-five Republicans and four Democrats support the Lodge reservations; in the second vote, thirty-seven Democrats and one Republican vote for the treaty.) Peace treaty with Bulgaria signed at Neuilly, November 27.

1920   Last American troops leave France, January 3. (American occupation of Germany ends in January 1923.) Soviet Russia signs treaty recognizing Estonian independence, February 2. Senate votes 49–35 to ratify Versailles treaty with reservations, March 19, falling seven votes short of the necessary two-thirds majority. Last U.S. troops leave

Vladivostok, April 1. (About 14,000 American soldiers serve in Russia, 1918–20, and about 400 are killed in action or die from other causes. Troops in North Russia engage in limited combat against Bolshevik forces, while troops in eastern Siberia fight skirmishes against Bolshevik partisans and Cossack bands.) At conference held in San Remo, Italy, April 19–26, British and French agree that France will receive League of Nations mandate for Syria (including Lebanon) and Britain will receive mandates for Iraq and Palestine (including territory that becomes Transjordan in 1923). Peace treaty with Hungary signed at Trianon, June 4. (Austrian, Bulgarian, and Hungarian treaties all incorporate the League of Nations covenant, and are never submitted to the Senate.) Soviets sign treaty recognizing Lithuanian independence, July 12. Peace treaty with Turkey is signed at Sèvres, August 10. (United States is not a signatory to the Sèvres treaty, which is replaced by Treaty of Lausanne in 1923.) Soviets sign treaty recognizing Latvian independence, August 11. Ratification of the Nineteenth Amendment is completed, August 18. Poland and Lithuania sign peace treaty, October 7. Warren G. Harding, Republican senator from Ohio, defeats James M. Cox, Democratic governor of Ohio, in presidential election on November 2, receiving 404 out of 531 electoral votes and 60 percent of the popular vote. Eugene V. Debs, who is still in federal prison, receives more than 3 percent of the popular vote. (Debs is released on December 25, 1921, after Harding commutes his sentence.) Congress repeals Sedition Act, December 13. (Remaining prisoners convicted under the Sedition Act are pardoned by President Calvin Coolidge in December 1923).

1921 Poland and Soviets sign treaty in Riga, March 18, ending their 1919–20 war. Harding signs congressional resolution ending state of war with Germany, Austria, and Hungary, July 2. United States signs separate peace treaties with Austria, August 24, Germany, August 25, and Hungary, August 29. Harding dedicates Tomb of the Unknown Soldier at Arlington National Cemetery, November 11.

More than 116,000 Americans died while serving in the armed forces during World War I; of these deaths, 53,000 were the result of hostile action and 63,000 were from noncombat causes. Battle deaths by service were approximately

50,500 in the army, 400 in the navy, and 2,500 in the marines; 26,000 of the battle deaths were men killed in the Meuse-Argonne campaign (September 26–November 11, 1918). It is estimated that 46,000 of the noncombat deaths were from influenza.

Great Britain and Ireland lost 744,000 military dead; India, 74,000; Australia, 62,000; Canada, 57,000; New Zealand, 18,000; South Africa, 7,000; and Newfoundland, 1,200. France lost 1,400,000 military dead, including 70,000 from its colonies; Russia, 1,800,000; Italy, 650,000; Romania, 336,000; Serbia, 278,000; and Belgium, 38,000. Germany lost 2,000,000 military dead; Austria-Hungary, 1,200,000; the Ottoman Empire, 770,000; and Bulgaria, 87,500. About 15,000 African soldiers died on both sides in African campaigns, along with an estimated 150,000 porters and laborers, mostly from disease and malnutrition. The total number of military dead from 1914 to 1918 is estimated at more than 9 million, while total civilian deaths from violence and war-related food shortages and epidemics (excluding the 1918 influenza pandemic) are estimated at 6 million, including 2,100,000 in the Ottoman Empire and 1,500,000 in Russia.

Biographical Notes

Jane Addams (September 6, 1860–May 21, 1935) Born in Cedarville, Illinois, the daughter of a mill owner and businessman who served in the state senate. Graduated Rockford Female Academy, 1881. With friend Ellen Gates Starr, founded Chicago settlement house Hull-House, a reclaimed mansion in the impoverished Nineteenth Ward, in 1889; resided there until her death. Achieved national recognition as a proponent of social reform, including woman suffrage and civil rights. Served as member of Chicago school board, 1905–9. Delegate to National Arbitration and Peace Congress in New York City in 1907. Helped found Woman's Peace Party and attended International Congress of Women held in The Hague, 1915; subsequently attended congress in Zurich that founded Women's International League for Peace and Freedom in 1919. Her many publications include *Democracy and Social Ethics* (1902), *The Spirit of Youth and the City Streets* (1909), the best-selling *Twenty Years at Hull-House* (1910), *Peace and Bread in Time of War* (1922), and *The Second Twenty Years at Hull-House* (1930). Awarded Nobel Peace Prize in 1931. Died in Chicago.

Hervey Allen (December 8, 1889–December 28, 1949) Born William Hervey Allen, Jr. in Pittsburgh, Pennsylvania, the son of an inventor and entrepreneur who worked in the steel industry. Entered U.S. Naval Academy in 1909, but was medically discharged the following year. Graduated from University of Pittsburgh in 1915 with degree in economics. Commissioned as second lieutenant in Pennsylvania National Guard in 1916 and served at El Paso, Texas, for several months. Published poetry collection *Ballads of the Border* (1916). Promoted to first lieutenant in the 111th Infantry Regiment in 1917. Arrived in France with 28th Division in May 1918. Saw action in the Second Battle of the Marne, the advance to the Vesle, and at Fismette, July–August 1918. Hospitalized in mid-August suffering from mustard gas exposure and "shell shock." Served as English instructor with French army. Returned to the United States in 1919 and settled in Charleston, South Carolina, where he taught English at the Porter Military Academy, 1919–21, and at Charleston High School, 1921–24. Published widely read war poem "The Blindman" in *The North American Review* (December 1919) and poetry collections *Wampum and Old Gold* (1921) and *Carolina Chansons: Legends of the Low Country* (1922), the latter a collaboration with DuBose Heyward. Taught English at Columbia University, 1924–25, and Vassar College, 1926–27. Published

Earth Mood and Other Poems (1925), war memoir *Toward the Flame* (1926, revised 1934), biography *Israfel: The Life and Times of Edgar Allan Poe* (1926), and, with Thomas Ollive Mabbott, *Poe's Brother: The Poems of William Henry Leonard Poe* (1926). Married Ann Hyde Andrews in 1927 and moved with her to Bermuda, where they lived until 1932. Published poetry collection *New Legends* (1929). Historical novel *Anthony Adverse* (1933), set in Napoleonic era, became major bestseller. Moved to farm in Talbot County on Eastern Shore of Maryland. Published *Action at Aquila* (1938), novel set in Civil War, and *It Was Like This: Two Stories of the Great War* (1940). Moved to Coconut Grove, Florida. Became co-editor of the "Rivers of America" series in 1943. Began writing *The Disinherited*, series of historical novels set in western Pennsylvania. Published *The Forest and the Fort* (1943), *Bedford Village* (1944), and *Toward the Morning* (1948). Died in Coconut Grove.

Newton D. Baker (December 3, 1871–December 25, 1937) Born in Martinsburg, West Virginia, the son of a doctor. Graduated from Johns Hopkins in 1892 and received law degree from Washington and Lee in 1894. Opened law practice in Martinsburg. Served as secretary to Postmaster General William L. Wilson, 1896–97. Joined law office in Cleveland, Ohio, in 1899. Appointed assistant law director of Cleveland, 1901, and law director, 1902. Married Elizabeth Wells Leopold in 1902. Elected city solicitor, 1903, and subsequently re-elected, serving until 1911. Won mayoral election in 1911 as Democrat and served January 1912–January 1916. Supported nomination of Woodrow Wilson at 1912 Democratic national convention. Appointed secretary of war by Wilson in March 1916 and served until March 1921. Returned to law practice in Cleveland. Published *Why We Went to War* (1936). Died in Cleveland.

Ray Stannard Baker (April 17, 1870–July 12, 1946) Born in Lansing, Michigan, the son of a land agent. Moved with family to St. Croix Falls, Wisconsin, in 1875. Graduated from Michigan Agricultural College (now Michigan State University) in 1889. Studied law at the University of Michigan. Reporter and editor for the *Chicago Record* newspaper, 1892–97. Married Jessie Irene Beal in 1896. Moved to New York, where he was managing editor of McClure's Syndicate, 1897–98. Associate editor of *McClure's Magazine*, 1898–1905, writing articles on popular science, labor unions, trusts, and railroads. Published *The Boy's Book of Inventions* (1899), *Our New Prosperity* (1900), *Seen in Germany* (1901), and *Boys' Second Book of Inventions* (1903). Left *McClure's* in 1906. Purchased *American Magazine* with Ida M. Tarbell, Lincoln Steffens, and several other journalists, and served as its editor, 1906–15. Published *Adventures in Contentment* (1907), first of nine volumes of essays written under the pen name David Grayson that would appear through 1942, *Following the Color Line: An Account of Negro Citizenship in the American Democracy* (1908), *New Ideals in Healing* (1909), and *The Spiritual Unrest* (1910). Supported Woodrow Wilson in 1912 and 1916 elections. Traveled to Britain, France, and Italy as special diplomatic commissioner, March–November 1918, sending confidential reports on public opinion and political developments to the Wilson administration while ostensibly serving as correspondent for *The New Republic* and the *New York World*. Served as head of the press bureau of the American delegation at the Paris peace conference, December 1918–June 1919. Returned to the United States with Wilson in July 1919. Published *What Wilson Did at Paris* (1919), *The New Industrial Unrest: Reasons and Remedies* (1920), *Woodrow Wilson and World Settlement* (3 volumes, 1922), *Woodrow Wilson: Life and Letters* (8 volumes, 1927–39), and two autobiographies, *Native American: The Book of My Youth* (1941) and *American Chronicle* (1945). Died in Amherst, Massachusetts.

Charles J. Biddle (March 13, 1890–March 22, 1972) Born at Andalusia, family estate in Bensalem Township, Pennsylvania, the son of a lawyer. Graduated from Princeton in 1911 and from Harvard Law School in 1914. Joined father's law practice. Began training in French aviation service in April 1917. Assigned to Escadrille N. 73 in July 1917, flying SPAD VII and, later, SPAD XIII fighter planes over Flanders. Transferred in January 1918 to American 103rd Aero Squadron and commissioned as captain in the U.S. Army. Served in Champagne region before returning to Flanders. Shot down by observer in German two-seater on May 15, 1918, and crashed in No Man's Land with wounded leg, but managed to reach British lines. Returned to duty in July 1918 with U.S. 13th Pursuit Squadron in Lorraine. Flew patrols over Meuse-Argonne during American offensive. Assigned command of 4th Pursuit Group on October 25, 1918, and promoted to major. Returned to United States in December 1918 credited with eight victories in aerial combat. Published memoir *The Way of the Eagle* (1919), drawn from wartime letters. Resumed legal practice with father. Married Katharine Legendre in 1923. Formed legal partnership Drinker, Biddle, and Reath in 1925 after his father's death. Served as general counsel to Philadelphia Contributorship insurance company and Drexel University. Retired from law practice in 1968. Died at Andalusia.

Nellie Bly (May 5, 1864–January 27, 1922) Born Elizabeth Jane Cochran in Cochran's Mills, Pennsylvania, the daughter of a mill owner. Raised in poverty after her father's death. Studied to be a teacher at Indiana State Normal School; dropped out within a year for financial reasons. Wrote anonymous letter to the *Pittsburgh Dispatch* in 1885, harshly criticizing the paper's condescending position on women seeking work outside the home; the paper offered her a job. Adopted the pseudonym "Nellie Bly" after a popular song. Traveled in Mexico for five months writing series of articles for the *Dispatch*, later collected in *Six Months in Mexico* (1888). Moved to New York in 1887. For the *New York World*, committed herself to lunatic asylum on Blackwell's Island in order to report on conditions there; her articles were collected as *Ten Days in a Mad-House* (1887). Wrote extensively for the *World* on social and political issues and human interest stories. Undertook 72-day trip around the world in emulation of Jules Verne's *Around the World in Eighty Days*, November 1889–January 1890; her newspaper accounts were collected as *Nellie Bly's Book: Around the World in Seventy-Two Days* (1890). Left journalism after her marriage in 1895 to 73-year-old industrialist Robert Livingston Seaman; she became president of his Iron Clad Manufacturing Company; set up first plant in the U.S. to manufacture steel barrels. Following her husband's death in 1904 she became embroiled in legal troubles due to employee embezzlement and the company's bankruptcy, and was indicted for obstruction of justice in 1914. Traveled to central Europe on business matters in August 1914; began writing dispatches for the *New York Evening Journal* from the Galician and Serbian fronts, twenty-one of which were published from December 1914 to February 1915. Remained in Austria during war; returned to the States in 1919. Reduced to difficult financial circumstances, having lost control of her steel barrel company to her siblings. From 1919 until her death wrote an advice column for the *Journal*. Died in New York City.

Mary Borden (May 15, 1886–December 2, 1968) Born in Chicago, Illinois, the daughter of a wealthy businessman with extensive holdings in real estate, mining, and dairy products. Graduated from Vassar in 1907. Married George Douglas Turner, a Scottish lay missionary, in 1908. Published two novels under pseudonym Bridget Maclagan, 1912–13. Used her inheritance to establish military hospital at Rousbrugge, Belgium, in July 1915; her nursing staff included the American volunteer Ellen N. La Motte. Served as director of hospital at Bray-sur-Somme, August 1916–February 1917, and at hospital in Mont-Notre-Dame during the 1917 spring offensive in Champagne, before returning to Rousbrugge. Published four poems in the *English Review*, August–December 1917. After divorce from her first husband, married Edward Spears, a British liaison officer who had served with the French army on the Somme. Lived in Paris, 1918–21, before moving to England. Published *The Forbidden Zone* (1929), collection of sketches and poems based on wartime experiences, nonfiction work *The Technique of Marriage* (1933), and numerous novels, including *Jane: Our Stranger* (1923), *Flamingo* (1927), and *Passport for a Girl* (1939). Organized field hospital in Lorraine in February 1940. Escaped from Bordeaux in late June 1940 and returned to England. Reorganized hospital unit and served with Free French forces in Syria, Lebanon, Egypt, and Libya, 1941–42, and in eastern France in 1945; spent remainder of the war with her husband, who served as the British envoy to Syria and Lebanon, 1941–44. Published memoir *Journey Down a Blind Alley* (1946), describing experiences in Second World War. Continued to write novels, including *For the Record* (1950) and *Martin Merriedew* (1952). Died in Warfield, Berkshire, England.

Randolph Bourne (May 30, 1886–December 22, 1918) Born in Bloomfield, New Jersey, the son of a salesman. Suffered facial deformity from forceps injury during birth and spinal tuberculosis at age four that left him short-statured and hunchbacked. Attended Columbia, where he studied with John Dewey and Charles Beard and became editor of *Columbia Monthly*. Awarded undergraduate degree in 1912 and MA in 1913. Published series of essays in *The Atlantic Monthly*, collected in *Youth and Life* (1913). Traveled in Europe, 1913–14, observing scenes of nationalist fervor in Germany at the outbreak of war. Contributed essays regularly to *The New Republic* and served as its education editor; broke with *New Republic* colleagues over their support for American entry into World War I. Wrote antiwar essays published in *The Seven Arts*. Began long essay on the modern state, left unfinished at his death and published posthumously as "The State." Died in New York in the influenza epidemic.

Alfred Bryan (September 15, 1871–April 1, 1958) Born in Brantford, Ontario, Canada. Attended the Collegiate Institute in London, Ontario. Worked as a reporter in Chicago. Moved to New York City around 1905 and established himself as an arranger and songwriter for music publishing firms. Wrote lyrics for many successful songs, including "Come Josephine in My Flying Machine" (1910), "Peg o' My Heart" (1913), and "Oui, Oui, Marie" (1918). Became charter member of ASCAP in 1914. "I Didn't Raise My Boy to Be a Soldier" (1915), with music by Al Piantadosi, was recorded by numerous artists and inspired several parodies (a successful plagiarism suit asserted that the melody was derived from the 1914 song "How Much I Really Cared"). Contributed songs to Broadway revues, including *The Shubert Gaieties of 1919* and *The Midnight Rounders of 1920*. Published poetry collection *Pagan Love Lyrics* in 1925. Moved to Hollywood in 1928 to write songs for films. Died in Gladstone, New Jersey.

William Jennings Bryan (March 19, 1860–July 26, 1925) Born in Salem, Illinois, the son of a lawyer and farmer. Graduated from Illinois College, 1881, and from Union College of Law, 1883. Married Mary Baird in 1884. Practiced law in Jacksonville, Illinois, before moving to Lincoln, Nebraska, in 1887. Served in Congress as a Democrat, 1891–95. Became editor of the *Omaha World-Herald* and a successful lecturer. Won Democratic presidential nomination in 1896 and 1900 but was twice defeated by William McKinley. Founded *The Commoner*, successful weekly newspaper, in 1901. Won Democratic nomination in 1908 but was defeated by William Howard Taft. Became secretary of state in the Wilson administration in 1913 and served until June 9, 1915, when he resigned, fearing that Wilson's response to the sinking of the *Lusitania* would lead to war with Germany. Published *The Commoner* as a monthly until 1923. Served as special prosecutor at the Scopes evolution trial in Dayton, Tennessee, in 1925. Died in Dayton five days after the trial ended.

Robert J. Casey (March 14, 1890–December 5, 1962) Born in Beresford, South Dakota. Graduated from St. Mary's College in Kansas in 1910. Married Marie Driscoll, 1910. Worked for the *Des Moines Register and Leader*, *Houston Post*, *Chicago Inter-Ocean*, *Chicago Evening Journal*, and *Chicago Evening American*. Enlisted in army in 1917 and was commissioned as captain. Commanded Battery C, 124th Field Artillery Regiment, 33rd Division, in the St. Mihiel and Meuse-Argonne campaigns. Returned to journalism and joined *Chicago Daily News* in 1920, becoming prominent feature writer. Published travel books, including *Land of the Haunted Castles* (1921), *The Lost Kingdom of Burgundy* (1923), *Baghdad and Points East* (1928), *Four Faces of Siva* (1929), about Cambodia, and *Easter Island* (1931); war memoir *The Cannoneers Have Hairy Ears* (1927), which initially appeared anonymously; and several mysteries, including *The Secret of the Bungalow* (1930), *News Reel* (1932), *Hot Ice* (1933), and *The Third Owl* (1934). Served as war correspondent during World War II in France, Belgium, Luxembourg, Britain, North Africa, the Pacific, and Germany. Published *I Can't Forget: Personal Experiences of a War Correspondent* (1941), *Torpedo Junction: With the Pacific Fleet from Pearl Harbor to Midway* (1942), *Battle Below: The War of the Submarines* (1945), and *This Is Where I Came In* (1945). After the death of his first wife, married Hazel MacDonald in 1946. Retired from the *Chicago Daily News* in 1947. Continued to write; later books include *The Black Hills and Their Incredible Characters* (1949) and *Give the Man Room: The Story of Gutzon Borglum* (1952). Died in Evanston, Illinois.

Willa Cather (December 7, 1873–April 24, 1947) Born in Back Creek Valley, near Winchester, Virginia, daughter of a sheep farmer. Parents and other relatives moved to the Nebraska Divide in 1883, ultimately settling in Red Cloud. Attended University of Nebraska, where she studied Greek, Latin, French, German, and English literature; graduated 1894. Published poetry and short fiction and began contributing reviews to *The Nebraska State Journal*. Worked in Pittsburgh as a magazine editor and reviewer for Pittsburgh *Leader*, and later as high school Latin teacher. Published poetry collection *April Twilights* (1903) and story collection *The Troll Garden* (1905). Moved to New York in 1906 as editor of *McClure's Magazine*; subsequently spent time in Boston and London, and frequently returned to Nebraska. First novel *Alexander's Bridge* published in 1912, followed by *O Pioneers!* (1913), *The Song of the Lark* (1915), and *My Ántonia* (1918). Traveled extensively in Southwest. Toured French battlefields to research novel *One of Ours* (1922), inspired by cousin G. P. Cather, who was killed at Cantigny in 1918. Later novels included *A Lost Lady* (1923), *The Professor's House* (1925), *My Mortal Enemy* (1926), *Death Comes for the Archbishop* (1927), *Shadows on the Rock* (1931), *Lucy Gayheart* (1935), and *Sapphira and the Slave Girl* (1940), along with story collections *Youth and the Bright Medusa* (1920), *Obscure Destinies* (1932), and *The Old Beauty and Others* (1945). Died in New York City.

Carrie Chapman Catt (June 9, 1859–March 9, 1947) Born Carrie Lane in Ripon, Wisconsin, the daughter of a farmer. Graduated from Iowa State Agricultural College in 1880. Taught school in Mason City, Iowa, 1881–83, and served as its superintendent of schools, 1883–85. Married Leo Chapman, a newspaper editor, in 1885, but was widowed in 1886. Became a professional lecturer. Worked as an organizer for the Iowa Woman Suffrage Association, 1889–92, and the National American Woman Suffrage Association, 1890–1900. Married George Catt, an engineer, in 1890, and settled in Brooklyn in 1892. Succeeded Susan B. Anthony as president of NAWSA, 1900–4. Helped found the International Woman Suffrage Association in 1902 and served as its president until 1923. Widowed in 1905. Traveled around the world, 1911–12, on behalf of the IWSA. Succeeded Anna Howard Shaw as president of NAWSA in 1915 and served until the ratification of the Nineteenth Amendment in 1920. Helped found the League of Woman Voters in 1919 and the National Committee on the Cause and Cure of War in 1925. Died in New Rochelle, New York.

John Jay Chapman (March 2, 1862–November 4, 1933) Born in New York City, the son of a stockbroker. Graduated from Harvard in 1884, and was admitted to the New York bar in 1888. Married Minna Timmins in 1889; after her death, he married Elizabeth Winthrop

Chanler in 1898. Became active in reform politics in New York City. Published *Emerson and Other Essays* (1898), *Causes and Consequences* (1898), *Practical Agitation* (1900), and a magazine, *The Political Nursery*, 1897–1901. Led public prayer meeting in Coatesville, Pennsylvania, in 1912 on first anniversary of the lynching of black steelworker Zachariah Walker. Later books included *William Lloyd Garrison* (1913), *Memories and Milestones* (1915), *Greek Genius and Other Essays* (1915), *Letters and Religion* (1924), and *New Horizons in American Life* (1932). Son Victor, a pilot in the Lafayette Escadrille killed in 1916, was the first American aviator to die in World War I. Died in Poughkeepsie, New York.

Victor Chapman (April 17, 1890–June 23, 1916) Born in New York City, the son of John Jay Chapman. Graduated from Harvard in 1913. Moved to Paris to study architecture at L'École des Beaux-Arts. Joined French Foreign Legion in August 1914 and was sent with his regiment to trenches in Picardy in December 1914. Began pilot training in French aviation service in September 1915. Joined Escadrille N. 124, fighter squadron with American volunteer pilots, in April 1916 (unit later became known as the Lafayette Escadrille). Began flying patrols in Nieuport 11 over Verdun sector in late May. Wounded in head during fight with German aircraft on June 17, but continued flying. Shot down and killed in battle with German Fokkers near Beaumont-en-Verdunois on June 23, 1916. A collection of his wartime letters was published posthumously by his father in 1917.

George M. Cohan (July 3, 1878–November 5, 1942) Born in Providence, Rhode Island, the son of vaudeville performers. Appeared on stage from an early age with parents and older sister in act billed as "The Four Cohans." Began publishing songs in 1893. Married Ethel Levey in 1899. Wrote hit Broadway musical *Little Johnny Jones* (1904), in which he also appeared with his family; show featured songs "Give My Regards to Broadway" and "The Yankee Doodle Boy." Subsequently created and produced over fifty Broadway shows, 1904–20, and wrote hit songs including "You're a Grand Old Flag," "Forty-Five Minutes from Broadway," and "Mary Is a Grand Old Name." After divorce from his first wife, married Agnes Nolan in 1907. "Over There" (1917), written in response to America's entry into World War I, was widely performed and recorded. Published autobiography *Twenty Years on Broadway and the Years It Took to Get There* (1925). Later appeared on Broadway in Eugene O'Neill's *Ah, Wilderness!* (1933) and the Rodgers and Hart musical *I'd Rather Be Right* (1937). Shortly before his death, expressed satisfaction with his on-screen portrayal by James Cagney in Warner Brothers film *Yankee Doodle Dandy* (1942). Died in New York City.

George Creel (December 1, 1876–October 2, 1953) Born in Lafayette County, Missouri, the son of a farmer. Reporter for *Kansas City World*, 1896. Freelance joke writer for newspapers and magazines in New York City, 1897–98. Co-founded *Kansas City Independent*, a weekly newspaper, in 1899 and served as its publisher and editor until 1909. Editorial writer for the *Denver Post*, 1909–10, and the (Denver) *Rocky Mountain News*, 1911–13. Married Blanche Bates, 1912. Supported Woodrow Wilson in 1912 presidential election. Served as reform police commissioner of Denver, 1912–13, before losing position in political power struggle. Wrote for magazines and published *Children in Bondage* (1914), study of child labor written with Edwin Markham and Ben Lindsay. Worked on Wilson's reelection campaign and published *Wilson and the Issues* (1916). Appointed chairman of the Committee on Public Information, government wartime propaganda organization, in April 1917 and served until its dissolution in June 1919. Published *Ireland's Fight for Freedom* (1919), *The War, The World, and Wilson* (1920), and *How We Advertised America* (1920). Moved to San Francisco in 1926. Published a history of Mexico, *The People Next Door* (1926), *Sam Houston: Colossus in Buckskin* (1928), and *Tom Paine: Liberty Bell* (1932). Defeated by Upton Sinclair in 1934 California Democratic gubernatorial primary. After death of his wife, married Alice Rosseter in 1943. Published *War Criminals and Punishment* (1944), autobiography *Rebel at Large* (1947), and *Russia's Race for Asia* (1949). Died in San Francisco.

E. E. Cummings (October 14, 1894–September 3, 1962) Born Edward Estlin Cummings in Cambridge, Massachusetts, the son of a Unitarian minister who taught sociology at Harvard. Began writing poetry at an early age. Graduated from Harvard in 1915. Volunteered for Norton-Harjes Ambulance Service in 1917. Along with William Slater Brown, a fellow volunteer, abandoned unit in Paris. Imprisoned for three months in Normandy with Brown on suspicion of sedition. Married Elaine Orr in 1924. *The Enormous Room*, a prose account of his incarceration in France, appeared in 1922, followed by poetry collections including *Tulips and Chimneys* (1923), *XLI Poems* (1925), *Is 5* (1926), *ViVa* (1931), and *No Thanks* (1935). *Collected Poems* appeared in 1938. Won Bollingen Prize in 1958. Died in North Conway, New Hampshire.

Leslie Davis (April 29, 1876–September 27, 1960) Born in Port Jefferson, New York. Graduated from Cornell University in 1898 and received law degree from George Washington University in 1904. Practiced law in Washington, D.C., and New York City, 1904–12. Joined State Department in 1912 and was appointed U.S. consul at Batum, Russia (now Batumi, Georgia). Married Catherine Carmen in

1912. Served at Batum until May 1914, when he was assigned to the Ottoman Empire and became consul in the neighboring cities of Harput and Mamouret-ul-Aziz (now Elâziğ) in eastern Anatolia. Sent series of dispatches to Ambassador Henry Morgenthau reporting on the course of the Armenian genocide in his province, April–December 1915. Sheltered as many as eighty Armenians in the consulate, and helped them escape to safer areas. Remained at post until May 1917, when he left the Ottoman Empire following break in diplomatic relations with the United States. Submitted detailed report on his service at Harput to the State Department in February 1918. (Report was published along with several of his 1915 dispatches as *The Slaughterhouse Province* in 1989.) Assigned as consul at Archangel, Russia, 1918; Helsinki, Finland, 1919; Zagreb, Yugoslavia, 1924; Patras, Greece, 1929; Oporto, Portugal, 1930; and Glasgow, Scotland, 1936. Retired from State Department in 1941. Died in Pittsfield, Massachusetts.

Richard Harding Davis (April 18, 1864–April 11, 1916) Born in Philadelphia, the son of newspaper editor Lemuel Clarke Davis and novelist Rebecca Harding Davis. Attended Lehigh University and Johns Hopkins. Began a career in journalism in 1886, reporting for the *Philadelphia Record* and the *Philadelphia Press*; in 1889 joined staff of New York *Sun*, also contributing frequent articles to *Scribner's Magazine*. Traveled widely as a correspondent, publishing books including *The Rulers of the Mediterranean* (1894) and *Three Gringos in Venezuela and Central America* (1896). Covered conflicts including the Greco-Turkish War, the Cuban revolution and Spanish-American War, the Boer War, and the Russo-Japanese War. Published several volumes of war reporting, including *Cuba in War Time* (1897), *With Both Armies in South Africa* (1900), and *Notes of a War Correspondent* (1910). A prolific writer of popular fiction and drama, Davis wrote nineteen novels and short story collections, including *Gallegher and Other Stories* (1891), *Soldiers of Fortune* (1897), *The King's Jackal* (1898), and *The Bar Sinister* (1903), and twenty-five plays, including *Ranson's Folly* (1904) and *Miss Civilization* (1906). Married Cecil Clark in 1899; after their divorce, married Elizabeth McEvoy in 1912. Reported on World War I from Belgium, France, Serbia, and Greece, publishing *With the Allies* (1914) and *With the French in France and Salonika* (1916). Died in Mount Kisco, New York.

Eugene V. Debs (November 5, 1855–October 20, 1926) Born in Terre Haute, Indiana, the son of a grocer. Began working in a railroad shop in 1870 and became a locomotive fireman. Helped found local lodge of the Brotherhood of Locomotive Firemen in 1875. Secretary-treasurer of the national Brotherhood, 1880–93. City clerk of Terre Haute, 1879–83. Elected as a Democrat to the Indiana house of representatives in 1884. Served during 1885 term and did not seek reelection. Married Katherine Metzel in 1885. Founded American Railway Union in 1893. Led strike against Pullman Company that resulted in an injunction that crippled the union. Served six-month sentence for contempt in 1895. Founded Social Democratic Party of America in 1897 and was its presidential candidate in 1900. Presidential candidate of the Socialist Party in 1904, 1908, and 1912, when he received 6 percent of the vote. Convicted under the Espionage Act in 1918 for making an antiwar speech and sentenced to ten years' imprisonment. Received more than 900,000 votes in the 1920 presidential election while in prison. Released in 1921 after President Harding commuted his sentence. Died in Elmhurst, Illinois.

W. A. Domingo (November 26, 1889–February 14, 1968) Born Wilfred Adolphus Domingo in Kingston, Jamaica. Joined National Club, political movement campaigning for Jamaican home rule. Co-wrote pamphlet *The Struggling Mass* (1910) with fellow Club member Marcus Garvey. Moved to Boston in 1910 and to New York City in 1912. Founding editor of *Negro World*, official newspaper of Garvey's Universal Negro Improvement Association, August 1918–July 1919; dismissed by Garvey for advocating socialism. Joined *The Messenger*, socialist magazine published by A. Philip Randolph and Chandler Owen, as contributing editor in 1919. Became member of the African Blood Brotherhood for Liberation and Redemption, radical group founded by Cyril Briggs, and contributed articles to Briggs's magazine *The Crusader*. Published *The Emancipator*, March–May 1920. Broke with Randolph and Chandler in 1923 over their criticism of West Indian immigration. Established business importing fruits and vegetables from the Caribbean. Essay "Gift of the Black Tropics" published in Alain Locke's anthology *The New Negro* (1925). Helped found Jamaica Progressive League, organization established in New York in 1936 to campaign for Jamaican self-government. Became active supporter of the People's National Party, founded in Jamaica in 1938. Arrested by British authorities on his arrival in Jamaica in June 1941 and imprisoned without charge under wartime emergency regulations until February 1943, when he was released after widespread protests. Broke with the PNP and returned to New York in 1947. Published *The British West Indian Federation: A Critique* (1956) and *Federation: Jamaica's Folly* (1958). Died in New York.

John Dos Passos (January 14, 1896–September 28, 1970) Born John Roderigo Madison in Chicago, Illinois, the natural son of Lucy Madison and John Randolph Dos Passos, a prominent corporation lawyer. Parents married in 1910. Graduated from Harvard in 1916. Served with Norton-Harjes Ambulance Corps in France, 1917, and Italy,

1918. Traveled in Spain and Portugal. Settled in New York City in 1920. Published war novels *One Man's Initiation* (1920) and *Three Soldiers* (1921). Traveled in the Middle East and the Caucasus, 1921–22. Published plays, poetry, travel writing, journalism, and novels *Manhattan Transfer* (1925) and the *U.S.A.* trilogy, consisting of *The 42nd Parallel* (1930), *1919* (1932), and *The Big Money* (1936). Married Katharine Smith in 1929. Returned to Spain in 1937 to help write film about the Civil War; learned that his longtime friend Jose Robles had been executed by Communists for alleged spying. Disenchantment with left-wing political movements was expressed in later novels including *Adventures of a Young Man* (1939), *Number One* (1943), *The Grand Design* (1949), *The Prospect Before Us* (1950), and *Midcentury* (1961); supported Senator Barry Goldwater in 1964 election. Following death of his wife in 1947, married Elizabeth Holdridge in 1949. Died in Baltimore.

W.E.B. Du Bois (February 23, 1868–August 29, 1963) Born William Edward Burghardt Du Bois in Great Barrington, Massachusetts, the son of a barber and a domestic servant. Entered Fisk University in 1885; spent summers teaching in the South; graduated Fisk 1888. Studied philosophy at Harvard, awarded BA cum laude in 1890, MA in history in 1891. Studied for two years in Berlin. Awarded PhD in history from Harvard in 1895. Taught at Wilberforce University, 1894–97. Married Nina Gomer in 1896. Published *The Suppression of the Africa Slave-Trade to the United States of America 1638–1870* (1896), *The Philadelphia Negro* (1899), and *The Souls of Black Folk* (1903). Professor of history and economics at Atlanta University, 1897–1910. Helped found National Association for the Advancement of Colored People in 1909 and edited its monthly magazine, *The Crisis*, 1910–34. Executive secretary of Pan-African Congress held in Paris in 1919. Later books included *John Brown* (1909), *Darkwater* (1920), *Black Reconstruction* (1935), and *Dusk of Dawn* (1940). Resigned from NAACP in 1934 in policy dispute. Professor of sociology at Atlanta University, 1934–44. Returned to NAACP in 1944 as director of special research, but was dismissed in 1948 for criticizing "reactionary, war-mongering" American foreign policy. Helped found Peace Information Center in 1950 and served as its chairman. Indicted in 1951 under Foreign Agents Registration Act for his role in the now-dissolved Center; charges were dismissed at trial later in the year. After wife's death, married Shirley Graham in 1951. Denied passport in 1952; after it was restored in 1958, visited Soviet Union and China. Settled in Ghana in 1961. Died in Accra.

Frederick Trevenen Edwards (July 11, 1892–October 6, 1918) Born in Cambridge, Massachusetts, the son of an Episcopal clergyman.

Attended Bowdoin College and the University of Wisconsin at Madison before graduating from Columbia University in 1915. Studied at the Episcopal General Theological Seminary until May 1917, when he volunteered for officer training. Commissioned as first lieutenant in 118th Field Artillery Regiment, 3rd Division. Arrived in France in May 1918. Served as gas officer and personnel adjutant at regimental headquarters in the Second Battle of the Marne and in the Marne-Aisne offensive, July 1918. Regiment returned to front in the St. Mihiel and Meuse-Argonne campaigns. Wound by German shellfire at Montfaucon on October 5, 1918, and died the next day in American military hospital at Fleury-sur-Aire.

Clyde D. Eoff (April 28, 1893–November 12, 1984) Born in Nebraska. Worked as taxi driver in Omaha in 1913. Landed in France in summer 1918 and served in St. Mihiel and Meuse-Argonne campaigns with 314th Mobile Ordnance Repair Shop, 89th Division. Returned to United States in 1919. Married Ruth Bundy in 1923. Died in Orange County, California.

James Reese Europe (February 22, 1880–May 9, 1919) Born in Mobile, Alabama; father was a Baptist minister, mother a teacher and church musician. Family moved to Washington, D.C., in 1889. Studied violin and piano. Joined the Memphis Students, New York–based troupe of black musicians and dancers, in 1905. Served as musical director for plays *The Shoo-Fly Regiment, The Black Politician, The Red Moon*, and *Mr. Lode of Koal*, 1906–10. Founded Clef Club, labor organization and booking agency for black musicians, in 1910. Organized members into the 125-piece Clef Club Orchestra, which in 1912 became the first African American ensemble to play at Carnegie Hall. Married Willie Angrom Starke in 1913. Became the first black bandleader to record in the United States, cutting "Down Home Rag," "Too Much Mustard," and six other sides for Victor, December 1913–February 1914. Left Clef Club and founded Tempo Club, new organization for black musicians. Served as music director for popular dance team of Vernon and Irene Castle, 1914–15, and helped innovate the fox-trot. Enlisted in the 15th New York, a black National Guard regiment, in September 1916, and was commissioned as a first lieutenant. Organized and led regimental band. Arrived in France in January 1918; served as rifle company commander when the regiment, now known as the 369th Infantry, went into combat with the French army in April. Led regimental machine-gun company in fighting in Champagne before being gassed in late July. Served as bandleader for remainder of war after returning for duty. Led band when the 369th Infantry, now known as the "Harlem Hellfighters," marched up Fifth Avenue in victory parade on February 17, 1919. Recorded twenty-eight sides with the "Hellfighters" band for Pathé, March–May 1919. Stabbed to death in Boston by one of the drummers in his band. Became the first African American to receive a public funeral in New York.

Bernice Evans Published thirteen poems under title "The Sayings of Patsy" in the Sunday supplement of the *New York Call*, a socialist newspaper, from September 23, 1917, until March 17, 1918.

Jessie Fauset (April 27, 1882–April 30, 1961) Born Jessie Redmon Fauset in Camden County, New Jersey, the daughter of an African Methodist Episcopal minister. After being denied entrance to Bryn Mawr because of her race, graduated from Cornell University in 1905. Taught French and Latin at M Street High School (later Paul Laurence Dunbar High School) in Washington, D.C., 1906–19. Became contributor to *The Crisis* in 1912. Received master's degree in French from University of Pennsylvania in 1919. Named literary editor of *The Crisis* by W.E.B. Du Bois in 1919 and moved to New York City. Her essay "The Gift of Laughter" was included in Alain Locke's anthology *The New Negro* (1925). Held Sunday teas and literary soirées that became gathering places for writers and intellectuals. Published novels *There Is Confusion* (1924), *Plum Bun* (1928), *The Chinaberry Tree* (1931), and *Comedy: American Style* (1933). Left *The Crisis* in 1926 and began teaching at DeWitt Clinton High School in New York. Married Herbert Harris in 1929. Retired from teaching in 1944 and moved to Montclair, New Jersey. Died in Philadelphia.

Norman Fenton (March 21, 1895–January 18, 1977) Born Norman Feinberg in New York City, the son of a doctor. Graduated from Harvard with a BA in psychology, 1917, and MA, 1918. Served in army medical corps in France at Base Hospital 117, established to treat cases of war neurosis. Married Jessie Chase in 1921. Taught at Arizona State Teachers College, 1922–26. Received PhD in psychology from Stanford in 1925. Published *Shell Shock and Its Aftermath* (1927), based on follow-up studies of patients from Hospital 117. Taught at Ohio University, University of Southern California, and Claremont College before becoming professor of education at Stanford in 1937. Published *The Delinquent Boy and the Correctional School* (1935) and *Mental Hygiene in School Practice* (1943). Appointed deputy director for treatment of the California Department of Corrections, 1944. Published *The Prisoner's Family* (1959). Died in Pacific Grove, California.

Dorothy Canfield Fisher (February 17, 1879–November 9, 1958) Born Dorothea Francis Canfield in Lawrence, Kansas; father was professor of political economy and sociology at University of Kansas, mother an artist. Traveled to Europe with mother in 1890 and attended French schools. Graduated from Ohio State University in 1899. Did graduate work at Sorbonne; received PhD in French literature from Columbia in 1904. Married John Fisher in 1907. Published novels *Gunhild* (1907), *The Squirrel-Cage* (1912), and *The Bent Twig* (1915), and story collections *Hillsboro People* (1915) and *The Real Motive* (1916), along with educational works expounding the views of Maria Montessori, whom she had met in Rome. Joined her husband in 1916 in France, where he was working in war relief; returned to home in Arlington, Vermont, after the Armistice in 1918. Published story collections *Home Fires in France* (1918), *The Day of Glory* (1919), *Raw Material* (1923), and *Made-to-Order Stories* (1925) and novels *The Brimming Cup* (1921), *Rough-Hewn* (1922), *The Home-Maker* (1924), *Her Son's Wife* (1926), *The Deepening Stream* (1930), *Bonfire* (1933), *Seasoned Timber* (1939), as well as volumes of fiction and history for children. Served as member of the Book-of-the-Month Club selection committee, 1926–51. Son James, an army surgeon serving with a Ranger battalion in the Philippines, was killed in the raid on the Cabanatuan prisoner-of-war camp in 1945. Died in Arlington, Vermont.

Robert Frost (March 26, 1874–January 29, 1963) Born in San Francisco, California, the son of a journalist. Family moved to New Hampshire in 1885 following father's death. Attended Dartmouth in fall 1892. Worked as schoolteacher, in woolen mill, and as newspaper reporter. Married Elinor White in 1895. Attended Harvard, 1897–99, before taking up poultry farming. Moved to England in 1912 and published poetry collections *A Boy's Will* (1913) and *North of Boston* (1914). Met Ezra Pound and William Butler Yeats; formed close friendship with English essayist and poet Edward Thomas. Returned to United States in 1915. Began teaching at Amherst in 1917 and at the Bread Loaf School of English in 1921; would also hold appointments at the University of Michigan and Harvard. Later collections included *Mountain Interval* (1916), *Selected Poems* (1923), *New Hampshire* (1923), *West-Running Brook* (1928), *Collected Poems* (1930), *A Further Range* (1936), *A Witness Tree* (1942), *Steeple Bush* (1947), and *In the Clearing* (1962). Poetry Consultant to the Library of Congress, 1958–59. Recited his poem "The Gift Outright" at the inauguration ceremony of John F. Kennedy in 1961. Visited Russia in 1962. Awarded Bollingen Prize shortly before his death in Boston.

Edmond C. C. Genet (November 9, 1896–April 16, 1917) Born in Ossining, New York, the son of a lawyer. Sought appointment to U.S. Naval Academy but failed mathematics examination. Enlisted in Navy in 1912 and served on battleship *Georgia* in the Atlantic and

Caribbean. Deserted in January 1915 and went to France. Enlisted in French Foreign Legion and fought in Champagne; suffered concussion from shell burst during attack on the Butte de Souain on September 28. Accepted for flight training by French aviation service in May 1916. Joined Escadrille N. 124 (Lafayette Escadrille) in January 1917. Shot down and killed by German anti-aircraft fire while flying Nieuport 17 near St. Quentin.

Floyd Gibbons (July 16, 1887–September 24, 1939) Born in Washington, D.C. Attended Georgetown University, 1905–6; expelled for gambling. Hired as police reporter by *Minneapolis News*, 1907. Moved to *Milwaukee Free Press*, 1909. Joined *Chicago Tribune*, 1912. Married Isabella Pehrman in 1914 (they were divorced in 1924). Covered deployment of National Guard to the Mexican border, 1914; interviewed Mexican revolutionary Pancho Villa, 1915; and reported on Pershing expedition hunting Villa, 1916. Survived sinking of British liner *Laconia* off Ireland by U-boat on February 25, 1917, in which two American passengers died; his account of the sinking was widely reprinted and read into the *Congressional Record*. Covered American Expeditionary Forces in France, 1917–18. Seriously wounded during Marine attack on Belleau Wood, June 6, 1918, losing left eye. Published *"And They Thought We Wouldn't Fight"* (1918). Reported on the Sinn Fein insurrection in Ireland, 1919; the Soviet-Polish War, 1920; the famine in the Ukraine and southern Russia, 1921; and the Rif rebellion in Morocco, 1925. Left the *Chicago Tribune* in 1926. Published *The Red Knight of Germany* (1927), biography of fighter pilot Manfred von Richtofen, and *The Red Napoleon* (1929), speculative novel about a future world war. Made daily national broadcasts for NBC, 1930. Reported for International News Service on Sino-Japanese conflict, 1932, the Italian-Ethiopian War, 1935, and the Spanish Civil War. Died in Stroudsburg, Pennsylvania.

Ernest W. Gibson (December 29, 1872–June 20, 1940) Born in Londonderry, Vermont, the son of a farmer. Graduated from Norwich University in 1894. Served as principal of high school in Chester, Vermont, 1894–98. Married Grace Hadley in 1896. Studied at the University of Michigan Law School, 1898–99. Admitted to the bar in 1899 and began legal practice in Brattleboro, Vermont. Deputy clerk of the U.S. district court, 1899–1906. Elected as Republican to the state house of representatives, 1906–8, and the state senate, 1908–10. Served as captain in 1st Vermont Infantry, National Guard regiment that guarded the Mexican border in the summer of 1916, and in the 57th Pioneer Infantry, 1918–19; landed in France in October 1918 but did not see action. State's attorney for Windham County, 1919–21. Elected as Republican to vacant seat in Congress in 1923 and served until 1933. Appointed to vacant seat in the U.S. Senate in 1933, elected in 1934, and served until his death in Washington, D.C.

Hugh Gibson (August 16, 1883–December 12, 1954) Born in Los Angeles, California; father was a banker and businessman, mother a schoolteacher. Attended Pomona College, 1900–1902. Graduated from the École Libre des Sciences Politiques in Paris, 1907. Joined U.S. foreign service in 1908. Held positions as secretary of legation in Honduras, 1908, second secretary in London, 1909–10, private secretary to the assistant secretary of state, 1910–11, and secretary of legation in Cuba, 1911–13. Appointed secretary of the legation in Belgium, 1914. Worked with Herbert Hoover in establishing Commission for Relief in Belgium. Unsuccessfully sought reprieve for Edith Cavell, British nurse shot by the Germans in 1915 for helping Allied soldiers escape. Left Belgium in 1916 and served in London, Paris, and Vienna, 1916–19. Published *A Journal from Our Legation in Belgium* (1917). U.S. minister to Poland, 1919–24. Married Ynés Reyntiens in 1922. Minister to Switzerland, 1924–27, and ambassador to Belgium, 1927–33. Served on American delegations to Geneva naval conference, 1927, and London naval conference, 1930. Ambassador to Brazil, 1933–36, and Belgium, 1937–38. Declined appointment as ambassador to Germany and retired from the foreign service in 1938. Published *Rio* (1937), *Belgium* (1939), and *The Road to Foreign Policy* (1944). Served on commissions for Polish and Belgian Relief, 1940–41. Became editor at Doubleday. Served as director of Intergovernmental Committee for European Migration, 1952–54. Died in Geneva, Switzerland.

Emma Goldman (June 27, 1869–May 14, 1940) Born in Kovno, Russia (now Kaunas, Lithuania), the daughter of a merchant; subsequently lived in Königsberg, Germany, and St. Petersburg. Emigrated to the United States in 1885, settling in Rochester, New York. After a brief failed marriage to Jacob Kershner (never legally dissolved), moved to New York City. Met anarchist Alexander Berkman, who became lover and lifelong friend. Worked for anarchist publications and became famous as public speaker. During Homestead Strike of 1892, Berkman and Goldman planned assassination of Henry Clay Frick, manager of Carnegie Steel factory. Berkman attacked Frick in his home on July 23, 1892; Frick survived, and Berkman was sentenced to twenty-two years in prison. In 1893 Goldman was convicted of inciting a riot after addressing a mass rally in New York's Union Square and served ten months of a one year sentence on Blackwell's Island. Studied nursing in Vienna, 1895–96. Traveled in Europe in 1899–1900 and met leading European anarchists. When Leon Czolgosz, assassin of President William McKinley in 1901, cited her as an inspiration, Goldman was arrested but released after two weeks. Protested enforcement of the

Anarchist Exclusion Act of 1903. Founded magazine *Mother Earth* in 1906. Published *Anarchism and Other Essays* (1910) and *Social Significance of the Modern Drama* (1914). Supported Margaret Sanger's birth control campaign and was jailed for two weeks in 1916 for distributing information on contraceptives. Helped found the No-Conscription League in May 1917. Arrested in June 1917 and convicted the following month of conspiring to obstruct the draft. Began serving two-year sentence in Missouri in February 1918. Released in September 1919. Deported to Russia, with Berkman and 247 other suspected radicals, in December 1919. After initially supporting the Bolshevik regime, became disenchanted and left Russia, moving to Berlin in 1922 and London in 1924. Published *My Disillusionment in Russia* (1923). Autobiography *Living My Life* published in two volumes in 1931. Visited Barcelona during Spanish Civil War at invitation of anarcho-syndicalist organizations. Died of a stroke in Toronto, Canada.

Martha Gruening (1889–October 25, 1937) Born in New York City, the daughter of a physician. (Older brother Ernest Gruening later served as U.S. senator from Alaska, 1959–69.) Graduated from Smith College in 1909. Arrested while supporting striking shirtwaist workers in Philadelphia in 1910. Lecturer for the National College Equal Suffrage League, 1911–12. Protested exclusion of black delegates from Atlanta meeting of the National American Woman Suffrage Association in 1912. Served as assistant secretary for public relations for the NAACP, 1911–14. Published article "Two Suffrage Movements" in *The Crisis*, September 1912, linking woman suffrage with struggle against black disenfranchisement. Received law degree from New York University in 1914. Supported No-Conscription League founded by Alexander Berkman and Emma Goldman. Traveled to East St. Louis and Houston in 1917 to investigate racial violence for the NAACP and reported on her findings in *The Crisis*. With her friend Helen Boardman, established progressive egalitarian school in Marlboro, New York, in 1918. Wrote articles and reviews for *The Crisis*, *The Nation*, *The New Republic*, *The New York Times*, *Hound & Horn*, and *The Brooklyn Daily Eagle*. Lived in Paris, 1923–31, and wrote for international edition of the *Herald Tribune*. Published children's book *The Story of Mining* (1931). With Boardman, wrote controversial article for *The Nation* in 1934 criticizing attorney Charles Hamilton Houston and the NAACP for their handling of George Crawford murder trial in Virginia. Died in Northampton, Massachusetts.

James Norman Hall (April 22, 1887–July 5, 1951) Born in Colfax, Iowa, the son of a farmer and grocer. Graduated from Grinnell College in 1910. Worked for the Massachusetts Society for the Prevention of Cruelty to Children in Boston while studying for a master's degree at

Harvard. While on vacation in England at the outbreak of World War I, enlisted in the 9th Royal Fusiliers by claiming to be Canadian. Landed in France in May 1915 and served as machine gunner at the Battle of Loos. Discharged in December 1915 on discovery of his nationality. Returned to Boston. Published *Kitchener's Mob: The Adventures of an American in the British Army* (1916). Sent to France by *The Atlantic* to cover the formation of an American squadron in the French Air Service. Volunteered for aviation training in October 1916. Joined the Lafayette Escadrille (Escadrille N. 124) in June 1917 and was shot down and wounded later in the month. Returned to the Lafayette Escadrille in October 1917. Commissioned as captain in the U.S. Army aviation service in February 1918. Served with the 103rd Aero Squadron and 94th Aero Squadron. Published *High Adventure: A Narrative of Air Fighting in France* (1918). Shot down and captured near Pagny-sur-Moselle in Lorraine on May 7, 1918, and was a prisoner until the Armistice. Collaborated with Charles Nordhoff on *The Lafayette Flying Corps* (1920), history of American pilots in French service. Traveled to Tahiti with Nordhoff in 1920 and settled there for the remainder of his life. Married Sarah Winchester in 1925. Collaborated with Nordhoff on series of novels, including *Falcons of France* (1929); the trilogy *Mutiny on the Bounty* (1932), *Men Against the Sea* (1934), and *Pitcairn's Island* (1934); *The Hurricane* (1936); *Botany Bay* (1941); and *Men Without a Country* (1942). Published numerous books written on his own, including *On the Stream of Travel* (1926), *Mid-Pacific* (1928), *Doctor Dogbody's Leg* (1940), *Lost Island* (1944), *The Far Lands* (1950), and *My Island Home* (1952). Died in Arue, Tahiti.

Warren G. Harding (November 2, 1865–August 2, 1923) Born in Blooming Grove, Ohio, the son of a farmer who became a homeopathic practitioner. Graduated from Ohio Central College in 1882. Became editor and publisher of the *Marion Star* in 1884. Married Florence DeWolfe in 1891. Elected as a Republican to the Ohio state senate and served, 1899–1903. Lieutenant governor of Ohio, 1904–05. Unsuccessful candidate for governor in 1910. Elected as a Republican to the U.S. Senate and served, 1915–21. Won the Republican presidential nomination in 1920 and defeated Governor James M. Cox. President of the United States from 1921 until his death. Died in San Francisco from a heart attack.

Hubert H. Harrison (April 27, 1883–December 17, 1927) Born on St. Croix, Danish West Indies. Immigrated to New York City in 1900 following the death of his mother. Worked as hotel bellman and telephone operator while attending school at night. Graduated from high school in 1907 and began working as postal clerk. Married Irene Louise Horton in 1909. Joined Socialist Party. Published letters in the

New York Sun in 1910 criticizing Booker T. Washington; lost post office job in 1911 due to retaliation by one of Washington's supporters. Became prominent lecturer, writer, and organizer in New York Socialist Party, 1911–14, before breaking with the party over its racial policies. Founded Liberty League of Negro-Americans in 1917 along with *The Voice*, a "newspaper for the New Negro" that called for enforcement of the Reconstruction amendments, federal antilynching legislation, and armed self-defense against racial violence. Published *The Negro and the Nation* (1917). After *The Voice* ceased publication, published short-lived newspaper *New Negro* in 1919. Became principal editor of *Negro World*, newspaper of Marcus Garvey's Universal Negro Improvement Association, in 1920. Published *When Africa Awakes* (1920). Contributed to *Negro World* until 1922, when he broke with Garvey. Became lecturer for New York Board of Education while continuing to write for the press. Died in New York City after undergoing appendectomy.

Ernest Hemingway (July 21, 1899–July 2, 1961) Born in Oak Park, Illinois. Reporter for *Kansas City Star*, 1917–18. Served as Red Cross ambulance driver and canteen worker with Italian army in World War I and was severely wounded in July 1918. Married Hadley Richardson in 1921. Traveled to France in 1921 as foreign correspondent for *Toronto Star*. First story collection *In Our Time* appeared in 1925, followed by novels *The Torrents of Spring* and *The Sun Also Rises* in 1926. After divorce from his first wife, married Pauline Pfeiffer in 1927. Returned to United States in 1928, settling in Key West in 1930. Subsequent fiction included *Men Without Women* (1927), *A Farewell to Arms* (1929), *Winner Take Nothing* (1933), and *To Have and Have Not* (1937); also published *Death in the Afternoon* (1932), about bullfighting, and *The Green Hills of Africa* (1935), about big game hunting. Covered Spanish Civil War as correspondent for North American Newspaper Alliance, 1936–37, an experience that helped inspire novel *For Whom the Bell Tolls* (1940). Settled in Cuba, 1939–40. After divorce from second wife, married war correspondent Martha Gellhorn in 1940 and traveled with her to China as correspondent for *PM*, 1941. War correspondent in northwest Europe for *Collier's*, May 1944–March 1945. After divorce from third wife, married former war correspondent Mary Welsh in 1946. Published *Across the River and Into the Trees* (1950) and *The Old Man and the Sea* (1952). Won Nobel Prize for literature in 1954. Committed suicide in Ketchum, Idaho.

Morris Hillquit (August 1, 1869–October 8, 1933) Born Moishe Hillkowitz in Riga, Russia (now Latvia), the son of a factory owner. Immigrated to New York City in 1886. Worked as cuff maker in shirt factory. Joined Socialist Labor Party of America in 1887 and became union organizer in garment industry. Graduated from New York University Law School in 1893 and became successful labor lawyer. Married Vera Levene in 1893. Led faction of Socialist Labor Party that merged with Social Democratic Party to form Socialist Party of America in 1901. Published *History of Socialism in the United States* (1903) and *Socialism in Theory and Practice* (1909). Ran for Congress in 1906, 1908, 1916, 1918, and 1920. Became counsel for International Ladies Garment Workers Union in 1913. Along with Algernon Lee and Charles Emil Ruthenberg, drafted antiwar resolution adopted by Socialist Party in spring 1917. Served as attorney for socialist publications censored by the post office. Ran for mayor of New York in 1917 and 1932. Elected national chairman of the Socialist Party in 1929. Died in New York City.

Oliver Wendell Holmes (March 8, 1841–March 6, 1935) Born in Boston, the son of the physician, poet, and essayist Oliver Wendell Holmes. Graduated from Harvard in 1861. Served as an officer with the 20th Massachusetts Volunteer Infantry, July 1861–July 1864, and was wounded at Ball's Bluff, Antietam, and the Second Battle of Fredericksburg. Graduated from Harvard Law School in 1866. Practiced law in Boston, wrote legal articles, and edited new edition of James Kent's *Commentaries on American Law*. Married Fanny Bowditch Dixwell in 1872. Published *The Common Law* in 1881. Served as an associate justice of the Massachusetts supreme judicial court, 1883–99, as its chief justice, 1899–1902, and as an associate justice of the U.S. Supreme Court, 1902–32. Died in Washington, D.C.

Herbert Hoover (August 10, 1874–October 20, 1964) Born in West Branch, Iowa, the son of a blacksmith. Graduated from Stanford in 1895. Married Lou Henry in 1899. Worked as a mining engineer in California, Nevada, Colorado, Australia, and in China, where he was trapped in Tientsin during the Boxer Rebellion. Served as chairman of the Commission for Relief in Belgium, 1914–20, U.S. Food Administrator, 1917–19, and director of the American Relief Administration, 1918–20; oversaw the distribution of food throughout Europe and the Near East. Secretary of Commerce in the administrations of Warren Harding and Calvin Coolidge, 1921–28. Won Republican presidential nomination in 1928 and defeated Governor Al Smith. President of the United States, 1929–33. Defeated for reelection by Franklin D. Roosevelt. Served as government coordinator for overseas food relief, 1946–47, and as chairman of commissions on government reorganization, 1947–49 and 1953–55. Died in New York City.

Carlos F. Hurd (September 22, 1876–June 8, 1950) Born in Cherokee, Iowa, the son of a Congregational minister. Graduated from

Drury College in 1897. Reporter for the *Springfield Leader* and *St. Louis Star* before joining *St. Louis Post-Dispatch* in 1900. Married Katherine Cordell in 1906. Witnessed rescue of survivors from the *Titanic* in April 1912 while a passenger on board the S.S. *Carpathia*; wrote 5,000-word story on the sinking that he delivered to editor on board tugboat in New York harbor, scooping the competition. Wrote eyewitness account of mob violence against African Americans during East St. Louis riot on July 2, 1917. Following death of his first wife, married Rachel Metcalfe in 1930. Published *Front Office Banker* (1943), biography of Charles Huttig. Wrote for *Post-Dispatch* until his final illness. Died in University City, Missouri.

Charles R. Isum (May 22, 1889–March 6, 1941) Born in California. Worked as bookbinder for the *Los Angeles Times*. Drafted into army and was assigned to the medical detachment of the First Battalion, 365th Infantry Regiment, 92nd Division. In June 1918 his regiment arrived in France, where it held the St. Die sector of the Lorraine front, August–September. Regiment was kept in reserve during opening of the Meuse-Argonne offensive before being sent to Marbache Sector along the Moselle in October. Served in battalion aid station at Pont-à-Mousson under heavy artillery fire, November 5–10, before being sent to Lesménils, where he was gassed on the night before the Armistice. Threatened with court-martial in January 1919 for violating order forbidding black soldiers from speaking with French women, but charges were dropped, and Isum was honorably discharged in March 1919. Returned to Los Angeles and job at the *Times*. Married Zellee Jones. Retired from work in 1930s as heart condition linked to wartime gassing worsened. Daughter Rachel, born 1922, began studying nursing in 1940 at UCLA, where she met star athlete Jackie Robinson and introduced him to her father shortly before his death. (Rachel Isum and Jackie Robinson married in 1946, the year before he joined the Brooklyn Dodgers.)

Henry James (April 15, 1843–February 28, 1916) Born in New York City, the son of the social and religious philosopher Henry James. Family traveled in England and France, 1843–45; returned to New York City. Educated in private schools and by tutors. Family moved between Europe and the United States, 1855–60, living in Newport, Rhode Island, and later Boston. Published first story in 1864 and first novel, *Watch and Ward*, in 1871. Traveled repeatedly to Europe, settling in London in 1876. Published novels including *Roderick Hudson* (1875), *The American* (1877), *Washington Square* (1880), and *The Portrait of a Lady* (1881). Published stories and criticism prolifically, along with novels including *The Bostonians* (1886), *The Princess Casamassima* (1886), and *The Tragic Muse* (1890). Aspired to a career as playwright; devastated by failure of his play *Guy Domville* (1895). Established residence at Lamb House in Rye, Sussex, in 1897. Later novels included *The Spoils of Poynton* (1897), *What Maisie Knew* (1897), *The Awkward Age* (1899), *The Sacred Fount* (1901), *The Wings of the Dove* (1902), *The Ambassadors* (1903), and *The Golden Bowl* (1904). Traveled through the United States, 1904–5, recording impressions in *The American Scene* (1907). Wrote prefaces for New York Edition of his fiction, 1906–8. Returned to United States in 1910 and remained for a year following the death of his brother William. Published autobiographies *A Small Boy and Others* (1913) and *Notes of a Son and Brother* (1914). Distressed by outbreak of war; participated in Belgian Relief and visited wounded soldiers in hospitals. Adopted British nationality in July 1915. Died in London.

James Weldon Johnson (June 17, 1871–June 26, 1938) Born in Jacksonville, Florida. Father was a hotel waiter, mother a schoolteacher. Graduated from Atlanta University in 1894. Principal of Stanton School in Jacksonville, 1894–1902. Published *Daily American* newspaper in Jacksonville, 1894–95. Studied law and was admitted to the Florida bar in 1898. Wrote lyrics to "Lift Ev'ry Voice and Sing," with music by brother J. Rosamond Johnson, in 1900. Moved to New York City in 1902 to write popular songs with Rosamond and performer Bob Cole. Served as U.S. consul in Puerto Cabella, Venezuela, 1906–9. Married Grace Nail in 1910. U.S. consul in Corinto, Nicaragua, 1910–12. Published novel *The Autobiography of an Ex-Colored Man* anonymously in 1912. Editorial writer for *The New York Age*, 1914–23. Named field secretary for the National Association for the Advancement of Colored People in 1916, and served as its secretary, 1920–30. Publications included poetry collection *Fifty Years* (1917), *God's Trombones: Seven Negro Sermons in Verse* (1927), *Black Manhattan* (1930), *Along This Way* (1933), and anthologies *The Book of American Negro Poetry* (1922) and *The Book of American Negro Spirituals* (1925). Killed when his car was struck at a railroad crossing near Wiscasset, Maine.

Vernon E. Kniptash (December 6, 1896–September 1987) Born in Terre Haute, Indiana, the son of a clerk for a dry goods wholesaler. Family moved to Indianapolis. Graduated from Manual High School in 1914. Became draftsman at architectural firm of Vonnegut and Bohn. (Firm was co-founded by Bernard Vonnegut, grandfather of the novelist Kurt Vonnegut.) Enlisted in April 1917. Landed in France in November 1917 with 150th Field Artillery Regiment, 42nd (Rainbow) Division. Assigned to regimental headquarters as wireless operator. Served in Lunéville and Baccarat sectors of the Lorraine front, February–June 1918, and in Marne-Aisne, St. Mihiel, and

Meuse-Argonne campaigns, July–November 1918. Discharged as corporal in May 1919. Returned to work at Vonnegut and Bohn. Married Maude Wolfe in 1920. Studied structural engineering. Lost job with Vonnegut and Bohn during the Depression. Worked for U.S. Army Corps of Engineers. Joined the Carl M. Geupel Company, major Indiana construction firm, in 1942 as consulting engineer. After the death of his first wife, married Margaret Kellenbach in 1946. Retired in 1967.

Ellen N. La Motte (November 27, 1873–March 2, 1961) Born in Louisville, Kentucky, the daughter of a businessman. Graduated from Johns Hopkins Training School for Nurses in 1902. Worked at Johns Hopkins, as private duty nurse in Italy, and at St. Luke's Hospital in St. Louis. Returned to Baltimore in 1905. Became expert on tuberculosis nursing; served as superintendent of the tuberculosis division of the Baltimore Health Department, 1910–13. Campaigned for woman suffrage. Reported from London on militant suffragist protests for the *Baltimore Sun,* 1913. Moved to Paris in fall 1913. Wrote *The Tuberculosis Nurse: Her Functions and Her Qualifications* (1915). Joined nursing staff of military hospital established by Mary Borden at Rousbrugge, Belgium, in July 1915 and remained there for a year. Wrote sketches collected in *The Backwash of War: The Human Wreckage of the Battlefield as Witnessed by an American Hospital Nurse* (1916). Traveled with companion Emily Chadbourne to Japan, China, Hong Kong, Indochina, Siam, and Singapore, 1916–17. Published travel book *Peking Dust* (1919) and *Civilization: Tales of the Orient* (1919). Campaigned against European involvement in the opium trade. Published *The Opium Monopoly* (1920), *The Ethics of Opium* (1924), and story collection *Snuffs and Butters* (1925). Lived with Chadbourne in England, Washington, D.C., and Stone Ridge, New York. Died in Washington, D.C.

Robert Lansing (October 17, 1864–October 30, 1928) Born in Watertown, New York, the son of a lawyer. Graduated from Amherst in 1886. Read law in father's office and was admitted to the bar in 1889. Formed family partnership in Watertown that lasted until father's death in 1907. Married Eleanor Foster in 1890; her father, John Watson Foster, was a lawyer and diplomat who served as secretary of state, 1892–93. (Lansing was uncle to John Foster Dulles, future secretary of state, and Allen Welsh Dulles, future director of the Central Intelligence Agency.) Through his father-in-law, Lansing began practice in international law, serving as American counsel to arbitration panels and claims commissions for the Bering Sea, the Alaskan boundary, and the North Atlantic fisheries. Helped found *American Journal of International Law* in 1907. Appointed Counselor for the State Department (the second-ranking position) in March 1914.

Succeeded William Jennings Bryan as secretary of state on June 9, 1915. Attended Paris Peace Conference in 1919. Disagreements with President Wilson over the League of Nations and tensions arising from Wilson's illness led to his dismissal on February 13, 1920. Resumed practice of international law. Published *The Peace Negotiations: A Personal Narrative* (1921) and *The Big Four and Others of the Peace Conference* (1921). Died in Washington, D.C.

Charles E. Lauriat, Jr. (August 4, 1874–December 28, 1937) Born in Swampscott, Massachusetts, son of a Boston publisher and bookseller. Worked in father's bookselling business. Married Marian Bullard in 1912. Survived sinking of the *Lusitania*; published *The Lusitania's Last Voyage* (1915). Following his father's death in 1920, became president of the Lauriat company. Died in Brookline, Massachusetts.

Algernon Lee (September 15, 1873–January 5, 1954) Born in Dubuque, Iowa, the son of a carpenter. Attended University of Minnesota, 1892–97. Joined Socialist Labor Party in 1895 and Socialist Party of America in 1901. Moved to New York City in 1899 to become editor of *The Worker*. Became educational director of the Rand School of Social Science in 1909. Along with Morris Hillquit and Charles Emil Ruthenberg, co-authored antiwar resolution adopted by Socialist Party in spring 1917. Left Socialist Party in factional split in 1936 and helped form Social Democratic Federation. Died in Amityville, New York.

Sam Lewis (October 25, 1885–November 22, 1959) Born Samuel M. Levine in New York City. Established career as songwriter beginning in 1912, writing lyrics (often in collaboration with Joe Young) for many hits including "Rock-a-Bye Your Baby with a Dixie Melody" (1918), "Dinah" (1925), "I'm Sitting on Top of the World" (1925), "In a Little Spanish Town" (1926), and "Just Friends" (1931). Was a charter member of ASCAP in 1914. "How You Gonna Keep Down on the Farm" (1919) was popularized by many recording artists, including Sophie Tucker, Nora Bayes, and James Reese Europe's 369th Infantry Band. Lewis died in New York City.

Ludwig Lewisohn (May 30, 1882–December 31, 1955) Born in Berlin. Came with family to United States in 1890 and was raised in Charleston, South Carolina. His Jewish parents were converts to Christianity and in his youth Lewisohn was an active Methodist. Graduated from College of Charleston and received MA degree from Columbia University in 1903. Married Mary Crocker in 1906. Taught at Ohio State University, 1911–19. Was an editor of *The Nation*, 1919–24. Returned to Judaism and became strong supporter of Zionism, publishing *Israel* (1925), *The Answer: The Jew and the World* (1939), and *The*

American Jew (1950). Published memoirs *Up Stream* (1922) and *Mid-Channel* (1929), and many novels including *The Broken Snare* (1908), *Roman Summer* (1927), *The Island Within* (1928), *Stephen Escott* (1930), *Trumpet of Jubilee* (1937), and *In a Summer Season* (1955). *The Case of Mr. Crump* (1926), an autobiographical novel recounting the difficulties of his unraveling marriage, was withheld from American publication until 1947 because of a threatened libel suit by Lewisohn's wife. He later married Edna Manley in 1940 and Louise Wolk in 1944. He was a prolific translator of German authors and published many critical works including *The Modern Drama* (1915) and *Expression in America* (1932). He edited *New Palestine*, 1944–48, and in 1948 was a founding faculty member of Brandeis, where he taught comparative literature until his death. Died in Miami Beach, Florida.

Walter Lippmann (September 23, 1889–December 14, 1974) Born in New York City, the son of an investor. Took annual holidays in Europe with his German-Jewish parents. At Harvard studied under George Santayana and William James, and was president of Harvard Socialist Club. Published *A Preface to Politics* (1913), *Drift and Mastery* (1914), and *The Stakes of Diplomacy* (1915). Became a founding editor of *The New Republic* in 1914. Supported reelection of Wilson in 1916 and American intervention in the war. Married Faye Albertson in 1917. Served as assistant to Secretary of War Newton D. Baker before becoming leading member of "The Inquiry," secret group of government advisors working on terms of peace settlement. Helped draft memorandum that served as a basis for Wilson's Fourteen Points. Commissioned as captain in military intelligence in 1918 and served in England and France, working on propaganda projects. Returned to United States in January 1919. Published *Public Opinion* (1922), influential study of modern communications technology and the dangers of mass manipulation, and *The Phantom Public* (1925). Left *The New Republic* and became editorial writer for the *New York World*, 1922–29, and its executive editor, 1929–31. Moved to *New York Herald Tribune* after the *World* ceased publication; syndicated column "Today and Tomorrow" began appearing in 1931 and ended in 1967. Following divorce from his first wife, married Helen Armstrong in 1938. His later books included *A Preface to Morals* (1929), *A New Social Order* (1933), *The Good Society* (1937), *The Cold War* (1947), and *Essays in the Public Philosophy* (1955). Awarded Pulitzer Prize for journalism in 1958 and 1962. Became public critic of American intervention in Vietnam in 1965. Died in New York City.

Henry Cabot Lodge (May 12, 1850–November 9, 1924) Born in Boston, the son of a successful merchant. Graduated from Harvard in 1871. Married Anna Cabot Davis in 1871. Graduated from Harvard

Law School in 1874; awarded a PhD in history and government by Harvard in 1876. Wrote numerous historical works, including biographies of Alexander Hamilton (1882), Daniel Webster (1883), and George Washington (1888). Elected to the Massachusetts house of representatives as a Republican and served 1880–81. Served in Congress, 1887–93, and in the Senate from 1893 until his death. Chairman of the Senate Republican conference, 1918–24, and the Foreign Relations Committee, 1919–24. Died in Cambridge, Massachusetts.

Edward C. Lukens (September 29, 1893–May 17, 1948) Born in Elizabeth, New Jersey, the son of an iron manufacturer. Graduated from Princeton in 1915. Joined army and became platoon commander in Company I, Third Battalion, 320th Infantry Regiment, 80th Division. Arrived in France in June 1918. Served in British trenches southwest of Arras, July–August, and in the St. Mihiel and Meuse-Argonne offensives. Awarded Silver Star for organizing patrols under fire, October 9–12, 1918; his older brother Alan, a captain in the 316th Infantry, 79th Division, was killed near Montfaucon on September 29, 1918, and posthumously awarded the Distinguished Service Cross. Returned to United States in 1919 with rank of first lieutenant. Attended University of Pennsylvania Law School. Began law practice in Philadelphia, 1920. Published *A Blue Ridge Memoir* (1922), account of his war service. Married Frances B. Day. Contributed articles to magazines and legal journals, and became active in Republican politics. Served as major in Allied military government in North Africa, Sicily, and France during World War II. Died in Philadelphia.

Henry A. May (July 25, 1874–June 21, 1960) Received medical degree from Columbian College in 1899. Commissioned in U.S. Navy medical corps in 1904. Served as lieutenant commander on board troopship USS *Leviathan* in 1918. Retired from navy with rank of captain. Died in Bethesda, Maryland.

Claude McKay (September 15, 1889–May 22, 1948) Born Festus Claudius McKay near Clarendon Hills, Jamaica, youngest of eleven children. Joined Jamaican Constabulary in 1909. Published poetry collections *Songs of Jamaica* and *Constab Ballads*, both 1912. Came to United States after winning poetry prize and enrolled at Tuskegee Institute; moved to New York City in 1914. Formed friendship with Max Eastman and published poems in his magazine *The Liberator*. Traveled to London in 1920 and to the Soviet Union in 1922 and 1923. Remained in Europe until 1934, settling in Marseilles. Published poetry collection *Spring in New Hampshire* (1920) and novels *Home to Harlem* (1928), *Banjo* (1929), and *Banana Bottom* (1933). After return to America, married Ellen Tarry in 1938. Worked for National Catholic Youth Organization in Chicago, where he died.

H. L. Mencken (September 12, 1880–January 29, 1956) Born Henry Louis Mencken in Baltimore, Maryland, son of a cigar manufacturer. Graduated from Baltimore Polytechnic Institute in 1896. Began reporting for the Baltimore *Herald* in 1899; covered election of 1900 and served as drama critic; became city editor of *Morning Herald*, 1903, and *Evening Herald*, 1904. After *Herald* ceased publication, became editor of the Baltimore *Sunday Sun* in 1906. Published *The Philosophy of Friedrich Nietzsche* (1908). Became editor of newly established Baltimore *Evening Sun* in 1910. Began daily column "The Free Lance," 1911. Became co-editor of *The Smart Set* with George Jean Nathan in 1914. Criticized anti-German propaganda in "The Free Lance" before ending the column in October 1915. Resigned editorship at the *Sun* in 1916. Reported on the war from Germany, January–February 1917. Published *A Book of Prefaces* (1917), *In Defense of Women* (1918), *The American Language* (1919), and *Prejudices: First Series* (1919), which was followed by five further volumes, 1920–34. Contributed weekly column to the *Evening Sun*, 1920–38, and the Sunday *Sun*. Left *The Smart Set* in 1923. Founded and edited *The American Mercury*, 1924–33. Covered Scopes evolution trial in 1925. Married Sara Powell Haardt in 1930. Published *Treatise on the Gods* (1930). Published memoirs *Happy Days* (1940), *Newspaper Days* (1941), and *Heathen Days* (1943). Resigned from *Sun* papers in 1941 because of his isolationism and opposition to the Roosevelt administration. Suffered debilitating stroke in 1948. Died in Baltimore.

Shirley Millard (November 25, 1890–March 4, 1977) Born Shirley Eastham, daughter of a socially prominent family in Portland, Oregon. Served as Red Cross nurse with French military hospital in 1918. Married Alfred Millard, Jr., in 1919; they were divorced in 1931. Published memoir *I Saw Them Die: Diary and Recollections of Shirley Millard* (1936). Died in Los Angeles, California.

Henry Morgenthau (April 26, 1856–November 25, 1946) Born in Mannheim, Baden, Germany, the son of a cigar manufacturer. Family immigrated to the United States in 1866 and settled in New York City. Graduated from Columbia Law School in 1877. Practiced law and successfully invested in real estate. Married Josephine Sykes in 1883. (Their son, Henry Morgenthau, Jr., would serve as secretary of the treasury under Franklin D. Roosevelt; their grandchildren included the historian Barbara Tuchman and longtime Manhattan district attorney Robert M. Morgenthau.) Left law practice in 1899 to become president of Central Realty Bond & Trust; founded Henry Morgenthau Company, real estate investment and development firm, in 1905. Supported numerous social reform and charitable organizations in New York City. Served as finance chairman of 1912 Democratic national campaign. U.S. ambassador to the Ottoman Empire, December 1913–February 1916; sent reports to State Department on the Armenian genocide. Returned to the United States to serve as finance chairman for President Wilson's reelection campaign and to raise funds for Armenian relief. Published *Ambassador Morgenthau's Story* (1918). Headed special U.S. diplomatic commission that investigated situation of the Jewish population of Poland, July–September 1919. Published autobiography *All in a Life-Time* (1922), written with French Strother. Served as chairman of the League of Nations Refugee Settlement Commission, established in 1923 to aid Greek refugees fleeing Turkey. Died in New York City.

Hugo Münsterberg (June 1, 1863–December 16, 1916) Born in Danzig, Prussia (now Gdansk, Poland). Father was a lumber merchant, mother an artist. Received PhD in psychology from University of Leipzig in 1885 and medical degree from University of Heidelberg in 1887. Married Selma Oppler in 1887. Taught at University of Freiburg, 1887–92. Accepted invitation from William James to serve as director of the Harvard psychology laboratory, 1892–95. Returned to Freiburg, then accepted appointment as professor of psychology at Harvard in 1897. Taught at University of Berlin, 1910–11; founded the American Institute in Berlin. Besides works on psychology written in German, published numerous books in English, including *American Traits from the Point of View of a German* (1901), *The Americans* (1904), *On the Witness Stand* (1908), *Psychology and Crime* (1908), *Psychology and Industrial Efficiency* (1913), *The War and America* (1914), and *The Photoplay: A Psychological Study* (1916). Defended German policies after outbreak of war, drawing widespread condemnation and calls for his dismissal from Harvard. (Münsterberg retained his German nationality and never became a naturalized American citizen.) Died of a stroke on lecture platform at Radcliffe College in Cambridge, Massachusetts.

George Norris (July 11, 1861–September 2, 1944) Born in York Township, Sandusky County, Ohio, the son of a farmer. Graduated from Northern Indiana Normal School at Valparaiso, 1880, and received degree from its law school, 1883. Established law practice in Beaver City, Furnas County, Nebraska, in 1885. Married Pluma Lashley in 1889. Elected county attorney in 1892 and served three terms; elected judge of Fourteenth District in 1895 and served until 1902. Moved to McCook, Nebraska, in 1899. Elected to Congress as a Republican and served, 1903–13. Following death of his first wife, married Ellie Leonard in 1903. Supported Progressive Party candidacy of

Theodore Roosevelt for president in 1912, the same year he was elected to the Senate as a Republican. Reelected in 1918, 1924, and 1930. Opposed American entry into World War I and U.S. membership in the League of Nations. Proposed Twentieth Amendment to the Constitution, changing presidential and congressional terms, in 1932. Introduced legislation creating the Tennessee Valley Authority, 1933, and sponsored Rural Electrification Act, 1936. Successfully campaigned for referendum creating unicameral Nebraska legislature, 1934. Supported Franklin D. Roosevelt for president, 1932 and 1936. Reelected to the Senate in 1936 as an Independent, but was defeated by Republican candidate in 1942; served in the U.S. Senate, 1913–43. Autobiography *Fighting Liberal* (1945) published posthumously. Died in McCook, Nebraska.

Walter Hines Page (August 15, 1855–December 21, 1918) Born in Cary, North Carolina, the son of a successful logger and builder. Graduated from Randolph-Macon College in 1875. Graduate fellow at Johns Hopkins University, 1876–77. Taught school in Louisville, Kentucky. Married Alice Wilson in 1880. Reporter and then editor with the St. Joseph (Missouri) *Gazette*, 1880–81. Wrote for the *New York World*, 1881–83. Edited the *Raleigh State Chronicle*, 1883–85, becoming advocate for public education and industrial development in the South. Returned to New York and wrote for the *Evening Post*, 1885–87. Joined staff of magazine *Forum*, 1887, and served as its editor, 1891–95. Joined publishing firm Houghton, Mifflin. Editor of the *Atlantic Monthly*, 1898–99. Founded publishing house Doubleday, Page, and Company with Frank N. Doubleday in 1900 and became editor of monthly magazine *The World's Work*. Published *The Rebuilding of Old Commonwealths* (1902), series of essays on education reform; *A Publisher's Confession* (1905), which appeared anonymously; and *The Southerner* (1909), a novel that appeared under pseudonym Nicholas Worth. Supported Woodrow Wilson in 1912 campaign. Appointed U.S. ambassador to Great Britain in April 1913. Resigned due to failing health in August 1918 and returned to the United States. Died in Pinehurst, North Carolina.

Frederick Palmer (January 29, 1873–September 2, 1958) Born in Pleasantville, Pennsylvania. Graduated from Allegheny College in 1893. Became London correspondent for *New York Press* in 1895. Reported on the Greco-Turkish War, Klondike gold rush, Philippine insurrection, Boxer Rebellion, Russo-Japanese War, First Balkan War, and Mexican revolution for a variety of newspapers and magazines. Traveled to Europe in 1914 to cover war and became sole American correspondent permanently accredited to cover the British Expeditionary Force. Served as chief press censor for the American

Expeditionary Forces, June–December 1917, and as staff officer at AEF headquarters. Published more than thirty books, including *America in France* (1918), *Our Greatest Battle* (1919), *The Folly of Nations* (1921), memoir *With My Own Eyes* (1933), and biographies of Newton Baker (1931), Tasker Bliss (1934), and Pershing (1948). Married Helen Runkle in 1924. Reported from Pacific during World War II and covered U.S. nuclear weapons tests at Bikini Atoll in 1946. Died in Charlottesville, Virginia.

John J. Pershing (September 13, 1860–July 15, 1948) Born in Laclede, Missouri, the son of a railroad foreman. Worked on family farm, taught school, and attended Kirksville Normal School before entering West Point in 1882. Graduated in 1886 and commissioned as second lieutenant. Served with 6th Cavalry Regiment in New Mexico, 1886–90, and South Dakota, 1890–91. Professor of military science and tactics at University of Nebraska, 1891–95; received law degree from the university in 1893. Served with African American 10th Cavalry ("Buffalo Soldiers") in Montana, 1896–97. Taught tactics at West Point, 1897–98. Fought in Cuba with the 10th Cavalry during Spanish-American War, 1898. Served in southern Philippines, 1899–1903, during campaign against Moro insurgents. Married Helen Frances Warren in 1905. Served as military attaché to Japan and observed Russo-Japanese War in Manchuria, 1905. Promoted from captain to brigadier general by President Theodore Roosevelt, 1906. Returned to the Philippines and served as military governor of Moro Province, 1908–13. Commanded troops in western Texas guarding Mexican border, 1914. Wife and three of their four children died in fire at Presidio army post in San Francisco, 1915. Commanded expedition into Mexico in pursuit of Pancho Villa, March 1916–February 1917. Appointed commander of American Expeditionary Forces in Europe, May 1917. Returned to United States in September 1919. Served as chief of staff of the U.S. Army, 1921–24. Published *My Experiences in the World War* (1931). Died in Washington, D.C.

Horace Pippin (February 22, 1888–July 6, 1946) Born in West Chester, Pennsylvania; grew up in Goshen, New York. Developed love of drawing and painting in childhood. Worked at various jobs including hotel porter, furniture crater, and iron molder. Joined the army in 1917 and was sent to France as part of 369th Infantry ("Harlem Hellfighters"). Was badly wounded in the right shoulder near Séchault on September 30, 1918, losing the full use of his arm. Received Croix de Guerre. Returned to United States in 1919 and settled in West Chester, living on odd jobs and his disability pension. Married Jennie Wade in 1920. Resumed activity as an artist, executing oil paintings using his left hand to assist his injured right arm; the first of these, *The*

End of the War: Starting Home (c. 1930), took over three years to complete. His work, focused on historical and political themes and scenes of African-American life, attracted local attention and was championed by painter N. C. Wyeth. Began exhibiting in galleries and major museums including the Carlen Gallery (Philadelphia), the Corcoran Gallery (Washington, D.C.), the Art Institute of Chicago, and the Museum of Modern Art. Died in West Chester.

Frederick A. Pottle (August 3, 1897–May 16, 1987) Born in Center Lovell, Maine, the son of a farmer. Graduated from Colby College in 1917. Enlisted in army in December 1917 and was assigned to the medical corps because of poor eyesight. Served in France as surgical assistant with Evacuation Hospital No. 8, June–November 1918, treating wounded from fighting at Belleau Wood, Château-Thierry, the Marne-Aisne, St. Mihiel, and the Meuse-Argonne. Taught history at Deering High School, Portland, Maine, 1919–20. Married Marion Starbird in 1920, the same year he began graduate studies at Yale. Taught at the University of New Hampshire in Durham, 1921–23. Published *Shelley and Browning: A Myth and Some Facts* (1923). Received PhD from Yale, 1925, and joined its English department. Published *The Literary Career of James Boswell, Esq.* (1928) and war memoir *Stretchers* (1929). Edited volumes 7–18 of the *Private Papers of James Boswell* (1931–34), a privately printed limited edition based on the Ralph Isham collection. Published *The Idiom of Poetry* (1941). Appointed Sterling Professor of English, 1944. Became editor of Yale edition of the Boswell papers in 1949. Published twelve volumes of selections from the journals, 1950–86. Retired from teaching in 1966. Published *James Boswell: The Earlier Years, 1740–1769* (1966) and *Pride and Negligence: The History of the Boswell Papers* (1982). Died in New Haven, Connecticut.

Ezra Pound (October 30, 1885–November 1, 1972) Born in Hailey, Idaho, the son of a federal land office register who later worked for the U.S. Mint. Studied at University of Pennsylvania, 1901–02; formed friendships with William Carlos Williams and Hilda Doolittle (H.D.). Graduated from Hamilton College in 1905. Moved to London, 1908. Published poetry collection *A Lume Spento* (1908). Named foreign editor of *Poetry*, 1912. Achieved recognition as a founder of the Imagist school; championed work of Robert Frost, James Joyce, and T. S. Eliot. Married Dorothy Shakespear in 1914. Published several poetry collections, including *Provença* (1910), *Cathay* (1915), and *Hugh Selwyn Mauberley* (1920). Moved to France in 1921 and to Italy in 1924, residing mainly in Rapallo. Published collected poems as *Personae* (1926) and *A Draft of XVI Cantos* (1925), first volume of lifelong work *The Cantos*. Became admirer of Benito Mussolini, with whom he had an audience in 1933. Visited the United States in 1939.

Broadcast series of pro-Fascist speeches over Radio Rome, January 1941–July 1943, marked by anti-Semitic invective and vilification of Roosevelt and other Allied leaders. Indicted for treason in July 1943. Captured by Italian partisans in May 1945 and interrogated by the FBI. Confined in a military stockade at Pisa for nearly five months before being flown to Washington, D.C., in November 1945 to face treason charges. In February 1946 a jury found Pound to be of "unsound mind" and unfit to stand trial, and he was committed to St. Elizabeth's, federal mental hospital in Washington. *The Pisan Cantos* (1948) was controversially awarded the Bollingen Prize in 1949. Released from hospital after treason indictment was dismissed in April 1958. Returned to Italy, 1958. Died in Venice.

John Reed (October 22, 1887–October 17, 1920) Born in Portland, Oregon, the son of an agricultural machinery salesman who later sold insurance. Studied at Harvard, 1906–10; moved in 1911 to New York where he worked at magazine *The American*. Became an editor of *The Masses*. Arrested for involvement in silk workers' strike in Paterson, New Jersey. Traveled to Mexico in November 1913 to report for *The Metropolitan*; met Pancho Villa; published *Insurgent Mexico* (1914). Went to Europe as war correspondent for *Metropolitan*, reporting from France, Germany, Greece, Serbia, Romania, and Russia. Published *The War in Eastern Europe* (1916). Married Louise Bryant in 1916. Traveled to Russia in 1917 and witnessed November revolution in Petrograd. Formed association with Lenin, Trotsky, Zinoviev, Radek, and other Bolshevik leaders. Returned to New York to stand trial with *Masses* colleagues on charges of conspiracy to obstruct draft; charges dismissed after two trials ended with hung juries. Account of Bolshevik revolution published as *Ten Days That Shook the World* (1919). Returned to Russia in fall 1919. Arrested in Finland in March 1920 while attempting to return to the United States and was imprisoned for three months. Attended Second Congress of the Communist International in Petrograd in July 1920. Contracted typhus and died in Moscow; buried in Kremlin Wall cemetery.

George E. Riis (February 22, 1877–October 7, 1928) Born George Edward Valdemar Riis in New York, son of social reformer Jacob Riis. In youth traveled to the West to be a cowboy; subsequently established career in journalism writing for *San Francisco Chronicle*; subsequently wrote for many years for *Brooklyn Eagle*; later employed by *Brooklyn Times*. Married Florence Moloso in 1905. Active in the progressive movement, forming friendships with Theodore Roosevelt and New York governor Charles Whitman. Sailed as observer on Henry Ford's Peace Ship in December 1915. Went to Denmark in June 1918 as American Director of Public Information; knighted (like his father and grandfather before him) for his services by King Christian X; returned to New York in March 1919. He was a frequent public speaker and in his later years taught at the Columbia School of Journalism.

Will Rogers (November 4, 1879–August 15, 1935) Born William Penn Adair Rogers to a family of partial Cherokee descent in Colagah, Indian Territory (later Oklahoma). Dropped out of school in the tenth grade and became a cowboy. Traveled to South Africa with Texas Jack's Wild West Show, making his first public appearance as an expert rope twirler; traveled in Australia and New Zealand with Wirth Brothers Circus. Performed on the vaudeville circuit in the United States, Canada, and Europe, 1904–15, becoming known as a unique humorist. Married Betty Blake in 1908. Appeared with the Ziegfeld Follies in 1917 and in films from 1918 on, in vehicles including *The Ropin' Fool* (1921), *They Had to See Paris* (1929), *A Connecticut Yankee* (1931), *State Fair* (1933), *Judge Priest* (1934), and *Steamboat 'Round the Bend* (1935), achieving major stardom in the early talkie period. He became a frequent radio performer and syndicated columnist, and published books including *Rogers-isms: The Cowboy Philosopher on the Peace Conference* (1919), *Rogers-isms: The Cowboy Philosopher on Prohibition* (1919), *Illiterate Digest* (1924), and *Letters of a Self-Made Diplomat to His President* (1926). Died in a plane crash in Point Barrow, Alaska, while flying with aviator Wylie Post.

Theodore Roosevelt (October 27, 1858–January 6, 1919) Born in New York City, the son of a wealthy investor and philanthropist. Graduated from Harvard in 1880. Married Alice Lee, 1880. Elected as a Republican to the New York state assembly in 1881 and served 1882–84. Published *The Naval War of 1812* in 1882, the first of many works of history, biography, and natural history. Raised cattle on ranch in the Dakota Badlands, 1884–86. After the death of his first wife, married Edith Carow in 1886. Served on U.S. Civil Service Commission, 1889–95, and on the New York City Police Commission, 1895–97. Assistant Secretary of the Navy in the McKinley administration, 1897–98. Commanded 1st U.S. Volunteer Cavalry (Rough Riders) in Cuba, 1898. Elected governor of New York in 1898 and served 1899–1900. Elected vice-president of the United States on the McKinley ticket, and became President on September 14, 1901, following the assassination of President McKinley. Defeated Alton B. Parker in 1904 election. President of the United States, 1901–9. Challenged President William Howard Taft for the Republican nomination in 1912, then ran as the Progressive candidate and was defeated by Woodrow Wilson. Wounded in assassination attempt during 1912 campaign. Became prominent advocate of the Allied cause during World War I; after the American entry into the war, all four of his sons served in France, where two were wounded and one was killed. Died in Oyster Bay, New York.

Damon Runyon (October 8, 1880–December 10, 1946) Born Alfred Damon Runyon in Manhattan, Kansas; family moved to Pueblo, Colorado, when he was seven. Left school after sixth grade. Employed by local newspapers and became reporter for *Pueblo Evening Press* in 1895. Enlisted in army during Spanish-American War. Worked for *San Francisco Post* and *Rocky Mountain News*; hired as sports reporter by *New York American* in 1911; became syndicated columnist in 1916. Published poems and short stories. Sent to Europe as war correspondent in 1918. Married Patrice Amati in 1932. Story collection *Guys and Dolls* appeared in 1931, followed by *Blue Plate Special* (1934), *Money from Home* (1935), *Take It Easy* (1938), and *Runyon à la Carte* (1944); newspaper columns collected in *My Old Man* (1939) and *My Wife Ethel* (1940). Died in New York City.

Charles Emil Ruthenberg (July 9, 1882–March 3, 1927) Born in Cleveland, Ohio, the son of a longshoreman. Worked as bookkeeper and sales manager for regional publishing company. Married Rosaline Nickel in 1904. Joined Socialist Party in 1909. Edited *The Cleveland Socialist*, 1911–13, and *Socialist News*, 1914–19. Along with Morris Hillquit and Algernon Lee, helped draft antiwar resolution adopted by Socialist Party in spring 1917. Convicted under Espionage Act for making antiwar speech on May 17, 1917, and sentenced to one year in prison; served almost eleven months before being released in December 1918. Indicted for role in 1919 May Day march in Cleveland that ended in riot, but was never convicted. Became executive secretary of Communist Party of America, one of several competing factions, in September 1919. Convicted in October 1920 of violating the New York State criminal anarchism statute and was imprisoned until April 1922. Became executive secretary of the Workers Party of America, newly unified Communist organization, in 1922. Died in Chicago.

George Santayana (December 16, 1863–September 26, 1952) Born Jorge Ruiz de Santayana y Borras in Madrid, Spain, of Spanish parents; mother was the daughter of a Spanish official, father a colonial civil servant. Parents separated; raised in Boston by his mother from age eight. Graduated from Harvard in 1886 and awarded PhD in philosophy from Harvard in 1889. Taught philosophy at Harvard, becoming full professor in 1907. Retired from Harvard in 1912 and lived in England and Paris before settling in Rome in 1925. Published collections of poetry and a series of philosophical works including *The Sense of Beauty* (1896), *The Life of Reason* (1905–6), *Three Philosophical Poets*

(1910), *Scepticism and Animal Faith* (1923), and *The Realms of Being* (1927–40). His novel *The Last Puritan* was a bestseller in 1935. During World War II took refuge in English convent in Rome, remaining there until his death.

William Seabrook (February 22, 1884–September 20, 1945) Born in Westminster, Maryland. Was reporter and city editor for *Augusta* (Georgia) *Chronicle*. Married Katie Edmunson, daughter of Coca-Cola executive; worked as an executive for advertising agency in Atlanta. In 1915 joined American Field Service No. 8 as ambulance driver; was gassed at Verdun; awarded Croix de Guerre; published *Diary of Section VIII* (1917). Became acquainted with English occultist Aleister Crowley, who stayed with him for a week at Seabrook's farm near Atlanta in 1920. Frequented literary circles in Greenwich Village. Traveled to Arabia in 1924 and published *Adventures in Arabia* (1927); subsequently traveled to Haiti, describing experiences in *The Magic Island* (1929). Travels in West Africa recounted in *Jungle Ways* (1930), in which Seabrook also claimed to have experimented with cannibalism, availing himself of human flesh from an accident victim, provided by a hospital intern. Published *Air Adventure* (1933) and *The White Monk of Timbuctoo* (1934). In France married expatriate Marjorie Muir Worthington, who had been his partner for several years, in 1935; she later published an account of their marriage, which ended in divorce, in *The Strange World of Willie Seabrook* (1966). Committed himself to Bloomingdale Asylum in White Plains, New York, for treatment of acute alcoholism; gave account of the experience in bestselling *Asylum* (1935). His later books included *Witchcraft: Its Power in the World Today* (1940) and *No Hiding Place: An Autobiography* (1942). He committed suicide, in Rhinebeck, New York.

Alan Seeger (June 22, 1888–July 4, 1916) Born in New York City, the son of a businessman. Moved with family to Mexico in 1900. Sent to Hackley School in 1902; in 1906 entered Harvard. Became an editor of the *Harvard Monthly*, where he published many poems. Went to live in Paris in 1912. After war broke out in 1914, enlisted in the French Foreign Legion. Mortally wounded during attack on Belloy-en-Santerre; awarded the Croix de Guerre and the Médaille Militaire. *Poems* (1916) published posthumously.

Elizabeth Shepley Sergeant (April 23, 1881–January 26, 1965) Born in Winchester, Massachusetts. Graduated from Bryn Mawr in 1903. Formed friendship with Willa Cather while writing in 1910 for *McClure's Magazine*, of which Cather was editor. Published travel book *French Perspectives* (1916). Went to France as war correspondent for *The New Republic* in 1917; gravely wounded in an accidental explosion while touring a former battlefield in 1918. She recounted her recuperation in *Shadow-Shapes: The Journal of a Wounded Woman, October 1918– May 1919* (1920). Moved to Taos, New Mexico, in 1920; published articles in *Saturday Review*, *Harper's*, and other magazines. Published essay collection *Fire Under the Andes* (1927) and novel *Short As Any Dream* (1929). Traveled to Europe, where she studied with Carl Jung. Later moved to Piermont, New York. Published *Willa Cather: A Memoir* (1953) and *Robert Frost: The Trial by Existence* (1960).

Elmer Sherwood (February 22, 1896–February 27, 1979) Born in Linton, Indiana, the son of a doctor. Enlisted in April 1917. Landed in France in November 1917 with Battery B, 150th Field Artillery Regiment, 42nd (Rainbow) Division. Served in Lunéville and Baccarat sectors of the Lorraine front, February–June 1918, and in Marne-Aisne, St. Mihiel, and Meuse-Argonne campaigns, July–November 1918. Returned to United States in April 1919 as corporal. Graduated from Indiana University in 1921. Served in Indiana house of representatives, 1921–22, and as clerk of Greene County, 1922–35. Published war memoirs *Rainbow Hoosier* (1922) and *Diary of a Rainbow Veteran: Written at the Front* (1929). Married Lucille Smith in 1924. Taught English at Linton High School. Worked in public relations and edited *National Legionnaire*, official publication of the American Legion. Served as public information officer at Fort Harrison, Indiana, during World War II. Founded Sherwood Associates, successful public relations firm, and was close adviser to George Craig during his term as governor, 1953–57. Convicted of bribery in 1958 as part of scheme to rig state highway contracts, and served three months in prison in 1961. Died in Sebring, Florida.

Herbert Bayard Swope (January 5, 1882–June 20, 1958) Born in St. Louis, Missouri, to German immigrants. Traveled in Europe after high school, then worked as reporter for *St. Louis Post-Dispatch*. Later worked for *Chicago Tribune*, *New York Herald*, and *New York Morning Telegraph*; joined *New York World* full-time in 1909, eventually becoming city editor (1915) and executive editor (1920–28). Married Margaret Powell in 1912. His articles from Germany during World War I won him first Pulitzer Prize for Reporting in 1917, and were collected in *Inside the German Empire* (1917). During World War I was commissioned in U.S. Navy and assisted Bernard Baruch on U.S. War Industries Board; afterwards served as *World's* chief correspondent at the Paris peace conference. Recruited notable contingent of columnists at the *World*, including Heywood Broun, Alexander Woollcott, Franklin P. Adams, and Laurence Stallings; initiated newspaper campaign against Ku Klux Klan that won Pulitzer Prize for Public Service in 1922. Served as chairman of New York State Racing

Board, 1934–45, and, during World War II, as consultant to Secretary of War Henry Stimson. Died in New York City.

Norman Thomas (November 20, 1884–December 19, 1968) Born in Marion, Ohio, the son of a Presbyterian minister. Graduated from Princeton in 1905. Worked at Spring Street settlement house in New York City. Attended Union Theological Seminary, 1908–11. Married Frances Violet Stewart in 1910. Ordained in 1911 and became pastor of East Harlem Presbyterian Church. Joined Fellowship of Reconciliation, a Christian pacifist group, and the American Union Against Militarism in 1916. Helped found Civil Liberties Bureau, precursor to the American Civil Liberties Union, in 1917. Resigned pastorate in 1918 and joined the Socialist Party. Editor of *The World Tomorrow*, journal of the Fellowship of Reconciliation, 1918–21. Became co-director of League for Industrial Democracy in 1922. Supported family through extensive lecturing and writing; published numerous books and pamphlets, including *The Conquest of War* (1917), *The Conscientious Objector in America* (1923), and *As I See It* (1932). Socialist candidate for president six times from 1928 to 1948; won 2.2 percent of the vote in 1932, less than 1 percent in other elections. Opposed U.S. intervention in World War II until attack on Pearl Harbor. Criticized internment of Japanese Americans. Helped found National Committee for a Sane Nuclear Policy in 1957. Opposed American involvement in Vietnam War. Died in Cold Spring Harbor, New York.

Harry S. Truman (May 8, 1884–December 26, 1972) Born in Lamar, Missouri, the son of a farmer. Graduated from high school in Independence in 1901. Worked as a railroad timekeeper and bank clerk, then returned to the family farm in Grandview in 1906. Commanded field artillery battery in France in 1918 and saw action in the Vosges, the St. Mihiel salient, and the Meuse-Argonne. Married Bess Wallace in 1919. Opened men's clothing store in Kansas City in 1919 that failed in 1922. Elected as a Democrat to the Jackson County Court (county commission) in 1922; served 1922–24, and then as presiding judge, 1926–34. Served in the Senate, 1935–45, and as vice-president of the United States from January 20 to April 12, 1945, when he became President following the death of Franklin D. Roosevelt. Defeated Thomas Dewey in 1948 election. President of the United States, 1945–53. Died in Kansas City, Missouri.

William M. Vaile (June 22, 1876–July 2, 1927) Born in Kokomo, Indiana, the son of a lawyer. Moved with family to Denver, Colorado, in 1881. Graduated from Yale University in 1898. Served with Connecticut volunteer artillery during Spanish-American War, May–October 1898, but did not leave the United States. Studied law at the

University of Colorado and Harvard Law School. Admitted to the bar in 1901. Joined father's law practice in Denver, representing the Denver & Rio Grande Railroad and other corporate clients. Married Luverne Hall in 1902. Served as county attorney for Jefferson County, 1911–14. Following divorce from first wife, married Katherine Varrell in 1915. Served on Mexican border as second lieutenant in Colorado National Guard, June–December 1916. Elected to Congress in 1918 as a Republican and served from 1919 until his death. Prominent supporter of restrictive 1924 immigration act. Published novel *The Mystery of Golconda* (1925), set in Rocky Mountain mining camps. Died from heart attack in Rocky Mountain National Park, Colorado.

Edith Wharton (January 24, 1862–August 11, 1937) Born Edith Newbold Jones in New York City. Family moved to Europe in 1860, and lived successively in England, Italy, France, and Germany before returning to America in 1872. Educated at home. Married Edward Wharton in 1885; they were divorced in 1913. Began publishing poems and stories; first novel *The Valley of Decision* published in 1902. Formed close friendship with Henry James. Built large house, The Mount, in Lenox, Massachusetts, dividing time between Europe and Lenox. Novels include *The House of Mirth* (1905), *Ethan Frome* (1911), *The Reef* (1912), *The Custom of the Country* (1913), *The Age of Innocence* (1920), and *The Glimpses of the Moon* (1922). During World War I, established American Hostels for Refugees and organized Children of Flanders Rescue Committee; reported on the war for *Scribner's*, and the articles were collected in *Fighting France, from Dunkerque to Belfort* (1915); edited *The Book of the Homeless* (1916). She was named Chevalier of the Legion of Honor in 1916. Bought a house in village of St. Brice-sous-Forêt outside Paris. Autobiography *A Backward Glance* published in 1934. She died at St. Brice.

Ashby Williams (June 18, 1874–May 31, 1944) Born John Ashby Williams in Stafford County, Virginia, the son of a farmer. Family moved to Washington, D.C., in 1892. Worked as clerk in government hydrographic office in Norfolk, Virginia, 1898–1901. Attended Oberlin College, 1901–3, and the University of Virginia, 1903–6, where he was awarded a law degree. Practiced law in Roanoke, Virginia, where he served on the board of aldermen, 1908–12. Published *Corporation Laws of Virginia* (1909), an annotated compilation. Married Eva Wallbridge in 1911. Arrived in France in May 1918, commanding Company E, Second Battalion, 320th Infantry Regiment, 80th Division. Trained behind British lines, June–July, and then served in trenches near Ransart, southwest of Arras, July–August. Assigned command of First Battalion, 320th Infantry Regiment, on August 28; led battalion at St. Mihiel and in the Meuse-Argonne offensive. Returned to the

United States in May 1919 as lieutenant colonel. Published *Experiences of the Great War: Artois, St. Mihiel, Meuse-Argonne* (1919). Moved to Washington, D.C., where he practiced law. After divorce from his first wife, married Lois Allee. Died in Washington, D.C.

Woodrow Wilson (December 28, 1856–February 3, 1924) Born Thomas Woodrow Wilson in Staunton, Virginia, the son of a Presbyterian minister. Graduated from the College of New Jersey (Princeton) in 1879. Admitted to the bar in Atlanta in 1882. Entered graduate school at Johns Hopkins in 1883. Married Ellen Axson in 1885. Published *Congressional Government* (1885), the first of several works on American history and politics. Awarded PhD in 1886. Taught at Bryn Mawr, 1885–88, and Wesleyan, 1888–90. Professor of jurisprudence and political economy at Princeton, 1890–1902, and president of Princeton, 1902–10. Elected as a Democrat to the governorship of New Jersey in 1910 and served 1911–13. Won Democratic presidential nomination in 1912 and defeated Theodore Roosevelt and William Howard Taft; defeated Charles Evans Hughes in 1916 to win reelection. President of the United States, 1913–21. Following the death of his first wife, married Edith Bolling Galt in 1915. Suffered stroke on October 2, 1919, that left him an invalid for the remainder of his term. Awarded Nobel Peace Prize in 1919. Died in Washington, D.C.

Joe Young (July 4, 1889–April 21, 1939) Born in New York City. Worked as singer and song plugger. Toured Europe entertaining the troops during World War I. Wrote lyrics, often in collaboration with Sam Lewis, for many successful songs including "Don't Blame It All on Broadway" (1914), "How You Gonna Keep 'Em Down on the Farm" (1919), "My Mammy" (1920), "I Kiss Your Hand, Madame" (1929), "In a Shanty in Old Shanty Town" (1932), "Lullaby of the Leaves" (1932), and "I'm Gonna Sit Right Down and Write Myself a Letter" (1935). Charter member of ASCAP in 1914. Died in New York City.

Note on the Texts

This volume collects early twentieth-century American writing about World War I and its immediate aftermath, bringing together newspaper and magazine articles, diary entries, letters, addresses, speeches, essays, memoranda, manifestos, diplomatic notes, judicial opinions, psychological studies, literary sketches, poems, songs, and excerpts from narratives and memoirs written by participants and observers and dealing with events in the period from June 1914 to November 1921. A coda collects three works—"Soldier's Home" (1925) by Ernest Hemingway, "my sweet old etcetera" (1926) by E. E. Cummings, and "The Body of An American," the concluding episode in *1919* (1932) by John Dos Passos—that are presented as examples of the literary response to the war by American writers who had experienced the conflict firsthand. Some of these documents were not written for publication, and some of them existed only in typescript or manuscript form during the lifetimes of the persons who wrote them. With six exceptions, the texts presented in this volume are taken from printed sources. In cases where there is only one printed source for a document, the text offered here comes from that source. Where there is more than one printed source for a document, the text printed in this volume is taken from the source that appears to contain the fewest editorial alterations in the spelling, capitalization, paragraphing, and punctuation of the original. In five instances where no printed sources (or no complete printed sources) were available, the texts in this volume are printed from typescripts or manuscripts. The lyrics for the song "On Patrol in No Man's Land" are taken from a recorded performance by its composer, James Reese Europe, that contains lyrics not found in the printed sheet music.

This volume prints texts as they appear in the sources listed below, but with a few alterations in editorial procedure. The bracketed conjectural readings of editors, in cases where original manuscripts or printed texts were damaged or difficult to read, are accepted without brackets in this volume when those readings seem to be the only possible ones; but when they do not, or when the editor made no conjecture, the missing word or words are indicated by a bracketed two-em space, i.e., [   ]. In cases where a typographical error or obvious misspelling in manuscript was marked by earlier editors with "[*sic*]," the present volume omits the "[*sic*]" and corrects the typographical error or slip of the pen. In some cases, obvious errors were not marked by earlier editors with "[*sic*]" but were printed and then followed by a bracketed correction; in these instances, this volume removes the brackets and accepts the editorial emendation. Bracketed editorial insertions used in the source texts to supply dates and locations have been deleted in this volume. In instances where canceled, but still legible, words were printed in the source texts with lines through the deleted material, this volume omits the canceled words.

The texts of the remarks by John J. Pershing to the officers of the 1st Division, the letter by Pershing to the Supreme War Council, and the speech to the court by Eugene V. Debs were presented as quoted material in the sources used in this volume, with quotation marks placed at the beginning of each paragraph and at the end of the text; this volume omits the quotation marks.

In *The Slaughterhouse Province: An American Diplomat's Report on the Armenian Genocide, 1915–1917* (1989), edited by Susan K. Blair, the texts of the dispatches sent by Leslie Davis to Henry Morgenthau on June 30 and July 11, 1915, are taken from the documents in the State Department records in the National Archives. The texts printed in *The Slaughterhouse Province* include parenthetical file number references that were added to the dispatches after they were forwarded from the American embassy in Constantinople to the Department of State in Washington, D.C. For example, at 155.5–6, "dispatches of April 19th, May 5th and June 2nd referred to" appears in *The Slaughterhouse Province* as "dispatches of April 19th, May 5th and June 2nd (file No. 840.1) referred to," and at 155.13, "in my cipher dispatch of June 24th I gave" appears as "in my cipher dispatch of June 24th (File No. 300/840.1/703) I gave." This volume prints the texts of the dispatches and omits the added parenthetical file number references.

The following is a list of the documents included in this volume, in the order of their appearance, giving the source of each text. The most common source is indicated by this abbreviation:

PWW   *The Papers of Woodrow Wilson*, ed. Arthur S. Link (69 vols., Princeton, NJ: Princeton University Press, 1966–1994). Volume 30 (1979), Volume 33 (1980), Volume 36 (1981), Volume 40 (1982), Volume 41 (1983), Volume 42 (1983), Volume 45 (1984), Volume 49 (1985), Volume 51 (1985), Volume 59 (1988), Volume 61 (1989), Volume 62 (1990), Volume 63 (1990). Copyright © 1979, 1980, 1981, 1982, 1983, 1984, 1985, 1988, 1989, 1990 by Princeton University Press. Used by permission of Princeton University Press via Copyright Clearance Center, Inc.

The New York Times: Heir to Austria's Throne Is Slain. *The New York Times*, June 29, 1914.

Hugh Gibson: from *A Journal from Our Legation in Belgium*. Hugh Gibson, *A Journal from Our Legation in Belgium* (Garden City, NY: Doubleday, Page & Company, 1917), 3–10.

Walter Hines Page: Memorandum, August 2, 1914. Burton J. Hendrick, *The Life and Letters of Walter H. Page*, vol. I (Garden City, NY: Doubleday, Page & Company, 1922), 301–3.

Hugo Münsterberg to the *Boston Herald*. *Boston Herald*, August 5, 1914.

Walter Hines Page to Woodrow Wilson, August 9, 1914. *PWW*, vol. 30, 366–94.

Woodrow Wilson: Statement on Neutrality, August 18, 1914. *PWW*, vol. 30, 393–94.

Richard Harding Davis to the *New York Tribune*, August 21 and 30, 1914. *New York Tribune*, August 24 and 31, 1914.

Theodore Roosevelt to Hugo Münsterberg, October 3, 1914. *The Letters of Theodore Roosevelt*, vol. VIII, ed. Elting E. Morison (Cambridge, MA: Harvard University Press, 1954), 822–25. Copyright © 1954 by the President and Fellows of Harvard College. Copyright © renewed 1982 by Elting Elmore Morison.

W.E.B. Du Bois: World War and the Color Line. *The Crisis*, November 1914.

Nellie Bly to the *New York Evening Journal*, October 30 and November 10, 1914. Nellie Bly, *Around the World in Seventy-Two Days and Other Writings*, ed. Jean Marie Lutes (New York: Penguin Books, 2014), 287–90, 296–99.

George Santayana: The Logic of Fanaticism. *The New Republic*, November 28, 1914.

Alfred Bryan: I Didn't Raise My Boy to Be a Soldier. "I Didn't Raise My Boy to Be a Soldier," lyrics by Alfred Bryan, music by Al Piantadosi (New York: Leo. Feist, 1915).

Edith Wharton: In Argonne. *Scribner's Magazine*, June 1915.

John Reed: Goutchevo and the Valley of Corpses. John Reed, *The War in Eastern Europe* (New York: Charles Scribner's Sons, 1916), 94–106.

Charles E. Lauriat, Jr.: from *The Lusitania's Last Voyage*. Charles E. Lauriat, Jr., *The Lusitania's Last Voyage: Being a Narrative of the Torpedoing and Sinking of the R.M.S. Lusitania by a German Submarine off the Irish Coast, May 7, 1915* (Boston: Houghton Mifflin Company, 1915), 7–34.

Woodrow Wilson: Address to Naturalized Citizens at Convention Hall, Philadelphia, May 10, 1915. *PWW*, vol. 33, 147–50.

The New York Times: Roosevelt for Prompt Action. *The New York Times*, May 12, 1915.

William Jennings Bryan to Gottlieb von Jagow, May 13, 1915. *Papers Relating to the Foreign Relations of the United States, 1915,*

Supplement, The World War (Washington, D.C.: Government Printing Office, 1928), 393–96.

Henry Morgenthau to William Jennings Bryan, May 25, 1915. *United States Official Records on the Armenian Genocide 1915–1917,* ed. Ara Sarafian (London: Gomidas Institute, 2004), 32–34.

W.E.B. Du Bois: Lusitania. *The Crisis,* June 1915.

Robert Lansing to Gottlieb von Jagow, June 9, 1915. *Papers Relating to the Foreign Relations of the United States, 1915, Supplement, The World War* (Washington, D.C.: Government Printing Office, 1928), 436–38.

John Reed: Zalezchik the Terrible. John Reed, *The War in Eastern Europe* (New York: Charles Scribner's Sons, 1916), 137–43.

Edith Wharton: In the North. *Scribner's Magazine,* November 1915.

Henry James to Herbert Henry Asquith, June 28, 1915. *Henry James Letters,* vol. IV, ed. Leon Edel (Cambridge, MA: The Belknap Press of Harvard University Press, 1984), 764. Copyright © 1984 by Leon Edel, editorial. Copyright © 1984 Alexander R. James, James copyright material.

Leslie Davis to Henry Morgenthau, June 30 and July 11, 1915. Leslie A. Davis, *The Slaughterhouse Province: An American Diplomat's Report on the Armenian Genocide, 1915–1917,* ed. Susan K. Blair (New Rochelle, NY: Aristide D. Caratzas, 1989), 143–55.

Henry Morgenthau to Robert Lansing, July 16, 1915. *United States Official Records on the Armenian Genocide 1915–1917,* ed. Ara Sarafian (London: Gomidas Institute, 2004), 55.

Jane Addams: The Revolt Against War. *The Survey,* July 17, 1915.

Richard Harding Davis to *The New York Times. The New York Times,* July 13, 1915.

Alan Seeger: Diary, September 16–September 24, 1915, and to Elsie Simmons Seeger, October 25, 1915. *Letters and Diary of Alan Seeger* (New York: Charles Scribner's Sons, 1917), 155–73.

James Norman Hall: Damaged Trenches. James Norman Hall, *Kitchener's Mob: The Adventures of an American in the British Army* (Boston: Houghton Mifflin Company, 1916), 159–71.

Henry Morgenthau to Robert Lansing, November 4, 1915. *United States Official Records on the Armenian Genocide 1915–1917,* ed. Ara Sarafian (London: Gomidas Institute, 2004), 316–19.

Theodore Roosevelt to William Castle, Jr., November 13, 1915. Typescript with manuscript additions, Gilder Lehrman Institute of American History, GLC 00782.19.

Emma Goldman: Preparedness, the Road to Universal Slaughter. *Mother Earth,* December 1915.

George E. Riis to *The Daily Brooklyn Eagle,* January 6, 1916.

Alan Seeger: I Have a Rendezvous with Death. Alan Seeger, *Poems* (New York: Charles Scribner's Sons, 1916), 144.

Ellen N. La Motte: Alone. Ellen N. La Motte, *The Backwash of War: The Human Wreckage of the Battlefield as Witnessed by an American Hospital Nurse* (New York: G. P. Putnam's Sons, 1916), 49–59.

Woodrow Wilson: Address to Congress, April 19, 1916. *PWW*, vol. 36, 506–10.

William B. Seabrook: from *Diary of Section VIII*. William B. Seabrook, *Diary of Section VIII, American Ambulance Field Service* (Boston: Thomas Todd Co. printers, 1917), 11–15.

Victor Chapman to John Jay Chapman, June 1, 1916. *Victor Chapman's Letters from France* (New York: The Macmillan Company, 1917), 182–86.

Mary Borden: Conspiracy. Mary Borden, *The Forbidden Zone* (London: Hesperus Press Limited, 2008), 79–81. Copyright © Patrick Aylmer 1929, 2008. Used by permission.

Herbert Bayard Swope: Boelcke, Knight of the Air. Herbert Bayard Swope, *Inside the German Empire in the third year of the war* (New York: The Century Co., 1917), 226–41.

Theodore Roosevelt: Speech at Cooper Union, November 3, 1916. *Americanism and Preparedness: Speeches of Theodore Roosevelt, July to November, 1916* (New York: The Mail and Express Job Print, 1917), 135–45.

John Jay Chapman to the *Harvard Alumni Bulletin*. *Harvard Alumni Bulletin*, January 4, 1917.

Robert Frost: Not to Keep. *The Yale Review*, January 1917.

Woodrow Wilson: Address to the Senate, January 22, 1917. *PWW*, vol. 40, 533–39.

H. L. Mencken: "The Diary of a Retreat": Berlin At Time of Break. *Baltimore Sun*, March 10, 1917.

Robert Lansing: Memorandum on the Severance of Diplomatic Relations with Germany, February 4, 1917. *PWW*, vol. 41, 118–25.

New York Tribune: Germany Asks Mexico to Seek Alliance with Japan for War on U.S. *New York Tribune*, March 1, 1917.

Edmond C. C. Genet: Diary, March 19–24, 1917. *An American for Lafayette: The Diaries of E.C.C. Genet, Lafayette Escadrille*, ed. Walt Brown, Jr. (Charlottesville: University Press of Virginia, 1981), 164–71. Copyright © 1981 by the Rector and Visitors of the University of Virginia. Used by permission of the University Press of Virginia.

Woodrow Wilson: Address to Congress on War with Germany, April 2, 1917. *PWW*, vol. 41, 519–27.

George Norris: Speech in the U.S. Senate, April 4, 1917. *Congressional Record*, 65th Congress, 1st Session, 212–14.

George M. Cohan: Over There. "Over There," words and music by George M. Cohan (New York: Leo. Feist, 1917).

Majority Report of the St. Louis Socialist Convention. *The American Socialists and the War: A Documentary History of the Attitude of the Socialist Party toward War and Militarism Since the Outbreak of the Great War*, ed. Alexander Trachtenberg (New York: The Rand School of Social Science, 1917), 39–43.

Walter Lippman: The World Conflict in Its Relation to American Democracy. *The Annals of the American Academy of Political and Social Science*, July 1917, 1–10.

Herbert Hoover: Introduction to *Women of Belgium*. Charlotte Kellogg, *Women of Belgium: Turning Tragedy into Triumph* (New York: Funk & Wagnalls Company, 1917), vii–xviii.

The New York Times: German Airmen Kill 97, Hurt 437 in London Raid. *The New York Times*, June 14, 1917.

Woodrow Wilson: Flag Day Address in Washington, D.C., June 14, 1917. *PWW*, vol. 42, 498–504.

Randolph Bourne: The War and the Intellectuals. *The Seven Arts*, June 1917.

Carlos F. Hurd to the *St. Louis Post-Dispatch*, July 3, 1917. *St. Louis Post-Dispatch*, July 3, 1917.

Norman Thomas: War's Heretics, a Plea for the Conscientious Objector. *The Survey*, August 4, 1917.

Jessie Fauset to *The Survey*. *The Survey*, August 18, 1917.

John Dos Passos to Rumsey Marvin, August 23, 1917. *The Fourteenth Chronicle: Letters and Diaries of John Dos Passos*, ed. Townsend Ludington (Boston: Gambit Incorporated, 1973), 91–93. Copyright © 1973 by Elizabeth H. Dos Passos and Townsend Ludington. Used by permission of Lucy Dos Passos Coggin.

Martha Gruening: Houston, an N.A.A.C.P. Investigation. *The Crisis*, November 1917.

Dorothy Canfield Fisher to Sarah Cleghorn, September 5, 1917. *Keeping Fires Night and Day: Selected Letters of Dorothy Canfield Fisher*, ed. Mark J. Madigan (Columbia: University of Missouri Press, 1993), 71–73. Copyright © 1993 by the Curators of the University of Missouri. University of Missouri Press, Columbia, Missouri 65201. Used by permission.

James Weldon Johnson: Experienced Men Wanted. *James Weldon Johnson: Writings*, ed. William L. Andrews (New York: Library of America, 2004), 630–32.

Carrie Chapman Catt: Votes for All. *The Crisis*, November 1917.

Mary Borden: Unidentified. *The English Review*, December 1917.

Charles J. Biddle: from *The Way of the Eagle*. Charles J. Biddle, *The Way of the Eagle* (New York: Charles Scribner's Sons, 1919), 124–31.

Bernice Evans: The Sayings of Patsy. *Rendezvous with Death: American Poems of the Great War*, ed. Mark W. Van Wienen (Urbana:

University of Illinois Press, 2002), 205–7. © 2002 by the Board of Trustees of the University of Illinois.

Woodrow Wilson: Address to Congress on War Aims, January 8, 1918. *PWW*, vol. 45, 534–39.

Shirley Millard: from *I Saw Them Die*. *I Saw Them Die: Diary and Recollections of Shirley Millard*, ed. Adele Comandini (New York: Harcourt, Brace & Company Inc., 1936), 9–16. Copyright © 1936 by Shirley Millard. Used by permission of Houghton Mifflin Harcourt Publishing Company. All rights reserved.

John J. Pershing: Remarks to the Officers of the 1st Division, April 16, 1918. John J. Pershing, *My Experiences in the World War*, vol. I (New York: Frederick A. Stokes Company, 1931), 393–95. Copyright, 1931, by John J. Pershing.

Shirley Millard: from *I Saw Them Die*. *I Saw Them Die: Diary and Recollections of Shirley Millard*, ed. Adele Comandini (New York: Harcourt, Brace & Company Inc., 1936), 35–45. Copyright © 1936 by Shirley Millard. Used by permission of Houghton Mifflin Harcourt Publishing Company. All rights reserved.

Floyd Gibbons: Wounded—How It Feels To Be Shot. Floyd Gibbons, *"And They Thought We Wouldn't Fight"* (New York: George H. Doran Company, 1918), 305–22.

Frederick A. Pottle: from *Stretchers*. Frederick A. Pottle, *Stretchers: The Story of a Hospital Unit on the Western Front* (New Haven, CT: Yale University Press, 1929), 98–114. Copyright 1929 by Yale University Press. Used by permission of Yale University Press.

James Weldon Johnson: "Why Should a Negro Fight?" *James Weldon Johnson: Writings*, ed. William L. Andrews (New York: Library of America, 2004), 632–36.

W.E.B. Du Bois: Close Ranks. *The Crisis*, July 1918.

Hubert H. Harrison: Why Is the Red Cross? Hubert H. Harrison, *When Africa Awakes: The "Inside Story" of the Stirrings and Strivings of the New Negro in the Western World* (New York: The Porro Press, 1920), 27–29.

Ernest Hemingway to His Family, July 21, 1918. *The Letters of Ernest Hemingway*, vol. I, ed. Sandra Spanier and Robert W. Trogdon (New York: Cambridge University Press, 2011), 117–19. The Letters of Ernest Hemingway copyright © 2015 by The Ernest Hemingway Foundation and Society (in the USA) and the Hemingway Foreign Rights Trust (outside the USA). Used by permission of Cambridge University Press.

Woodrow Wilson: Statement on Lynching, July 26, 1918. *PWW*, vol. 49, 97–98.

James Reese Europe: On Patrol in No Man's Land. "On Patrol in No Man's Land," vocal by Lieut. Noble Sissle, accompanied by Lieut.

Jim Europe's 369th Infantry ("Hellfighters") Band. Pathé Frères Phonograph Co., 22089 B, 1919. Recording accessed at https://youtu.be/wpFCuZ-B4jo, August 18, 2016.

Shirley Millard: from *I Saw Them Die*. *I Saw Them Die: Diary and Recollections of Shirley Millard*, ed. Adele Comandini (New York: Harcourt, Brace & Company Inc., 1936), 78–81. Copyright © 1936 by Shirley Millard. Used by permission of Houghton Mifflin Harcourt Publishing Company. All rights reserved.

Hervey Allen: from *Toward the Flame*. Hervey Allen, *Toward the Flame: A War Diary* (New York: Farrar & Rinehart Incorporated, 1934), 200–277. Copyright © 1926, 1934 by Hervey Allen. Used by permission of the University of Nebraska Press.

Ernest Hemingway to His Family, August 18, 1918. *The Letters of Ernest Hemingway*, vol. 1, ed. Sandra Spanier and Robert W. Trogdon (New York: Cambridge University Press, 2011), 130–33. The Letters of Ernest Hemingway copyright © 2015 by The Ernest Hemingway Foundation and Society (in the USA) and the Hemingway Foreign Rights Trust (outside the USA). Used by permission of Cambridge University Press.

Frederick Trevenen Edwards to Frederick Edwards, September 12, 1918. *Fort Sheridan to Montfaucon: The War Letters of Frederick Trevenen Edwards* (DeLand, FL: E. O. Painter Printing Co., 1954), 262–66. Copyright, 1954, by Elizabeth Satterthwait.

Eugene V. Debs: Speech to the Court, September 14, 1918. David Karsner, *Debs: His Authorized Life and Letters* (New York: Boni and Liveright, 1919), 48–54.

Willa Cather: Roll Call on the Prairies. *The Red Cross Magazine*, July 1919.

Ashby Williams: from *Experiences of the Great War*. Ashby Williams, *Experiences of the Great War: Artois, St. Mihiel, Meuse-Argonne* (Roanoke, VA: The Stone Printing and Manufacturing Co., 1919), 78–79.

Edward C. Lukens: from *A Blue Ridge Memoir*. Edward C. Lukens, *A Blue Ridge Memoir* (Baltimore: Sun Print, 1922), 59–65.

Horace Pippin: from "Autobiography, First World War." "Horace Pippin's Autobiography, First World War." Manuscript, Archives of American Art, Smithsonian Institution, Washington, D.C.

Ernest W. Gibson: from "History of First Vermont and 57th Pioneer Infantry." *Biennial Report of the Adjutant, Inspector and Quartermaster General of the State of Vermont for the Two Years ending June 30, 1920* (Rutland, VT: The Tuttle Company, 1920), 27–29.

Henry A. May: from *History of the U.S.S. Leviathan*. *History of the U.S.S. Leviathan, Cruiser and Transport Forces, United States Atlantic Fleet, compiled from the Ship's Log and data gathered by the*

History Committee on board the ship (Brooklyn, NY: Brooklyn Eagle Job Department, n.d. [1919]), 159–63.

Woodrow Wilson: Address to the Senate on Woman Suffrage, September 30, 1918. *PWW*, vol. 51, 158–61.

Ashby Williams: from *Experiences of the Great War*. Ashby Williams, *Experiences of the Great War: Artois, St. Mihiel, Meuse-Argonne* (Roanoke, VA: The Stone Printing and Manufacturing Co., 1919), 131–33.

Damon Runyon: Runyon Sees Return of Lost New York Battalion. *New York American*, October 13, 1918.

Woodrow Wilson: Second and Third Peace Notes to Germany, October 14 and 23, 1918. *Papers Relating to the Foreign Relations of the United States, 1918, Supplement 1, The World War, Volume I* (Washington, D.C.: Government Printing Office, 1933), 358–59, 381–83.

John J. Pershing to the Supreme War Council, October 30, 1918. John J. Pershing, *My Experiences in the World War*, vol. II (New York: Frederick A. Stokes Company, 1931), 366–67. Copyright, 1931, by John J. Pershing.

Harry S. Truman to Bess Wallace, November 10 and 11, 1918. Manuscript, Harry S. Truman Library, Independence, MO.

Robert J. Casey: from *The Cannoneers Have Hairy Ears*. Anonymous, *The Cannoneers Have Hairy Ears* (New York: J. H. Sears & Company, Inc., 1927), 326–30. Copyright, 1927, by J. H. Spears & Co., Incorporated.

Elizabeth Shepley Sergeant: from *Shadow-Shapes*. Elizabeth Shepley Sergeant, *Shadow-Shapes: The Journal of a Wounded Woman, October 1918–May 1919* (Boston: Houghton Mifflin Company, 1920), 170–86.

Sam M. Lewis and Joe Young: How 'Ya Gonna Keep 'Em Down on the Farm? "How 'Ya Gonna Keep 'Em Down on the Farm?," words by Sam M. Lewis and Joe Young, music by Walter Donaldson (New York: Waterson, Berlin & Snyder Co., 1919).

Oliver Wendell Holmes: Opinion in *Schenck v. United States*. *Schenck v. United States*, 249 U.S. Reports 47 (1919), 48–53.

Ray Stannard Baker: Diary, March 8, April 3–5, and April 7, 1919. *A Journalist's Diplomatic Mission: Ray Stannard Baker's World War I Diary*, ed. John Maxwell Hamilton and Robert Mann (Baton Rouge: Louisiana State University Press, 2012), 294–99, 321–24, 325–28. Copyright © 2012 by John Maxwell Hamilton and Robert Mann. Used by permission of Louisiana State University Press.

Vernon E. Kniptash: Diary, March 30–April 1 and April 18–19, 1919. Vernon E. Kniptash, *On the Western Front with the Rainbow Division: A World War I Diary*, E. Bruce Geelhoed (Norman: University of Oklahoma Press, 2009), 192–93, 204–5. Copyright © 2009 by the University of Oklahoma Press. Used by permission of University of Oklahoma Press.

Elmer W. Sherwood: Diary, April 18–21, 1919. *A Soldier in World War I: The Diary of Elmer W. Sherwood*, ed. Robert H. Ferrell (Indianapolis: Indiana Historical Society Press, 2004), 160–63. © 2004 Indiana Historical Society Press. Used by permission of the Indiana Historical Society Press.

Clyde D. Eoff to Josephine Eoff, April 28, 1919. Typescript, Clyde D. Eoff World War One correspondence collection (2014.023.w), Center for American War Letters Archives, Chapman University, CA. Used by permission.

W.E.B. Du Bois: Returning Soldiers. *The Crisis*, May 1919.

Charles R. Isum to W.E.B. Du Bois, May 17, 1919. Typescript, W.E.B. Du Bois Papers (MS 312). Special Collections and University Archives, University of Massachusetts Amherst Libraries.

Will Rogers: from *Rogers-isms: The Cowboy Philosopher on the Peace Conference*. Will Rogers, *Rogers-isms: The Cowboy Philosopher on the Peace Conference* (New York: Harper & Brothers, 1919), 2–4, 20, 21–22, 27, 41–42.

Woodrow Wilson: Memorial Day Address at Suresnes, May 30, 1919. *PWW*, vol. 59, 606–10.

Claude McKay: The Little Peoples. *The Liberator*, July 1919.

George Creel: The "Second Lines." George Creel, *How We Advertised America: The First Telling of the Amazing Story of the Committee on Public Information that Carried the Gospel of Americanism to Every Corner of the Globe* (New York: Harper & Brothers, 1920), 3–15.

Woodrow Wilson: Address to the Senate on the League of Nations, July 10, 1919. *PWW*, vol. 61, 426–36.

Newton D. Baker and Woodrow Wilson: An Exchange, July 23–July 31, 1919. *PWW*, vol. 61, 611, and vol. 62, 69.

Henry Cabot Lodge: Speech in the U.S. Senate, August 12, 1919. *American Speeches: Political Oratory from Abraham Lincoln to Bill Clinton*, ed. Ted Widmer (New York: Library of America, 2006), 327–55.

W. A. Domingo and Claude McKay: "If We Must Die." *The Messenger*, September 1919.

Woodrow Wilson: Speech at Pueblo, Colorado, September 25, 1919. *PWW*, vol. 63, 500–513.

Oliver Wendell Holmes: Dissenting Opinion in *Abrams v. United States*, November 10, 1919. *Abrams v. United States*, 250 U.S. Reports 616 (1919), 624–31.

William N. Vaile: Before the Buford Sailed. *The New York Times*, January 11, 1920.

Ezra Pound: from *Hugh Selwyn Mauberley*. *Hugh Selwyn Mauberley by E. P.* (London: The Ovid Press, 1920), 12–13.

Norman Fenton: from *Shell Shock and Its Aftermath*. Norman Fenton, *Shell Shock and Its Aftermath* (St. Louis, MO: The C.V. Mosby Company, 1926), 91–94. Copyright, 1926, by The C.V. Mosby Company.

Frederick Palmer: from *The Folly of Nations*. Frederick Palmer, *The Folly of Nations* (New York: Dodd, Mead & Company, 1921), 315–23.

Ludwig Lewisohn: Myth and Blood. Ludwig Lewisohn, *Up Stream: An American Chronicle* (New York: Boni and Liveright, 1922), 198–219.

Warren G. Harding: Address at the Burial of an Unknown American Soldier. *Address of the President of the United States at the Ceremonies Attending the Burial of an Unknown American Soldier in Arlington Cemetery, November 11, 1921*, Senate Documents Vol. 9, 67th Congress, 1st Session (Washington, D.C.: Government Printing Office, 1921), 3–6.

CODA

Ernest Hemingway: Soldier's Home. Ernest Hemingway, *In Our Time* (New York: Charles Scribner's Sons, 1930), 89–101. Used by permission of Scribner, a division of Simon & Schuster, Inc., from *In Our Time* by Ernest Hemingway. Copyright © 1925, 1930 by Charles Scribner's Sons, renewed 1953, 1958 by Ernest Hemingway. All rights reserved. Used in the United Kingdom by permission of The Random House Group Limited.

E. E. Cummings: my sweet old etcetera. E. E. Cummings, *is 5* (New York: Liveright, 1996), 70. Copyright © 1926, 1954, 1991 by the Trustees for the E. E. Cummings Trust. Copyright © 1985 by George James Firmage, from *Complete Poems: 1904–1962* by E. E. Cummings, edited by George J. Firmage. Used by permission of Liveright Publishing Corporation.

John Dos Passos: The Body of An American. John Dos Passos, *1919* (New York: Harcourt, Brace and Company, 1932), 467–73. Copyright, 1932, by John Dos Passos. © renewed 1959 by John Dos Passos. Used by permission of Lucy Dos Passos Coggin.

This volume presents the texts of the printings, typescripts, and manuscripts chosen as sources here but does not attempt to reproduce features of their typographic design or physical layout. In the texts that have been printed from manuscript, the beginnings of sentences have been capitalized and punctuation at the end of sentences and closing quotation marks have been supplied. The texts are printed without alteration except for the changes previously discussed and for the correction of typographical errors. Spelling, punctuation, and capitalization are often expressive features, and they are not altered, even when inconsistent or irregular. The following is a list of typographical errors corrected, cited by page and line number: 10.28, Jaurés; 26.2, beseiged; 31.16, opinon,; 35.2, Curassiers; 39.6, Some, were; 48.19, than; 48.28, dispair; 110.6, gives; 139.38, dust discomfort; 155.10, schools In; 161.32, it going; 166.33, among; 167.34, intent; 187.25, separted; 212.10, proposes; 214.24, anykind; 218.2–3, unscruplous; 219.13, up and; 220.4, phenominally; 223.14, artifically.; 230.23, subime; 237.21, 1915.; 262.32, the the days; 272.5, George III.; 282.28, sharpened; 288.8, *Lokal-Anzeiger*;; 297.11, preceeding; 312.2, definate; 335.28, "defense",; 355.6, stedfast; 361.13, hospital."; 362.16, winudow; 364.17, over the; 370.13, its; 389.7, weer; 389.16, an another; 392.28, through; 393.12, weer; 420.39, allleged,; 442.7, wont; 471.1, Germans; 478.14, eye lid; 482.22, its; 496.30, this a; 499.31, off; 502.12, Christans; 528.11, was was; 559.20, rap stand; 599.20, predelections; 601.21, posesses,; 608.12, cpm; 608.15, dacks; 611.28, throwers came; 611.31, Whitlesey; 621.30, comming; 665.27, accomplishes The; 666.33, biding; 668.1, at and; 668.32, that; 669.6, way;; 675.12, there there; 763.15, Czecko-Slovaks; 786.3, civilizations; 791.9, 1919; 791.10, brute.'; 791.15, 1919; 791.25, again; 792.5, beastiality.; 801.37, multilate; 818.12, Kreb's.

Notes

In the notes below, the reference numbers denote page and line of this volume (the line count includes headings, but not rule lines). No note is made for material included in the eleventh edition of *Merriam-Webster's Collegiate Dictionary*. Biblical references are keyed to the King James Version. Quotations from Shakespeare are keyed to *The Riverside Shakespeare*, ed. G. Blakemore Evans (Boston: Houghton, Mifflin, 1974). Footnotes and bracketed editorial notes within the text were in the originals. For further historical background, references to other studies, and more detailed maps, see John Keegan, *The First World War* (New York, NY: Alfred A. Knopf, 1999); Hew Strachan, *The First World War* (New York, NY: Viking, 2004); David Stevenson, *Cataclysm: The First World War as Political Tragedy* (New York, NY: Basic Books, 2004); Edward M. Coffman, *The War to End All Wars: The American Military Experience in World War I* (Lexington, KY: The University Press of Kentucky, 1998); David M. Kennedy, *Over Here: The First World War and American Society* (New York, NY: Oxford University Press, 1980); Jennifer D. Keene, *World War I: The American Soldier Experience* (Westport, CT: Greenwood Press, 2006); Michael S. Neiberg, *The Path to War: How the First World War Created Modern America* (New York, NY: Oxford University Press, 2016); A. Scott Berg, *Wilson* (New York, NY: G. P. Putnam's Sons, 2013); Martin Gilbert, *The Routledge Atlas of the First World War*, Third Edition (New York, NY: Routledge, 2008).

2.9–10   Francis Ferdinand . . . Duchess of Hohenberg,] Archduke Franz Ferdinand (1863–1914) became heir to the throne of Austria-Hungary in 1896 and married Countess Sophie Chotek (1868–1914) in a morganatic union in 1900. Sophie was made Duchess of Hohenberg in 1905.

2.17–18   Archduke pushed it . . . his arm] The bomb may have bounced off the folded-down roof of the car.

2.21   Col. Morizzi] Lieutenant Colonel Erik von Merizzi (1873–1917) was adjutant to Oskar Potiorek, the governor of Bosnia-Herzegovina. Merizzi served during the war as a staff officer in Serbia and Galicia before becoming commander of an artillery brigade on the Italian front, where he died.

2.25   Gabrinovics] Nedeljko Čabrinović (1895–1916), a Bosnian Serb who worked as a typesetter. Čabrinović died of tuberculosis on January 20, 1916, while imprisoned at the fortress of Theresienstadt (now Terezín, Czech Republic).

2.28   the Mayor] Fehim Ćurčić (1886–1916), a Bosnian Muslim.

3.6   Gavrio Princip] Gavrilo Princip (1894–1918), a Bosnian Serb student.
Princip died of tuberculosis at Theresienstadt on April 28, 1918.

3.12   Konak] The residential palace of the governor of Bosnia-Herzegovina.

3.32   Ischl,] Bad Ischl, a spa town about 130 miles west of Vienna.

3.36   Archduke . . . head of the army] Franz Ferdinand was made inspector
general of the Austro-Hungarian army in 1913.

4.3–4   Emperor visited . . . annexation, in 1908] The Congress of Berlin
(1878), held after the Russo-Turkish War of 1877–78, placed the Ottoman provinces of Bosnia and Herzegovina under Austro-Hungarian occupation and administration. Austria-Hungary annexed Bosnia and Herzegovina in 1908. The
annexation was opposed by Serbia and caused an international crisis that was
resolved in early 1909 when the Russian government decided not to risk war
with Austria-Hungary. Emperor Franz Joseph visited Bosnia-Herzegovina, May
30–June 4, 1910. During his visit, a young Serbian student from Herzegovina,
Bogdan Žerajić, unsuccessfully tried to assassinate the governor of Bosnia-
Herzegovina, then committed suicide. At their trial Princip and Čabrinović
cited Žerajić's actions as an inspiration for their decision to kill Franz Ferdinand.

4.9   last Wednesday] June 24, 1914.

4.9–13   the Servian minister . . . the Archduke.] Jovan Jovanović, the
Serbian minister to Austria-Hungary, met with Leon Biliński, the Austro-
Hungarian finance minister, on June 5, 1914, and warned him that it would be
dangerous for Franz Ferdinand to visit Sarajevo, especially on June 28, the anniversary of the Serbian defeat by the Ottoman Turks at the battle of Kosovo
in 1389. Jovanović outlined a scenario in which a Serb conscript participating
in the maneuvers might shoot the Archduke. Biliński contacted the civil authorities in Sarajevo, who expressed concern about the security arrangements
for the visit, but was rebuffed by Oskar Potiorek, the military governor of
Bosnia.

4.22   recent Balkan war] In the First Balkan War, October 1912–May 1913,
Serbia, Montenegro, Greece, and Bulgaria fought and defeated the Ottoman
Empire; in the Second Balkan War, June–July 1913, Serbia, Montenegro,
Greece, Romania, and the Ottoman Empire fought and defeated Bulgaria.
Serbia increased its population by about 50 percent and nearly doubled its ter-
ritory as a result of the two wars.

5.13–14   coat of silk strands . . . bullet] A design for body armor made from
woven silk was patented by the Polish inventor Casimir Zeglen in 1897 and
marketed in Europe and the United States. It is not known if Franz Ferdinand
owned a Zeglen coat.

5.33   Glumex] Chlumetz, now Chlumec nad Cidlinou in the Czech Republic.

5.35   Duke of Cumberland] Ernst August (1845–1923), a cousin of George V and the exiled heir to the throne of Hanover. His English title was revoked in 1919 after he supported Germany in the war.

5.39–6.2   Archduke Charles Francis Joseph . . . Princess Zita] Karl Franz Joseph (1887–1922), a nephew of Archduke Franz Ferdinand, married Princess Zita of Bourbon-Palma (1892–1989) in 1911. Karl succeeded Franz Joseph as emperor of Austria and king of Hungary on November 21, 1916. He renounced all participation in Austrian state affairs on November 11, 1918, and died in exile on Madeira.

7.16–18   the tragedy . . . the Hapsburgs.] Maximillian (1832–1867), a younger brother of Emperor Franz Joseph, was made emperor of Mexico by Napoleon III in 1864. He was overthrown by the forces of President Benito Juárez and executed in 1867. Crown Prince Rudolf (1858–1889), the emperor's son and heir, shot himself at the Mayerling hunting lodge outside Vienna in 1889 as part of an apparent suicide pact with Baroness Mary Vetsera (1871–1889). Karl Ludwig (1833–1896), Franz Joseph's younger brother, died of typhoid allegedly caused by drinking water from the Jordan River during a pilgrimage to the Holy Land in 1896; his death made his son Franz Ferdinand heir to the throne. Empress Elizabeth (1832–1898) was fatally stabbed by an Italian anarchist in Geneva, Switzerland, in 1898.

8.19   Gabrinovics . . . River Miljachka] The river was at low water because of the summer weather, and Čabrinović fell onto a sand bank.

9.4–5   the bomb . . . came from Belgrade] The assassination plot was organized by Lieutenant Colonel Dragutin Dimitrijević (1876–1917), alias Apis, the chief of Serbian military intelligence and one of the founders of Union or Death, a secret Serbian nationalist society also known as the Black Hand. Dimitrijević's aide, Major Voja Tankosić (1880–1915), recruited Princip, Čabrinović, and a third Bosnian Serb, Trifko Grabež (1895–1916) in Belgrade, supplied them with six bombs and four pistols, and arranged for them to be smuggled into Bosnia. They were joined in Sarajevo by Danilo Ilić (1891–1915), a member of the Black Hand who had recruited three other Bosnians into the plot. Although all seven conspirators were deployed along the motorcade route on June 28, only Čabrinović and Princip took action. The Austro-Hungarian authorities arrested six members of the assassination team by July 3 (one of the men recruited by Ilić escaped to Montenegro and then Serbia). The six assassins were tried in Sarajevo for high treason, October 12–28, 1914, along with nineteen men accused of assisting them. Princip, Čabrinović, and Grabež were sentenced to twenty years in prison. (Under Austrian law, defendants under the age of twenty could not receive the death penalty.) Ilić and two other men were sentenced to death and hanged on February 3, 1915, while thirteen defendants received sentences ranging from three years to life; nine of the accused were acquitted. Tankosić was killed in action during the invasion of Serbia in autumn 1915. Dimitrijević was arrested in 1917 by the Serbian government-in-exile in Salonika, Greece, as part of a purge of the Black Hand.

He was accused of attempting to assassinate Prince-Regent Alexander, court-martialed, and shot.

9.8   M. Potiorek, Governor of Bosnia] Lieutenant General Oskar Potiorek (1853–1933) was the governor of Bosnia-Herzegovina, 1912–14. He led three unsuccessful invasions of Serbia, August–December 1914 (see Chronology), before resigning his command on December 21, 1914.

10.33   Jaurès] Jean Jaurès (1859–1914) was a member of the chamber of deputies, 1885–89, 1893–98, 1902–14, a founder and leader of the S.F.I.O., the French Socialist Party, 1905, and editor of the socialist newspaper *L'Humanité*, 1904–14. An opponent of militarism who had sought to make the international socialist movement a force for preserving peace, Jaurès traveled to Brussels, July 29–30, 1914, to meet with German Socialists in an attempt to prevent the outbreak of war. He then returned to Paris, where he was assassinated on the evening of July 31 by a right-wing French nationalist.

11.8   the Minister] Brand Whitlock (1869–1934) was the independent reform mayor of Toledo, Ohio, 1906–13, before serving as U.S. minister to Belgium, 1913–19, and ambassador to Belgium, 1919–21. A prolific author of fiction and nonfiction, Whitlock published *Belgium: A Personal Narrative* in 1919.

12.8   Colonel Falls] Dewitt Clinton Falls (1864–1937) had served as a military observer in the Balkans in 1912–13. In 1914 he was the regimental adjutant of the 7th New York with the rank of captain.

12.12   Millard Shaler] A graduate of the University of Kansas, Shaler (1880–1942) worked as an engineer in the Congo, Angola, and South Africa. He served on the Commission for Relief in Belgium, 1914–19.

13.1–2   Germans . . . crossed the frontier] The first German troops crossed the Belgian frontier on the morning of August 4.

13.40   Mexico loomed large] General Victoriano Huerta (1850–1916) over-threw President Francisco Madero on February 18, 1913, and had Madero assassinated on February 22. His seizure of power resulted in an insurrection by the Constitutionalists, under the leadership of Venustiano Carranza (1859–1920), the governor of Coahuila. After his army suffered major defeats at Zacatecas, June 23, 1914, and Orendáin, July 6–8, Huerta resigned the presidency on July 15 and fled the country five days later. Francisco Carvajal, Huerta's foreign minister, became interim president and began negotiations with the Constitutionalists for the peaceful surrender of Mexico City. On August 20 Carranza entered the capital and became the provisional president of Mexico.

14.2   Albania] Great Britain, France, Italy, Germany, Austria-Hungary, and Russia agreed in 1913 that Albania would be removed from Ottoman rule and become an autonomous principality under the supervision of an international control commission. The six powers chose William of Wied (1876–1945), a German prince, as the sovereign of the new state. William began his reign on March 7, 1914, but soon faced rebellions by Greek separatists in southern Albania and by Muslim peasants in the central region. In July 1914 William appealed unsuccessfully to the six powers for military and financial aid. The outbreak of war in August caused the collapse of the international control commission, and on September 3 William left the country. During World War I various regions of Albania were occupied at different times by Italy, Greece, Serbia, Montenegro, Austria-Hungary, Bulgaria, and France.

14.3 Thibet] Tibet.

14.10–11 the Marseillaise] The French national anthem, written in 1792 by Claude Joseph Rouger de Lisle (1760–1836), a French army officer.

14.21–22 von Below] Karl Konrad Claus von Below-Saleske (1866–1939) was the German minister to Belgium, 1913–14. He had previously served in Beijing and Istanbul and as minister to Bulgaria, 1910–12.

14.32 *Le Soir*] A Belgium evening newspaper, founded in 1887.

15.19 Herrick] Myron T. Herrick (1854–1929) was U.S. ambassador to France, 1912–14 and 1921–29. He had previously served as the Republican governor of Ohio, 1904–6.

15.24 Squier] Lieutenant Colonel George Squier (1865–1934), an officer in the Signal Corps, was the U.S. military attaché in London, 1912–16. He later served as the Chief Signal Officer of the U.S. Army, 1917–23.

16.11 Home Rule quarrel] In April 1912 the Liberal government led by Prime Minister Herbert Henry Asquith introduced a Home Rule bill establishing an Irish parliament with limited powers. Opposed by the Conservatives and Unionists, the bill passed the House of Commons twice in 1913 with the support of the Irish Parliamentary Party, but was defeated twice in the House of Lords. Division over Home Rule led to the formation in 1913 of two opposing paramilitary organizations in Ireland, the Ulster Volunteer Force and the nationalist Irish Volunteers. The House of Commons passed the bill for a third time in May 1914, making it eligible for royal assent without the approval of the Lords. Fearing that its implementation would cause civil war in Ireland, the Asquith government introduced an amending bill that would allow for the temporary exclusion of Ulster counties from Home Rule. After the outbreak of the war the amending bill was replaced with a measure that suspended the implementation of Home Rule for the duration of the conflict, and on September 18, 1914, both the Home Rule and suspensory bills received the royal assent.

18.11 When England . . . had the right] The neutrality of the Grand Duchy of Luxembourg was guaranteed by the 1867 Treaty of London, signed by Austria, Belgium, France, Great Britain, Italy, the Netherlands, Prussia, and Russia. After German troops occupied Luxembourg on August 2, 1914, Chancellor Theobald von Bethmann Hollweg (1856–1921) justified the action as a defensive measure intended to protect railroads under German administration from possible French attack.

18.22 France went through . . . first] Reports in the German press on August 3, 1914, falsely claimed that French airmen had flown over Belgium and Dutch territory on their way to Germany, and that French officers dressed in German uniforms had crossed the Dutch-German border.

18.38–39 proclamation . . . Emperor Franz Josef] The Austro-Hungarian declaration of war against Serbia, issued by Emperor Franz Joseph on July 28, 1914.

19.37–39 Russia knew . . . wounds of the Japanese war] The Russian defeat in the Russo-Japanese War of 1904–5 led to a series of revolutionary uprisings in 1905–6 that threatened the tsarist regime.

20.1 revenge itself for Alsace] France ceded the provinces of Alsace and Lorraine to Germany following its defeat in the 1870–71 Franco-Prussian War.

20.11 Four times he . . . Czar] Nicholas II and Wilhelm II exchanged ten telegrams, July 29–August 1, 1914, all written in English and signed "Nicky" and "Willy." In his messages Wilhelm defended the Austro-Hungarian war against Serbia and warned the Tsar not to undertake mobilization measures.

20.13 urge Austria to new negotiations.] German chancellor Bethmann Hollweg urged Austria-Hungary on July 29 to halt its military action against Serbia and accept mediation, and Wilhelm II made a similar appeal in a message to Emperor Franz Joseph on July 30. Count Leopold von Berchtold (1863–1942), the foreign minister of Austria-Hungary, replied on July 30 that military operations against Serbia could no longer be halted.

20.24–25 punitive expedition against Mexico] President Wilson refused to recognize the government of Victoriano Huerta (see note 13.40) and imposed an arms embargo on his regime. On April 9, 1914, nine American sailors from the USS *Dolphin* were briefly detained in the port of Tampico by forces loyal to Huerta. Although the Mexican authorities apologized to Admiral Henry Mayo (1856–1937), the commander of the U.S. squadron stationed off Tampico, Mayo demanded that the Mexicans honor the American flag by firing a full twenty-one-gun salute. Wilson supported Mayo's demand, and decided to take military action. On April 21 a force of 800 Marines and sailors landed at Veracruz with orders to seize the customhouse, beginning three days of fighting in which nineteen Americans and more than 150 Mexicans were killed. The invasion was condemned by Huerta's opponents and brought the United States and Mexico close to full-scale war. Wilson accepted an offer by Argentina, Brazil, and Chile to mediate the dispute. Although the subsequent proposal by the "ABC Powers" for establishing a new Mexican government was rejected by Huerta, it contributed to his decision to resign as president on July 15. U.S. forces would remain in Veracruz until November 23, 1914.

21.21–22 flight of Italy . . . deserted its allies] Italy had declared its neutrality on August 2, 1914, despite its 1882 Triple Alliance with Austria-Hungary and Germany. The Italian government asserted that because the alliance was strictly defensive, it did not oblige Italy to join a war caused by the aggression of Austria-Hungary.

21.28–29   Roumania and Japan] Romania had associated itself with the Triple Alliance in 1883, but chose to remain neutral in August 1914. It declared war on Austria-Hungary on August 27, 1916. Japan declared war on Germany on August 23, 1914.

23.24   Sir Edward Grey] Grey (1862–1933) was foreign secretary of Great Britain, 1905–16.

24.9   Mr. Kent] Fred I. Kent (1869–1954), vice-president of Bankers' Trust and an expert on foreign exchange.

25.16   Austrian ambassador] Count Albert Mensdorff (1861–1945) was the Austro-Hungarian ambassador to Great Britain, 1904–14.

25.21   Austria had not given . . . for war.] Great Britain declared war on Austria-Hungary on August 12, 1914.

25.35   the German Ambassador] Prince Karl Max von Lichnowsky (1860–1928) was the German ambassador to Great Britain, 1912–14. In 1916 Lichnowsky wrote and privately circulated a memoir, *Meine Londoner Mission 1912–14*, in which he attributed the outbreak of the war to reckless German support for Austria-Hungary. His memoir was published in March 1918 without his permission and was widely circulated by the Allies, resulting in his expulsion from the upper chamber of the Prussian parliament.

26.4   Princess Lichnowsky] Princess Mechtilde Lichnowsky (1879–1958).

26.14   Laughlin's] Irwin B. Laughlin (1871–1941) served as secretary of the London embassy, 1912–17, and counselor of the embassy, 1916–19. He was later U.S. minister to Greece, 1924–26, and ambassador to Spain, 1929–33.

26.31–32   Chandler Anderson] Anderson (1866–1936), an attorney with extensive experience in international law, served as counselor for the State Department, 1910–13.

26.33   Skinner . . . McCrary] Robert Peet Skinner (1866–1960) was consul-general at the London embassy, 1914–24. He later served as minister to Greece, 1926–32, minister to Lithuania, Latvia, and Estonia, 1931–33, and ambassador to Turkey, 1933–36. Lieutenant Commander Frank R. McCrary (1879–1952) later became a naval aviator and was the first lighter-than-air pilot in the U.S. Navy.

27.6   the Tennessee] The armored cruiser USS *Tennessee* sailed from New York on August 6, 1914, carrying $5,867,000 in gold to be used for the financial relief of stranded American travelers.

28.18   the King] George V (1865–1936), king of Great Britain and Ireland and emperor of India, 1910–36.

29.19–20   canal tolls victory] Congress had passed legislation in 1912 lowering or abolishing tolls on American ships using the Panama Canal. Britain protested that preferential treatment for U.S. shipping violated the 1901 Hay-Paunceforte Treaty, an Anglo-American agreement giving the United States exclusive rights to build a Central American canal, and in February 1914 Wilson called for the exemption to be repealed. The repeal measure passed the House, 247–162, on March 31, and the Senate, 50–35, on June 11, 1914.

34.1–2   swollen waters . . . Johnstown.] The collapse of the Conemaugh Reservoir dam on May 31, 1889, flooded Johnstown, Pennsylvania, killing 2,200 persons.

35.1   Burgomaster Max] Adolphe Max (1869–1939) was mayor of Brussels, 1909–39. Max was arrested on September 26, 1914, for resisting demands for food requisitions and was imprisoned in Germany for the remainder of the war.

37.11   General von Lutwitz] Arthur von Lüttwitz (1865–1928).

37.19–20   As for a week . . . occupied Louvain] The Germans occupied Louvain on August 19, 1914.

38.14–16   Father Damien . . . Stevenson wrote] Born Joseph De Veuster, Father Damien (1840–1889) trained for the priesthood in Louvain before going as a missionary to the Hawaiian Islands, where he served in the leper colony on Moloka'i, 1873–89. Stevenson defended Damien against criticism by a Presbyterian missionary in *An Open Letter to the Reverend Dr. Hyde of Honolulu* (1890).

38.22   destroy Vera Cruz] See note 20.24–25.

39.35   makes a wilderness . . . war] Cf. Tacitus, *Agricola* (c. 98 c.e.): "To robbery, murder and pillage they give the false name of empire, and when they make a wilderness they call it peace."

43.29–30   Admiral Diederichs at Manila] Otto von Diederichs (1843–1918), the commander of the German Asiatic Squadron, arrived with his flagship in Manila Bay on June 12, 1898, while Commodore George Dewey was blockading the city. Dewey became apprehensive that the Germans were planning to intervene in the Philippines, although the stated purpose of their naval presence was the protection of German nationals and property. The German squadron began to withdraw after the surrender of Manila on August 13.

43.37   Kiaochow] Jiaozhou, a town on the Shantung peninsula in northeast China. In 1898, Germany obtained concessions on the peninsula, including control of the port of Tsingtao (Qingdao), railways, mines, and the right to station troops.

45.29   Godoy] Manuel de Godoy (1767–1851), prime minister of Spain 1792–98 and 1801–8, became known as "the prince of the peace" after negotiating the Treaty of Basel in 1795, under which Spain ceded Santo Domingo to France while regaining Catalonian territory occupied by the French.

48.27 "Germany above . . . the world."] Cf. the hymn "Deutschland, Deutschland über Alles" (1841) by August Heinrich Hoffman (1798–1874): "Deutschland, Deutschland über alles, über alles in der Welt" (Germany, Germany above all, above all else in the world).

48.35 essential humanity . . . twenty years ago] Du Bois was a student at Friedrich Wilhelm University in Berlin, 1892–94, and traveled throughout Germany during his stay.

49.6–9 a proclamation . . . Wundt] "An die Kulturwelt! Ein Aufruf" (To the Civilized World! An Appeal) was published on October 4, 1914, and signed by ninety-three "representatives of German science and art." The appeal protested against "the lies and calumnies" being used "to stain the honor of Germany," and denied ("it is not true") that Germany was guilty of causing the war, violating Belgium neutrality, killing Belgian civilians without justification, destroying Louvain, disregarding international law, or engaging in destructive militarism. It concluded with a pledge to "fight this war to the end as a civilized people to whom the legacy of Goethe, Beethoven, and Kant are as sacred as hearth and home." Among its signers were the theologian and church historian Adolf von Harnack (1851–1930), art historian Wilhelm von Bode (1845–1929), dramatist Gerhardt Hauptmann (1862–1929), novelist and dramatist Hermann Sudermann (1857–1928), physicist Ernest Roentgen (1845–1923), composer Engelbert Humperdinck (1854–1923), and psychologist Wilhelm Wundt (1832–1920), as well as the chemist Fritz Haber (1868–1934) and physicist Max Planck (1858–1947).

49.10–11 sneering at "Mongrels and Niggers."] In refuting the accusation that Germany disregarded international law, the appeal asserted: "Those who have allied themselves with Russians and Serbs, and who present the world with the shameful spectacle of inciting Mongolians and Negroes against the white race, have the very least right to portray themselves as the defenders of European civilization."

50.24 Przemyśl] See Chronology, September–November 1914, March and June 1915.

50.27–30 Baron Mednyanszky . . . Herr Hollitzer's] László Mednyánszky (1852–1919), a Hungarian painter; Lieutenant Cesare Santorre, an Italian naval officer and correspondent for the journal *Aero Marittima*; Alexander Exax (1896–1994), a photographer who served with the military press office in Galicia, Serbia, and on the Italian front, 1914–17; and Carl Leopold Hollitzer (1874–1942), a singer and sketch artist serving with the military press office.

54.2 famous lady . . . turned to look!] Lot's wife; see Genesis 19:26.

54.34 kino] Film, motion picture.

55.9 the Astoria] A hotel in Budapest.

55.10 Dr. MacDonald] Charles B. MacDonald (1873–1936), a surgeon with the U.S. Army, served as a Red Cross volunteer at hospitals in Vienna and Budapest, 1914–15.

55.23   Mr. Schriner] George A. Schreiner (1875–1942), a German-American correspondent for the Associated Press who reported on the war from Germany, Austria-Hungary, the Balkans, and the Ottoman Empire, 1914–17.

56.35   von Leidenfrost] Adolf von Leidenfrost, a Hungarian-American relief worker.

64.1   great conflict of September] The German advance to, and subsequent retreat from, the Marne River. See Chronology, August–September 1914.

64.39   an army . . . of a division,] A French division had about 15,000 men at full strength. Two or three divisions made up a corps, and from two to five corps made up an army. There were eight French armies deployed along the Western Front in February 1915; Châlons-sur-Marne was the headquarters of the Fourth Army.

65.7   "torpedo" racers] Streamlined race cars.

65.17   "éclopés"] Disabled, crippled..

66.32–33   "La France . . . guerrière."] France is a warlike nation.

67.28   "Seventy-fives."] French field artillery gun that fired shells 75mm (2.95 inches) in diameter that weighed twelve pounds. It had a maximum range of more than four miles (7,400 yards).

69.23   Sister Gabrielle Rosnet,] Marie Rosnet (1872–1927) entered the Daughters of Charity in 1891 and took the name Sister Gabrielle. She later joined the Sisters of Saint Vincent de Paul and served at the hospital in Clermont-en-Argonne throughout the war. In 1916 she was made a Chevalier of the Legion of Honor.

69.33   "à coups de crosse"] With rifle butts.

70.1   "ces satanés Allemands"] Those devilish Germans.

70.3–4   fierce September days] After the French army retreated from Clermont-en-Argonne on September 4, 1914, the Germans shelled the town for several hours, and then occupied it that night. The Germans withdrew from Clermont-en-Argonne on September 14, and French troops returned there later that day.

70.9   "Et ils étaient tous comme ça"] And they were all like that.

70.15   obus] Howitzer shell.

71.3–4   Vauquois . . . first importance] Observation posts on the hill of Vauquois allowed the Germans to shell the railway running from Ste. Menehould to Verdun.

71.14–16   retake it . . . securely established there] The fighting in the ruins of

Vauquois became stalemated in March 1915. Both sides then engaged in extensive tunneling operations, detonating more than 500 mines on or beneath the hill of Vauquois from February 1915 to April 1918. The entire hill was captured by American troops on the first day of the Meuse-Argonne offensive, September 26, 1918.

71.27   *médecin-chef*] Chief doctor.

72.35–36   "*Sauvez, sauvez . . . pas!*"] Save, save France, do not abandon her!

73.8   Varennes . . . Bois de la Grurie,] Varennes was captured by the Germans on September 23, 1914. French attempts to retake the village in December 1914 and January 1915 failed, and it remained in German hands until its capture by American troops on September 26, 1918. Le Four de Paris, a crossroads hamlet six miles southwest of Varennes, came under German attack in February 1915 but remained in French possession. Le Bois de Gruerie, on the western edge of the Argonne Forest, was the scene of prolonged and inconclusive fighting in 1915.

73.31   "permis de séjour"] Residence permit.

74.24   *infirmière major*] Head nurse.

75.27–28   Les Eparges, . . . desperate struggle] French troops assaulted German positions on the high ridge east of Les Éparges on February 17, 1915. After weeks of costly fighting the battle ended in a stalemate in late April, with neither side having full possession of the ridge.

76.34–35   Verdun . . . the road to Bar-le-Duc] In 1916 the road served as the main route for supplies and reinforcements being sent to the battle of Verdun (see Chronology, February–December 1916). It became widely known in France as the *Voie Sacrée* (Sacred Way).

77.2–3   St. Mihiel . . . armour!] The Germans captured St. Mihiel on September 25, 1914, forming a salient that cut the main railway supplying Verdun from the south and threatened to turn the French line along the Meuse. A French offensive in the spring of 1915 failed to retake the St. Mihiel salient, which remained in German hands until its elimination by the American Expeditionary Forces, September 12–16, 1918.

78.23   *sous-officiers*] Noncommissioned officers.

79.23   *estafettes*] Couriers, dispatch riders.

80.6   *Jéna*] Napoleon defeated a Prussian-Saxon army in the battle of Jena-Auerstedt, fought in Saxony on October 14, 1806.

80.32–34   Suippes . . . Beauséjour] A series of French attacks in March 1915 made limited gains in Champagne.

81.31   Losnitza . . . Goutchevo Mountain] Loznica, a town in northwest Serbia, across the Drina River from Bosnia; Gučevo Mountain.

81.34–35 the second invasion] See Chronology, August–December 1914. Austro-Hungarian troops crossed the Drina River on September 8 and reached the summit of Gučevo by September 11.

82.4–5 third invasion . . . rout at Valievo] Austro-Hungarian forces began a general offensive on November 6 that forced the Serbs to retreat from Gučevo. The Austro-Hungarians captured Krupanj on November 9 and occupied Valjevo on November 16 as the Serbs retreated across the Kolubara River. On December 3 the Serbs launched a counteroffensive that recaptured Valjevo on December 9 and drove the Austro-Hungarians across the Drina on December 13.

82.8 *comitadji*] Serbian guerrillas.

82.33 *rackia*] Rakija, plum brandy.

84.35 Svornik] Zvornik, in Bosnia-Herzegovina.

86.17 "*Haide!*"] Come on!

86.19 Robinson] Boardman Robinson (1876–1952), Canadian-American illustrator and painter who accompanied Reed on his travels in the Balkans and Eastern Europe in 1915.

86.25 Voyvoda Michitch, . . . King Peter] Živojin Mišić (1855–1921) served as deputy to Radomir Putnik, the chief of the Serbian general staff, from the outbreak of war until November 1914, when he took command of the Serbian First Army. Mišić played a key role in the counteroffensive that ended the third Austro-Hungarian invasion, December 3–15, 1914. *Voivode*, literally meaning "war chief" or "war lord," was the highest rank in the Serbian military. Peter I (1844–1921) was king of Serbia, 1903–18, and king of the Serbs, Croats, and Slovenes, 1918–21.

86.31 Johnson] The name Reed used in *The War in Eastern Europe* for the guide assigned to him by the Serbian press bureau. Reed described him as a former lecturer in comparative literature at the University of Belgrade and wrote that "Johnson" was "a literal translation of his name."

89.4 Nish] Niš, the wartime capital of Serbia, 1914–15.

90.3 *Charles E. Lauriat, Jr.*] Lauriat dictated the narrative excerpted here in London on May 12, 1915.

90.35 Mr. and Mrs. Elbert Hubbard] Elbert Hubbard (1856–1915) was the owner of the Roycroft Printing Shop in East Aurora, New York, editor and publisher of the monthly journal *The Philistine* (1895–1915), and a prolific writer best known for the inspirational tract *A Message to Garcia* (1899), based on an incident in the Spanish-American War. Alice Moore Hubbard (1861–1915) was a writer whose works included *Woman's Work* (1908), *Life Lessons* (1909), and *The Basis of Marriage* (1910).

91.4–5 "Who Lifted the Lid Off Hell"] In his essay, Hubbard wrote that

"William Hohenzollern" had "a shrunken soul," "a mind that reeks of ego-mania," and was "a mastoid degenerate of a noble grandmother" (Wilhelm II was a grandson of Queen Victoria). Hubbard concluded by predicting that the defeat of Germany would be followed by disarmament and the creation of a "World Federation."

91.14–15   second explosion . . . a boiler] The *U-20* fired only one torpedo at the *Lusitania*. While the cause of the second explosion is uncertain, it was most likely the result of a steam line rupture.

92.3   the Hubbards . . . again.] The bodies of Elbert and Alice Hubbard were never identified, and may never have been recovered.

92.10   Captain Turner and Captain Anderson] Captain William Turner (1856–1933), commander of the *Lusitania*, and Staff Captain James Anderson (1865–1915), his second in command. Anderson's body was recovered after the sinking.

95.30–31   about 60 fathoms . . . 755 feet long.] The *Lusitania* sank in fifty fathoms (300 feet) of water and was 785 feet long.

96.11   Camp Asquam] A summer camp for boys on Squam Lake in New Hampshire, founded as Camp Harvard in 1885 and renamed Camp Asquam in 1887. The camp closed in 1912.

96.24   a seaman] Leslie Morton (1896–1968), who had served on sailing ships since 1910, was making his first voyage on the *Lusitania*.

96.28   G——] Frederic Gauntlett (1870–1951), an English-born American who was traveling on business for the Newport News Ship Building Company.

98.20   B——] James Brooks (1875–1956), an American salesman for a tire chain company.

98.35–38   a woman; her husband] Margaret Gwyer (born c. 1889), who had married Herbert Gwyer (1883–1960), a clergyman in the Church of England, on April 15, 1915.

100.34–36   McM—— . . . the Republic] The British liner *Republic* collided with the Italian passenger ship *Florida* in a fog bank fifty miles south of Nantucket Island on January 23, 1909. Three persons on the *Republic* were killed or fatally injured in the collision; the remaining passengers and crew were safely evacuated before the ship sank on January 24.

102.24   Mr. Mayor] Rudolph Blankenburg (1843–1918), a naturalized citizen born in Germany, was elected mayor of Philadelphia on a reform independent-Democratic ticket in 1911 and served December 1911–January 1916.

108.22–24   China . . . the theory] Roosevelt had previously argued that China invited foreign aggression and encroachment by being unwilling to build up its army and navy.

108.34–35   the message . . . strict accountability] On February 10, 1915,

Secretary of State Bryan sent a diplomatic note warning the German government that sinking American ships, or ships carrying American passengers, would be considered "an indefensible violation of neutral rights" and that the United States would hold Germany to "a strict accountability" for its naval actions. The note was drafted by Robert Lansing, the counselor for the State Department, and President Wilson.

110.15   Hague Conventions] The Hague Conferences of 1899 and 1907 resulted in conventions on the peaceful settlement of international disputes, the laws of war on land and sea, the opening of hostilities, and the rights and duties of neutral powers in wartime.

110.20   number of American ships . . . torpedoed] At the time Roosevelt was writing, the only American ship to have been torpedoed was the tanker *Gulflight*, which was attacked in the Irish Sea on May 1, 1915. Although the *Gulflight* did not sink, two crewmen jumped overboard and drowned, and the ship's captain died of a heart attack later in the day.

111.21–23   those who guide . . . the Huns] In a speech delivered at Bremerhaven on July 27, 1900, to German troops who were being sent to China to suppress the Boxer Rebellion, Wilhelm II said: "Should you encounter the enemy, he will be defeated! No quarter will be given! Prisoners will not be taken! Whoever falls into your hands is forfeited. Just as a thousand years ago the Huns under their King Attila made a name for themselves, one that even today makes them seem mighty in history and legend, may the name German be affirmed by you in such a way in China that no Chinese will ever again dare to look cross-eyed at a German."

111.25   Louvain and Dinant] See pp. 33–41 in this volume.

111.35–36   peace when there is no peace] Jeremiah 6:14, 8:11; Ezekiel 13:10.

113.4   *Gottlieb von Jagow*] Jagow (1863–1935) was the German secretary of state for foreign affairs from January 1913 to November 1916, when his opposition to resuming unrestricted submarine warfare led to his resignation.

116.4–6   recently published . . . a formal warning] The warning was published on May 1, 1915, the day the *Lusitania* sailed from New York.

119.2   Turkish Revolution] A military uprising in Macedonia in July 1908 forced Sultan Abdul Hamid II (1842–1918) to restore parliamentary rule. An attempted counterrevolution in April 1909 by supporters of the sultan failed, and Abdul Hamid was deposed in favor of his brother Mehmed (1844–1918). Political instability continued as the Ottoman Empire suffered defeat in its war with Italy, 1911–12, and in the First Balkan War, 1912–13. In June 1913 the nationalist Committee of Union and Progress, which had played a prominent role in the 1908 revolution, seized power and established single-party rule.

119.11   Adana Massacre in 1909] In April 1909, Turkish soldiers and civilian mobs killed an estimated 20,000 Armenians in the city of Adana and the surrounding region of Cilicia.

119.17   Alexandretta] Iskenderun.

119.23   Mr. Consul Jackson] Jesse B. Jackson (1871–1947) served as the U.S. consul in Alexandretta (Iskenderun), 1905–8, and in Aleppo, 1908–17 and 1919–23.

119.29   Dr. Dodd] William S. Dodd (1860–1928), an American Presbyterian minister, missionary, and physician, was the director of the American Hospital at Konia (Konya), 1911–16.

120.2–3   Armenian insurrection . . . Van] In April 1915, Cevedet Bey, the new governor of Van province in eastern Anatolia, ordered the Armenian population to surrender its weapons while sending Circassian and Kurdish irregulars to raid Armenian villages in the region. Armenians in the city of Van refused to disarm, built barricades, and fought back when Ottoman forces attacked on April 20. The fighting continued until May 17, when the Turks withdrew as Russian forces approached the city. Most of the surviving Armenian population of Van accompanied the Russians when they retreated from the province in August 1915.

120.4   Pastermadjian] Karekin Pastermadjian (1872–1923), more widely known by his nom de guerre Armen Garo, was a member of the Armenian Revolutionary Federation (Dashnak). As a deputy in the Ottoman parliament, 1908–12, Garo supported proposals to build railways in eastern Anatolia using American capital. In the fall of 1914 he helped form and led a unit of Armenian volunteers fighting with the Russians in the Caucasus against the Turks. Garo later served as the envoy to the United States of the provisional Armenian republic, 1918–20, and helped organize the assassination of former Ottoman leaders involved in the Armenian genocide. He died in exile in Switzerland.

120.20   arrest and exile . . . Armenians] On April 24, 1915, Turkish authorities arrested more than 250 prominent Armenians in Istanbul. The detainees, including members of parliament, clergymen, lawyers, doctors, journalists, educators, writers, and businessmen, were sent into the interior of Anatolia, where most of them were killed.

121.14–15   recent expulsion measures . . . Bosphorus] The Ottoman government ordered the expulsion of all Christians and Jews from the upper Bosphorus on May 15, 1915.

122.22   2,732 American citizens lynched] Statistics kept by the Tuskegee Institute recorded the lynching of 2,727 African Americans from 1882 to 1914.

122.28   "lesser breeds without the law"] From "Recessional," poem (1897) by Rudyard Kipling (1865–1936).

131.21   Pole] Pula, a port city on the northern Adriatic coast, now in Croatia.

133.36   Novo Seidlitz] Novoselitsa (now Novoselytsya, Ukraine), a town on the north bank of the Prut River that was divided by the border between Russia and Austria-Hungary. Reed's driver was from Russian Novoselitsa.

134.3 Li Hung Chang] Li Hongzhang (1823–1901), Chinese statesman who had negotiated peace with Japan after the Chinese-Japanese War, 1894–95, and with the Western powers after the Boxer Rebellion, 1900–1901.

135.16 Doullens] Town in northeastern France, about seventeen miles north of Amiens.

135.31 mitrailleuses] Machine guns.

137.15 St. John's Ambulance] The St. John Ambulance Brigade, a volunteer organization founded in England in 1887 to provide first aid services.

137.17 Pall Mall] Street in Westminster, London, the location of several prestigious gentlemen's clubs.

138.15 "War and Peace"] Novel (1869) by Leo Tolstoy (1828–1910).

138.31 Angel . . . Bottomless Pit] Revelation 9:1–12.

139.20 Poperinghe] Town in Belgium, about eight miles west of Ypres.

139.26 Phidian] Characteristic of Phidias, a Greek sculptor of the fifth century B.C.E.

140.22–23 Badonviller, Raon-L'Étape] Towns in Lorraine.

141.27 Belgium's Foreign Minister . . . *ne regrette rien*] Julien Davignon (1854–1916) was foreign minister of Belgium, 1907–16. Charles de Broqueville (1860–1940), prime minister of Belgium, 1911–18, wrote in a telegram to French premier René Viviani on October 13, 1914: "As the President of the Chamber of Duties said on August 5th, Belgium has sacrificed all to defend honesty, honor, and liberty; she regrets nothing." Frans Schollaert (1851–1917) was president of the chamber, 1901–8 and 1911–17. Wharton used the phrase *La Belgique ne regrette rien* as the epigraph for her poem "Belgium," published in December 1914 in *King Albert's Book: A Tribute to the Belgian King and People from Representative Men and Women Throughout the World*.

141.34 miraculous snow-fall . . . legend] According to an Italian legend from the thirteenth century, a wealthy Roman husband and wife in the fourth century had vowed to donate their possessions to the Virgin Mary and prayed for guidance as to where to leave their property. On the night of August 4–5, at the height of summer, snow fell in the shape of a square on the Esquiline Hill on what became the site of the Basilica de Santa Maria Maggiore.

141.35 Taube] A two-seat monoplane used by the German air service for reconnaissance, 1914–15.

143.4–6 "Your country . . . by strangers."] Isaiah 1:7.

144.14–15 siege gun of Dixmude] A long-range German naval gun used to shell Dunkirk in 1915 from a position near Dixmude. It fired shells 380mm (15 inches) in diameter.

145.2–4 "Admiral Ro'narch!" . . . Dixmude] Rear Admiral Pierre Ronarc'h (1865–1940) commanded a brigade of French marine fusiliers that fought alongside Belgian troops in the defense of Dixmude, October 16–November 10, 1914. Many of the men in the brigade were territorials (reservists) from Brittany.

145.19–20 lost Dixmude—for a while] The town was captured by the Germans on November 10, 1914, and recaptured by the Belgians on September 29, 1918.

146.31 St. George, Ramscappelle, Peryse] Villages south of Nieuport.

147.10 "au repos"] At rest.

148.17 "bain-de-mer"] Place to go swimming in the sea.

149.6 David's statue of Jean Bart] Completed in 1845, the statue by French sculptor David d'Angers (1788–1856) depicted the French privateer and naval commander Jean Bart (1650–1702). A native of Dunkirk, Bart successfully defended the port against English attack in 1694–95.

149.38 *The Broken Heart*] Play, published in 1633, by John Ford (1586–c. 1639).

150.13 call of Roland's horn] In the medieval French epic poem *La Chanson de Roland*, depicting a battle in the Pyrenees between Charlemagne's warriors and the Saracens.

150.20–21 cluster of villas . . . two hearts] In October 1914 King Albert and his consort, Queen Elizabeth (1876–1965), chose to remain on Belgian territory at La Panne while the Belgian government relocated to the French city of Le Havre.

152.2 *Herbert Henry Asquith*] Asquith (1852–1928) was elected to the House of Commons as a Liberal in 1886 and served as Home Secretary, 1892–95, Chancellor of the Exchequer, 1905–8, and Prime Minister, 1908–16.

153.4 "a poor thing . . . own."] Cf. *As You Like It*, V.iv.57–58: "an ill-favor'd thing, sir, but mine own."

153.11 Edmund Gosse] A close friend of James's since the 1880s, Gosse (1849–1928) was a prolific critic, essayist, biographer, and poet. James's other sponsors were James Pinker (1863–1922), his literary agent, and George Prothero (1848–1922), a historian and the editor of *The Quarterly Review*.

155.40 Syrians] Assyrian Christians. In 1915–16 at least 150,000 Assyrian Christians were killed, or died from hunger and disease, in massacres and deportations in the Ottoman Empire.

156.39–40 my attempted trip to America] In the summer of 1914 Davis received leave to return to the United States and see his ailing parents. He traveled overland from Harput to Beirut and then went to Alexandria, Egypt, where he received orders from the State Department to return to Harput on account of the outbreak of the war.

157.23 the Vali] Sabit Bey was the *vali* (governor) of Mamouret-ul-Aziz, 1914–16. He was imprisoned on Malta by the British after the armistice in 1918, but was later released and appointed governor of Erzerum in 1921 by the new Turkish government.

158.25 Mr. Riggs to Mr. Peet] The Rev. Henry H. Riggs (1875–1943), an American missionary, had served as president of Euphrates College, a coeducational secondary school in Harput, 1903–10. Riggs returned to Harput in 1912 and remained there until 1917. His account of the genocide, written in 1918, was published as *Days of Tragedy in Armenia: Personal Experiences in Harpoot, 1915–17* (1997). William W. Peet (1851–1942) was the treasurer of the Istanbul office of the American Board of Commissioners for Foreign Missions.

159.37 Kaimakam] An Ottoman official in charge of a provincial district.

169.25 Protests as well as threats] Morgenthau had transmitted to the Ottoman leadership the joint declaration issued by the governments of Britain, France, and Russia on May 24, 1915, describing the massacre of the Armenians as "new crimes of Turkey against humanity and civilization" and warning that the Allies would "hold personally responsible for their crimes all members of the Ottoman government and those of their agents who are implicated in such massacres." During the Allied occupation of Istanbul in 1919–20, a Turkish military tribunal held a series of trials relating to the Armenian massacres. Three defendants were hanged, another fifteen were condemned to death in absentia, and several others were sentenced to prison. All of those convicted had their verdicts overturned by the new government of Mustafa Kemal in 1923. More than one hundred former Ottoman officials were detained on Malta by the British in 1919–21, but none of them were tried for crimes against the Armenians due to lack of evidence and legal questions regarding jurisdiction. The Malta detainees were released in 1921 in exchange for British prisoners captured in Anatolia by Kemal's forces.

169.27 Capitulations] Agreements between the Ottoman Empire and foreign powers that granted foreign nationals residing in Ottoman territory certain economic privileges and special extraterritorial legal status. The Ottoman government announced on September 9, 1914, that it was unilaterally abrogating the capitulations, an action the United States refused to recognize as legally valid.

171.23–24 Dr. Shaw] Anna Howard Shaw (1847–1919), president of the National American Woman Suffrage Association, 1904–15. The first woman ordained as minister by the Methodist Protestant Church, Shaw received an MD from Boston University Medical School in 1886 but never practiced.

171.28 three days and a half] The Congress met from April 28 to May 1, 1915.

172.3 twelve different countries] Austria, Belgium, Canada, Denmark, Germany, Great Britain and Ireland, Hungary, Italy, the Netherlands, Norway, Sweden, and the United States.

172.12–14 a woman from the side . . . the neutral nations] The committee was composed of Chrystal Macmillan (1872–1937) from Great Britain, Rosika Schwimmer (1877–1948) from Hungary, Cor Ramondt-Hirschmann (b. 1871) from the Netherlands, and Emily Greene Balch (1867–1961) from the United States.

172.24–25 the vice-president and the president] Aletta Jacobs (1854–1929) of the Netherlands and Addams. They were accompanied by Alice Hamilton (1869–1970) of the United States and Frederika Wilhelmina van Wulfften Palthe-Broese van Groenou (1875–1960).

173.36 our resolutions] The Congress called for a negotiated end to the war without forced annexations, the arbitration and conciliation of future international disputes, democratic control over foreign policy, and the enfranchisement of women.

183.6 the Pope] Benedict XV (1854–1922) was pope from 1914 until his death.

183.25–26 one of the prime ministers of Europe] Karl von Stürgkh (1859–1916), minister president (prime minister) of Austria, 1911–16. An advocate of war with Serbia in July 1914, Stürgkh was assassinated in Vienna by an antiwar Socialist on October 21, 1916.

184.5–6 this prime minister, . . . without power] Stürgkh was one of five members of the common ministerial council of Austria-Hungary, along with the minister president of Hungary and the joint ministers of war, finance, and foreign affairs.

184.17–18 if they have conscription in England] By the summer of 1915 the possibility of adopting conscription was being debated in Britain, and on July 5 a bill was introduced in Parliament to establish a national register of available manpower. The Military Service Act, passed on January 27, 1916, instituted conscription in Great Britain (Ireland was exempted).

188.8 General Joffre] Joseph Joffre (1852–1931) was appointed chief of the general staff in 1911 and served as commander-in-chief of the French army from the outbreak of war until December 1916, when he was replaced by General Robert Nivelle.

188.16–18 Canadians at Ypres . . . on the Aisne] Canadian troops fought their first major engagement of the war in the Second Battle of Ypres, April 22–May 25, 1915, and played a key role in stopping the initial German attack. Australian troops landed on the Gallipoli peninsula, April 25, 1915, as part of a campaign designed to open the Dardanelles. British and French forces fought the Germans along the Aisne River, September 13–28, 1914, following the German retreat from the Marne.

189.25 Plancher–Bas] A village behind the lines in Alsace, northwest of Belfort, where Seeger's regiment had been resting and training since mid-July 1915.

189.31   *musettes*] Haversacks.

189.32   *Tirailleurs* and Zouaves] Seeger was assigned to the Moroccan Division, which included regiments from the Foreign Legion, Tirailleurs (light infantry) from Tunisia and Algeria, and Zouaves from Algeria.

190.11–12   "*blessés assis*" or "*blessés couchés*"] Literally, "sitting wounded" or "lying wounded," i.e., walking wounded or stretcher cases.

190.15   *Champagne pouilleuse*] Literally, "lousy Champagne"; a region of Champagne that was difficult to cultivate because of its chalky soil and used mostly for grazing sheep.

190.22   *fusées . . . pose*] Signal rockets; rest break.

190.32   *2me Etranger*] The 2nd Regiment of the Foreign Legion, in which Seeger served.

190.36   Vouziers] A town on the Aisne, about twenty miles north of Suippes.

190.37   *Etat-Major*] Headquarters.

191.9   *fusées éclairantes*] Flares, star shells.

191.16   Perthes-les-Hurlus] A village about five miles northeast of Suippes.

191.18   210s] A German howitzer that fired shells 210mm (8.2 inches) in diameter that weighed 252 pounds. It had a maximum range of almost six miles (10,300 yards).

191.22   *boyau*] Communication trench.

192.7   *rapport*] Report, briefing.

192.27   Ferme de Navarin] Navarin's Farm.

193.9   Somme-Suippe] A village five miles east of Suippes.

193.14   *génie*] Engineering corps.

193.15   Décauville engines] Small locomotives used on narrow-gauge railways.

193.27–28   plateau of Craonne . . . Lille] Both rumors were false. The plateau of Craonne, about fifteen miles northwest of Reims, was at the eastern end of the Chemin de Dames, a ridge that overlooked the Aisne from the north for more than twenty miles. First occupied by the Germans on September 1, 1914, the plateau of Craonne was captured by the French, May 4–6, 1917, recaptured by the Germans on May 27, 1918, and finally retaken by the French on October 12, 1918. The city of Lille was occupied by the Germans on October 13, 1914, and retaken by the British on October 17, 1918.

194.7   *Elsie Simmons Seeger*] Seeger (1861–1940), born Elsie Simmons Adams, was the mother of Alan Seeger and his brother, the musicologist Charles Louis Seeger (1886–1979), and the grandmother of the folksinger and political activist Pete Seeger (1919–2014).

194.12   Compiègne] A town about twenty-five miles west of Soissons.

194.19   Souain] A village three miles north of Suippes.

194.30   *tranchées de depart*] Trenches of departure, first-line trenches.

194.35   *Baïonnette au canon*] Bayonets fixed.

194.36   *tirailleurs*] Skirmishers.

195.14   *guerre de tranchées*] Trench warfare.

196.1   *les salauds!*] The bastards!

196.7   *blessure heureuse*] Lucky wound.

196.10   *postes de secours*] Dressing station, first aid post.

196.17   *sac au dos*] Rucksack, backpack.

196.19–20   their 77s] German field gun that fired high-explosive and shrapnel shells 77mm (3 inches) in diameter that weighed fifteen pounds. It had a maximum range of more than three miles (6,000 yards).

196.27   the 1*er Etranger*] The 1st Regiment of the Foreign Legion, which was also assigned to the Moroccan Division.

197.1–2   *troupes de poursuit*] Pursuit troops.

197.29–30   serious turn that affairs . . . Balkans] The invasion of Serbia by Germany, Austria-Hungary, and Bulgaria. See Chronology, October 1915.

197.34   *guerre d'usure*] War of attrition.

198.3   Marsouins] Colonial infantry, i.e., troops stationed near ports in metropolitan France for deployments overseas. Before 1900 the colonial infantry were designated as marine infantry and were known informally as "marsouins" (porpoises).

198.8   "Nous les avons eus.] We got them.

198.13   "Gott mitt uns" . . . und Vaterland] God is with us; For King and Fatherland.

199.1   Thwing] The son of the president of Western Reserve University, Francis Wendell Butler-Thwing (1891–1964) attended Harvard and New College, Oxford. Butler-Thwing became a naturalized British subject and was commissioned as an officer in the Coldstream Guards in July 1915. He was wounded at Ypres in 1916 and at Cambrai in 1917.

200.22   our first night] The 9th Royal Fusiliers were sent into the front line near the village of Hulloch on September 30, 1915, as part of the 36th Brigade, 12th (Eastern) Division.

202.9   bayonets were saw-edged] Saw-edged bayonets were issued to German field engineers and machine-gun crews and used to clear away brush.

202.12 "*Gott . . . herein.*"] "Come in with God and bring luck with you."

202.18 "Krieg-Zeitung,"] "War Newspaper."

203.30 Gardner's] Hall used pseudonyms for the men in his unit who became casualties.

204.33 'ap'worth o' 'ate] Halfpenny worth of hate.

207.28 The Sultan] Mehmed V (1844–1918), sultan of the Ottoman Empire, 1909–18.

207.29 Iradés] Decrees, edicts.

207.30 Grand Vezier] Said Halim Pasha (1865–1921), grand vizier of the Ottoman Empire, 1913–17. He was assassinated in Rome in 1921 by a member of the Armenian Revolutionary Federation.

208.2–8 Dr. Nazim . . . Beha-ed-din Chakir] A physician, Mehmed Nâzım (1870–1926) was an influential ideologist on the Central Committee of the Committee of Union and Progress Party (CUP), a leader of its paramilitary Special Organization, and a principal architect of the Armenian genocide. Nâzım fled to Germany in 1918 but returned to Turkey in 1922. He was hanged in 1926 for allegedly conspiring to overthrow Mustafa Kemal. Mithat Şükrü (1872–1956) was secretary general of the Committee of Union and Progress Party, 1911–17. Mehmed Talât (1874–1921) was minister of the interior, 1913–17, minister of finance, 1914–17, and grand vizier, 1917–18. Talât fled to Germany in 1918 and was assassinated in Berlin in 1921 by a member of the Armenian Revolutionary Federation. Ismail Enver (1881–1922) was minister of war and commander-in-chief of the Ottoman army, 1914–18. He fled to Germany in 1918 and was killed by the Red Army in 1922 while fighting with anti-Bolshevik insurgents in Soviet Central Asia. Along with Talât and Enver, Ahmed Cemal (1872–1922) formed the dominant political triumvirate in the Ottoman Empire during the war. Cemal (or Djemal) served as minister of the navy, 1914–18, and as commander of the Fourth Army in Syria, 1914–17, where he brutally repressed the Arab nationalist movement. He fled to Germany in 1918 and was assassinated by the Armenian Revolutionary Federation in Tbilisi, Georgia, in 1922. Ayoub Sabri, a close friend of Talât, was interned by the British on Malta during the war. In his memoir *Ambassador Morgenthau's Story* (1918), Morgenthau wrote that Talât's failure to secure his friend's release was "a constant grievance and irritation" to the Ottoman leader. Halil Bey (1874–1948) served as foreign minister, 1915–17. Hadji Adil Bey (b. 1866) was governor of Edirne before becoming speaker of the chamber of deputies. Bahaeddin Şakir (1874–1922), a physician, was the leader of the Special Organization during the Armenian genocide. Şakir fled Turkey in 1918 and was assassinated in Berlin by the Armenian Revolutionary Federation.

208.29–30 Kiamal Pasha . . . Abdul Hamid] Mehmed Kâmil (1833–1913) served as grand vizier, 1885–91, and for brief periods in 1895, 1908–9, and

1912–13. Adbul Hamid II (1842–1918) was sultan of the Ottoman Empire, 1876–1909.

208.30   Ahmed Riza Bey] Ahmed Riza (1859–1930), one of the founders of the Committee of Union and Progress, resigned from its central committee in 1910. He served as speaker of the chamber of deputies, 1908–11, and in the Ottoman senate, 1912–18.

209.24–27   Djavid Bey . . . Bustany Effendi] Mehmed Djavid Bey (1875–1926) served as minister of finance in the Ottoman government, 1909–14. Djavid (or Cavit) was hanged in 1926 for allegedly plotting the overthrow of Mustafa Kemal. Dönmehs were the descendants of the Ottoman Jews who had followed Sabbatai Zevi in converting to Islam in the seventeenth century. Osman Nizami (1856–1939) was the Ottoman ambassador to Germany, 1908–13, and minister of posts and telegraphs, 1913–14. Çürüksulu Mahmud (1864–1931) was minister of the navy, 1913–14, and was serving as minister of public works when he resigned at the outbreak of the war. Suleiman al-Bustani (1856–1925) was minister of agriculture, 1913–14.

210.28   four big nations] Italy had declared war on the Ottoman Empire on August 21, 1915.

210.30   English fleet was not unconquerable] The Royal Navy lost two obsolete battleships to mines during a failed attempt to force passage of the Dardanelles on March 18, 1915. A third obsolete battleship was sunk by a Turkish destroyer on May 13.

213.21–22   Metropolitan Magazine . . . the Hague Treaties] "International Duty and Hyphenated Americanism," *Metropolitan*, October 1915.

213.24   Dr. James Brown Scott] A former professor of law at Columbia, Scott (1866–1943) served as solicitor of the Department of State, 1906–11, and as the head of the division of international law at the Carnegie Endowment for International Peace, 1911–40. He was a member of the U.S. delegation to the Hague Conference in 1907 and later published *The Hague Peace Conferences of 1899 and 1907* (1909). Roosevelt described Scott as "our foremost international lawyer" in his *Metropolitan* article.

214.4–5   two Hague Conferences . . . Geneva Conventions] For the Hague Conferences, see note 110.15. The Geneva Convention of 1864 established rules for the treatment of sick and wounded soldiers in land warfare, and the Geneva Convention of 1906 covered the treatment of the wounded, sick, and shipwrecked in naval warfare.

214.10–11   the Somerset Club] A private social club in Boston, founded in 1852.

215.15–16   "I Didn't Raise . . . Soldier."] See pp. 61–62 in this volume.

215.36   Dave Goodrich] David Goodrich (1876–1950) was a director of the

B. F. Goodrich tire company, which had been founded by his father, Benjamin Franklin Goodrich (1841–1888). In the Spanish-American War Goodrich had served as a lieutenant under Roosevelt in the 1st U.S. Volunteer Cavalry ("Rough Riders").

216.15   "not only in deed but in thought"] Cf. President Wilson's statement on neutrality, August 18, 1914, pp. 30–32 in this volume.

216.25   Wilson's note to England] The note, sent on October 21, 1915, and signed by Secretary of State Robert Lansing, protested "ineffective, illegal, and indefensible" British blockade practices that restricted American trade with neutral European nations.

216.27   sinking of the Ancona] Nine Americans were killed when the Italian passenger ship *Ancona* was sunk off Tunisia on November 7, 1915, by the *U-38*, a German submarine flying Austro-Hungarian colors. Austria-Hungary accepted liability for the sinking on December 29, 1915, and agreed to pay compensation.

216.28–29   blowing up of our munitions plants.] Beginning in January 1915 a series of fires and explosions occurred at American plants manufacturing war materials for the Allies. On December 1, 1915, Secretary of State Lansing declared two German diplomats, Franz von Papen, the military attaché, and Karl Boy-Ed, the naval attaché, persona non grata after evidence linked them to sabotage plots.

218.30   its Garrisons, its Daniels] Lindley M. Garrison (1864–1932), a lawyer and chancery judge from New Jersey, was secretary of war from March 1913 to February 1916. Josephus Daniels (1862–1948), editor and publisher of the *Raleigh News and Observer*, served as secretary of the navy, 1913–1921.

220.6–8   Woodrow Wilson, . . . beaten than ostracized."] In his speech to the Daughters of the American Revolution given in Washington, D.C., on October 11, 1915, Wilson said: "I would a great deal rather be beaten than ostracized. I would a great deal rather endure any sort of physical hardship if I might have the affection of my fellow-men. We constantly discipline our fellow-citizens by having an opinion about them. That is the sort of discipline we ought now to administer to everybody who is not to the very core of his heart an American."

220.35–36   Jefferson . . . which governs least;] The phrase "the best government is that which governs least" has been widely attributed to Thomas Jefferson, but has not been found in his writings. Its first known appearance was in the initial number of the *United States Magazine and Democratic Review*, founded in 1837 by John L. O'Sullivan (1813–1895).

220.37–39   David Thoreau] In his posthumously published essay "Civil Disobedience" (1866), Henry David Thoreau (1817–1862) wrote: "I heartily accept the motto,—'That government is best which governs least'; and I should like to see it acted up to more rapidly and systematically. Carried out, it finally amounts to this, which also I believe,—'That government is best which governs not at all'; and when men are prepared for it, that is the kind of government which they will have."

221.13–19 Major General O'Ryan . . . pistol in hand."] John F. O'Ryan (1874–1961), a lawyer, was appointed commander of the New York National Guard in 1912. O'Ryan commanded the 27th Division in Belgium and France in 1918, fighting with the British army in Flanders and Picardy. *The New York Times* reported on October 21, 1915, that in a recent speech to the Technology Club in New York City O'Ryan had said:

> The recruit does not know how to carry out orders. His mental state differs from that of the trained soldier, who obeys mechanically. We must get our men so that they are machines, and this can be done only as the result of a process of training.
>
> When the feeling of fear—the natural instinct of self-preservation— comes over a man there must be something to hold him to his duty. We have to have our men trained so that the influence of fear is overpowered by the peril of an uncompromising military system, often backed up by a pistol in the hands of an officer. We must make the men unconsciously forget their fear. All these matters of standing at attention and "Sir, I have the honor to report," are valuable to put him through the biological and social process by which he becomes a soldier.
>
> That is the reason why we cannot have any military force simply by having dinners and entertainments. The recruits have got to put their heads into the military noose. They have got to be "jacked up"—they have got to be "bawled out."

221.21 Treitschke or Bernhardi] Heinrich von Treitschke (1834–1896), German historian and political writer who became a prominent advocate for authoritarian nationalism, militarism, and colonial expansion. General Friedrich von Bernhardi (1849–1930), German military writer best known for *Germany and the Next War* (1911), which defended the right of Germany to wage war in order to establish itself as a world power.

221.28 Samuel Gompers] Gompers (1850–1924), president of the American Federation of Labor, 1886–94 and 1896–1924, first endorsed the preparedness campaign in January 1916.

222.2 Ludlow?] In September 1913 thousands of coal miners went out on strike against the Colorado Fuel and Iron Company, which was owned by the Rockefeller family. After being evicted from their company-owned houses, the strikers and their families set up makeshift tent settlements. On April 20, 1914, a gunfight broke out between strikers and the Colorado National Guard at the Ludlow tent colony. Six strikers were shot to death, and two women and eleven children died in an underground shelter after Guardsmen and mine company gunmen set fire to the camp.

223.29–30 Carl Liebknecht] Liebknecht (1871–1919), a member of the

German Social Democratic Party, was sentenced to eighteen months' imprisonment in 1907 for writing *Militarism and Anti-Militarism*. In September 1914 Liebknecht accused the German government of waging a "capitalist war of expansion," and in December he became the first deputy in the Reichstag to vote against further war credits. Liebknecht was imprisoned in 1916 after participating in an antiwar demonstration on May Day. Released in October 1918, he joined the left-wing Spartacist uprising in Berlin in January 1919 and was murdered by right-wing officers after its failure.

227.5 single-taxers] Supporters of the single tax on land advocated by the American reformer Henry George (1839–1897).

227.13–14 Mme. Schwimmer] Rosika Schwimmer (1877–1948).

228.14–15 Senator Helen Ring Robinson] A progressive Democrat, Robinson (1860–1923) was elected to the Colorado state senate in 1912 and served one term, 1913–17. She was the first woman state senator in Colorado and the second in the nation.

228.29–30 Louis Lochner, . . . Jenkin Lloyd Jones] Lochner (1887–1975) was an organizer for the American Peace Society. He later served as a Berlin correspondent for the Associated Press, 1924–41. Charles F. Aked (1864–1941) was the minister of the Fifth Avenue Baptist Church in New York, 1907–11, and the First Congregational Church in San Francisco, 1911–15. Jenkin Lloyd Jones (1843–1918) was a Unitarian clergyman, social reformer, and editor of the weekly journal *Unity*.

228.31–32 carries a big stick . . . softly.] Cf. "Speak softly, and carry a big stick—you will go far," phrase first publicly used by Theodore Roosevelt in a speech at the Minnesota State Fair, September 2, 1901.

229.32–35 Judge Lindsey . . . Bethea] Ben B. Lindsey (1869–1943), a county judge in Denver, Colorado, 1901–27, became nationally famous as an advocate for reform of the juvenile justice system. Louis B. Hanna (1861–1948), a Republican, served in the North Dakota house of representatives, 1895–97, in the state senate, 1897–1901 and 1905–9, in the U.S. house of representatives, 1909–13, and as governor of North Dakota, 1913–17. Samuel S. Marquis (1866–1948), an Episcopalian clergyman, was dean of St. Paul's Cathedral in Detroit, 1908–15, and an adviser to the Sociology Department of the Ford Motor Company. Andrew J. Belthea (1879–1945), a Democrat, was lieutenant governor of South Carolina, 1915–19.

230.15 Lord Rosebery] Archibald Primrose, fifth Earl of Rosebery (1847–1929), a Liberal, served as foreign secretary, 1892–94, and prime minister, 1894–95. *The New York Times* reported on November 17, 1915, that in a recent speech in London Rosebery had said: "I know nothing more disheartening than the announcement recently made, that the United States—the one great country left in the world free from the hideous, bloody burden of war—is about to embark upon the building of a huge armada destined to be equal or second to our own."

233.24–25   gas gangrene . . . poisonous shells.] Gas gangrene is caused by infection by *Clostridia*, a genus of anaerobic bacteria, and not by chemical warfare agents.

234.3   *Médecin Chef*] Chief doctor.

235.3   *Cela pique! Cela brule!*] It stings! It burns!

235.39   *picqures*] Injections.

236.40   *C'est triste! C'est bien triste!*] It's sad! It's very sad!

241.5   ARABIC] The British passenger liner was sunk without warning off the coast of Ireland by the *U-24* on August 19, 1915, with the loss of forty-four lives, including two Americans.

244.14   Mourmelon] A town in Champagne, about eight miles west of Suippes.

244.21   poilus call a "*mauvais coin*."] Literally "hairy ones," popular name for French infantrymen; bad spot.

247.3   soixante-quinze] Seventy-five; see note 67.28.

248.22   that Greek chap] The legendary hero Theseus.

248.27   the Captain] Captain Georges Thenault (1887–1948), commander of the Lafayette Escadrille (Escadrille N. 124), from its formation in April 1916 to January 1918, when its American pilots were transferred to the 103rd Aero Squadron of the U.S. aviation service.

249.3   Douaumont] French fortress about four miles northeast of the town of Verdun. It was captured by the Germans on February 25, 1916, and retaken by the French on October 24, 1916.

249.5   Nieuports] French single-engine, single-seat biplane fighter aircraft. The Nieuport 11, flown by the Lafayette Escadrille, had a top speed of 97 mph and was armed with a single machine gun mounted on the aircraft's top wing that fired over the arc of the propeller.

249.7–8   Farman or Caudron] French biplane used for reconnaissance.

249.11   *réglage*] Artillery spotting.

249.15   Fokkers] German single-engine, single-seat monoplane fighter aircraft. The Fokker E. III had a top speed of 87 mph and was armed with a single machine gun synchronized to fire through the propeller arc.

249.20   Prince] Norman Prince (1887–1916), a graduate of Harvard Law School who played a leading role in founding the Lafayette Escadrille. Prince was fatally injured on October 12, 1916, when the landing gear of his Nieuport struck a high-tension wire.

249.25–26   *mitrailleuse . . . rouleau*] Machine gun, ammunition magazine (literally, "roller"). The Lewis machine gun used to arm the Nieuport 11 had a top-mounted, pan-shaped magazine that held forty-seven rounds.

249.39 L. V. G.] German single-engine, two-seat biplane reconnaissance aircraft.

250.12 Avions] Aircraft.

250.23 reservoirs] Fuel tanks.

250.26 Poincaré] Raymond Poincaré (1860–1934), president of France, 1913–20.

250.32–33 Luxeuil] Luxeuil-les-Bains in the Vosges Mountains, where the La-fayette Escadrille had trained in the spring of 1916 before moving to the Verdun sector.

250.37–38 Lion Vert] A hotel in Luxeuil-les-Bains.

254.19–20 Hindenburg, . . . of the U-9] General Paul von Hindenburg (1847–1934) was recalled from retirement on August 22, 1914, and given com-mand of the Eighth Army in East Prussia, with General Erich Ludendorff (1865–1937) assigned to serve as his chief of staff. Although Ludendorff was the dominant figure in their military partnership, Hindenburg became a popular hero in Germany following the defeat of the invading Russians at Tannenberg, August 24–31, and the Masurian Lakes, September 7–13. Hindenburg and Lu-dendorff assumed command of the German forces on the Eastern Front on November 1, 1914, and succeeded in driving the Russians out of Poland in 1915. Following the dismissal of Erich von Falkenhayn as chief of the general staff, Hindenburg and Ludendorff assumed command of the German army on all fronts August 29, 1916. General August von Mackensen (1847–1945) led the German Eleventh Army in its breakthrough at Gorlice-Tarnow, May 2–4, 1915, and in the subsequent campaign that drove the Russians from Galicia (see Chronology, June 1915). Mackensen later successfully commanded the in-vasion of Serbia in October 1915 and of southern Romania in September 1916. Karl von Müller (1873–1923), commander of the light cruiser *Emden*, success-fully raided Allied commerce in the Indian Ocean in the opening months of the war and sank a Russian cruiser and French destroyer off Penang. On No-vember 9, 1914, the Australian cruiser *Sydney* engaged the *Emden* in the Cocos and forced Müller to run his ship onto a reef and surrender. Otto Weddigen (1882–1915), commander of the *U-9*, sank the British cruisers *Hogue*, *Aboukir*, and *Cressy* off the Dutch coast on September 22, 1914, and the cruiser *Hawke* off Scotland on October 15. Weddigen later took command of the *U-29* and was killed on March 18, 1915, when his submarine was rammed in the North Sea by the British battleship *Dreadnought*.

254.27–28 his twentieth victory . . . early in October] Boelcke scored his twentieth aerial victory on September 2, 1916, bringing down a British D.H. 2 fighter flown by Captain Robert Wilson.

254.29–30 Somme Battle . . . since June 23] The preliminary bombardment began on June 24, 1916, and the Allied infantry began their assault on July 1.

258.4 Lieutenant Immelmann] Max Immelmann (1890–1916) was credited with fifteen aerial victories while flying Fokker monoplanes from August 1915 to June 1916. He was killed on June 18, 1916, during an aerial engagement with British fighters near Arras.

259.27 Ambassador Gerard] James W. Gerard (1867–1951), a Democratic lawyer and judge from New York, served as U.S. ambassador to Germany, 1913–17.

259.33 case of Captain Fryatt] Charles Fryatt (1872–1916), the captain of the unarmed British passenger ship *Brussels*, was praised for his bravery after he attempted to ram a surfaced U-boat in the North Sea on March 28, 1915. The *Brussels* was captured by German torpedo boats off the Dutch coast on June 22, 1916, and Fryatt was taken prisoner. Accused of having unlawfully engaged in combat as a civilian during his 1915 ramming attempt, he was tried by a naval court-martial and shot on July 27, 1916.

259.36–37 Ronald Walker . . . C. Smith] Walker and Smith were never tried.

262.4–5 Mr. Hughes] Charles Evans Hughes (1862–1948), the Republican nominee, had served as governor of New York, 1907–10, and as an associate justice of the U.S. Supreme Court, 1910–16. He later served as secretary of state, 1921–25, and as chief justice of the U.S. Supreme Court, 1930–41.

264.29–30 When Lincoln accepted . . . he spoke] In his letter of May 23, 1860, formally accepting the nomination.

265.36 a recent speech at Long Branch] President Wilson gave the speech to an audience of farmers at Long Branch, New Jersey, on October 21, 1916.

266.14–16 his Secretary of War . . . bandit chiefs of Mexico] Newton D. Baker (1871–1937) served as secretary of war from March 1916 to March 1921. *The New York Tribune* reported that in a speech in Jersey City on October 16, 1916, Baker said: "We had a revolution, and from the beginning to the end of that revolution the conditions of this country were so like Mexico that it is perfectly astounding to read. Washington's soldiers on the march to Valley Forge stole everything they could lay their hands on. They stole the silver vessels from the churches and melted them up to buy things to drink. They drove ministers of the Gospel and preachers of churches out of their churches and out of the country."

267.22–23 On last Saturday afternoon] Wilson spoke in Long Branch on the afternoon of October 28, 1916.

268.3–4 speech last Thursday . . . be neutral!] In a speech at Cincinnati on October 26, 1916, Wilson said: "We must have a society of nations, not suddenly, not by insistence, not by any hostile emphasis on the demand, but by the demonstration of the needs of the time. The nations of the world must get together and say, 'Nobody can hereafter be neutral as respects the disturbance of the world's peace for an object which the world's opinion cannot sanction.' America must hereafter be ready as a member of the family of nations to exert her whole force, moral and physical, to the assertion of those rights throughout the round globe."

269.9　Shadow Lawn] A rented oceanside estate in Long Branch, New Jersey, where Wilson stayed from the beginning of September 1916 through the election.

269.17–18　Boyd and Adair and their troopers] Captain Charles F. Boyd (1870–1916) and First Lieutenant Henry R. Adair (1882–1916), two white officers, and ten black troopers from the 10th Cavalry Regiment were killed at Carrizal, Chihuahua, Mexico, on June 21, 1916, in a battle with federal troops loyal to President Venustiano Carranza. Boyd was leading a scouting mission searching for Pancho Villa (see Chronology, March 1916) and advanced on the Mexican positions after being denied permission to pass through Carrizal.

271.13–17　proposed memorial . . . cause of the Allies.] The monument eventually took the form of the Memorial Church in Harvard Yard, which was dedicated on November 11, 1932. Inscribed on its walls are the names of 372 Harvard men who died in the war while serving either with the United States or the Allies. There are also the names of four men who died fighting for Germany, accompanied by an inscription in Latin that reads: "Harvard has not forgotten her sons who under opposite standards gave their lives for their country 1914–1918."

271.27–29　Charles Francis Adams . . . Robert E. Lee] In "Shall Cromwell Have a Statue?," an address delivered to the Phi Beta Kappa Society of the University of Chicago on June 17, 1902. Charles Francis Adams (1835–1915), the grandson of John Quincy Adams and a former Union cavalry officer, was president of the Massachusetts Historical Society, 1895–1915.

282.23　*Tageblatt*] The *Berliner Tageblatt*, influential daily newspaper published 1872–1939.

282.34　Dr. Bernstorff] A career diplomat who had previously served as a counselor in London and Cairo, Johann Heinrich von Bernstorff (1862–1939) was the German ambassador to the United States, 1908–17, and the Ottoman Empire, 1917–18.

283.1　back to Berlin from Vilna] Mencken had left Berlin on January 27 to visit the front along the Dvina River. He returned on January 31, 1917.

283.4　Raymond Swing] Swing (1887–1968) was Berlin correspondent for the *Chicago Daily News*, 1912–17.

283.5　*Gamaschen*] Leggings.

283.8　Novo Aleksandrowsk] Now Zarasai, in northeast Lithuania.

283.11   *Exeunt omnes!*] Exit all!

283.12   Oswald Schütte] a German-American born in Milwaukee, Schuette (1882–1953) was a Berlin correspondent for the *Chicago Daily News*, 1915–17. He continued to report on the war from Switzerland after he left Germany.

283.23   *Lokal-Anzeiger*] *Die Berliner Lokal-Anzeiger*, daily newspaper published 1883–1945.

283.29   Admiral von Scheer] A strong advocate for the resumption of unrestricted U-boat warfare, Reinhard von Scheer (1863–1928) was the commander of the High Seas Fleet from January 1916 until August 1918, when he became chief of the naval staff.

284.5   *Feldgrau*] German soldiers, from "field gray," the color of the German uniform.

284.9–10   Falkenhayn . . . Danish frontier] The rumor was false. Erich von Falkenhayn (1861–1922) succeeded Helmut von Moltke as chief of the general staff on September 14, 1914, and served until August 29, 1916, when he was replaced by Hindenburg and Ludendorff. Falkenhayn then assumed command of the German and Austro-Hungarian forces in Transylvania, defeated the Romanians, and occupied Bucharest on December 6. In July 1917 Falkenhayn was given command of the Turkish forces in Palestine, but was relieved in February 1918 following the British capture of Jerusalem.

284.19   North German Lloyd] A German shipping company.

285.24–25   Dr. Roediger] Conrad Roediger (1887–1973) worked for the German foreign ministry from 1914 until 1945 and became an adviser on international law during World War II. He later served on the West German constitutional court, 1951–55.

286.3   Consul-General Thiel] Fritz Thiel (1863–1931), a former consul-general in Tokyo, was the chief of the German information service.

287.32   Herr Gutmann] Eugen Gutmann (1840–1925) was the founder of the Dresdner Bank and its chairman, 1872–1920.

288.17   Total . . . 2,634,879] C. E. Fayle, *Seaborne Trade*, volume III (1924), one of the volumes in the British official history of the war, records the loss of 2,327,326 tons of merchant shipping in 1916.

288.18–19   gossiped . . . 1,000,000 tons a month.] Henning von Holtzendorff (1853–1919), the chief of the German naval staff, September 1915–August 1918, sent a secret memorandum to Hindenburg on December 22, 1916, in which he projected that an unrestricted U-boat campaign that sank 600,000 tons a month would force Britain to sue for peace after five months.

290.8–9   the public statement . . . note of December 18th] Lansing told reporters on December 21, 1916, that Wilson's note asking the belligerents to state their peace terms had been sent because "the situation is becoming increasingly critical. I mean by that that we are drawing nearer the verge of war ourselves, and therefore we are entitled to know exactly what each belligerent seeks, in order that we may regulate our conduct in the future." His statement angered the President, who instructed Lansing to tell the press that he had been "radically misinterpreted."

291.20 Polk and Woolsey] Frank Polk (1871–1943), counselor for the State Department, 1915–19, and undersecretary of state, 1919–20, and Lester Woolsey (1877–1961), who served as a legal adviser to Lansing, 1915–17, and as solicitor of the State Department, 1917–20.

291.28 Sweet] Richard Sweet, clerk to the secretary of state.

291.35 picture of Secretary Day . . . peace with Spain] Secretary of State William R. Day (1849–1923) and Jules Cambon (1845–1935), the French ambassador who was representing Spain, signed the preliminary peace treaty at the White House on August 12, 1898. The signing became the subject of a painting (1899) by French artist Théobald Chartran (1849–1907).

293.23–24 Senator Hitchcock . . . Senator Stone] Gilbert M. Hitchcock (1859–1934), Democratic senator from Nebraska, 1911–23; William J. Stone (1848–1918), Democratic senator from Missouri, 1903–18.

293.35 Col. House] Edward M. House (1858–1938), a successful businessman from Texas, met Wilson in November 1911 and became his closest adviser, although House held no formal position in the administration. (The title "Colonel" was honorific.)

295.2 Secretary Wilson, and Burleson] William B. Wilson (1862–1934) was a Democratic congressman from Pennsylvania, 1907–13, and secretary of labor, 1913–21. Albert S. Burleson was a Democratic congressman from Texas, 1899–1913, and postmaster general, 1913–21.

295.4 McAdoo and Houston] William G. McAdoo (1863–1941), a railroad executive, managed Wilson's campaign in 1912 and served as secretary of the treasury, March 1913–December 1918. He married Eleanor Wilson, the youngest daughter of the President, in 1914. David F. Houston (1866–1940) was secretary of agriculture, 1913–20, and secretary of the treasury, 1920–21. A professor of political science, Houston had served as president of Texas Agricultural and Mechanical College, 1902–5, president of the University of Texas, 1905–8, and chancellor of Washington University, 1908–13.

296.37 Tumulty] Joseph Tumulty (1879–1954), a lawyer and former state assembly member from New Jersey, served as Wilson's personal secretary, 1911–12 and 1913–21.

297.1 Phillips] A career diplomat, William Phillips (1878–1968) served as third assistant secretary of state, 1914–17.

298.27 Zimmermann] Arthur Zimmermann (1864–1940) was state secretary for foreign affairs, November 1916–August 1917.

298.33 von Eckardt] A career diplomat who had previously served in Cuba and Montenegro, Heinrich von Eckhardt (1861–1944) was the German ambassador to Mexico, 1914–19.

300.18 Bethmann-Hollweg was declaring . . . "authentic"] Theobald von Bethmann Hollweg (1856–1921) was chancellor of Germany from July 1909 until July 1917, when he was replaced by Georg Michaelis. Bethmann-Hollweg made the quoted remarks in a speech to the Reichstag on February 27, 1917.

300.35–36 celebrated report of Jules Cambon] Cambon (1845–1935) served as ambassador to the United States, 1897–1902, to Spain, 1902–7, to Germany, 1907–14, and as secretary general of the French foreign ministry, 1915–17. The French foreign ministry released on December 1, 1914 a collection of documents relating to the outbreak of the war. The first chapter of the French "Yellow Book," titled "Warnings," included three messages that Cambon sent from Berlin in 1913, as well as a memorandum, dated April 2, 1913, in which Eugène Étienne, the minister of war, alleged that Germany planned to "stir up trouble" in North Africa and Russia.

301.17–18 Carranza's recent proposal . . . be cut off] The Mexican government sent a note to the United States, Argentina, Brazil, Chile, Spain, Norway, and Sweden on February 12, 1917, proposing that neutral nations embargo the shipment of food and munitions to the belligerents in Europe if the warring powers refused to end the war by mediation.

301.37 Luis Cabrera] Luis Cabrera Lobato (1876–1954) was the Mexican minister of finance, 1914–17 and 1919–20.

302.4–5 American-Mexican Joint Commission] After the battle of Carrizal (see note 269.17–18) the Carranza government proposed the creation of a joint commission to negotiate the withdrawal of U.S. troops from Mexico and develop measures for securing the border against future incursions. The commission first met on September 4, 1916, and dissolved on January 16, 1917, without reaching any formal agreement.

302.19–20 Niagara mediation conferences] Following the American occupation of Veracruz (see note 20.24–25), representatives from Argentina, Brazil, and Chile met with envoys from Mexico and the United States at Niagara Falls, Canada, from May 20 to July 2, 1914.

303.14–15 Captain Boy-Ed . . . Captain von Papen] See note 216.28–29.

303.30 Foreign Minister Aguilar] Candido Aguilar Vargas (1889–1960) was foreign minister of Mexico, March–November 1916 and February–November 1918.

304.10 Count Kalman Votkanya] Kálmán de Kánya (1869–1945) was the Austro-Hungarian ambassador to Mexico, 1914–18. He later served as foreign minister of Hungary, 1933–38.

305.15–16 Council of National Defense . . . an appeal] The appeal was issued by the Advisory Commission to the Council of National Defense. Its seven members, appointed by Wilson in October 1916, were Daniel Willard (1861–1942), president of the Baltimore and Ohio Railroad, Samuel Gompers (1850–1924), president of the American Federation of Labor, Franklin H. Martin (1857–1935), founder of the American College of Surgeons, Bernard Baruch (1870–1965), a leading New York financier, Hollis Godfrey (1874–1936), president of the Drexel Institute, Howard E. Coffin (1873–1937), an automobile engineer and manufacturer, and Julius Rosenwald (1862–1932), president of Sears, Roebuck and a leading philanthropist.

306.13   *Mon. 19* 959] March 19, 1917, was 959 days after August 3, 1914, when Germany declared war on France.

306.14   MacConnell . . . Parsons] James McConnell (1887–1917) worked as a railroad agent in North Carolina before volunteering in 1915 for ambulance service in France. In May 1916 McConnell became one of the original pilots in the Lafayette Escadrille. He wrote a series of articles for *World's Work* that was published as *Flying for France* (1917). Edwin Parsons (1892–1968) joined the Lafayette Escadrille in January 1917. He remained in the French aviation service until the end of the war and was credited with eight aerial victories.

306.15   Ham] Town on the Somme, about ten miles southwest of St. Quentin.

306.26   biplace] Two-seater.

307.3   St. Just] Saint-Just-en-Chaussée, about thirty miles southwest of Ham.

307.6   Lufberry and Lt. de Laage] Gervais Raoul Lufberry (1885–1918) joined the Lafayette Escadrille in May 1916 and later flew with the U.S. 94th Aero Squadron. Lufberry was credited with seventeen aerial victories before being shot down and killed on May 19, 1918. Alfred de Laage de Meux (1891–1917), a French pilot assigned to the Lafayette Escadrille, was killed in a flying accident on May 23, 1917.

307.8   Spads] French single-engine, single-seat biplane fighter aircraft.

307.14   the Commandant] See note 248.27.

307.17–18   French and English . . . few losses] The Allies were advancing following the German withdrawal to the Hindenburg Line; see Chronology, March 1917.

307.23   Thaw] William Thaw (1893–1934) flew with the Lafayette Escadrille and the U.S. 103rd Aero Squadron. He was credited with the destruction of four enemy aircraft and one observation balloon.

307.36–37   The French . . . new cabinet] On March 20, 1917, a new ministry headed by Alexandre Ribot (1842–1923) replaced the government of Aristide Briand (1862–1932), who had served as premier since October 1915. Ribot served until September 12, 1917, when he was succeeded by Paul Painlevé (1863–1933).

308.16 Major Parker . . . Paul Rockwell] Major Frank Parker (1872–1947), a West Point graduate, served as an observer and liaison officer with the French army, 1916–17. Parker commanded the 18th Infantry Regiment, January–July 1918, the 1st Brigade, July–October 1918, and the 1st Division, October–November 1918. Walter Lovell (1884–1937), a former ambulance unit volunteer, flew with the Lafayette Escadrille, February–October 1917. Paul Rockwell (1889–1985) enlisted in the Foreign Legion in August 1914 and was wounded in December. Rockwell remained in France after his medical discharge and became a correspondent for the *Chicago Daily News.* His brother Kiffin Rockwell (1892–1916) also served in the Foreign Legion before becoming one of the original pilots in the Lafayette Escadrille. He was shot down and killed on September 23, 1916.

308.18 Rocle] Marius Rocle (1897–1967) served in the Foreign Legion, 1914–16, and as an observer-gunner in the French air service, 1917–18.

308.20 Mother] Martha Rodman Fox Genet (1858–1931).

308.28 Gertrude] A young woman Genet had known since childhood who had corresponded with him until August 1916.

309.11–12 Mrs. Wheeler . . . David] David Wheeler (1872–1918), a physician, served as a Red Cross volunteer, 1914–15, before joining the French Foreign Legion. Badly wounded in September 1915 during the Champagne offensive, he served in hospitals in France and England, 1916–17, before joining the U.S. Army as a surgeon. Wheeler was killed in action near Soissons on July 18, 1918, while serving with the 16th Infantry Regiment, 1st Division.

309.13 Hoskier, Ronald's] Ronald Hoskier (1896–1917) joined the Lafayette Escadrille in December 1916. He was shot down and killed near St. Quentin on April 23, 1917.

309.14 Dugan] William Dugan (1890–1924) served with the Foreign Legion, 1915–16, with the Lafayette Escadrille, March 1917–January 1918, and with the U.S. 103rd Aero Squadron.

309.16 the G.D.E.] Groupement des Divisions d'Entrainement (Training Divisions Group), the French aviation training center at Plessis Belleville.

309.30 Willis] Harold Willis (1890–1962) served in France with a volunteer ambulance unit in 1915 before volunteering for aviation training. He flew with the Lafayette Escadrille from March 1917 until August 18, 1917, when he was shot down and captured. In October 1918 Willis escaped from his prison camp and made his way to Switzerland.

309.37 Haviland and Hinkle] Willis Haviland (1890–1944) served as ambulance driver in Alsace, 1915–16, and with the Lafayette Escadrille, October 1916–September 1917, before becoming a pilot in the U.S. Navy. Edward Hinkle (1877?–1967) flew with the Lafayette Escadrille, March–June 1917, before being removed from flight duty due to illness.

310.3 Bigelow] Stephen Bigelow (1894–1939) served with the Lafayette Escadrille from February 1917 until August 23, 1917, when he was wounded in
action.

310.9 Johnson] Charles Chouteau Johnson (1889–1969) flew with the Lafayette Escadrille from May 1916 to November 1917 before becoming a flight
instructor with the U.S. air service.

310.15 Soubiran] Robert Soubiran (1886–1949) served with the Foreign Legion in 1915 and was wounded in the fall offensive in Champagne. He flew
with the Lafayette Escadrille, October 1916–February 1918, and with the U.S.
103rd Aero Squadron.

310.18 motherly marriane] A "marriane de guerre" (godmother for the war)
was a woman who wrote letters and sent packages to a soldier at the front.

310.24 Rivers] Genet's brother, Rivers Genet (1889–1922).

311.6 Mrs. Weeks] Alice S. Weeks (1877–1940), an American woman living
in Paris who opened her home to American volunteers in the Foreign Legion,
ambulance corps, and the aviation service. Her son, Kenneth Weeks (1889–
1915), was killed while serving in the Foreign Legion.

312.2 Mr. Grundy] Frederick P. Grundy, a Paris correspondent for the Associated Press.

321.11–17 Government to receive Count Tarnowski . . . authorities at
Vienna.] Adam Tarnowski (1866–1946) arrived in New York on February 1,
1917, but was not formally received by the Wilson administration. Austria-
Hungary broke diplomatic relations with the United States on April 8, 1917, and
Tarnowski left the country on May 8. The United States declared war on Aus-
tria-Hungary on December 7, 1917, but never went to war with Bulgaria or the
Ottoman Empire.

328.35–329.9 Regarding the war . . . actual war.] This quotation had appeared in "Do the People Want War?," an antiwar statement, dated March 3,
1917, that was printed as an advertisement in several newspapers. Signed by the
lawyer and Progressive Party activist Amos Pinchot (1873–1944), Randolph
Bourne (see Biographical Notes), radical journalist Max Eastman (1883–1969),
and sociologist Winthrop D. Lane (1887–1962), it called for a national advisory referendum to be held before war was declared. The quotation was
attributed to a "weekly letter of a Baltimore firm, a member of the New York
Stock Exchange."

330.39 Mr. REED] James A. Reed (1861–1944), Democratic senator from
Missouri, 1911–29.

341.21 in May, 1916, the President made a speech] Wilson addressed a meeting of the League to Enforce Peace in Washington, D.C., on May 27, 1916.

344.5–6 Anglo-German agreement of June, 1914] In 1899 the Ottoman

Empire granted a German company the concession to build a railroad linking Istanbul with Baghdad and the Persian Gulf. The Anglo-German agreement signed on June 15, 1914, protected British interests in the Gulf by stipulating that the (still unfinished) railroad would extend no further south than Basra.

344.8 Professor Rohrbach] Paul Rohrbach (1869–1956), German writer on politics and economics whose works include *Der Krieg und die deutsche Politik* (1914), translated as *Germany's Isolation: An Exposition of the Economic Causes of the Great War* (1915).

345.15 naval agreements with France] Britain and France agreed in 1912 that in the event of war, the British navy would protect the Channel coast, allowing the French to concentrate their naval forces in the Mediterranean.

356.4–5 Mrs. Kellogg . . . her husband] Charlotte Hoffman Kellogg (1874–1960), author of *Women of Belgium: Turning Tragedy to Triumph* (1917) and *Bobbins of Belgium: A Book of Belgian Lace, Lace-Workers, Lace-Schools and Lace-Villages* (1920). Vernon Lyman Kellogg (1867–1937), a professor of entomology at Stanford, directed the Brussels office of the American Commission for Relief in Belgium, 1915–16.

356.29–30 "*Mes petites, il n'y en a plus,*"] My little ones, there is no more.

357.20–21 KILL 97, HURT 437] The final toll from the raid of June 13, 1917, was 162 killed in London, Essex, and Kent, and 432 wounded.

357.27–29 ONE PLANE DOWNED . . . Only Three Visited] All fourteen of the German aircraft that bombed London on June 13 returned to their airfields in Belgium near Ghent.

358.38 Taubes] The bombers were Gotha G.IVs, twin-engined biplanes with a crew of three and a top speed of 83 mph. They could carry up to 880 pounds of bombs.

359.23 Hendon] An airfield in north London.

360.13 Bonar Law] Arthur Bonar Law (1858–1923), a Conservative, was chancellor of the exchequer in the coalition government headed by David Lloyd George, 1916–19, and prime minister, 1922–23.

361.27 children in a school] Eighteen children were killed at the Upper North Street School in Poplar.

362.13 Archies] Anti-aircraft guns.

365.3 Dr. Hugh H. Young] Young (1870–1945), a prominent surgeon and urologist, would be put in charge of efforts to control venereal disease in the American Expeditionary Forces.

370.3–4 guns of German warships . . . Constantinople] The German battle cruiser *Goeben* and light cruiser *Breslau* were in the Mediterranean when the war broke out. They eluded their British pursuers and reached the Dardanelles on August 10, 1914, and were later transferred to the Turkish navy, although they retained their original crews and remained under a German admiral.

374.20–21 famous manifesto . . . German colleagues] See note 49.6–9.

374.23 Bernhardi] See note 221.21.

376.38–377.1 Veblen's "Imperial . . . Policies;"] *Imperial Germany and the Industrial Revolution* (1915) by the economist Thorstein Veblen (1857–1929); *Culture and War* (1916) by Simon Patten (1852–1922), professor of economics at the Wharton School of the University of Pennsylvania; *German Philosophy and Politics* (1915) by the philosopher John Dewey (1859–1952); and *American World Policies* (1917) by Walter Weyl (1873–1919), a journalist and social economist.

378.31 League to Enforce Peace] The League was founded in Philadelphia in June 1915 with William Howard Taft as its president. Its program called for the creation of an international agreement establishing a world court and a commission for the resolution of disputes. Nations that entered into the agreement would be subject to economic and military sanctions if they resorted to the use of force in a dispute instead of submitting it to either the court or the commission.

381.5–8 Britain's tory premiers . . . to Russia.] Arthur Balfour (1848–1930) was the Conservative prime minister of Great Britain, 1902–5. He became foreign secretary in the coalition government in December 1916 and led a British mission that visited Washington, D.C., April–May 1917. President Wilson sent Elihu Root (1845–1937) on a special mission to Russia, June–July 1917. Root had served as secretary of state under Theodore Roosevelt, 1905–9, but had supported Taft over Roosevelt for the 1912 Republican nomination.

385.28 St. Bartholomew's night] The massacre of French Huguenots in Paris, August 24–25, 1572.

388.21 Winchester] A Winchester rifle.

391.33 Col. Stephen O. Tripp] Tripp (1860–1938) was the assistant quartermaster-general of the Illinois National Guard. The special committee of the U.S. House of Representatives appointed to investigate the riot submitted a report to Congress on July 15, 1918, that strongly criticized Tripp for failing to take immediate, forceful action against the mob upon his arrival in East St. Louis on the morning of July 2. It described him as "ignorant of his duties, blind to his responsibilities and deaf to every intelligent appeal that was made to him."

392.30–31 Mollman harness . . . the mayor] The harness shop was owned by the family of Fred Mollman, the Democratic mayor of East St. Louis.

394.26 Dr. Paton] In a letter sent to *The New York Times* on July 10, 1917, Stewart Paton (1865–1942), a psychiatrist and lecturer in neurobiology at

Princeton, wrote: "We cannot now, as a nation, afford to be lenient in our dealings with the 'Conscientious Objector,' for this type of personality representing a form of egotism which marks an attempt to restore the balance destroyed by a gnawing sense of personal as well as social inadequacy gives rise to the accumulation and subsequent liberation of undesirable impulses."

396.22–25   John Dewey . . . Conscience and Compulsion] The article appeared in *The New Republic* on July 14, 1917.

396.35–37   Edward T. Devine's . . . Charities and Corrections] Devine (1867–1948) was a professor of social economy at Columbia and secretary of the Charitable Organizations Society of New York. He made his remarks at a meeting of the National Conference of Charities and Correction held in Pittsburgh, June 6–13, 1917.

396.38–40   Christian denomination . . . inhuman and unchristian."] The General Assembly of the Presbyterian Church of the United States of America, in a resolution adopted on May 22, 1917.

397.20   big Berthas] German siege howitzers that fired shells 420mm (16.5 inches) in diameter that weighed 1,800 pounds. They had a maximum range of almost eight miles (13,670 yards). "Big Bertha" guns were used against Belgian fortresses in 1914 and at Verdun in 1916.

397.37–38   being recently discovered by H. G. Wells] Wells published *God the Invisible King*, a work of theology, in May 1917.

400.4   William English Walling] A social reformer and journalist, Walling (1877–1936) left the Socialist Party in 1917 to support the war.

401.28   recent amazing letter Prof. Stewart Paton] See note 394.26.

402.16–17   "conscription of wealth" . . . Amos Pinchot] In the spring of 1917 Pinchot (see note 328.35–329.9) proposed a 100 percent tax on all income above $100,000 as a means of financing the war.

402.37–38   Fellowship of Reconciliation] A Christian pacifist organization founded in 1915; Thomas was a member.

405.35–37   Civil Liberties Bureau . . . Roger Baldwin] Baldwin (1884–1981), a social reformer and antiwar activist, founded the Civil Liberties Bureau in 1917 to assist conscientious objectors. In 1920 Baldwin transformed the Civil Liberties Bureau into the American Civil Liberties Union and served as its director until 1950.

407.16–17   Mr. Gompers . . . reply to Colonel Roosevelt] At a public meeting held in New York City on July 6, 1917, to welcome a visiting Russian delegation, Theodore Roosevelt said that the "appalling brutality" of the St. Louis riot had left "a stain on the American name." Gompers responded by reading a message from the Illinois Federation of Labor blaming the riot on the hiring of black strikebreakers by employers. Roosevelt shook his fist at Gompers and accused him of seeking to excuse "the infamous brutalities visited on the colored people of East St. Louis," a charge Gompers denied.

408.10 Chester and Youngstown] After a white man was fatally stabbed in an altercation with four African Americans on the night of July 24, 1917, white mobs began attacking black residents in Chester, Pennsylvania. Three whites and one African American were killed before the riot ended on July 29. White soldiers attacked black residents of Youngstown, Ohio, on July 27, 1917.

409.30 battery of 220s] French howitzer firing a shell 220mm (8.6 inches) in diameter and weighing 220 pounds. It had a maximum range of almost seven miles (11,810 yards).

410.10 great advance of the 21st of August] The French launched a limited offensive at Verdun on August 20, 1917, and by August 24 had succeeded in retaking Le Mort Homme and Côte 304, two hills on the left (west) bank of the Meuse that the Germans had captured in the spring of 1916 after weeks of costly fighting.

410.20–21 Jane Addams . . . *rum* & ether] See pp. 184.32–185.3 and pp. 187–88 in this volume.

411.12 C'était rigolo, mon vieux!] It was comical, my man.

411.13 brancardiers] Stretcher bearers.

415.7 Fort Ben] Fort Bend County southwest of Houston, the site of the Central State Prison Farm at Sugar Land.

418.3–5 Major Snow . . . Baltimore be returned] Major Kneeland S. Snow, the commander of the Third Battalion, 24th Infantry, succeeded in having Corporal Charles Baltimore released. Baltimore left camp later that night and was charged with participating in the mutiny. He was found guilty and hanged on December 11, 1917.

419.8 Sparks has been indicted] Sparks was acquitted.

420.24 Houston eighteen lives] The mutineers killed fifteen people, all white, including four police officers and one army officer; a fifth police officer later died from his wounds. Four soldiers also died, some of whom were shot by mistake.

421.20–21 bayoneting of Captain Mattes] Captain Oliver W. Mattes (1875–1917) of the 2nd Illinois Field Artillery was shot to death after mutineers mistook him for a police officer. The undertaker who prepared his body testified that he saw no evidence of bayonet wounds.

421.24–27 All the men . . . sufficiently punished] A total of 118 men were court-martialed in three separate trials, resulting in 110 convictions. Of those found guilty, twenty-nine were sentenced to death, fifty-three to life terms, and twenty-eight defendants received terms ranging from two to fifteen years. Thirteen of the condemned were hanged on December 11, 1917, and another six men were executed in the fall of 1918, while ten of the death sentences were commuted by President Wilson. All of the men sentenced to prison were released by 1938.

421.32   Governor Ferguson] James Ferguson (1871–1944) was the Democratic governor of Texas, 1915–17.

423.14   Crouy-sur-Ourcq] A village about fifteen miles west of Château-Thierry.

424.1   Journal letters] "War Journal of a Pacifist," the title used by Cleghorn for the series of letters she sent to Fisher, April–September 1917.

424.11   Jimmy] Her son, James Fisher (1913–1945), later killed in action in the Philippines.

424.15   Sally] Her daughter, Sally Fisher Scott (1909–1978).

424.16   lynching of Little] Frank Little (1879–1917), an organizer for the Industrial Workers of the World, was taken from his hotel room in Butte, Montana, and hanged from a railway trestle on August 1, 1917.

424.32   suppression of the socialist-press] Postmaster General Albert Burleson had used his powers under the Espionage Act of 1917 to ban several socialist publications from the mail.

425.10   blue glass craze . . . the Montessori system] Chromotherapy, the belief that illness can be treated by colored light; a method of self-motivated early childhood education, named after Maria Montessori (1870–1952).

428.31   four crack regiments] The 9th and 10th Cavalry and the 24th and 25th Infantry.

428.40   *line officers*] Officers with the rank of second lieutenant, first lieutenant, or captain.

429.1   *field officers*] Officers with the rank of major, lieutenant colonel, or colonel.

432.12   the picket prisoners] Protestors arrested outside the White House for "obstructing traffic." There were 218 arrests made from June to November 1917, and ninety-seven women were sent to either the District of Columbia jail or the Occuquan workhouse in Virginia.

439.11   chasse] Pursuit.

439.34   renversement] Reversal, an aerial maneuver in which the pilot reverses direction by doing a half-roll followed by a downward half-loop.

440.11–12   my sad experience with the single-seater] In a letter written on November 23, 1917, Biddle described how he had damaged a German fighter plane. He attributed his failure to destroy his target to having been "too hasty in my shooting."

440.17   both my machine guns] Biddle was flying a French SPAD XIII fighter armed with two machine guns mounted on the engine cowling and synchronized to fire through the propeller arc.

443.18   "Disparu,"] Missing.

445.27   Oyster Bay,] Town on the north shore of Long Island where Theodore Roosevelt lived.

446.13   "Timeo Danaos et dona ferentes,"] Virgil, *Aeneid*, II.49: I fear the Greeks even when they bear gifts.

449.1–2   Resolutions of the German Reichstag . . . July last,] On July 19, 1917, the Reichstag adopted a peace resolution, 212–126, calling for "a peace of understanding and international reconciliation" and disavowing "forced acquisitions of territory and political, economic, and financial violations."

449.22   Mr. Lloyd George has spoken] David Lloyd George (1863–1945), prime minister of Great Britain, 1916–22, had addressed British war goals in a speech in London on January 5, 1918.

456.6–7   supply *camions* and ammunition *caissons*] Supply trucks and ammunition wagons.

457.30   tetanus . . . poison from gas and explosives] Tetanus is caused by infection with the *Clostridium tetani* bacterium.

458.22–23   *Roses are blooming in Picardy*] Cf. "Roses of Picardy," British song (1916) with lyrics by Frederick Weatherley (1848–1929) and music by Haydn Wood (1882–1959).

460.23   General Bullard] A West Point graduate who had served in the Philippines, Robert Lee Bullard (1861–1947) commanded the 1st Division, December 1917–July 1918, III Corps, July–October 1918, and the Second Army from October 1918 until after the Armistice.

464.33   Absolument jamais!] Absolutely never!

465.12   Mon Petit *and* Mon Vieux] My little one; my pal.

466.19   *macquillage*] Makeup.

466.22   *vicomtesse*] Vicountess.

466.30   mondaine] Worldly.

468.7   Madelon] Song (1914) about a barmaid, with words by Louis Bousquet and music by Camille Robert, that became very popular among French soldiers.

471.13   American divisions] The 2nd and 3rd Divisions.

471.28   Omar Bundy] A West Point graduate who had fought in Cuba and the Philippines, Bundy (1861–1940) commanded the 2nd Division, November

1917–July 1918, VI Corps, July–September 1918, and VII Corps, September–October 1918.

471.31 Brigadier General Harbord] Harbord (1866–1947) was chief of staff of the American Expeditionary Forces, May 1917–May 1918, commander of the 4th Marine Brigade, May–July 1918, of the 2nd Division, July 1918, and of the Services of Supply, August 1918–May 1919.

471.40 *Mairie*] Town hall.

472.4 Lieutenant Oscar Hartzell] Arthur E. Hartzell (1891–1940), a press officer at AEF headquarters.

472.12 Colonel Neveille] Wendell Neville (1870–1930) commanded the 5th Marine Regiment, January–July 1918, and the 4th Marine Brigade, July 1918–19. A veteran of the Spanish-American War, the Boxer Rebellion, the Philippines, and the Veracruz expedition, Neville later served as commandant of the Marine Corps, 1929–30.

473.23 "Corned Willy"] Corned beef.

474.8 Major John Berry] Benjamin S. Berry (1882–1942) commanded the 3rd Battalion, 5th Marine Regiment.

484.15 beautiful green lawn] Pottle's unit, Evacuation Hospital No. 8, was set up in the Collège de Juilly, a Catholic boarding school founded in 1638.

486.18 Dakin solution] An antiseptic solution containing sodium hypochlorite, developed in 1915 by British biochemist Henry Drysdale Dakin (1880–1952).

502.10–11 a Swiss infidel] Henry Dunant (1828–1910), the Swiss businessman who inspired the founding of the International Committee of the Red Cross in Geneva in 1863, was raised in a devout Calvinist household. It was reputed that in later life Dunant became an agnostic and grew hostile to organized religion.

502.31 cannot cite . . . Negro woman as a nurse.] The Red Cross did not accept any black nurses for overseas service throughout the war. About two dozen black nurses served in army hospitals in the United States at the height of the influenza epidemic in late 1918.

503.23 the "silent" protest parade] The NAACP had organized a silent protest parade down Fifth Avenue in New York City on July 28, 1917. Between 8,000 and 10,000 African Americans marched to the sound of muffled drums to protest the East St. Louis riot and other recent incidents of racial violence.

503.31–36 Which I wish . . . free to maintain] From "Plain Language from Truthful James" (1870), by Bret Harte (1836–1902).

504.19 Brummy] Theodore Brumback (1894–1955), a fellow Red Cross volunteer who had traveled with Hemingway to Italy. Brumback had previously served as a volunteer ambulance driver in France for four months in 1917 before becoming a reporter at the *Kansas City Star*, where he met Hemingway.

504.21 Capt. Bates] Robert W. Bates (1888–1978), the director of the American Red Cross ambulance service in Italy.

504.23 first American wounded in Italy] Lieutenant Edward M. McKey (1877–1918), an American Red Cross canteen worker, had been killed by an Austro-Hungarian artillery shell near Fossalta di Piave on June 16, 1918.

505.1–2 That is wise don't you think Dad?] Clarence Edmonds Hemingway (1871–1928) was an obstetrician.

505.36 the medal] The Silver Medal of Military Valor.

510.21 minnenwerfer] German trench mortar; the word is used here to refer to the shell the *minenwerfer* (mine launcher) fired.

514.17 the company] Allen served in Company B of the 111th Infantry Regiment.

515.40–516.1 relieve the 112th infantry] The 111th Infantry Regiment, 112th Infantry Regiment, and 109th Machine Gun Battalion made up the 56th Brigade, one of two brigades in the 28th Division.

517.35 Having occupied the town . . . "Fritz"] The Germans had captured Fismes on May 27, 1918.

521.10 *Hôtel de Ville*] City hall.

522.29 *Die Woche*] *The Week*, popular illustrated weekly magazine published in Berlin, 1889–1944.

522.31 King of Saxony] Frederick Augustus III (1865–1942) was King of Saxony from 1904 until his abdication on November 13, 1918.

524.6–7 Alan Seeger speaks . . . in 1914] Seeger described marching through Fismes in a diary entry from October 28, 1914, printed in *Letters and Diary of Alan Seeger* (1917)

524.24–25 potato-masher bombs] German hand grenades.

525.2–3 *Cher Adolph: . . . ici, nous*] Dear Adolph, spring has come here, we.

526.26 a 6-inch shell] A shell 150mm (5.9 inches) in diameter and weighing 93 pounds, fired from a howitzer with a maximum range of more than five miles (9,400 yards).

527.39 French *Chauchat* automatic rifle] The Chauchat, introduced into French army service in 1916, fired a bullet 8mm in diameter, was fed from a twenty-round magazine, had an effective range of 220 yards, and weighed twenty pounds.

531.40 *citron grenades*] Lemon grenades, so called because of their shape.

536.36–37   Glendenning . . . saw *him* alive] Second Lieutenant Frank M. Glendenning (1889–1918) was killed in action on August 12.

541.32   Captain Law . . . had been killed] In his preface to the first edition of *Toward the Flame* (1926), Allen wrote that some of the personal names in his narrative had been slightly changed. "Law" was the name Allen used for Captain Edmund W. Lynch, who was killed in action on August 10, 1918.

545.5–6   last time I ever saw Dan Brooks] Second Lieutenant Daniel W. Brooks (1891–1918) was killed in action near Fismes on September 6.

549.31–32   Thompson . . . either him or Fletcher] Captain Orville R. Thompson was killed in action on August 11, 1918; First Lieutenant Lee C. Fletcher was killed in action on September 1, 1918.

549.37   the French Army Commander] General Jean Degoutte (1866–1938), commander of the French Sixth Army, June–November 1918.

549.39–40   Bullard's Memoirs . . . August 28, 1918.] In *Personalities and Reminiscences of the War* (1925), Robert Lee Bullard (see note 460.24) wrote that he had ordered the evacuation of the Fismette position but had been overruled by Degoutte, who wanted the bridgehead enlarged by aggressive action. On August 27, 1918, a sudden German attack overran the Fismette position; of the 236 defenders from the 112th Infantry, 75 were killed, 127 captured, and 34 escaped across the Vesle. Bullard included in his memoirs a letter sent to Pershing on August 28, 1918, in which he cited an earlier, almost successful German attack as convincing evidence that Fismette could not be held. The mid-August attack Bullard cited is the incident that concludes Allen's narrative; see pp. 552–53 in this volume.

553.14   *Here ends this narrative*] In the preface to the 1934 edition of *Toward the Flame*, Allen wrote:

> It was not the object of this book merely to relate a personal adventure. I tried, insofar as anyone can, to eliminate the big "I" of little ego and to substitute for it only the first person singular of the fellow who happened, under certain circumstances, to be around. Hence, I ended the story with the night attack on the village of Fismette, when most of the defenders of that place had ceased to exist. If I did not inflict upon my readers certain personal sufferings and physical indignities that followed, it was because I felt that they were important to me alone. In other words, I meant this to be a report of what I saw on the battle line, and when the fighting ends the story stops.
>
> In answer, however, to many letters and innumerable questions as to what *did* happen to me, I can now, after sixteen years, "hasten to add" that in the early morning hours after the attack, and in the company of one sergeant, I managed to return to headquarters where I was promptly tagged by our regimental surgeon and sent to a base hospital.
>
> To him, and to that surgeon, whoever he was, who in a certain field

hospital saved my eyes from the effect of mustard gas and tended other injuries, I should like at this time to express what the word "gratitude" only too coldly conveys. But that is another story.

554.14   The Oak Leaves and the opposition] The *Oak Leaves* was a local newspaper published in Oak Park, Illinois; "the opposition" probably refers to its competitor, the *Oak Parker*.

554.19–20   hell . . . Gen. Sherman's time] In a speech to a reunion of Union veterans in Columbus, Ohio, on August 11, 1880, General William Tecumseh Sherman (1820–1891) said: "There is many a boy here today who looks on war as all glory, but, boys, it is all hell."

557.15   Ma Petengill . . . home fires burning!"] In "Red Gap and the Big-League Stuff," a story in the June 15, 1918, number of *The Saturday Evening Post* by the American humorist Harry Leon Wilson (1867–1939) featuring his recurring character Ma Pettengill.

557.18   Helmles] A family who lived in Oak Park.

559.12   the Colonel] Albert S. Fuger (1880–1972), commander of the 118th Field Artillery Regiment.

560.27   hundreds of tanks, whippets] The Whippet was a British tank similar to the French Renault FT used by American tank units at St. Mihiel and the Meuse-Argonne. The first tank design to have a fully rotating turret, the Renault FT weighed seven tons, had a two-man crew, a maximum speed of four miles per hour, armor ranging in thickness from 8 to 22mm, and was armed with either a 37mm gun or a 7.92mm machine gun.

563.1   names of two noble women] Kate Richards O'Hare (1876–1948) and Rose Pastor Stokes (1879–1933), two Socialists imprisoned under the Espionage Act for making antiwar statements and whom Debs had praised in his speech at Canton. O'Hare was tried in North Dakota in December 1917 and sentenced to five years in prison, but was released after fourteen months when President Wilson commuted her sentence. Stokes was convicted in Missouri in June 1918 and sentenced to ten years. Her conviction was overturned on appeal in March 1920 on the grounds that the trial judge had shown prejudice in his charge to the jury, and her case was never retried.

563.21–22   preferred to go to prison] In 1895 Debs served a six-month sentence for contempt of court for defying an injunction during the 1894 Pullman railroad strike.

567.26–33   'He is true . . . the race.'] James Russell Lowell, "On the Capture of Fugitive Slaves near Washington" (1845).

568.26–27   first Liberty Loan] The first sale of Liberty Bonds to finance the war began on April 28, 1917, with an offering of $2 billion of bonds with a 3.5 percent rate of return. Bonds were sold in denominations ranging from $50 to $10,000, and the sale of "War Thrift Stamps" made it possible to purchase $50 bonds on the installment plan. There were more than four million subscribers to the loan.

568.34 Cantigny] The 1st Division won the first American offensive victory of the war when it captured the French village of Cantigny and defended it against German counterattacks, May 28–31, 1918.

570.5 Hoover] Herbert Hoover served as U.S. Food Administrator, 1917–19.

572.24 Sarka Herbkova] Šárka Hrbková (1878–1948), a native of Cedar Rapids, Iowa, was chairman of the department of Slavic languages and literature at the University of Nebraska, 1908–19.

572.28–29 Women's Council for National Defense] The Women's Committee of the Council for National Defense (see note 305.15–16) was created on April 21, 1917, with the suffragist leader Anna Howard Shaw as its chairman; other members included Carrie Chapman Catt and the journalist Ida M. Tarbell (1857–1944).

573.11 the Y hut] An entertainment hut sponsored by either the YMCA or YWCA.

575.1 "The Education of Henry Adams"] The first trade edition of the book was posthumously published in September 1918.

580.12 Dead Man's Hill] Le Mort Homme; see note 410.10.

583.5 buzzer station] A station for sending signals over wires in the form of buzzing tones.

583.26 Chauchat] See note 527.39.

585.18 bomb] Hand grenade.

586.2–3 Luger revolvers] German 9mm semiautomatic pistols.

593.21 epistaxis] Bleeding from the nose.

595.19 E.R.S. 2] E Room Section 2.

597.28–29 CCS . . . SC-2] Chief Commissary Steward; Ship's Cook 2nd Class.

600.10–11 Great Britain . . . justice to women] The Representation of the People Act, passed on February 6, 1918, abolished almost all property qualifications for male voters over twenty-one and enfranchised women over thirty who paid rates (local taxes) or were married to ratepayers. Legislation passed in 1928 extended suffrage to all women over twenty-one.

604.1 Major Emory] A lawyer from Baltimore, Major German Horton Hunt Emory (1882–1918) commanded the Third Battalion, 320th Infantry Regiment. He was killed in action on November 1, 1918, near Sommerance.

605.18 Lieutenant France] First Lieutenant James W. France, commander of L Company, Third Battalion, 320th Infantry, was killed on October 11, 1918.

607.16–17   Polyglots a Siege of] It is likely that this phrase is the result of a setting error by the *New York American*.

608.1–2   Hudson Dusters . . . Gophers] New York City street gangs that flourished on the West Side of Manhattan at the beginning of the twentieth century. The Hudson Dusters were based in Greenwich Village, while the Gophers controlled Hell's Kitchen.

608.8   Yaphank] An army training camp on Long Island.

608.18   Plattsburg] A training camp for volunteer army officers was established at Plattsburg, New York, in 1915 as part of the "preparedness" movement.

609.2   Charles Whittlesey] A graduate of Williams College and Harvard Law School, Major Charles Whittlesey (1884–1921) was the commander of the First Battalion, 308th Infantry Regiment, 77th Division. Whittlesey was awarded the Medal of Honor and returned to New York City, where he practiced law, became active in the Red Cross, and assisted distressed veterans and their families. As a recipient of the Medal of Honor, Whittlesey attended the dedication of the Tomb of the Unknown Soldier on November 11, 1921. He disappeared from a ship bound for Havana on November 26 and is believed to have jumped overboard.

609.28–30   six companies with him . . . battalions of his regiment.] The force commanded by Whittlesey on October 2 also included two sections from the 306th Machine Gun Battalion. On the morning of October 3 the force was joined by a company from the Third Battalion, 307th Infantry, 77th Division.

609.31–32   Captain George R. McMurtry] McCurtry (1876–1958) was the commander of the Second Battalion, 308th Infantry. He was awarded the Medal of Honor for his leadership during the siege.

611.4–5   man who was sent back . . . note demanding surrender] Private Lowell R. Hollingshead (1899–1966) was one of eight men who crossed the lines without permission to search for food packages dropped by American aircraft. Four of the men were killed, while Hollingshead and the other three were captured.

615.17–18   a separate reply . . . Austria-Hungary] The government of Austria-Hungary had offered on October 7, 1918, to conclude an armistice and negotiate peace on the basis of the Fourteen Points. Wilson replied on October 19 that while the Fourteen Points had envisioned "the peoples of Austria-Hungary" being "accorded the freest opportunity of autonomous development," the United States now recognized the legitimacy of Czechoslovak and Yugoslav aspirations for full independence. Austria-Hungary accepted Wilson's new conditions on October 29 and signed an armistice in November 3.

615.19   Accept [etc.]] The text printed here is taken from *Papers Relating to the Foreign Relations of the United States, 1918, Supplement 1, The World War,*

Volume I (1933), which uses "[etc.]" to abbreviate standard diplomatic closings, in this case "Sir, the renewed assurances of my high consideration."

615.37   address of the 27th of September] Speaking in New York City, Wilson declared that "there can be no peace obtained by any kind of bargain or compromise" with the Imperial German government.

616.34–36   constitutional changes . . . 20th of October] Wilhelm Solf (1862–1936) was foreign secretary in the new government formed by Max of Baden on October 3, 1918. In his note to Wilson, Solf wrote that future German governments would be formed or dismissed by a majority vote of the Reichstag, and that the consent of the Reichstag would be required "for decisions on war and peace." (The power to appoint and dismiss governments and to declare war had previously been the prerogative of the kaiser.)

617.7–8   the King of Prussia] Wilhelm II, who was both king of Prussia and emperor of Germany.

618.12   Allied Supreme War Council] Formed in November 1917, the Supreme War Council was composed of the heads of government of Great Britain, France, Italy, and the United States, or their civilian representatives; each nation also appointed a permanent military representative to advise the Council. Lloyd George and French premier Georges Clemenceau attended the meeting where Pershing's letter was read, along with Italian foreign minister Sidney Sonnino and Wilson's special representative, Edward M. House.

621.3   *Bess Wallace*] Truman wrote to Bess Wallace (1885–1982) at her family home on 219 North Delaware Street in Independence, Missouri. After their marriage in 1919, Truman moved into the house, which would be his Missouri home for the rest of his life.

621.17   Boxley] Fred A. Boxley (1877–1936), a lawyer from Kansas City Truman had met in the Missouri National Guard.

621.19   Morgan and Company] In the fall of 1916 Truman had become a partner in the Morgan Oil & Refining Company, a venture that bought and sold oil leases in Kansas, Oklahoma, Texas, and Louisiana. The company failed in 1917.

621.27   Foch] General Ferdinand Foch (1851–1929), the Allied supreme commander, had presented the Armistice terms to a German delegation on November 8.

621.36   Lizzie] The car Truman had purchased in 1914, a five-seater built by the Stafford Company in Kansas City.

622.4   sausage balloons] Observation balloons.

623.15   big 155 battery] The AEF was equipped with French artillery, including howitzers that fired shells 155mm (6.1 inches) in diameter that weighed 100 pounds and had a maximum range of seven miles (12,400 yards).

623.39 Mrs. Wells] Maud Gates Wells (1864–1934), Bess Wallace's maternal aunt.

624.4 "Stars & Stripes"] U.S. Army newspaper that was published weekly in France from February 8, 1918, until June 13, 1919.

626.1 the 77s] See note 196.19–20.

627.8 150s] See note 526.26.

627.10 Gen. Hall] Brigadier General Herman Hall (1864–1928), commander of the 178th Infantry Brigade, 89th Division.

627.16 Whiz-bang] A German 77mm shell.

627.20 G. I. cans] "Galvanized Iron Cans," slang term for German shells.

627.21 Romagne] A heavily shelled town in the Meuse-Argonne, captured by American troops on October 14, 1918.

629.29–30 Blue Devil] Chasseurs Alpins, elite French mountain infantry, known as "Blue Devils" after their distinctive blue uniforms.

629.33 *Société des Nations*] League of Nations.

629.34 *Fédération Ouvrière des Mutilés* and the C.G.T.] Fédération Ouvrière des Mutilés de la Guerre, Worker's Federation for the War Disabled; Confédération Générale du Travail, General Confederation of Labor.

629.35 *Populaire*] French socialist newspaper, published 1918–70.

630.6 George Washington] The USS *George Washington*, a former German ocean liner converted for use as an American troopship, was bringing President Wilson to France.

630.11 *Journal du Peuple*] French socialist newspaper, founded in 1916.

630.12 Jaurès,] See note 10.33.

630.18–19 M. Clemenceau and M. Poincaré] Georges Clemenceau (1841–1929), premier of France, November 1917–January 1920, and Raymond Poincaré, president of France, 1913–20.

630.24 Miss O.] The name Sergeant used for one of her nurses, a Red Cross volunteer from North Dakota.

630.28 Rick] The name Sergeant used for Sidney Howard (1891–1939), an American bomber pilot with the 20th Aero Squadron who had flown combat missions over St. Mihiel and the Meuse-Argonne. Howard later became a successful playwright and screenwriter whose work includes the play *They Knew What They Wanted* (1924) and the screenplay for *Gone with the Wind* (1939).

631.24 Lippmann, Merz, R. Hayes] Walter Lippmann (see Biographical Notes); Charles Merz (1893–1977), a former Washington correspondent for *The New Republic* now serving in military intelligence; Ralph Hayes

(1894–1977), a former assistant to Secretary of War Newton Baker, also now serving in military intelligence.

632.27   *Fermée par cause de frousse*] Closed on account of fear, closed on account of jitters.

633.4–5   the Madeleine!] Neoclassical Roman Catholic church in central Paris, consecrated in 1842.

634.5   King of Italy] Victor Emmanuel III (1869–1947), king of Italy, 1900–1945.

634.6   *femme de ménage*] Cleaning woman.

634.14–15   "'*Je t'assure, . . . pas deux haies.*'"] "'I assure you, mama,' she told me, 'it was nothing special, they didn't even have two lines.'"

634.31   Joffre] See note 188.8.

634.32   *Débats*] *Le Journal des Débats*, French newspaper published 1789–1944.

634.35–37   old soldier . . . spring of 1917] Joffre made a goodwill tour of the United States, April–May 1917.

635.7   the A.R.C.] The American Red Cross.

635.31   pinard] Wine.

636.4   M. Gauvain's] Auguste Gauvain (1861–1931), French diplomat and writer on international affairs for *Le Journal des Débats*.

636.10   Amy Lowell] American poet and critic (1874–1925) known as an exponent of Imagism.

636.13   "*Heureux Noël!*"] Happy Christmas!

636.23   *Vieux Marc*] Old brandy made from the skin and stems of grapes.

636.27   Ernest] An officer serving with military intelligence, Ernest Angell (1889–1973) was the husband of Sergeant's sister Katharine, later Katharine Sergeant White (1892–1977) and father of the writer Roger Angell (b. 1920).

636.34   "*Encore du chocolat . . . chasseur*] "More chocolate?"; see note 629.29–30.

637.12   the Guildhall] Wilson spoke at Guildhall in London on December 28, 1918.

638.6   *La question . . . question terrible.*"] The question of the peace is an enormous one.

638.11   speech in the *Chambre*] Clemenceau spoke about the peace conference in the Chamber of Deputies on December 29, 1918.

638.16   Ebert Government is tottering] Friedrich Ebert (1871–1925), the leader of the Majority Social Democrats, became chancellor of Germany on November 9, 1918, the same day that Wilhelm II abdicated. The following day Ebert became co-chairman of the Council of People's Deputies, a revolutionary government formed by the Majority Social Democrats and the more radical Independent Social Democrats. Street fighting in Berlin between army troops and radical sailors on December 24 caused the Independent Socialists to withdraw from the Council of People's Deputies on December 29. In January 1919 Ebert and the Majority Social Democrats allied themselves with right-wing nationalist officers and repressed an uprising by the radical Spartacist League. Ebert became president of the newly established Weimar Republic in February 1919 and served until his death.

642.11 Schenck] The secretary of the Philadelphia branch of the Socialist Party, Charles Schenck was convicted in December 1917 and sentenced to six months in prison.

642.32 defendant Baer] A practicing physician, Elizabeth Baer was sentenced to ninety days.

644.34–35 *media concludendi*] Means of concluding.

645.6–7 amending Act of May 16, 1918] Also known as the Sedition Act of 1918; see Chronology.

646.23–24 Attorney General Gregory] A lawyer from Texas, Thomas Gregory (1861–1933) served as attorney general from August 1914 until March 5, 1919, when he was succeeded by A. Mitchell Palmer (1872–1936).

646.24–25 Metropolitan meeting] Wilson addressed a public meeting held in support of the League of Nations at the Metropolitan Opera House in New York on March 4, 1919.

647.1 Judge Daniel Cohalan] Cohalan (1867–1946), a judge of the New York State Supreme Court, 1911–23, opposed the League of Nations after the Paris peace conference failed to support Irish self-determination.

647.40 Dmowski] Roman Dmowski (1864–1939), leader of the Polish National Democratic Party and the chief Polish delegate at the peace conference.

649.4 thirty-seven of the round robin] See Chronology, March 4, 1919.

649.9 Dr. Grayson] Cary T. Grayson (1878–1938), a naval officer who served as the White House physician.

649.18 Weir Mitchell] Silas Weir Mitchell (1829–1914).

650.11–13 A.G. Gardiner's . . . *War Lords*] Arthur George Gardiner (1865–1946), a British journalist and essayist whose works include *Prophets, Priests and Kings* (1908) and *War Lords* (1915).

650.15 David Grayson!] A pen name used by Ray Stannard Baker (see Biographical Notes).

652.22–23 Signor Orlando . . . Ante Trumbić] Vittorio Orlando (1860–1952), prime minister of Italy, 1917–19; Ante Trumbić (1864–1938), foreign minister of the Kingdom of Serbs, Croats, and Slovenes (Yugoslavia), 1918–20.

652.23 The Four] Wilson, Clemenceau, Lloyd George, and Orlando.

653.1 Fiume] The Italian claim to Fiume, an Adriatic port that had formerly been part of Austria-Hungary, was strongly opposed by the Kingdom of Serbs, Croats, and Slovenes. (Fiume was not part of the territory promised to Italy by the Allies in 1915; see Chronology, April–May 1915.) In November 1920, Italy and the Kingdom of Serbs, Croats, and Slovenes signed a treaty making Fiume a free state. The city was annexed to Italy in 1924 but became part of Yugoslavia in 1945 and is now Rijeka in Croatia.

653.1 Italians . . . unredeemed provinces] The conference had agreed that the South Tyrol and Trentino would be ceded to Italy by Austria.

654.24 Mr. White] Henry White (1850–1927) had served as first secretary at the U.S. legation in London, 1886–93 and 1897–1905, and as ambassador to Italy, 1905–7, and to France, 1907–9.

655.16 Bavaria . . . Soviet Republic] A Soviet republic was proclaimed in Bavaria on April 6, 1919. It was brutally repressed by government troops and right-wing paramilitary forces on May 3.

655.17 Dr. Nansen] Fridtjof Nansen (1861–1930), a famous arctic explorer, would later organize the repatriation of former prisoners of war from Soviet Russia, 1920–22, and manage the Red Cross famine relief program in Russia, 1921–23.

656.32 Close] Gilbert Close (1881–1952), a stenographer and private secretary to the President.

656.37 Crillon] The Hôtel Crillon, the main headquarters of the American delegation to the peace conference.

657.5 Klotz] Louis-Lucien Klotz (1868–1930), French minister of finance, 1917–20.

657.18 the Saar] After Wilson and Lloyd George blocked French attempts to annex the Saar basin, the conference agreed that the region would be placed under League of Nations administration for fifteen years while its coal fields would be controlled by France. In 1935 the inhabitants of the Saar voted in a plebiscite to rejoin Germany.

660.13 A. of O.] Army of Occupation.

660.16 Gen. Gatley] Brigadier General George Gatley (1868–1931) commanded the 67th Artillery Brigade, July 1918–April 1919.

660.18 Col. Bob] Colonel Robert Tyndall (1877–1947) commanded the 150th Field Artillery Regiment, August 1917–May 1919.

660.23 Heth] Lieutenant Colonel Clement C. Heth (1884–1930) led the 150th Field Artillery, February–March 1919, while Tyndall was ill with pneumonia.

661.5 killed an American soldier in Coblenz] An American soldier was stabbed to death in Gulz, a suburb of Coblenz, on March 16, 1919, after a street fight broke out between three soldiers and a group of German civilians.

661.21 Divisions on board] Kniptash was returning to the United States on the troopship USS *Leviathan*.

662.15 the Lincoln] Kniptash had sailed to France in October 1917 on board the USS *President Lincoln*, a former German liner that had been seized and converted into a troopship. The *President Lincoln* was torpedoed and sunk by the *U-90* on May 21, 1918, while returning to the United States from France.

663.27 Smiles] Song (1917) with music by Lee S. Roberts (1884–1949) and lyrics by J. Will Callahan (1874–1946).

664.7–11 Ambassador Sharp . . . Hitchcock] William Graves Sharp (1859–1922), U.S. ambassador to France, 1914–19; George W. Read (1860–1934), commander of II Corps, June 1918–February 1919; Samuel Davis Sturgis (1861–1933), commander of the 87th Division, August 1917–November 1918, and the 80th Division, November 1918–April 1919; Douglas MacArthur (1880–1964), commander of the 84th Infantry Brigade, 42nd Division, later General of the Army; Oscar T. Crosby (1861–1947), assistant secretary of the treasury, 1917–18; Frank Hitchcock (1867–1935), postmaster general, 1909–13.

664.18 T.H. and MP] Transportation Headquarters and Military Police.

665.22 "Life"] American weekly magazine, founded in 1883 and purchased in 1936 by Henry Luce.

665.38 A.L.A.] American Library Association.

667.15 Romagne,] See note 627.21.

674.5 Ambrieres, Mayenne] Isum was billeted in northwestern France, away from the former battle zone.

674.37 Colonel George McMaster] A native of South Carolina, McMaster (1869–1950) took command of the 365th Infantry after the Armistice.

676.19–20 Brig. Gen. Gehardt] Charles Gerhardt (1869–1950) commanded the 183rd Infantry Brigade, 92nd Division, December 1918–March 1919. Gerhardt was born in Maryland and admitted to West Point from North Carolina.

679.10–11 Pres Wilson . . . Boston speech] In a speech delivered in Boston on February 24, 1919, Wilson said: "One of our American humorists, meeting the criticism that American soldiers were not trained long enough, said, 'It takes only half as long to train an American soldier as any other, because you only have to train him one way, and he did only go one way, and he never came back until he could do it when he pleased.'"

680.8   Lafollette] A Republican, Robert M. La Follette (1855–1925) was a congressman from Wisconsin, 1885–91, governor, 1901–6, and a senator, 1906–25.

681.12   Mr. Ambassador] Hugh Wallace (1863–1931), U.S. ambassador to France, 1919–21.

687.17   SECRETARY BAKER points out] In a speech given in Washington, D.C., on November 29, 1918, printed as a foreword to *How We Advertised America* (1920), from which "The 'Second Lines'" is taken.

690.6   National Board of Historical Services] The National Board for Historical Services was founded on April 29, 1918.

690.14–15   the Blue Devils, Pershing's Veterans] Soldiers from the Chasseurs Alpins (see note 629.29–30) and AEF veterans who toured the United States to promote the sale of Liberty Bonds.

691.24   plate-matter service] A service that supplied stories and illustrations to small newspapers in the form of stereotype plates.

691.32–33   "Pershing's Crusaders," . . . Four Flags"] Documentary films released in May, July, and November 1918, respectively.

691.40   Tuckerton] A radio station in New Jersey operated by the U.S. Navy.

696.12   Mr. Gillett] Frederick H. Gillett (1851–1935), a Republican from Massachusetts, served in the House of Representatives, 1893–1919, as Speaker of the House, 1919–24, and in the Senate, 1925–31.

696.19   Mr. Mondel of Wyoming] Frank W. Mondell (1860–1939), a Republican from Wyoming, served in the House of Representatives, 1895–97 and 1899–1923.

696.20   Initiative and . . . me in 1912] Creel wrote editorials for the (Denver) *Rocky Mountain News*, 1911–13.

699.15   we had associated ourselves] In 1917 Wilson had defined the United States as an "associated power" in the war against Germany because the U.S. had not signed a formal alliance with the Allied Powers.

699.18–19   our associates . . . the sea] Cuba and Panama declared war against Germany on April 7, 1917, and were followed by Brazil on October 26, 1917, Guatemala on April 23, 1918, Nicaragua on May 8, 1918, Costa Rica on May 23, 1918, Haiti on July 12, 1918, and Honduras on July 19, 1918.

702.2   action at Château-Thierry] See Chronology, June 1918.

704.37–40   the Saar . . . distant date] See note 657.18.

705.4   a State] Poland.

708.23–24   a special treaty with France] At the peace conference Clemenceau had sought to establish an independent buffer state in the Rhineland to protect

France against future German invasion. Lloyd George and Wilson rejected the idea, and the conference agreed that the Rhineland would be occupied for fifteen years and permanently demilitarized thereafter. As an additional measure to guarantee French security, the United States and Great Britain pledged on June 28, 1919, to defend France against unprovoked German aggression. Wilson submitted the treaty with France to the Senate for ratification on July 29, 1919, but it was never acted upon. Under its terms, the American failure to ratify the agreement released Great Britain from its obligations.

708.24–25 temporary protection of France] The treaty would end once the League of Nations was capable of guaranteeing French security.

713.19 the Essays of Elia,] *The Essays of Elia* (1823) by Charles Lamb (1775–1834).

713.33 treaty of Utrecht] A series of treaties was signed at Utrecht, 1713–14, at the end of the War of the Spanish Succession.

713.34–714.1 a project . . . the Abbé de Saint-Pierre] Charles-Irénée Castel (1658–1743), *Le projet de paix perpétuelle* (1713).

714.14–15 Kaunitz . . . Leopold] Prince von Kaunitz (1711–1794) was state chancellor of Austria, 1753–92; Leopold II (1747–1792) was grand duke of Tuscany, 1765–90, and Holy Roman Emperor, 1790–92.

714.24 Emperor Alexander] Alexander I (1777–1825) was Tsar of Russia, 1801–25.

714.38 treaty of Tilsit] A treaty between France and Russia signed in 1807.

715.2 Baroness von Krudener] Barbara Juliane von Krüdener (1764–1824), the widow of a Russian diplomat, underwent a religious conversion in 1804. She met Alexander I in Switzerland in 1813 and became his religious adviser and confidante.

716.4 Lord Castlereagh] Viscount Castlereagh (1769–1822) was the foreign secretary of Great Britain, 1812–22.

716.10 Troppau and Laibach] The Congress of Troppau was held in 1820 and the Congress of Laibach in 1821.

716.13 Congress of Verona] Held in 1822.

716.14 George Canning] Canning (1770–1827) was foreign secretary, 1807–9 and 1822–27, and prime minister, April–August 1827.

716.37 Metternich] Prince von Metternich (1773–1859) was foreign minister of Austria, 1809–48.

717.40–718.2 Canning . . . of the old."] In a speech made in the House of Commons on December 12, 1826, Canning said: "I called the New World into existence, to redress the balance of the Old."

718.6 Mr. William Alison Phillips, says] Walter Alison Phillips (1864–1950), professor of modern history at Trinity College, Dublin, 1914–39, in "The Congresses, 1815–22," in *The Cambridge Modern History*, Volume X, *The Restoration* (1907).

718.9   "in itself . . . to mankind."] This phrase does not appear in "The Congresses, 1815–22."

719.18   Paderewski] Jan Paderewski (1860–1941) was prime minister of Poland, January–November 1919.

722.21   cession . . . Shantung] The Treaty of Versailles ceded to Japan the German concessions on the Shantung peninsula, including control of the port of Tsingtao (Qingdao), railways, mines, and the right to station troops.

723.1   King of the Hedjaz] Sharif Hussein ibn Ali (c. 1854–1931), the emir of Mecca from 1908 to 1916, became king of the Hejaz in 1916 at the beginning of the Arab revolt against the Ottoman Empire and ruled until his defeat in 1924 by Ibn Saud.

723.4   Emir Abdullah] Abdullah (1882–1951), a son of Hussein, was later emir of Transjordan, 1921–46, and king of Jordan, 1946–51.

723.5–6   Kurma . . . Ibn Savond] Al-Khurma, an oasis about 150 miles east of Mecca; Ibn Saud (c. 1880–1953), the sultan of Nejd, conquered the Hejaz in 1926 and united it with the Nejd in 1932 to form the kingdom of Saudi Arabia, which he ruled until his death.

723.21–24   Great Britain . . . Mosquito Coast] The British maintained a protectorate on the Mosquito Coast, 1687–1783 and 1816–60.

725.7–8   school laws . . . international dispute?] The decision by the San Francisco board of education in 1906 to segregate Japanese schoolchildren caused a crisis in Japanese-American relations. It was resolved in 1907 when President Theodore Roosevelt reached a "gentlemen's agreement" with the Japanese government, under which the segregation policy was ended in return for severe restrictions on Japanese immigration to the continental United States.

727.6–7   England . . . seven] The original members of the league included Great Britain, Canada, Australia, South Africa, New Zealand, and India.

728.23   M. Lausanne] Stéphane Lauzanne (1874–1958) was co-editor, and later editor, of *Le Matin*, 1901–44.

730.14   John Quincy Adams] Adams (1767–1848) served as secretary of state during the Monroe administration, 1817–25.

731.20   the unhappy tool] The Emperor Maximilian; see note 7.16–18.

731.33–35   Mr. Olney] Richard Olney (1835–1917) was secretary of state, 1895–97. In a note sent to the British government on July 20, 1895, regarding the border dispute between Venezuela and British Guiana, Olney wrote: "Today the United States is practically sovereign on this continent, and its fiat is law upon the subjects to which it confines its interposition."

731.35–39 Theodore Roosevelt . . . international law."] In "Bring the Fighting Men Home," published posthumously in *Metropolitan* in March 1919, Roosevelt criticized the Wilson administration for the "hideous" condition of Mexico, then wrote: "We are in honor bound to remedy this wrong and to keep ourselves so prepared that the Monroe Doctrine, especially as regards the lands in any way controlling the approach to the Panama Canal, shall be accepted as immutable international law."

736.16–17 eminent Senators . . . the Philippines] Under the terms of the Treaty of Paris, signed on December 10, 1898, Spain ceded the Philippines to the United States. The treaty was ratified by the Senate, 57–27, on February 6, 1899.

741.19 "*Post equitem sedet atra cura*,"] Horace, *Odes*, III.I.40: "Behind the rider sits dark care."

743.17–18 Washington . . . Chicago] On July 18, 1919, a white woman in Washington, D.C., reported that two black men had tried to rob her. Mobs of white servicemen began attacking black residents the next day, beginning four days of rioting that ended after 2,000 federal troops were deployed on July 22. At least four black and three white persons were killed during the violence. Rioting began in Chicago on July 27 when a black teenager drowned in Lake Michigan, reportedly after being struck in the head by a rock thrown by a white man. The violence continued until order was restored on July 31 by 6,000 troops from the National Guard. Twenty-three African Americans and fifteen whites were killed during the riot.

743.19–20 President Wilson . . . unstinted force,"] In a speech delivered in Baltimore on April 6, 1918, Wilson said: "Germany has once more said that force, and force alone, shall decide whether justice and peace shall reign in the affairs of men, whether right as America conceives it or dominion as she conceives it shall determine the destinies of mankind. There is, therefore, but one response possible from us: Force, force to the utmost, force without stint or limit, the righteous and triumphant force which shall make right the law of the world and cast every selfish dominion down in the dust."

744.22–23 "Those who live . . . the sword,"] Cf. Matthew 26:52.

747.37–38 very severe settlement with Germany] Under the terms of the Treaty of Versailles, Germany was to have an army of 100,000 men, without tanks, aircraft, or heavy artillery, and a navy of 15,000 men, without submarines, battleships, or battle cruisers. Military conscription was prohibited, the Rhineland was to be demilitarized, and all prewar German colonies were made into League of Nations mandates under the administration of various Allied states. Germany lost 13 percent of its prewar territory, ceding land to France, Belgium, Poland, and, after a plebiscite in 1920, Denmark. The treaty also required Germany to pay an undetermined amount of reparations for war damages and costs; in 1921 a commission fixed the amount at $33 billion, of which about $4.5 billion was eventually paid.

748.7–8 first of several treaties] See Chronology, September 1919–August 1920.

748.30–31 international charter . . . rights of labor.] Article XXIII of the Covenant of the League of Nations provided that member states "will endeavour to secure and maintain fair and humane conditions of labour for men, women, and children, both in their own countries and in all countries to which their commercial and industrial relations extend, and for that purpose will establish and maintain the necessary international organisations."

752.17 General Botha and General Smuts] Louis Botha (1862–1919) and Jan Smuts (1870–1950) were both prominent Boer commanders in the Second Boer War, 1899–1902. Botha served as prime minister of the Transvaal, 1907–10, and as the first prime minister of the Union of South Africa, 1910–19. He returned to South Africa after signing the Treaty of Versailles and died there on August 27, 1919. Smuts led troops against German forces in South-West Africa, 1914–15, and in East Africa, 1916, then went to Great Britain, where he served as a minister without portfolio in the War Cabinet, 1917–19. He served as prime minister of South Africa, 1919–24 and 1939–48.

752.27 figures . . . came from India] India was represented at the peace conference by Edwin Samuel Montagu (1879–1924), secretary of state for India, 1917–22; Sir Ganga Singh (1880–1943), the Maharaja of Bikaner; and Satyendra Prassano Sinha (1863–1928), first Baron Sinha of Raipur, the undersecretary of state for India in 1919.

753.22–23 Article X? . . . its language] Article X of the Covenant of the League of Nations read: "The Members of the League undertake to respect and preserve as against external aggression the territorial integrity and existing political independence of all Members of the League. In case of any such aggression or in case of any threat or danger of such aggression the Council shall advise upon the means by which this obligation shall be fulfilled."

754.3–4 Japan . . . Shantung] See note 722.21.

754.17 John Hay] Hay (1838–1905) served as ambassador to Great Britain, 1897–98, and as secretary of state, 1898–1905.

754.33–35 Russia and Japan . . . Portsmouth] The Treaty of Portsmouth, signed on September 5, 1905, concluded the 1904–5 Russo-Japanese War.

756.35–757.5 Theodore Roosevelt: . . . capacity."] In article published in *The New York Times* on October 18, 1914, under the title "Theodore Roosevelt Writes on Helping the Cause of World Peace," Roosevelt wrote: "The one permanent move for obtaining peace, which has yet been suggested, with any reasonable chance of attaining its object, is by an agreement among the great powers, in which each should pledge itself not only to abide by the decisions of a common tribunal but to back with force the decision of that common tribunal. The great civilized nations of the world which do possess force, actual or immediately potential, should combine by solemn agreement in a great World League for the Peace of Righteousness. A court should be created—a changed and amplified Hague Court would meet the requirements—composed of representatives from each nation; these representatives being sworn to act in each case as judges, pure and simple, and not in a representative capacity."

757.6–10 "The nations . . . these rights."] Roosevelt wrote: "The nations should agree on certain rights that should not be questioned, such as their territorial integrity, their rights to deal with their own domestic affairs, and with such matters as whom they should or should not admit to residence and citizenship within their own borders. All should guarantee each of their number in the possession of these rights."

762.32 the intervention in Russia] See Chronology, August 1918.

763.15–16 Czecko-Slovaks . . . Bolsheviki] In March 1918 the Bolsheviks agreed to allow the Czechoslovak Legion, a military force of about 40,000 men recruited largely from among former prisoners of war and deserters from the Austro-Hungarian army, to leave Russia by way of Vladivostok and join the Allies fighting in France. An altercation at Chelyabinsk between members of the Legion and released Hungarian prisoners of war on May 14, 1918, resulted in Leon Trotsky issuing an order for the Legion to be disarmed. The Legion rebelled, and by the late summer of 1918, Czechoslovak troops had seized control of the Trans-Siberian railroad from the Urals to the Pacific.

765.3 *Schenck, Frohwerk* and *Debs*] The Supreme Court decided *Schenck* on March 3, 1919 (see pp. 641–45 in this volume) and the appeal of Eugene V. Debs (see pp. 562–67) on March 10. In *Frohwerk v. United States*, also decided on March 10, the Court upheld 9–0 the conviction of Jacob Frohwerk, a Missouri newspaper editor, under the Espionage Act of 1917. Holmes wrote the opinion in all three cases.

766.22–24 sentences of twenty years . . . the defendants] Jacob Abrams (1886–1953), Mollie Steimer (1897–1980), Samuel Lipman, and Hyman Lachowsky were arrested in August 1918 and convicted in October. Abrams, Lipman, and Lachowsky were sentenced to twenty years in prison, and Steimer to fifteen. Their sentences were commuted in 1921 after they agreed to be deported to Russia. Abrams left the Soviet Union in 1925 and settled in Mexico in 1926; Steimer was deported from the Soviet Union in 1923 and settled in Mexico in 1941; Lipman was shot during the 1937–38 purge; Lachowsky is believed to have been murdered by the Nazis in 1941–42.

768.19 *Alexander Berkman*] Berkman (1870–1936) was born in Vilna, Russia (now Vilinius, Lithuania), and immigrated to the United States in 1887. After nine striking workers were killed during the Homestead steel strike in 1892,

Berkman tried to assassinate Henry Clay Frick, the plant's general manager. Sentenced to twenty-two years, Berkman was released in 1906 and began collaborating with Emma Goldman in editing the anarchist publication *Mother Earth*. In 1917 Berkman was convicted along with Goldman of conspiring to obstruct the draft and sentenced to two years in prison. Berkman left Russia in 1921 and settled in France in 1925.

768.31   Mr. Hoover] J. Edgar Hoover (1895–1972) joined the Justice Department in 1917. Hoover served as chief of the General Intelligence Division, 1919–21, assistant director of the Bureau of Investigation, 1921–24, and director of the Bureau of Investigation (after 1935, the Federal Bureau of Investigation), 1924–72.

769.19   "none but Americans on guard"] "Put none but Americans on guard tonight," an order allegedly issued by George Washington during the Revolutionary War.

769.30   Peter Blanky] Peter Bianki (1891–1930), general secretary of the anarcho-syndicalist Union of Russian Workers and co-editor of its publication *Khleb I Volya* (Bread and Freedom). Born in Odessa to Italian parents, Bianki immigrated to the United States around 1907. He joined the Soviet Communist Party in 1924 and was killed in Siberia in 1930 by peasants rebelling against forced collectivization.

769.32–34   Seattle . . . general strike] The general strike, February 6–11, 1919, was called by the Seattle Central Labor Council in solidarity with an unsuccessful strike for higher pay by Seattle shipyard workers, January 21–February 19.

771.13–18   "aliens who are . . . destruction of property"] From the Immigration Act of 1918, signed into law by President Wilson on October 16.

772.2   "Kropotkin's Memories of a Revolutionist"] *Memoirs of a Revolutionist* (1899) by Prince Pyotr Kropotkin (1842–1921).

773.15–16   Chairman Johnson] Albert Johnson (1869–1957), a Republican congressman from Washington, 1913–33, served as chairman of the House Committee on Immigration and Naturalization, 1919–31.

774.2   Dora Lipkin and Ethel Bernstein] Lipkin was one of 184 members of the Union of Russian Workers deported on the *Buford*. Ethel Bernstein (1898–after 1970) was romantically involved with Samuel Lipman (see note 766.22–24) and married him after his deportation to Russia in 1921. She was arrested during the Stalin era and spent ten years in a labor camp.

774.29   "catching the . . . first beam."] Cf. the second verse of "The Star-Spangled Banner."

777.13   pro domo] For home.

777.21   pro patria . . . et decor] "For the country, neither sweetly nor gloriously," an adaptation of Horace, *Odes*, III.ii.13: "dulce et decorum est pro patria mori" ("It is sweet and glorious to die for one's country").

782.8   astasia-abasia] An inability to either stand or walk in a normal manner as a result of conversion hysteria.

782.13   Southard] Elmer Ernest Southard (1876–1920), professor of neuro-pathology at Harvard Medical School, was the director of the Psychopathic Department at Boston State Hospital, 1912–20.

785.19   Greek Deputy] In the first chapter of *The Folly of Nations* Palmer re-called meeting a "platitudinous Greek Deputy" in a café in Larissa during the Greco-Turkish War of 1897. The deputy made a series of bellicose pronouncements while claiming that his governmental responsibilities prevented him from going to the front.

785.29   Landstürm] German third-line reserves, for men from thirty-nine to forty-five years of age.

785.31–32   our pioneer division] The 1st Division.

787.2–3   So I elided . . . correspondents' accounts] The Associated Press, in a story dated October 29, 1917, reported that the "first prisoner of war taken by the American expeditionary forces" had been shot on the night of October 27 and later died in a field hospital despite "the combined efforts of several surgeons"; the story made no mention of a bayonet wound.

787.6   A few days later . . . a night raid] The Germans carried out a raid near the town of Bathelémont in Lorraine on the night of November 2–3, 1917, kill-ing three American soldiers, wounding five, and capturing twelve prisoners.

787.17–18   divisional operations officer] Captain George C. Marshall (1880–1959) was the operations officer of the 1st Division, June 1917–July 1918. Mar-shall later served as chief of staff of the U.S. Army, 1939–45, as secretary of state, 1947–49, and as secretary of defense, 1950–51.

787.30   "hymn of hate"] "Hymn of Hate Against England," poem written and published shortly after the outbreak of war in 1914 by Ernst Lissauer (1882–1937).

789.32–33   "Little Hayti"] President Wilson ordered U.S. Marines to land in Haiti in July 1915 after President Vibrun Guillaume Sam was killed by a mob, beginning an occupation that would last until 1934. An insurrection against American rule, 1918–20, was defeated by the Marines and U.S. trained gen-darmes in fighting that killed as many as 2,000 Haitians.

790.5–6   Amritsar or Balbriggan] At least 379 Indian protestors were shot and killed by British troops in Amritsar, Punjab, on April 13, 1919. British "Black and Tans" (special police) murdered two men and burned fifty-four houses and a factory in the Irish town of Balbriggan on the night of Septem-ber 20–21, 1920.

790.36   A Private of the Guards] Memoir (1919) by the British journalist and travel writer Stephen Graham (1884–1975).

790.39–791.1   blockade . . . "illegal and indefensible,"] See note 216.25.

791.11   Grand Division] In *The New York Times*, July 31, 1918, this appeared as "Guard Division."

791.19   Heimat] Homeland.

791.20–21   An English Wife in Berlin] *An English Wife in Berlin: a private memoir of events, politics and daily life in Germany throughout the War and the social revolution of 1918* (1920) by Evelyn Mary Füstrin von Blücher von Wahlstatt (1876–1960).

791.23   Lissauer . . . Serment] For Lissauer, see note 787.30. French poet Henri de Régnier (1864–1936) wrote "Le Serment" (The Oath) in September 1914; its first line was translated in 1915 as "I swear to cherish in my heart this hate."

791.24   The Beast of Berlin] Film, released in March 1918, directed by Rupert Julian and starring Julian as Kaiser Wilhelm II.

791.25–26   Thackeray . . . lecture on George III] Published in *The Four Georges* (1860).

793.38   Eucken] Rudolf Christoph Eucken (1846–1926), professor of philosophy at the University of Jena, 1874–1920, and the 1908 Nobel laureate in literature. Eucken was a guest lecturer at Harvard and New York University, 1912–13. In 1914 he was one of the signers of the appeal "To the Civilized World" (see note 49.6–9).

794.7–8   Black and Tans] Former British soldiers recruited to serve in the Royal Irish Constabulary during the Irish War of Independence, 1920–22.

795.2–4   Matthew Arnold . . . the saving remnant] In "Numbers; or The Majority and the Remnant," published in *Discourses in America* (1885).

795.20–22   La faccia . . . l'altro fusto.] *Inferno*, Canto XVII.10–12: "The face was as the face of a just man, / Its semblance outwardly so benign, / And of a serpent all the trunk beside" (translation by Henry Wadsworth Longfellow).

798.27–28   Franz Werfel and Walter Hasenclever] Werfel (1890–1945) published four volumes of poetry from 1911 to 1919. His later works include *Die vierzig Tage des Musa Dagh* (1933), a historical novel about the Armenian genocide. Werfel fled Germany in 1938 and died in exile in California. Hasenclever (1890–1940) published a volume of poetry and four plays from 1913 to 1919, including the Expressionist drama *The Son* (1914). He committed suicide in the south of France in 1940 to avoid capture by the Nazis.

798.33   Stinnes . . . Simon] German industrialist Hugo Stinnes (1870–1924), whose business interests included mines, factories, power plants, river and ocean shipping, insurance, and newspapers; Walter Simons (1861–1937), foreign minister of the Weimar Republic, June 1920–May 1921.

799.24–25 president of the university] William Oxley Thompson (1855–1933), a Presbyterian minister, was president of Ohio State University, 1899–1925.

799.37 Dehmel] Richard Dehmel (1863–1920), German poet and dramatist.

800.19 ninety-three German intellectuals] See note 49.6–9.

800.26 I had published a little book] *The Spirit of Modern German Literature* (1916).

801.5 Zona Gale's excellent story] *Miss Lulu Betts* (1920), a novel by Zona Gale (1874–1938).

803.35 Mary's] Mary Arnold Crocker Lewisohn (1861–1946). She and Lewisohn were married in 1906, separated in 1922, and divorced in 1935.

804.23–24 "beat the gong . . . plot and conspire"] From "Song of Myself," Canto 23.

805.23 MR. SECRETARY OF WAR] John W. Weeks (1860–1926) was a Republican congressman from Massachusetts, 1905–13, a U.S. senator, 1913–19, and secretary of war, 1921–25.

807.30–31 demonstration of modern warfare] Harding observed U.S. Marines conduct maneuvers on the Civil War battlefield of the Wilderness, October 1–2, 1921.

825.34 slum] Army stew.

825.36–37 shortarm inspection] Inspection for symptoms of venereal disease.

828.1 Hamilton Fish, Jr.] Fish (1888–1991), a Republican congressman from New York, 1920–45, had sponsored the resolution authorizing the burial of the Unknown Soldier at Arlington. During the war Fish had served as the commander of Company K in the 369th Infantry Regiment, the "Harlem Hellfighters."

Index

*This book is set in 10 point ITC Galliard, a face
designed for digital composition by Matthew Carter and based
on the sixteenth-century face Granjon. The paper is acid-free
lightweight opaque that will not turn yellow or brittle with age.
The binding is sewn, which allows the book to open easily and lie flat.
The binding board is covered in Brillianta, a woven rayon cloth
made by Van Heek–Scholco Textielfabrieken, Holland.
Composition by Dedicated Book Services.
Printing and binding by Edwards Brothers Malloy, Ann Arbor.
Designed by Bruce Campbell.*

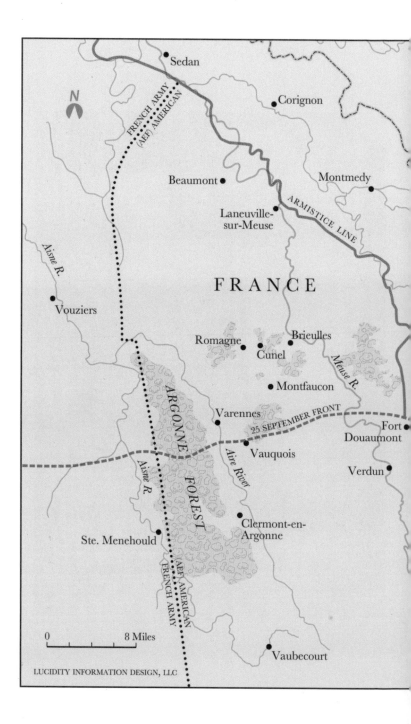

N

Sedan

Corignon

Beaumont

Montmedy

FRENCH ARMY
(AEF) AMERICAN

ARMISTICE LINE

Laneuville-
sur-Meuse

Aisne R.

Vouziers

FRANCE

Romagne

Brieulles

Cunel

Meuse R.

Montfaucon

Varennes

ARGONNE

25 SEPTEMBER FRONT

Fort
Douaumont

Aisne R.

Aire River

Vauquois

FOREST

Verdun

Ste. Menehould

Clermont-en-
Argonne

(AEF) AMERICAN
FRENCH ARMY

0   8 Miles

Vaubecourt

LUCIDITY INFORMATION DESIGN, LLC